Social Work in Health Settings

The most comprehensive book of its kind, *Social Work in Health Settings* presents a "practice in context" framework which is then applied in 31 casebook chapters, covering a great variety of health care settings from working with survivors of domestic violence through supporting people with HIV to services for military personnel.

Reflecting the enormous changes in policy, health care delivery, insurance systems, and the diagnosis and treatment of many conditions, this third edition features all-new case chapters. Each chapter considers the impact on the client situation of dimensions of context—including policy, technology, and organization—and then explores the key practice decisions that structure the helping relationship:

- definition of the client;
- determining goals, objectives, and contract;
- meeting place;
- use of time;
- strategies and interventions;
- stance of the social worker;
- use of resources outside of the social worker/client relationship;
- reassessment and evaluation;
- transfer or termination.

This thought-provoking volume thoroughly integrates social work theory and practice, and provides an excellent opportunity for understanding particular techniques and interventions. In this era of managed care, downsizing, and moving away from hospital-based work, the approach taken in *Social Work in Health Settings* proves more salient than ever before.

Toba Schwaber Kerson, D.S.W., Ph.D., is Mary Hale Chase Professor in the Graduate School of Social Work and Social Research at Bryn Mawr College in Bryn Mawr, Pennsylvania.

Judith L. M. McCoyd, Ph.D., is an Assistant Professor at the Rutgers University School of Social Work in New Brunswick, New Jersey.

Social Work in Health Settings

Practice in context

Third edition

Toba Schwaber Kerson,
Judith L. M. McCoyd and Associates

Routledge
Taylor & Francis Group

LONDON AND NEW YORK

First edition published 1989 (revised) by Haworth Press Inc

Second edition published 1997 by Haworth Press Inc

This edition published 2010
by Routledge
2 Park Square, Milton Park, Abingdon, Oxon, OX14 4RN

Simultaneously published in the USA and Canada
by Routledge
270 Madison Avenue, New York, NY 10016

Routledge is an imprint of the Taylor & Francis Group, an informa business

© 2010 Toba Schwaber Kerson, Judith L. M. McCoyd and Associates

Typeset in Baskerville by
Pindar NZ, Auckland, New Zealand
Printed and bound in Great Britain by
TJ International Ltd, Padstow, Cornwall

British Library Cataloguing in Publication Data
A catalogue record for this book is available from the British Library

Library of Congress Cataloging in Publication Data
Social work in health settings : practice in context / [edited by] Toba Schwaber Kerson, Judith L.M. McCoyd, and associates. — 3rd ed.
     p. ; cm.
  Includes bibliographical references and index.
  1. Medical social work—United States. 2. Public health—United States. I. Kerson, Toba Schwaber. II. McCoyd, Judith L. M.
  [DNLM: 1. Health Facilities—United States. 2. Social Work—United States. 3. Delivery of Health Care—United States. 4. Professional-Patient Relations—United States. 5. Social Work Department, Hospital—United States. W 322 S67355 2010]
  HV687.5.U5K48 2010
  362.1'0425—dc22   2009031227

ISBN10: 0-415-77845-X (hbk)
ISBN10: 0-415-77846-8 (pbk)
ISBN10: 0-203-85973-1 (ebk)

ISBN13: 978-0-415-77845-9 (hbk)
ISBN13: 978-0-415-77846-6 (pbk)
ISBN13: 978-0-203-85973-5 (ebk)

Contents

Figures

Tables

Contributors

Shauna P. Acquavita, Ph.D., L.C.S.W.-C., is a social worker in Baltimore.

Annick Barker M.S.S., M.L.S.P. is a therapist case manager at Health Care for the Homeless in Baltimore.

Patricia A. Barry, B.S., is a domestic violence counselor for the Lutheran Settlement House in Philadelphia.

Jennifer Bell, M.S.W., L.G.S.W., is a social worker in the skilled nursing facility of a not-for-profit continuing care skilled nursing facility in Baltimore.

Caryl Blackwood, M.S.W., L.C.S.W., currently works in the area of pregnancy and HIV in the OB/GYN Diagnostic and Treatment Center's Infectious Disease Program at the Mount Sinai Hospital in New York City. She is the social worker for the case described in her chapter.

Betsy C. Blades, M.S.W., is a social worker in a for-profit renal dialysis unit in Baltimore.

Laura Boyd, M.S.W., is a social worker at The Center for Children with Special Health Care Needs located in St. Christopher's Hospital for Children in Philadelphia.

Michelle K. Brooks, M.S.S., L.C.S.W., is Director of Social Services, Keystone Hospice, Philadelphia.

Bettina Campbell, L.M.S.W., is Executive Director of YOUR Center, a faith-based HIV/AIDS prevention organization in Flint, Michigan.

TaMara Campbell, M.S.Ed., is Director of Health and Wellness and training and curricula specialist for the YOUR Blessed Health Project in Flint, Michigan.

Helaine Ciporen, M.S.W., L.C.S.W., is a social worker at Mount Sinai Medical Center, New York, working at the Hall Family Center for Pediatric Endocrinology and Diabetes, and in the Pediatric Pulmonary Center, Cystic Fibrosis division.

Nick Claxton, Q.C.S.W., is a social worker at the Philadelphia Department of Public Health, Division of Maternal, Child and Family Health.

Renee C. Cunningham-Ginchereau, M.S.S., is Associate Director of Center in the Park, a nationally accredited senior center in northwest Philadelphia.

Susan E. Dawson, M.S.S., Ph.D., is Professor of Social Work in the Department of Sociology, Social Work and Anthropology at Utah State University in Logan, Utah.

Kathleen Desmond, M.S.W., is the Chief Executive Officer of Best Nest, Inc. a social service agency that provides foster care and adoption services to children with special health care needs and their families in Philadelphia.

Helen Dombalis is an M.S.W./MPH student at the University of North Carolina at Chapel Hill. She served as a social work intern at the adolescent parenting program described in this case.

Emily Beil Duffy, M.S.S., L.S.W., is the Pediatric Behavioral Health Consultant for Eleventh Street Family Health Services of Drexel University's Primary Care Department, Philadelphia.

Kathleen "Casey" Durkin, M.S.S.A., L.I.S.W.-S, B.C.D., has a private practice serving individuals ages 3 to 93, groups, couples and families and serves in the capacity of Assistant Director of the Beech Brook Orange City Schools Partnership in Pepper Pike, Ohio.

Jennifer L. Fenstermacher, M.S.S., L.C.S.W., is a social worker on the general pediatrics service at the A. I. duPont Hospital for Children in Wilmington.

Patricia A. Findley, Dr.PH., M.S.W., L.C.S.W., is Assistant Professor of Social Work at Rutgers University School of Social Work, New Brunswick, New Jersey.

Kim Lyons Garver, L.C.S.W., B.C.D., is a social worker in the Center for Development, Behavior and Genetics at SUNY Upstate Medical University in Syracuse.

Anne P. Hahn, Ph.D., L.C.S.W.-C, is a social worker in the Johns Hopkins Burn Center, Johns Hopkins Bayview Medical Center, Baltimore.

Gretchen Clark Hammond, M.S.W., L.S.W., TTS, serves as the Grant Writer for Amethyst, Inc. (Columbus, Ohio) and as Project Coordinator for their Integrated Tobacco Treatment Program. Gretchen has worked at Amethyst since 1999 and served as the practitioner in the case described in her chapter.

Phyllis Braudy Harris, L.I.S.W., Ph.D., is Professor and Chair of the Department of Sociology and Criminology and Director of the Aging Studies Program at John Carroll University, Cleveland.

Kathy J. Helzlsouer, M.D., M.H.S., is Director in the Prevention and Research Center at Mercy Medical Center and Adjunct Professor in the Department of Epidemiology at the Johns Hopkins Bloomberg School of Public Health in Baltimore.

Lori Hendrickson, M.S.W., is the Associate Director of Best Nest, a social service agency that provides foster care and adoption services to children with special health care needs and their families, and she is the supervisor on the case described in her chapter.

Wendy Emerson Hinch, M.S.S., L.S.W., is a school social worker for a Regional Special Services School District in Southern New Jersey.

Martha G. Hudson, M.S.W., is a social worker in the Center for Fetal Diagnosis and Treatment and the Neonatal Intensive Care Unit at the Children's Hospital of Philadelphia.

Toba Schwaber Kerson, D.S.W., Ph.D., is Mary Hale Chase Professor in Social Sciences and Social Work and Social Research at the Bryn Mawr College Graduate School of Social Work and Social Research in Bryn Mawr, Pennsylvania.

Bozena Lamparska, M.M., M.Ed., is the supervisor for the Philadelphia Department of Public Health, Division of Maternal, Child and Family Health's CAPTA program, Philadelphia.

Sue Livingston, B.S., is Education Coordinator for the Epilepsy Foundation of Eastern Pennsylvania in Philadelphia.

Gary E. Madsen, Ph.D., is Professor Emeritus of sociology in the Department of Sociology, Social Work and Anthropology at Utah State University in Logan, Utah.

Judy Mason, M.S.W., is the Social Work Manager for the Department of Obstetrics and Gynecology at Mt. Sinai Hospital in New York.

Katherine C. Maus, M.S.S., A.C.S.W., L.S.W., is the Director of the Division of Maternal, Child and Family Health for the Philadelphia Department of Public Health.

Sarah L. Maus, L.C.S.W., is the Manager of Geriatrics at the Muller Center for Senior Health at Abington Memorial Hospital in Abington, Pennsylvania.

Judith L. M. McCoyd, L.C.S.W., Ph.D., is Assistant Professor of Social Work at Rutgers University School of Social Work, New Brunswick, New Jersey and maintains a small clinical practice in Bala Cynwyd, Pennsylvania.

Regina Miller, M.S.S., is the social worker on the lung transplant team in the Penn Transplant Institute at the University of Pennsylvania Health System in Philadelphia.

Arden Moulton, M.S.W., is Program Coordinator of "Woman to Woman" in the Division of Gynecologic Oncology at the Mount Sinai Hospital Medical Center, New York.

Navami Naik, M.S.S., is a social worker working globally on outreach efforts for cancer education.

Vanessa Norris, L.C.S.W., is a social worker/advanced clinician at the Center for Special Studies, a comprehensive care center dedicated to the treatment of adult patients with HIV/AIDS in New York City.

Julianne S. Oktay, M.S.W., Ph.D., is Professor in the School of Social Work at the University of Maryland, Baltimore.

Carol Perrot, R.N., is Community Liaison for the Visiting Nurse Association of Greater Philadelphia.

Kevin J. Robinson, M.S.W., M.H.A., Dr.PH., is the Alexandra Grange Hawkins Assistant Professor at Bryn Mawr College, Graduate School of Social Work and Social Research in Bryn Mawr, Pennsylvania.

Kathleen Rounds, M.S.W., M.P.H., Ph.D., is Professor and Chair of the Doctoral Program at the School of Social Work at the University of North Carolina at Chapel Hill.

Susan A. Scarvalone, M.S.W., L.C.S.W., is Clinical Research Therapist in The Prevention and Research Center at Mercy Medical Center, in Baltimore, and she is the social worker in the case described in her chapter.

Jessica Scott, M.G.C. and C.G.C., is a genetic counselor in the Prevention and Research Center at Mercy Medical Center, in Baltimore.

Laurie Stewart, M.S.S., is a social worker in the neonatal intensive care unit at St. Christopher's Hospital for Children in Philadelphia.

Barbra Teater, Ph.D., is Lecturer in the Department of Social & Policy Sciences at the University of Bath in Bath, United Kingdom.

Virginia Walther, L.C.S.W., is Associate Director of Social Work for Women and Children's Health at the Mount Sinai Hospital in New York, and is Assistant Professor in the Departments of Community and Preventive Medicine; Obstetrics, Gynecology and Reproductive Science; and Pediatrics at the Mount Sinai School of Medicine.

Traci L. Wike, M.S.W., is a doctoral student at the School of Social Work, University of North Carolina at Chapel Hill.

Nancy Xenakis, L.C.S.W., M.S., is the Program Coordinator at the Initiative for Women with Disabilities at NYU Hospital for Joint Diseases in New York.

Acknowledgments

I would like to thank all of the superb practitioners, educators and researchers who contributed to this volume. Several of the authors have been involved with this enterprise since 1979 when the first edition was conceived. Now, with the third edition, written 30 years later, the world of social work in health care is a very different one especially in terms of the elements of context that shape the work. My work has been greatly enhanced and enlightened with the addition of co-editor, Judith L. M. McCoyd. I would like to thank, in particular, Peggy Robinson and Jessica Fenton for their technical assistance, and Jennie Kerson Pritzker, Larry Kerson, and David M. Schwaber for their devotion to me and respect for my work.

Toba Schwaber Kerson
Bryn Mawr, Pennsylvania

I too want to thank all the contributors to this edition, with a special thanks to Toba Schwaber Kerson who allowed me to join her in this important and wonderful work. She has been a wonderful mentor and support. I also want to thank Kathleen J. Moyer, Ph.D., my mother, who lit the way to a scholarly life. Finally, I thank "my boys," Patrick McCoyd, my husband, and Ryan and Ian, my sons, who keep me grounded in the world of sports, needs and life while still encouraging me to fly with my dreams.

Judith L. M. McCoyd
Drexel Hill, Pennsylvania

1 Practice in context

The framework

Toba Schwaber Kerson

Social Work in Health Settings presents a framework called "practice in context" that I have used for the past 30 years as a tool for teaching and evaluation. The primary subject of the framework is the relationship between social worker and client. Only through trustworthy, strong, knowledgeable and skill-based relationships with clients and others can social workers help clients to reach their goals (Beresford, Croft & Adshead, 2007; Kerson & McCoyd, 2002). As a concept, relationship can be interpreted in diverse ways. It is an association or involvement, a connection by blood or marriage, or an emotional or other connection between people. Other synonyms for relationship include dependence, alliance, kinship, affinity, or consanguinity, but each of these words suggests a different meaning based on a distinctive bond and duration. People can be related who have never met and never will; for example, people who have a common membership in a religious or fellowship group or a common profession may feel or act more "related" than first cousins.

The definition of the social worker/client relationship used here is based on the work of others. Sociologist Erving Goffman, and anthropologist Gregory Bateson theorize about some structural aspects of relationship such as the interactional focus, the connection of a relationship to its milieu, and the rules that inform or govern a relationship. Bateson uses the word *interaction* and Goffman, the word *encounter* to be as precise as possible about their subjects. For this framework, interaction and encounter are seen as factors in a broader concept.

Goffman suggests that when studying interaction, the proper focus is not on the individual and his or her psychology, but rather the syntactical relations among the acts of different persons who are mutually present to one another (Goffman, 1981). To understand interaction, one must understand not the separate individuals but what occurs between them. Goffman (1966) further alludes to the special mutuality of immediate interaction:

> When two persons are together, at least some of their world will be made up of the fact (and consideration for the fact) that an adaptive line of action must always be pursued in this intelligently helpful or hindering world. Individuals sympathetically take the attitude of others present, regardless of the end to which they put the information thus acquired. (p. 16)

Thus, in interaction, there is always a shared sense of situation and a capacity, in some way, to be in the place of the other, no matter what each participant's purpose in the interaction.

Goffman places relationship in context when he develops the notion of a "membrane" that "wraps" the interaction and, to some extent, separates it from its surroundings. "Any social encounter," he writes, "any focused gathering is to be understood, in the first instance, in terms of the functioning of the 'membrane' that encloses it cutting it off from a field of properties that could be given weight" (Goffman, 1961b, p. 79). Still, while the relationship can be viewed and defined in its own right, it remains intimately related to the world outside of it. Thus, Goffman says, "An encounter provides a world for its participants, but the character and stability of the world is intimately related to its selective relationship to the wider one" (Goffman, 1961b, p. 80). This reflects the membrane that surrounds and identifies the social worker and client relationship within health care.

The rules that inform a relationship, and the uses that the participants make of those rules, are also part of Goffman's and Bateson's analyses of relationship. According to Bateson, interaction is the "process whereby people establish common rules for the creation and understanding of messages" (Bateson, n.d., p. 3). Goffman adds to this definition by noting that, in encounters, rules are considered and managed rather than necessarily followed. Rules may shape interaction, but they also may be influenced by the participants. He writes,

> Since the domain of situational proprieties is wholly made up of what individuals can experience of each other while mutually present, and since channels of experience can be interfered with in so many ways, we deal not so much with a network of rules that must be followed as with rules that must be taken into consideration, whether as something to follow or carefully to circumvent. (Goffman, 1966, p. 42)

This foreshadows many of the relationships written about in this book. Part of taking rules about organization, professional roles, and ethics into consideration is viewing them in the service of the client's wellbeing and goal accomplishment and therefore flexing them to meet these needs.

Social work educator Helen Harris Perlman adds a sentient dimension to the more structural views of relationship posed by Goffman and Bateson. She defines relationship as "a person's feeling or emotional bonding with another" (Perlman, 1979, p. 23). Elaborating on the psychological dimension, Perlman says the relationship between social worker and client is "a catalyst, an enabling dynamism in the support, nurture, and freeing of people's energies and motivations toward problem solving and the use of help" (Perlman, 1979, p. 2). Thus, the relationship affirms and motivates the client. To these dimensions, social worker Carol Meyer adds *purpose*. The social worker/client relationship, she says, is not an end in itself but a tool for moving the problem situation forward (Meyer, 1976, 1983). It is formed for the purpose of meeting goals. In this book, the word *client* stands for any notion of a client unit; that is, an individual, family, program, organization, or advocacy effort that engages, or has some other entity pay for, the services of a social worker who will help this entity to reach its goals.

Thus, for this framework, the relationship between social worker and client is defined with the help of both sociological and psychological ideas. The sociological contributions have to do with structure; the focus is on interaction rather than on individual participants, on the use of rules, on the relationship's connection to (or separation from) its surroundings, or context. The psychological contributions are the purposive, feeling, catalytic, and enabling dimensions. Here, the relationship of social worker and client involves one or more purposive encounters, intended to be catalytic and enabling, where structure and rules for interaction are set by dimensions of context as well as by decisions made by the participants.

Practice-in-context framework

According to this framework, then, the two basic elements that structure the relationship between social worker and client are (1) the "context" in which the relationship occurs, and (2) the "practice decisions," that social worker and client make about the form and nature of the relationship. Context and practice decisions act as a matrix for the relationship, a supporting and enclosing structure. By determining many of the rules by which the work of social worker and client proceeds, context and practice decisions define the possibilities for relationship. Although elements such as personality, nature and degree of illness, psychosocial assessment, and cultural background contribute to the social worker/client relationship, they are characteristics of the individuals involved and not the interaction.

This approach or framework is not a generic practice theory because it is not a system of ideas meant to explain certain phenomena or relations. Nor is it a model, because it does not show proportions or arrangements of all of its component parts. Here are simply described elements of context and practice that structure the relationship between social worker and client. The framework has three overarching purposes that help the social worker to: (1) clarify the work, (2) understand alterable and unalterable dimensions of practice and context, and (3) evaluate work in light of these dimensions. Each is meant to support the decisions and actions of the social worker. With client participation, the social worker understands and tries to influence context and constructs the relationship in ways that will help meet client goals. Thus, *Social Work in Health Settings* is about the craft of social work; that is, the skill with which social workers manage dimensions of practice.

Context

To assume that possibilities for the work are completely determined within the social worker/client relationship is unrealistic, and may contribute to disappointment and a sense of failure on the part of the participants, evaluators of service, and funding sources. To a great extent, dimensions of context determine many of the rules for the helping relationship (Kerson, 2002). Context means the set of circumstances or facts that surround a particular event or situation, the surrounding conditions that form the environment within which something exists or takes place. Gregory Bateson defines context as a "collective term for all those events which tell the organism among what set of alternatives he must make his next choice" (Bateson, 1975, p. 289). He adds to this the notion that "however widely *context* be defined, there may always be wider contexts a knowledge of which would reverse or modify our understanding of particular items" (Bateson, n.d., p. 16). While context is a limitless concept, and focusing on certain dimensions means ignoring others, to intervene effectively means that one has to be able to consider and assess the enabling situational conditions under which one is working (Brett, Behfar & Kern, 2006).

The present framework addresses three dimensions of context that I continue to think have the most direct and describable consequences for the relationship between social workers and clients in health care settings: policy, technology, and organization. These elements are considered most important because of the ways in which each affects the structure of and possibilities for the social worker/client relationship. Policies increasingly provide rules specifying the services clients may receive, who may provide them, and under what conditions. Organizations are also rule-makers, setting the structure for service delivery and defining the nature of service often at the behest of policymakers. Finally, in this era when the means of communication continue to expand and change and technological interventions have us questioning definitions of life and death, the impact of technology on the relationship between social worker and client is immeasurable. Social workers' understanding of and comfort with a great range of technologies enhance their roles as "translators" for their clients, their opportunities for empathy, as well as their general relational capacities. In addition, computer-assisted technologies and the internet have altered and expanded the ways in which we communicate and receive information. Thus, technology contributes to the content of the relationship, expands possibilities and may also constrain it. The salience of each dimension, and the ways in which dimensions are related, depend on the particular setting. In effect, these contextual factors may at most determine or at least contribute to the rules of the game. As these factors change, the constraints and possibilities for action are altered as well.

Policy

Policies are explicit and definite sets of principles or courses of action that guide a range of actions in specific situations. They are always related to the political economy; that is, the ways in which a government manages its material resources (McClelland & Rivlin, 2009). Policies address entitlements and restrictions. They provide rightful claim, privileges or prerogatives, and/or they impose limitations and constraints. To think of policies in these ways demonstrates the need for social workers to understand all of the policies that may affect their clients. Social workers' understanding can help clients interpret policies and gain access to services. To be an effective client advocate, one must excel at understanding the policies that shape clients' entitlement and restrictions.

The status of the populations with which social work is most concerned, and the status of the social work profession itself are, to a great extent, reflections of the political economy and the social policies of any particular period in U.S. history (Mechanic, 2004). Understanding health disparities is critical in this regard (Emlet & Poindexter, 2004; Kawacki, Daniels & Robinson, 2005; Levenson, 2004). Peter Drucker notes that every 10 years or so, society reorganizes its world view, basic values, political and social structure, arts, and major institutions (Drucker, 1990). Thus, social policy is dynamic, fluid, and responsive to many powerful forces within and outside of a particular community or society. This bodes to be a time of enormous social reform in the United States, and hopes are high for reforming the health care system (Barr, 2007, 2008; Blank & Borau, 2007; Bodenheimer & Grumbach, 2009; Buyx, 2008; Epstein, 2008; Little, 2007; Stevens, Rosenberg & Burns, 2006).

The basis for policy is the law, which in the form of legislation, administrative regulations, and/or court decisions affects every dimension and nuance of social work practice in any health setting (Kerson, 2002). Dickson (2004) identifies the following aspects of the health and human services permeated by the law:

1   The entrance into and exit from health and human services delivery systems
2   The criteria used to determine eligibility for treatment, benefits, or services
3   The rights to which patients and clients are entitled
4   The rights to which professionals and staff are entitled
5   The way health and human services programs are administered and regulated
6   The relationship between the professional and the patient or client
7   The practice of the health and human services professional (p. 3).

Therefore, in order to understand the policies that shape their practice, social workers must know and understand the laws that affect the policies.

No matter whether they work on the individual, group, community, or policy level, social workers must be able to contribute to, interpret, and influence policy in order to advocate for their clients and the profession (Clark, 2009; Social workers introduce …, 2009). Decisions regarding which populations to serve, allocation of resources, planning, and programming are too often made before social work practitioners become involved, and it is far easier to affect the structure of a program before it is instituted rather than after (Vladeck, 2003). These activities are also most beneficial to clients when clients and social workers advocate together. In addition, involvement in policy formulation helps the social work profession to broaden and strengthen its influence and to fulfill its ethical mission to advocate for social justice (Denis & Clancy, 2006). When policy has a negative effect on clients or the profession, a united and concerted lobbying effort can stem the tide.

Historically, the presence of social work has been strongest in areas such as maternal and child health, as well as services to veterans, where social workers have been involved in developing policy on national, state, and local levels (Cox, 1999; Handel, 2009; Harris, 2008; Kerson, 1985a, 1980). To a great extent, which policies that social workers must understand depends on the populations with whom they work and the institutions for whom they work. At this time, primary foci of health-related social policy seem to be on trying to control and cap costs and to incorporate new knowledge and the development of new technologies into the notion of cost control (Arrow *et al.*, 2009; Mas & Seinfeld, 2008; Miller & West, 2009). Two such examples that affect social work in health care are diagnostic-related groups and managed care.

Diagnostic-related groups

In order to try to control the costs of Medicare, the federal government created diagnostic-related groups or DRGs, a prospective payment system in which Medicare and participating insurers pay hospitals according to case diagnosis rather than cost (Mayes & Berenson, 2007; Oberlander, 2003). Formerly, the hospital charged the insurer for costs incurred to care for the patient, plus a small percentage in addition. Now, the insurer pays the hospital based on the patient's diagnosis. According to the DRG classification, if the diagnosis indicates four days of hospitalization, the hospital will be paid for four days of hospitalization only. The rationale for the DRG schema is that some patients will leave earlier than four days. Yet, if the patient stays in the hospital longer, the hospital must absorb the extra cost. Consequently, there is great pressure on the hospital to discharge the patient and great pressure on the social worker to make prompt and appropriate arrangements for the patient to return to the community. Thus, a social worker who previously may have had weeks to develop a relationship with, and an adequate discharge plan for, a patient now may have a matter of days or less in which to accomplish the same task. More and more, the focus of the health care facility is for the social worker to discharge the patient as soon as the physician can no longer justify the stay, or, even more important, before the insurer will begin to deny payment for services rendered.

Managed care

For several decades, managed care—which promises both service efficacy and cost containment—has become a focal point for influencing policy formulation and advocating for clients and the profession (Golensky & Mulder, 2006; Pecukonis, Cornelius & Parrish, 2003). This is not a new idea. In 1869, the Sisters of Charity of the Incarnate Word offered a pre-paid health plan wherein, for 25 cents a week or $13.00 a year, one could be assured care in their infirmary. Closer to today's realities was the 1932 Elk City Cooperative, a true pre-paid health maintenance organization that focused on prevention, understood the economic and other devastating effects of serious illness, and supported group practice (Anderlik, 2001). For now, "Whatever motivated the turn to managed care, and no doubt the motives are mixed, reducing costs is clearly a major objective in the current wave of health care reform. Whatever the ultimate judgment of the cost issue, managed care has come to dominate health care" (Anderlik, 2001, p. 11). Approximately 90% of medical expenses are directed by managed care organizations (U.S. Census Bureau, 2000).

At this point, the term *managed care* is used for almost any strategy or structure put forth to manage the quality or cost of health care. Broadly defined, managed care encompasses any measure that, from the perspective of the purchaser of health care, favorably affects the price of services, the site where the services are received, or their utilization. As such, it represents a continuum—from plans that, for example, do no more than require prior authorization of inpatient stays, to the staff model HMO (health management organization) that employs its doctors and assumes risk for delivering a comprehensive benefit package. Ideally, managed care should not simply seek to reduce costs; rather it should strive to maximize value, which includes a concern with quality and access.

Iglehart (1992) says a managed care system integrates the financing and delivery of appropriate medical care by means of the following features: (1) contracts with selected providers who supply a comprehensive set of health services to enrolled members, generally for a predetermined monthly premium; (2) patient financial incentives to use providers who have contracted with the plan; (3) quality and utilization controls, which contracting providers have accepted; and (4) the assumption of a varying degree of financial risk by the providers "thus fundamentally altering their role from serving as agent for the patient's welfare to balancing the patient's needs against the need for cost control"(p. 742).

Now, managed care is forcing social work to re-examine our practices and also the values that support the missions of organizations (Schwartz & Weiner, 2003). It is critical that social workers in health care see this current panacea-like solution as a series of complex strategies viewed by important and powerful interest groups as ways to control the costs of health care (Managed Care, 2009). Managed care is not the enemy of social work, nor is it a simple way to solve deep, complicated problems. It is not even an entity. The fact that managed care is altering roles and tasks for social workers in many settings again underscores the importance of social workers' ability to interpret policy and advocate for clients (Bolen & Hall, 2007; Bransford, 2005; Lens, 2002; Neuman & Ptak, 2003). Nowhere will social workers see more efforts in this direction than in Medicaid managed care, its carve-outs, and other special situations (Gray, Lowery & Godwin, 2007; Hurley & Zuckerman, 2003; Iglehart, 2007; Smith & Moore, 2008; Spitz, 2007).

Technology

For contemporary health care, the development and cost of technology relate directly to policy formulation. Technology and the organizations that house and/or distribute it account for a good deal of the astronomical costs of medical care today (Aaron, 2007; Ehrenhof, 2009; Goyen & Debatin, 2009; Little, 2007; Pauly, 2007). The United States' passion for, rapid acceptance of, and diffusion of "high-tech" solutions means hospitals, health professionals, patients, and families demand what they believe to be the best available technology regardless of the cost. And, in the same way policy and the law provide parameters for practice, so does technology. As Jasanoff (2008) says:

As prime custodians of the "is" and the "ought" of human experience, science and the law wield enormous power in society. Each plays a part in deciding how things are in the world, both cognitively and materially; each also helps shape how things and people should behave, by themselves and in combination (p. 767).

Technology is applied science—the ways in which a social group satisfies its material needs. In the broadest sense, technology means the concrete, practical solutions people invent or discover. In the present framework, technology primarily refers to medical/scientific inventions that are used for diagnosis or treatment: medication, surgical techniques, life-sustaining machinery, ways of viewing or measuring bodily functions and, in addition, ways in which we collect, manage and disseminate information and new possibilities for interaction in relation to both diagnosis and treatment (Starr, 2000; West & Miller, 2009; Wheeler & Goodman, 2007). It is through the development of technology, as well as management of lifestyle issues such as diet, that we are expanding possibilities for treating illness and extending life (Hossain, Kawar & Nahas, 2007; Steinbrook, 2009; Sturm, 2002). Because of technological development, for example, we are able to respond to conditions in-utero, keep people alive who would otherwise die, and redefine many conditions from fatal to chronic.

Technology also means information management, the rise of electronic record keeping, and the computerization of all imaginable kinds of data (Tjora & Scambler, 2009). It can also be said that new communication technology is transforming the social work profession just as it is affecting many others. For example, one only has to think of the enormous amount of research Gary Holden has been able to present to social workers in health care; through Gopher Resources for Social Workers, World Wide Web Resources for Social Workers, and now the professional news services—Information for Practice (IP) (Holden, 2009). Says NASW Web Designer Ebony Jackson, "Social media technology, texting via phone and email messaging are revolutionizing the way people communicate" (Sfiligoj, 2009). This refers to e-clinical work, e-therapy, social networking websites, chat rooms, distance learning, as well as other virtual efforts. (Serafini, Damianakis & Marziali, 2007) and new learning techniques such as e-health, telehealth, interactive video, videoconferencing, and social work rooms on the Web (Matusitz & Breen, 2008; McCarty & Clancy, 2002; Rosenthal Gelman & Tosone, 2008).

The development of life-sustaining technology has also raised perplexing ethical and legal problems in health care (Callahan & Wasunna, 2006; Morrison & Monagle, 2009). Sometimes, the extension of life can mean greatly diminished life quality. In other situations, medical solutions may be dehumanizing and/or produce negative side-effects. Each raises new questions related to confidentiality, privacy and record keeping. Current concerns about confidentiality stem from these technological developments. Determining who has the right to access information—the individual or group paying for the care, the individual receiving the care, the individual with access to the computer system, etc.—has yet to be resolved satisfactorily although the Health Insurance Portability and Accountability Act of 1996 (HIPAA) Privacy Rule is a beginning (HIPAA, 1996). This is particularly critical in the areas of medical uncertainty that technology creates. An exemplar is the ability to identify certain genetic conditions and/or vulnerabilities when the diagnoses are often only "risk potentials." When the results are placed on a database that employers, insurers and others may see, it opens the possibility that the individuals will not be hired or insured when it is not even certain that they will experience the given condition. Similar concerns about privacy of data exist when diagnoses range from clinical depression to HIV infection to cancer.

For social workers, sometimes the lack of medical means to intervene in an illness creates opportunities for psychosocial intervention. Historically, social workers had important roles in the care of people with venereal diseases and tuberculosis, in part because medical interventions were inadequate to treat the illnesses. Before the discovery of penicillin permitted treatment of syphilis at an early stage with a single injection, treatment required many outpatient visits over a period of 18 months. The social worker's role was to ensure that patients returned for prolonged outpatient treatment, and to educate patients and others in their social circles who may have been infected. Contemporary situations provide similar epidemiological and educational opportunities. With diseases such as AIDS and Alzheimer's for which there are not yet adequate medical treatments, social workers help garner the social support needed to live with the illness. With other conditions, such as end-stage renal disease and severe burns, technology provides life support, and the social worker helps the patient and family to live with both the illness and the technology. Each of these circumstances provides opportunities for social work. In these ways, the presence or absence of technological solutions shapes the parameters of the relationship between social worker and client.

Organization

An organization is a sociological entity: thus, it sets certain patterns of, and expectations about, interaction. It is defined here as a body of people structured for some end or work, and the administrative personnel or apparatus of an agency, business, or institution. In the grand scheme of the delivery of health care, even the simplest organization has close ties to very large and complex networks of service. Therefore, every organization must attend to aligning itself with its external environment. In order to maintain order and stability and to develop, organizations must continuously respond to and integrate internal and external demands (Ivery, 2007; MacKenzie *et al.*, 2008). Increasingly, to understand organizational context requires knowledge about multiple, complex systems involving varied funding streams, auspices, professional and nonprofessional providers, and public, not-for-profit, and for-profit agencies with varied degrees of authority (Globerman, White, Mullings & Davis, 2003). Insensitivity towards these demands or to contextual issues will inhibit the service effectiveness (Preston, 2004).

It is also critical that social workers understand and be capable of influencing how their organizations, programs and services are being evaluated (Kerson, 2002). We often find ourselves in the position of being evaluated by others who may not understand or value the unique contributions of social work. Thus, part of understanding one's organization as an element of the context that shapes the relationship between social worker and client means incorporating evaluation into all of the work and engaging the evaluators if they come from outside of the organization (Neumann, Jacobson & Palmer, 2008).

To compete in today's health care arena, most health care organizations are in the midst of transforming themselves in order to become more efficient and to attract a broad insurance mix (Burke & Cooper, 2008; French & Bell, 2005; Institute of Medicine, 2001). For professional social workers, there can be no more hiding out in an office, seeing individual clients, and acting as if there is no world encroaching from outside. Organization also structures practice. It is essential for social workers to understand how the formal dimensions of their organizations affect health care delivery and the relationship between them and their clients. Here, I mean size, division of labor, degree of bureaucratization, degree of centralization of control, and role structure and the relationship of one's organization to others and to larger systems. Role structure is especially important in understanding social work's place and authority in the organization (Kerson, 2002). Changes in structure and design carried out in the name of efficiency and cost-effectiveness can enhance or restrict services and creativity (Austin, Brody & Packard, 2009; Lukas *et al.*, 2007; Sandberg, 2008).

One county agency told to spend less money, fired all of its first-line supervisors, saying their tasks could be carried out by two or three administrators. The following year, problems with staff morale and poor, undirected practice caused an almost 100% turnover in line staff. Informal dimensions include mores, which are the unwritten rules about behavior that people know implicitly but rarely discuss, such as how to relate to members of other professions and whether it is acceptable to have a meal at a client's home. When supervised by other social workers, one has appropriate socialization to professional mores and ethics. When administrators of other disciplines supervise, workload may be attended to, but professional socialization and support suffer. "In the era of managed care, we can no longer afford to ignore the effects of organizations on conduct and character, or the location of transactions between individuals within a social matrix" (Anderlik, 2001, pp. 13–14).

Also important are the networks, collaborative alliances, teamwork and partnerships that people develop within and outside of the formal organizational structure in order to accomplish tasks (Abramson & Mizrahi, 2003; Bronstein & Abramson, 2003; Drach-Zahavy & Baron-Epel, 2006; Kitchen & Brock, 2005; Solheim, McElmurry & Kim, 2007). The establishment of such a network requires us to enlist those with expertise or power regarding matters that are critical to clients. Such power does not necessarily reside with high office. Sometimes it can be held by a chief of service, other times by a clerk. Although it is generally easier to make exceptions or bend the rules in a smaller organization, those who work for large, highly bureaucratized organizations also learn to develop informal networks. Intimate knowledge of an organization increases the possibility of making it more responsive to clients' needs.

In conclusion, understanding context is about understanding the rules of the game. You can't play the game without understanding the rules, and you can't take advantage of, exploit, bend, or go around the rules unless you fully understand them. For health-related social workers, the most critical elements of context are policy, technology and organization—what regulations and laws, elements of technology, organizational dimensions and issues influence the work. An additional critical skill of social work in context is the ability to assess what aspects of context are alterable through advocacy and which are "givens" for any particular case. Then, within context sits the relationship between social worker and client. So, context determines parameters and also creates the nesting space where the relationship is established which will help the clients to reach their goals.

Decisions about practice

Within the constraints of context is located the relationship between social worker and client. The framework maintains that specific elements in the context (policy, technology, and organization) structure the relationship between social worker and client. Similarly, the framework suggests that specific elements within the relationship, which are to a degree determined by the participants in that relationship, provide structure and regulate interaction (Goffman, 1981). In the framework, the elements are called practice decisions because they are often determined by decisions made by social worker and client that set the pattern for their relationship. Practice decisions provide the process whereby the participants themselves have the power to create the vehicle that will enable them to accomplish their goals. The term stresses the dimensions of activity, judgment, and responsibility implicit in such choices (Banach, 2000).

In some situations, practice decisions may be constrained by elements of context. For example, in order to receive funding, an organization may have to adhere to policies set by a funding source regarding use of time or even goals. The organization would therefore constrain its social workers in those ways. Also, practice decisions are not always discrete and can recur as the relationship evolves. Alterable, they act as a flexible structure that can guide the relationship and help the participants to judge the quality of their work. The 10 practice decisions in this framework are: (1) definition of the client; (2) goals, objectives, and outcome measures; (3) use of contract; (4) meeting place; (5) use of time; (6) strategies and interventions; (7) stance of the social worker; (8) use of outside resources; (9) reassessment; and (10) transfer or termination.

Definition of the client

Defining the client involves the choice of a client unit; that is, deciding with whom one works in a situation (Turner, 2005). The client can be any unit, such as an individual, family, couple, parent and child, group, committee, housing project, clinic, or even a whole neighborhood (Fischer, 2009; Hartman & Laird, 1983). While a case is open, the definition of the client can change as needs change. Sometimes, one may intervene with the most troubled people in the situation, and in other instances, the social worker may work on the client's behalf. For example, the person who is most dependent or troubled may be too young, demented, or ill to be directly involved. At times, broadening the definition of the client from an individual to a larger unit enhances the social support of the ill person and strengthens the whole (Kerson, 2002).

Goals, objectives and outcome measures

The words "goals," "objectives" and "outcome measures" all refer to aspirations that social workers, clients, programs, organizations and funding sources want to attain. As social workers, we hope that these reflect the needs and desires of the client. In the best of worlds, they should be owned by the client with the social worker collaborating to clarify, articulate and help set the course for attainment. With the client's help, the social worker then uses the rest of the practice decisions to structure the relationship in ways that would support the work. When this is not the case, as when goals and objectives have been formulated by the social worker or other staff, funding sources, or family members and not by the client, it is much more difficult to attain goals. To work most effectively, this relationship has to be a partnership.

I see this part of the work as operating on two levels, at least. Overarching is the notion of "lending a vision," that is to say, "helping the client to envision a better life, better times, a more positive future" (Berman-Rossi, 1994). This is the "goals" level where wishes and dreams are articulated. The social worker holds the hope of this vision for clients whose hope has been dashed. This "lending" of hope can be a powerful element of the relationship and of the work.

The second level is the more pragmatic one in which social worker and client divide the work into steps and objectives. These measureable outcomes tell them concretely about their progress in their work together. This is the key to both assessment and evaluation (Kerson, 2002). Assessment in relation to measurable outcomes or objectives, means that one has determined the criteria for evaluation.

The relationship between social work goals and objectives and certain diagnoses is also important here. Diagnosis is often made by another profession, usually medicine, with which social work collaborates. In some ways, when a diagnosis is imposed, it becomes part of context, an organizational issue that informs social work practice. However, a diagnostic term such as diabetes, arthritis, or epilepsy is a label that provides very little information about functional capacity, and it is often that capacity with which social work concerns itself. For example, the question for the social worker is not whether the patient has multiple sclerosis, but whether her symptoms make it impossible for her to care for her children. If social workers employ this kind of information to limit the use that they think a client can make of the relationship, or even to discard certain clients into a category that receives no service, they are allowing diagnosis to restrict their work.

Objectives may be as concrete as obtaining an apartment or a prosthesis. Because objectives are, by definition, measurable, it is imperative that social workers think in these terms because they provide social workers, clients, funders and the organization the means for assessing progress (Kerson, 2002). Being able to call attention to some success such as "arriving at work or school on time nearly every day" or "going to the senior center three times a week" is helpful in encouraging a client to continue to work in the relationship. Increasingly, funding sources are asking social workers and other helping professionals for outcome measures. They must specify concrete measures by which they will evaluate their work and the work of the clients. Through articulating objectives and outcome measures, and achieving success in reaching a certain percentage or number of these measures, social workers will be able to help clients to see their progress. They can show their results and their economic value to the organization and the funding sources. Thus, goals are clients' wishes, to which social workers and clients aspire, and objectives and outcome measures are the realistic, attainable, concrete ways social workers and clients can measure their own progress and prove their worth to organizations and funding sources.

Use of contract

Contract refers to the agreement between social worker and client about the means used to obtain goals, as well as the description of the goals themselves. It is the keystone, cynosure, and linchpin of the social worker/client relationship and of this framework. Comprising mutually agreed-upon obligations and expectations, a contract is a way of establishing norms for the relationship (Goffman, 1972). Norms also exist for the relationship between client and agency. Increasingly, there are contracts between funding source, agency, and client. For example, many drug-abuse treatment centers require that clients sign agency-formulated contracts stipulating the conditions of treatment.

Whether verbal or written contracts are more effective remains a matter for debate, and most probably depends on the nature of the agency, work, and clients. Certainly, written formats clarify the agreement, and having all participants sign adds formality and perhaps importance to the matters at hand. This written form is very common in drug and alcohol programs, and often the conditions for the contract are set by the courts or the state. Some argue that this very formality stultifies the interaction, interfering with creativity, transference, or other aspects of the relationship. Others say that it lends clarity that protects everyone involved. Because contracting requires that each party articulates goals and norms, it includes each of the elements of relationship structure. Participants in a helping relationship always have some expectations of each other. The process of developing a contract ensures that the expectations of all parties are explicit and helps prevent misunderstanding.

Meeting place

Meeting place refers to the physical space in which the relationship happens. Often, decisions about meeting place are determined by the rules of the setting and the needs of the clients. Most work occurs in the social worker's institution/agency, or in the client's home. Increasingly, meeting place is determined by the organization rather than by the needs of the clients. The major portion of some services such as home care, foster care, and hospice occur in the home, while other services such as dialysis and discharge planning are generally offered in the institution (Beder, 1998; Moody, 2004). There is a renewed trend to place social work services back in the community with the increase in a range of case management services, intensive or otherwise, occurring wherever the client is (Brorson, 2005; Ferguson, 2008; Jonsson, 2005).

Meeting place can influence assessment by limiting or increasing the amount of information made available about the client. One's social scene provides some information about his or her identity (Goffman, 1959, 1972). When meetings take place outside of the client's habitat, the social worker relies on the person's appearance and the details he or she provides about his or her life. The sight of an institutionally gowned person lying in bed in a hospital room provides no clues to individual identity. Personality, memories, experiences, and style are all obscured. Often in such situations it is easy for social workers to assume knowledge of their clients that in fact they do not have.

When the client is seen at home, the social worker learns something about the client's means, organizational abilities, values, neighborhood, and, perhaps, his or her relationships with family members and neighbors (Paris, Gemborys, Kaufman & Whitehill, 2007). No other means compare to home visits for assessing the life of a client or, sometimes, for empowering him or her (Morris, 2003; Paris, 2008). One sees the impact of problems, illnesses, and disabilities on daily living. Through home visits, social workers can help collaborating professionals and aides to understand a client's life and problems. Many organizations think that home visits are too expensive and as a result do not allow them; however, denying social workers the opportunity to see their clients in their home environments, if the clients are willing, limits the ability of the social workers to assess client capacities and resources.

The telephone is another "place" in which to help people who cannot come to the organization and whom the social worker cannot visit. It has proven effective as a means of support and treatment for isolated clients (Heiney *et al.*, 2003; Mohr, Hart, Fonareva & Tasch, 2006). As mentioned earlier, social work will continue to make greater use of e-techniques as well (Drumm, McCoy & Lemon, 2003; Kanani & Regehr, 2003; Parker-Oliver & Demiris, 2006; Santhiveeran, 2009; Santhiveeran & Grant, 2005).

Two important aspects of meeting place are space and privacy. Where none exists, social workers can create private space for themselves and their clients by using undivided attention, eye contact, voice quality, and body language. When other professionals ignore the need for privacy, social workers have to educate them in order to protect their clients and foster the work.

Use of time

Decisions about time relate to the duration of the relationship and the duration and spacing of each meeting. Since use of time is a means of structuring the relationship, sharing this information with clients empowers them. In the broadest sense, orientation in time and space "is felt as a protection rather than a straitjacket, and its loss can provoke extreme anxiety" (Mead & Bateson, 1942). Time is just as important in single-encounter work in a hospital emergency room as it is in group work or long-term psychotherapy (Budman, Gurman & Wachtel, 2002).

In many instances, the use of time is determined by the organization or funding source. For example, policy may determine the duration of a session, how many sessions a client may be seen, or the number of days a patient is hospitalized. The critical question is how best to use the time that you have (Budman, 1995). Time is also an important dimension of contract. No matter who determines duration, using time to structure the relationship, and having the client participate in the structure, aids the work.

Strategies and interventions

Strategies and interventions refer to the selection of particular methods of care that are most appropriate for specific clients in particular situations (Kerson, 2002). In every situation, the social worker makes decisions about the ways the client can best be helped. These decisions involve choices about orientation, modality, technique, and intervention. To some degree, choice of strategies and interventions relates to definition of client and client unit. Thus, designating an individual as the client might indicate that one would do individual work, while designating the family as the client would indicate family work. However, the more general decision to work with a certain client unit opens the possibility for a plethora of decisions regarding particular theoretical orientations such as a psychodynamic, cognitive, or behavioral approach. Such orientations often reflect beliefs and world views of the social worker, which may relate little to particular client problems. For example, because it is common in our society to believe that elderly people are not amenable to psychodynamic work, these approaches are unusual in work with the elderly; yet programs for the elderly report excellent work that is sometimes entirely psychodynamic or, at other times, in combination with case management (Choi & Kimbell, 2009; Hill & Brettle, 2006). This practice decision reminds social workers to choose treatment modalities that reflect needs and goals of clients rather than their own world view or beliefs.

The choice of a particular theoretical orientation and treatment modality brings one to decisions regarding use of specific techniques or interventions, such as ritual, or narrative therapy (Laird, 2000). These techniques bring a theoretical model to life. Monitoring their use offers the social worker another way to assess ongoing work because strategies such as these tend to have specified outcomes. At times, interventions are different from ones that had been anticipated because a client's needs may be redefined as the work progresses. Social workers must be clear about how their preferred theoretical orientation and skill set meet the needs of the client. Treatment method is also sometimes determined by dimensions of context such as organization or funding policy. For example, one facility may extol a particular form of family therapy to treat an illness such as bulimia and another may use a specific form of individual therapy to treat the same illness. These choices arise from differing beliefs about etiology or cure or both.

At times, the nature of the illness or disability affects the choice of modality (Desselle & Proctor, 2000). For example, an illness or disability that leaves an individual physically dependent, such as advanced rheumatoid arthritis or emphysema, may require that the social worker work with family members as well as the ill person. In the case of advanced Alzheimer's disease or with a seriously ill infant, the social worker may work only with family members.

Case or care management

One modality that has resumed its important place in social work practice is case or care management, which is sometimes referred to as advanced or intensive case management

(Buck & Alexander, 2005; Coffey, 2003). The expression "care management" seems to be more palatable to clients because the word "case" suggests to some that they are passive in the role, without voice or full participation. Developed for client groups such as the frail elderly, chronically mentally ill, the developmentally disabled and foster children, this modality is one response to the complexity of service delivery systems (Cambridge, 2008; Casado *et al.*, 2008; Selander & Marnetoft, 2005). It rests on notions of comprehensiveness, a full array of services, on longitudinality (service over a relatively long period of time), and on a special, dependable, therapeutic relationship with another individual (Bedell, Cohen & Sullivan, 2000; Naleppa & Reid, 2000). It can be used to organize the services of an entire agency, a national program of immense proportions, or a single caseload; but, properly defined, case management should never exclude clinical work. In fact, case management is both a concept and a process. One can view it as a system of relationships between direct service providers, administrators, funders and clients. However, it is also an orderly, planned provision of a range of services that are directed at a specific problem area and are intended to help clients function as normally as possible within their communities (Gursansky, Harvey & Kennedy, 2003).

There are many approaches to case management as a strategy or intervention for the social work practitioner (Ferry & Abramson, 2005; Hall *et al.*, 2002; Manfred-Gilham, Sales & Koeske, 2002). These approaches vary in terms of the direct involvement of the social worker. They range from a brokering role, in which the social worker links clients to services, advocates for clients, and monitors client activities, to clinical or advanced case management, in which the managers act as primary therapists as well as monitors, advocates, and brokers. In these latter positions, the social workers carry a great deal of authority in the system of services that the client requires. Clinical case managers often work in teams, especially when working with clients with serious and persistent chronic illness; nevertheless the special one-to-one relationship of clinical case manager and patient continues to be paramount. Case management has a special appeal to managed care approaches because such services are generally based in the community rather than in institutions, and they can serve a utilization review function if given the authority to approve or deny services to prevent their unreasonable or unnecessary use.

Integrative, pragmatic and eclectic approaches

Practitioners generally suggest that their approaches are integrative, pragmatic and eclectic. They do what they must depending on the circumstances, needs, and capabilities of their clients, and they tend to draw from many modalities and techniques (Lundy, 2008; Pavlek, 2008). Sometimes it is difficult to distinguish between style of the social worker and choice of treatment modality. Those who are more comfortable in a listening/supporting mode may report their orientation as psychoanalytic. Those who are highly structured and/or directive may say they use short-term solution-focused work or a task-oriented approach. In some ways, this is like self-typecasting. One plays the ingénue or bad guy because it is comfortable. Again, the allusion to an art form is meant to underscore the notion that conscious decisions about modality are ideally based on the client need, rather than the style of the social worker.

Stance of the social worker

Stance of the social worker is closest to the old-fashioned term "conscious use of self," which is an understanding of one's self, motivations, place in, and impact on relationships. It implies that the social worker has sufficient self-awareness, experience, and discipline to be able to choose how to behave in a particular client situation. Unlike some other practice decisions shared with the client, the social worker is totally responsible for this choice. Experience and self-awareness provide the social worker greater mastery of stance so that, within realistic limits, the social worker can be what the client and situation need him or her to be. Just as an actor learns to assume a role, the social worker adapts and refines his or her stance according to the needs of the client situation.

Some elements of stance are the worker's degree of activity or passivity, amount of advice-giving, use of authority, self-disclosure, and touch (Goffman, 1961a, 1961b). Other elements such as transference and counter-transference, prejudices, and false assumptions (which may support action that is different from the needs of the client situation) are part of the stance of the social worker as well (Farnham, 2008; Friedman, 2008; Thomas, 2008).

Use of outside resources

Outside resources are the services used by client and social worker that are outside of the relationship, often external to the agency, and that further the work of the relationship (Dawson & Berry, 2002). These services can range from the protective work of a state or county child welfare or aging agency, to assistance with obtaining an apartment, walker, or prosthesis, to referral to a mutual aid group. Determination of the client's ability to broker his or her own services is an issue in the use of outside resources. Sometimes, the client and/or family can grow stronger by managing outside resources themselves; in some instances, the social worker can enhance the relationship by arranging services; and, at other times, the social worker must procure outside resources because the client/family is unable to manage.

Mapping devices: ecomaps and organigraphs

We have encouraged case chapter authors to include a mapping device that sets out the ecological system in which they are working and draws the boundaries that define a lifespace (Hartman, 1978; Iversen, Gergen & Fairbanks, 2005; Kerson, 2002). Such representations are useful for assessment, evaluation, and helping clients to set priorities and make decisions about altering relationships with individuals and organizations. One can present very complicated relationships on a single page, giving client and social worker some sense of control of a situation. Many chapters have chosen to use ecomaps, others have sought a more specific drawing tool, and some use no mapping device.

In the ecomap, a large center circle generally includes the client's nuclear family, with circles surrounding that one representing people and organizations with whom the client interacts. In this book, a strong relationship is drawn as an unbroken line. The flow of energy is either depicted as going back and forth between both parties, with an arrow at either end, or as going from only one to the other, with an arrow pointing at the party who is receiving the energy. A tenuous relationship is depicted as a light, broken line, while a stressful relationship is drawn as a heavy, broken line. A circle with a name in it and no line drawn to it means that there is no relationship between the client and the person or agency named in the circle. Like a snapshot, an ecomap captures a static moment in the client's life. Updated regularly, the map suggests the direction of the work, can demonstrate progress, and can be used for evaluation. On p. 16 is an example drawn from Patricia Findley's chapter, "Returning veterans, traumatic brain injury, and Veterans' Administration services: A War Related Illness and Injury Study Center."

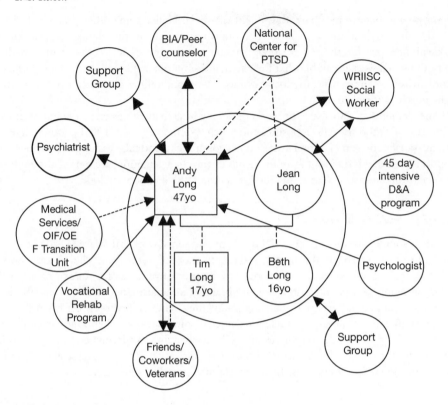

Figure 1.1 Illustrative ecomap.

Reassessment

Reassessment presents an opportunity for social worker and client to evaluate their work during the course of the relationship. Like artists, they are asked to step back from their work and examine it. Reassessment is the process of re-examining the dimensions of the framework as well as other issues that participants have deemed important. It can be made part of the pattern of each meeting or set aside to be brought into the work at certain intervals. The technique can be as simple as discussing how the work is going, or as sophisticated as using standardized measures of success (Fischer & Corcoran, 2007). Also, reassessment can be a way to reactivate a stalled relationship or to slow one that seems to be speeding along almost out of control. Schwartz's questions, "Are we working?" and "What are we working on?" are helpful here (Schwartz & Zalba, 1971). Finally, reassessment provides the social worker an opportunity to assess and obtain feedback about his or her performance.

Transfer or termination

Transfer and termination mark the end of the relationship between client and social worker. After this occurence they will not be meeting in this way any longer (Baum, 2007). Goffman notes that greetings and farewells are ritual displays that mark a change in degree of access (Goffman, 1972). Now, social worker and client will not have the same kind of access to each other as they would have had if the work continued. Ideally, termination is a decision that social worker and client make together because goals have been accomplished and their work is finished. Often, when clients terminate before the social worker is ready, it is because the client has perceived work more positively than the social worker has (Mirabito, 2006). Even when the client wants to terminate before the social worker thinks work is finished, it is important to end the relationship positively so that the client may return to the agency (or to another one) if he or she needs further help (Gelman *et al.*, 2007; Siebold, 2007). Sometimes, termination signals the end of the relationship between client and agency. At other times, the social worker is leaving the organization, and the client will continue with another social worker. Vacations also evoke issues about termination. Often a difficult period, termination has great potential for growth through the use of the relationship and review of gains that the client has made during the work. Termination work can also identify potential hazards to maintaining the client's goal accomplishment.

Case conclusion

Conclusion refers primarily to outcome and current functioning of the client. Client and social worker summarize their work together so that each can leave the relationship with knowledge of accomplishments. In addition, they finish in a positive manner that will allow the client to seek help again, if necessary.

Differential discussion

In a differential discussion, all of the previous framework decisions are reviewed in order for the social worker to analyze his or her work. Differential discussion allows the social worker to be a "Monday morning quarterback," that is, to look back on the case to decide which elements would remain the same the next time he or she worked with a client with similar capacity, personality, and problems. Differential discussion encourages the social worker to generalize from a specific client to a category of like cases with which he or she can use similar structure and techniques. It also reinforces evaluation as a routine part of practice. In retrospect, the social worker may decide he or she was too confrontational with a client, the coldness of the meeting place might have been a detriment, or the client may have been asked to coordinate more resources than he or she was able to manage. Emphasis on the social worker's ability to (1) generalize from a particular case and (2) alter elements in the relationship between social worker and client makes differential discussion the most useful dimension of the framework. This step moves the social worker out of the present relationship and on to the next. This resembles Kaplan and Norton's discussion of closed loop management systems in which one begins with strategy and ends with a test and adaptation process (Kaplan & Norton, 2008).

Practice in context

A review of the overarching conception of practice in context brings the framework full circle. Constraints on the setting, the influence that these constraints have had on the relationship, and the series of decisions that determine the structure of the relationship enable social workers to map their work and, as a result, enhance action. This review also helps to identify areas of advocacy and social action for the social worker (Freddolino, Moxley & Hyduk, 2004).

Using the framework described above, *Social Work in Health Settings* acts as a casebook, a collection of real cases in settings described by, and reflecting the style of, each experienced social work practitioner. Altogether, 31 health settings are examples of the great range of

Table 1.1 Practice-in-context template

Differential Discussion Practice in Context Grid

CONTEXT

	Change	How
Policy		
Technology		
Organization		

PRACTICE DECISIONS

	Change	How
Definition of the Client		
Goals/Objectives/Outcome Measures		
Use of Contract		
Meeting Place		
Use of Time		
Strategies and Interventions		
Stance of the Social Worker		
Use of Outside Resources		
Reassessment		
Transfer or Termination		

health-related social work activity. Each setting article follows the practice-in-context framework as its outline. The case chapters are organized in two sections: (1) individual and family (beginning with maternal and child health, then children and adolescents, adults, and the elderly), and (2) group, program and advocacy foci.

Ideally, the format for this book would be a three-ringed notebook in which case/setting articles and dimensions of context and practice could be arranged and rearranged for teaching purposes. One could then use these case/settings to discuss issues around settings and populations, such as short-term and long-term care; institutional and home care; physical and mental health; services for children, adults, and the elderly; or trauma and disease. In addition, one can examine a particular practice decision, such as use of contract or stance of the social worker, across 31 practice settings. Overall, *Social Work in Health Settings* has one primary purpose: to help social workers to clarify and explicate practice in context in order to best ply their craft.

The chapters that follow are generally written in the first person, although some chapters have multiple authors. This format was used to enhance the notion that the practitioner is speaking about his or her work. The names of all clients and some organizations have been changed in order to preserve confidentiality, and, in some cases, this is true for the names of institutions and systems, as well.

Overall themes from the case chapters

Just as the practice-in-context framework is circular, so is this chapter since I conclude my introduction with themes that I have drawn from reading all of the case chapters. The central theme is that of "lending a vision," holding out hope for an individual, family, program, or advocacy effort that others misunderstand, undervalue or think is impossible to attain. To do this, social workers have to motivate clients, and sometimes clients' families, to share the vision and objectives in order to further the work. They also have to remain flexible, altering their views about the definition of the client, where the work can happen, who can be included, and what the timeframe is. In addition, they understand that they have to enlist the help of other professionals, organizations, friends and family members in order to make things happen or, sometimes, to protect the client. They are careful not to "claim turf," but to encourage all helpers who can contribute to the client's goals. This notion unites social workers no matter what the context.

A second, closely related theme is the incredible persistence and tenacity of the social workers in helping their clients to reach their goals. It seems as if social workers never give up. Associated with this is the idea of boundary spanning; being willing to view the larger picture and, on behalf of the client, go beyond what may be written in one's job description. This particular theme means sometimes taking two kinds of risks: (1) becoming personally involved and then having to find a way to step back, and/or (2) stepping into zones of authority where others may think that one doesn't belong. The first risk reaffirms how much social workers in all contexts must remain self-aware and involve team members in their work. The second underscores the importance of understanding how policies and formal and informal elements of systems and organization inform one's work. Thus, to be excellent boundary spanners and advocates, these case examples show that social workers must understand themselves and the systems in which they work. In turn, this relates to the chapter authors' very proud view of their own institutions. In general, they are drawn to the mission and work of each of their organizations. When this is not the case, when the mission or value system of the organization differs from the social worker's, the work becomes even more difficult and much less satisfying.

Another theme has to do with the overall relationship of social work practice to technology. The chapter authors embrace the many kinds of technology that enhance the lives of their clients; however, those innovations that allow clients to live longer but do not necessarily guarantee life-quality raise ethical and moral dilemmas for them. Perhaps social workers are especially concerned with these dilemmas because they are concerned with their clients' functional capacity, the course of their disease or disability and how their clients will be able to manage their lives. Further, social workers are often in the position of providing support to clients when the "promise" of technology provides uncertainty rather than clear prognosis.

In addition, the authors demonstrate not only professionalism and persistence but humility. They often choose to write about very difficult cases with whom they may have worked differently if they had been able to begin again. This affirms the place of the differential discussion at the end of every case. In their differential discussion, social workers evaluate each case in terms of what they would keep the same and what they would do differently when they encounter similar situations. Chapter authors critically and thoughtfully consider their creative use of each practice decision, including flexing their professional boundaries.

Each case chapter has affirmed the utility of the practice-in-context framework. The context of social work in health care has three primary dimensions: policy, technology, and organization. Together these elements provide parameters for the practice decisions that social workers and clients make to determine the structure of their work. In sum, a large measure of the art of social work is the ability to structure the relationship between social worker and client in ways that maximally support the work. Thus, another critical theme that emerges in every chapter is the power of relationship to support, advocate for, expand options of, and make a difference in the life of the client. Relationship is the ultimate area of expertise, the catalyst through which adaptation and change can happen for clients. With superb relationship skills, anything is possible.

References

Aaron, H. J. (2007). It's health care stupid! Why control of health care spending is vital for long-term fiscal stability. In Little, J. S. (ed.). *Wanting it all: The challenge of reforming the U.S. health care system* (pp. 183–206). Boston: Federal Reserve Bank of Boston.

Abramson, J. S. & Mizrahi, T. (2003). Understanding collaboration between social workers and physicians: Application of a typology. *Social Work in Health Care*, 37 (2): 71–100.

Anderlik, M. R. (2001). *The ethics of managed care: A pragmatic approach*. Bloomington: Indiana University Press.

Arrow, K., Auerbach, A., Bertko, J., Brownlee, S., Casalino, L. P., Cooper J., *et al.* (2009). Toward a twenty-first century health care system: Recommendations for health care reform. *Annals of Internal Medicine*, 150 (7): 493–499.

Austin, M. J., Brody, R. P. & Packard, T. (2009). *Managing the challenges in human service organizations: A casebook*. Thousand Oaks: Sage.

Banach, M. (2000). Influences on decision making in child welfare. *Journal of Law and Social Work*, 10 (1, 2): 143–63.

Barr, D. A. (2007). *Introduction to U.S. health policy: The organization, financing, and delivery of health care in America*. Baltimore: Johns Hopkins University Press.

Barr, D. A. (2008). *Health disparities in the United States: Social class, race, ethnicity and health*. Baltimore: Johns Hopkins University Press.

Bateson, G. (nd). *The natural history of an interview*. Unpublished manuscript.

Bateson, G. (1975). *Steps to an ecology of mind*. New York: Ballantine.

Baum, N. (2007). Therapists' responses to treatment termination: An inquiry into the variables that contribute to therapists' experiences. *Clinical Social Work Journal*, 35 (2): 97–106.

Bedell, J. R., Cohen, N. L. & Sullivan, A. (2000). Case management: The current best practices and the next generation of innovation. *Community Mental Health Journal*, 36 (2): 179–94.

Beder, J. (1998). The home visit revisited. *Families in Society*, 79 (5): 514–21.

Beresford, P., Croft, S. & Adshead, L. (2007). 'We don't see her as a social worker': A service user case study of the importance of the social worker's relationship and humanity. *British Journal of Social Work*, 38 (7): 1388–1407.

Berman-Rossi, T. (ed.). (1994). *The collected writings of William Schwartz*. Itasca: F. E. Peacock Publishers.

Blank, R. H. & Borau, V. (2007). *Comparative health policy* (2nd ed.). New York: Palgrave Macmillan.

Bodenheimer, T. S. & Grumbach, K. (2009). *Understanding health policy: A clinical approach*. (5th ed.). New York: McGrawMedical.

Bolen, R. M. & Hall, J. C. (2007). Managed care and evidence-based practice: The untold story. *Journal of Social Work Education*, 43 (3): 463–79.

Bransford, C. L. (2005). Conceptions of authority within contemporary social work practice in managed mental health care organizations. *American Journal of Orthopsychiatry*, 75 (3): 409–20.

Brett, J., Behfar, K. & Kern, M. C. (2006). Managing cultural teams. *Harvard Business Review*, (November): 84–91.

Bronstein, L. R. & Abramson, J. S. (2003). Understanding socialization of teachers and social workers: Groundwork for collaboration in the schools. *Families in Society*, 84 (3): 323–30.

Brorson, K. (2005). The culture of a home visit in family intervention. *Journal of Early Childhood Research*, 3 (1): 51–76.

Budman, S. (ed.). (1995). *Forms of brief therapy* (2nd ed.). New York: Guilford Press.

Budman, S. H., Gurman, A. S. & Wachtel, P. L. (2002). *Theory and practice of brief therapy* (3rd ed.). New York: Guilford Press.

Buck, P. & Alexander, L. B. (2005). Neglected voices: Consumers with serious mental illness speak out about intensive case management. *Administration and Policy in Mental Health and Mental Health Services Research*, 33 (4): 470–81.

Burke, R. J. & Cooper, C. L. (2008). *Building more effective organizations: HR management and performance in practice*. Cambridge, MA: Cambridge University Press.

Buyx, A. M. (2008). Personal responsibility for health as a rationing criterion. Why we don't like it and why we should. *Journal of Medical Ethics*, 34 (12): 871–4.

Callahan, D. & Wasunna, A. (2006). *Medicine and the market: Equity vs. choice*. Baltimore: Johns Hopkins University Press.

Cambridge, P. (2008). The case for a new 'case' management in services for people with learning disabilities. *British Journal of Social Work*, 38 (1): 91–116.

Casado, B. L., Quijano, L. M., Stanley, M. A., Cully, J. A., Steinberg, E. H. & Wilson, N. L. (2008). Healthy IDEAS: Implementation of a depression program through community-based case management. *The Gerontologist*, 48 (6): 828–38.

Choi, N. G. & Kimbell, K. (2009). Depression care need among low-income older adults: Views from agency service providers and family care givers. *Clinical Gerontologist*, 32 (1): 60–76.

Clark, E. (2009, April). Clinical social workers have clinical expertise that would be an asset in the development of the *DSM-V. NASW News*, 5.

Coffey, D. S. (2003). Connection and autonomy in the case management relationship. *Psychiatric Rehabilitation Journal*, 26 (4): 404–12.

Cox, J. (1999). The role of social work in policy practice. In Daley, J. G. (ed.), *Social work practice in the military* (pp. 165–77). New York: Haworth.

Dawson, K. & Berry, M. (2002). Engaging families in child welfare services: An evidence-based approach to best practices. *Child Welfare*, 81 (2): 293–317.

Denis, M. & Clancy, C. M. (2006). *Ethical dimensions of health policy*. New York: Oxford University Press.

Desselle, D. & Proctor, T. (2000). Advocating for the elderly hard-of-hearing population: The deaf people we ignore. *Social Work*, 45 (3): 277–81.

Dickson, D. (2004). *Law in the health and human services: A guide for social workers, psychologists, psychiatrists and related professionals*. New York: The Free Press.

Drach-Zahavy, A. & Baron-Epel, O. (2006). Health promotion teams' effectiveness: A structural perspective from Israel. *Health Promotion International*, 21 (3): 181–90.

Drucker, P. (1990). *Managing the non-profit organization: Practices and principles*. New York: HarperCollins.

Drumm, R. D., McCoy, H. V. & Lemon, A. (2003). Technology trauma: Barriers to increasing technology utilization. *Social Work in Health Care*, 37 (4): 39–56.

Ehrenhof, D. W. (2009). Options for controlling the costs & increasing the efficiency of health care. Washington, DC: CBO Testimony. Retrieved 5/5/09, from http://cbo.gov/ftdocs/100xx/doc10016/Testimony1.1.shtml

Emlet, C. A. & Poindexter, C. C. (2004). Unserved, unseen and unheard: Integrating programs for HIV-infected and HIV-affected older adults. *Health and Social Work*, 29 (2): 86–95.

Epstein, S. (2008). Patient groups and health movements. In Hackett, E. J., Amsterdamska, O., Lynch, M. & Wajcman, J. (eds.). *The handbook of science and technology studies* (3rd ed., pp. 499–539). Cambridge, MA: The MIT Press.

Farnham, B. C. (2008). When professionals weep: Emotional and counter transference responses in end-of-life care. *Journal of Social Work in End-of-Life Palliative Care*, 4 (1): 79–81.

Ferguson, H. (2008). Liquid social work: Welfare interventions as mobile practices. *British Journal of Social Work*, 38 (3): 561–79.

Ferry, J. L. & Abramson, J. S. (2005). Toward understanding the clinical aspects of geriatric case management. *Social Work in Health Care*, 42 (1): 35–56.

Fischer, J. (2009). Childbirth at a crossroads: Advocacy and support for childbearing families. Presented at "Liberty and Justice for All: Perinatal Social Workers Promoting Care Choices and Equity," the annual conference of the National Association of Perinatal Social Workers, Philadelphia, PA.

Fischer, J. & Corcoran, K. (2007). *Measures for clinical practice*. New York: Oxford University Press.

Freddolino, P. P., Moxley, D. P. & Hyduk, C. A. (2004). A differential model of advocacy in social work practice. *Families in Society*, 85 (1): 119–28.

French, W. H. & Bell, C. H. (2005). *Organization development and transformation: Managing effective change* (6th ed). New York: McGrawHill/Irwin.

Friedman, F. B. (2008). Borderline personality disorder and hospitalization. *Social Work in Mental Health*, 6 (1–2): 67–84.

Gelman, C. R., Fernandez, P., Hausman, N., Miller, S. & Weiner, M. (2007). Challenging endings: First year M.S.W. interns' experiences with forced termination and discussion points for supervisory guidance. *Clinical Social Work Journal*, 35 (2): 79–90.

Globerman, J., White, J. J., Mullings, D. & Davis, J. M. (2003). Thriving in program management environments: The case of social work in hospitals. *Social Work in Health Care*, 38 (1): 1–18.

Goffman, E. (1959). *Presentation of self in everyday life*. New York: Doubleday.

Goffman, E, (1961a). *Asylums: Essays on the social situation of mental patients and other inmates*. New York: Doubleday & Co.

Goffman, E. (1961b). *Encounters: Two studies in the sociology of interaction*. New York: Macmillan.

Goffman, E. (1966). *Behavior in public places*. New York: The Free Press.

Goffman, E (1972). *Relations in public*. New York: Harper and Row.

Goffman, E. (1981). *Interaction ritual: Essays in face to face behavior*. New York: Pantheon.

Golensky, M. & Mulder, C. (2006). Coping in a constrained environment: Survival strategies of nonprofit human organizations. *Administration in Social Work*, 30 (3): 5–24.

Goyen, M. & Debatin, J. F. (2009). Health care costs for new technologies. *European Journal of Medical Molecular Imaging*, 39 (Suppli. 3): 139–43.

Gray, V., Lowery, D. & Godwin, E. K. (2007). The political management of managed care: Explaining variations in state health maintenance organization regulations. *Journal of Health Politics, Policy and Law*, 32 (2): 457–96.

Gursansky, D., Harvey, J. & Kennedy, R. (2003). *Case management: Policy, practice and professional business*. New York: Columbia University Press.

Hall, J. A., Carswell, C., Walsh, E., Huber, D. L. & Jampoler, J. S. (2002). Iowa case management: Innovative social casework. *Social Work*, 47 (2): 132–41.

Handel, G. (2009). *Social welfare in western society*. New Brunswick, NJ: Transaction.

Harris, G. (2008). *Dynamics of social welfare policy: Right vs. left*. Lanham, M.D.: Rowman & Littlefield.

Hartman, A. (1978). Diagrammatic assessment of family relationships. *Social Casework*, 59 (8): 465–76.

Hartman, A. & Laird, J. (1983). *Family-centered social work practice*. New York: Free Press.

Heiney, S. P., McWayne, J., Walker, S., Bryant, L. H., Howell, C. D. & Bridges, L. (2003). Evaluation of a therapeutic group by telephone for women with breast cancer. *Journal of Psychosocial Oncology*, 21 (3): 63–80.

Hill, A. & Brettle, A. (2006). Counseling older people: What can we learn from research evidence? *Journal of Social Work Practice*, 20 (3): 281–97.

HIPAA (Health Insurance Portability and Accountability Act of 1996 Privacy Rule). Retrieved 3/17/09, from http://www.hhs.gov.ocr/privacy/index.html

Holden, G. (2009). Information for Practice (IP). Retrieved 6/3/09, from http://blogs.nyu.edu/socialwork/ip/

Hossain, P., Kawar, B. & Nahas, M. E. (2007). Obesity and diabetes in the developing world—A growing challenge. *New England Journal of Medicine*, 356 (3): 213–15.

Hurley, R. E. & Zuckerman, S. (2003). Medicaid managed care: State flexibility in action. In Holahan, J., Weil, A. & Weiner, J. M. (eds.). *Federalism & health policy* (pp. 215–48). Washington: The Urban Institute Press.

Iglehart, J. K. (1992). The American health care system: Managed care. *New England Journal of Medicine*, 327: 742–7.

Iglehart, J. K. (2007). Medicaid revisited—Skirmishes over a vast public enterprise. *New England Journal of Medicine*, 356 (7): 734–40.

Information for Practice. Retrieved 4/8/09, from http://www.nyu.edu/socialwork/ip/

Institute of Medicine (2001). *Crossing the quality chasm*. Washington: National Academy Press.

Iversen, R. R., Gergen, K. & Fairbanks, R. P. II (2005). Assessment & social construction: Conflict & Co-creation? *British Journal of Social Work*, 35 (5): 689–708.

Ivery, J. M. (2007). Organizational ecology: A theoretical framework for examining collaborative partnerships. *Administration in Social Work*, 31 (4): 7–19.

Jasanoff, S. (2008). Making order: Law and science in action. In Hackett, E. J., Amsterdamska, O., Lynch, M. & Wajcman, J. (eds.). *The handbook of science and technology studies* (3rd ed., pp. 761–86). Cambridge: The MIT Press.

Jonsson, L. E. (2005). Home, women and children: Social services home visits in postwar Sweden. *Home Cultures*, 2 (2): 153–73.

Kanani, K. & Regehr, C. (2003). Clinical, ethical & legal issues in E-therapy. *Families in Society*, 84 (2): 155–62.

Kaplan, R. S. & Norton, D. P. (2008). Mastering the management system. *Harvard Business Review*, (January): 63–77.

Kawacki, I., Daniels, N. & Robinson, D. (2005). Health disparities by race and class: Why both matter. *Health Affairs*, 24 (2): 343–52.

Kerson, T. S. (1980). *Medical social work: The pie-professional paradox*. New York: Irvington.

Kerson, T. S. (1985a). Responsiveness to need: Social work's impact on health care. *Health and Social Work*, 10 (4): 300–7.

Kerson, T. S. (1985b). *Understanding chronic illness: The medical and psychosocial dimensions of nine diseases*. New York: The Free Press.

Kerson, T. S. (2002). *Boundary spanning: An ecological reinterpretation of social work practice in health and mental health systems*. New York: Columbia University Press.

Kerson, T. S. & McCoyd, J. L. M. (2002). The power of the relationship between the social worker and the client system. In Kerson, T. S. *Boundary spanning: An ecological reinterpretation of social work practice in health and mental health systems* (pp. 143–198). New York: Columbia University Press.

Kitchen, A. & Brock, J. (2005). Social work at the heart of the medical team. *Social Work in Health Care*, 40 (4): 1–18.

Laird, J. (2000). Theorizing culture: Narrative ideas and practice principles. *Journal of Feminist Family Therapy*, 11 (4): 99–114.

Lens, V. (2002). Managed care and the judicial system: Another avenue for reform? *Health & Social Work*, 27 (1): 27–35.

Levenson, J. (2004). *The secret epidemic: The story of AIDS and black America*. New York: Pantheon Books.

Little, J. (2007). (ed.).*Wanting it all: The challenge of reforming the U.S. health care system*. Boston, MA: Federal Reserve Bank of Boston. http://www.bos.frb.org

Lukas, C. V., Holmes, S. K., Cohen, A. B., Restuccia, J., Cramer, I. E., Shwartz, M. & Charns, M. P. (2007). Transformational change in health care systems: An organizational model. *Health Care Management Review*, 32 (4): 309–20.

Lundy, M. (2008). An integrative model for social work practice: A multi-systemic, multi-theoretical approach. *Families in Society*, 89 (3): 394–406.

MacKenzie, R., Capuano, T., Dunshin, L. D., Stern, G. & Burke, J. B. (2008). Growing organizational capacity through a systems approach: One health network's experience. *The Joint Commission Journal on Quality and Patient Safety*, 34 (2): 63–73.

Managed Care (2009). Retrieved on 5/15/09, from http://www.nlm.nih.gov/medlineplus/managedcare .html

Manfred-Gilham, J. J., Sales, E. & Koeske, G. (2002). Therapist and case manager perceptions of client barriers to treatment participation and use of engagement strategies. *Community Mental Health Journal*, 38 (3): 213–21.

Mas, N. & Seinfeld, J. (2008). Is managed care restraining the adoption of technology by hospitals? *Journal of Health Economics*, 27 (4): 1026–45.

Matusitz, J. & Breen, G. M. (2008). E-health: A new kind of telemedicine. *Social Work in Public Health*, 23 (1): 95–113.

Mayes, R. & Berenson, R. A. (2007). *Medicare prospective payment and the shaping of U.S. health care*. Baltimore: The Johns Hopkins University Press.

McCarty, D. & Clancy, C. (2002). Telehealth: Implications for social work. *Social Work*, 47 (2): 153–61.

McClelland, M. & Rivlin, A. M. (2009). *Building a healthier America*. Retrieved 4/30/09, from http:// buildingahealthieramerica.com

Mead, M. & Bateson, G. (1942). *Balinese character*. New York: Academy of Sciences.

Mechanic, D. (2004). Policy challenges in addressing racial disparities and improving population health. *Health Affairs*, 24 (2): 335–42.

Meyer, C. (1976). *Social work practice*. New York: The Free Press.

Meyer, C. (1983). Selecting important practice methods. In A. Rosenblatt & D. Waldfogel (eds.), *Handbook of clinical social work* (pp. 731–49). San Francisco: Jossey-Bass.

Miller, E. A. & West, D. M. (2009). Where's the revolution?: Digital technology & health care in the internet age. *Journal of Health Politics & Law*, 34 (2): 261–84.

Mirabito, D. M. (2006). Revisiting unplanned termination: Clinicians' perceptions of termination from adolescent mental health treatment. *Families in Society*, 87 (2): 171–80.

Mohr, D. C., Hart, S. L., Fonareva, I. & Tasch, I. S. (2006). Treatment of depression for patients with multiple sclerosis in neurology clinics. *Multiple Sclerosis*, 12 (2): 204–8.

Moody, H. R. (2004). Hospital discharge planning: Carrying out orders? *Journal of Gerontological Social Work*, 43 (1): 107–18.

Morris, J. (2003). The home visit in family therapy. *Journal of Family Psychotherapy*, 14 (3): 95–9.

Morrison, E. E. & Monagle, J. F. (2009). *Health care ethics: Critical issues for the 21st century*. Sudbury: Jones & Bartlett.

Naleppa, M. J. & Reid, W. J. (2000). Integrating case management and brief-treatment strategies: A hospital-based geriatric program. *Social Work in Health Care*, 32 (4): 1–23.

Neuman, K. M. & Ptak, M. (2003). Managing managed care through accreditation standards. *Social Work*, 48 (3): 384–91.

Neumann, P. J., Jacobson, P. D. & Palmer, J. A. (2008). Measuring the value of public health systems: The disconnect between health economists and public health practitioners. *American Journal of Public Health*, 98 (12): 2173–80.

Oberlander, J. (2003). *The political life of Medicare*. Chicago: University of Chicago Press.

Paris, R. (2008). "For the dream of being there … " Voices of immigrant mothers in a home visiting program. *American Journal of Orthopsychiatry*, 78 (2): 141–151.

Paris, R., Gemborys, M., Kaufman, P. H. & Whitehill, D. (2007). Reaching isolated new mothers: Insights from a home visiting program using paraprofessionals. *Families in Society*, 88 (4): 616–26.

Parker-Oliver, D. & Demiris, G. (2006). Social work informatics: A new specialty. *Social Work*, 51 (2): 127–34.

Pauly, M. V. (2007). It's technology (and what it is or isn't worth), stupid. Comments on Aaron's, "It's health care stupid! Why control of health care spending is vital for long-term fiscal stability." In Little, J. S. (ed.). *Wanting it all: The challenge of reforming the U.S. health care system* (pp. 207–12). Boston: Federal Reserve Bank of Boston.

Pavlek, M. (2008). Paining out: An integrative pain therapy model. *Clinical Social Work Journal*, 36 (4): 385–393.

Pecukonis, E. V., Cornelius, L. & Parrish, M. (2003). The future of health social work. *Social Work in Health Care*, 37 (3): 1–15.

Perlman, H. H. (1979). *Relationship, the heart of helping people*. Chicago: The University of Chicago Press.

Preston, M. S. (2004). Mandating management training for newly hired child welfare supervisors: A divergence between management research and training practice. *Administration in Social Work*, 28 (2): 81–95.

Rosenthal Gelman, C. & Tosone, C. (2008). Teaching social workers to harness technology and interdisciplinary collaboration for community service. *British Journal of Social Work.* Retrieved 6/2/09, from http://www.bjsw/oxfordjournals.org

Sandberg, J. (2008). *Managing understanding in organizations.* Thousand Oaks: Sage.

Santhiveeran, J. (2009). Compliance of social work e-therapy websites to the NASW Code of Ethics. *Social Work in Health Care,* 48 (1): 1–13.

Santhiveeran, J. & Grant, B. (2005). Use of communication tools and fee-setting in e-therapy: A website survey. *Social Work in Mental Health,* 4 (2): 33–47.

Serafini, J. D., Damianakis, T. & Marziali, E. (2007). Clinical practice standards and ethical issues applied to a virtual group intervention for spousal caregivers of people with Alzheimer's. *Social Work in Health Care,* 44 (3): 225–43.

Schwartz, J. & Weiner, M. B. (2003). Finding meaning in medical necessity. *Social Work,* 48 (3): 392–400.

Schwartz, W. & Zalba, S. (eds.). (1971). *The Practice of Group Work.* New York: Columbia University Press.

Selander, J. & Marnetoft, S. U. (2005). Case management in vocational rehabilitation. *Work,* 24 (3). Retrieved on 4/25/09, from http://iospress.metapress.com/content/yaqbubnkvd00dfxx

Siebold, C. (2007). Everytime we say goodbye: Forced termination revisited, A commentary. *Clinical Social Work Journal,* 33 (2): 91–5.

Sfiligoj, H. (2009, April). New technology transforming profession: Evolving tools are changing how social workers and their clients communicate. *NASW News:* 4.

Smith, D. G. & Moore, J. D., (2008). *Medicaid, politics and policy.* New Brunswick: Transactions Publishers.

Social workers introduce hospice credential (2009). Retrieved 5/1/09, from http://www.socialwkers.org/pressroom/2008/110408.asp

Solheim, K., McElmurry, B. J. & Kim, M. J. (2007). Multidisciplinary teamwork in United States primary health care. *Social Science & Medicine,* 65 (3): 622–34.

Spitz, B. (2007). Medicaid agencies as managed care organizations: An "actuarially sound" solution? *Journal of Health Politics, Policy and Law,* 32 (2): 379–414.

Starr, P. (2000). Health care reform and the new economy. *Health Affairs,* 19 (6): 23–32.

Steinbrook, R. (2009). Health care and the American Recovery & Reinvestment Act. *New England Journal of Medicine,* 360 (11): 1057–60.

Stevens, R. A., Rosenberg, C. E. & Burns, L. R. (eds.). (2006). *Healing & health policy in the United States: Putting the past back in.* New Brunswick: Rutgers University Press.

Sturm, R. (2002). The effects of obesity, smoking and drinking on medical problems and costs. *Health Affairs,* 21 (2): 245–54.

Thomas, B. (2008). Seeing and being seen: Courage and the therapist in cross-racial treatment. *Psychoanalytic Social Work,* 15 (1): 60–8.

Tjora, A. H. & Scambler, G. (2009). Square pegs in round holes: Information systems, hospitals and the significance of contextual awareness. *Social Science and Medicine,* 68 (3): 519–25.

Turner, L. M. & Shera, W. (2005). Empowerment of human service workers: Beyond intra organizational strategies. *Administration in Social Work,* 29 (3): 79–94.

U.S. Census Bureau (2000). Current population survey. Washington, D.C.

Vladeck, B. (2003). Where the action really is: Medicaid and the disabled. *Health Affairs,* 22 (1): 90–100.

West, D. M. & Miller, E. A., (2009). *Digital medicine: Health care in the internet era.* Washington: The Brookings Institution.

Wheeler, D. P. & Goodman, H. (2007). Health and mental health social workers need information literacy skills. *Health & Social Work,* 12 (3): 235–7.

Part 1.1

INDIVIDUAL AND FAMILY WORK

Maternal and child health

2 Fetal surgery

A new setting for social work intervention

Martha G. Hudson

Context

Since the 1970s, ultrasounds have become a routine part of pregnancy care, allowing the diagnosis of fetal malformations to be made prenatally. It is now the standard of care to do a full fetal anatomical survey between 18 and 24 weeks of gestation, sometimes leading to the unexpected discovery of fetal anomalies. Because of this, women increasingly have to make difficult decisions about their unborn babies.

The Center for Fetal Diagnosis and Treatment at the Children's Hospital of Philadelphia evaluates about 750 women a year with fetal diagnoses that have been referred after their obstetrician has found a problem. For many of these women, we are the last hope that something can be done. Many of those fetuses have anomalies that are best handled after birth, but will require close monitoring during the remainder of the pregnancy. Other babies' conditions are determined to have problems that are not correctable and will either be chronic or lethal. A third group is found to have conditions that evolve during gestation and therefore may be mitigated by a prenatal surgical intervention.

There are two types of fetal surgery: fetoscopic procedures and open fetal surgery. In a fetoscopic procedure, the fetal surgeon inserts a scope through a small incision into the uterus using ultrasound guidance and performs a temporizing or corrective procedure. This intervenes in the progression of the problem and allows the baby to develop until delivery. Examples of this would be to keep a laser placental division for twin-to-twin transfusion syndrome or to put a shunt in a fetus to drain the bladder in cases of a urinary blockage.

Open fetal surgery is a more complicated situation. It requires the mother to undergo a hysterotomy, surgery in which the uterus is opened. The baby, while attached to the placenta, is partially removed from the uterus for the corrective procedure, and then returned. Open fetal surgery carries significant risk and is only offered in cases where the baby has a high risk of death or morbidity if nothing is done, or as part of a clinical trial. Examples of this would be a prenatal spina bifida closure or the removal of a lung mass when the baby is showing signs of hydrops fetalis, an abnormal accumulation of fluid in two or more fetal compartments, which is considered to be an end-stage process (Adzick, 2003; Kitano & Adzick, 1999; Howell, Miesnik & Young, 2007).

Policy

In the United States, fetal surgery is generally covered by insurance and Medicaid. Since 1999, many of these procedures have been considered standard of care by The Technology Evaluation Center of Blue Cross Blue Shield (Howell, Johnson & Adzick 2006). Medicaid generally covers fetal intervention, as well. Fetal surgery is always time sensitive and a few days can make a big difference in outcome. It is our policy to proceed without insurance approval if it is felt that the delay will further compromise the baby, and we seek charity care if necessary.

Much has been written about the ethical policies that have been generated by the advances in fetal procedures (Flake, 2001; Chervenak & McCullough, 2001). They mostly revolve around the conflict between maternal and fetal interests. While fetal surgery is undertaken to benefit the baby, we consider the mother to be the primary patient and will decline a fetal procedure if it is felt that the mother will be at too much risk. By the same token, all procedures are voluntary and mothers may decline a procedure without impunity (Belkin, 2001). All patients undergoing open fetal surgery must agree to stay within the Philadelphia area for the duration of the pregnancy and are required to have another adult stay with them for support, as the mother must remain on bed-rest for much of the pregnancy (McCann, 1999). Each family who is a candidate for surgery undergoes a social work assessment prior to finalizing the surgical plan. This assessment is done to determine psychosocial risk factors and to strategize solutions with the patient. In rare cases, surgery may be denied on a psychosocial basis if it is felt that the issues may adversely affect outcome or increase the risk to the mother.

All referrals are seen as soon as possible within the context of the diagnosis. If the baby is thought to be hydropic, for example, the woman can be seen in a few days. The age of infant viability is generally considered to be between 23 and 25 weeks gestation (Pignotti & Donzelli, 2008), and this is the latest age at which a termination can be legally preformed. Gestational age may also be used in determining certain treatment modalities. If a woman is close to 24 weeks gestation at the time of referral, the genetic counselor/coordinator will determine if a termination of pregnancy is an option for her. If it is, we will make every attempt to evaluate her before that time. While we do not perform terminations, we strive to give the woman accurate, detailed information so that she can make an informed decision (Minnick, Delp & Ciotti, 2000). The guidelines of Family Centered Care, as mandated within the bureau of Maternal & Child Health, are adhered to during all phases of the family's evaluation and treatment (Children's Hospital Times, 2007).

Technology

With the current media and political focus on termination, some women reject amniocentesis, which may be perceived as giving information that potentially forces difficult decisions. Ultrasounds, however, do not carry this stigma. Today, most women undergo an ultrasound to find out the gender or to simply get a picture of the baby. The baby's first ultrasound has, in fact, become a milestone in a healthy pregnancy. This is usually the first indication that something is wrong and is generally when the referral to our center occurs.

We complete the full evaluation in one day so that that family can review all their options. The evaluation consists of a two-hour, high-resolution ultrasound, and, depending on the diagnosis, a fetal echocardiogram and an ultrafast fetal MRI. The ultrasound evaluates the entire baby, takes fetal measurements, Dopplers and an amniotic fluid level. The echocardiogram functions not only to check for heart anomalies, but to assess heart function under the stresses of the identified defect. The fetal MRI is used in the evaluation of brain and spinal anomalies as well as issues involving masses in the lungs, lower back and neck. After the tests are completed, the family sits down with the fetal obstetrician, genetic counselor/coordinator and, possibly, pediatric surgeon to review the studies, clarify the implications and determine care options (Howell, Johnson & Adzick, 2006). Types of anomalies evaluated fall into the following groups:

- congenital diaphragmatic hernias
- lung lesions (CCAM, BPS, CHAOS)
- gastro-intestinal disorders (gastroschisis, omphaloceles, intestinal atresias)
- neurological malformations (hydrocephalus, spina bifida, brain anomalies)
- neck masses (cervical teratoma, cystic hygroma)
- sacrococcygeal teratoma (mass at lower spine)
- twins (Twin to Twin Transfusion Syndrome, TRAP sequence)
- urinary tract disorders (obstruction, renal anomalies)
- miscellaneous (chromosomal, skeletal, multiple anomalies).

Fetal surgery, while a major breakthrough in treatment, can pose significant risk to the mother. In both fetoscopic and open procedures, there is risk for chorio-amniotic membrane separation in which the amniotic fluid leaks into the space between the amnion and chorion. This can cause preterm rupture of membranes. Prematurity and all its complications is the most common risk factor in all fetal procedures. Because of this, each woman who is offered an open procedure must meet with a neonatologist prior to the surgery. When undergoing open procedures, the woman is advised that she must have a planned caesarean-section for all subsequent pregnancies. She will also be at risk for uterine rupture in future pregnancies and is cautioned to wait at least a year after delivery before conceiving again (Wilson, 2008).

If a fetal procedure is offered, it generally must be done promptly. I usually meet with the family at this point to clarify their understanding of both the diagnosis and surgery. Often, they are still in shock about the diagnosis and may have failed to grasp the details, risks or even the potential outcomes, with which the social worker needs to be familiar. Families frequently state their desire to undergo the procedure, to "cure" the baby regardless of risk. Informed consent is vital at this stage of treatment.

Organization

While our center is a division of the Children's Hospital of Philadelphia, all references to the organization will be limited in scope to The Center for Fetal Diagnosis and Treatment (CFDT). The Center was started in 1995 with the mission to provide multidisciplinary care for the mother and fetus with a genetic or anatomic abnormality (Howell & Adzick, 2003). The focus has always been on providing a continuum of care for the mother and the baby that starts at diagnosis and continues into the neonatal course. The center has grown to include four pediatric/fetal surgeons, four specialty obstetricians, three general obstetricians, seven midwives, one OB nurse practitioner, one ultrasonographer, one genetic counselor/coordinator, one nurse/coordinator, and two social workers, in addition to the specialized practitioners in nursing, neonatology, anesthesia, cardiology, radiology and other medical and surgical sub-specialists.

In 2008, we opened the Garbose Special Delivery Unit, an eight-bed obstetrical unit within the Children's Hospital of Philadelphia, for women who have been given a fetal diagnosis. This unit allows constant access to the Neonatal Intensive Care Unit (NICU) or Cardiac Intensive Care Unit (CICU) and reflects our philosophy of keeping mothers and babies together as much as possible at this stressful time. Women who are undergoing fetal surgery are also hospitalized on this unit, which is staffed by specialized nurses, midwives and obstetricians. Our goal is to create a warm and sensitive environment for the families at this crisis point in their lives.

All the evaluations are completed in one day and the CFDT is committed to providing all services in a timely manner. Patients from the entire country as well as overseas are seen and every effort is made to accommodate any psychosocial and financial needs. The social worker performs a detailed assessment prior to surgery to identify any psychosocial barriers to care, as well as to determine what ongoing supports and referrals will be needed.

After the evaluation, all options are presented to the family using nondirective counseling techniques and the family is supported in whatever decision is right for them (Howell & Adzick, 2003). The social worker assists with any issues that are barriers to the care option that the family has chosen. If the family is having a fetal intervention, the social worker remains involved throughout the pregnancy, delivery and NICU course. There is a strong emphasis on this level of continuity and it affords a very significant, long-term social work/client relationship.

There is a strong research ethos present and the center is involved in both multi-center clinical trials, and individual studies. All team members participate in research. It is felt that the publication of these studies is an approach to obtain systematic information about pregnancy outcomes with specific fetal diagnoses, related costs and the effects on family and society (Howell & Adzick, 2003).

Decisions about practice

Definition of client

While the CFDT uses the mother/baby dyad in defining the client, for the social worker in this setting, the client is always the mother and her partner. During the fetal intervention and definitely after the delivery, the baby becomes the primary client for the rest of the team. While the mother always remains primary for the social worker, the focus of the relationship may change to helping the mother shift her focus from being the patient to being the mother. Advocacy in this area may also change as the social worker in this setting always has a responsibility to assure a safe discharge for the baby. If concerns arise in this area, a change in primary client, from the mother to the baby, may become necessary towards discharge.

Many of our families live a distance from the hospital; it is common to work with the extended family who may also offer support for the mother, according to the mother's wishes. We also have a diverse ethnic population and will draw on outside cultural/religious organizations as needed to better understand the family perspective.

Fathers are also a big focus of the social worker. Whether or not they are legally married to the mother, they are afforded all the rights to participate in counseling, and receive information about the baby. While fathers are always encouraged to participate in decision making, the final decision about undergoing a fetal procedure is always that of the mother, as she must undergo the surgery. A large part of the social work assessment is in looking at how the family has come to its decision; we want to guard against the mother's being pressured or coerced by the father and ascertain that he understands the necessity of ongoing support while the mother's activity is restricted.

The following situation demonstrates this ongoing dyad. Caitlin is a married, 35-year-old, stay-at-home mother. She and her husband, Noah, 37, have two daughters: Carrie, five, and Danielle, three. Both parents have advanced degrees and have been married for eight years. They are Roman Catholic and live about 500 miles from the hospital. At Caitlin's routine 20-week ultrasound, the baby was noted to have a large congenital cystic adenomatoid malformation (CCAM) in his left lung. Although this type of benign cystic lung mass is relatively rare, we see about 75 per year, 12% of which require fetal surgery (Howell, 2009). The severity varies, but most of these lesions need to be removed surgically, either pre- or postnatally. In Caitlin's case, the CCAM was pressing on the baby's heart, causing it to shift from its normal position.

As the nature of this type of anomaly can change quickly, Caitlin and Noah were seen here the following week. At their evaluation, the mass was noted to be enlarging causing the baby to develop hydrops. This condition is life-threatening for the baby and, if untreated, can cause maternal mirror syndrome, a condition in which the mother develops symptoms that mimic those of the baby, similar to pre-eclampsia. If maternal mirror syndrome occurs, the only treatment is immediate delivery of the baby, regardless of viability (Kitano & Adzick, 1999).

Goals

The initial social work goals all revolve around enabling the family to make good decisions, especially as they are in crisis. For Caitlin and her husband, this meant helping them understand both the diagnosis and their options, with the long-term implications for their family. The options given to them were: (1) do nothing and let nature take its course, (2) termination of pregnancy, (3) a short trial of steroids to try and shrink the mass, and (4) open fetal surgery (fetal lobectomy). Each had both positive and negative aspects and some carried significant risk to the mother.

Once a treatment decision has been made, the secondary goals involve helping the couple with arrangements, resources and overall planning. As in any crisis situation, the goals must be fluid to meet any unexpected changes in status. For example, if Caitlin had an unexpected fetal demise, the goals would then shift to bereavement interventions.

Contracting and developing objectives

As all patients in this setting are essentially in shock, I generally take the lead in developing objectives. Most families look to my specific knowledge-base, in an area that is foreign to them, in helping them determine their needs. The first objective is always to answer concrete questions about the evaluation and help to clarify the diagnosis and implications of each option they have been given by the medical staff. Once a medical treatment decision is made, the family and I can work together in implementing the plan from a psychosocial point of view.

Caitlin and Noah had initially rejected the possibility both of doing nothing and having a termination of pregnancy. However, as they developed a better understanding of the risk factors associated with fetal surgery, Noah began to consider a termination of pregnancy as a viable option. He expressed concern about his wife's health in undergoing open fetal surgery and was also able to state his fear about having a permanently disabled child. The strengths of this couple were noted. They were articulate and able to communicate openly with each other. They had a strong marriage without any previous major stressors. In stating his concern about his wife, Noah also expressed his feeling that he had no part in this decision, as she would have to undergo the surgery and take all the risks. This is a theme I hear often from fathers who are struggling with the enormity of the situation and feeling removed from the mother-baby dyad. Caitlin felt strongly that she did not want a termination of pregnancy. She expressed anticipated guilt about doing nothing and felt they had to try an intervention. Ultimately, they decided to try a short course of steroids followed by open fetal surgery, if needed.

Meeting place

Initially, I meet with families in a consultation room in the outpatient section of the Special Delivery Unit. The room has a round table, with a computer and telephone on an adjacent desk. There is a large flat screen on the wall for viewing images and a printer for downloading educational information. I always sit around the table with the family. Generally, all prenatal meetings take place in this room. Once the baby is delivered, I meet with the family in their private hospital room, or, for casual encounters, at the baby's bedside in the NICU. Once the baby is in the NICU, all scheduled meetings are held in my private office on the unit.

Use of time

My initial assessment is generally done after the medical evaluation is complete. If the family is in major crisis, or if the medical situation requires an immediate decision, I will meet with them that day. However, I prefer to do a full assessment a day or two later, if possible, when the ability to help the family sort out their situation is optimized. The duration of the relationship is very specific to the nature of the medical problem. If the family is having a fetoscopic procedure, for example, I may only work with them for a week with the focus being on their ability to manage around the procedure. In an open fetal surgery, however, much time is spent initially in helping the family look at their individual situation, strengths and resources to prepare them for a significant expenditure of emotional capital. The relationship is likely to require fairly extensive interaction initially, followed by shorter, but frequent meetings during the hospitalization. Unless medical complications develop, meetings from this point until delivery tend to be brief encounters. The relationship continues through the birth, NICU stay, baby's discharge, and, in certain cases, outpatient follow-up. If their baby survived, Caitlin and Noah would be followed in our Pulmonary Hypoplasia Program, which I also cover.

Strategies and interventions

Once the treatment decision has been made, the social worker is able to help the family investigate the longer-term issues. Many families have limited outside supports, as well as financial and work issues. Childcare can be another obstacle. Single mothers without partners present another challenge. We have also cared for families with mental health or pre-existing legal issues.

The trial of steroids was not effective so, five days after coming to Philadelphia, Caitlin and Noah decided to undergo open fetal surgery. We met on the day this decision was made. While still very anxious, they were no longer in major crisis and were now able to focus on plans and strategies needed to maximize the outcome. Caitlin would have to remain in Philadelphia on bed-rest for at least four months. The couple had adequate resources for their standard of living, but could not manage this length of time without Noah returning to work. He was eligible for FMLA, but could not afford to take the 12 weeks unpaid. They were anxious to have their other children remain in their normal environment, but were aware that they may be frightened about Caitlin's absence. They were also struggling with what to tell the children about the baby. Caitlin had a large, close-knit, extended family who would be able to help out; however, she and Noah felt the need for some distance from them during this time and wanted to do things as a couple as much as possible. At the same time, they were fearful of creating hurt feelings.

The couple spoke to their family by phone and Caitlin's parents and several siblings came to the hospital with the two children to allow Caitlin to spend time with them before surgery. It was decided that the children would return home with one of their aunts and that Caitlin's mother, Ruth, would remain with her for the duration of the pregnancy. This was not an easy decision. While they had a good relationship, they would now be sharing a room at Ronald McDonald House with little privacy. Our patients are, of course, always used to being independent and this can be quite an adjustment. While not the case with this family, I have had to contract formally with other families to establish roles and boundaries between the mother and support person (Hudson, 2004).

In keeping with our Family Centered Care focus, I arranged for a Child Life therapist to meet with the family about the siblings. The Child Life therapist and I agreed with the family that it was best to have the children continue as much of their normal routine as possible. The decision was then made to have Noah return home once Caitlin was discharged, and have the children remain with him. They were both in school and their aunts agreed to take turns caring for them until Noah returned home at night. Later in the pregnancy, they would be able to visit Caitlin at Ronald McDonald House. In cases where there are several support people involved, formal contracting may also become necessary. Fear about the care of their other children is probably the most common stressor our mothers express.

As we do in all open fetal surgery cases, a full team meeting was held the day before surgery. This meeting is attended by all staff participating in the procedure: primary pediatric/fetal surgeon, fetal obstetricians, anesthesiologists, nurse practitioner, scrub nurses, fellows, social workers, nurse coordinator and both parents. The couple generally determines who else they wish to be present, but in this case, we restricted the rest of the family. The diagnosis, surgical procedure and follow-up care are again discussed in detail. The family is told of the maternal risks as well as the potential of fetal death. Fetal surgery is not a guarantee of a good outcome.

Stance of the social worker

In this setting it is important to allow the family sufficient leeway in the initial meeting to express their perceived needs. However, as virtually no one seeking our assistance has any prior experience with such a diagnosis, it is frequently necessary to become more directive in helping people move to a point that enables them to ask the right questions. One of the earmarks of fetal treatment is, in fact, the lack of a pre-conceived expectation on the part of the parent or extended family (Hudson, 2008).

The main social work modality starts out as crisis intervention, but generally develops into a task-centered focus. This was the case with Caitlin and Noah. Once the treatment decision had been made and logistics were worked out, they functioned quite well. While they were grateful for their family's assistance, they continued to feel the need for some private time throughout this process. To prevent a rift within the family, I advocated within the team to restrict overnight visiting and medical meetings to Caitlin and Noah alone.

Resources outside of the helping relationship

Depending on the issues determined in the initial social work interview, local supports may be explored to help the family cope while they are here. I have used local Alcoholic Anonymous groups to continue rehabilitation and the local VA Hospital for treatment needed by the support person, a veteran. Ongoing mental health treatment is a special issue, as insurance rarely covers this outside their home area. Depending on the situation, we have established a behavioral health consultation system within the hospital, to use as needed, in conjunction with our obstetrical staff. If families have strong religious faith, and need additional reassurance, they are encouraged to consult with their clergy person, especially when in the decision-making phase. We make every effort to connect them with an appropriate religious service while they are here. Bed-rest, itself, is another stressor. I loan each mother a copy of *Days in Waiting*, and provide them with a list of support groups and additional internet resources.

Reassessment and evaluation

After the surgery is completed, families may feel relieved that the worst is over. Extended family members return home and the patient is discharged to the Ronald McDonald House. This can be a time of major stress reduction or, if supports are not adequate, a second crisis point. Caitlin was having some difficulty with what she perceived as her mother being overbearing. At the same time, she was grateful for her assistance and feeling guilty that this was an issue for her. Ruth felt the need to try and entertain her daughter and was very focused on her restrictions. Caitlin just wanted to be left alone for a period. While Caitlin was able to express her needs, other mothers have gotten into major disputes with their support person and this has sometimes caused the support person to leave. I continued to meet with Caitlin during her weekly visits to the center and she was able to reflect and strategize with me about the issue. To afford her some privacy, we had the medical team see her alone, asking Ruth to wait in the

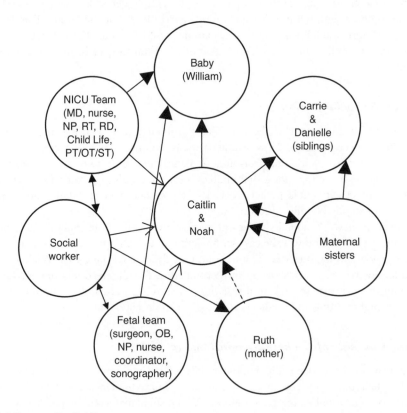

Figure 2.1 Ecomap for Caitlin.

waiting room. While Caitlin was with the medical team I casually met with Ruth, encouraging her to go out, spend some time with the other families at Ronald McDonald House and help out with some jobs there. As time went on, Caitlin was able to encourage her mother to do this, herself, and Ruth derived great satisfaction in helping the other families.

Transfer and termination

Although Caitlin had done well post-operatively she had premature rupture of membranes leading to delivery at 30 weeks gestation. As the baby was still recovering from the hydrops, he was critically ill and placed on a ventilator in the NICU. Caitlin and Noah named him William. The patient-social worker relationship now shifted to helping the couple cope with their fears about their baby. They brought Carrie and Danielle in, after having a sibling preparation by Child Life. They also had the baby baptized. The staff on the fetal team that had been their main supports for the last eight weeks were now in the background. They were developing relationships with the neonatologists and nurses in the NICU. In our structure, the social worker and primary surgeon are the only constants in this process. Having an al-ready established therapeutic relationship is a significant advantage when supporting a family through this new crisis point.

Case conclusion

William had a difficult NICU course but was able to go home at 12 weeks of age with naso-gastric tube feedings and home oxygen. Our therapy team (PT, OT and ST) had been working with him through most of his hospitalization and continued to have some concerns about his developmental status. Early Intervention services were set up in his area, as was his sub-specialty care. The family planned to bring him back to the Pulmonary Hypoplasia Program every three months for ongoing follow-up.

Caitlin remained in Philadelphia for the duration of the hospitalization. Noah, however, maintained his work schedule and continued to care for Carrie and Danielle at home. After the immediate period around the birth, he appeared distant from the baby, continuing to fear a permanently disabled child. There was some strain between them at this point and I continued to meet with them actively during this period. Noah was able to acknowledge that he missed his old life and was fearful that his marriage would be permanently altered. He wondered when he would be able to "have fun again." As William began to improve, however, Noah's attachment grew and the couple was able to work together once again in planning his discharge.

Differential discussion

By all measures, Caitlin and Noah were the ideal couple to undergo fetal surgery. They had a strong relationship, open communication, realistic understanding of the medical issues and an involved family. However, the stresses brought on by this level of intervention cannot be overstated. Mothers must live away from their home while feeling the responsibility of main-taining it. Although they have a support person with them, they are removed from all their normal supports: friends, co-workers, religious community. Many families have significant financial issues, even if they were stable financially before. Mothers may have difficulty in being less active or in letting others do things for them. Their other children may resent the mother's absence and develop behavioral problems. Extended family may be unreliable or financially unable to help. They may also be, as in this case, overbearing.

I have rarely met with families who have heard of their diagnosis previously. In addition, they cannot draw on the experience of their mothers, sisters or friends. Even their referring obstetricians may have little information about these diagnoses or treatments. Often, families come here for a "cure" or to have us "save" their baby, and may not be prepared for the long-term implications. Educating the family thoroughly, both about the diagnosis and treatment process, is vital. The focus of many of our interventions is to improve the outcome or allow the fetus to develop to the point of being treated postnatally. Curing the baby may or may not be an option, even with surgery. It is important that families understand this throughout the process.

Social workers have a significant role to play in this setting. By completing a comprehensive assessment early in the evaluation process, issues as well as family strengths can be identified and acted upon. Family needs change along with the medical situation and interventions must be fluid. The ability to continue the social work relationship through the entire course of treatment is vital in giving quality care to the family. This area of medicine continues to evolve, creating new challenges as well as new hope for families. It is an area that presents similar challenges for the social worker.

References

Adzick, N. S. (2003). Management of fetal lung lesions. *Clinics in Perinatology*, 30: 481–92.

Belkin, H. R. (2001). Legal considerations in fetal treatment. In *The Unborn Patient* (3rd ed. pp. 27–36). Philadelphia: W. B. Saunders Company.

Chervenak, F. A. & McCullough, L. B. (2001). Ethical considerations. In *The Unborn Patient* (3rd ed.), pp. 19–25). Philadelphia: W. B. Saunders Company.

Children's Hospital Times (2007, May/June). Retrieved 6/8/09, from http://stokes.chop.edu/programs/cpt/plcb/times.pdf

Flake, A. W. (2001). Prenatal interventions: Ethical considerations for life-threatening and non-life-threatening anomalies. *Seminars in Periatric Surgery*, 10 (4): 212–21.

Howell, L. J., 2009, personal communication.

Howell, L. J. & Adzick, N. S. (2003). Establishing a fetal therapy center: Lessons learned. *Seminars in Pediatric Surgery*, 12 (3): 209–17.

Howell, L. J., Johnson, M. P. & Adzick, N. S. (2006). Creating a state-of-the-art center for fetal diagnosis and treatment: Importance of a multidisciplinary approach. *Progress in Pediatric Cardiology*, 22: 153–165, 121–7.

Howell, L. J., Miesnik, S. B. & Young, K. B. (2007). Fetal surgery, In *Nursing Care of the Pediatric Surgical Patient* (2nd ed. pp. 153–65). Sudbury: Jones and Bartlett Publishers.

Hudson, M. G. (2004, November 10).Challenges to families undergoing fetal diagnosis and treatment. *Fetal Diagnosis and Treatment: The Future is Now*. Cherry Hill: Delaware Valley Association of Neonatal Nurses.

Hudson, M. G. (2008, March 27). Difficult choices: Psychosocial aspects of decision making in complicated twin pregnancies. *Update on Prenatal Diagnosis and Treatment of Fetal Anomalies*. Philadelphia, Pa.

Kitano, Y. & Adzick, N. S. (1999). New developments in fetal lung therapy. *Current Opinion in Pediatrics*, 11: 193–9.

McCann, M. A. (1999). *Days in Waiting: A Guide to Surviving Pregnancy Bedrest*. St. Paul: deRuyter-Nelson Publications.

Minnick, M. A., Delp, K. J. & Ciotti, M. C. (2000). *A Time to Decide, A Time to Heal* (4th ed.). Sarasota: Pineapple Press.

Pignotti, M. S. & Donzelli, G. (2008). Perinatal care at the threshold of viability: An international comparison of practical guidelines for the treatment of extremely preterm births. *Pediatrics*, 121 (1): E193–E198.

Wilson, R. D. (2008). In utero therapy for fetal thoracic abnormalities. *Prenatal Diagnosis*, 28 (7): 619–25.

Websites

Center for Fetal Diagnosis and Treatment, www.fetalsurgery.chop.edu
Pregnancy From the Shadows, www.about.com: pregnancy from the shadows
Pregnancy Weekly, www.pregnancyweekly.com
Sidelines National Support Network, www.sidelines.org

3   Intimate partner violence in the NICU

Laurie Stewart and Patricia A. Barry

Introduction and context

St. Christopher's Hospital for Children is a 161-bed pediatric facility in north Philadelphia. The privately owned hospital provides a full range of inpatient and outpatient services for children and young adults 21 and younger. Forty of St. Christopher's 161 beds are dedicated to the care of newborns; 30 beds for critically ill infants in the neonatal intensive care unit (NICU) and 10 beds for less critical infants in the continuing care nursery (CCN). Combined, these two units admit approximately 300 patients a year. The average length of a NICU/CCN hospitalization is 33 days.

St. Christopher's NICU is one of two Level III (the most critical and comprehensive) nurseries in southeastern Pennsylvania. All babies are transferred to St. Christopher's as the hospital does not have a labor and delivery unit. Most patients are from Philadelphia and the immediate surrounding area, but the NICU receives multiple admissions each year from New Jersey and rural counties outside of the metropolitan area. Eighty to 85% of NICU babies are covered under a Medicaid HMO based on family income.

About half of the babies are born to parents who are married or currently in a relationship. In 2008, the age of parents at the time of their children's admission ranged from 13 to 46. The patient population is also diverse in terms of race, ethnicity and religion. Ten percent of our families speak Spanish only. In the past few years the NICU has admitted more babies born to parents from Russia and the countries of West Africa as more families from these countries settle in Philadelphia.

St. Christopher's primarily cares for patients in Philadelphia and the surrounding counties. Thus, social workers at St. Christopher's frequently form relationships with, and use the services of, area agencies to assist families with meeting a full range of medical and non-medical needs. One such relationship is with the Children and Mom's Project (CAMP) of Lutheran Settlement House (LSH), a nonprofit agency based in Philadelphia which, through its Bilingual Domestic Violence Program, has been serving intimate partner violence (IPV) survivors since 1977 and whose mission is "To empower individuals, families and communities to achieve and maintain self sufficiency through an integrated program of social, educational and advocacy services." LSH provides a full-time IPV advocate to the hospital. A result of this unique partnership places an IPV counselor on site in the hospital to assist with those cases that require more in-depth intervention regarding intimate partner violence. Thus, this chapter describes the collaborative work of two social workers, Patti Barry, the IPV counselor, and Laurie Stewart, the St. Christopher's social worker.

While this chapter focuses on the intervention portion of the CAMP program, CAMP is a comprehensive IPV training, research and intervention program located at St. Christopher's.

It has multiple components, is collaborative in its efforts, and is designed to identify families experiencing IPV, to minimize adverse effects of childhood IPV exposure and to prevent child abuse. Innovative features of the program include the presence of an onsite IPV counselor, IPV screening support from attending physicians and pediatric resident "champions" as well as IPV screening prompts in the patient charts. The CAMP program began in 2005 as a way to support child abuse prevention efforts at the hospital.

Nationally, nearly one-third of all women will be a victim of a physical or sexual assault by an intimate partner in their lifetime (Commonwealth Fund, 1999; Ellsberg, Janson, Heise, Watts & Garcia-Moreno, 2008; Tjaden, 2002) and between five and 15 million children witness violence between their parents (Fantuzzo & Mohr, 1999; McDonald, Jouriles, Ramisetty-Mikler, Caetano & Green, 2006). The American Academy of Pediatrics (AAP) Committee on Child Abuse and Neglect (1998) links lifelong negative mental and physical health outcomes to childhood exposure to IPV, stating that the abuse of women is a pediatric issue (1998). According to the AAP, "Each year up to 15 million children are exposed to intimate partner violence, and 33 to 77% of these children are, or will become victims of child abuse." (1998) Long-standing, adverse effects of IPV exposure include post-traumatic stress disorder, behavior and school problems, risk-taking behaviors, and violence perpetration (American Academy of Pediatrics, 1998; Barnett, Miller-Perrin & Perrin, 2005; Dutton, 2006; Tjaden, 2002). In 2006, the four zip codes surrounding St. Christopher's accounted for more than 13,000 incidents of IPV, or 20% of all IPV-related crime in Philadelphia.

I, Patti Barry, have been the IPV advocate since the program started. During this time, I have received more than 300 referrals for families in need of IPV counseling, advocacy, resources and safety planning and have trained more than 1,500 health care professionals and presented nationally on the topic of IPV and health care (Barry, 2008; Barry & Bledsoe, 2008; Barry & Cruz, 2007; Giardino, Cruz & Barry, 2007; McColgan, Barry & Cruz, 2007). At St. Christopher's I present to the nursing staff at the new nurses' orientation as well as their mandatory annual in-service training courses. Also, twice a year, I arrange conferences for the medical residents and I assist them in preparing trainings on IPV that they give to the rest of the medical staff during their clinic hours. I also provide an introduction to the CAMP program for all St. Christopher's employees at new employee orientation.

Policy

The CAMP program has written treatment guidelines for working with families affected by IPV and these guidelines allow for an outside agency to provide IPV counseling and support in the hospital. I am available on-site Monday through Thursday and via pager on Friday. My responsibilities include responding to IPV referrals by providing crisis and ongoing counseling and advocacy for victims of IPV. I also provide training and support to pediatric residents, faculty, social workers and other staff. Although the initiative focuses on the outpatient clinic, I respond to referrals from all areas of the hospital including the NICU.

Because I am not a St. Christopher's employee, due to the constraints of HIPAA, I do not have access to medical charts either to write in them, or to read what other health care professionals have written. Also, I do not document discussions between myself and IPV victims or discuss the information with physicians unless requested or approved by the IPV victim. Female caregivers who disclose IPV but decline to speak with me are offered other resources including the Philadelphia Domestic Violence Hotline card (see Resources section at the end of the chapter). As mandated by law, any concerns for child abuse are reported to child protection services in the client's state of residence (Pallitti, Campbell & O'Campo, 2005; Renner, Slack

& Berger, 2008). In these ways, I can keep my interactions with families out of the medical record. This is important as both mother and father have access to the medical record.

Nationwide, about one in 10 infants are admitted to a NICU or ICN (intensive care nursery) within 24 hours of delivery. Premature birth (defined as an infant born before the 37th week of pregnancy) occurs in 12.5% of all live births nationally (March of Dimes, 2005) and in 11.9% of births in Pennsylvania. In Philadelphia County, the rate of premature births is 14.7%. Prematurity and resulting complications, including pulmonary disorders, abdominal distention, infection and brain bleeds are common reasons for admission to the NICU. Reasons for admission of full-term infants include infection, respiratory distress syndrome and transient tachypnea of the newborn (TTN) (Bohlin, Jonsson, Gustafsson & Blennow, 2008).

Most infants from Pennsylvania who are admitted to the NICU meet the state disability guidelines for Medical Assistance (Medicaid). Unlike other states, Pennsylvania has expanded upon the federal Medicaid program established by Congress through Title XIX of the Social Security Act in 1965. In this state, children who meet medical requirements qualify for medical assistance (MA) regardless of parental income, assets or whether children have primary insurance under their parents (Costlow & Lave, 2007). Thus, few families are left with outstanding hospital bills at the end of their child's hospitalization, notable because the average daily NICU cost at St. Christopher's is $2,000.

Technology

Pennsylvania's Medicaid policy also ensures that, in almost every case, St. Christopher's receives payment for NICU stays. With proper payment comes the ability for the hospital to invest in costly NICU technology. For example, a typical three- to eight-day course of extracorporeal membrane oxygenation (ECMO) costs, on average, $1 million. Similar to heart-lung bypass, ECMO allows oxygen to be delivered to blood outside of the body. Because of the risks associated with ECMO, it is only used when absolutely necessary; about 12 times a year at St. Christopher's. More common machines in the NICU include ventilators, continuous positive airway pressure (C-PAP), monitors that continuously evaluate pulse, oxygenation and blood pressure, isolettes and pumps to administer medications and fluids. Hyperalementation, also called total parenteral nutrition (TPN), provides intravenous nutrition for babies too sick to eat by mouth.

Organization

The St Christopher's social work department includes 25 full-time workers and 15 part-time and on-call workers. At the hospital, each inpatient unit has at least one dedicated social worker exclusive to the unit. I, Laurie Stewart, cover both the NICU and CCN. I meet with infants' parents within a few days (ideally within 48 hours) of admission to conduct a complete psychosocial assessment in order to identify the immediate and long-term social work goals of the patient and family and to develop, in conjunction with the parents, a plan to reach these goals. Goals are wide-ranging, from obtaining a breast pump for home, applying for Social Security Income on behalf of the child, securing transportation for parents to be able to visit their child, supporting siblings and working through death and dying of a child. Parents identify and prioritize these goals; I work to facilitate this process, not to identify and set their goals for them.

I also provide support to parents as needed during the NICU period, a time parents have reported as being "the most stressful thing" that has happened in their lives. Parents describe this period as being filled with fear, grief, guilt and loss. Loss relates to more than what families feel when a newborn dies in the NICU. Parents also report feelings of loss related to not having a typical pregnancy, not having a healthy infant and not having a baby to bring home at the end of the mother's hospitalization after delivery (Dyer, 2005).

NICU-related loss is compounded by other life stressors already in place prior to the birth of an infant who requires intensive care. I work with families to address the needs outside of parenting an infant in the NICU. After the initial assessment, I continue to work with families to reach these goals throughout the hospitalization and after discharge, if necessary.

When social workers at St. Christopher's are consulted to see a family for any reason, ideally the mother and some fathers are screened for IPV. Constraints on the screening process include lack of privacy in the hospital setting, the presence of the partner during assessment, and the presence of a patient/child old enough to understand screening. In these cases, I try to speak to the parent alone or will return to the bedside after the partner leaves.

If the parent screens positive for IPV, I then tell the parent about CAMP and ask what further information, support and assistance can be provided. Some parents feel they will be at greater risk if they pursue CAMP services or even if they accept the phone number for Philadelphia's IPV hotline. Thus, the parent decides the safest course of action for herself. If parents would like to participate in the CAMP program, they are referred to Patti.

Decisions about practice

Client definition and description

Baby Maria Brown was born prematurely at 30 weeks of pregnancy weighing 3 pounds 7 ounces. It was anticipated she would stay in the NICU for at least six weeks. Maria is the youngest of seven children born to Crystal Brown, 39, and Kevin Morales, a couple who lived together with their children in Philadelphia. Crystal and Kevin's children range in age from nine to one. Two of the couple's other children were also premature. Maria was admitted to St. Christopher's from the delivery room of the birth hospital primarily due to respiratory distress. A ventilator supported her immediately after birth. Caffeine, TPN and nasojejeunal tube feeds were part of her NICU treatment course.

We knew that we would be working cross-culturally with the Brown family. The Browns are Puerto Rican, and we are both Caucasian. Due to the immediate safety needs of this family, this was not a dynamic discussed in the first interventions with the family, and, in fact, it never became a focus or a barrier in our work. St. Christopher's does have many families and patients from Puerto Rico. While a language barrier was not a focus in our work with the Browns (Patti fortunately speaks fluent Spanish), issues such as primary family supports living in Puerto Rico, being new to Philadelphia and differing cultural norms do arise with other families.

When Maria was born, Kevin worked full-time as a manager at a retail store while Crystal was a full-time mom. All of Maria's older siblings were in good health except for her seven-year-old brother, Joshua. St. Christopher's neurology team diagnosed Joshua with ADHD and he also displayed frequent aggressive and violent behavior toward his siblings and mother. His diagnosis was exacerbated by his witnessing the abuse of his mother.

While Kevin's presence in the hospital made me nervous, he never acted out in the NICU and his visits allowed Crystal to talk to me more freely about their relationship. She noted that his calmness at Maria's bedside was a show for me and for hospital staff as he was hoping that his calm behavior would challenge Crystal's credibility. In the course of these conversations, I learned that Kevin drank on a daily basis. He would binge drink on days he had off, and on days when he worked he'd drink a few drinks in the morning, have a few more at lunch and then drink once he got home. He would drink anything, she said, but whiskey was his drink of choice. Most of the abuse happened while he was drunk, Crystal said, but he also abused her while sober. He raped her often and prohibited her from using birth control, leading to her multiple pregnancies. On the few occasions that Crystal managed to obtain birth control, he destroyed it.

We got to know Crystal well during Maria's time in the NICU. She was clearly bonded with her children and even while the family was living in two rooms of a shelter, Crystal truly enjoyed being with her children. She was their sole caregiver and had a very limited support system, yet she almost always had a story to tell about how one of her kids made her laugh that day. Even while living in the shelter, Crystal got all of her kids to routine medical and dental checkups. All seven would arrive with Crystal on time, neatly dressed and with all insurance in place. We encouraged Crystal to take care of herself and to take time out alone whenever it was remotely possible. Her kids were her priority, but we worried about just how much one mom could handle in the midst of what some would consider chaos.

I (Laurie) met Crystal and Kevin at Maria's bedside the day after her admission and provided them with my contact information. An emergency with another NICU patient took me away from the bedside before a full consult could be completed. The next day I received a phone call from Crystal who told me, in detail, that Kevin choked her that morning until she blacked out. She explained that Kevin had done this before, the abuse was physical, sexual and emotional in nature. She'd been hospitalized previously because of the abuse, he blamed her for the premature birth of three of their children, and she was prepared to leave him permanently (she had left once before a few years earlier). However, she was unsure what her next move should be. She called me because Kevin, over time, had isolated her from her family and friends. The few who initially offered support were quickly overwhelmed by the needs of her large immediate family.

Due to the physically violent nature of the abuse, Crystal was recovering physically as well as emotionally from being assaulted when we met. Like many survivors of assault and abuse she was having trouble sleeping, eating and maintaining a routine in her life with her children. IPV can have serious effects on victims' physical and mental health (CDC, 2006; Loue, 2002). Survivors cite headaches, back pain and digestive issues as common problems (Campbell, 2002; Campbell *et al.*, 2002). Compounding her physical need for recovery was Maria's stay in the NICU. Remarkably, all of her older children are healthy and well cared for—an amazing display of Crystal's hard work and dedication to her children.

Emotionally, Crystal was exhausted. She felt embarrassed, ashamed, frustrated, angry and sad about the breakup of her family. Like many IPV survivors, she was furious that her partner had treated her this way, angry at herself for staying so long and confused about why, in spite of all this, she still missed Kevin. IPV during pregnancy is not unique; between 3.9 and 26% of all live births are impacted in this way (Boy & Salihu, 2004).

Goals and objectives

When Crystal first called me (Laurie), she did so with clear and definitive goals: to leave her abusive relationship, take her children, to do so safely and permanently and to establish a stable life for herself and her children. When she called, she did so with bags packed: one for each of the kids and one for herself that included the children's birth certificates, medical records, social security cards and insurance information. She explained that Kevin had begun drinking the night before and was currently passed out from his drinking. Her goal was to leave

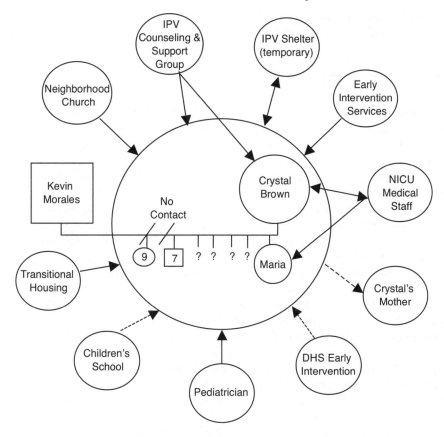

Figure 3.1 Ecomap for Crystal and Maria Brown.

unnoticed with her children before her husband woke up. Unsure of supports in Philadelphia for her and her children, she called me.

I, in turn, called Patti for assistance and a plan developed to have the family leave the home immediately to enter the shelter system. In Philadelphia, one shelter exists specifically for victims of domestic violence and their children, leaving the Browns with this as their only realistic short-term option. Crystal walked with her children and their few belongings to the city bus and headed to the domestic violence shelter. Kevin continued to call her cellphone. At first he was angry and aggressive and then was apologetic and pleaded for her to come back home. Crystal did not tell him where she was going but she did tell him that she had reported him and he was going to be arrested. Crystal shared that Kevin had a criminal history although she declined to elaborate on the nature of his offenses. We both hypothesized that his criminal history was keeping him from trying to find Crystal or to do anything that might get him arrested. Crystal did tell us that Kevin said he was scared to get locked up again.

Because Crystal set her goals on her own, we immediately helped her focus on solutions. Objectives were prioritized by immediate safety (leaving the home, getting to shelter) with the longer-term goals of more permanent housing and having Maria discharged from the NICU into a safe home environment. Many of Crystal's initial conversations with Patti focused on the immediate safety needs of Crystal and her family because that was the most pressing issue at the time. Kevin continued to call multiple times a day and Crystal and Patti created a plan that Crystal would just not answer the phone and let him leave messages.

Measures of success and interventions

Meeting the goals Crystal set for herself and her family was an important measure of her success. She quickly left Kevin and the house, immediately entered the shelter and, within a few weeks, obtained free, long-term, transitional housing for her family through the domestic violence shelter. Crystal and her children had to transition to a new neighborhood, a new school and a new daycare and she reported that a few months went by before she and her kids truly felt comfortable and safe in her new home. In addition, her children began to develop coping skills. Joshua entered therapy at the Children's Crisis Treatment Center, and Crystal's nine-year-old daughter, formerly a protector to her younger siblings, began playing, coloring and even performed in a talent show at her new school. Crystal also began seeking out resources specifically for herself entering individual counseling and also beginning to attend tutoring sessions with the goal of obtaining her GED.

Crystal began attending individual counseling sessions at LSH. Because of Crystal's need to maintain confidentiality and her need for childcare, it was decided that she would get counseling at LSH because Lutheran Settlement House has the staff to assure that someone could care for her children while she spent the time with her counselor. Also, because Patti is the only person at St. Christopher's from her agency, this service could not be provided at the hospital. Crystal began attending weekly counseling sessions at LSH and eventually joined a support group. Because Crystal was physically safe, her counselor was able to explore the impact of violence in Crystal and her family's life. Although Crystal attended counseling at LSH, Patti continued to provide supportive counseling through telephone conversations and during Crystal's visits to St. Christopher's with her children.

Crystal bonded with Maria throughout her NICU hospitalization even while living in the shelter with her older children. Several days a week, she'd bring her children to the social work office at a scheduled time. We (Patti and Laurie) and any other social worker who was available would arrange age-appropriate activities for Maria's brothers and sisters, allowing Crystal to visit the baby for several hours a week. The children struggled with adjusting to their new surroundings and missing their father. Kevin would still call and ask to speak with the children. When he did, the children were normally willing to talk with him. After a few weeks, however, it frustrated them that he was not following through on his promises to call on their birthdays or send cards and presents. Some of the older children went through phases where they didn't even want to talk to him.

After about three weeks in the NICU and three additional weeks in the CCN, Maria was discharged from St. Christopher's. She went home on a monitor to alert Crystal to periods of apnea and on caffeine to stimulate respiration. Despite a brief admission to the medical floor of the hospital a few days after discharge from the CCN, Maria has grown and met developmental milestones in a timeframe more typical of a full-term baby than of a 30-weeker.

Use of time and length of relationship

The hectic and frequently emergent nature of the NICU and CCN makes scheduling appointments with social work difficult. Medical emergencies arise quickly, and a family that is calm one minute finds itself in crisis the next. Thus, social work meetings usually happen when time allows on an as-needed basis, most often in person but occasionally over the phone. I, Laurie, met with Crystal at Maria's bedside and in my office on just about every visit she made to the nursery. These meetings lasted anywhere from five minutes to an hour, depending on childcare arrangements for her older kids and on the nature of the conversation.

After Maria's discharge from the NICU and CCN, she and her siblings were followed regularly by St. Christopher's ambulatory clinic, allowing us to continue working with the family. For approximately a year, we, Patti, Laurie and Crystal, worked together on issues including obtaining wrap-around services for Joshua, early intervention services for Maria, counseling for Crystal and the children and securing furniture, clothing, and toys for the family's new apartment. This relationship continued for about a year after Maria's NICU discharge.

Stance of the social worker

While Maria was in the NICU, I learned that some of the baby's medical caregivers felt that Crystal had too many children and should not have had Maria, especially since she had two previous premature deliveries. They commented out loud that Crystal should be spending upward of eight hours a day at Maria's bedside and that she should not continue to have her children with her while living in a shelter. These staff members were unaware of the history of IPV and of the major life changes Crystal had made for herself and her children just after Maria's birth. They also did not know about Crystal's history of sexual abuse and her lack of choice regarding the number of children she would have.

Because both parents have equal access to their child's medical records, the specifics of IPV and resulting plans are not documented for safety reasons. Thus, not every medical caregiver knows the family's complete story. With Crystal's permission, I told Maria's hospital caregivers the family's story and they began supporting Crystal instead of judging her. I also brought this issue to the attention of a NICU administrator in the hopes that, in the future, we would be able to prevent obvious and open negative judgment of families, regardless of their circumstances.

Termination and case conclusion

Ultimately, the Browns left their new home after about one and a half years in order to ensure their continued safety from Kevin as a series of anonymous phone calls alluded to the possibility that Kevin was closing in on the family's whereabouts. Crystal worked with the transitional housing program to transfer out of county. Crystal and her family were frustrated that they had to move again but also felt that Kevin was a real threat and that they couldn't relax and start a life until they were further away. After their move, Patti helped Crystal connect with a primary care pediatrician for her kids and with a neurologist for Joshua. While we receive occasional updates from Crystal, neither of us continues to provide direct services to the family.

Differential discussion

IPV during pregnancy is not uncommon and women are often at greatest risk for IPV prior to and immediately after delivery, increasing the risk for pregnancy-related morbidity, including pre-term labor. This, in turn, increases the likelihood of the newborn requiring care in a NICU (Silverman, Decker, Reed & Raj, 2006). Therefore, positive IPV screens are common in the NICU. However, moms often opt out of accepting CAMP services, citing their sick newborn as their main source of stress and primary concern. Weeks can go by before these moms are willing to discuss IPV and services in more detail, and often moms decline services completely.

Crystal's case stands out because she sought social work assistance on her own and had already decided to leave Kevin by the time she met us. Crystal also quickly relocated her seven children permanently and safely, a process that often takes months to years. Ready to make a permanent change, she made her decision independently of us. Instead, we supported her and guided her toward appropriate resources that helped her meet her self-directed goals.

References

American Academy of Pediatrics (1998). Committee on Child Abuse and Neglect. Retrieved 6/13/09, from http://www.aap.org/sections/scan/

Barnett, O. W., Miller-Perrin, C. L. & Perrin, R. D. (2005). *Family violence across the life span: An introduction* (2nd ed.). Thousand Oaks: Sage Publications.

Barry, P. (2008). *Talking the talk: Using research for education.* National Coalition Against Domestic Violence Conference, Washington DC.

Barry, P. & Bledsoe, V. (2008). *Changing a culture: Maintaining a grassroots perspective in a medical setting.* National Coalition Against Domestic Violence Conference, Washington DC.

Barry, P. & Cruz, M. (2007). *Addressing intimate partner violence in a pediatric setting: The CAMP screening and intervention model.* Family Violence Prevention Fund, San Francisco.

Bohlin, P. K., Jonsson, B., Gustafsson, A.-S. & Blennow, M. (2008). Continuous positive airway pressure and surfactant. *Neonatology*, 93: 309–15.

Boy, A. & Salihu, H. (2004). Intimate partner violence and birth outcomes: A systematic review. *International Journal of Fertility and Women's Medicine*, 49 (4): 159–63.

Campbell, J. C. (2002). Health consequences of intimate partner violence (a review). *Lancet*, 359 (9314): 1331–6.

Campbell, J. C., Jones, A. S., Drenemann, J., Kub, J., Scollenberger, J., O'Campo, P., Gielen, A. C. & Wynne, C. (2002). Intimate partner violence and physical health consequences. *Archives of Internal Medicine*, 162 (10): 1157–63.

CDC (Center for Disease Control and Prevention) (2006). *Understanding Intimate Partner Violence.* Retrieved 3/2/09, from http://www.cdc.gov/ncipc/dvp/ipv_factsheet.pdf.

Commonwealth Fund (1999). *Health concerns across a woman's lifespan: 1998 survey of women's health.* Retrieved 3/2/09, from http://www.endabuse.org/content/action_center/detail/754.

Costlow, M. & Lave, J. (2007). *Faces of the Pennsylvania Medicaid Program.* Retrieved 3/2/09 from www.pamedicaid.pitt.edu/documents/facesofmedicaid.pdf

Dutton, D. G. (2006). *Rethinking domestic violence.* Vancouver: University of British Columbia Press.

Dyer, K. (2005). Identifying, understanding, and working with grieving parents in the NICU, part II: Strategies. *Neonatal Network*, 24 (4): 27–40.

Ellsburg, M., Jansen, H. A., Heise, L., Watts, C. H. & Garcia-Mareno, C. (2008). Intimate partner violence and women's physical and mental health in the WHO multi-country study on women's health and domestic violence. *Lancet*, 371 (9619): 1165–72.

Fantuzzo, J. W. & Mohr, W. K. (1999). Prevalence and effects of child exposure to domestic violence. *The Future of Children*, 9 (3): 21–32.

Giardino, A., Cruz, M. & Barry, P. (2007). *Implementing pediatric domestic violence screening.* Pediatric Academic Societies, Toronto.

Loue, S. (2002). *Intimate partner violence: Societal, medical, legal and individual responses.* New York: Kluwer Academic Publishers.

March of Dimes (2005). *Pennsylvania preterm birth overview.* Retrieved 2/25/09, from www.marchofdimes.com/peristats.

McColgan, M., Barry, P. & Cruz, M. (2007). Referral patterns for victims of intimate partner violence identified in a pediatric hospital (poster). Pediatric Academic Societies, Toronto.

McDonald, R., Jouriles, E. N., Ramisetty-Mikler, S., Caetano, R. & Green, C. E. (2006). Estimating the number of American children living in partner-violence families. *Journal of Family Psychology*, 20 (1): 137–42.

Pallitti, C. C., Campbell, J. C. & O'Campo, P. (2005). Is intimate partner violence associated with unintended pregnancy: A review of the literature. *Trauma Violence Abuse* 6 (3): 217–35.

Renner, L. M., Slack, K. S. & Berger, L. M. (2008). A descriptive study of intimate partner violence and child maltreatment: Implications for child welfare policy (pp. 154–73). In Lendsey, D. & Shlonsky, A. (eds.). *Child Welfare Research*. New York: Oxford University Press.

Silverman, J., Decker, M., Reed, E. & Raj, A. (2006). Intimate partner violence victimization prior to and during pregnancy among women residing in 26 U. S. states: Associations with maternal and neonatal health. *American Journal of Obstetrics and Gynecology*, 195: 140–8.

Tjaden, P. G. (2002). *Extent, nature and consequences of intimate partner violence*. Washington, DC: U.S. Department of Justice, Office of Justice Programs, National Institute of Justice.

Resources

Childlink: Early intervention service coordination program for children birth to age three with developmental delays and disabilities. www.phmc.org (accessed 3/23/09).

Children's Crisis Treatment Center. www.cctckids.org (accessed 3/23/09).

Domestic Violence Hotline: a nationwide toll-free hotline will provide immediate crisis intervention, counseling and referrals to emergency shelters and services. Phone number—800-799-SAFE.

4 Social work in a perinatal AIDS program

Caryl Blackwood, Judy Mason,
and Virginia Walther

Context

Description of the setting

The Maternal-Child Health HIV/AIDS Prevention and Treatment Program began in response to the rising number of HIV-infected women and their perinatally infected newborns when New York had the highest HIV seroprevalence rate among childbearing women (.67) in the U.S. (Kirschenbaum, Hirty & Correale *et al.*, 2004; Lindau, Jerome & Miller *et al.*, 2006). New York State (NY) still has the highest percentage of cumulative AIDS cases of all ages in the U.S. (16% of the total), and New York City (NYC) has 12.5% of all HIV/AIDS cases in the country (New York State HIV/AIDS, 2007). In NY, there are 172,051 cumulative AIDS cases, and in NYC, 138,251. Women of childbearing age make up 27% of all persons living with HIV/AIDS in the U.S., and 91% of females in the city living with HIV/AIDS are in that age range (Center for Disease Control and Prevention [CDC], 2006). About one-third of HIV-infected individuals are women and, of those women, 79% are African American or Latina (NYC HIV/AIDS, 2007). Transmission risks for women of childbearing age are: heterosexual contact only (32%); injection drug use (20.1%), perinatal exposure (4.5%), and self-reported unknown causes thought to be a combination of heterosexual contact and injection drug use (41%). While the transmission rate from mother to child was 2.8% in 2004, at our hospital, it was 1.2% in 2008.

The Medical Center comprises a school of medicine and a 1,100 bed multi-specialty tertiary care hospital. Approximately 5,500 births occur here each year, and almost 1,500 of the mothers participate in our prenatal clinical program, which provides continuity of care to predominantly poor, minority women. According to Health Status 2010, the AIDS case rate in Northern Manhattan, the location of this medical center, is nearly 50 times the national rate, and the HIV death rate among women in New York is 10.2 compared with 2.3 nationally. Due to early identification and intervention programs in OB/GYN clinical settings as well as maternal and newborn anti-retroviral treatments, however, the rate of perinatal transmission has been drastically reduced to approximately 1.2% of all births to HIV-infected women. Here, social workers provide HIV prevention programs for all pregnant women registering for prenatal services, regardless of individual risk behaviors. Voluntary HIV testing is also offered, and approximately 98% of all women have been HIV pretest counseled and tested prior to their deliveries (Patterson, Leone & Fiscus *et al.*, 2007). Pregnant women who are identified as HIV positive, and women known to be HIV positive who are referred for prenatal care and elect to continue their pregnancies, are followed by the Department of Obstetrics and Gynecology's Perinatal Infectious Disease Team which includes a licensed clinical social worker. Following delivery, the mother's primary care is provided by the AIDS Designated Treatment Center, while newborns, both affected and infected, are referred to the center's Pediatric HIV/AIDS Team where they are followed for at least 18 months or throughout their childhood if they are HIV positive or are diagnosed with AIDS. All women delivering at the hospital—including those who have received minimal or no prenatal care—receive HIV counseling and testing, if requested. A funded, intensive community follow-up program that includes home visits is available to help engage "hard to reach" clients.

Policy

Early in the epidemic, legislation providing guidelines for confidentiality, disclosure, testing, treatment, and reporting was enacted in every state and DC. On the federal level, the CDC recommends guidelines for regulating practices, but states and local departments of health can choose to adopt or modify these guidelines. In addition, the CDC mandates that all states report collected coded AIDS information to them. In 1999, our state legislators passed successful but controversial, legislation that requires people with HIV to be listed by name on a confidential state registry and that included voluntary reporting of known sexual and needle-sharing partners of infected individuals (New York HIV Reporting/Partner Notification Law). This surveillance contributes to understanding the pathogenesis and epidemiology of the disease. Also, individual states now have laws that protect patients' health information and Public Health Law, article 27–F provides civil penalties for disclosing unauthorized information that identifies an individual's serostatus in this state.

The CDC has rewritten multiple HIV counseling and testing guidelines, and states' requirements for HIV testing in health care settings have been revised. With 40,000 new infections (CDC HIV/AIDS Surveillance Report, 2001) occurring annually since 1998, governments remain concerned that people do not know they are infected until they are seriously ill and unknowingly pass the infection on to others. Currently the CDC recommendations include testing for the virus early in pregnancy and in the third trimester as part of other routine screenings with an opt-out provision (CDC, 2006) thus, separating the process of counseling the patient and obtaining voluntary informed consent from the provision of HIV testing. This separation has been controversial for many HIV/AIDS activists and civil liberties groups who fear that testing will be less voluntary or even mandatory. Concerns exist that physicians may test patients without a true process of informed consent and/or there may be missed opportunities to provide risk reduction counseling and to educate patients about prevention.

Some states have passed laws preventing the disconnection of counseling and testing, preventing a full adoption of the CDC's 2006 recommendations. In NY, all pregnant women are advised to have voluntary testing for HIV early and, again, in the third trimester. Counseling content guidelines have been abbreviated, and the HIV consent form simplified. In addition, counseling and testing occurs on the labor and delivery floors for those whose HIV status is unknown, and HIV testing has been incorporated into routine newborn screens. Currently the American College of Obstetricians and Gynecologists recommends routinely screening all women aged 19 to 64 for HIV regardless of individual risk factors. In the OB/GYN Diagnostic and Treatment Center, routine HIV services are provided to every woman entering prenatal care, and a majority of women who begin care at the OB clinic accept HIV testing services.

Also, health insurance is of grave concern to this special needs population. In NY, they are covered not by managed care Medicaid, but rather by an enhanced Medicaid program, the Prenatal Care Assistance Program (PCAP), insuring that all women entering prenatal care, including HIV-infected women, receive medical coverage and comprehensive care.

Technology

Understanding available technology allows perinatal social workers to help women and their families, including those who are HIV positive, to cope and make good decisions for themselves and their children (Cooper, Charurat & Mofenson, 2002). Technological advances include assisted reproductive technologies to combat infertility, prenatal diagnosis, intrauterine surgery, and the human genome project. Computer-assisted learning, digital media, and centralized databases enhance accessibility to scientific advances, and internet networking allows us to communicate with scientists and professionals around the world. New epidemiological information helps providers to modify interventions. Direct consumer access to on-line information helps to empower populations to advocate for themselves. In addition, electronic medical records enhance tracking patients' course of illness and treatment. Testing now yields immediate results, and care for the infected pregnant women can begin immediately. Increased access means all professionals must be vigilant in protecting patients' privacy and assuring that information-sharing advances do not have negative consequences. Here it is interesting to note that the epidemic has sent social workers back to their public health roots to focus on broad-based education and prevention. We have always partnered with others around prevention as well as treatment, and this is particularly important given the horizontal and vertical transmission of HIV.

Organization

The Mount Sinai Hospital Diagnostic and Treatment Center's OB/GYN Associates sees women who have sought care at the hospital, have been transferred from affiliates or referred by community agencies or clinics, or other programs in the hospital. The focus here is on HIV education, screening and treatment, and risk reduction counseling for patients who are HIV negative but report high risk behaviors. Such counseling is also employed with HIV positive clients to lower risk of secondary HIV transmission to negative partners. The client unit includes the pregnant woman, her partner, her unborn child and, perhaps, her other children. Partners of the OB/GYN patients are offered free HIV counseling and testing services. Services for fathers include support for young fathers as well as group and individual counseling services for HIV positive male partners, caretakers of children or partners, and partners who are members of discordant couples in whom the HIV negative men are partnered with HIV positive pregnant women.

The professional team always balances the needs of the mother with those of the unborn child. Thus, together, Pediatric and Adult Infectious Disease clinicians and Obstetrical Infectious Disease clinicians hold weekly interdisciplinary team meetings to plan treatment and to discuss psychosocial issues that impact care, and plan for follow-up for the baby. Issues related to decisions to continue a pregnancy to term, medication adherence, family planning, and available and appropriate maternal treatments are of vital importance. We provide mothers with the best care and options for long-term medical treatment and reduce risk for HIV transmission.

Decisions about practice

Description of the client

Ms. Jackie Smith, a 26-year-old African American single woman who has a four-year-old daughter, is the eldest of two children raised by her mother, a single parent. She reveals a history of depression, with counseling services as an adolescent, due to conflict with her mother and fueled by her own acting-out behavior at that time. A high school graduate with some college credits who had worked primarily as a secretary or a clerk, she had recently lost her job. During her care in the Obstetrics Infectious Disease clinical program, Ms. Smith received Medicaid, cash assistance and food stamps from Public Assistance and, frustrated with that system, she said frequently that she wanted to re-enter the workforce as she felt she could more adequately provide financially for herself and child. Her identity was strongly associated with being independent, and she was suffering from that loss and the dependency that resulted from unemployment.

Ms. Smith's first prenatal visit occurred at 18 weeks of pregnancy, upon referral and discharge from the antepartum inpatient service where she had first presented with vaginal bleeding. During her social work screening, a routine aspect of entry into care, she said that until recently she and her daughter lived with her mother and brother but stayed frequently with Ray, the father of the baby, a man who was abusing her but who was not the father of her daughter (Silverman, Deeker & Niranjan *et al.*, 2003; Wu, El-Bassel, Witte *et al.*, 2003). She reported a one-year history of verbal and physical abuse, but an incident of physical violence while she was pregnant made her "draw the line" and enter the city's shelter system for abused women and their children. The loss of a relationship—even one with an abusive partner—can involve yet another loss; of the wished for non-violent relationship. Thus, a chaotic and desperate situation fraught with losses led to her entering the shelter system. At her initial prenatal appointment, Ms. Smith received HIV counseling as part of the social work screening process and denied concerns about HIV risks. One year ago, at a neighborhood health center, she had tested negative.

Although Ms. Smith denied concerns about being at risk for exposure to HIV, she accepted HIV testing services at that initial visit and her result was positive. At the HIV post-test counseling session, Ms. Smith was tearful but generally accepting of her HIV status. She had a positive outlook, indicated that she knew people living with HIV, was knowledgeable about the ways HIV is transmitted and was also aware that not all babies who were HIV exposed were infected with the virus. Still, she worried about possible risk of HIV transmission to her baby. After a discussion about the medical treatment and care for HIV positive pregnant women, Ms. Smith indicated that she would do whatever was necessary to take care of herself and her baby (Siegel, Karus, Raveis & Hagen, 1998).

Ms. Smith had known Ray for two and a half years and had filed an order of protection when she left him. Initially, she adamantly reported that she wanted no contact with him. However, at times during the prenatal period, she minimized the violence between her and Ray and expressed a desire for him to be a part of the baby's life. Clearly she was ambivalent about the relationship, wishing the violence to end, and the relationship to continue. Additional stresses at that time included court involvement as Ms. Smith took the father of her daughter to court for child support. She also consented to have her daughter HIV tested and received negative results.

Ms. Smith was aware that people with HIV could live a long time with the virus and felt that there was no benefit in disclosing her status to her family at this time because she was "healthy" and felt some family members would "disown" her if they knew of her HIV diagnosis. The threat of more loss of significant others due to the stigma associated with HIV was too great a challenge for her. A cousin's HIV positive status was known but not discussed in the family. Because of domestic violence issues, partner notification of her HIV status was deemed a risk to Ms. Smith's safety. Disclosure and secrecy are issues that HIV positive clients contend with throughout their lives and social workers need to address on an ongoing basis.

Preparing for disclosure of one's HIV status requires first that the individual come to terms with the diagnosis. Thinking about disclosing to others involves weighing the possible positive and negative outcomes in relation to safety issues and possible loss of social supports. In addition, determining who to disclose to, and how to initiate and conduct that conversation requires preparation and planning because of the stigma attached to the diagnosis. In NY, clients can use partner notification assistance services that protect client confidentiality, but that may have endangered Ms. Smith. Thus, Ms. Smith's not being ready to disclose her status was normal in light of a new diagnosis and the risks of disclosure.

Definition of the client

The OB/GYN ID team client is generally a single woman of minority status who lives in one of the boroughs of New York City, primarily East Harlem and another poor urban area in the city. The client is the mother and child dyad principally, especially given the fact that the mother's HIV positive status will have profound implications for the serostatus of the baby. However, using a family-centered model of care, this view of the client is often expanded to include the father of the baby and can be further expanded or revised based on information about additional risks, involvement or lack of involvement of partners, and the inclusion of siblings and other relatives playing significant roles within a family. In this case, the client unit included Ms. Smith, her four-year-old daughter and the unborn child.

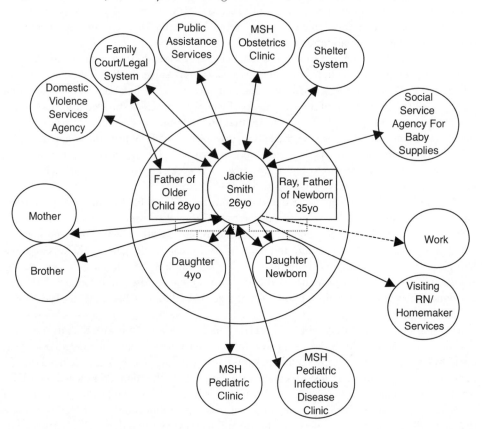

Figure 4.1 Ecomap for Jackie Smith.

Goals, objectives, and outcome measures

With the overall goal of a successful postnatal outcome for herself and her newborn, the objectives for Ms. Smith were to: accept her HIV positive status, enroll in appropriate comprehensive biopsychosocial prenatal care, and promote her adherence to care. To help the client to reach these objectives, I assess the implications of the diagnosis within the patient's psychosocial and cultural contexts and address impediments to meeting the objectives. For Ms. Smith, confronting and mastering addressing her multiple losses was critical.

In the perinatal setting, while the needs and wishes of the pregnant woman are of paramount importance, I must simultaneously attend to population-based program mandates to provide primary and secondary HIV education, counseling, and prevention service to all pregnant women. Broad-based risk reduction counseling involves engaging the woman in a mutual assessment of her relationships and testing history, partner history, condom use, and substance use. Following this intervention, with my assistance, the individual will articulate goals for her continued medical and social work intervention in the arena of perinatal AIDS. In the case of pregnancy, a diagnosis of HIV or AIDS forms a powerful context under which the patient's goals for herself and her unborn child are developed. Using the underpinnings of the trans-theoretical framework of the "stages of change" (Prochaska, Norcross & DiClemente, 1994), stage-base behavior counseling is instituted. The woman is given a behavioral diagnosis, behaviors are targeted, and appropriate interventions are formulated. These may be as focused as making decisions regarding changing one's risk behavior or disclosing to one's partner, and as broad-based as coming to emotional and pragmatic terms with this life-threatening diagnosis and its potentially dire consequences for the future of the unborn child. Given the uncertainties of the course of HIV progression for both mother and baby, it is particularly important that I set treatment goals based on the client's ability to tolerate the realities and multiple implications of the diagnosis within her own social context and in keeping with her capacities to use a variety and wide range of available services, which may change over the course of pregnancy. A woman's response to the HIV diagnosis is categorically different depending on her awareness of her status when entering pregnancy care. The social work interventions will be shaped by this contextual issue. In addition, the pregnancy itself demands a family-focused approach to all goal setting, as the definition of client is shifted from the individual woman to the maternal child dyad.

The effectiveness of social work service delivery is measured by an increase in knowledge of HIV issues geared to maternal transmission on the part of an entire population of pregnant women; the ability to engage patients and families in an individually focused counseling process; and the coordination of specialized medical and case-management services opted for by patients, based on their goals.

Use of contract

In the OB ID program, the contract is defined by a variety of regulatory agencies, funding sources, the hospital, and departmental policies and standards. In working with the client the social work practitioners in the OB/GYN DTC perinatal HIV program are also informed by ethical standards of the social work profession and utilize well-founded social work practices and principles in working with clients toward mutually identified goals. All practitioners in health care settings including social workers have to abide by HIPAA regulations as they relate to the patient's protected health information. Specifically the client's right to protection regarding her HIV-related and other medical information is protected by state and federal laws.

Ms. Smith was referred to the OB/GYN clinic from the Labor and Delivery floor's antepartum program and upon entering care at the OB clinic went through the same evaluation process that is provided to all new clinic patients. An in-depth psychosocial assessment was completed by the screening social worker and HIV counseling and testing was provided. Ms. Smith denied any ambivalence about the pregnancy, but as noted she did not begin prenatal care until she was 18 weeks pregnant, in her second trimester. She reported financial concerns, domestic violence and the resulting admission to a domestic violence shelter as her psychosocial stressors (Campbell, Baty, Ghandour *et al.*, 2008). During the early part of her care following her diagnosis Ms. Smith indicated that she hoped to retest for HIV following her pregnancy because many illnesses were present during pregnancy like "gestational diabetes and high blood pressure" and were not present following delivery. This makes her initial acceptance of her diagnosis seem more as an attempt at coping with the unexpected but when that coping mechanism faltered, she expressed doubt about the diagnosis and voiced the "wish" that the condition was only temporary or would be found to be in error. In addition to expressing denial at times of her diagnosis, Mrs. Smith also reported sleep and appetite changes and a depressed mood. These symptoms of depression were discussed, but she denied and refused further mental health evaluation and subsequently reported improved mood as she was able to better integrate the diagnosis and began to address the multiple issues that were of concern to her. Throughout her pregnancy Ms. Smith was found to have an undetectable viral load and good CD4 count (CDC, 2006). Some of the identified goals of social work interaction included conducting an assessment of Ms. Smith's coping and adaptation to her new diagnosis, providing education and support to facilitate reducing the risk of secondary and mother to child transmission, helping Ms. Smith to cope with her losses and plan for managing these stressors, as well as transitioning mother and child to postpartum care.

Meeting place

The setting for social work interaction with pregnant women is the OB/GYN Diagnostic and Treatment Center. Clients are seen for medical appointments in the Infectious Disease specialty clinic that incorporates management and care of both Obstetrical and Infectious Disease issues by the same physician. This integrated form of care supports better treatment adherence, follow-up and continuity. Clients do not have to feel stigmatized or worry about confidentiality issues as the OB Infectious Disease clinic operates as a specialty clinic during regular clinic operation when general clinic functions are being performed. I meet with clients in a private office, and we have frequent telephone contact. There is also ongoing collateral contact with the numerous agencies providing services to our clients and their families.

Ms. Smith was not working during the time she received prenatal care in the clinic, but she plans to return to work following her delivery so she can provide financially for herself and her children. She missed very few clinic appointments, had frequent face-to-face and telephone contacts with me and was open and verbal about her concerns. Ms. Smith had received prenatal care and delivered her first child at the hospital and was glad she did not have to transfer care now that she had an HIV diagnosis.

She was also very comfortable with continuing to receive care in the same clinic and hospital with which she had a long history and indicated that her four-year-old daughter was receiving care in the hospital's pediatric clinic.

Use of time

By its very nature, the time structure of perinatal social work is limited by the gestation of pregnancy and its immediate postpartum period. The use of time may either be constricted or structured depending on the gestational stage of the patient as she enters care, regulatory and insurance requirements, and individual medical and social needs corresponding to the stage of HIV/AIDS disease progression. If the patient begins obstetric care late in the pregnancy, the engagement process and social work interventions are compromised and constricted by time factors inherent in late initiation of prenatal care. Furthermore, the mandates of funding sources set time parameters. At their best, they have enhanced the focus and timeliness of interventions in relation to counseling, testing, and case management services. At worst, they make it difficult for the program to continue beyond the provision of "soft" monies. Finally, the clinical manifestations and emotional and social needs engendered by perinatal AIDS heighten the use of time in the patient and social work relationship. Each stage of the infection has its own set of psychosocial stressors. These social work services offered will be in response to the severity of medical and psychosocial needs which advance with time and disease progression.

Work with Ms. Smith took place for the duration of her pregnancy and during the postpartum period for a total of 27 weeks. Presenting for care during the eighteenth week of gestation, she delivered at 39 weeks and remained involved with me and the OB Infectious Disease Team until her 6th week postpartum appointment when she was transitioned into our Adult-Pediatric Infectious Disease Program.

Intervention

Family-centered clinical case management consists of rapid assessment, crisis and short-term treatment, psychiatric consultation, resource management, and outreach services to all family members, with a flexible definition of family provided by the consumer. Case approaches that are family-centered place me in the role of case manager on an interdisciplinary team and protect integrated, continuous care. The program, in keeping with a family focus, also has a co-located program for HIV-infected and affected fathers and to-be fathers at risk from HIV.

Consideration of racial, cultural, ethnic, and socioeconomic diversity is essential in planning and implementing programs. Bilingual social workers and other staff members as well as bilingual educational materials are essential, given the demographic makeup of the clinic population. Because diversity among staff and clients influences service utilization, staff members represent the diverse populations served in the program. For example, many staff members who live in the community bring local concerns to clinic care. In addition, Latino social workers help minimize language barriers and provide culturally attuned continuing education for social workers and staff (Walther & Mason, 1994). Program communication is maintained through a weekly, multidisciplinary staff meeting led by the medical director and attended by members of the OB/GYN Infectious Disease team and the Pediatric HIV/AIDS program. Content includes scientific updates and staff education, and planning and discussion of patient care (Mason, Preisinger & Donohue, 1995).

When we care for clients who are affected by HIV and AIDS, it is important to take into account all stressors, the nature of HIV transmission, ongoing risks for secondary transmission and disease progression as it relates to client functioning for people who are poor and whose lives are affected by violence, social isolation, and substance use/abuse. The HIV-infected client is part of a family and community, and my family-centered approach helps focus on all issues affecting client functioning. Recognition of the place of these biopsychosocial issues in clients' lives makes case management a desirable modality for providing care to this population. Case management works with the client and the various systems that impact that client and seeks to reduce the effects of those stressors on client and family. It also connects the numerous service providers who are involved with the family and helps me to identify gaps in service that need to be addressed. Although the client's time in the perinatal clinic is limited, case management services can be transitioned to adult and pediatric services, or to a community case management agency that can continue to provide services to the client and family as needed after the perinatal care has ended. As HIV is now considered a long-term manageable illness, rather than a fatal one, the benefits of ongoing case management services are even more apparent.

In addition to case management there is also the opportunity for other treatment modalities, including individual, couple and/or group services in order to deliver care to the client and to address issues brought forward by the client or identified in the client/social worker relationship. As the timeframe for working with women during pregnancy is limited, social work emphasis on focused, achievable objectives and use of short-term modalities is essential.

Stance of the social worker

Deliberation about value and ethical dilemmas is inherent in social work practice in a perinatal AIDS program setting. A social worker's conscious or unconscious behavioral, cognitive, or emotional responses to the circumstances, emotions, or behaviors presented by clients can cause blurring of ethical and professional boundaries. I am required to manage complex, ambiguous questions and must be aware of my own and others' biases. For example, I must contend with health providers' overt or subtle opinions about infected women's continuation or termination of pregnancy. Providers may promote the use of sterilization to guard against future pregnancies without regard to values important to the client in her own context. Since providers have variable understanding of infected women's pregnancy-related decisions, I must be comfortable in exploring issues, options, and resources to support the client's decisions. HIV infection linked to maternal substance abuse raises complex legal and ethical questions for the professional, especially as related to issues of child welfare and protection. Working with HIV-infected mothers and children can evoke anxiety, touch deep feelings, and challenge deeply rooted attitudes and professional beliefs, and I am challenged to intervene in a positive, creative, and nonjudgmental manner.

Reassessment

HIV is a continually changing and evolving illness that necessitates ongoing assessment of the medical, social and emotional needs of those persons whose lives it touches. During every clinical encounter, the levels of physical, social, and emotional functioning of the client as well as the existing environment stressors and familial supports need to be assessed. As the case is re-evaluated, new contracts are established accordingly.

Case conclusion and differential discussion

Ms. Smith is a resourceful and capable woman who used social work services well to deal with her HIV diagnosis and plan for herself and her baby. At times, however, she minimized the effects that intimate partner violence and HIV had on her life as she attempted to adjust to these losses. Studies have shown a link between domestic or intimate partner violence and the risk for HIV infection. Women who are being abused have little ability to negotiate safer sex practices. Additionally, the stigma associated with both having HIV and being a victim of domestic violence which Ms. Smith experienced kept her from some family support that she might have used. As the ecomap shows, she and her daughters had a variety of support systems. She was adept at identifying needs for herself and seeking out or requesting, assistance to obtain services. However, upon reflection, there are areas that may have been managed differently or, time allowing, addressed further. Ms. Smith did not disclose her HIV status and did not involve family members in her care. While she used me for support she may have benefited from exploring availability of an extended support network in her circle of family and friends.

Would she have benefited from seeking out support from family and/or friends or was she correct in her assessment that she would be disowned? Was she correct in her assumption that the need for disclosure was unnecessary because she was "healthy"? Later, when a family member was faced with a medical problem Ms. Smith disclosed her HIV status in order to provide that family with hope about their situation. Ms. Smith also moved back to her mother's home during her pregnancy due to frustration with the shelter system. She subsequently had contact and negative interaction with the father of her baby that resulted in her having concerns about her safety and the safety of her children. Her work with the domestic violence agency and her self-advocacy eventually led her to move away from her mother's apartment, and obtain safe housing that was away from the father of the baby. Ms. Smith's baby received care at the hospital's Pediatric Infectious Disease clinic, and the baby was found not to be infected with the HIV virus. How do the low mother-to-child transmission rates affect women's attitudes toward parenting, childbearing, and family planning? With improved medications and treatment, people who have HIV are living longer and healthier. What implications does that have in terms of disclosure of HIV status? We are living in times when many people who are of childbearing age have never lived without the specter of HIV/AIDS. What does this mean in terms of their attitudes toward HIV and other sexually transmitted infections? How does that affect choices regarding behaviors, risks, feelings about HIV and how do these choices impact on their lives? Are people more accepting of HIV as "just another sexually transmitted infection"? Is the stigma of HIV/AIDS any less different for people who have always had HIV/AIDS around than it is for people who lived through the nascence of HIV/AIDS?

Many children who were perinatally infected at birth have transitioned from pediatric to adolescent to adult care and are themselves of childbearing age. What implications are there for care of those young people regarding parenting, family planning, permanency planning, goal setting, and disclosure to sexual partners? When should discussion of sexuality begin for this cohort?

References

Campbell, J. C., Baty, M. L., Ghandour, R. M., Stockman, J. K., Francisco, L. & Wagman, J. (2008). The intersection of intimate partner violence against women and HIV/AIDS: A review. *International Journal of Injury Control and Safety Promotion*, 15 (4): 221–31.

Center for Disease Control (CDC) (2001). *HIV/AIDS Surveillance Report*. 13 (2). Atlanta, GA: U.S. Department of Health and Human Services.

Center for Disease Control and Prevention (CDC) (2006). Revised recommendations for HIV testing of adults, adolescents and pregnant women in health care settings. *Morbidity and Mortality Weekly Report*, 55 (RR 14), 1–17.

Cooper, E. R., Charurat, M., Mofenson L., *et al.* (2002). Combination antiretroviral strategies for the treatment of pregnant HIV-1 infected women and prevention of perinatal HIV-1 transmission. *Journal of Acquired Immune Deficiency Syndrome*, 29 (5): 484–94.

Kirshenbaum, A., Hirky, A. E., Correale, J., Goldstein, R. & Johnson, M. (2004). "Throwing the dice": Pregnancy decision-making among HIV-positive women in four U.S. cities. *Perspectives on Sexual and Reproductive Health*, 36 (3): 106–13.

Lindau, S. T., Jerome, J., Miller, K., Monk, E., Garcia, P. & Cohen, M. (2006). Mothers on the margins: Implications for eradicating perinatal HIV. *Social Science & Medicine* 62 (1): 59–69.

Mason, J., Preisinger, J. & Donohue, M. (1995) Women and their families: Psychosocial stages of HIV infection. In P. Kelly, S. Holman, R. Rothenberg, S. P. Holzemer (eds.) *Primary care of women and children with HIV infection: A multidisciplinary approach* (pp. 173–88). Boston: Jones and Bartlett Publishers.

New York State Department of Health (2007). HIV/AIDS. Retrieved 2/17/09 from, http://www.health.state.ny.us/nysdoh/hivaids/hivpartner/intro.htm

Patterson, K. B., Leone, P. A., Fiscus, S. A., Kuruc, J., McCoy. S. I., Wolf, L., Foust, E. B., Williams, D. B., Eron, J. A. & Pitcher, C. D. (2007). Frequent detection of acute HIV infection in pregnant women. *AIDS*, 21 (17): 2303–8.

Prochaska, J. O., Norcross, J. C. & DiClemente, C. C. (1994). *Changing for good. A revolutionary six-stage program for overcoming bad habits and moving your life positively forward.* New York: Avon Books.

Siegel, K., Karus, D., Raveis, V. & Hagen, D. (1998). Psychological adjustment of women with HIV/AIDS: Racial and ethnic comparisons. *Journal of Community Psychology*, 26: 439–55.

Silverman, J. G., Decker, M. R., Niranjan, S., Balaiah, D. & Raj, A. (2008). Intimate partner violence and HIV Infection among married Indian women. *Journal of the American Medical Association*, 300 (6): 703–10.

Walther, V. & Mason, J. (1994). Social work field instruction in a perinatal AIDS setting. *The Clinical Supervisor*, 12 (1): 33–52.

Wu, E., El-Bassel, N., Witte, S. S., Gilbert, L. & Chang, M. (2003). Intimate partner violence and HIV risk among urban minority women in primary health care settings. *AIDS and Behavior*, 7 (3): 291–301.

5 Social work practice in an adolescent parenting program

Kathleen Rounds, Traci L. Wike,
and Helen Dombalis

Context

The last 15 years have seen a consistent decline in the rates of adolescent pregnancies in the United States. From 1990 to 2004, rates among adolescents aged 15–19 years dropped from an all-time high of 11.6% to 7.2%, representing a 38% overall reduction in the number of pregnancies experienced by adolescents (Ventura, Abma, Mosher & Henshaw, 2008). Although the stability of the decline in teen pregnancy rates is good news, the actual birth rate for adolescents increased 3% in 2006 for the first time since 1991 (Martin *et al.*, 2009). It is unknown whether this trend will continue. Regardless, the long-term social and economic consequences associated with adolescent childbearing continue to be pressing societal concerns.

In 2004, the cost related to adolescent pregnancy and parenting was estimated at 9.1 billion dollars (Hoffman, 2006). This includes costs associated with health care, child welfare, public assistance, and criminal justice. Costs experienced by young women who bear children in adolescence include decreased educational attainment, decreased marital stability, and increased financial stress (Brien & Willis, 1997; Nock, 1998). Children of adolescents are less likely to be on par with their peers at school entry in the areas of cognition and knowledge, language and communication, emotional wellbeing and social skills, and physical wellbeing and motor skill development (Terry-Humen, Manlove & Moore, 2005), and are more likely to be poor, experience abuse and neglect, and enter the child welfare system (Hoffman, 2006).

The intergenerational impact of teen childbearing is particularly concerning, as daughters of teen mothers are more likely to become teen mothers themselves. Approximately one-third of female adolescents born to a teenage mother became teen mothers themselves compared with 11% of those whose mothers were age 20–1 at the time of their first birth (Hoffman, 2006). Also, adolescents who give birth before age 15 are more likely to experience a second pregnancy during adolescence than those who give birth to their first child later in adolescence (Boardman, Allsworth, Phipps & Lapane, 2006). Thus, it becomes important not only to work toward preventing a first pregnancy, but also to support adolescents who do become parents in preventing a second pregnancy and avoid perpetuating the cycle of intergenerational childbearing.

This chapter focuses on social work services provided to pregnant and parenting adolescents under the auspices of the North Carolina Adolescent Parenting Program (APP) that aims to prevent a second pregnancy during adolescence and to promote high school graduation among adolescent parents. Among all states in 2006, North Carolina's birth rate for adolescents aged 15–19 years was 49.7 per 1,000 teens (Martin *et al.*, 2009), ranking it 37th in the nation with 50 being the highest (National Campaign to Prevent Teen and Unplanned Pregnancy, 2009).

In 2007, 29% of adolescent pregnancies in North Carolina were repeat pregnancies, making a program such as the Adolescent Parenting Program critically important in preventing a second pregnancy (Adolescent Pregnancy Prevention of North Carolina [APPNC], 2008).

Description of the setting

The APP is a secondary pregnancy prevention program that has served pregnant and parenting teens in North Carolina for over 20 years. It is one part of the two-part, statewide North Carolina Teen Pregnancy Prevention Initiative (TPPI), which aims to reduce the state's high teen pregnancy rate. The other part, the Adolescent Pregnancy Prevention Program (APPP), focuses on primary prevention of teen pregnancy. The APP is a program partially funded by a federal initiative, administered and funded at the state level by the North Carolina Department of Health and Human Services, Division of Public Health, and implemented at and with some financial contribution from the local level. The program is designed to provide services at the county level in various agency settings, such as public health departments, mental health centers, schools, departments of social services, and private non-profit agencies. Currently, there are 29 APP programs operating in 28 of North Carolina's 100 counties (North Carolina Department of Health and Human Services [NCDHHS], 2008). Each local APP offers case management and other services to participants. The APP described in this chapter is located in a school in a county that is a mix of both rural and small-town residents.

Policy

Federal legislation to reduce the incidence of teen pregnancies has focused mostly on efforts toward preventing a first pregnancy and less on preventing a second. These efforts have primarily taken the form of abstinence-only education interventions funded heavily through programs such as Community-Based Abstinence Education (CBAE) and Title V of the 1996 Welfare Reform Law. Federal policies that impact youth who are already pregnant and parenting include Temporary Assistance to Needy Families (TANF) and Title XX of the Public Health Service Act, the Adolescent Family Life Act (AFLA).

As part of the 1996 welfare reform effort, TANF includes special provisions addressing minor parents who are required to live with a parent, caregiver, or in an adult-supervised setting and participate in education leading to a high school diploma or its equivalent (Hummel & Levin-Epstein, 2005; Levin-Epstein & Hutchins, 2003). Generally, the TANF legislation limits the amount of time one can receive federal aid and mandates work requirements in order to discourage chronic dependence on government assistance (Levin-Epstein & Hutchins, 2003). By specifically featuring minor parents, TANF intends to address and break the cycle of inter-generational teen childbearing. A 2007 report by The National Campaign to Prevent Teen and Unplanned Pregnancy indicated that none of the welfare reform legislation directed at adults has shown any positive effects on preventing their children from becoming teen parents; however, these studies did not evaluate the legislation directly affecting minor parents and, specifically, effects of the TANF provisions for minor parents are unknown (Kirby, 2007).

Enacted in 1981, the AFLA contains not only a prevention component supporting abstinence-based education but also one supporting comprehensive health, education, and social services to pregnant and parenting adolescents, their children, family members, and young fathers. Although this legislation has important implications for adolescent parenting programs, it leaves program design and implementation to the discretion of state and local authorities. Because all program participants are minors and most do not have private insurance, programs are able to bill Medicaid for many case management and psychosocial counseling services.

School-based policies can significantly impact pregnant and parenting teens' ability to achieve the goal of finishing high school which will ultimately affect their self-sufficiency and economic stability. For example, flexible school policies, offering an evening class schedule or GED classes for adolescent parents, or having an on-site daycare can make a difference in whether an adolescent completes high school.

Technology

To provide accurate data on how well a program is serving its clients and on the degree to which the program is meeting its goals, the TPPI implemented a web-based data entry system in 2000. Each APP must enter data on clients using several forms regarding client intake, individual service, group activity, goals (initial, periodic update, and review), and case closure (see https://tppi.its.state.nc.us/info/tppi.htm). The system was originally developed so that the state agency could monitor as well as track service delivery across all programs. A recent evaluation noted that more oversight is required to ensure data completion and validation, and further development of the system is needed to allow program coordinators to analyze their own data and develop reports that would be useful in local community outreach (Gruber, 2008). In addition to using the internet for data entry, the APP programs use a range of internet health information resources (see Resource List). With the use of web-based meeting technology, the state TPPI program staff meet with local program coordinators across the state to disseminate new guidelines and best practices. Local programs can use this format as well as list-serves and social networking sites for sharing information on strategies that work.

Organization

TPPI provides statewide administration and funding for all local APP programs, each of which is under the auspices of a health and human service organization such as a public health department, local nonprofit agency, department of social services (DSS), or school system. The sponsoring organization applies to TPPI for a four-year, annually renewable grant to support the program, provides matching community funds and physical space for the program, and hires and supervises the program coordinator. Under this arrangement, each local APP coordinator reports to the sponsoring agency and to the state TPPI director who establishes guidelines regarding participant eligibility, case load sizes, mandated services, data collection requirements, and community advisory council. State-level TPPI program staff support local program coordinators through regular statewide meetings and conferences about best practices and an annual graduation conference for clients and staff of the programs. The organizational culture of each program is heavily determined by its physical location and sponsoring agency; an APP located in a DSS office has a different organizational culture than one located in a high school.

A full-time coordinator—in many programs an M.S.W.—administers each program and provides direct services. As part of their administrative role, coordinators engage in a range of activities such as planning, implementing, and evaluating the program; recruiting, screening, training, and supervising volunteer mentors; developing and maintaining partnerships with other agencies; conducting community outreach and education; and collaborating with other parties to advocate for services for pregnancy prevention and teen parenting. Coordinators organize community advisory councils that meet at least four times a year and include representatives from agencies and community groups that will support the program in developing linkages the coordinator can tap into for client services, fund-raising, and marketing.

Coordinators carry a case load of 12–20 clients. As direct service providers, coordinators conduct initial individual assessments, work with clients to set goals and objectives and ways to reach those goals, provide case management and psychosocial counseling, and organize peer education and support groups. They must spend at least 20% of their total work time per month offering and arranging family planning services, such as community education and outreach, classroom presentations, peer-leadership activities, teen and parent workshops, counseling and referrals, and developing and researching educational and informational materials. To increase the impact of the program, APP coordinators match volunteer mentors with participants to serve as role models and to help them navigate the social service, health care, and school systems.

Decisions about practice

Definition of the client

First-time pregnant and parenting teens, female or male, may participate if they are 17 or younger, eligible for Medicaid, and they do not experience a second pregnancy while participating in the program. They are typically referred by teachers, guidance counselors, and public health department Maternity Care Coordinators but also by friends and/or siblings who are current or former program participants. Adolescent parents are not considered emancipated minors in North Carolina; although program participation is voluntary, parental consent is required.

Description of the client

Tanya Smith, 16 years old and Caucasian, is the mother of three-year-old Sean. Tanya and Sean live in a small two-bedroom apartment with Tanya's mother Danielle, age 32, who is employed at a local fast food restaurant. A high school student (10th grade) who enjoys learning and performed well academically, Tanya was a cheerleader prior to her pregnancy. While Tanya is at school and Danielle is at work, Sean spends the day at a family-home daycare near Tanya's school.

A middle school teacher referred Tanya to the Adolescent Parenting Program when she discovered Tanya was pregnant at age 13; Tanya was afraid to tell her mother about her pregnancy. She wanted to enroll in the program but could not do so without parental consent. When I first met Tanya, I needed to deal with my own reaction to working with such a young pregnant teen. While I had been working with parenting teens for at least two years, for the most part they were 15 years of age and older. Tanya and I conducted a role-play in which Tanya practiced telling her mother about her pregnancy, and I prepared her for her mother's possible responses. Ultimately, Tanya chose not to tell her mother in person but rather through a handwritten letter placed on her pillow before leaving the house one morning for school. Danielle was initially upset, deeply disappointed, yet supportive. She became a teenage mother at 16 when she gave birth to Tanya and had always hoped that her own daughter would at least finish high school before becoming a parent.

After completing enrollment paperwork for the program, Tanya and I discussed her options: parenting, adoption, and termination of the pregnancy. When Tanya chose to continue with the pregnancy and to become a parent, Tanya's boyfriend—Sean's father—quickly disassociated himself from her and their relationship ended. Danielle and I became her primary supports throughout her pregnancy. Meeting with both Tanya and her mother helped me to better understand the cultural context of this family and why Tanya had decided to go ahead with the pregnancy and parenting at such a young age. In accordance with her family's religious beliefs, Tanya would not have terminated the pregnancy. She was part of a large extended family in which teen parenting was not unusual and in which family members supported teens in raising their children. As Danielle said to me, "This is not how I would have had it for my daughter—but we will make the best of this."

As Tanya's pregnancy progressed, she became embarrassed to be in school surrounded by middle school classmates who frequently commented on her changing body. Her grades suffered, and a week before her due date, Tanya went on homebound status, which meant that a teacher came to her home to provide assignments and tutoring. Following Sean's birth, Tanya remained on homebound status for six weeks, the maximum time allowed by her school.

Upon her return to school, her world rapidly changed. Tanya's typically high grades gradually worsened because she had less time available for studying and assignment completion; she was severely sleep-deprived for the first five months postpartum. During her pregnancy, Tanya dropped off the cheerleading squad and she could not return to cheerleading or any extracurricular activities because of parenting responsibilities after school. Tanya noted that whereas her friends spent their evenings doing homework, talking on the phone, and watching television, she spent her evenings feeding and bathing Sean and putting him to bed. Fortunately, in the first year of Sean's life, Danielle assisted with these tasks. For the first two years of Sean's life, Tanya was an active participant in the Adolescent Parenting Program, and both the program and her mother helped Tanya as she learned to juggle school and parenting. Although she faced challenges and her grades moved up and down, Tanya used program supports effectively.

As Tanya moved into high school, Danielle's perception of her changed from that of a teenager needing help to that of an adult, fully capable of independently raising a child and running a household. Danielle increased her time at work into evening hours, and Tanya became responsible not only for caring for her son but also for housework; she cooks, cleans, shops, and pays bills. Meanwhile, Danielle became less involved in her family's life and more involved in her relationship with her boyfriend who stays overnight at the apartment several nights a week, offering less time to spend with Tanya and less support for her as well. Recently the household responsibilities have overwhelmed Tanya. Her grades are plummeting and her relationship with Danielle continues to worsen. Tanya reports that when she asks her mother for help or explains that her responsibilities are more than she can handle, she is told to "grow up" and to "act your age." Tanya feels that her mother and her mother's boyfriend criticize her constantly and do not understand how overwhelmed she feels.

For the past six months Tanya has had a boyfriend, a senior at her school who is attentive to her and her son. Since he is not Sean's father, he cannot enroll in the program or receive APP services, but he can and does attend peer group meetings when invited by Tanya. Few participants in her program are in relationships and even fewer have support at meetings from boyfriends. Tanya reports that she is struggling to find time to be with her boyfriend.

Despite fluctuations in her grades and parental support, Tanya's participation in the program has rarely wavered. She visits my office a couple of times per week for counseling on life management; we discuss such issues as her arguments with her mother, financial hardships, frustrations with teachers, and poor grades. She also attends the monthly peer group meetings, which provide an opportunity for all program participants to socialize and to learn information and skills from presenters on topics including parenting, stress management, children's language development, and adolescent advocacy.

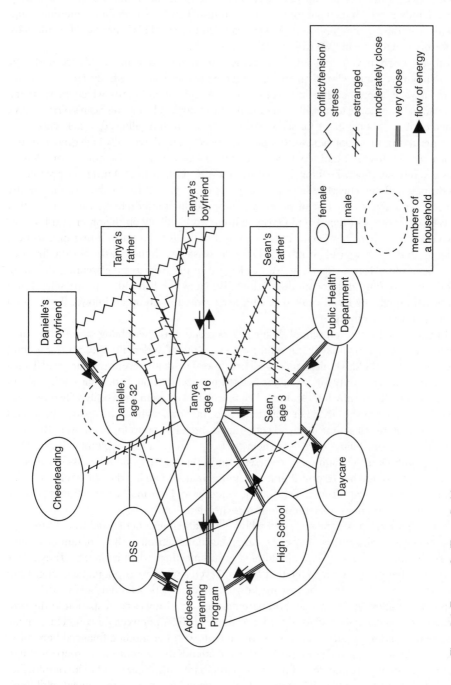

Female ◯ male ▭

- - - members of a household

conflict/tension/ stress

estranged

moderately close

very close

→ flow of energy

Danielle's boyfriend

Tanya's father

Tanya's boyfriend

Sean's father

Danielle, age 32

Tanya, age 16

Sean, age 3

Public Health Department

Cheerleading

DSS

Adolescent Parenting Program

High School

Daycare

Figure 5.1 Ecomap for Tanya Smith.

Goals

The primary aim of APP is to increase the likelihood that young parents will obtain self-sufficiency and be better able to provide a positive, stable foundation for their children. We are mandated to focus on eight goals with participants, with the first two of these being the most critical: 1) preventing a second pregnancy while participating in the program; 2) remaining in high school or an equivalent program with the goal of graduation or completion; 3) applying appropriate health care for self; 4) applying appropriate health care for the child; 5) enhancing parenting abilities; 6) preparing for employment through learning job readiness skills/vocational development; 7) enhancing life skills (e.g. budgeting, time management); and 8) eliminating substantiated referrals of abuse and neglect (NCDHHS, 2008).

Participants work with their coordinators to develop additional goals based on individual situations.

Contract and objectives

Upon entering the program, Tanya met with me to develop an individual plan that includes goals, objectives, and activities to meet these goals; we formally review and update this plan at least every six months. Tanya updated her goals and objectives at our most recent meeting. This process is similar to a contracting process; we contract as to how and when goals and objectives will be accomplished. The following is an example of the objectives for three goals that we established in our most recent meeting.

Goal one: Delay a second pregnancy

- At the next peer group meeting, Tanya will participate in the session on birth control methods; she will invite her boyfriend to this meeting.
- At a session to be scheduled with me after the peer group meeting Tanya will role-play how to negotiate condom use with her boyfriend.
- In the next week, Tanya will schedule a doctor's appointment to discuss having an intrauterine device (IUD) implanted; she will notify the coordinator when she does this.
- Tanya will consistently use condoms in addition to her other chosen method of birth control.

Goal two: Graduate from high school

- For the next month Tanya will have no unexcused absences.
- In the case of a necessary absence (e.g. M.D. appointment), Tanya will submit the necessary paperwork (i.e. doctor's note) to have the absence excused.
- At each scheduled meeting, Tanya and I will review her progress and discuss any need for academic support or tutoring. Prior to each meeting, I will contact Tanya's teachers to obtain their assessment of her progress.

Goal three: Improve her relationship with her mother

- The coordinator will schedule a counseling session within the following two weeks with Tanya and her mother to discuss their relationship and Tanya's sense of feeling overburdened.

- To prepare for this meeting, Tanya will keep a week-long daily log of how she is spending her time.
- Prior to the session, the coordinator will meet with Tanya to role-play how she will tell her mother about how she feels overburdened with household responsibilities and how she would like to spend more time with her mother.

Meeting place

The APP discussed in this case is located in a high school, which is ideal for frequent contact between the participants and me. Tanya regularly drops in to see me, and I have easy access to Tanya's teachers. I also use a school classroom for afterschool peer group meetings. This makes these group meetings much more accessible to participants as they are already at school. I am mandated to meet with Tanya in her home at least eight out of the 12 monthly required formal visits. The volunteer mentor, who is assigned to Tanya, frequently picks her up after school for activities or to take her to appointments.

Use of time

On average Tanya and I meet three to five times per month. One of these meetings is scheduled for about an hour, during which we review her progress in meeting her goals. Many meetings occur when Tanya drops in to talk with me or are scheduled as needed when Tanya is having a problem at school or at home. I spend a fair amount of time checking in with providers such as the daycare and the public health department who are helping Tanya and Sean.

Strategies and interventions

I use various interventions in my work with clients including crisis intervention, case management, case level advocacy, group work using a psycho-educational approach, and brief solution-focused work by developing "short-term goals and contracting within a long-term relationship" (Kerson, 2002). The primary goal of these interventions is to educate, support, and empower teens to manage their lives and effectively solve problems as they arise. I use my knowledge of adolescent development and a risk and resiliency framework (Fraser, 2004; Rounds, 2004) to adapt interventions to the cognitive, psychological, and social capabilities of my clients and to the context of their lives. In addition, I advocate at the case level (e.g. advocating with the school for a change in class sections for a student) and the class level. As noted earlier, I also engage in macro level social work interventions such as class level advocacy (e.g. participating in a legislative action day to increase funding for adolescent pregnancy prevention), community outreach, and collaborating with other community agencies.

Stance of the coordinator

I use a problem-solving and empowerment approach. Through modeling, I teach Tanya how to seek help and advocate for herself and her son. I focus on relationship building and collaboration with staff from other agencies, and I am very skilled at developing a network of helping agencies I can call on when clients need resources and when I need community support for the program.

Uses of resources outside of the coordinator/client relationship

In order for the APP to be successful and for me to secure needed resources for the teens in the program, I am heavily dependent upon collaborative working relationships with staff of local agencies including the sponsoring agency. Because the program is located in a school and program emphasis is on school success, I meet frequently with school counselors and individual teachers. One of my key responsibilities is to develop a network within the community to support the program and individual clients. I frequently call on members of the advisory council to help me develop and maintain these relationships. Additionally, I have developed an active volunteer mentoring program to extend the program's services. To network with community groups, I serve on a local community board composed of representatives from social services, mental health, public health, and other key community agencies. My participation on this board provides me with invaluable insight into the workings of various community agencies and I use these meetings to promote awareness of the APP and the problems of teen pregnancy. I also enlist community speakers, leaders, and trainers to conduct educational sessions at the peer group meetings on topics such as early child development, how to protect oneself from sexually transmitted infections, and how to complete a job application.

Reassessment and evaluation

I participate in reassessment at both the individual client level and the program level. As noted earlier, I meet with Tanya at least every six months to formally review and update her goal plan. To evaluate the program, I also ask program participants to complete an evaluation form on the educational component of each peer group meeting. I use this feedback on speakers and content to assist with planning of future meetings. In addition, at the quarterly advisory council meetings I ask members to provide feedback and to assess program performance and development. Finally, as mandated by the state, I enter client level and program data into the web-based data entry system used by the state to formally evaluate each APP and the overall Teen Pregnancy Prevention Initiative (TPPI).

Transfer or termination

Tanya can stay in the program until she graduates from high school or completes her GED and as long as she does not become pregnant again. She has been an active program participant, and I hope that she will continue and develop into one of the role models and leaders. During Tanya's senior year, she and I will focus our work on preparing Tanya for the transition to employment or further education and on ensuring adequate support is in place for this transition. Her graduation from the program will be marked by a statewide graduation program.

Differential discussion

In reviewing my work with Tanya, I realize I have learned much from our work together. At first, I was dismayed when Tanya came in to the program at age 13; I had not worked with a pregnant teen so young. In order to be effective, I needed to quickly update my knowledge of development of young teens and locate additional resources to address the issues for this age group.

Looking back, as additional younger teens entered the program, I wonder if I should not have developed separate peer group meetings for the younger girls in the program. Because I did not have the resources to run separate groups, I tried to ensure that issues concerning the younger teens were addressed and that they felt they could speak up in the group meetings. I also plan to use my APP coordinators network to learn how others are addressing the increase in pregnancy among very young teens.

Because the APP is located in the local high school and not in the middle school, I neither have the same relationships with, nor access to, teachers and the school counselor as I had at the high school. This made it more difficult for me to advocate for Tanya during her pregnancy and the first years of parenting. I realize I need to foster closer relationships to the middle school, as I am receiving more referrals of middle school age girls. I plan to raise this challenge with my Advisory Council at our next meeting to get their input. I would like to open a satellite office at the middle school, but I realize this is a politically and culturally sensitive issue that would need school board, middle school staff, teachers and parental support.

I also realize how important it is to fully engage a young teen early on in the program and to work on retention issues, including pregnancy prevention and school success. I feel I have been successful with Tanya because we developed a close relationship early on in the process, and I have been able to match Tanya with an excellent volunteer mentor who has made a long-term commitment to her. I was not as successful with two other young clients who left the program after their second year; one became pregnant and the other dropped out of school.

Finally, reviewing my work with Tanya has made me realize how important the teen's relationship is with her family. While I spent a great deal of time with both Tanya and Danielle during the first year or so of Tanya's time in the program, over the last year my focus has shifted to helping Tanya finish high school and prepare for employment or additional education. While this is appropriate, I wish I had also paid more attention to Tanya's relationship with her mother. Tanya is only 16 and, while a parent herself, is developmentally an adolescent and still needs and wants the involvement of, and guidance from, her mother. In looking forward to Tanya's eventual graduation from the program and transition to becoming more independent, I realize that Tanya's relationship with her mother will continue to be critical.

References

Adolescent Pregnancy Prevention of North Carolina (APPNC) (2007). *2007 North Carolina repeat pregnancies, ages 15–19*. Retrieved 1/4/09: http://www.appcnc.org/statistics.html

Boardman, L. A., Allsworth, J., Phipps, M. G. & Lapane, K. L. (2006). Risk factors for unintended versus intended rapid repeat pregnancies among adolescents. *Journal of Adolescent Health*, 39 (4): 597.e1-7.

Brien, M. J. & Willis, R. J. (1997). The costs and consequences of early fatherhood: The impact on young men, young women, and their children. In R. A. Maynard (ed.), *Kids having kids: Economic costs and social consequences of teen pregnancy*. Washington, DC: Urban Institute Press.

Fraser, M. W. (ed.). (2004). *Risk and resilience in childhood: An ecological perspective*. Washington, DC: NASW Press.

Gruber, K. J. (2008). *Evaluation of the Adolescent Parenting Program. A report to the N. C. Department of Health and Human Services, Division of Public Health, Teen Pregnancy Prevention Initiative (TPPI)*.

Hoffman, S. (2006). By the numbers: The public costs of teen childbearing. *National Campaign to Prevent Teen Pregnancy*. Retrieved 4/21/07: www.teenpregnancy.org/costs/default.htm

Hummel, L. & Levin-Epstein, J. (2005). *A needed transition: Lessons from Illinois about teen parent TANF rules*. Retrieved 5/3/07: www.clasp.org

Kerson, T. S. (2002). *Boundary spanning: An ecological reinterpretation of social work practice in health and mental health systems*. New York: Columbia University Press.

Kirby, D. (2007). *Emerging answers 2007: Research findings on programs to reduce teen pregnancy and sexually transmitted diseases*. Washington, DC: National Campaign to Prevent Teen and Unplanned Pregnancy.

Levin-Epstein, J. & Hutchins, J. (2003). *Teens and TANF: How adolescents fare under the nation's welfare program.* Retrieved 6/13/07: www.clasp.org

Martin, J. A., Hamilton, B. E., Sutton, P. D., Ventura, S. J., Menacker, F., Kirmeyer S. & Matthews, T. J. (2009). Births: Final data for 2006. *National Vital Statistics Reports*, 57 (7): 1–102.

Nock, S. L. (1998). *Marriage in men's lives.* New York: Oxford University Press.

National Campaign to Prevent Teen and Unplanned Pregnancy. (2000). Retrieved 11/04/09, from www.thenational

North Carolina Department of Health and Human Services (NCDHHS). (2008). *Teen pregnancy prevention initiatives.* Retrieved 1/4/09: http://www.teenpregnancy.ncdhhs.gov/app.htm

Rounds, K. A. (2004). Preventing sexually transmitted infections among adolescents. In M. W. Fraser (ed.), *Risk and resilience in childhood: An ecological perspective* (pp. 251–79). Washington, DC: NASW Press.

Terry-Humen, E., Manlove, J. & Moore, K. A. (2005). *Playing catch up: How children born to teen mothers fare.* Washington, DC: National Campaign to Prevent Teen Pregnancy.

Ventura, S. J., Abma, J. C., Mosher, W. D. & Henshaw, S. K. (2008). Estimated pregnancy rates by outcome for the United States, 1990–2004. *National Vital Statistics Reports*, 56 (15): 1–26.

Resource list

Bright Futures: Infant, Child and Adolescent Health Promotion and Disease Prevention Information for Health Professionals, Families, and Communities http://brightfutures.aap.org/

ETR's Resource Center for Adolescent Pregnancy Prevention http://www.etr.org/recapp/

The March of Dimes http://www.marchofdimes.com

The Maternal and Child Health Bureau http://mchb.hrsa.gov

Zero to Three http://www.zerotothree.org

Part 1.2

INDIVIDUAL AND FAMILY WORK

Children and youth

6 Managing asthma from a social work perspective in a center for children with special health needs

Laura Boyd

Context

Policy

Asthma is the leading serious chronic illness affecting children in the United States with an estimated 6.8 million children under 18 years old having asthma in 2006. According to the American Lung Association (ALA) (2008), asthma is an inflammatory condition of the bronchial airways. These changes produce airway obstruction, chest tightness, coughing and wheezing. If severe, this can cause severe shortness of breath and low blood oxygen. Asthma exacerbations are preventable and each individual suffers a different level of severity. Virtually all children with asthma, however, do experience a reversal of symptoms until something triggers the next episode.

Statistics show that asthma rates of mortality and morbidity are disproportionately higher amongst low-income populations, minorities and children living in the inner city (Segoris Love & Spiegel, 2006; Stephen, 2006). In 1991, the National Cooperative Inner-City Asthma Study (NCIAS) received funding, and in 2000 the Inner-City Asthma Intervention (ICAI) was awarded additional funding to develop a coordinated, focused, evidence-based intervention program for children with asthma (NCIAS, 2006; Katten *et al.*, 2006; Spiegel *et al.*, 2006). The unique part of this intervention was that rather than focus on only the medical component, the programming used a masters-level social worker to develop a fine-tuned, comprehensive approach for families to effectively create environments in which children's asthma would be best managed outside of the medical setting (Parker, 2005). The focus was on prevention, and while the children faced many challenges, the results demonstrate that such a multifaceted approach was often successful. This emphasizes the importance in the medical team of the social worker, whose goal is to weave medical management into the fabric of the patient's life outside of the medical setting.

If asthma is indeed something that can largely be controlled, why does it make such a profound impact on our youth? Why does it so often prevent children from enjoying typical activities and result in many hospitalizations? Why is it that asthma can so greatly impact a child's education? For example, the Center for Disease Control and Prevention (CDC) found that asthma is one of the most common causes of school absenteeism (CDC, 2007). In 2003, children aged five to 17 years who reported at least one asthma attack in the previous year missed 12,800,000 school days due to the disease (CDC, 2006).

Why? Knowledge of, Impact on quality of life, Comparison between "well" people *controlled ≠ not there* (handwritten annotation)

Technology

Due to medical advances, asthma can largely be controlled with preventative medications, specialized treatments for exacerbations, lifestyle and environmental changes. With these advances in technology and improved understanding of asthma triggers, it seems, with a coordinated approach, children's asthma can be better managed, allowing them to attend school just as regularly as other children and to enjoy all activities without having asthma frequently prevent participation. The disproportionate rate of asthma among impoverished communities in the inner city and minorities is concerning because it indicates there is an unjust allocation of resources and education to prevent this rising public health concern. The best intervention and rectification of this inequity is a multifaceted systems approach that is tailored to the needs of the family (Evans *et al.*, 1999).

→ do they really? (handwritten annotation)

Organization

Jose, the child on whom I focus here, is a patient at The Center for Children with Special Health Care Needs (The Center) in St. Christopher's Hospital for Children located in north Philadelphia. Center staff comprises two physicians specializing in primary care for children with special needs, a nurse care coordinator, administrative office staff, and a social worker. Our mission is to encourage recommended medical management for children at risk due to a variety of health issues and to support stability within the family by providing resources, coordination, health education, and intense follow-up.

   We know when there is instability at home, caregivers struggle to manage their children's medical needs, and the result is increased emergency room visits and hospitalizations. It can be challenging to remember a child's medication schedule and appointments with specialists, and to recognize a child's signs and symptoms before the child is in a health crisis. It can be increasingly challenging to coordinate all of the above when the caregiver is struggling with social issues such as inappropriate housing, domestic violence, neighborhood violence, mental health issues, and substance use within the family (Walker *et al.*, 2008). Often, preventative medical care goes by the wayside (American Academy of Pediatrics, 2009).

Description of the client situation

Jose, an 11-year-old Hispanic male, lives at home with his mother, Evelyn, and his nine-year-old sister, Sara. Carlos, his 21-year-old brother, is in and out of the family's life. Jose has been diagnosed with severe, persistent asthma and a learning disability, chronic conditions that severely affect his lifestyle at school and at home.

   When Carlos was living at home he often stayed out very late, bringing home friends who were involved in the drug trade and who were often under the influence, loud, and occasionally violent. In the past, Carlos has been incarcerated.

   Evelyn became so worried for his safety that she would sometimes leave the house, leaving both of her younger children sleeping, to follow Carlos through the streets of north Philadelphia and protect him. This often left Evelyn tired, angry and depressed the following day and meant she didn't always have the patience necessary for her other two children, their school meetings, and their medical appointments.

   About five years ago, Evelyn left her husband, the father of all three of her children, after enduring years of physical violence, emotional turmoil, and financial control as well as the rollercoaster ride of living with a crack cocaine user. After she left him, he never again physically hurt Evelyn or the children but they took his threats seriously, and Evelyn continued living in fear of bumping into him in their neighborhood. She has few people whom she trusts and who help her. To avoid further threats and harassment, Evelyn agreed that their father could see Jose and Sara on the weekends without court involvement.

Unfortunately, Jose's father's lifestyle was not conducive to the consistency needed to raise children, especially a child with a learning disability and a serious medical condition. Their father rarely remembered to give Jose his medication. In fact, both parents determined that an 11-year-old should be able to manage his own medication often saying, "He's old enough to figure it out and to deal with the consequences if he doesn't. It's his [Jose's] problem." Both parents have asthma, and it did not seem out of the ordinary to them that Jose's asthma prevented him from many outdoor activities and being a carefree child. Additionally, Jose has a learning disability resulting in him spending half of his school day in special education for his core academic classes. Managing his asthma became an enormous responsibility for this child.

Sadly, due to many other issues occurring at both his mother and father's homes, as well as a lax attitude towards the severity and controllability of asthma, many preventative measures were ignored. Jose did not regularly take medication at home, his parents did not create an asthma action plan, and the recommended routine medical appointments with his pulmonologist did not occur. Much of Jose's medical management came during an asthma attack when he was already in a health crisis. The family often ended up in the emergency room and Jose was hospitalized on several occasions including twice in intensive care.

When Jose came to us, he frequently said he was not feeling well and he was failing school. His mother, Evelyn, seemed frustrated with the medical and educational systems. As their social worker, I noted that Evelyn appeared consistently sad—she often cried in the office and couldn't tell us why, other than to say she was tired—and was seemingly angry with Jose. Evelyn often yelled at Jose in our office telling us he knew to take his medication and to tell her when he wasn't feeling well but because he was "a bad kid and always getting into trouble" he wouldn't do it. Evelyn explained that he was "old enough to figure this out."

[handwritten: Parents can also be ½ of the problem]

Decisions about practice

Definition of the client

Jose is our client because he is the identified patient in our program. However, our philosophy is that in order for Jose to receive the care we medically recommend, we have to look at the global picture and note that other stressors in the household could potentially distract the family, preventing them from focusing on Jose's medical needs. Therefore, Jose remains at the center of any care plan but it is with the understanding that, at times, my intervention may seem to be focusing more on other family members or global family issues.

Goals

Our goal at The Center is to work with the family to provide resources to prevent any barriers from providing the child, our patient, with medical care. Our assistance may come in the form of educational sessions with caregivers, community resources, forming a relationship with the school system to build consistency with medical management, or troubleshooting problems to alleviate the burden from the family. Our goals with this case were to figure out how to better stabilize the family situation so that they could concentrate on Jose's care. To determine these goals, I had to hear from the family what they needed in order to have the patience and means to focus on Jose's asthma. We had to build our care plan with Jose at the center to achieve comprehensive asthma management across the systems to ensure his safety and wellbeing.

Developing objectives and contracting

Jose's physician and I met often to figure out what to do about this situation that seemed dysfunctional and dangerous for Jose. I first spoke with Evelyn about what she thought the challenges were to medical management and she listed her current barriers: (1) My son, Carlos, is on and off the streets and might be using drugs. At the very least, he's dealing. It's making me crazy; (2) Jose won't take his medicine; (3) My ex-husband sees the kids and he never remembers Jose's medicine; (4) I don't like Jose's school. They're always calling me and complaining about Jose. There's nothing that I can do. I don't know what they want from me; (5) I'm tired and frustrated. I don't want to deal with this mess any more.

Evelyn's responses provided me with our framework. We developed an intervention to assist with stabilizing the outlying factors affecting Evelyn's ability to therapeutically help Jose both medically and educationally. While it appears my client focus has shifted from our patient, Jose, to his mother, Evelyn, I must assist the adult caregiver with whom he spends the most time. Children come with guardians and it is very difficult to provide intervention for a child without consideration of, and assistance to, the adults making decisions in his life.

Meeting place and use of time

Our meetings took place within our clinic during Jose's follow-up or sick visits. During clinic visits, much of my time with the family depended on the physician's structure of Jose's visit. I would be able to meet with the family before or after the physician had completed the exam. This also depended on the family's schedule that day, and whether or not they might be able to spend additional time after Jose's appointment to meet with me. I had to be quite flexible to best support the family. At times, Evelyn and I made appointments together so that we could speak privately. Additionally, I spent time attending a series of school meetings and supporting the family by phone.

Strategies and interventions

I began by clarifying with Evelyn that our program's help with other issues in the family's life originated from our concern and hers that Jose's asthma management was not optimal. I formed my social work intervention based on concrete services I could provide to ease some of the stress in their lives. We discussed her concerns about Carlos at length, how Jose and Sara perceive Carlos, and how his lifestyle affects the rest of the family. Through lengthy discussions about how scared Evelyn said she was about the fate of her oldest son, she was able to see that her feelings about this tenuous situation were similar to her younger children's feelings about Carlos. Evelyn said she could see they were scared and sad even though she was trying so hard to protect them from Carlos's lifestyle and struggles. Evelyn further explained she was overwhelmed by her eldest son's problems, and that they often took up all of her energy so she couldn't dedicate nearly as much time to her younger children. While identifying behavior and patterns does not eliminate them, Evelyn could begin to understand that events and actions were linked and causal rather than completely out of her control and merely a series of tragic coincidences.

Through discussions over the course of months, Evelyn determined that Carlos's behavior put his life at great risk, and she began to take action. Evelyn made one of the most difficult decisions for a mother to make and agreed to collaborate with the police in assisting them in prosecuting her son, resulting in his incarceration.

During this time, Evelyn seemed calmer and it appeared to me that making this decision was not solely about protecting her son, but about regaining control as the matriarch of the family. Evelyn came into our clinic and I assisted her with the phone call to her son's parole officer reporting Carlos's whereabouts and schedule. While his arrest and subsequent court hearings made the family stressed and sad, Evelyn said she felt more at ease, knowing her eldest son would be safer now.

During the months of the above intervention, we also worked to reinforce asthma education, realizing both Evelyn and Jose would need to take ownership for managing Jose's asthma. Initially, I had thought that Evelyn assumed the mother's role, and Jose the child's. I began to notice, however, that Evelyn's expectations of Jose in everything related to his medical needs were that he was no longer a child, but rather someone developmentally able to fully manage his medical needs. While Jose should begin taking greater ownership over his asthma management in this stage of his life, it remains developmentally inappropriate for an 11-year-old to take full responsibility for his medical needs. Additionally, Jose's learning disability affected his ability to competently understand the complexity of health, medication, and outcomes.

The physician, the nurse, and I coordinated our approach and delivered a consistent message to the family: we must work with Jose to teach him about asthma, but it remains an adult's responsibility to manage and redirect him as he continues to gain comfort in taking on this role. We reinforced this message with every medical appointment and follow-up phone call with the goal of Evelyn accepting that she held agency in this situation.

We worked with Evelyn to define what Jose's role should be with his asthma and directed her to verbalize what her asthma plan was for him. Should he always remember all of his medications? What happens if he forgets his medication? Is there a rewards system to encourage and reinforce this behavior? Should he report every sign and symptom without prompts from her? If he does report that he's not feeling well, what would she then do? Does she know what the next steps are? Coaxing this information from Evelyn helped her process these concepts. Most importantly, I had full support from the medical team, pediatrician and nurse, so that we all reinforced these topics with the family. Both Evelyn and Jose were urged to verbalize their knowledge of asthma, their medical management plan, and their frustrations.

To focus on Evelyn's hope that Jose would manage his own preventative medication, I met with Evelyn and Jose separately and together to develop realistic expectations for Jose's role in his health care. Evelyn said she wanted Jose to take all of his preventative medication and be responsible for it, including noticing when he was running out of medication and remembering every dose. He reported that he took his medication, but "sometimes forgot." Developmentally, Jose was unable to fully connect cause and effect. While working on his understanding of the reasons behind taking preventative medicine to improve his quality of life and lessen his symptoms, it was important that we implement a concrete, age-appropriate intervention.

I worked with Jose to figure out how to include taking medication into his daily routine. We began by looking at his daily schedule. We reviewed what he routinely did every single day regardless of going to school or his mood. From here, Jose took control and formed his own plan. He would need to explain his plan to Evelyn and implement it with her assistance signifying that both he and his mother controlled their individual roles in this plan. Jose determined that if he were to remember his asthma medication, he would need to keep it on the sink in the bathroom. He recognized that it could never be put away because then he wouldn't remember it. He also realized that, to keep him on target, he needed to put a sign—which he made himself—on the wall of the bathroom. Jose took charge and explained his plan to his mother with the physician and me present. We reviewed the plan as a team and realized this would ensure consistency with medication five days out of the week, but he may still struggle on the weekends when with his father. I spoke with Evelyn and Jose about what they could do to prevent inconsistency with medications while Jose visited his father, who seemingly did not agree with a focused medical management plan for asthma and often put up barriers to care. Provided Jose took his medication regularly during the school week and as consistently as possible at the weekends, with Evelyn's reminders, he would still reduce his chances of symptoms.

Use of resources outside of the relationship

When looking at concrete services that could be provided to this family, I referred them to an asthma educational outreach program. The community program provides families with asthma education via phone and is able to troubleshoot some frequently asked questions through the anonymity of the telephone. The program also reviews asthma triggers within the child's home such as wall-to-wall carpeting, curtains, rodents and insects, pets, cleaning agents, dust and paint chips, safety tips for storage of medications and tracking usage. It then provides the family with resources and ideas on how to eliminate these risk factors from their child's lifestyle and environment (Leading Healthy Communities, 2008).

While we provided much of this information to the family in our pediatric office, it was greatly reinforced by this outside agency that the family deemed as non-intrusive because of the contact by phone. To me, the more times Evelyn heard the facts in varying formats, the more she might retain further information on asthma, its impact, and its prevention. An additional goal was that, as a byproduct of assisting Jose, this information would benefit anyone in the family struggling with asthma, including Evelyn herself.

We then focused on Jose's elementary school. Despite Jose's placement in special education, he was doing very poorly and reports showed that he was often in the school nurse's office complaining of his asthma. At times, his asthma caused him to miss recess and physical education. When I called the school nurse and the teacher, they described Jose's asthma as a crutch; he would report that his chest was tightening resulting in an automatic visit to the nurse. This behavior seemed to happen often during his academic subjects. The school further reported that while Jose's asthma symptoms were real, he had a high level of anxiety around them. He often began by reporting his symptoms. If he wasn't given a nebulizer treatment immediately, he would become increasingly anxious, further exacerbating his asthma, until—regardless of the way they had begun—his symptoms would quickly worsen.

The school had tried behavior modification. They attempted to work with Jose to diminish his fears, lessen his anxiety, and teach him composure so his asthma symptoms would stabilize, as opposed to spiking with increased anxiety. One should always be cautious when using behavior modification in connection with a child's health concern of any kind. It would, for example, be difficult to discern what was true asthma, what was anxiety, or what was an "excuse" to avoid participation. Such an intervention would need a meeting of all parties involved, including Jose.

I coordinated the meeting with the school, the family, and my team, and we had two successful meetings at the school. I attended both of them and our nurse care coordinator attended one. The teachers, nurse, guidance counselor, principal, mother, child, and I met to review everyone's concerns. Jose was present, and we made sure we spoke in an age-appropriate manner and that he answered questions and provided us with feedback. Jose's asthma exacerbations were frequent, and the school wondered if some of his symptoms were more behavioral rather than true symptoms of asthma. In response, the school would call Evelyn frequently, frustrating her because it seemed to her to be another problem she could not fix.

Meeting with the school led to great insight into Jose's academic abilities and challenges. When he struggled, instead of asking for help, he misbehaved. As a team interested in Jose's success, we were able to reframe this meeting from being about how Jose overreacted and mismanaged his asthma to one about what additional strategies the school could use to assist him in better comprehending the most difficult subjects, potentially increasing his comfort while at school. The school recognized that this family took the issues seriously enough to work closely with their medical team in advocating for Jose's needs.

Additionally, by verbalizing that this child was failing educationally and medically, we all saw how closely health, behavior, academic performance, and family dynamics were intertwined. How could Jose concentrate if he was anxious about having an asthma attack? How could he learn if he was constantly in the nurse's office? Was his anxiety about certain academics a trigger to shortness of breath and nerves that appeared as if they were symptoms of asthma? Was much of what would calm Jose down closely linked with receiving individualized attention from the school nurse? In relation to his asthma, the school team had reported that they noted increased anxiety in Jose whenever he showed any signs of asthma. While asthma and anxiety are closely linked, the ALA (2008) notes that:

> a common misbelief is that children with asthma have a major psychological problem that has caused the asthma … Emotional stress itself (anxiety, frustration, anger) can trigger asthma, but the asthmatic condition precedes the emotional stress … Many children with asthma suffer from severe anxiety during an episode as a result of suffocation produced by asthma. The anxiety and panic can then produce rapid breathing or hyperventilation, which further triggers the asthma.

According to the school's reports, Jose's anxiety affected his behavior. Potentially, many of the behavioral problems the school reported could be stabilized if Jose felt better. Possibly, Jose would improve his concentration in school if he were not anxious about his symptoms flaring up and if he were regularly taking his medication. Maybe Jose would feel more positively about school if he could consistently participate in all activities.

These cycles would not easily be broken without consistent and fine-tuned interventions. Because Jose spent a large portion of his time in school, school would be an ideal and necessary place to intervene. Much of our success can be attributed to our nurse's providing further asthma education for the teachers, and the school's making accommodations in Jose's Individualized Education Plan (IEP) for additional educational supports for his most challenging subjects. For the first time, Jose participated in school meetings and could see that everyone, including his mother, was communicating and making a plan with him rather than for him.

Throughout this process, Evelyn continued to struggle; however, she struggled less than when she worried about Carlos and when she was frustrated that the school didn't take her seriously. Now, we had open communication between family, school, and medical team. Once we were able to stabilize her noted concerns, we could begin to speak about what therapeutic assistance Evelyn needed for herself. I had gained her trust due to the success of the other interventions and knew we could continue building progress for her children and the family as a whole.

Stance of the social worker

When I reflect on this case, I note the importance of a multi-systems approach. It seems finding the barriers to obtaining medical care, identifying the strengths of the family and the individual, and then coordinating care between all of the players involved creates a more successful approach. Furthermore, this approach empowers the family in disease management. The focus shifts away from how the professionals expect a family to medically care for a child and moves towards how a family will manage their child's needs through the medical team and the school. The parent is able to manage the key players in the child's life. Children are encouraged to share with us the signs and symptoms they are feeling, that adults will then react accordingly, and that we trust children to be a part of our team to manage their needs. My goal for any case is that families continue on this trajectory until they are requesting specific assistance from our team, coordinating meetings between the professionals, and that eventually, as children mature, they are the ones dictating their care needs to us. Families should become the central players in the care plan. Professionals will not always be consistent figures in the children's lives. Physicians leave, nurses change positions, children graduate and social workers may or may not continue to be involved. It would be a great service to adults if, throughout their youth, we encouraged them to take on developmentally appropriate responsibilities of care so they could successfully manage their disease over their lifetime.

Use of resources outside of the helping relationship

Much of this intervention depended on systems outside of the family: the medical team, the school, and the community asthma education program. At times, my role was primarily as a coordinator and communicator between parties. I depended on working with a physician who agreed with the importance of intervention in this case and who dedicated time and energy to educating the family. Additionally, I depended on the physician and nurse to reinforce the importance of medical management, providing positive feedback to the family when they were appropriately managing care and redirecting them when they faltered. The school also became an active part of this series of interventions by amending Jose's educational plan, meeting directly with Jose to create a plan to eliminate his asthma triggers, and conducting an open dialogue with mother and child to create a working, functional relationship.

Reassessment and evaluation

In reassessing Jose's case, I realized I had to be very flexible and that interventions had to be continually reconfigured in order to meet the needs of the family in each period. One of the greatest aspects of this case was the cooperation between systems. The school's interest in and dedication to Jose was remarkable. The school team created a comprehensive plan, supported Jose through his struggles with his medical management without promoting dysfunctional behavior, and noted his academic needs, which may have been previously masked as behavior around asthma. I have not formally spoken with the family about how fewer hospital visits and better controlled asthma have affected their lives. In the future, it would be valuable in my evaluation to review progress with the family. Also, in time, individual and family therapy might enable this family to explore past trauma, and improve their current dynamic and management of chronic illness.

Transfer and termination

Jose's case will remain ongoing. Our center sees patients until they are 21 years old, and we will continue to shape our care plan to Jose's needs. This family continues to struggle. Their medical management, while improved, remains inconsistent. The foundation for good medical management and multi-systems communications has been built so that when there are inconsistencies of care, we have something to which we can return.

Case conclusion

Jose has had far fewer sick visits and emergency room visits, and has had no hospitalizations in the past year for his asthma. He continues to struggle with asthma, but not to the same extent. Evelyn now coordinates meetings with the school when she has concerns. She also took on the responsibility of inviting our medical team to participate in the meetings with the school. While Jose still struggles in school and admits to not always taking his medication, the reduced rate of overall hospital visits around asthma indicates that the family has improved its medical management of his chronic health condition at home.

Differential discussion

While there have been successes and setbacks with Jose's case, the key element seems to be working across systems while empowering the caregiver and the child to take on this responsibility themselves. However, if the medical team or the school system had been unwilling to take part in these discussions, Jose may never have received the necessary coordination to stabilize his asthma. Jose's case further illustrates the challenges of managing chronic illness at any point, but especially when difficult mental health, domestic violence and addiction problems bar the caregiver from providing care. Jose's asthma was not the family's utmost concern and management of it consistently came second.

I wonder what would have happened in Jose's care if the medical team had reached out to the school earlier or if social services had become involved sooner. While the family did have some help in the past, our allowing for a long time period to manage and reconstruct this intervention contributed greatly to its success. Much depended on the family's connection with our team and a level of trust that led to disclosure of the barriers to managing Jose's asthma. Fortunately for this case, I was not given a time period or a deadline, but rather permitted to continually work with the family.

References

American Academy of Pediatrics (2009). The National Center of Medical Home Initiatives for Children with special Needs. Retrieved 1/8/09, from http://www.medicalhomeinfo.org

American Lung Association (ALA) (2008). *Childhood asthma overview*. Retrieved January, 2009, from http://www.lungusa.org

CDC (2006, December 29). Center for Disease Control and Prevention. *National Center for Health Statistics, Advance Data from Vital and Health Statistics. The State of Childhood Asthma, United States, 1980–2005* (Number 381). Retrieved January 2009, from http://www.cdc.gov/nchs/data/ad/ad 381.pdf

CDC (2007, December). National Center for Chronic Disease Prevention and Health Promotion. *Healthy youth! Health topics: Asthma*. Retrieved 1/10/09, from http://www.cdc.gov/healthyyouth/asthma/index.htm

Evans, R. III, Gergen, P. J., Mitchell, H., Kattan, M. Kercsmar, C., Crain, E. Anderson, J., Eggleston, P.,

Malveaux, F. J. & Wedner, J. (1999). A randomized clinical trial to reduce asthma morbidity among inner-city children: Results of the National Cooperative Inner-City Asthma Study. *The Journal of Pediatrics*, 135 (3): 332–8.

Katten, M., Stearns, S. C., Crain, E. F., Stout, J. W., Gergen, P. J. & Evans, R. III. (2006). Cost-effectiveness of a home-based environmental intervention for inner-city children with asthma. *Journal of Allergy & Clinical Immunology*, 116 (5): 1058–63.

Leading Healthy Communities (2008). Child Asthma Link Line. Retrieved 1/8/09, from http://www.leadinghealthycommunities.com

NCIAS (1995). National Cooperative Inner City Asthma Study. Retrieved 6/8/09, from http://grants.nih.gov/grants/guides/ifa-files/RFA-A1-95-007.html

Parker, O. (2005). Asthma management: A role for social work. *Health & Social Work*, 30 (2): 167–70.

Segoris Love, A. & Spiegel, J. (2006). The inner-city asthma intervention tool kit: Best practices and lessons learned. *Annals of Allergy, Asthma, and Immunology*, 97 (1): 536–9.

Spiegel, J., Segoris Love, A., Wood, P. R., Griffith, M., Taylor, K. R., Williams, S. G. & Redd, S. (2006). The inner city intervention: Description of a community-based implementation of an evidence-based approach to asthma management, *Annals of Allergy, Asthma and Immunology*, 97 (1): SUP 1:S6–S10.

Stephen C., M.D. (2006). The Inner-City Asthma Intervention: description of a community-based implementation of an evidence-based approach to asthma management. *Annals of Allergy, Asthma, and Immunology*, 97: 6–10.

Walker, J., Lewis-Land, C., Kub, J., Tsonkleris, M. & Butz, A. (2008). The effect of violence on asthma: Are our children facing a double-edged sword? *Journal of Community Health*, 33 (6): 384–8.

7 Social work in the pediatric endocrinology and diabetes clinic

Fighting the new epidemic of type 2 diabetes in children

Helaine Ciporen

Context

Epidemic levels of type 2 diabetes mellitus (T2DM) are currently being observed in children (Caprio *et al.*, 2008). This new epidemic is mainly attributed to the environmental factors of our modern lifestyle. Once called adult onset diabetes, T2DM had to be renamed because over the past 20 years, it affects younger and younger individuals. While this type of diabetes is associated with a genetic predisposition, the trigger that activates the gene is obesity (Laurence, Liese *et al.*, 2008; Ogden, Carroll & Flegan, 2008). A complex web of environmental, economic, political, cultural, genetic, and psychological factors have changed our modern lifestyle into one that promotes obesity. While type 2 diabetes is currently more prevalent in certain ethnic, economic and regional groups, the epidemic crosses all of these boundaries, threatening many segments of our population. Emerging first in the United States, this epidemic is now a worldwide concern (Popkin, Conde, Hou & Monteiro, 2006).

Fast foods, cutbacks in physical education programs at school, trading active playtime for TV and computer time and lack of access to fresh fruits and vegetables in certain neighborhoods, are a few of the factors that have contributed to creating the problem. Agricultural policy may be another force driving the proliferation of junk foods, with three subsidized crops—wheat, corn and soybeans—being the main ingredients in these processed packaged foods (Polan, 2007). The "cure" must be addressed on all levels, from political to personal. Education is a primary weapon to deploy if a lasting lifestyle change and reversal of this trend is to be achieved.

Increasingly, hospitals have been called on to address this epidemic. Social workers acting as educators, advocates and therapists in this setting have a unique and creative opportunity to play a role in the battle to reverse the T2DM epidemic. Meaningful lifestyle changes can be initiated through individual, family, group and outreach educational approaches that address the maladaptive behavioral, family system and psychological issues.

The Hall Family Clinic for Pediatric Endocrinology and Diabetes was established, as a new facility, at the Mount Sinai Medical Center, a major, urban hospital complex, in 2006, but this specialty has always existed as a distinct service within the pediatric department. At its inception, the department served patients with a variety of hormonal disorders, primarily type 1, or juvenile diabetes, but also hyperthyroidism, premature or delayed puberty and growth issues. Today, there are also many young patients seen for the prevention and treatment of type 2 diabetes. The area served by the hospital, and its immediate neighborhood of East Harlem, has one of the highest prevalence rates of T2DM in the city and in the state.

We all require the hormone insulin in order to break down the carbohydrates we eat.

Insulin is produced as needed, by the pancreas, in proportion to the amount and type of food we ingest. Type 2 diabetes occurs when the body develops a resistance to insulin and no longer uses it properly. As the need for insulin rises, the pancreas gradually loses its ability to produce sufficient amounts needed to regulate the blood sugar. T2DM is associated with a genetic predisposition, but in order to manifest in youngsters, its onset is triggered by obesity. It is distinct from type 1 diabetes, which is not reliant on genetic predisposition or obesity, and occurs when the pancreas ceases to function completely.

Formerly, the average onset of T2DM occurred in middle or old age, when the body's organs, including the pancreas, slow their function. Increasingly, people develop T2DM at younger ages, as excessive weight gain make it difficult for the pancreas to keep up with increased demands for insulin. Despite genetic predisposition, T2DM will not be activated at a young age if an appropriate weight is maintained. Once T2DM is established, the persistence of obesity interferes with the response to treatment and therefore, regulating weight remains an important goal.

Type 2 diabetes is generally diagnosed through presentation of clinical symptoms, including excessive thirst, polydipsia; excessive urination, polyuria; and excessive hunger, polyphagia. In addition, when blood sugars reach very high levels, symptoms commonly mistaken for flu, such as stomachache, vomiting and weight loss may occur. Acanthosis nigrocans, a darkening of the skin, typically around the neck, is another common indicator. Diagnosis is confirmed through blood glucose testing. An elevated CPEPTID level signals a resistance to insulin, indicating a higher risk for potentially developing T2DM.

Obesity trends in our national adult population have gone from 11.5% in 1980 to 25.6% in 2006 and an astounding 60.5% of the adult population in the United States was overweight by 2005 (CDC, 2007). We see a similar trend in children, with the number of 6–11-year-olds at the 95th percentile of BMI (body mass index, a ratio of height and weight) at 7% in 1980 and 15.3% in 2000. Children, ages 12–19 with a BMI in the 95th percentile, jumped from 5% in 1980 to 15.5% in 2000 (NCHS, 2005). In New York City, 24% of elementary school children are categorized as obese, with an additional 19% considered overweight. In every grade, K through 5th, more than 20% of the class is obese. It is already a serious problem in kindergarten with 21% of the children categorized as obese (Kim, Berger & Matte, 2006). This translates nationally to more than six million children who are overweight and therefore at risk for a multitude of related medical problems, including heart and kidney disease, sleep apnea, exacerbation of asthma, and cardiovascular problems leading to blindness and amputation (Kaufman, 2002).

Policy

Although it is now in its second decade of existence, governmental bodies are just beginning to address the T2DM phenomenon in children. Diabetes has become a popular topic in political speeches and yet, to date, no coherent national policy has emerged. The epidemic levels of this illness suggest severe implications for our national medical and insurance infrastructure. The increase in per capita Medicare spending can also be measured by weight. For a normal weight adult, medical costs are approximately $3,500 per year. For an overweight adult, annual costs are $4,000 and for an obese adult, costs jump to more than $5,000. At the same time, life expectancy goes down, from 70+ years for a 20-year-old male with a BMI of 24, to only 50+ years for a 20-year-old male with a BMI greater than 45 (CDC, 2007). By every societal measure, the cost of obesity is great, including the personal cost, where the effects of having a chronic illness can be devastating.

The government of New York City has taken a leadership role in establishing aggressive policies to reverse the trend. Trans fats have been banned as an ingredient in prepared foods, calorie counts are mandated to be listed on menus, school menus are being revamped and fruit-selling green carts have been opened in poor neighborhoods (Lucadamo, 2008). On a statewide level, a tax on sugared soda is being considered. Much like the cigarette tax, this new "obesity tax" is intended to reduce the consumption of highly caloric drinks while it raises money for health programs (Chan, 2008). Health insurers are considering new policies as well, as they try to limit their costs of care per subscriber. Like auto insurers who offer incentives for good driving records, health insurers may someday tie rates to healthy, or lowered, BMIs. In the private sector, the Robert Wood Johnson Foundation has devoted itself to abolishing obesity in children by the year 2015 by offering a wide range of grant support to creative initiatives and research throughout the country. Despite its chronic nature, T2DM is not considered a disability and therefore those who have it do not qualify for SSI or other supplemental entitlements or benefits.

Technology

Continual developments in pharmacological, technological and surgical interventions mean we know far more about the management of diabetes than we did even 10 years ago. Theoretically, no one need suffer the devastating side-effects—such as blindness or amputation of lower limbs—which were viewed as inevitable just a generation ago. The development of long- and short-acting insulin makes the careful regulation of blood sugars possible. If the disease is less severe, Glucophage, the only oral medication approved for pediatric use, may suffice.

Improved technology makes it possible to get nearly instant blood glucose level readings from a tiny drop of blood. Computer technology allows for these readings to be stored within the meter, so personal trends can be monitored, insulin needs calibrated and medication levels adjusted for more accurate control. Patients now have a choice of insulin delivery systems, such as ports or pumps inserted on the abdomen or thigh, which only need to be changed every other day, replacing multiple injections per day.

When lifestyle changes or pharmacological interventions fail to produce the desired results, various bariatric surgical interventions such as gastric bypass or gastric banding can be considered to control obesity. This surgery has been used successfully with adults, but is considered a last resort for teens who suffer multiple complications related to T2DM. There are stringent guidelines for both the medical team and the teenage patient, including six months of lifestyle modification and a psychosocial evaluation to ensure appropriate family support and medical adherence after surgery (Endocrine Society, 2008). This intervention has various risks and side-effects and is in the early stages of being offered to older teens.

Ironically, it may be the low-tech intervention that proves to be the safest, least costly and most effective—that is a simple lifestyle change. However, this change has managed to be the most elusive one. Our national obsession with dieting has not helped to lower our collective BMI. In fact, our cultural view of beauty and the diet industry it has spawned may be one of the factors contributing to the problem. Yet it is here, in the "low-tech" solution, that social workers can be most effective. Social workers can explore the psychosocial factors that impede treatment and develop pragmatic plans to overcome them. Social workers are trained to address the psychological and motivational issues that are too often overlooked. I have successfully used individual psychotherapeutic work with children, psycho-educational work with families, group work, and outreach education events as interventions to meet these goals.

Organization

Patients are generally referred to this specialty clinic by their pediatrician or pediatric emergency room. A multi-disciplinary team of endocrinologists, nurse practitioner, nutritionist and social worker meet with patients and their families to develop appropriate treatment plans. Social work clinical practice in endocrinology and diabetes requires a working knowledge of current medical practice, features of various treatment options and technologies, and access to local resources in order to facilitate the family's decision-making process. It also requires strong clinical skills, especially in understanding the effects of chronic illness on the patient and family.

Description of the client situation

John is a 12-year-old Hispanic boy who was referred to the clinic by his pediatrician for evaluation of obesity and risk for type 2 diabetes. He lives with his parents, two younger sisters and paternal grandmother, in the vicinity of the hospital. There is a strong family history of type 2 diabetes, with both his father and grandmother, among others, affected. John presented with a BMI in the 92nd percentile and acanthosis nigricans, a skin disorder characterized by dark, thick velvety skin in body folds and creases, visible around his neck. We will follow John as he and his family proceed through the interventions described below.

Decisions about practice

Definition of the client

In a pediatric setting, the patients being treated are minors, newborns through 21 years of age. They are accompanied by their caregivers—most often their mothers, but also other family members or guardians. Teens returning to the clinic for routine follow-up may arrive independently. The child and primary caregiver are thought of as a unit and are, as such, the "patient." When this dyad is part of a larger family unit, the entire family should be considered the patient, even when they are not being treated directly. It is likely that the lifestyle modifications being called for will, to some extent, affect all family members. It is also likely other family members are overweight and at risk for T2DM but may not recognize this in themselves. This is true for John's family, where his father, paternal grandmother and two younger sisters are all overweight.

There is often a multi-generational familial awareness of T2DM because it is genetically linked. It is important to explore the family's preconceptions about T2DM; their personal experiences and possible idiosyncratic misconceptions may exist as hidden barriers to treatment. Family members may have varying points of view on how to treat illness. These opinions may differ, between generations represented, or between the main decision makers, the parents. Consideration must be given to the family's cultural and religious background, as well as their economic and educational status in developing effective plans. John's mother was very worried about her children getting T2DM; she saw its devastating effects on her husband and mother-in-law. She was motivated to help her children in any way she could. However, John's father had not taken an active stance in controlling his own weight or blood sugars, considering T2DM inevitable. John's grandmother was depressed by the complications she had already suffered. This sense of hopelessness was perceived by the children and may have triggered a level of anxiety they then attempted to quell by overeating.

In the pediatric setting, responsibility for executing treatment plans falls to the parents or caregivers and educational efforts are largely aimed toward them. Caregivers are also the ones who buy, prepare and serve the family meals. They can be empowered to make needed changes by reminding them that, in the same manner they have taught their children to brush their teeth and cross the street safely, they are also teaching them how to make diet and exercise choices, either directly or by example. Establishing the right habits early in life is the best prevention for a host of future health problems related to or exacerbated by obesity.

Receiving a diagnosis of T2DM is life altering, and can be anxiety provoking, even traumatic, for a parent. They may feel guilt about transferring a condition with a genetic component. Children's reactions are often cued by their parents' response to the diagnosis; therefore helping parents to cope by providing the "permission" they need to attend to their own needs can also be beneficial in mediating the children's adjustment process. Type 2 diabetes, once contracted, becomes a lifelong consideration in daily living, and so prevention, or forestalling of onset, is well worth the effort. By informing John's parents of the latest developments in diabetes care, I was able to motivate his mother and peak his father's interest in exploring lifestyle changes that could benefit the whole family.

A family's coping style may be shaped by its cultural or religious heritage. For instance, parents had a heightened need for confidentiality because they felt their child's future prospects for marriage would be compromised if the child's condition was known within their community. Another family initially rejected pharmacological solutions due to religious teachings, another due to its cultural preference for herbal remedies. Ethnicity also plays a large role in the type of foods the family cooks and eats, creating resistance to change and making this topic difficult to discuss. When John's mother met with our nutritionist, they were able to make slight adjustments to treasured family recipes, reducing the fat content and increasing the quantity of vegetables used. The family was also encouraged to switch, first to 2% milk, then later to 1%, so the taste difference would hardly be noticed. Making one small change at a time is a surer routine to lasting lifestyle changes than is crash dieting which eventually wears out one's willpower, leading only to frustration and failure.

Poverty, lack of disposable income, educational status, poor access to resources and chaotic family life can pose serious obstacles to making fitness changes. There are many creative options that can be considered, including free activities sponsored by the local parks department, volunteering for gardening or dog walking duties, sports leagues or simple family walks after dinner. Other economic considerations include access to and cost of food. Many poor neighborhoods do not have adequate supermarkets and rely on small shops where choices are limited to expensive prepared foods. There may be limited access to farmers' markets and families may not be familiar with the array of available fruits and vegetables. John's mother was introduced to the hospital's newly established farmer's market and was motivated to use it when she learned of the special discount coupons and recipes available there. A family may run out of food stamps before the end of the month and fall back on a diet of what they perceive as less expensive, but high carbohydrate, foods, such as rice and beans. Education on alternative food options and assistance in planning family menus can be a helpful solution.

The effects of poverty can be far reaching on very personal levels. For instance, our staff expressed their concern that the daughters of one family, headed by a single mother, were watching too much TV and therefore not getting enough physical activity. The mother did not attempt to hide her contempt when she explained why she was happy to know her girls were safe at home. She had lost her teenage son to the lures of the street and gang violence and had no intentions of allowing the girls to stray. She felt misunderstood and frustrated in resolving her daughters' health issues, which seemed less important than other potential dangers she and they faced. Now she also felt abandoned by our staff in resolving her problems. In letting her know that her circumstances were understood and helping her prioritize and deal with other issues, such as her daughters' school placements, I was able to establish a better partnership with her and devise a more reasonable health plan with them.

Interventions

I employ four distinct forms of intervention and will talk about each separately: working individually with children, working with the family unit, group work and outreach education efforts. Within these sections I will address the goals, contracting, meeting place, use of time

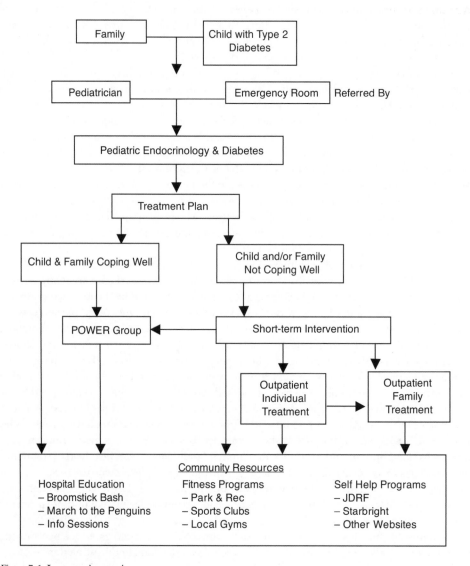

Figure 7.1 Intervention options.

and resources, social work stance, reassessment and transfer needs that are unique to each situation.

Common to all four of these formats is a family-centered approach. A family is a natural "team." It follows, according to the American Medical Association (AMA), that family-based weight-management programs work best; they take advantage of this pre-existing, cohesive support network. Recommendations on food and fitness are beneficial to all family members, regardless of weight. It is important not to single out overweight children, which could make them feel deprived or judged as a result of their health needs. It is recommended that the families eat together, eat the same healthy foods, and exercise as a family, whenever possible.

Working individually with children

The decision to work therapeutically with children is made based on their adjustment to the diagnosis and their coping ability. Their need for intervention will usually manifest in a variety of acting-out behaviors, such as a change in school performance or peer relationships, tearfulness, volatility, or loss of interest in their usual activities. They may experience a loss of their age-appropriate sense of invulnerability and feel they are now "broken." There are several goals in working with children individually: facilitate adjustment to the diagnosis, uncover and address any psychological issues that would impede adherence to medical treatment and enlist the child's active participation in developing and executing the treatment plan. A parent's permission and cooperation must be obtained before intervening with the child and it is best to meet with parents at regular intervals to ensure continuity of care. Children's participation is key to the success of the treatment plan and, more importantly, to their future wellbeing as adults. This is a "teaching moment" when positive attitudes and good habits can be established.

Among attitudes and concerns to be explored with children are: the effect of the diagnosis on self-image; their understanding of the diagnosis and the treatment needs; their relationship to family members, especially parents; communication styles within the family; needs for privacy and their plans to share information with others. Children often feel they are limited to "eavesdropping" on their parents to learn about their medical information. I encourage children to feel free to ask questions and express their feelings, both at home and at the clinic.

Children can be very concrete in their thinking and so I attempt not to take any detail for granted. John, upon hearing that he was now at risk for T2DM, began to cry inconsolably, terrified that he was about to die. With further support, he articulated this fear: "Why else would they call it *die*-abetes?" This aspect of concrete thinking must be taken into consideration on every level. For instance, in devising a weekly exercise or snack plan, a child will be familiar with the concept of a "week," but not necessarily know that it consists of seven days. It is safest to provide a calendar or other age-appropriate, concrete or visual supports for the child to use.

The full range of child therapy interventions, including play therapy, should be considered. It is important to assess the child's maturational, as well as chronological, age, interests and skill levels. Keeping a diary, for instance, may be a good tool for a teenage girl, but not for one who has a reading disability and/or is uninterested in writing. Teaching hypnotherapy or relaxation techniques can be very effective in assisting the child in managing the fear or pain of injections and finger pricks.

Children see themselves as members of a family system, identifying with their culture, religion and other family traits. For instance, children may dream of growing up and joining the same profession as their parents. While this is often positive, it can sometimes work in a negative way. In John's case, he assumed T2DM was his unavoidable fate, mirroring an attitude expressed by his father. He was terrified because he had seen his grandmother's complications, including amputation of lower limbs. I explained that these side-effects are now avoidable, due to improved medical technology. His relief was palpable when his misconceptions were addressed. John had no underlying psychopathology and only short-term intervention was needed to assist him. In partnership with our medical team, he learned to forestall the onset of T2DM by making healthier decisions. John transformed from being a belligerent resister who quelled his anxieties with food, to a full partner, enlisting his mother's and our support in the plan he helped devise to stay healthy.

It is important to help children think through their attitudes towards privacy. Even children who seem to be adjusting well and want to share information about their diabetes with friends may not be prepared for the variety of responses they may encounter. For instance, some friends may fear that diabetes is contagious; some may be repulsed by the possible need for daily injections; while others may consider it heroic. It is best to prepare children, in advance, for these types of questions and reactions. Unanticipated over-exposure to public scrutiny may interfere with children's adherence to treatment. They may become reluctant to go to the school nurse before lunchtime or consume inappropriate snacks along with their friends after school in an effort to conceal their medical needs.

The relationship between children and clinic generally lasts many years. I begin to make plans for transfer to an adult service a year prior to their aging out of pediatrics, at 21 years of age. We discuss the transition of disengaging from a trusted, long-term relationship with our staff to re-engaging with a new support team who will expect them to behave as autonomous adults. This new expectation accounts for the major differences in adult and pediatric treatment style. Changes, similar to those a teen may feel when going off to college for the first time, are echoed in the transition to adult service.

Working with the family

The medical team views the parent as the adult responsible for overseeing adherence to the treatment plan. My goal is to ease parents through the first stage of coping with the new diagnosis and then help them integrate the demands of the treatment plan into the family's existing routine. My approach is non-judgmental and pragmatic. I frame the series of desired adjustments as small, manageable steps. Children are still growing and should not be on restrictive diets; this may trigger an eating disorder. Instead, establishing moderate habits and healthy choices should be fostered. Often, the objective is simply for children not to gain additional weight. As they grow in height, their BMI will automatically be reduced. Small changes, such as switching to 1% milk, giving up sugared drinks, or adding 15 extra minutes of daily physical activity may be all that is needed.

Meetings with individuals or families take place in my office. The clinic itself is a new facility offering a pleasant and cheerful atmosphere for children and families, but the hospital is a large, imposing facility, often associated with health crises and stressful times for families. The duration of an individual session will be between 30 minutes and one hour, depending on the situational needs. Patients are scheduled for routine follow-up clinic visits four times per year, but more frequent visits will occur as required, especially after a new diagnosis. At this time or during crises, I may see patients as often as once or twice per week. Patients are free to see the social worker during any clinic visit and I make it a practice to use each encounter to reassess the family's current needs and make appropriate adjustments or interventions.

In family work, I am often in the role of "go-between" between the family and the medical staff. As I explore what has transpired, I re-word medical explanations to be more easily understood by the various family members. I also urge them to bring any questions to the appropriate team professional. I explained to John, in terms he could understand, how high blood glucose levels contribute to circulatory problems and in turn, provoke the consequences his grandmother suffered. He could understand that these problems were avoidable if he used the technology available to him today to keep his blood sugars stable. I advise the staff of these conversations, both in patient chart notes and during our twice-weekly medical rounds, so they can be better prepared for their next patient encounters.

In our urban community, we are fortunate to have a variety of resources for family referrals. I keep lists, including local playgrounds and parks, with classes and other activities offered there, important informational websites, lo-cal snack recipes, self-help groups, etc., and distribute them as needed. John eventually decided to pursue his interest in soccer and I was able to direct him to a local league and secure a waiver for his fees and uniform. His father has enjoyed watching his son's games and may become more involved with the league himself. There are also a number of resources within the hospital, including the Adolescent Health Center, child psychiatry and other specialty clinics to which I may refer. Referrals often go beyond the immediate medical needs related to T2DM, to include social, legal, employment, education, housing or other services. Such assistance helps build a partnership with the family. As other, possibly more pressing, family stressors are relieved or resolved, there is more capacity to focus on health issues.

Working with groups: the POWER Program

I established the POWER Group (Parent Power Over Weight, Eating Right) with the goal of empowering parents to protect their families from the avoidable health risks associated with obesity, including T2DM. In addition to information about nutrition and fitness, we discuss the behavioral, environmental, and motivational issues the families face. The twice-monthly program is free and open to any parent or caregiver who wants to attend. Enrollment is open and revolving. The mix of participants varies in each session. Members of the group are mostly mothers of clinic families from the neighborhood who are free to attend during the weekday. Randomly, the group may or may not be cohesive in its ethnic, economic or geographical make-up, but the one factor that unites the members is their concern for their children. This has proven to be a powerful bond, allowing seemingly disparate parties to communicate with each other effectively. Those who have attended six or more sessions seem to benefit most in adapting and implementing new approaches to their family's health needs.

Group members are able to talk and listen to each other in powerful ways. My stance in group work is to promote a level of comfort by introducing the participants, helping them identify a subject or theme and then taking a back seat to their spontaneous discussion, intervening only when needed. I always learn something new which will often lead to new ideas for more effective interventions. In this setting, John's mother was able to explore various behavioral issues that were undermining her efforts to improve the family's health. Excessive TV and snacking are common concerns for many of the mothers. They encouraged each other to set time limits on TV viewing and together we devised a multi-stepped plan of first switching to healthier snacks, then limiting portions, and finally substituting some TV time with family activities such as preparing healthy snacks together. Synergistically, I was able to address John's TV habits with him in our individual sessions and enlist his cooperation in limiting his viewing time. As his fear of diabetes subsided and his sense of mastery grew, his need to quell his anxiety through overeating also diminished.

Outreach education

The goal of outreach education is to raise awareness of preferred nutritional and physical fitness habits. The Broomstick Bash, a candy-less Halloween party, and March to the Penguins, a family exercise experience, are enjoyable ways to learn about health. Each event employs both experiential and interactive learning components. These high "entertainment value" events have proven to be an effective means of reaching people, attracting as many as 800 participants at a time. Children with type 1 or type 2 diabetes are invited and the events are also advertised through diabetes organizations and to the general public.

The Broomstick Bash takes place in the large public lobby of a main campus building, festively decorated for the occasion. Children are rewarded with non-edible treats, such as stretchy skeletons, day-glo bracelets, and vampire teeth as they complete each activity. Family goody bags that include educational resource materials, farmer's market food coupons, recipes, free gym passes and other pertinent gifts are distributed. Families are gathered in small groups and escorted through the event by a trained "team host." Each group is led through three educational stations: "Freaky Foods" to investigate healthier food choices, "Monster Moves" to explore incorporating fitness into one's daily routine, and "Pumpkin Pledges" to activate their motivation and set goals for themselves. Members of our clinic staff use an interactive approach, engaging the children directly in games and conversation about the given subject. Appealing and engaging visual aids are used to support the interaction.

An inclusive "good, better, best" approach is employed to encourage children and families to examine current practices and take small steps towards developing better habits. For instance, one game "swaps" fast food options to make healthier choices. Trading large for regular size French fries, eliminating cheese from a hamburger or adding a salad are all small, realistic decisions that result in better outcomes. Lessons are graphic, concrete and appropriate for a range of ages. For instance, faced with a table set with many small cups filled with one tablespoon of sugar each, children appear startled to discover how many tablespoons (eight or more) are in their drinks, like soda. They develop a more concrete understanding of the hidden calories they are consuming and can make smarter choices. John, who had come to this event with his sisters and a few classmates, was overheard debating with them about their food choices and who had guessed correctly in some of the games they played. My hope is that this sort of healthy competition will be reactivated at school and will nudge them into choosing healthier snacks.

After participants complete all three educational stations, there are other activities such as Monster Mash dance exercises (led by local youth karate instructors), broomstick and mask decorating, and face painting. Children are eligible for additional raffle prizes when they drink and submit their emptied water bottle, received earlier at the "hydration station." There is a vegetable soup making demonstration and tasting. Children are surprised to learn they actually do like vegetables. Families are encouraged to repeat this at home; they receive the recipe and food coupons to spend at the local farmer's market.

The spring event, March to the Penguins, has a similar format, but with an emphasis on exercise. Families are gathered in small groups and led through the three educational stations to explore food, exercise and goal-setting options. Then, they are outfitted with a penguin logo backpack filled with lunch, water bottle, educational materials and a pedometer. Taking advantage of the hospital's geographic location, the experiential segment of this event consists of each group walking, parade style, through Central Park to its zoo, where families gain free entry. The walk is broken into four 15-minute segments, with a short session of exercises, such as jumping jacks, at each stop. At the last stop, we eat our picnic lunch and participate in a final round of group exercise, using fitness bands that participants keep as motivational awards. Upon reaching the zoo, families are free to enjoy the rest of the afternoon on their own.

Differential discussion

Is it possible to change a culture? Is it possible to alter a lifestyle that makes fast food and other timesaving conveniences a necessity but leaves no time for cooking nutritious meals or exercise? In a word, yes. We have good examples of society making major, previously unimaginable shifts. A case in point is the shift in our societal attitude towards cigarette smoking. Through the combined and concerted efforts of health professionals, educators, legislators and concerned individuals, what was once considered "cool" is now decidedly unacceptable. Likewise, major perceptual shifts and concurrent changes in policy and behaviors have taken place in our attitudes towards driving while intoxicated and wearing seatbelts.

While none of these problems have been completely eradicated, they reveal our societal ability to reverse harmful, unhealthy trends. Unfortunately, these efforts have succeeded less well in marginalized segments of our society. It is important not to "ghettoize" a health issue as important as obesity. The food industry has been adroit in adapting to and exploiting the latest trends, as there is a clear economic advantage for them to provide newly packaged "lite" foods. Likewise, television, with shows like *Biggest Loser* and *Dietribe*, which focuses on weight issues in teens and young adults, is keen to capitalize on trends of interest to their viewers. Governmental agencies and legislators tend to enact change at a slower pace. A constellation of broad measures, from all sectors, public, private and personal, will be needed to reverse this trend. The "tipping point" (Gladwell, 2002) for this change appears to be close at hand.

References

Caprio, S., Daniels, J. R., Drewnowski, A., Kaufman, F. R., Palinkas, L. A., Rosenbloom, A. L., Schwimmer, J. B. (2008). Influences of race, ethnicity and culture on childhood obesity: Implications for prevention and treatment: consensus statement of shaping America's health and the obesity society. *Diabetes Care*, 31:2211–21.

Center for Disease Control and Prevention (CDC) (2007). *Adult Obesity Trends*, Atlanta, Ga. Retrieved 12/15/08: http://www.cdc.gov.nccdphp/dnpa/obesity/trends/maps

Chan, S. (2008, Dec. 17). Tax on many soft drinks sets off a spirited debate. *New York Times*. p. A 36.

Endocrine Society, The (2008). *Prevention and treatment of pediatric obesity: Clinical practice guideline based on expert opinion*. Chevy Chase: Self-published.

Gladwell, M. (2002). *The tipping point*. New York: Little, Brown and Company.

Kaufman, F. R. (2002). Type 2 diabetes in children and young adults: A "New Epidemic." *Clinical Diabetes*, 20:217–18.

Kim, M., Berger, D. & Matte T. (2006). *Diabetes in New York City: Public health burden and disparities*. New York: New York City Department of Health and Mental Hygiene.

Lawrence, J. M., Liese, A. D., Lui, L., Dabelea, D., Anderson, A., Imperatore, G. & Bell, R. (2008). Weight-loss practices and weight-related issues among youth with Type 1 or Type 2 diabetes. *Diabetes Care*, 31:2251–7.

Lucadamo, K. (2008, Nov 14). Diabetes takes a grim toll on N.Y. *The Daily News*. p. 12

National Center for Health Statistics (NCHS) (2005). Prevalence of overweight among children and adolescents: United States, 1999–2000. Retrieved 12/15/08: http://www.cdc.gov/nchs/products/pubs/pubd/hestats/overwght99.htm

Ogden, C. L., Carroll, M. D. & Flegan, K. M. (2008). High Body Mass Index for age among U.S. children and adolescents, 2003–6. *Journal of the American Medical Association*, 299 (20):2401–5.

Polan, M. (2007/04/22). You are what you grow. *New York Times Magazine*. Retrieved 12/15/08: http://

www.nytimes.com/2007/04/22/magazine/22wwlnlede

Popkin, M., Conde, W., Hou, N. & Monteiro, C. (2006). Is there a lag globally in overweight trends for children compared with adults? *Obesity*, 14:1846–53.

Websites

American Diabetes Association: www.diabetes.org
Juvenile Diabetes Research Foundation: www.jdrf.org
International Diabetes Federation: www.idf.org
Starlight Children's Foundation: www.starbright.org

8 Foster care for children with special health care needs

Kathleen Desmond and Lori Hendrickson

Context

Description of the setting

A community-based social service organization, Best Nest, Inc. is a part of Pennsylvania's county-administered and state-supervised child welfare system and is licensed by the State of Pennsylvania Department of Public Welfare (DPW). The agency has contracts with the Philadelphia Department of Human Services (DHS) and the surrounding counties for the provision of placement and prevention services. Best Nest annually serves approximately 100 children in foster care, 85% of whom have been diagnosed with a special health care need.

The foster care system in the United States evolved as a means of providing protection and shelter for children who require out-of-home placement (American Academy of Pediatrics, 2002; Simms, 1991). Foster care is meant to be a short-term intervention with the goal of reunifying families once the abuse or neglect is remedied. When reunification is not a viable option, adoption options are explored. In Philadelphia the average length of stay for children in foster care who are being reunified is 21 months, compared with a national average of 15 months (Philadelphia Department of Human Services, 2008). When a child in foster care has a special health care need, the length-in-care increases, and the likelihood of reunification decreases.

Despite significant legislative advances, there has been an unprecedented rise in the number of children in foster care over the last two decades (Chipungu & Bent-Goodley, 2004; Ringeisen, Casanueva, Urato & Cross, 2008). A disproportionate number of children placed in foster care come from the most marginalized families (ACYF, 1999; American Academy of Pediatrics, 2002; Simms, Dubowitz & Szilagy, 2000). Poverty is not only the largest risk factor for poor health and wellbeing, it is also the primary risk factor for entry into the foster care system (Case & Paxson, 2006; Chipungu & Bent-Goodley, 2004). It is not surprising to find that children entering the foster care system are often in poor health. It is estimated that 30–60% of children in foster care have chronic health conditions (Ringeisen, Casanueva, Urato & Cross, 2008).

Policy

The federal government's Social Security Act of 1935 established the Aid to Dependent Children Program, which later became known as Aid to Families with Dependent Children (AFDC). No longer considered an entitlement, Temporary Aid to Needy Families (TANF) now provides cash assistance to families in need. This legislation also provided funding to states for the purpose of establishing child protective services including foster care. Amendments to the Social Security Act of 1935 made children in foster care eligible to receive Medicaid benefits.

In 1974, The Child Abuse Prevention and Treatment Act encouraged states to pass laws requiring mandatory reporting of child abuse and to establish procedures for investigating reports of maltreatment (Schene, 1998). This law established a minimum definition of child abuse and neglect, which states then used as a guide when developing their child protective service laws.

The two final pieces of federal legislation that govern child welfare services are The Adoption Assistance and Child Welfare Act of 1980 and the Federal Adoption and Safe Family Act of 1997. The Adoption Assistance and Child Welfare Act provides fiscal incentives to states to reduce the unnecessary placement of children in foster care (Adoption and Safe Families Act, 1997; Juvenile Law Center, 2007). The law mandates that states must make reasonable efforts to prevent the placement of children into foster care by providing prevention services to families, i.e. parenting education classes, family preservation services or other in-home protective service programs. Additionally, this law mandates periodic (six month) judicial review to determine the appropriateness and feasibility of the permanency goal and to measure progress.

The Adoption and Safe Families Act of 1997 (ASFA) shifted the emphasis towards children's health and safety concerns and away from a prioritizing reunification with birth parents (Adoption and Safe Families Act, 1997). ASFA defines certain circumstances under which a court may determine that family reunification efforts are not required (Juvenile Law Center, 2007). In addition, ASFA establishes a timeframe in which parents must make reasonable efforts at eliminating the causal factors that led to placement. If a child remains in care for 15 out of 22 consecutive months then a petition can be filed to terminate parental rights.

The Pennsylvania Juvenile Act, passed in 1972, delicately balances the right of children to be protected, against the right of families to be free from state intrusion. It enables the Commonwealth to intervene to protect dependent children. The Pennsylvania Child Protective Service Law (CPSL) was enacted in 1975. The CPSL integrates the reporting, investigating, and recording of child abuse and provides for the prompt delivery of protective services to children in need. The CPSL mandates that counties provide General Protective Services intended to keep children at home and to provide temporary and permanent placement resources as needed (Juvenile Law Center, 2007).

Technology

Many of the children served by Best Nest have one or more medical diagnoses that render them technology-dependent, meaning they rely on one or more pieces of electronic medical equipment and/or medication to monitor and support their physical health. Many children, including those who are HIV-infected or those who have had organ transplants, require life-sustaining medication several times a day. Others require medication to manage symptoms associated with their illnesses. In addition to complex medication regimens, many children must adhere to strict dietary requirements.

The client in this chapter has recently been diagnosed with diabetes mellitus type 1. The diabetic treatment regimen is complex and includes multiple daily injections, blood glucose monitoring several times a day, dietary considerations, exercise, and careful attention to the timing and coordination of all these tasks (Auslander, Bubb, Rogge & Santiago, 1993). Chronic illness affects all aspects of family life (Ashton, 2004). All families go through a developmental process as they learn to cope with the demands of a chronic illness. When a child with a chronic illness is in foster care, that developmental process is interrupted. Birth parents do not have the same opportunity to adjust to all of the changes a chronic illness brings, yet they are still expected to demonstrate a command of the information and skill necessary to care for their child.

Organization

Founded in 1987 in response to the HIV/AIDS epidemic, Best Nest was one of the first agencies in Pennsylvania willing to address the complex placement needs of HIV-infected children and their families. Originally, the intent was to develop a transitional group home for infected children and their mothers, based on the expectation that the recruitment of foster families would be difficult given the stigma and fear regarding HIV/AIDS at that time. Vast community opposition to this effort included town meetings, petitions, and appeals to legislators. Paradoxically, the publicity generated by this resistance engendered an outpouring of community support for these children and their families, including many inquiries from potential foster parents. Best Nest revised the original plan and focused instead on developing a foster care program as a resource for this population. During the same time, the "boarder baby" phenomenon created by the crack cocaine epidemic was also creating great stress on the child welfare system. The agency's response to this epidemic, coupled with the original goal of meeting the needs of children infected with HIV, shaped Best Nest's vision of creating a specialized foster care system for children with an array of special health care needs.

Our ability to effect change within individuals, systems, or communities depends on the integrity and authenticity with which we enter and navigate our relationships with these entities. As social workers, we recognize that families' culture and ethnicity frame their patterns of beliefs, practices, and perceptions about: health/illness; the nature of the relationship with the health care provider; health care seeking behaviors; and the use of complementary and alternative therapies (Gee & Payne-Sturges, 2004). We model and teach parents effective ways of communicating with health care professionals in regard to their cultural beliefs.

A crucial element in the provision of quality social services is a skilled and well-trained staff. A workforce trained and sustained through supervision, in-service training, outside consultation and continuing education will be more successful in meeting the needs of families. Our supervisory relationships provide powerful opportunities for collaboration, professional development, and skill acquisition. Best Nest uses the social work model of supervision that integrates administrative, educational, and supportive components (Kadushin, 2002). Working with families experiencing many stressors is hard work, and supervision helps to guide and transform these experiences through the use of a theoretical framework, shared problem solving, stress management techniques, support and care.

Description of the client situation

Corrina, a six-year-old African American female, was born to a 14-year-old mother named Latisha who was residing in foster care at the time of Corrina's birth. Both mother and daughter continued to reside together in mother/baby foster care placement for approximately two years, at which point Latisha made the decision to leave care. Little is known about Corrina's history while she was living with her mother. Latisha's arrest when Corrina was five years old and the lack of familial resources necessitated Corrina's coming into foster care. Corrina was with a previous foster care agency for 14 months during which time she resided in four different foster homes. Her last placement was disrupted when Corrina was hospitalized and subsequently diagnosed with Diabetes Mellitus Type 1 (Jee, Barth, Szilagzy, Aida & Davies, 2006).

At the time of her hospital admission, Corrina was suffering from a life-threatening complication of her diagnosis, known as Diabetic Ketoacidosis, and she was hospitalized for 40 days. Best Nest received Corrina's referral from the Philadelphia Department of Human Services (DHS) because the prior agency was not a provider of medical foster care. Upon identification of a foster parent, and in conjunction with the medical providers attending to Corrina, Best Nest established a training schedule for the foster parent. The Best Nest intake worker participated in the training along with the foster parent. While in the hospital, Corrina established a strong attachment to her medical providers, most notably her nurses. The day of her discharge was therefore difficult, as she yet again experienced the loss of primary caretakers. After making the rounds to say goodbye to both staff and patients with whom she had formed relationships, a visibly upset Corrina told us that her "eyes were sweating." While Corrina and her new foster parent had established a connection, Corrina had made it clear that she wanted to go home to her mother or remain in the hospital.

Corrina's mother grew up in foster care without ever having the security of a permanent family. Since Corrina's placement into foster care, Latisha's involvement has been sporadic at best. Like many children who age out of the foster care system, Latisha was ill-equipped to

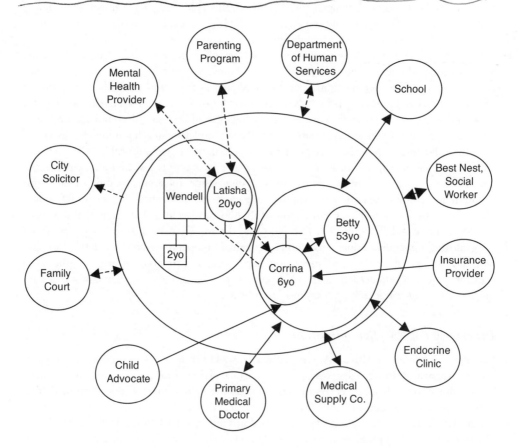

Figure 8.1 Ecomap for Corinna.

manage the demands of daily living and lacked the supports necessary to adequately care for herself and her young daughter. She loves her daughter but she lacks an adequate frame of reference for parenting and becomes easily overwhelmed by her daughter's needs.

Latisha's relationship with Corrina became more complicated as a result of her recent marriage to Wendell, a move into a new home, and the assumption of the primary caretaker role of Wendell's two-year-old son. Since her marriage, Latisha has seen Corrina even less. Wendell occasionally accompanies Latisha to visits with Corrina but he does not engage with Corrina. Latisha's absence has created confusion, anger, and an increased sense of loss for Corrina. The metabolic changes caused by this stress make it difficult to manage her diabetes.

Corrina's current foster parent is Betty, a 53-year-old African American woman who is divorced and semi-retired after working as a teacher for 23 years. She is employed part-time at a bank and is the mother of two grown children. While she has worked with children with special needs, this is her first experience with foster parenting. She successfully completed Best Nest's home study, orientation, and training process and she is fully certified as a foster care parent in the state of Pennsylvania. Corrina is a bright, spirited, and insightful little girl who readily expresses her feelings and thoughts. Betty's energetic, playful demeanor enables her to easily engage with Corrina. Despite their connection, Corrina's primary attachment is with her mother. She calls her mom every night before she goes to bed and gets angry with Betty if her mother is not available. She believes her diabetes will go away if only she could go home.

Decisions about practice

Definition of the client

Best Nest identifies the client as the child who is placed in foster care, the birth parent(s), and/or another extended family member identified as a permanency resource. In this case, Corrina, Latisha, and Wendell are the clients. Our interventions with parents are focused on identifying and then ameliorating the problems that precipitated placement through community resources, the development of coping strategies, and the enhancement of parenting abilities. While Best Nest does provide support, counseling, education and training to foster parents they are not clients. Rather, they are part of the service providing team who are expected to meet the physical, emotional, social, and spiritual needs of the children in their care. In short, they are expected to love the children as if they were their own, and advocate on their behalf with the numerous service providers involved in their lives. As if that were not enough, Best Nest expects them, whenever possible, to act as supports and mentors to birth parents.

Goals

The primary goals of foster care are to provide for the safety and wellbeing of vulnerable children and to mitigate the circumstances that led to protective custody. DHS in conjunction with the family establishes a Family Service Plan (FSP) for every family receiving protective services. The FSP establishes the service goal for children in care and identifies objectives that parents must attain in order to successfully reunify with their child or children. The permanency goal for the majority of children entering foster care is reunification with a birth parent. DHS identified the following goals that Latisha must accomplish in order for reunification to occur:

- To attend and actively engage in all regularly scheduled medical appointments;

- To attend Diabetes training classes offered by hospital;
- To demonstrate the knowledge and ability to meet Corrina's special medical needs by creating meal plans that reflect Corrina's dietary restrictions; and appropriately using all medical equipment;
- To be able to explain disease process and identify the signs and symptoms of disease complication;
- To secure safe housing;
- To maintain supervised weekly visits with Corrina at the Best Nest office and demonstrate positive parenting practices;
- To attend and complete parenting education classes for parents of children with chronic illness;
- To participate in individual therapy.

Latisha recently attained safe housing but has not yet met any of the other goals identified in the FSP. In addition, her recent marriage means the FSP will need to be modified to include goals and objectives for Wendell.

Contracting and developing objectives

The quality and effectiveness of Best Nest's service intervention is directly linked to the quality of the comprehensive assessment we conduct with families, which must take into account the Safety and Risk Assessments, and the Family Service Plan provided by DHS. Family involvement in the assessment and service planning process is critical to ensuring successful outcomes. Best Nest engages family members, other key familial supports, health care and other service providers with whom the family is currently or recently involved in order to gather information. This is vital for assessing parental protective capacity, family strengths, and the resources that the family can contribute to the management of child safety.

The comprehensive assessment is used to develop a culturally sensitive individual service plan (ISP) that acts as a written contract and outlines an intervention strategy. The ISP identifies goals that help to build the behavioral, cognitive, and emotional protective capacity of parents. Additionally, it includes goals and objectives for every member of the triad and timeframes in which the goals are to be attained in order to achieve the permanency objective. The ISP, like the FSP, is re-evaluated every six months to monitor progress and efficacy and serves as the blueprint for service delivery.

Face-to-face visitation between parent and child in foster care is considered the primary intervention for maintaining and enhancing the development of parent-child relationships necessary for successful reunification (Haight, Kagle & Black, 2003). Latisha currently has supervised weekly visits with Corrina at the agency. Visits are held in the early evening to enable Latisha to participate in meal preparation, glucose monitoring and administration of insulin.

Meeting place

Foster care services occur in a variety of venues with the client. I can meet with the child and resource parent in the foster home, at school or medical appointments, agency social events such as "Best Nest Fest" (springtime games and activities), the birth parent's home, the Agency for supervised visits, and scheduled Court dates. Thus, in Corrina's foster home, I observed Corrina being very active and talkative. Corrina feels comfortable and in charge of this environment and is a proud hostess, showing me how she does her homework and what she eats for dinner. This is a good indicator that the foster placement is providing Corrina with some control—an essential need for Corrina since she lacks control in so many other aspects of her life.

At the yearly holiday party, Corrina was able to make crafts, run, play basketball, go on a fire engine ride for the first time, and eat lunch with a new group of children and adults. She enjoyed this new experience but with less confidence than she displays at her foster home. Throughout the afternoon, I observed that Corrina is much more at ease relating to adults than to the other children at the event. I can act as observer and participant, simultaneously making note of and easing Corrina's fears as she faces these new activities. Accordingly, this novel experience for Corrina both enhances my working picture of her functioning and associated needs, and enhances our relationship.

At Best Nest, Corrina and Latisha can choose between quiet, private visit rooms with sofas, toys and books, or a larger open (gymnasium-like) area where there is comfortable seating and bikes to ride. Latisha chooses the smaller, private area and Corrina chooses to run between the small room and the larger area. Trust is established and nurtured across time by creating this routine at Best Nest. Corrina knows where to find her favorite toys and where my office is; she checks with me frequently. She knows where to find the bathroom, water fountain and kitchen.

Latisha also requires, and finds, a place where her own unique set of needs can be met. She passively allowed me to control the early visits and took no initiative in interacting with, supervising, directing activities, or limit-setting for her daughter. I incorporated these observations and built a relationship with her across many visits. Sensitively and systematically, I continue to model the skills necessary for effective parenting, leaving many openings for Latisha to join in. She is slowly beginning to assume a slightly more active parental posture in the visits. Her progress is halting and requires me to expend great sustained effort and modeling to achieve the slightest gain. She needs ideas for developmentally appropriate activities; she never had an unencumbered childhood and does not know how to play with her daughter. We have discovered that Latisha enjoys coloring pages at least as much as Corrina!

Use of time

Consistency is a true cornerstone of the work with the client in foster care services. Neither Latisha nor Corrina has experienced consistent caregivers in her life. Unfortunately, they have also been subject to many changes in social workers/agencies. When I inform parents I will meet them at a doctor's appointment for their children, for example, it is of utmost importance that I be present at the arranged time, ready and waiting to support the parent/child dyad. While this may seem an absurdly obvious point, it cannot be underscored enough. The social worker's consistency serves multiple functions. As I model the appropriate parental attitude towards routines, schedules and special appointments, I increase both the parent's and child's trust. In addition, my active participation allows direct access and full availability to translate any confusing or potentially frightening information or procedures the parent or child may receive from the doctors. I try to demonstrate through my actions how I value the relationship to each of them as individuals with innate worth and dignity.

Agendas can be another essential tool in the social worker's kit, providing focus, structure, goals and timelines to the processes involved in a home visit to the child or parent. It helps both the social worker and the client for them to meet prepared, confident, and purposeful. When the child or parent knows what to expect, the utility of the visit is enhanced and all parties feel a sense of mutual respect. The agenda maximizes the team's use of time via a clear outline of purposes, goals and interventions. It can serve as an evolving document of the family's progress, providing clear direction; both for the worker's case activity log and for questions requiring further collateral action, consultation and supervision.

During one home visit, first on my agenda was helping Corrina open up and talk about being in foster care, and second was to discuss her upcoming medical appointments with Betty, her foster mother. When I arrived at the foster home with my agenda it was clear that the purpose of the visit—and accordingly, the agenda—had to be changed. Betty was distressed because Corrina's blood sugar levels were extremely high. My behavioral assessment of Corrina indicated no immediate areas for concern. Having thus obtained an initial impression of Corrina's immediate stability relative to her blood sugar and ketone levels, I acknowledged Betty's distress, allowed her to process Corrina's day, diet, exercise and then problem-solved with her how to address the problem. Betty had already checked for ketones exactly as she'd been trained to do in cases such as this one. The support I provided helped Betty gain confidence in her own capacity to assess, intervene and consult on behalf of the child. I could reassure her that not only had she done nothing wrong but also that she had done everything right. Finally, the visit ended with calls to the child's doctor, providing the foster parent with further reassurance and relief.

The original agenda was saved and introduced at a later date when there was ample time to focus on those goals. Because the interrupting crisis had been resolved (and for Betty, this had indeed been experienced as a crisis), the foster parent was better able to respond to the issues in the agenda. This temporary modification of my agenda shows the utility of a flexible approach, accommodating to the immediate needs presented in any given situation. Social workers quickly learn that adaptability is a key to good practice.

Strategies and interventions

Theory serves as the basis for our practice with families, and we draw primarily from the following frameworks: the human ecology/ecological systems theory (Kerson, 2002), self-efficacy theory (Bandura, 1977); and attachment theory (Bowlby, 1998). These focus our attention/efforts in the following ways: an ecological approach underscores the need for a thorough assessment of the social environment that parents live in; the identification of stressors, and needed health and human service interventions, and the need for linkage of the family with formal community services. Self-efficacy theory emphasizes our need to focus on identifying and reinforcing family strengths and healthy behaviors; establishing realistic goals and behavioral objectives that can be achieved; and teaching problem solving skills. Attachment theory reminds us to develop close and empathic relationships with our families; understand a parent's beliefs and attitudes about parenting so that we can help change unhealthy practices; and promote sensitive and responsive parenting.

Latisha seems to be suffering from a significant clinical depression, likely due to her multiple unresolved losses and internalized feelings of helplessness. I have created many opportunities for her to continue to play an active role in decision making regarding her daughter. At the time of placement, I facilitated a conversation between Latisha and Betty, Corrina's foster mother, in which Latisha was able to talk about her Muslim background and beliefs and express her desire that Corrina continue observing dietary guidelines by not eating pork. Latisha is also encouraged and expected to actively participate in medical and educational appointments for Corrina. Despite our efforts to help Latisha remain involved and connected, she remains on the periphery of Corrina's life.

Stance of the social worker

Best Nest starts with the assumption that all people aspire to reach their true potential but some may lack the road map to get there. As social workers, we recognize that we have a unique opportunity/responsibility to create environments to support an individual's optimal personal development and that this is done primarily through the use of the relationship we establish with clients. We approach all of our professional relationships with warmth, positive regard, and authenticity in the service of the work with our clients.

Use of resources outside of the helping relationship

It does take a whole village to raise a child and Best Nest, along with DHS, is responsible for mobilizing that village on behalf of children and families. The diagram (see Figure 8.1, page 100) shows other service systems involved with Corrina. Much of our work with families is focused on identifying and then ameliorating the problems that precipitated placement through the use of community resources, the development of coping strategies, and the enhancement of parenting abilities. The ongoing health and stability of families depend on their ability to identify and utilize community resources. One of the most significant resources mobilized on Corrina's behalf was her elementary school. Corrina's diagnosis requires maintaining normal glucose levels in her blood. It was imperative for Best Nest to engage the school in the medical monitoring process. We located a school with a full-time nurse on site and arranged for the nurse from the endocrine clinic to come out to the school to train both the classroom teacher and the nurse. Best Nest provided the school with Corrina's supplies, arranged a schedule for Corrina's snacks, and ensured that the teacher had a supply of sugar-boosting snacks for any hypoglycemic episodes.

Reassessment and evaluation

Best Nest workers are responsible for continuously evaluating the needs, strengths and progress of families. Assessments and subsequent ISPs are reviewed every six months at an inter-disciplinary team meeting that includes the family. The ISP is then revised to reflect any major change in goal identification or family circumstance. Through the use of individual supervision, peer supervision, utilization meetings, and other forms of quality assurance, Best Nest monitors the quality and efficacy of the services families are receiving, offers solutions for eliminating service delivery obstacles, and makes recommendations for additional linkages with other service providers.

Case conclusion

Corrina remains in the medical foster home. She has been in foster care for approximately 22 months of which the last eight months have been spent under our supervision. Latisha has made little progress towards attaining the goals outlined in the FSP and has still not come to terms with Corrina's diagnosis. There is concern that she will be unable to monitor the complex dietary and scheduling regimen necessary for managing diabetes. This case is due for a judicial review in two months and DHS will convene a meeting of all involved parties at which point a decision will be made about changing the permanency goal to adoption.

Differential discussion

Reunification is always the preferred permanency option. In an effort to ameliorate the conditions that caused the placement of a child, every available resource is mobilized to support family functioning. Careful guidelines and timeframes are put in place to ensure remedial action is quickly focused on restoring the family. To be successful, reunification requires a concerted and coordinated effort of all parties involved in the provision of services to children and their families. Parents need not be perfect in their attainment of individual service plan goals or be the epitome of good parenting, but they must be "good enough."

Corrina's situation is important to consider because alongside the child/parent strengths—chief among them the unbreakable attachment and powerful love they share—the child and her family are beset by many other difficulties. Corrina's mother is suffering from the insidious effects of chronic poverty, apparent gaps in early and basic education, untreated depression, the inexperience of extreme youth, and her own history of inadequate parenting. These factors, along with Latisha's incarceration contributed to Corrina's original out-of-home placement. Adding more recent life stressors such as the multiple foster placements prior to Best Nest's involvement, Corrina's recent diagnosis of Juvenile Diabetes, and Latisha's acquisition of a new family, complete with the demands of a very young child, complicates the work. In essence, Corrina was placed outside the home for one set of difficulties that had not been adequately addressed prior to her re-placement with Best Nest, due to her medical condition.

In the best of circumstances, juvenile diabetes presents many problems for a family, shaking its foundation and affecting its capacity to function. It is not always possible to create enough resources within the family system to accommodate the basic requirements of daily care for a child with juvenile diabetes. As can be seen in Corrina's situation, the addition of multiple pre-existing and chronic problems hinders her family's ability to meet Corrina's basic physical needs. Corrina's case outcome remains to be determined. Her story serves as a lens through which to view both current shortfalls in social work practice in child welfare and the multiple complex systems that must be able to work together to ensure the wellbeing of children and families with medical conditions.

References

ACYF (Administration for Children, Youth, and Families). (1999). *Child welfare statistical stat book*. Washington, DC: U.S. Office of Human Development Services.

Adoption Assistance and Child Welfare Act of 1980, Pub. L. 96–272, 42 U.S.C. §§ 608, 621–6, 628, 670–6.

Adoption and Safe Families Act of 1997, Pub. L. 105–89, 42 U.S.C. §§ 101–7, 201–3, 301–8, 401–6.

American Academy of Pediatrics Committee on Early Childhood, Adoption, and Dependent Care. (2002). Health care of young children in foster care. *Pediatrics*, 109 (3): 536–41.

Ashton, J. (2004). Life after the shock! The impact on families caring for young children with chronic illness. *Australian Journal of Early Childhood*, 29 (1), 22+. Retrieved 12/10/08, from http://www.questia.com/PM.qst?a=o&d=5008170894

Auslander, W., Bubb, J., Rogge, M. & Santiago, J. (1993). Family stress and resources: Potential areas of intervention in children recently diagnosed with diabetes. *Health and Social Work*, (18)2, 101+. Retrieved 10/8/08, from http:www.questia.com/PM.qst?a=o&d=5000182195.

Bandura, A. (1977). Self-efficacy: Toward a unifying theory of behavioral change. *Psychological Review*, 84: 191–215.

Bowlby, J. (1998). *Attachment and Loss*. New York: Pimlico.

Case, A. & Paxson, C. (2006). Children's health and social mobility. *The Future of Children*, 16 (2), 151+. Retrieved 7/22/08, from http://www.questia.com/PM.qst?a=o&d=5021925770

Chipungu, S. & Bent-Goodley, T. (2004). Meeting the challenges of contemporary foster care. *The Future of Children*, 14 (1), 74+. Retrieved 11/8/08, from http://www.questia.com/PM.qst?a=o&d=5002650969

Gee, G. C. & Payne-Sturges, D. C. (2004). Environmental health disparities: A framework for integrating psychosocial and environmental concepts. *Environmental Health Perspectives*, 112 (17): 1645–53.

Haight, W., Kagle, J. & Black, J. (2003). Understanding and supporting parent-child relationships during foster care visits: Attachment theory and research. *Social Work*, 48 (2), 195+. Retrieved 06/22/08, from Questia database: http://www.questia.com/PM.qst?a=o&d=50019118931

Kadushin, A. (2002). *Supervision in Social Work* (4th ed.). New York: Columbia University Press.

Kerson, T. S. (2002). *Boundary spanning: An ecological reinterpretation of social work practice in health and mental health care.* New York: Columbia University Press.

Jee, S., Barth, R., Szilagzyi, M., Aida, M. & Davis, M. M. (2006). Factors associated with chronic conditions among children in foster care. *Journal Health Care Poor Underserved*, 17 (2): 328–41.

Juvenile Law Center (2007). *Child abuse and the law.* Compiled by Shah, R., Darcus, J. & Kadushin, A. (2002). *Supervision in Social Work* (4th ed.). New York: Columbia University Press.

Ringeisen, H., Casanueva, C., Urato, M. & Cross, T. (2008). Special health care needs among children in the child welfare system. *Pediatrics*, 122: e232–e241

Schene, P. (1998). Past present and future roles of child protective services. *Future of Children*, 8 (1): 23–38.

Simms, M. (1991). Foster children and the foster care system. *Current Problems in Pediatric & Adolescent Health Care*, 21: 297–321.

Simms, M., Dubowitz, H. & Szilagy, M. (2000). Health care needs of children in the foster care system. *Pediatrics*, 106 (4): 909–18.

Website

Philadelphia Department of Human Services website: PhillyStat presentation (retrieved: 2008). http://dhs.phila.gov/dhsphilagovp.nsf

9 Social work in a pediatric hospital

Managing a medically complex patient

Jennifer L. Fenstermacher

Context

Description of the setting

Nemours is one of the nation's largest health systems dedicated to the health of children. One of its largest providers is the Alfred I. duPont Hospital for Children (AIDHC) located in Wilmington, Delaware. Originally founded as an orthopedic facility, it is now a 180-bed hospital that encompasses all the specialties of pediatric medicine in a spacious, family-focused facility. Children from birth through age 17 with acute, chronic and complex health problems benefit from the threefold mission established by the founders—excellence in patient care, education, and research (http://www.nemours.org/hospital/de/aidhc/about.html). The Patient and Family Services Department comprises master's level social workers. Social workers are assigned to specific services and are responsible for both the inpatient and outpatient needs of that service.

Policy

Many policy arenas affect social workers in hospital settings. Following are three examples: the accrediting process for hospitals and other health organizations, the protection of patients' privacy regarding health information, and one effort to control costs through payment by diagnosis. An independent, non-profit group that sets standards for hospitals and issues accreditation based on a hospital's compliance and efforts to improve (http://www.jointcommission.org), the JC sends a team of surveyors to a hospital every few years for an on-site inspection to ensure that the hospital is in compliance with the standards and regulations. As part of the inspection, social workers are expected to be aware of and able to answer questions regarding key standards. Social workers are often included in "tracer" cases, where the surveyors follow a patient over the course of several hours and interview every team member who interacts with them. When the inspection is complete, the hospital receives accreditation and a report of areas in which to improve.

In regard to the second, the right to privacy, HIPAA (1996), the Health Insurance Portability and Accountability Act of 1996 primarily affects the social worker in the area of protected health information (PHI). Title II of HIPAA includes the Privacy Rule, which states:

> a major goal of the Privacy Rule is to assure that individual's health information is properly protected while allowing the flow of health information needed to provide and promote high quality health care and to protect the public's health and well being. The

Rule strikes a balance that permits important uses of information, while protecting the privacy of people who seek care and healing. (http://www.hhs.gov./ocr/hipaa)

A hospital may use and disclose PHI in three areas without an individual's authorization: treatment, payment and health care operations. Treatment includes the provision, coordination and management of health care and related services including consultations and referrals. This means a social worker does not need to have a release of information (ROI) signed every time a referral is made to a durable medical equipment (DME) company or a home health care (HHC) agency for skilled nursing visits. This certainly helps to expedite discharges. Payment includes obtaining or remitting any form of payment from insurance companies or other health care providers. Finally, health care operations include such things as quality improvement projects, performance evaluations, accreditations or business planning.

In regard to the third, the effort to manage costs and patient care, my work is particularly affected by DRGs (diagnostic-related groups), a system by the United States Department of Health and Human Services through which hospitals are paid not according to what they spend to care for a patient but according to the diagnosis for which the patient is hospitalized (Dranove, 2000; NASW, 2005). Thus, the social worker involved in discharge planning is pushed to make suitable post-hospitalization arrangements for a patient before the insurance approved time span has elapsed. As the costs of hospitalization rise, hospitals are placed under greater fiscal pressure, and in turn, they pressure the social worker to plan discharge with greater efficiency. Even if the necessary services or resources are not available, the social worker is still expected to use her skills and knowledge to expedite a safe and appropriate discharge plan. Coordinating services for patients with multiple needs in a short time period can be challenging. Discharge planning has been referred to as one of the most time-consuming services provided by social workers (Kayser, Hansen & Groves, 1995). This and other efforts are justified by the promise that they will reduce the costs of care without sacrificing quality.

Technology

Technology is ever present and always changing in a pediatric hospital. It is the social worker's responsibility to be aware of the technology (medications, equipment, etc.) that her patients use in the hospital and assist in obtaining them for the patient to use at home, if appropriate. This can range from helping a family navigate a financial assistance program in order to obtain medications, to acquiring a hospital-grade infant warmer. Using the internet to do research, speaking with doctors, and consulting any supporting agencies (DME, HHC, etc.) are avenues to pursue when doing our job. Social workers need to find value in their work because it can be a thankless job; patients, families and colleagues are often unaware of the effort it takes to accomplish these tasks.

Another area of technology that affects a social worker's daily routine is electronic record-keeping. With the advent of HIPAA and managed care, electronic documentation has become the norm. Documentation in social work serves several functions: (1) assessment and planning; (2) service delivery; (3) continuity and coordination of services; (4) supervision; (5) service evaluation; and (6) accountability to clients, insurers, agencies, other providers, courts, and utilization review bodies (Kagle, 2008; Luepker & Norton, 2002; Reamer, 2003). It is critical that the social worker be aware of the content of the documentation, the language and terminology and the credibility of the document (Reamer, 2005). Social workers often joke that if it is not written down, then it did not happen.

Organization

The A. I. duPont Hospital for Children (AIDHC) is an organization whose motto is doing "whatever it takes" to ensure the best treatment for the children in our care. The hospital is divided into divisions, departments, services, and teams. As a social worker, I find the motto can be difficult to live up to, as the expectations placed upon us by families, colleagues, and ourselves can become a burden.

Patient and Family Services performs as a team both within its department and the assigned services. Social workers attend an interdisciplinary team meeting each morning (known as screening) with a member of the utilization review team, nursing and an attending physician to discuss the patients and their needs (medical, social, financial, etc.). This provides each social worker with a comprehensive picture of the daily census and allows the social worker to ask any questions or share important information with the members of the team. Early identification of patients who need a social work assessment is integral to effective discharge planning. It is important to recognize that while everyone's goal is the maximization of health for each patient, each team members' objectives and responsibilities to achieve that goal vary.

I am the social worker assigned to the General Pediatrics service. I am responsible for all of the general pediatric patients on a 22-bed unit and half of their patients on a 20-bed unit. This means I could be actively working with up to 30 patients at any given time. My typical caseload is around 15 patients and their diagnoses range from asthma to gastroenteritis, cyclic vomiting to failure to thrive, or from meningitis to an ear infection. The patients' and families' needs vary just as widely: nebulizers to enteral feeding set-ups, applying for insurance to transportation home, or sitting with a parent after he has received a difficult diagnosis. It is a fast-paced service with short stays and quick responses required.

I also have a handful of patients on the Diagnostic Referral Service who have more complex diagnoses that require longer hospital stays, a slower pace and more social work involvement. The patient described in the rest of this chapter comes from the Diagnostic Referral Service (DRS).

Description of the client situation

Benjamin (Ben) is a 12-year-old boy who has been treated at AIDHC for the past seven years and lives with his mother, father and younger brother. Ben is seen by the hospital's Diagnostic Referral Service team due to his complex diagnosis and multi-system disorder, and I have been his social worker for almost three years. He has Tetrasomy 18p, a rare chromosomal disorder. Symptoms include craniofacial malformations; varying degrees of developmental delays, speech difficulties, malformation of the spine, hands, and feet, difficulty coordinating movements and altered muscle tone. In addition to his genetic condition, Ben also faces the diagnosis of cyclic vomiting syndrome (CVS). His particular type is called Sato's variant and involves elevated blood pressure and behavior changes. There is also a large anxiety component to CVS and because of his developmental delays, it has been difficult to use stress reduction/relaxation techniques with him. Ben has been in the hospital almost continuously for two-and-a-half years. Despite numerous adjustments in medications, implantation of a vagal nerve stimulator and a medically induced prolonged sedation, he has shown little improvement.

Due to the anxiety and behavioral issues associated with his diagnoses, Ben responds to stress with agitation and receives constant one-to-one care while in the hospital. This also provides relief for the family and allows them to feel safe leaving him and going home. Ben has not been in school since I met him. He is unable to handle even the most restrictive environment that his school district can provide, due to his anxiety and behavioral issues. He is not home often enough for homebound instruction and usually does not feel well enough for in-hospital school during his numerous admissions.

His family and I have been looking for residential placements that would be appropriate for Ben, but have been unsuccessful so far. The facilities state that he is either not technology-dependent enough or they are unable to handle his behavioral needs. There is also the matter of who will fund the placement, with state agencies pointing fingers at each other and none of them taking responsibility. This has led to great frustration about what the future holds for Benjamin.

Decisions about practice

Definition of the client

Ben was referred to social work services due to his complex medical diagnosis. One might assume that would make him the client. I have discovered over the course of my involvement with him that the client has changed from him to his family, to the medical team working with him, to the staff caring for him and back to the patient himself.

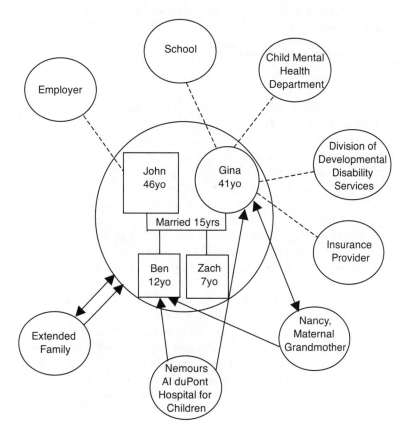

Figure 9.1 Ecomap for Ben.

When Ben is feeling well, he is a delightful, funny, engaging young man who loves vacuum cleaners, laughing, dogs and 1980s dance music. When he is ill and active in a vomiting cycle, it is his family who becomes the focus of my attention and support. Due to the lack of effective treatment and outside resources, his family often needs a person to listen to their concerns, frustration and anger about what their loved one is going through, when it is going to stop, and their fears about how they will handle his disorder as he ages. While his family is understandably discouraged, so are the medical teams and staff who care for him. I have seen them with their heads in their hands and tears in their eyes wondering why the latest treatment is not working and if there is more they can do. This is my opportunity to support them and reflect back that they are doing the very best they can with what they know and what they have available to them.

Goals

The goals in pediatric hospital discharge planning vary from the small and concrete (obtaining a home nebulizer) to the large and intangible (avoiding social isolation). The treatment team and Ben's family have established three goals for him: 1) increase independence; 2) avoid social isolation; and 3) remain at home or in a residential setting, instead of being an inpatient at the hospital. His parents have additional responsibilities outside of the hospital, including working and caring for their other child. Their goal of achieving a balance between Ben's illness and the needs of their family is not easy and is often accompanied by guilt.

Contracting and developing objectives

Utilizing the goals mentioned above, the family and I have created a plan that is flexible and changes with each admission or new development and challenge. This has not been a stress-free process. The objectives to help Ben increase his independence include learning to dress himself and walking on his own. Ben receives physical and occupational therapy to help him achieve these goals and objectives during his inpatient stays and on an outpatient basis on those rare occasions when he is home long enough.

Enrolling Ben in an appropriate educational program has been our objective to help him achieve his goal of avoiding social isolation. This has proven to be quite difficult due to his anxiety issues and inability to utilize stress reduction/coping techniques due to his developmental delays. When Ben is placed in a new situation with too many people, he becomes anxious, feels the physical sensations in his stomach and before any solutions can be put in place, the vomiting begins and a cycle starts. He is never home long enough for homebound instruction to take hold and the hospital school program is unable to work with him when he is in the midst of a cycle.

The third goal boils down to keeping Ben out of the hospital for as long as possible. Two months is the longest time span that he has been at home continuously in the last three years. I have spent a large portion of my time working to acquire private duty nursing for Ben in his home. Having a nurse 12 hours per day, seven days per week would allow the family more freedom and enable them to see Ben as a family member, not a patient. Insurance benefits cover this service but the nursing agencies are unwilling to take his case because they cannot guarantee their nurses consistent hours, due to his history of increasingly short home stays.

Meeting place

Meeting places take on many shapes and sizes in a hospital. They range from large lecture halls to huddling in a hallway trying to form an area of privacy in a public space. Due to Ben's medical issues, when he is admitted, he has one of the few single rooms. This allows his family to have their privacy and gives me a place to be present with them and Ben. Sometimes there are things that need to be expressed out of Ben's earshot and that is when we use my office, the attending physician's office, and the cafeteria, wherever the family feels most comfortable at the time. The telephone is a very important tool in my practice. Ben's mother knows she can call anytime, and I will respond in a timely manner. The hospital is moving towards all private rooms, which will enhance patients' comfort level, control over their environment and improve the quality of interaction and communication.

Use of time

The majority of my discharge planning cases are short-term, brief interventions with patients I may never see again. These revolve around obtaining a piece of medical equipment, a nursing visit, a sleep room in the family resource center, and various other things. There is a marked difference in the investment of time, self and energy between these cases and Benjamin and his family.

Working with a patient and his family for several years has many positives but there are areas to be sensitive to, as well. Spacing and duration of visits is one. When Ben is in the hospital, I see him and his family every day and sometimes several times per day, from an hour in his room discussing plans with his family, to a few minutes in the hallway when he's on his way to physical therapy. This can create too much familiarity, and boundaries can become diffused. I have to be very careful with this as Ben's mother and I are the same age and could easily be friends outside of the hospital. I admit the lines have blurred on occasion and sometimes our conversations have become too intimate. We are both aware of this. It is my responsibility to pull back and put the boundaries in place again when it happens.

Another consideration is the length of the relationship. I have wondered if I can still be objective after three years of seeing a patient and his family more than I see my own family. Recently, Ben's family has decided to take him to another hospital for a second opinion, as they were feeling frustrated and thought maybe the medical team could no longer be objective because they were so comfortable with Ben, his condition, his behaviors and his family.

Strategies and interventions

According to the NASW Standards for Social Work Practice in Health Care Settings (2005), intervention and treatment plans are steps identified by the health social worker, in collaboration with the client and with other members of the team, to achieve the objectives identified during assessment (pp. 21–2). These intervention or treatment plans may include: information, referral and education; individual, family or group counseling; psychoeducational support groups; financial counseling; case management and discharge planning; interdisciplinary care planning and collaboration; and client and systems advocacy.

I consider myself to be a generalist, which means I will "approach every client and situation in a manner open to the use of various models, theories, and techniques and will focus on several levels of intervention, from micro to macro" (Landon & Feit, 1999). In the hospital setting, I must be prepared to work with a variety of different clients one-on-one, with a whole family, a support group, committees and outside resources, to name just a few. The strategies and interventions I use are determined by the needs of my clients and the hospital (or funding source). The theories I regularly use are General Systems, Behavioral and Strengths-Based.

Interventions I use the most include active listening, self-disclosure and humor. Active listening is a process in which the social worker must pay attention to both the verbal and non-verbal messages the client is sending and reflect those messages back to the client so he knows he is being understood. Several skills are used during the active listening process: 1) verbal and non-verbal prompts to encourage the client to continue talking; 2) asking questions that encourage the client to clarify his statements; 3) paraphrasing or rephrasing the literal meaning of the client's statement; 4) reflecting the feelings of the client's statements; 5) summarizing the literal and feeling components of several statements; and 6) exploring extended silences without changing the topic (Shulman, 2006).

Another helping skill is self-disclosure. Self-disclosure is when a social worker makes statements that reveal some of her own thoughts, feelings or life experiences. This skill should not be used in the early rapport-building stage and one's statements should always have a connection with the client's current concern. Positive effects of self-disclosure include making it easier for clients to discuss sensitive things and putting clients at ease when they feel that they know something about you as a person and not just a social worker. If too much is shared, self-disclosure can cause clients to question a worker's emotional stability and professional competence and it can cause a client to feel manipulated. Revealing too much of oneself is especially difficult when interacting with a client who is similar. We must always keep boundaries in mind and be certain it is the client's need that is being met and not our own.

Humor is my favorite helping tool and one that can be used with clients or colleagues. People need to have fun. As social workers, we see clients who are in truly dire circumstances and our resources with which to help them are sometimes inadequate, at best. Humor can be used to counterbalance all the frustration and sadness experienced in our daily work. Social workers are often concerned that our expressions of humor could be misunderstood as insensitivity. Shulman (1991) observes:

> … macabre humor is often noted in high stress situations. Workers can joke about events in a way that would shock the public. This humor is often a defense against the pain of the client's problems. It also provides a release for many stresses in the peer system. Unfortunately, when humor becomes a substitute for facing client pain and self-pain … it can be a maladaptive form of coping. (p. 145)

There are risks associated with using humor at work but without it, social work practice can be unbearable.

Using humor with clients can also be risky and should be viewed like any other technique, realizing that what may be helpful, appropriate and effective with one client may be offensive to another. It is of the utmost importance that social workers never laugh at a client, although laughing with a client may be helpful. A client or family's sense of humor should always be affirmed and supported, no matter how odd it might seem to you as the social worker.

Stance of the social worker

After introducing myself to a patient and his family and explaining the function of social work in the hospital, my goal is to partner with them in seeking the best care for their child.

Partnering can be accomplished through several different roles: advocate, discharge planner, counselor and mediator, to name a few.

As an advocate, I speak up and reach out to other resources to access the most appropriate services for what the patient and family need. As a discharge planner, I research insurance benefits, locate in-network providers, obtain the necessary services from said providers, arrange for the delivery of equipment and supplies and any training that needs to be done. As a counselor, I listen to the patient and his family and provide emotional support during his hospital stay. As a mediator, I am the bridge between the patient, family and the medical team. I seek clarification and try to get any questions the family has answered effectively.

In all of these roles it is important to have an understanding of one's self, motivations, place and impact on relationships (Baldwin, 2000; Reupert, 2007). It is a conscious use of self that allows me to bring my personality to each of these roles and interactions. For me that includes organization, teamwork and a large dose of humor.

Use of resources outside the helping relationship

I have been a hospital social worker for almost eight years and in that time I have compiled a notebook of resources and useful information. By referring to my notebook, I may save myself or a colleague valuable time in resolving an issue. Part of my job is to learn to navigate systems and services as effectively as possible. In Ben's case, I have reached out to many different sources including his school and state agencies. Due to Ben's puzzling combination of diagnoses, I have also written to Dr. Oz of the *Oprah* show at the family's request. I haven't heard back yet, but nothing ventured, nothing gained.

The internet has proven to be a great source of information and access to support groups such as the Cyclic Vomiting Syndrome Association (www.cvsaonline.org). Ben's mother has been open to the opportunity to speak with other parents at our hospital whose children are diagnosed with CVS. It has allowed her to share her experience and knowledge with other families who are just beginning their journey.

Using outside resources as a social worker is part of the bigger case management picture. Strengths-based case management is a specific implementation of the overall strengths perspective, combining a focus on client strengths and self-direction with three other principles: (1) promoting the use of informal helping networks, (2) offering assertive community involvement by case managers, and (3) emphasizing the relationship between client and case manager. Each principle supports the resource acquisition activities that characterize case management (Brun & Rapp, 2001; Siegal *et al.*, 1997). The notebook and family-to-family support are examples of informal helping methods. Maintaining the relationship with my patients' families is the central factor in being a positive and successful hospital social worker.

Reassessment and evaluation

While working on the section regarding objectives I became discouraged when I realized how far we still have to go. Although Ben has great moments of triumph and there are glimmers of hope when the plan finally appears to be coming together, it never comes to fruition. Two steps forward, one step back is our unofficial motto. The plusses are that Ben is making strides in dressing himself, and physical therapy has helped him greatly with ambulation, although he still requires a wheelchair for any kind of distance. The minuses are that he still does not have an appropriate educational situation, and he is currently in a hospital waiting for placement in a residential setting.

With Ben's frequent admissions, there is ample time for reassessment and evaluation. Through the process of looking back, the family decided that it was time to alter the direction of his treatment and requested a second opinion.

Transfer and termination

Prior to Ben's family requesting a second opinion, I had begun to consider asking my supervisor to have another social worker assigned to his case. This was not because of my relationship with the family but because I felt that I had become too close and comfortable with the situation and issues and was unable to see other options besides the ones I had already tried. The thought of explaining this to him and his family weighed heavily on me.

Luckily for me, Ben's family decided to have him admitted to another hospital after his last discharge from AIDHC and I never had to ask for that reassignment. Ben's transfer was difficult for all involved. His mother had a lot of guilt about going somewhere else and expressed the feeling that she was betraying all of the people who had taken such good care of her son. I was able to listen to her and give her what she needed—permission to do what she thought was best for her son and assurance that we would continue to be a support to her and her family even if he was not technically our patient. Ben's mother continues to stay in touch with me and his attending physician via telephone. It has been a big change not seeing Ben every day or knowing how he is doing.

I did not realize how much I needed a respite from this case until Ben was gone for a while and I was speaking with his physician. We both disclosed that, although we missed him and his family, not having the stress and responsibility for his treatment and discharge plan was a relief. I had begun to question myself and my abilities because I could not find the solution to the puzzle that is Benjamin.

Case conclusion

Ben is currently admitted to another children's hospital. He has been there over a month and is being treated in the same manner as at AIDHC. The family remains frustrated and concerned about the future of their son. I have been in touch with his current social worker and have shared the resources I have tried and the knowledge I have gained regarding Ben and his family over the past three years. The plan is for Ben to be placed in a residential setting as soon as an appropriate one can be located and funding can be obtained. Recently, the Delaware Children's Mental Health Unit has denied the request to help pay for residential treatment asserting that his issues are more medical than behavioral. His family has decided to appeal this decision.

Differential discussion

Being a hospital social worker can be an overwhelming job. There are moments of great joy and great sadness. Being present during these intimate family times is a privilege but can become a burden. Occupational stress is real in the social work profession, especially in hospitals. In stressful hospital organizational cultures, social workers often experience high-volume and high-acuity caseloads, quick patient turnaround (leaving little time for intervention and planning), devaluation and the challenging of social work within a medical model, and professional territory and responsibility disputes. We are also exposed to patients who have experienced traumatic events or illnesses and we need to address our patients' pain and trauma as well as our own reactions and feelings. This can be difficult in a hospital environment that allows little time for processing these reactions and frequently precludes meeting personal needs because of the fast pace of the job (Dane & Chachkes, 2001; Gregorian, 2005; Pockett, 2003).

I feel the difficulty increases because my patients are children and have done nothing to warrant the diagnoses they receive. They have not had the opportunity to live a life of their choosing, only a life that their diagnoses allow. It is often harder for us, the treatment team, because we are aware of all that life has to offer and have something to compare it to; Ben only knows that life revolves around vomiting and frequent admissions to the hospital.

The majority of my caseload is high-volume and fast-paced which presents a different stress than what I experienced in Ben's case. With Ben it was a chronic, constant, pervasive stress, which on occasion even crept into my dreams at night. I did not always keep my boundaries firm and that only increased the level of my discomfort. Ben became very ill this past summer and was admitted to the PICU (Pediatric Intensive Care Unit) where he was intubated and remained on a ventilator for almost two weeks. During this time, there were moments of crisis where Ben's future was uncertain and I provided his mother with my personal cellphone number in case something happened while I was not in the hospital. Luckily, Ben came through that episode but his mother did call my cellphone number on several occasions. It became an unnecessary stress I placed on myself and I felt obligated to answer her calls no matter the time or what I was doing. I could not be upset with her because I was the one who had crossed the boundary. I had good reasons for doing this; I wanted to be informed and support the family but it was also selfish of me to think that I was the only one who would be able to provide Ben and his family with what they needed when any of my colleagues would have done a fine job. I do not believe I will do this again but I cannot say for certain.

My empathy for Ben's family came at the price of my own self-protection. Even though I am able to cognitively "put myself in another's shoes," it does not mean I should take that so literally. Feeling physically exhausted and emotionally drained can be side-effects of social work. It is paramount to remember that your job is what you do and not who you are. It is okay, and necessary, to leave your patients at the hospital. Self-care has to be a constant and can include absolutely anything that recharges your physical, mental and emotional batteries. Most social workers learn this lesson early in their careers. I guess I was due for a refresher course. I hope that my involvement with Ben is not finished. Wherever he ends up, whether at his family home or a residential program, I would like to continue to be a resource for his family. It has been my honor and privilege to know Ben and his family.

Even as I write this, I am asking myself why I still want to be a resource for Ben and his family. Do I really want to be a resource? Do I want updates on his condition and discharge plan or is it that I want to maintain contact with this family? If I don't receive a call from the other facility's social worker or Ben's family, will I contact them? These are interesting questions to ask and difficult ones to answer. I saw Ben and his family almost every day for two-and-a-half years and it was easy to become too familiar and too included. I know, because of Ben and his family, that I give more thought to the information I disclose about myself and am more aware of the amount of time I spend with any one patient. The line between professional and personal boundaries can be very thin at times, and I believe that Ben's family's decision to transfer him to another facility happened at the right time and saved us all from some difficult times ahead.

References

Baldwin, M. (2000). *The use of self in therapy* (2nd ed.). Binghamton: The Haworth Press.

Brun, C. & Rapp, R. (2001). Strengths-based case management: Individuals' perspectives on strengths and the case manager relationship. *Social Work*, 46 (3): 278–300.

Dane, B. & Chachkes, E. (2001). The cost of caring for patients with an illness: Contagion to the social worker. *Social Work in Health Care*, 33: 31–50.

Dranove, D. (2000). *The economic revolution of American health care*. Princeton: Princeton University Press.

Gregorian, C. (2005). A career in hospital social work: Do you have what it takes? *Social Work in Health Care*, 40 (3): 1–14.

HIPAA (Health Insurance Portability and Accountability Act of 1996), Pub. L. No. 104–91. Title II, Privacy Rule.

Kagle, J. (2008). *Social work records* (3rd ed.). Long Grove, IL: Waveland Press.

Kayser, K., Hansen, P. & Groves, A. (1995). Evaluating social work practice in a medical setting: How do we meet the challenges of a rapidly changing system? *Research on Social Work Practice*, 5 (4): 485–500.

Landon, P. & Feit, M. (1999). *Generalist social work practice*. Dubuque: Eddie Bowers Publisher.

Luepker, E. & Norton, L. (2002). *Record keeping in psychotherapy and counseling: Protecting confidentiality and the professional relationship*. New York: Brunner-Routledge.

National Association of Social Workers. (2005). *NASW standards for social work practice in health care settings*. Washington, DC: Author.

Nemours—About Nemours. (n.d.). Retrieved 11/10/08, from http://www.nemours.org/about.html

Pockett, R. (2003). Staying in hospital social work. *Social Work in Health Care*, 36 (3): 1–24.

Reamer, F. (2003). *Social work malpractice and liability: Strategies for prevention* (2nd ed.). New York: Columbia University Press.

Reamer, F. (2005). Documentation in social work: Evolving ethical and risk-management standards. *Social Work*, 50 (4): 325–34.

Reupert, A. (2007). Social worker's use of self. *Clinical Social Work Journal*, 35 (2): 107–16.

Shulman, L. (1991). *Interactional social work practice*. Itasca: F. E. Peacock.

Shulman, L. (2006). *The skills of helping: Individuals, families and groups*, (5th ed.). Itasca: F. E. Peacock.

Siegal, H. A., Rapp, R. C., Li, L., Saha, P. & Kirk, K. (1997). The role of case management in retaining clients in substance abuse treatment: An exploratory analysis. *Journal of Drug Issues*, 27: 821–31.

Sulman, J., Savage, D. & Way, S. (2001). Retooling social work practice for high volume, short stay. *Social Work in Health Care*, 34 (3–4): 315–32.

10 Family-focused care of an adolescent with a burn

A multidisciplinary approach

Anne P. Hahn

Context

Description of the setting

The Johns Hopkins Burn Center is situated within The Johns Hopkins Bayview Medical Center, part of the Johns Hopkins Medical Institutions. Accredited by the American Burn Association, the burn center treats patients age 15 and over for all types of burn injuries and also other skin conditions requiring complex wound care. Here, a multidisciplinary team of medical and psychosocial providers comprehensively cares for burn injury in all of its complexities.

Policy and reimbursement variables

Reimbursement issues are a major challenge for burn centers due to the high cost of acute care and the need for long-term follow-up. Survivors often need rehabilitation and multiple surgeries for reconstruction, and they and their families may need psychological follow-up for extended periods (Phillips, Fussell & Rumsey, 2007). Limited insurance or lack of insurance present challenges to obtaining follow-up care.

The American Burn Association, National Burn Repository (2007) reports in its analysis of insurance status for burn units that a significant group of burn patients are uninsured. For those who are insured, many insurance companies do not understand the complexity of wound care and healing. Reimbursement for acute hospital care varies from state to state, and social workers need to be aware of these variances.

— cost drives care —

Reimbursement: implications for social work

Because burn unit services are very costly, a major focus for me must be to ensure the patient has coverage for care and hospital reimbursement, so the initial assessment of the patient includes insurance coverage. I can assist with patient/family referral to the hospital's financial counseling office. A major reimbursement issue, consistent with national policy concerns, is that of undocumented immigrants (Herman, 2008) for whom only limited financial assistance is available. Emergency medical assistance can be authorized for the acute phase but does not cover additional care needs such as rehabilitation or reconstruction services. Reimbursement for, and access to, follow-up mental health care is often a challenge, particularly in rural areas.

Burn injury

A large burn is a major assault to the body and all its systems (Herndon, 2007). The human skin is a large organ whose major function is to act as a barrier to an inhospitable environment, maintain body fluids, and regulate body temperature. The loss of fluid and temperature control can cause other organs, such as lungs and kidneys, to malfunction. A combination of internal mediators and external treatments can cause a cascade of events that can lead to multi-system failure. The treatment of a large burn is not just focused on the burned skin but on all systems of the body.

Patients are first evaluated and stabilized in the emergency department where the source of the injury, and the depth and the size of the burn are determined. It is important to know the source of the burn in order to decide on treatment. For example, in a chemical burn, the exact chemical components must be obtained to properly treat the burn; grease and/or steam burns are often deeper than on initial presentation, and an electrical burn will have an entrance and exit wound.

The depth of the burn is assessed. If a burn involves all layers of the skin and destroys hair follicles, nerves and sweat glands it is determined to be a full thickness burn or third degree. This deep burn is not painful because nerve endings are destroyed, but it requires surgical treatment and will not heal on its own. A second degree or partial thickness burn can generally heal without surgery in several weeks. These burns are very painful. A first degree burn is similar to a sunburn and does not destroy skin layers. Most large burns are usually a combination of all three burn depths. In calculating the size of the burn or total body surface area (TBSA), only full or partial thickness depth burns are considered.

Patients are also assessed for inhalation and trauma injuries. When the patient breathes significant amounts of smoke, irritants can cause swelling of the airway. If an inhalation injury is identified or suspected, an endotracheal tube is inserted. Any delay may result in the patient's airway swelling, precluding the placement of a breathing tube. If the burn injury involves any type of trauma, patients are evaluated for fractures, and particularly for spinal cord injuries.

The assessment phase also consists of a history. The team looks at age, existing medical conditions such as neurological and cognitive impairments, cardiovascular diseases, renal failure and other chronic conditions such as diabetes, and alcohol/drug and psychiatric disorders. Any pre-existing condition can complicate wound healing and the burn plan of care. Age is a major factor in prognosis. Generally, advancing age (>50) and a large burn (50% total body surface area) are associated with increased mortality, but this has not been proven by rigorous examination (http://www.ameriburn.org).

Technology

The burn center is a specialized surgical intensive unit. Patients are monitored in ways that require lines and catheters to monitor internal functions. A feeding tube may be inserted to provide nutrition during the time the patient is in an induced coma. An important part of initial treatment of a large burn is fluid resuscitation. Patients lose fluid when skin is damaged or lost, yet care must be taken not to overload the patient with too much replacement fluid, which could result in respiratory or kidney failure.

The most important part of burn therapy is wound care. All patients are bathed daily in a specialized tub room. Patients are sedated and the wounds are washed, dead skin removed, and the wounds covered with creams and bandages. Advances in the types of dressings can now promote faster healing, and some wound care products can be left on for several days thus avoiding wound care pain and facilitating earlier discharge.

Other specialists also treat the patient. Physical therapy begins with range-of-motion exercises to promote conditioning and prevent contractures. Occupational therapy works with upper extremities and may place splints to maintain positioning and minimize stiffening of arms and hands. The nutritionist initiates the proper diet for optimal wound healing. The bedside nurse assesses and treats pain. Other team members who assist include representatives from pharmacy, psychology, psychiatry and palliative care. Pain rounds are conducted weekly and pain regimes, updated as needed.

Infection is a constant threat and challenge. Patients are frequently cultured for any sign of infection and lines changed at specific intervals. Infectious disease specialists determine which antibiotics to prescribe. Hand washing is enforced and all staff and visitors gown and glove before entering a patient's room.

Burn patients are surgically treated by transplanting tissue from one part of the body to another, skin grafting. The grafting procedure requires viable skin on one part of the body (donor site) that can be used as graft tissue (auto graft.) If none is available, cadaver skin is used (allograft) but this is only temporary, for as long as the patient's own skin cannot be used. Multiple grafting procedures may be necessary in large burns. A successful skin graft results in faster healing, shorter hospital stay, better function and cosmetic effect.

Several advances assist in the success of a graft. One is the use of cell cultured epithelial auto graft (CEA), in which skin cells from the patient are grown in a laboratory that produces skin cell sheets. These sheets are applied as temporary coverage if the patient lacks enough donor sites. Unfortunately, these often do not take and are very expensive. Vacuum assisted closures (VAC) are devices used to assist with closure of large wounds. The vacuum unit creates negative pressure through a system of foam, tubing and bandages that seal the edges of the wound. It draws out excess blood and fluids that help to maintain cleanliness, reduce infection, promote the development of new blood supply, and increase the success of the wound graft.

Treatment and technology: implications for social work

I am often the first person families meet, and they are usually frightened and bewildered. They have no idea what to expect. Patients with a life-threatening burn injury can sometimes walk to the ambulance and talk to families in the emergency department. This can give families the false impression that the injury is minor and easily overcome. They do not realize that the critical nature of the injury will manifest itself in the first 24 hours. It is part of my responsibility to prepare the family for the realities of the injury; that is, the patient may become critically ill from respiratory or infection issues. Patients may be intubated and sedated and unable to communicate with them, or they may look very distorted—bloated from an infusion of fluids and attached to multiple lines and machinery. I educate families about the course of care and about the members of the multidisciplinary team, the roles they play, and how to have access to them. Referral is provided to such agencies as the American Red Cross, financial counseling and other community resources. At the same time, I am gathering important information about the patient that can affect the course of care. A careful history includes asking about previous medical and psychiatric illnesses, as well as the patient's and family's previous experience with crisis situations and how they dealt with them. This gives me an idea of how the family will cope and what kinds of assistance they will need.

Organization

The burn center consists of a 10-bed surgical intensive care unit, an intermediate care unit for patients who are recovering from critical burns or for those with less serious burns, and its own rehabilitation suite and tub room. The operating rooms are nearby. Our multidisciplinary team has expanded over the last years to include intensivists and physicians' assistants who specialize in critical care and are responsible for the day-to-day management of critically ill patients in the burn and surgical intensive care units and work closely with the burn surgeons to improve the quality of care and reduce mortality.

Leadership is provided by two attending burn surgeons. Two burn fellows assist the surgeons and are key players in providing consistent care and tending to the technical aspects of burn care. The nurses are cross trained to work in the acute critical care burn or surgical units as well as the intermediate unit to accommodate the fluid bed census. Physical and occupational therapists are assigned to the burn center but rotate through other services. I am assigned full-time to the center and am an integral part of the team, and I am part of a centralized Department of Social Work. Other team members include a senior psychologist and two fellows, a nurse case manager, and a nutritionist. There is continuity of staff, many of whom have worked in the burn center for years, despite the emotional distress sometimes associated with this type of work (Murji *et al.*, 2006). Newly hired nurses are mentored by a senior nurse who trains them and introduces them to the culture of the center. The team approach is supported through a variety of rounds which everyone attends.

The burn center is also a community of interdependent and equal professionals who could not accomplish their work without each other (Kerson, 2002). The sense of community has developed from a core group of individuals who were part of the center at its inception, and who have the sense of both its history and its future that is essential to a sense of community. There is a shared ethos of good patient care.

Organization: implications for social work

It is imperative that social workers analyze and understand the context of their practice to be effective (Kerson, 2002). A social worker who is isolated and cannot work effectively with the team will not be successful with patients. This requires that I understand my role, function, and place on the team as well as what other team members do. Mintzberg and Van der Heyden (1999) refer to this as an organization with operational fluidity and high collaboration. This requires mutual and reciprocal respect among disciplines.

I can assist the team in conflict-resolution in relation to ethical issues by promoting communication and collaboration and minimizing confrontation. For example, burn surgeons may interpret "good patient care" as being as aggressive as possible to save a life while other team members may view "good patient care" as evaluating quality of life and/or providing comfort care. An ethics consultation might be suggested as a way to unblock communication, remove blame, and energize the team to arrive at a decision.

Visibility is very important. Just as community organizers work within the community to promote change and meet needs, I must be a visible and viable member of the burn/critical care team to inspire and increase productivity, which in this case is good patient care (Drucker, 1999).

Decisions about practice

Patient's injury

Charlie was a 15-year-old boy admitted to the burn center with burns to both legs. These burns covered 15% of the total body surface area and were assessed as partial thickness or second degree. Skin grafting was not necessary, but debridement (removal of dead skin) and wound care were. Pain was a major issue for him because nerve endings were exposed. He was also confined to bed and non-ambulatory to promote healing to the lower extremities.

The injury occurred when Charlie and a friend set a fire with gasoline for "fun." He was burned when he tried to stomp out the fire with his feet. Charlie came from a rural part of the state. I met him on day three of his admission because he was in too much pain to talk with me earlier. Charlie was an attractive, smiling young man who looked older than his age and who did not appear to be in distress, though he had little to say. He did not have a good explanation for the accident and admitted it was "stupid." His injury was complicated by diabetes. He had been diagnosed with Type I, insulin dependent diabetes at age 10, and it was never well controlled.

Definition of the client

After meeting Charlie, I spoke to his parents who provided background information and details about the accident and Charlie's non-adherence to his diabetic regime. Charlie lived with his mother and younger brother, age 12. His mother's extended family (her parents and siblings) lived nearby. Charlie's parents had been divorced for five years, at the same time Charlie was diagnosed with diabetes. His father lived in Michigan where the family had lived prior to the divorce. Following the divorce, his mother moved with her two sons to be closer to her family. Charlie's father and his parents remained involved in the boys' lives. His father came to the burn center as soon as he learned of his son's injury and visited his son for a week. Charlie's parents were amicable, taking care not to blame one another for what had occurred. They expressed their distress over the injury, and their primary concern was their son's healing from the burn and total recovery.

Both were very concerned about Charlie's behavior. Charlie was described as impulsive, rebellious and non-adherent to his diabetic regime. His parents' efforts to redirect his behavior were not successful. His behavior issues predated their divorce but had worsened since. Charlie had been in counseling, as well as family therapy, but it had not been effective. His school and pediatrician were all aware of the behavior issues and were trying to be helpful, but nothing seemed to be effective.

Charlie's mother described what she knew of the circumstances surrounding the injury. She was concerned Charlie was socializing with friends who were not a good influence. They were older than Charlie but accepted him into their circle because he appears older. She also thought he was using marijuana and occasionally drinking. He was with one of these friends when the injury occurred.

Charlie's parents and I discussed discharge issues. Since we knew that he would not be hospitalized long, we needed to establish plans for home care. Charlie's mother was prepared to take a leave of absence from her job to care for her son until he could return to school. His father was returning to Michigan and would not be available to assist. It became clear the after-care for Charlie would fall to his mother who was concerned for her own job and finances. Charlie had good health coverage through his mother's employment.

We discussed referrals for diagnosis and treatment of Charlie's behavior issues. Both agreed he needed some help but it was not clear to either how this could be arranged. His mother was pessimistic Charlie would cooperate in counseling. She was familiar with outpatient psychiatric resources in her area because of her background as a social worker. She said few resources were available. I told the parents the burn center's psychologist would evaluate Charlie and we would work together to find some resources and assist Charlie to accept the referral. Charlie's pediatrician also spoke to me about her concerns; she felt Charlie's mother was not taking sufficient responsibility for the management of Charlie's diabetes. She had considered a referral to child protective services because his mother missed pediatric appointments and did not follow through on the doctor's recommendations.

From my ongoing assessment, I knew the definition of the client was much more than just Charlie. Multiple strained relationships existed in Charlie's life. It became clear to me that assisting Charlie to heal physically, emotionally and socially from his burn injury would require an interdependent endeavor.

Goals

Setting a goal for social work intervention is based upon the definition of the problem, which is often a moving target that can change over time and may be dependent upon one's perspective. In Charlie's case, the goal from the burn center's perspective was to heal his wounds and minimize permanent impairment. From my perspective as the social worker, the goal was to assist the family to address Charlie's diabetes management and behavior issues. From the pediatrician's standpoint, the goal was to change the mother's behavior. The mother's goal was to maintain her own equilibrium and deflect judgments about her as an uncaring mother while caring for her son. Charlie's goal seemed to be noninvolvement with his issues, including family dynamics.

In order to adequately address the goals, we had to determine priorities. The first goal was related to the problem for which the patient and family sought help, burn treatment. The second goal, diabetes management, related to the first. Unless Charlie's diabetes could be managed, he would not heal properly from his burns. The burn occurred while the patient was participating in risky and impulsive behavior, which by history was a pattern and not an isolated incident; therefore, a third goal was acceptance of a referral for psychiatric diagnosis and treatment. My work was to facilitate the identification, acceptance and completion of these goals by all involved: patient, family and multi-disciplinary team.

Contract and objectives

Contracts, particularly in a hospital setting, are flexible and often informal, as the needs may change. After my initial meeting with Charlie and his family, I returned to discuss identified problems, Charlie's burn healing and after-care, diabetes management and mental health care. I explained how I could assist them with referrals to home care resources, consultations with a pediatric social worker about diabetes referrals, and assistance with identifying mental health care and follow-up. We agreed to work toward achieving the following objectives: discharge to home with follow-up appointments, information and referral for a pediatric endocrinologist and education resources, and referral for diagnosis and treatment of behavior issues.

While working with the family, I observed the mood, body language, and voice inflections. Charlie was outwardly cheerful and agreeable to all suggestions but he said very little. His father was often angry and overbearing, criticizing Charlie for his reckless behavior. Although verbally supportive of the objectives, he provided no specific offers of how he would assist. Charlie's mother agreed with the objectives but brought up barriers to achieving them, such as lack of resources in her rural area, long waiting lists for psychiatric care, and her own work schedule. I recognized everyone's frustration and acknowledged that the objectives might not all be achievable at once, but we could prioritize one. We agreed to work on locating resources for diabetes management.

Meeting place

Sessions with Charlie and his family were held in a number of places including the patient's room, my office and the burn center conference room. This is typical of my work with patients and families.

Use of time

Charlie was hospitalized in the burn unit for 17 days. I saw the patient and his mother almost every day but not necessarily for a therapeutic intervention. Often it was a brief conversation to inquire how things were going. This is typical. Most of my interactions take place at the time of admission and at the time of discharge. The middle phase is often more task-related, unless the family contracts with me for more intense and structured counseling.

Much can be accomplished in a short period of time if the intervention is clear and the family agrees. Families are usually in crisis and more open to admitting to underlying problems and accepting assistance due to the rising tension (Parad & Parad 2006; Pollin, 1995). Inner resources can often be mobilized to seek long-needed help.

Interventions

Social workers in intensive care units participate in multiple activities (McCormick, Engleberg & Curtis, 2007). Often patients are too ill to participate in the assessment and pre-discharge planning phases and interventions are thus often directed toward the families. Although the first intervention is assessment, this can also be therapeutic for families because it is not only about information-gathering but also education about the burn center's organization, treatment protocols, and referrals to resources. Charlie's burn injury was a symptom of a bigger problem, an undiagnosed psychiatric disorder within the context of a fractured family. His mother was overwhelmed, felt blamed and judged by others, and his father was physically and emotionally absent. In addition, the intervention also had to address burn healing and management of a chronic illness.

My interventions are guided by crisis intervention theory, family systems and psychosocial medicine (McDaniel, Hepworth & Doherty, 1997; Rolland, 1994). More recent evidence about reactions and adjustments to burns comes from the psychological literature (Esselman, Thombs, Magyar-Russell & Fauerbach, 2006; Fauerbach, Bresnick & Smith, 2007; Fauerbach, Pruzinsky & Saxe, 2007, Thombs, Fauerbach & McCann, 2005). Patients and family members can experience symptoms of depression such as loss of self-esteem and self-efficacy (Doctor, Mancuso, Bishop, Blakeney, Robert & Gaa, 2003). Poor functioning prior to the burn injury can complicate coping and be a predictor of a longer adjustment period (Landolt, Grubermann & Muell, 2002). The degree of distress can be associated with the size of the burn and how much it affects appearance (Williams, Davey & Klock-Powell, 2003).

Families are usually willing to engage with the social worker during the assessment phase because they are in crisis. They may then shut down as they begin to experience feelings of loss, shame, or guilt. These feelings may be heightened when other family members arrive to be supportive but may add to the tension if there is a history of poor family relationships. The assessment phase needs to be ongoing, as families' moods and behaviors can change from the initial evaluation.

Stance of the social worker

Charlie's case presented a challenge. I believed that focusing on the mother was important to meet the agreed objectives. The mother was the primary parent in Charlie's life. I sensed as the hospitalization continued that the mother became less engaged and more superficial in her interactions with me. About the same time, I received a call from Charlie's pediatrician. The pediatrician was concerned the mother was not accepting responsibility for Charlie's diabetes management.

This was difficult for me because the mother was a professional social worker. I wondered if the mother might feel judged by me as an inadequate mother; perhaps I was embarrassed about confronting her with our concerns. We met several days before Charlie's impending discharge. The mother asked what the psychologist thought about Charlie. I suggested we all meet to discuss her concerns because I thought an additional team member might promote communication. Prior to the meeting with the mother, the psychologist and I met. We went over the data we had gathered: Charlie's non-adherence and impulsive behavior, possible neglectful mother, absent father, concerned pediatrician, and lack of community resources. We decided to take an open and non-judgmental approach. We wanted to hear the mother's assessment of the situation both as a parent and a professional social worker. This was successful. We met in a comfortable and private conference room. The mother opened up about her son's violent behavior, her attempts to deal with it, and the poor relationship she had with the children's father.

At one point, I asked her if it would help her if we made a referral to Child Protective Services. She did not want this because she felt Charlie might get lost in the system and never receive the help he needed. She admitted to feeling very sad about her mothering and believed that her husband's family thought she was an inadequate parent. However, she felt her children were better off with her than with their father, who lacked the emotional resources to deal with them. By the end of the session, the psychologist and I saw a caring mother who was overwhelmed by multiple stressors: an out-of-control adolescent with a serious health problem, another son to protect, minimal social support, and financial issues. We acknowledged that she was a caring mother who was doing the best she could but needed help and had the courage to ask for it.

Use of outside resources

Following the meeting, the psychologist and I discussed how Charlie's wounds were almost healed and that the other equally important issues needed to be addressed. We could not accomplish this in our unit. We worked, with the help of the attending physician, to have Charlie transferred to the main hospital's pediatric unit. The psychologist spoke to Charlie about the plan and his agreement to participate. I followed up with Charlie and his mother to support the plan, discuss ambivalent feelings and assist with the technical aspects of the transfer. Once Charlie was transferred, he was able to receive evaluation and treatment for his behavior and diabetic issues. He was diagnosed with a mood disorder and ADHD and referred to the adolescent psychiatric day program. From there he was transferred to a similar program closer to his home. He was stabilized on a diabetes regime and appointments were arranged for him with a community pediatric specialist and a nurse diabetes educator. Charlie's pediatrician was made aware of the referrals. I informed the pediatrician that the burn team did not think the mother was negligent but overwhelmed, and I explained that the mother could benefit from the pediatrician's support for Charlie's ongoing care at these community resources.

Charlie did not need any other services for his burn injury. He and his mother returned to the burn clinic once for follow-up and he was discharged to the care of his pediatrician. Appearing happy and relaxed, they visited the in-patient burn center and thanked everyone for his care. Charlie was back at school, participating in outpatient psychiatry visits and his mother had returned to work.

Evaluation

The review of Charlie's case was positive, in that all goals were met. Charlie's burns were treated, his diabetes better managed, his behavior and psychiatric issues assessed and treatment had begun. Additionally, we were able to support his mother, validating that she was a caring mother, and at the same time relieving her of the burden of finding the appropriate care for her son and trying to make him adhere to the plan. We advocated with the pediatrician so she could be a source of ongoing support.

Differential discussion

This case is representative of the types of burns and cases seen in our center. The burn injury often occurs in the context of pre-existing poor functioning and chronic psychosocial problems. Admission to the burn center may have the effect not only of treating the burn but also of addressing the underlying issues and providing assistance.

Burn units have the luxury of a multidisciplinary team and more time to address issues because burn patients often have longer than usual acute stays. The burn team can be mobilized to assess and intervene with the patient and family, and the critical nature of the burn can mobilize the patient and family to address underlying conditions and accept assistance. The role of the social worker is twofold: assessment of the patient and family for underlying issues, and communication with the multidisciplinary team. The positive outcome in Charlie's case was due to assessment, relationship building with the family, and collaboration with the psychology team. The social worker must quickly be able to form relationships with patients and families while working with the team and be willing to share the work with others with the goal of good patient care.

In reviewing Charlie's case, it is not clear if anything else could be done differently. It is likely that the timing of events was consistent with the mother's comfort level with me, in addition to her anxiety as Charlie's discharge was approaching. The involvement of the pediatrician was a key factor. Once she understood the pressures the mother was under and the mother's willingness to work with us, she became a willing support for the mother.

Each case is different. The multidisciplinary team is a vehicle to address complex medical and psychosocial problems, and I contribute to the teamwork by remaining open and flexible, in order to use myself as a resource for patients and families.

128   *A. P. Hahn*

References

American Burn Association (2007). National Burn Repository. Retrieved 11/25/08, from http:// www. Ameriburn.org/2007NBR AnnualReport.pdf

Doctor, M. E., Mancuso, M. G., Bishop, S., Blakeney, P., Robert, R. & Gaa, J. (2003). Impact on the family: Psychosocial adjustment of siblings of children who survive serious burns. *Journal of Burn Care and Rehabilitation*, 24 (2): 109–18.

Drucker, P. (1999). *Management challenges for the 21st century*. New York: Harper Business.

Esselman, P. L., Thombs, B. D., Magyar-Russell, G. & Fauerbach, J. (2006). Burn rehabilitation: State of the science. *American Journal of Physical Medicine Rehabilitation*, 85 (4): 383–413.

Fauerbach, J. A., Bresnick, M. G. & Smith, M. T. (2007). Coping with burn injury: Research summary and a new model of the influence of coping on psychological complications. In E. Matz & H. Livneh (eds.), *Coping with chronic illness and disability: Theoretical, empirical and clinical aspects* (pp. 173–90). New York: Springer.

Fauerbach, J. A., Pruzinsky, T. & Saxe, G. N. (2007). Psychological health and function after burn injury: Setting research priorities. *Journal of Burn Care and Research*, 28: 587–92.

Herman, L. D. (2008). Reimbursement of medical care for immigrants. *Virtual Mentor*, 10 (4): 224–8.

Herndon, D. N. (ed.) (2007). *Total burn care*. Philadelphia: W. B. Saunders.

Kerson, T. S. (2002). *Boundary spanning: An ecological reinterpretation of social work practice in health and mental health systems*. New York: Columbia University Press.

Landolt, M. A., Grubermann, S. & Muell, M. (2002). Family impact: Greatest predictors of quality of life and psychological adjustment in pediatric burn survivors. *Journal of Trauma Injury, Infection and Critical Care*, 53 (6): 1146–51.

McCormick, A., Engelberg, R. & Curtis, J. R. (2007). Social workers in palliative care: assessing activities and barriers in the intensive care unit. *Journal of Palliative Medicine*, 10 (4): 929–37.

McDaniel, S. H., Hepworth, J. & Doherty, W. (1997). *The shared experience of illness: Stories of patients, families and their therapists*. New York: Basic Books.

Mintzberg, H. & Van der Heyden, L. (1999). Organigraphs: Drawing how companies really work. *Harvard Business Review*, September—October: 87–94.

Murji, A., Gomez, M., Knighton, J. & Fish, J. S. (2006). Emotional implications of working in a burn unit. *Journal of Burn Care and Research*, 27 (1): 8–13.

Parad, H. J. & Parad, L. G. (2006). *Crisis intervention book 2: The practitioner's source book for brief therapy* (2nd ed.). New York: Fenestra Books.

Phillips, C., Fussell, A. & Rumsey, N. (2007). Considerations for psychosocial support following burn injury—a family perspective. *Burns*, 33 (8): 986–94.

Pollin, I. (1995). *Medical crisis counseling*. New York: W. W. Norton & Co.

Rolland, J. (1994). *Families, illness and disability: An integrative treatment model*. New York: Basic.

Thombs, B., Fauerbach, J. & McCann, U., (2005). Stress disorders following traumatic injury: assessment and treatment considerations. *Primary Psychiatry*, March: 51–5.

Williams, N. R., Davey, M. & Klock-Powell, K. (2003). Rising from the ashes: Stories of recovery, adaptation and resiliency in burn survivors. *Social Work in Health Care*, 36 (4): 53–7.

11 Longing to belong

Finding a sense of acceptance and community at a Special Services School District

Wendy Emerson Hinch

Context

The eight Special Service School Districts in New Jersey (NJ) are county-based and designed to provide a wide range of programs and services to meet the needs of the students in the region. They enroll about 4,500 of the state's most severely disabled students in regionalized public school programs especially designed to meet their educational needs. Most have multiple disabilities, autism, behavioral disorders, physical impairments or severe cognitive impairments (Joint Council, 2009; Schmidt & Heybyrne, 2004). Our district provides a comprehensive array of academic, health and extracurricular resources needed to educate special needs students. Our students require very specialized teaching and care; such as low student/teacher ratio classes, one-to-one instruction, classroom and even personal aides. In addition, as part of their school day, many require therapy and medical services (Joint Council/NCLB, 2009).

Public education is a right of every child in the United States. State law requires each public school district to have a process in place for the "location, identification, evaluation, determination of eligibility, development of an individualized education program and the provision of a free appropriate, public education to students' disabilities" (NJAC, 2006, p. 10). In NJ, the school district's Child Study Team (CST) carries out this process. Core members include a school psychologist, learning disabilities teacher-consultant, and school social worker. A parent or teacher who suspects a student is having a learning problem refers the child to the CST, which meets with the teachers and parents to determine whether the child should be evaluated. If the CST determines the child is eligible for special education and related services, the team, family, and teachers develop an Individualized Education Plan (IEP), a written report of the child's educational goals, assessment measures, supports and the services needed to implement the plan. For the student discussed here, the local school district did not have an educational environment adequate to meet her needs. Ultimately, she was sent to us for her education.

Policy

Policies related to special education include federal and state legislation. Romano (1998, p. 55) says:

> The Individual with Disability Education Act (IDEA) "mandates that all states make available to handicapped children a 'free and appropriate public education' and extensive 'due process' procedures." This federal act and the regulations of the United States Department of Education establish procedures by which handicapped children are

evaluated, their classifications are determined, and an appropriate program of special education and related services is developed and implemented.

In addition, states are mandated to establish policy and procedures for local school districts (Fischer & Sorenson, 1996). IDEA requires that every state issue rules or regulations that provide guidance on its implementation of IDEA. At a minimum, state regulations must provide all the protections contained in IDEA (NCLD-IDEA, 2004). Also important is the NJ Administrative Code (NJAC); Title 6A, Chapter 14, Special Education, commonly known as the "Special Ed Code," "Code," or "NJAC 6A: 14," that establishes standards against which the NJ Department of Education determines district implementation of and compliance with the law (http://www.state.nj.us/education/Walther). The overarching result of these statutes is to create access and equal rights to a public education for students regardless of disability. Not eligibility but type and quantity of services provided are the usual issues, and I advocate for appropriate services despite budgetary concerns and limited school district resources.

Technology

Many tools are used to diagnose, treat and monitor students with special needs (Pierangelo, 2003; Roban, 2006). Standardized assessments are used to measure a student's ability compared with others of the same age and/or grade. Results that differ from the norm can be indicators that the child has a disability. With standardized assessments, we use informal measures such as interviews of the parent, teacher and/or student, and classroom observation of the student provides additional information to determine the student's level of functioning. Social workers are typically responsible for completing the parent interview. We explore the student's developmental, medical, educational, and family history and during the interview process we determine whether additional standardized assessments are needed to appraise the student's level of functioning in activities of daily living. Most social workers use the Vineland Adaptive Behavior Scales (VABS). One needs an adequate level of training to administer the test and interpret results.

Organization

Working in a special services school district comes with its own set of politicized rules and guidelines. We are designed as a county-based regionalized program incorporating many stakeholders. Our district is governed by a school board and superintendent. The difference between ours and local boards is that our county freeholders appoint our board members. The design of the school board makes our school district inherently political. Justification for a special services school district is primarily financial in that "it is inefficient, expensive and often impossible for each local community to offer the full range of services that may be needed by only a few students" (Murray, 2005, 1).

By design, our school district has a fluid response to the needs of the local communities. Early in its development, our district was designed to provide service to approximately 250 to 300 students. Now, we have grown to include an elementary, middle and high school program, a career transition program and a specialized program for students with autism. Some programs included in the original design for the district have closed or consolidated. Our district now serves approximately 500 students.

We are called a "receiving school district;" that is, we provide educational services to students on a contractual basis with other local school districts. As a "receiving district" we do not serve one local community; rather, local school district Child Study Teams notify us when they have a student they would like us to consider for one of our programs. Once determined that the referral is appropriate, the sending district contracts to pay tuition to our district. This is our primary source of funding. Each district pays from $40,000 to $100,000 per year to send a student to our school with the cost varying depending on the quantity and intensity of services needed to educate a student.

Trust is an element in the districts' contractual relationship. Sending districts have to trust that, as service providers, we act in the best interest of both their student and district. Dilemmas ensue when the services needed for the student and the financial resources of the sending district are in conflict. The key to effective service provision is our interdisciplinary team: the special education teacher, middle school vice principal and myself. Other treatment providers are included as needed. As a social worker it is absolutely imperative that I establish a professional rapport with administrators, special education teachers and other professionals who work with our students. Unilateral decision making is ineffective. Team decisions provide the most appropriate, comprehensive and effective services to our students. This format also minimizes the likelihood of inappropriate service provisions to students.

Decisions about practice

Description of the client situation

Jackie Larsen, a 15-year-old Caucasian female, is an only child who lives with her parents, who own a family business and are active in obtaining services to meet her chronic medical, educational, social, and emotional needs. For many students with special needs, parental availability to address medical and educational needs requires that families find a way to manage on one income or governmental assistance, and the flexibility of Jackie's parents' work has been helpful here. Jackie and I began our work together when she was in seventh grade, and we continued until she was in ninth grade. Her strengths include a willingness to learn and a natural curiosity about her environment. She is assertive, independent and persistent. While she has a strong work ethic and takes pride in her accomplishments, she struggles in the areas of communication and peer relationships.

Medical, educational and cultural history

Due to severe medical conditions and a history of developmental delays, Jackie received special education services from the time that she was three, and she has been with us since kindergarten. Upon entry into special education, Jackie had a medical diagnosis of Encephalopathy (unspecified), Mild Cognitive Impairment, Global Developmental Delays, Expressive Language Delays (which later was changed to Severe Verbal Apraxia), Mild to Moderate Hearing Loss, Food Allergies, Asthma and Social Anxiety. She was primarily non-verbal, and the few words she used were unintelligible to those who were not familiar to her. Throughout the course of early language development, Jackie and her immediate family created a sign language system of 30 to 40 words through mimes and gestures which could only be understood by them and was her primary means of communication. We introduced assistive technologies over the years, but Jackie preferred to use her unique sign system. With this in mind, the Child Study Team, along with her parents, decided to place Jackie in a classroom that contained students who were deaf or hard of hearing and used "total communication" for teaching.

Total communication is "not necessarily a method but rather a philosophy of trying any method (or language) and any combination of methods and languages to meet the individual needs of the particular child" (Medwid & Weston, 1995, 84). In this classroom, total communication integrated both sign language and speech. The goal was to give Jackie a proper sign language base to use as her primary mode of communication because someone using sign language as a form of communication has access to a culture with a unique history (Medwid & Weston, 1995). While integrating and identifying oneself as a part of deaf culture is a source of support and pride for many individuals, it was not for Jackie. When Jackie's mom and I talked about Jackie's move to this classroom, Mrs. Larsen expressed her hope that Jackie could find some comfort in deaf culture. While Jackie's parents did all they could to establish a social network for their daughter, Jackie felt uncomfortable in the deaf community. Jackie preferred being with hearing children only. The Child Study Team and family met to see what options were available. Due to Jackie's significant learning and social skill deficits, the team supported Jackie's choice to leave the program for children who are deaf or hard of hearing and try the middle school program for students with multiple disabilities because although she is diagnosed with Bilateral Mild to Moderate hearing loss, Jackie uses her hearing as her primary mode of receptive language. She identifies herself as a hearing person and everyone in her immediate family is hearing.

Definition of the client and goals

Jackie is the primary client, although I also work with her family and the school system. I provide case management and counseling services. Goal setting is part of the IEP process. The NJ Core Curriculum Content Standards (NJCCCS) drive our client goals. Each year, the student and I review progress and choose appropriate Standard goals for the upcoming year. Because our students are minors, their parents have the final decision of what goals to work on in school. Parents usually rely on our professional judgment to determine what goals are most appropriate. Jackie's goals were in Health and Physical Education and Career Education, Consumer, Family and Life Skills: (1) the learner will be able to identify factors that improve and maintain mature, loving, healthy relationships, and (2) the learner will model interpersonal and effective conflict resolution skills.

Contracting and developing objectives

The IEP is a legally binding contract that states goals for the upcoming school year. Within the IEP, I provide what are referred to as related services. If counseling is needed, the type of counseling, frequency, duration and location of services are written into the IEP. IEP goals are discussed at monthly review meetings. Jackie was scheduled for individual counseling one time per week for 20 minutes and group counseling one time per week for 20 minutes. When individual counseling is recommended, it "usually means that the child would benefit from a more intimate therapeutic situation with emphasis on control, insight, cause and effect awareness, special attention, and developing a trusting relationship with an authority figure" (Blum, 1998, 150). A recommendation of group counseling "means that the child would benefit from a group situation that emphasizes interpersonal relations, social skills, cooperative play and interaction, interdependence, social delay of gratification, peer feedback, and social connections" (Blum, 1998, 150). Social workers understand the difference between school counseling and therapy; even if we have the training and experience to offer psychotherapy services to the family, it may not be appropriate or in the child's best interest to address these issues in the school setting.

Table 11.1 Counseling and therapy services

Counseling	Therapy
Addresses preventative and developmental concerns.	Addresses serious disorders and personality problems.
Addresses conscious concerns.	Addresses unconscious concerns as well as conscious concerns.
Assists with educational, career, and decision-making problems.	Assists with personality reconstruction and other serious problems.
Uses teaching methods.	Uses healing methods.
Makes referrals to parents for students with serious problems to receive help from professionals outside of school with clinical training.	Provides ongoing therapy to students referred by school counselor to parents.

Source: Blum, 1998, 47.

Meeting place

Within the school, many locations are used to work on counseling goals. When I first began counseling services with Jackie, we met in my office. There is sufficient space and privacy for Jackie to feel comfortable. In addition, services are provided to Jackie in the group counseling room and integrated settings such as the classroom, cafeteria or gymnasium.

Use of time

In addition to Jackie's weekly scheduled time, I also train students to use social work request forms that are brightly colored orange so our non-readers can identify the form by color rather than the words on the paper. Students write their name on the form to access services. Once counseling is requested, the school staff notifies me to meet with the student. Jackie had access to these forms at any time to address difficulties that might have occurred during the school day.

Strategies and interventions

Evidence-based practice research geared to developmental disabilities is limited; the most recognized area is behavior therapy (Perry & Weiss, 2007). Most clinical interventions, derived from mental health research and from medical models, are often inappropriate for developmental disabilities where adaptation is the goal (Franklin, Harris & Allen-Meares, 2006; House, 2002).

> Treatments or interventions are often used to eliminate or reduce the intensity of specific symptoms, not the disability in general. To this end, it is critical that we consider what is needed in the field in terms of knowledge transfer and training in evidence-based practice. It is well established that the existence of the knowledge or of best practice guidelines does not necessarily translate into practice. (Barwick *et al.*, 2005)

I assessed Jackie's transition and performance in our program within 30 days of her arrival. I schedule at least one observation per week, and in order to maintain consistency in my evaluation of students, I use two different observational scales to record the behaviors

Table 11.2 Treatment plan

Jackie's Treatment Plan

Problem: *Difficulty with peer relationships and social skills.*

Behavioral Definitions	Long-term Goals
Refuses to initiate or maintain social relationships with peers in school resulting in isolation.	Develop essential social skills that will enhance the quality of interpersonal relationships.
Is a scapegoat or picked on by peers.	Establish and maintain long-term (i.e. six months) interpersonal or peer friendships outside of the immediate family.
Refuses to accept responsibility for socially inappropriate behavior and tends to blame others for the resulting consequences.	Demonstrate appropriate social interaction, assertiveness, confidence in self and initiation in social contact.
Immature social skills and lack of age-appropriate social behavior.	Believe in self as being likable, capable, and socially accepted.
	Develop conflict management skills to use at home, school, and in the community.

Short-term Objectives	Therapeutic Interventions
1 Identify positive personal qualities that are important for successful social interaction.	1 Jackie will develop written list of positive personal attributes. Create social skills journal. 2 Process questions and answers from the personal information sheet. Have student explain responses to assess possible causes of low self-esteem or relationship difficulties. Materials: Blank Social Skills journal Location: Individual counseling
2 Identify existing positive relationships and significant others who offer acceptance and friendship.	1 Develop ecomap. Materials: Ecomap, Social Skills journal Location: Individual counseling

3 List methods of establishing friendships.
   1 Assist student in listing methods of establishing friendships.
     Materials: "Art of Creating and Maintaining Friendships" activity.
   2 Read role-plays and techniques for making and keeping friends. Role-play with student various examples.
     Materials: *School counseling and school social work homework planner* (Knapp, 2003).
     Making and keeping friends (Schmidt, 1997). *Teaching social skills to youth* (Dowd & Tierney, 2005).
     Location: Individual Counseling.

4 Practice skills with school peers.
   1 Assist student in developing plan for using skills. Observe and assist student as needed in implementing knowledge and skill set.
     Materials: none
     Location: Integrated settings—Classroom, Cafeteria and Gym

5 Participate in counseling group focusing on teaching social skills and techniques for resolving conflicts.
   1 Create six week counseling groups with activities for role-play and game play.
     Materials: Games, Music CDs, *Scholastic Choices* Magazine, *Teaching social skills to youth* (Dowd & Tierney, 2005).
     Location: Group Counseling

6 Express feelings directly and assertively.
   1 Peer mediation as needed to resolve peer conflict.
     Materials: Peer Mediation materials
     Location: Mid School Conference Room

7 Participate in peer mediation to demonstrate the ability to work toward mutually acceptable solutions.
   1 Peer mediation as needed to resolve peer conflict.
     Materials: Peer Mediation materials
     Location: Mid School Conference Room

8 Report and document progress.
   1 Self-report by student on progress.
   2 Consult with teachers and aides on progress.
   3 Record my observations of student in various settings.
   4 Document incidents of peer mediation sessions.
   5 Document disciplinary reports.
   6 Document Social Work referrals.
   7 Assessment summary to be completed a minimum of once every marking period.

of students in the classroom. Depending on the setting, I use both the Structured and Unstructured Observation Forms (Blum, 1998, 109–10). I began individual counseling to establish rapport and discuss the changes Jackie experienced in her new school setting, reviewed educational records, observed Jackie in a minimum of four settings, assessed consistency in collateral information from Jackie's teachers and aides, and developed IEP goals and objectives and select students appropriate for group counseling sessions during this first month.

Assessment indicated that Jackie has significant difficulties in her social relationships with peers. She often isolates herself or seeks out the company of adults. When redirected to interact with her classmates, she remains independent. Jackie's current communication abilities include one to two word voice expressions, gesturing, miming, signing and use of an assistive communication device. A full-time sign language interpreter voices for her. During my observations, Jackie did not access her interpreter or assistive communication device to communicate with peers. Rather, she would often stare at others or stand next to them without using any type of communication to get their attention.

Jackie's medical diagnosis at entry into our program was the same as when she entered our district in kindergarten. Her educational diagnosis was Multiply Disabled including signs of Mild Cognitive Impairment. Entering seventh grade, Jackie had mid-second grade skills in math, beginning second grade skills in reading and mid-first grade skills in writing. Included in her diagnosis of Global Developmental Delay were weaknesses in fine motor skills and signs of severe verbal apraxia. Her bilateral hearing loss was unaided but monitored by an audiologist. Asthma and food allergies had minimal impact in the school environment. Social anxiety was evident through her social isolation and maladaptive peer interactions. Jackie's current medication regimen includes: Advair, Zyrtec, Singulair daily for asthma and an Epi-pen, as needed, for food allergy. She was prescribed Zoloft for anxiety. After completing my assessment I designed Jackie's treatment plan, adapted from Knapp and Jongsma (2002).

Jackie worked readily during individual counseling to create a list of positive personal attributes. Once we completed the ecomap and discussed the skills necessary to establish relationships, I used role-play and classroom observations to assess whether Jackie had a skill deficit or performance deficit. A skill deficit is when a student cannot perform the skill itself (e.g. walking up to another student and introducing herself). A performance deficit is when the student can perform the skill but for some reason does not use it consistently during daily activities. For a majority of the skills, Jackie had performance deficits. She could explain and model the skill when working with me during individual counseling but she could not consistently use the skill with her peers. In individual counseling, Jackie and I continued to discuss her difficulty with expressive language and the ways she could overcome these barriers with her peers. She was certain she did not want to use the sign language interpreter or assistive communication device. Since Jackie still had difficulty being understood, she decided she would carry pens and a piece of paper to communicate if she could not be understood by her peers during socialization times.

Stance of the social worker

While most interventions require more active approaches, work with Jackie required me to step back from the situation to see where the intervention's evolution would take both her and the system. In school we benefit from the gift of time. Most clients attend our program for four to six years. With Jackie, there is a balancing act between over- and under-involvement. If I were extremely accessible to Jackie as a counselor, she would rely heavily on her relationship with me to determine each step taken with her peers. Yet, if I allowed too much time between observations or sessions, Jackie would slip back into previous patterns of frustration and isolation. My consistent monitoring of client and environment helped Jackie to generalize the skills she learned in counseling to the school environment.

Peer and clinical supervision were necessary for me in working with Jackie. I found my commitment to her care often exceeded that of others. When I met Jackie, I felt sorry for her. She

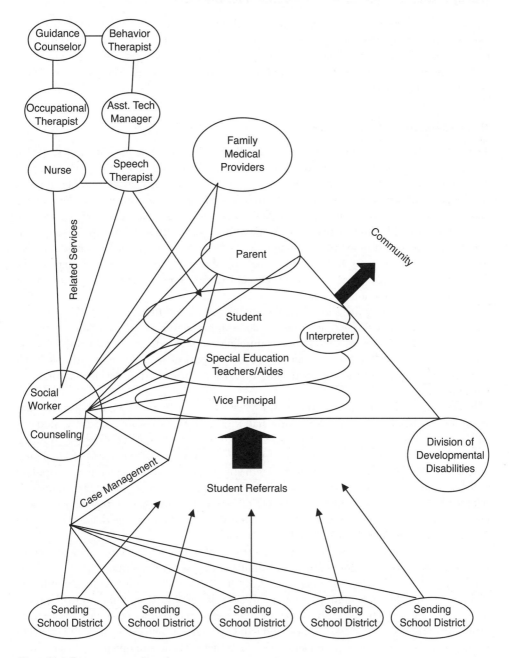

Figure 11.1 Program organigraph.

seemed so sad and lonely. I remind interns that we are human beings first; our fears, doubts and worries are a natural extension of caring for those we serve. Countertransference issues will arise, and recognizing and admitting that we need additional support creates appropriate boundaries in our work.

Use of resources outside of the helping relationship

I work in an environment where the team includes the special education teacher, teacher's aide, social worker, speech-language specialist, occupational therapist, assistive technology program manager, behavioral therapist, parents, special services program administrator, guidance counselor, school nurse, and the child study team case manager. Many resources were available and employed.

Reassessment and evaluation

Throughout the course of our first school year together, there were significant setbacks. Jackie was in a classroom with several students who were socially higher functioning than she. Her maladaptive attempts to befriend them led her to be the object of ridicule, and her use of a sign language interpreter led other students to believe she was deaf. Throughout the year, we had a minimum of three to four peer mediations per marking period attempting to resolve the conflicts. In addition, I increased my work with the other students to help educate them about acceptance and differences amongst themselves. At times, Jackie became extremely frustrated with the process and refused to look to other students who were willing to offer acceptance and friendship. She became preoccupied with three students and would stare at them for excessive amounts of time.

Individual counseling was successful. We established a good rapport and Jackie accepted constructive feedback. She was inconsistent about using new strategies but could verbalize the need to change her approach. Group counseling was somewhat successful; it gave Jackie one time per week where she was guaranteed to be a part of a social group. Although the students involved stated they enjoyed the group, friendships did not develop beyond our meeting time.

In addition to the current interventions, I believed the other special education classroom would be a better fit for Jackie. Mrs. Moss had proven to be successful with many students with significant social difficulties. She had a very structured schedule and integrated group and individual behavior modification systems within the classroom. She developed and integrated a social skills curriculum that included the use of peer leadership techniques based on individual student strengths. I talked with Mrs. Moss about Jackie's situation, explaining the significant communication difficulties and use of various technologies supporting Jackie and discussed Jackie's lack of real social progress. Mrs. Moss agreed, and, together, we requested that Jackie move to Mrs. Moss' room the next school year.

At the start of our second year together, Jackie's goals remained the same. The new classroom was a positive intervention; there was significantly less tension among classmates. Mrs. Moss' approach to behavior management kept conflict between students to a minimum, and her social skills curriculum promoted cohesion. Jackie and I were able to work proactively rather than reactively. Within three months, Jackie successfully generalized skills from counseling sessions to the classroom, cafeteria and gym classes. She used paper and pencil to communicate when she was not understood. The students Jackie attempted to befriend were more tolerant when some of her attempts appeared unusual.

Mrs. Moss reported that Jackie never used her interpreter or assistive communication device spontaneously in the classroom. Jackie listens to all lectures, raises her hand and voices the best she can with answers. I asked about clarity in voice response; although Mrs. Moss misunderstood Jackie sometimes, Jackie willingly repeated her responses. This new information created a dilemma. Jackie's primary mode of communication was slowly shifting from signing to voicing. I contacted the treatment providers and asked for reports about the clarity of Jackie's communication. Jackie's voice production had increased, but her clarity remained inconsistent; she was experiencing a burst of language development. All providers reported that when asked to repeat information, Jackie slowed her response and increased her effort in producing her sentences.

I had several thoughts about her current status. My primary concern was Jackie's ability to communicate with those unfamiliar to her. Having access to a sign language interpreter and augmentative communication device ensured that Jackie could communicate when needed. From a developmental perspective, I was concerned about Jackie's ability to increase her level of independence in preparation for employment as an adult. Having worked with students in the area of transition to the workplace for over 15 years, I knew it would be extremely difficult for Jackie to find employment if she relied on a sign language interpreter or assistive technology for communication. When I met with Jackie in counseling to discuss her use of the interpreter and assistive communication device, Jackie insisted she did not want to use them. In collaboration with the Vice Principal, we decided to call an interdisciplinary team meeting to review Jackie's case. As a result of the meeting, a data form was created to document Jackie's use of the sign language interpreter. And we also decided to explore other assistive technology devices. After a 60-day assessment, we reconvened and determined that Jackie no longer needed the sign language interpreter or assistive communication device. She had developed enough language and adaptive strategies to function within her academic setting. Once the communication needs were assessed and resolved, Jackie and I continued our work on improving her social skills. In April, Jackie had a birthday party and invited many of her new friends to her party. Five school friends came to her house to help celebrate. At year-end, Jackie and I reviewed the significant progress she had made throughout the year.

During our third year together, we continued to work on improving Jackie's social skills. Suddenly in November, Jackie was hospitalized with a diagnosis of diabetes. She was devastated! My feelings echoed her words when she screamed out "Why me?" during one of our sessions. With Jackie's newest medical complications, we had to adjust our objectives to include emotional adjustment, acceptance and management of diabetes. Due to my own emotional reaction, I sought peer supervision and support from the Guidance Counselor who also has diabetes. She agreed to develop a diabetes support group that would benefit several other students who had the same diagnosis. With a new plan in place, I used psycho-education to help assess and increase Jackie's understanding of diabetes, and I asked the school nurse to notify me of any concerns related to the diabetes management. As Jackie stabilized both physically and emotionally, we refocused on social skills. The gains Jackie made prior to her hospitalization were maintained. While Jackie met with some success in developing and maintaining social skills, she continued to need support in developing relationships outside of school.

Transfer and termination

Terminating with Jackie was difficult for me. I knew she had worked hard to maintain the gains she had made. Transfer and termination of service came as the result of my mid-year maternity leave. When I returned at the end of the school year, Jackie was doing well socially and academically. After three years, she moved on to our high school program. While our direct work together was finished, I still had the opportunity to see her in our school community.

Case conclusion

I have had the opportunity to briefly observe Jackie in the cafeteria and vocational areas. She appears to be maintaining the social skills we worked on last year. Academically, teachers report that Jackie is maintaining the two years' growth in reading and math she achieved last year, as well. Jackie does not yet engage in ongoing dialogue with her peers. She sits near them and this allows her to be a part of their social interactions. This small gesture of acceptance is meaningful to her. Jackie receives individual counseling with the high school social worker. Small group social skills counseling is impossible due to the academic schedule variances between students at the high school level. She continues to work with the school nurse and guidance counselor in managing her diabetes. The guidance counselor reports that she is more engaged and contributes more during group counseling. Her verbal communication continues to improve. She perseveres in using her voice and uses a pen and paper to clarify when others do not understand her.

Differential discussion

As my work with Jackie came to an end, I reflected on the extensive support that was needed to help her develop appropriate friendships. Jackie's case helped me clarify how individual, group and integrated therapy can benefit students. The process of teaching Jackie social skills in an isolated setting provided the space for us to practice, model and evaluate social skills, and the small group structure allowed me to create an appropriate mix of students who would support Jackie's growth. Other students in Jackie's group were able to model appropriate social behaviors while accepting that Jackie was still going to make some mistakes. Jackie developed the ability to generalize skills to the overall school setting. This model of intervention provided a map for future work with other students. My work with the guidance counselor led to a health group for children with diabetes. The group has now been in existence for two years and is led by both the guidance counselor and school nurse.

A question that should always remain in the school social worker's mind is whether or not Jackie could be educated in her local school district with typically developing peers. Although I do not believe that Jackie would benefit from a change to her local district, I could have advocated more strongly for her involvement in extracurricular activities with her regular education peers.

References

Barwick, M. A., Boydell, K. M., Stasiuus, E., Ferguson, B., Blasé, K. & Fixson, D. (2005). *Knowledge transfer and evidence-based practice in children's mental health.* Toronto: Children's Mental Health Association.

Blum, D. (1998). *The school counselor's book of lists.* Paramas, NJ: The Center for Applied Research in Education.

Dowd, T. & Tierney, J. (2005). *Teaching social skills to youth: A curriculum for child-care providers* (2nd ed.). Boys Town: The Boys Town Press.

Fischer, L. & Sorenson, G. P. (1996). *School law for counselors, psychologists and social workers* (3rd ed.). White Plains (NY): Longman Publishers USA.

Franklin, C., Harris, M. B. & Allen-Meares, P. (2006). *The school services sourcebook: A guide for school-based professionals.* Oxford: Oxford University Press.

House, A. E. (2002). *DSM-IV Diagnosis in the schools.* New York: The Guilford Press.

Joint Council of County Special Services School Districts (2009). Retrieved 6/8/09, from http://www.njspecialservices.org/services

Joint Council of County Special Services School Districts/NCLB (2009). Retrieved 6/8/09, from http://www.njspecialservices.org/services_Highly_Qualified_JV.php

Knapp, S. E. (2003). *School counseling and social work homework planner.* Hoboken: John Wiley & Sons.

Knapp, S. E. & Jongsma, Jr., A. E. (2002). *The school counseling and school social work treatment planner.* Hoboken, NJ: John Wiley & Sons.

Medwid, D. & Weston, D. C. (1995). *Kid-friendly parenting with deaf and hard of hearing children.* Washington D. C.: Gallaudet University Press.

Murray, C. (2005). *Testimony before the Assembly Budget Committee-NJ Administrative Code: Title 6A, Chapter 14, Special Education.* NJ State Board of Education.

NCLD-IDEA 2004 Parent Guide. Retrieved 6/8/09, from www.ncld.org

NJ Administrative Code: Title 6A, Chapter 14, Special Education (2006). NJ State Board of Education.

Perry, A. & Weiss, J. A. (2007). Evidence-based practice in developmental disabilities: What is it and why does it matter? *Journal on Developmental Disabilities,* 13 (1): 167.

Pierangelo, R. (1995). *The special education teachers book of lists.* West Nyack (NY): The Center for Applied Research in Education.

Roban, W. (1998). *Forms for helping the oppositional child.* Plainview: Childswork/Childsplay.

Romano, J. L. (1998). *Legal rights of the catastrophically ill and injured: A family guide* (2nd ed.). Norristown: Joseph L. Romano, Esq.

Schmidt, J. J. (1997). *Making and keeping friends.* West Nyack (NY): The Center For Applied Research in Education.

Schmidt, C. & Heybyrne, B. (2004). *Autism in the school-aged child.* Denver: Autism Family Press.

Part 1.3

INDIVIDUAL AND FAMILY WORK

Adults

12 Helping a man who had been living in a ventilator assistance facility to receive a new lung

Regina Miller

Context

Description of the setting

The Hospital of the University of Pennsylvania (HUP) is a 700-bed, university-affiliated teaching hospital whose Lung Transplant Program (LTP) leads the region in the number of transplants performed and is ranked among the top 10 multi-organ transplant centers in the country. Established early and highly experienced, the LTP has performed more than 600 procedures since 1991 and completed 163 transplants between the years 2004 and 2007 (OPTN, 2003). Nationally, there are 17,857 lung transplantations to date and 249 transplants that account for living lobar-lung donations (OPTN, 2003). The LTP survival rates outrank the nationally expected average of 80% for one year and 65% for three (SRTR, 2009), and it is one of a few centers in the nation performing multi-organ transplantation, such as lung/liver and heart/lung.

Policy

Regarding policy, the Department of Health and Human Services (DHHS) oversees the Health Resources and Services Administration (HRSA), which gives direction to the Office of Special Programs which controls the Department of Transplantation, which, in turn, regulates the Scientific Registry of Transplant Recipients (SRTR), along with the Organ Procurement Transplant Network (OPTN). The OPTN operates the national network for organ procurement and allocation and promotes organ donation through education and sound policy. The OPTN, whose role was created by the National Organ Transplantation Act of 1984 (NOTA, 1984), provides a multiplicity of oversight, including: organ match and placement; developing policies and procedures for organ recovery, distribution, and transportation; collection and management and dissemination of data; professional and public education; management of wait lists; oversight of transplant centers; and oversight of Organ Procurement Organizations (2009).

While highly publicized public debates about ethical dilemmas related to organ transplant continue, collegiality and trust among the decision makers, along with the presence of the United Network for Organ Sharing (UNOS), helps support a high level of professional and governmental oversight of the enterprise (Levine, 2006; Ornstein & Weber, 2006; UNOS, 2008). For example, in 2006, a swift response by the Centers for Medicare and Medicaid Services (CMS) to specific questions surrounding organ allocation, questionable program statistics, and death rates for those on a transplant list resulted in active monitoring of heart, liver, lung, and intestine transplant programs. In 2007, new regulations established a single set of requirements and periodic reviews for all Medicare-approved transplant programs (GAO, 2008).

All organ transplant programs must be located in a hospital with a Medicare-provider agreement and must comply with both transplant and hospital Conditions of Participation (specified in 42 CFR 482.1 through 482.57) (CMS, 2009). CMS can visit any transplant center, without notice, to assure that standards are being met. Mandated reporting includes: changes in key staff members, decreases in the number of transplants performed or a program's survival rates, the termination of an agreement between the hospital and the Organ Procurement Organization, and inactivation of the transplant program.

Policies related to costs and reimbursement

Transplantation is unaffordable to most transplant recipients without adequate insurance. A rough estimate places lung transplant, without complications, in the hundreds of thousands of dollars. Post-operatively, the non-reimbursed cost of a one-month supply of medicine can reach over $4,000. Lung transplant recipients can expect to take immunosuppressant medications for their entire lifespan. If a candidate is underinsured, due to a cap or a cost-sharing percentage, then obtaining transplant medications may be difficult. The improper use of immunosuppressant medications could result in poor outcomes, or rejection. Rejection of a solid organ is a real consequence and the inability to obtain immunosuppressant medications following a solid organ transplant can be viewed as a crisis by the transplant team.

Lung transplantation is covered by Medicare, Medicaid, and private health insurance plans. If the plan is on par with the corresponding center, the coverage of solid organ transplant extends from insurance to relocation to childcare and beyond. Medicare recipients are free to go to any National Center of Excellence. Additional insurance, beyond Medicare A & B, is necessary to be secured to cover the out-of-pocket expenses not reimbursed by Medicare B; or 20% of the total costs of doctors' visits, rehabilitation, pulmonary therapies, labs, radiologic testing, home IV nursing services, and pharmaceuticals, which can become all-encompassing in lung transplant programs. The PLT Center is listed as a 'Center of Excellence,' and insurers review and negotiate contracts annually. Medicare reimbursement policy sets the bar and is a template for private insurance companies.

At Penn, financial counselors meet with all potential recipients pre-transplant to determine coverage. While at some centers social workers also act as financial counselors, at Penn the roles are separate, but social work is consulted in complicated situations and must understand the nuances of and relationships between all of these kinds of health insurance. What follows is a very cursory discussion of this arena which must be successfully negotiated by recipients, family members and staff. Generally, procedures are planned ahead, and a potential candidate risks denial of transplant services if there is no payer. All members of the health care team express frustration when a transplant candidate's health care is jeopardized due to economics, and the transplant team, candidates, and recipients turn to the social worker for direction and support. At times, Penn social workers have fielded calls from local council representatives who are at a loss for a solution to their constituent's financial conundrum.

Some lung transplant candidates have a more acute lung condition; the prediction by the medical team is that this illness will cause a precipitous drop in function, potentially forcing them onto disability quickly. This scenario causes tremendous stress, as there is little time for financial planning and causes hardship for many, especially when the recently diagnosed person holds the medical insurance for an entire family.

Recently, President Obama signed the American Recovery and Reinvestment Act. Its primary goals are job creation and economic restoration, but it contains important revisions applying to Consolidated Omnibus Budget Reconciliation Act (COBRA)-involved employers. While short-lived, this subsidy will still help employees (Bracewell & Guiliani, 2009). Also, the National Transplant Assistance Fund (NTAF) provides information about the lifelong costs associated with transplantation, educates those who are interested in finding solutions to the financial difficulties experienced due to transplant cost, and guides families and support persons in successful fundraising efforts (NTAF, 2009).

The business of transplant is daunting, especially in this precarious economic time. Insurance companies continue to tighten reins and find reasons to deny claims. Some transplant candidates are wondering if their insurance company plans to re-contract with the corresponding transplant center and, if not, where they will go or, more likely, how their out-of-network costs will apply. Out-of-pocket costs in health care continue to increase and often exceed savings. Occasionally, a solid organ transplant candidate expresses the need to forgo transplant until fundraising is explored, or avoids listing to prevent causing economic harm to loved ones.

Long-term disability is a cushion, but it is not often available through employee benefits or private disability policies. Social Security Disability Insurance (SSDI) and Social Security Insurance (SSI) are both awarded based on disability status. The difference is that SSDI requires predetermined work credits based upon a candidate's age, whereas SSI is based on the income of the applicant. At times, a person can be both eligible for SSDI and SSI. In addition, candidates can be eligible for both Medicare and Medicaid, in which case Medicare is the primary insurance. If SSDI is approved, the candidate is entitled to Medicare 24 months after the first SSDI payment, or upon turning age 65. If SSDI is denied, due to work credit shortage or a higher functional status, appeals may be possible. In some cases, it may be necessary to find help from a social security lawyer or law clinic.

Technology

The first successful heart/lung, single lung and double lung transplants were carried out in the 1980s (Couture, 2001). The most common diagnoses leading to transplant include: Chronic Obstructive Pulmonary Disease (COPD); Idiopathic Pulmonary Fibrosis, and Non-Specific Interstitial Pneumonia; Cystic Fibrosis and other Causes of Bronchiectasis; Idiopathic Pulmonary Arterial Hypertension, and Pulmonary Langerhans Cell Histiocytosis (Orens *et al.*, 2006). The Penn Lung Transplant Center does both bilateral and single lung transplants.

The greatest technologic limitation is the organ shortage, which some predict will worsen over time. Today, 100,658 persons await a solid organ transplant. Between 1/08 and 10/08, 23,288 transplants were performed with only 11,813 donors recovered in the same period (UNOS, 2008). Gaps persist between donor organ availability and necessary organs needed to supply the waitlist. Educational campaigns, policy changes, and creative strategies to increase donations, have not closed the gap.

Ethical issues persist in relation to transplantation. Centers and teams answer organ-specific questions to overarching ethical dilemmas to suit each population. For example, should we re-transplant recipients? If so, how many times, and how many organs? How much co-morbidity can be tolerated at the time of listing? What should the age limit be? Should we list a candidate who presents with a potential addiction to prescription drugs as medically appropriate, while under his local physician's care? Should recipients know the social history of the donor? (Vermeulen *et al.*, 2007, 2008).

Organization

The Penn Lung Transplant (PLT) service has three clinical directors, including a pulmonologist, a surgeon, and a nurse practitioner. In addition, there are four transplant pulmonologists, three nurse coordinators, additional surgeons, a social worker, a registered dietician, a financial counselor, a pharmacist, a respiratory therapist, and a physical therapist, with other available consultants, as needed.

UNOS delineates all vital roles and services for any solid organ program including psychosocial services. Each center identifies a staff member for this role. Psychosocial services include psychosocial evaluation of potential living donors and recipients; substance abuse evaluation, treatment, referral, monitoring; counseling and crisis intervention, support groups and newsletters; patient care conferences; advocacy; patient and family education; referral to community services such as vocational rehabilitation, housing; knowledge of available social services, regulations; and death, dying, and bereavement counseling; team building; running department meetings such as process improvement; participation in organ donation awareness initiatives; and community advocacy efforts (OPTN). Penn recognizes that this role should be filled by qualified master's prepared social workers.

The organization requires a two-step process in application for a lung transplant. First, it must be determined whether the patient is a candidate for listing; that is, whether he is medically and psychosocially healthy enough to be considered. After a three-day evaluation period, a listing meeting is held to decide whether the person is ready for listing, needs to do some work before being considered, or cannot be listed. A follow-up appointment is scheduled for the patient to learn the results. If the person is ready, he or she is listed on the National Living Transplant waiting list through UNOS. Factors such as blood type, lung size and severity of illness determine priority for transplantation.

When called about a transplant, candidates must get to Penn within two hours. All logistical arrangements will have been completed with the social worker prior to listing. On arrival, the candidate is prepped, and the OR team awaits the final decision by the chief surgeon on the appropriateness of the organ. Post-operatively, the recipient is taken to the Surgical Intensive Care Unit (SICU), and remains there until removal of the breathing tube and other medical clearance. After time on a step-down floor, the patient is discharged following a total hospitalization of between 10 and 14 days. Upon discharge, the recipient returns three days a week for 12 weeks of rehabilitation, and must continue to be followed at the facility for a year and hopefully continue care in the region after that.

Decisions about practice

Client description

Sam Kerollis, 60 years old, has been living in a ventilator assistance facility for three years as a result of his end-stage chronic obstructive pulmonary disease (COPD). He worked as a bus driver for 30 years but had to retire because of his pulmonary disability. Before living in the facility, Sam was living alone in a New Jersey apartment. In the mid-1980s he successfully completed an outpatient program for illegal drug use and had no other significant history of addictions. He has Medicare and New Jersey Medicaid. Three adult children visit inconsistently. Noted on all of his health documents is that his daughter, Theresa, has his power of attorney. Sam consented to contacting Theresa and said it would be best that I made the initial contact.

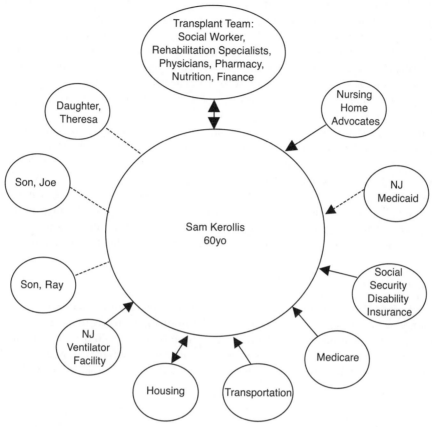

Figure 12.1 Ecomap for Sam Kerollis.

Sam requested a lung transplant to improve his quality of life. He resided two hours from the center and, at the time of listing, required a ventilator for over 12 hours in the evening to sustain his life. He demonstrated improvement by remaining off the ventilator during the day, tolerating a trach collar (Lewis *et al.*, 2007, 543). Sam survived multiple medical complications and multiple admissions at local hospitals in NJ, including a requirement of a feeding tube for substantial weight loss and an IV line sepsis.

Goals

The initial evaluation and subsequent listing meeting determined work on medical, nutrition, and social goals that needed to be addressed prior to listing. The pulmonologists felt Sam had enough time to address these issues. Among the problems to be addressed was Sam's inability to adhere to the follow-up requirements. At the meeting, the assigned respiratory therapist from the nursing home and his adult sons were present. Both sons suggested that Sam could move in with them both pre- and post-transplant, although they lived farther from the transplant center, or out of state, which could jeopardize Sam's NJ Medical Assistance. Among the things I learned was that Sam was able to communicate effectively, through speech, when he altered his trach cuff. It is atypical for a transplant team to evaluate an individual living in a ventilator facility, but Sam advocated for himself remarkably well (Nelson, 2000; Wayne, 2000).

My role, here, is to assess the candidate's understanding and ability to cope and to build a long-term, supportive relationship. Sam's pre-existing anxiety and depression was being treated by pharmacological agents, along with bi-monthly visits to the nursing home psychologist who "cleared" Sam for readiness to manage the transplant process (Blumenthal *et al.*, 2006). He became capable enough to schedule and plan his appointments. At times, the transplant team's direct communication with Sam caused stress for the nursing home care team who were, after all, legally responsible for his care. This, in turn, caused some tension for Sam, but the issues were eventually resolved.

Poor social supports are related to poor outcomes, so it is critical for patients to work to enhance their social support networks before transplantation (Cetingok, Hathaway & Winsett, 2007; Dobbels *et al.*, 2007; Goetzmann *et al.*, 2007; Myaskovsky *et al.*, 2006; Ortega, 2007). Sam knew he had to identify significant supports in the community, as the physicians were not so willing to accept a client returning to a nursing home due to the increased risk of infection. I worked with Sam on the telephone in this regard as is my common practice, since most candidates awaiting transplant do not return to the clinic for three months (Blumenthal *et al.*, 2006). Sam's telephone support was limited due to a lack of privacy within the nursing home.

Use of contract

A verbal contract was initiated at the first meeting to define reciprocity and to acknowledge Sam, and his support group, as a member on the transplant team. Written contracts are not typically used in transplantation—with the exception perhaps of informed consent documents—although extensive verbal agreements are made and, seemingly, most are kept (Penn Medicine News, 2008). There is an understanding that the team members are available and promptly return calls.

Meeting place

In a hospital, high volumes limit space, especially in the clinic, and teams or individual staff vie for privacy. Sam was seen in the clinic, in the physical therapy gym, in his hospital room, or spoken to on the telephone depending on the situation. The transplant social workers do not have an office for clients, per se, although more spaces should be available in the Center for Advanced Medicine, which is under construction. Interruptions are too frequent in hospitals, and relationship-building can be difficult. All members of the transplant team understand the importance of the social work role, and each helps to facilitate privacy and therapeutic space.

Use of time

Time is renegotiated constantly in hospitals. Sam was flexible and demonstrated a healthy response to change. The initial evaluation was a formal meeting, and appointments were scheduled. Occasionally, an outpatient visit was scheduled to include social work, finance, nutrition, or pharmacy, with the pulmonary appointment the central focus of the visit. Social workers do have the right to call a meeting or schedule an appointment with the understanding that another team member—physician and/or nursing—will be present for both support and education, if necessary. Transplant candidates can be listed for long periods of time, or over a year, depending upon a person's diagnosis, oxygen requirements, and functional status. The goal is not to plan to list a candidate who then faces a prolonged wait time—although this can occur due to medical status or insignificant changes in an allocation score. Once transplanted, recipients remain with Penn for a year; they can then negotiate a move to providers who are closer to home, if desired.

Strategies and interventions

Sam developed a long-standing relationship with the transplant team after being followed for 18 months from the transplant evaluation date to the listing date. This is not always the case, as potential candidates may arrive at Penn very ill, or with a quickly progressing disease. Sam waited an additional seven months prior to receiving a transplant. There were no addiction issues to resolve, and there had been no smoking since 2005.

Helping Sam to talk to his children was more complicated. Sam asked me to call his daughter Theresa, who held his power of attorney, to begin the conversation about the need for his family's support. Theresa became irate that a transplant social worker would request a family member to engage her in a discussion about support systems available to her father. Theresa's response pointed to caretaker burnout; she was taking care of her mother, or Sam's ex-wife, and refused to be the caretaker for two parents, along with her young children. Sam's response to his children's ambivalence to physical caretaking was indifference, as he was able to separate his feelings about their emotional support from his need for care. Eventually, he expressed guilt because he had caused them enough grief in their lives, saying that he hoped to end this cycle. Both sons reassured Sam, in face-to-face meetings, that transplantation and caretaking wouldn't be a problem, although follow-up conversations, away from their father, yielded much different results. I knew Sam was alone in his transplant journey, despite all the people physically present in his life. The initial plan for Sam to potentially leave the nursing home and find a host home in NJ to maintain benefits, through the Hosts for Hospitals non-profit organization, and for his son to be available and stay in the host home until Sam could take care of himself, proved to be unrealistic. If Sam left the nursing facility, his bed would become unavailable. The team was informed, and the next step was to begin negotiations with the nursing home facility. Psychosocial supports as predictors of a better quality of life post-transplant can be found in the literature, with a call for additional studies (Cetingok, Hathaway & Winsett, 2007; Dobbels *et al.*, 2007; Goetzmann *et al.*, 2005, 2007).

By late winter, Sam was still not listed because of unresolved psychosocial issues. Now that the transplant team clearly understood that his adult children were unable to physically provide himself the support he needed, a conference call was arranged that included Sam's social workers, psychologists, pulmonologist, and both sons. At this conference, it was discovered that Sam would be unable to return to his original bed, in the vent facility, if he was successfully transplanted and weaned, and regardless, his bed-hold would last 10 days, and then he would be treated as any other admission. This information was alarming to the transplant team. At this meeting, his sons were confronted with this information and they both agreed again, in front of multiple members of both care teams, that they would be available to meet his needs. In addition, a nursing assistant (a staff member from the nursing home) offered her own private home for Sam to reside in. His sons would pick Sam up at her home in NJ to transport him to Penn. At this meeting, the transplant team, the nursing home, and Sam felt all issues were resolved and it was a breakthrough for him in his care. I requested that his sons attend the next office visit in May to confirm and assess these findings. One son attended and confirmed his availability and commitment and, shortly thereafter, Sam was listed for transplantation. He received his single lung transplant that summer.

Upon my initial in-hospital assessment post-transplant, I discovered that Sam's three children visited over the weekend, and I felt relieved. Sam understood my role on the team, although he never discussed outstanding issues or a change in the post-operative plan. It became evident, as the days passed, that his children were neither returning phone calls to any members of the team, nor to the nursing home administrators. Essentially, through Sam's voice, I understood that the original plan, documented and reiterated, was never a plan at all, but rather a reflection of a support system that was unable or unwilling to perform duties and tasks required to list their father. My concern was that this family felt coerced, or that they imagined transplantation would benefit their father, regardless of a continued stay inside a nursing facility, and told us what we needed to hear for listing.

Stance of the social worker

Initially, I felt defeated by the fact that Sam was surrounded by so many people, and not one really wanted to or could take full responsibility for his caretaking. I soon understood, through discussions with his nursing home team, that Sam is fiercely independent, an attribute that can become a curse in so many systems that require extensive networking and a physical presence of someone other than self. In addition, Sam's family may have been agreeing with the team, while never fully investing into his post-operative follow-up plan. This feeling was confirmed upon hearing from the nursing home that the one nurse at his facility was backpedaling and reneged on her verbal agreement, as documented in the nursing home's case notes. My team turned to me for answers, and initially, there were no solutions. In addition, the Director of Nursing at the nursing home communicated disbelief and concern that the plan failed.

Prior to discharge, I needed to quickly develop a plan, and negotiate this, with clear obligations to Sam. Our team would send explicit written instructions to the nursing home care team after every inpatient admission or outpatient visit, in order to avoid medication errors, or missed appointments. Sam would need a private room in the nursing home to prevent infections. He would need transportation, very early in the morning, and the transporters could never leave him alone in a stretcher and he should preferably come by wheelchair van or car. A nursing home employee with an understanding of the complexity of a large university teaching hospital must accompany Sam, and have the ability to act as an advocate until he proved capable. Sam must be provided lunch and his meds must be sent with him to each hospital visit.

Sam would call me to complain that he did not like the lunches sent by his nursing home, or he felt there was too much fuss being made and how he disliked the attention. His feelings of disappointment were validated, and his concerns about control were explored. I understood the hardships this would place on the administrators, the care team and the clients in this nursing facility, but especially the difficulty Sam expressed about the need to return to another wing within the same nursing home, post-transplant.

Sam completed his 12 weeks of outpatient pulmonary rehab. By the end of his program, he was independent, traveling to the hospital by van, without an escort. He explained that the social worker in the nursing home is in the process of developing plans for a move to an apartment through a disability waiver, and he would relocate close to his son's home, although remain in NJ, and would obtain case management for this transition (Howell, Silberberg, Quinn & Lucas, 2007). All team members appreciated this plan.

Resources outside of the helping relationship

Resources available to post-lung transplant patients are extensive. Occasionally, a recipient may require nursing services in the home; for example, IV infusion for an infectious process, or oxygen could be required at the time of discharge. In addition, the recipients attend pulmonary rehabilitation sessions, where a helping relationship exists, but the goal is to educate the recipient on necessary skills to carry with them for their lifetime. PLT is committed to long-standing psycho-educational support groups, and there are numerous outside support groups. The Second Wind Organization developed a telephone mentoring program for potential lung transplant candidates, or recipients and their caretakers, and a screening process for volunteers is in place (Second Wind, 2009).

Reassessment, transfer or termination

For me, reassessment encompasses discussion, behaviors, timing, and underlying motivation, on the part of the candidate, or recipient, and this entails a lot of reflection on my part. For example, even the most mundane phone call or request for concrete resources can elicit more meaningful exploration. Termination occurs slowly in transplantation, as transplant recipients are welcome to remain at the center for a lifetime. Conversely, a team member may express the need for a transplant recipient to seek local care for uncomplicated health care, due to the distance from the transplant center. Termination is non-threatening, or a non-issue in transplant services, unless it is related to death. Bereavement services are available but not very sophisticated within transplant communities. Specifically, the Penn lung transplant team reaches out to transplant caretakers with a phone call, an invitation for the caretakers to meet with the physician, and then a potential social work referral outside of our system.

Case conclusion

Sam successfully graduated from his outpatient 12-week physical therapy treatment plan and his trach was removed. He told the transplant team that he was welcome in his son's home, but would transition to his own apartment. In retrospect, the team's concern that Sam did not have one person to commit to him wholeheartedly was a bit misguided. The multi-year commitment of his excellent nursing home care team supported this fine outcome. Sam's commitment to self, and the achievement of every goal placed before him by members of the medical team, was met. There was no other medical barrier to prevent transplant listing. The collaboration among the teams enabled Sam to have the hope of a better and more independent life.

Differential discussion

Sam's social worker at the nursing facility remained optimistic. I raised potential barriers, and together, we spent a lot of time on the phone brainstorming ideas to get Sam listed.

Other outlying concerns were insurance related, as Sam was enrolled in an MA plan, which included intensive case management. The fear from the top administrators of social services in NJ was that a change in address outside of the state would cause Sam to be dropped from his Medical Assistance Plan and thus lose case management; case management would assist longer term in transitioning him out of the nursing home while maintaining his health insurance. If Sam left the nursing home without plans to return, his bed would become unavailable and he would essentially be homeless. If he moved in with his son or took a host home in Philadelphia, his insurance benefits could be jeopardized because there would be a change in address, along with an increase in household income, or no address. The only solution was to find a host home in NJ to maintain his benefits. This never came to fruition. The initial referral made to a Penn doctor and, in turn, Penn's transplant pulmonologist, came from Sam's physician in the nursing home. This unusual referral set off a sequence of events that led to a successful single lung transplant. Interestingly, if this physician had known the psychosocial barriers Sam would confront, a referral may never have been initiated. Sam's insistence that he be evaluated certainly facilitated the process.

I wonder how many other potential transplant candidates have been overlooked in the setting of nursing home or ventilator facilities due to a lack of transplant education or underestimation of what can be accomplished by teams. Finally, lung transplant researchers now underscore the use of quality of life indicators to measure outcomes, versus survival rates alone; thankfully, the lung transplant community realizes and celebrates better outcomes throughout the past two decades affording this change in measurement.

References

Berg, E. R. (2009). *New York Organ Donor Network: Donate Life*. Retrieved 3/2/09, from http://www.hods.org/English/ppt/Elaine%20Berg.ppt.

Blumenthal, J., Babyak, M., Carney, R., Keefe, F., Davis, D., LaCaille, R., Parekh, P. I., Freedland, K. E. & Trulock, E. (2006). Telephone-based coping skills training for patients awaiting lung transplantation. *Journal of Consulting and Clinical Psychology*, 74 (3): 535–44.

Bracewell & Guiliani LLP, International Law Firm (2009). *Financial Industry Task Force*. Retrieved 3/2/09: http://www.bgtaskforce.com/2009/02/20/president-obama-signs-stimulus-plan-with-cobra-expansion/

Cetingok, M., Hathaway, D. & Winsett, R. (2007). Contribution of post-transplant social support to the quality of life of transplant recipients. *Social Work in Health Care*, (45) 3: 39–56.

CMS (Centers for Medicare & Medicaid) (2009). Certification and compliance: Transplant. Retrieved 3/2/09, from http://www.cms.hhs.gov/CertificationandComplianc/20_Transplant.asp.

COBRA (*Consolidated Omnibus Budget Reconciliation Act*). United States Department of Labor. Employee benefits security administration. Retrieved 2/21/09: http://www.dol.gov/ebsa/faqs/faq_consumer_cobra.HTML

Couture, K. A. (2001). *The lung transplantation handbook* (2nd ed.). Victoria, BC: Tafford Publishing.

Dobbels, F., Vanhaecke, J., Nevens, F., Dupont, L., Verleden, G. & Van Hees, D. (2007). Liver versus cardiothoracic transplant candidates and their pretransplant psychosocial and behavioral risk profiles: Good neighbors or complete strangers? *Transplant International*, 20 (12): 1020–30.

GAO. (2008, April). -08-412, a report to the Ranking Member, Committee on Finance, U.S. Senate: Accountability, Integrity, Reliability. Organ transplant programs. Federal agencies have acted to improve oversight, but implementation issues remain. *United States Government Accountability Office*. Retrieved 3/2/09: http://www.asts.org/Tools/Download.aspx?fid=684

Goetzmann, L., Klaghofer, R., Wagner-Huber, R., Halter, J., Boehler, A., Muellhaupt, B., Schanz, U. & Buddeberg, C. (2007). Psychosocial vulnerability predicts psychosocial outcome after an organ transplant: Results of a prospective study with lung, liver, and bone-marrow patients. *Journal of Psychosomatic Research*, 62 (1): 93–100.

Goetzmann, L., Scheuer, E., Naef, R., Vetsch E., *et al.* (2005). Psychosocial situation and physical health in 50 patients >1 year after lung transplantation. *Chest*, 127 (1): 166–70.

Howell, S., Silberberg, M., Quinn, W. V. & Lucas, J. A. (2007). Determinants of remaining in the community after discharge: Results from New Jersey's nursing home transition program. *The Gerontologist*, 47 (4): 535–47.

Levine, S. (2006, June 6). Organ transplant centers face federal scrutiny. *Washington Post*, B01.

Lewis, S., Heitkemper, M., Dirksen, S., O'Brien, P. & Bucher, L. (2007). *Medical-surgical nursing: assessment and management of clinical problems* (7th ed.). Missouri: Mosby-Elsevier.

Myaskovsky, L., Dew, M. A., McNulty, M. L., Switzer, G. E., DiMartini, A. F., Kormos, R. L. & McCurry, K. R. (2006). Trajectories of change in quality of life in 12-month survivors of lung or heart transplant. *American Journal of Transplantation*, 6 (8): 1939–47.

Nelson, W. (2000). Injustice and conflict in nursing homes: Toward advocacy and exchange. *Journal of Aging Studies*, 14 (1): 39–62.

NOTA (National Organ Transplant Act 1984): § 301 (c) (2) of NOTA, 42 U.S.C. § 274e (c) (2).

NTAF (National Transplant Assistance Fund). (2009). http://www.transplantfund.org/.

OPTN: Center Data. (2003). Richmond, VA. United Network of Organ Sharing, Department of Health and Human Services. Retrieved 1/21/09: http://www.optn.org

Orens, J. B., Estenne, M., Arcasoy, S., Conte, J. V., Corris, P., Egan J. J., *et al.* (2006). Int. guidelines for the selection of lung transplant candidates: 2006 update—A consensus report from the pulmonary scientific council of the International Society for Heart and Lung Transplantation. *Journal of Heart and Lung Transplantation*, 25 (7): 745–55.

Ornstein, C. & Weber, T. (2006, October). Transplant monitor lax in oversight: U.S. organ network routinely fails to detect problems. *Los Angeles Times*. Retrieved 3/2/09: http://www.latimes.com/news/printedition/la-me-transplant22oct22,1,2125146.story?ctrack=1&cset=true.

Ortega, F., Covadonga, V. & Ortega, T. (2007). Quality of life after solid lung transplantation. *Transplantation Reviews*, 21 (3): 155–70.

Penn Medicine News (2008, July). Penn research proposes major changes to informed consent for transplantation. http://www.uphs.upenn.edu/news/News_Releases/2008/06/organ-transplant-risk-disclosure.html.

Second Wind. (2009). Retrieved 6/12/09: http://www.2ndwind.org.

SRTR (2009). *Patient survival after transplant.* (2009). Retrieved 1/21/09: http://www.ustransplant.org/csr/current /publicData.aspx?facilityID=PAUPTX1LU&t=11&r=pennsylvania.

UNOS. (2008). *Transplantation in the United States*. UNOS scientific registry data.

Vermeulen, K. M., van der Bij, W., Erasmus, M. E. & TenVergert, E. M. (2007, Feb.). Long-term health related quality of life after lung transplantation: Different predictors for different dimensions. *Journal of Heart and Lung Transplantation*, 26 (2): 188–93.

Vermeulen, K. M., TenVergert, E. M., Verschuuren, E. A. M., Erasmus, M. E. & van der Bij, W. (2008, June). Pre-transplant quality of life does not predict survival after lung transplantation. *Journal of Heart and Lung Transplantation*, 27 (6): 623–7.

Wayne, N. (2000). Injustice and conflict in nursing homes: Toward advocacy and exchange. *Journal of Aging Studies*, 14 (1): 39–61.

13 Following her lead

A measured approach to providing case management and mental health treatment to homeless adults

Annick Barker

Context

Housed in a modest brick building in downtown Baltimore, Health Care for the Homeless, Inc. (BHCH) is an unassuming place. Founded in 1985, the Baltimore-based clinic is one of over 200 Health Care for the Homeless projects around the country. Among its services BHCH offers outpatient medical care, substance abuse treatment, mental health services, case management, client education, street outreach, and public policy advocacy. The Baltimore City clinic employs 115 staff and serves 6,000 people a year. HCH serves an additional 6,000 individuals through purchase-of-service agreements with organizations in other parts of the state. The organization strives to meet the highest standards of care and is the first freestanding HCH project in the country to receive accreditation from the Joint Commission.

Policy

Affordable Housing Shortage and Supportive Housing Programs

The rise of homelessness during the last 30 years is a symptom of the diminishing value of median incomes, the dramatic increase in housing costs, and the deterioration of the basic safety net (HCH Clinicians' Network, 2005). In Baltimore City, 30,000 residents lack stable shelter during the course of a year (Lindamood & Singer, 2008). The Baltimore Mayor's Office of Homeless Services estimates 3,002 individuals lived in shelters or on the streets on a typical night in 2007 (Baltimore Homeless Services, 2008).

People with physical and mental health disabilities suffer as a result of these trends (Baltimore Homeless Services and Baltimore City Health Department, 2007; Culhane, Metraux & Hadley, 2002; Draine, Salzer, Culhane & Hadley, 2002; Interagency Council on Homelessness, 2006). The National Low Income Housing Coalition reports that there is not one jurisdiction in the country where a disabled person who relies exclusively on Supplemental Security Income (SSI) can afford a studio apartment in the private rental market. In Baltimore City, the fair market rate for a one-bedroom apartment ($844/mo) is more than four times what the client described here could reasonably afford ($191/mo) with the income she receives from SSI ($637/mo) (National Low Income Housing Coalition, 2008). Subsidized housing in Baltimore is also in short supply, with over 16,000 households on the waiting list (Newman, 2005).

Supportive housing programs designed for severely mentally ill people who are homeless provide subsidized housing and social services with funding coming primarily from the federal McKinney-Vento Homeless Assistance Act of 1987. Many people who enter such programs remain housed and are less likely to be hospitalized, need emergency shelters, or spend time in jail or prison (Culhane *et al.*, 2002; SAMHSA, 2003). Because historically supportive housing required individuals to show that they were "housing ready," that is, they could comply with mental health treatment plans, achieve psychiatric stability, and maintain abstinence from drugs and alcohol, the most severely impaired and chronically homeless individuals were excluded from the programs' criteria (Gulcur, Stefancic, Shinn, Tsemberis & Fischer, 2003; Stefancic & Tsemberis, 2007).

SSI and the Representative Payee Program

It is difficult for people with active symptoms of schizophrenia to meet the basic demands of most jobs without significant support. Many adults rely on income from the Supplemental Security Income (SSI) program to meet their needs. Approval for SSI gives them Medicaid benefits and access to health care. In 2007, 40% of SSI recipients had mental health diagnoses other than mental retardation (SSA, 2007). Once awarded SSI benefits, people with a serious mental illness (SMI) often struggle to manage their finances. More than a third of SSI beneficiaries participate in the Social Security Administration (SSA) Representative Payee program, which enlists a third party to administer the beneficiary's monthly SSI funds (SSA, 2007). SSA prefers family members or friends as Representative Payee but SSA offices report difficulty identifying appropriate Representative Payees for at-risk beneficiaries (National Research Council, 2007). If this is not possible, SSA assigns an organization to carry out this role; thus, in response, BHCH provides Representative Payee services to a small number of severely impaired clients.

Maryland's Medicaid programs

Like many states, Maryland has carved out mental health care and administers the program through a single vendor. They serve Maryland residents who are uninsured or underinsured, have low incomes and require treatment for a mental illness, including those who are homeless (MAPS-M.D., 2008; Oliver, 1998). Consequently, everyone who receives mental health care at HCH is eligible to participate in Maryland's public mental health care program. Clients receiving mental health care at HCH may have physical health care needs and are potentially eligible for the Medicaid HealthChoice program. Establishing eligibility for HealthChoice demands a high level of organization on the part of applicants. They must provide proof of identity, citizenship, income, housing expenses, and inability to maintain employment due to a disability. The MCO enrollment process alone can be a barrier to medical treatment for severely mentally ill individuals.

Technology

Treatment of SMI has improved with the advent of new medications and methods of administration. Yet for people with schizophrenia, adherence to anti-psychotic medications is a persistent challenge. The rate of medication non-adherence among patients with schizophrenia is approximately 50% (Glazer & Byerly, 2008). Second generation atypical anti-psychotic medications reduce a number of the symptoms of schizophrenia without some of the troublesome side-effects of older anti-psychotic medications (Keith, 2009). In 2003, a long-acting injectable form of risperidone, an atypical anti-psychotic, was introduced as an alternative to oral risperidone, which must be taken daily. Second generation anti-psychotics have produced modest increases in adherence rates, and administration through long-acting injection has a positive impact as well (Davis, Chen & Glick, 2003; Keith, 2009).

Motivational techniques and engagement of other clinicians and family members in a patient's treatment also improve medication adherence (Davis *et al.*, 2003; Glazer & Byerly, 2008). For chronically homeless people with SMI, a tailored and flexible approach to prescribing and administering psychiatric medication is particularly important in promoting adherence (McMurray-Avila, Gelberg & Breakey, 1999).

Organization

HCH treatment providers include general internists, nurse practitioners, physician assistants, registered nurses, psychiatrists, addictions counselors, social workers, professional counselors, and outreach staff, among other disciplines. Providers are assigned to function-specific teams (medical, mental health case management, addictions, etc.) that meet regularly and make their own decisions about how best to provide services to clients. Monthly case conferences and co-located offices promote coordination of client care and client referrals between teams. HCH has also created staff positions that bridge different disciplines, including Therapist Case Managers, who provide both mental health therapy and case management.

HCH promotes coordination of care between members of different teams by articulating a philosophy of care for all providers, regardless of discipline. Based on the harm reduction approach (Denning, 2000), HCH's philosophy of care encourages staff to focus on the quality of their relationships with clients, to recognize that clients may not be ready to change behavior right away, and to understand that change happens in small steps, so success should be measured accordingly. HCH works to create an environment that fosters a client's motivation to change rather than judging compliance with recommended treatment. This incremental, person-centered approach is consistent with the recommendations of those who have studied models of care for people who are chronically homeless (Homeless Resource Center, 2008; McMurray-Avila, *et al.*, 1999; SAMHSA, 2003).

Case description

Ms. Harper is a 40-year-old white woman with a history of paranoid schizophrenia. A clinic outreach worker first identified Ms. Harper as a prospective client while she was living on the streets of downtown Baltimore several years ago. Notable for her striking physical appearance, Ms. Harper walked with a heavy dark coat draped over her head, obscuring most of her face and upper body. She appeared frightened and moved away when others approached. Outreach workers made attempts over a period of two years to make contact with her, offering tangible items such as snacks and toiletries. After about two years, Ms. Harper came into the clinic building for the first time. An intake worker interviewed her and she was able to take a shower. Following this, the intake worker referred Ms. Harper to a Therapist Case Manager. This was the beginning of our relationship.

At our first meeting, Ms. Harper said she had been staying in a local women's shelter but was asked to leave because "the other women said I was doing things to them." Ms. Harper was often asked to leave emergency shelters due to behavior deemed inappropriate by shelter staff. After venting her frustration, Ms. Harper asked for help with identification, alternative shelter and income. I made phone calls to shelters and helped Ms. Harper obtain a Disability Photo Identification card from the Maryland Transportation Authority (MTA). With no shelter beds available, I gave Ms. Harper two tokens so she could ride local buses, a form of shelter for many homeless people lacking alternatives. I explained that accessing housing would take time, but might be expedited if she maintained contact with HCH.

A few days later, Ms. Harper called me from a local hospital psychiatric unit after an involuntary admission. After a week, she was discharged with anti-psychotic medications to an emergency shelter and returned to HCH asking to see me. I responded to her requests for help with identification, food, clothing, toiletries, shelter and bus tokens. With her permission, I also contacted the state Disability Entitlement Advocacy Program (DEAP) to begin the application process for Medical Assistance, Food Stamps, and Social Security Disability benefits. Ms. Harper complained of side-effects from the medications prescribed by the hospital and an HCH psychiatrist conducted a brief evaluation and provided her with samples of a different medication.

Ms. Harper's symptoms during our first month of work included flat affect, paranoid thoughts, hypervigilance, disorganization, and dysthymia. She denied having auditory or visual hallucinations, but frequently appeared to respond to internal stimuli, laughing inappropriately and whispering to herself. During one of our encounters, she became very agitated. Although initially resisting my requests to lower her voice so we could talk, she eventually quieted and became tearful and despondent. I encouraged her to use our meetings as a safe place to address her fears and other intense feelings.

Ms. Harper was again involuntarily admitted to a hospital psychiatric unit and then discharged with anti-psychotic medication and referred to a local shelter. She returned to HCH, saying she wanted to continue her psychiatric care there. I scheduled another appointment with the staff psychiatrist and helped Ms. Harper contact a women's drop-in center for a place to go during the day. Soon after, Ms. Harper disappeared and did not return to HCH for four months. Ms. Harper traveled to another state where her family of origin lived and had a psychiatric hospitalization there. Upon her return, she was homeless, frequently agitated and had difficulty staying in the clinic building for longer than a few minutes. I arranged a psychiatric appointment and told her that she had been awarded Medical Assistance and Food Stamps and that Safe Haven—a low-demand shelter for homeless adults with SMI—had a bed available. Ms. Harper declined saying it was too far away.

Ms. Harper returned the next day. She was too agitated to stay long enough to meet with the psychiatrist. Ms. Harper's requests focused on getting some hot coffee, a change of clothes and toiletries, checking her mail (we agreed she could use HCH's address), and obtaining her Medical Assistance card. Ms. Harper refused to enroll in a Managed Care Organization (MCO) and was automatically assigned to an MCO that did not include HCH as an authorized provider. While this did not impede her access to mental health services at HCH, she was initially unable to access medical services. Later, the MCO added HCH to its provider list and she began medical treatment at HCH.

The ensuing months were marked by rare and brief encounters with Ms. Harper. When she did come into the clinic I focused on her goals, checking her mail and providing her with clothing. Late in 2005, she was approved for Supplemental Security Income (SSI). We went to the local Social Security Administration office, and she learned she needed a Representative Payee. Ms. Harper designated HCH as her Representative Payee; HCH assigned me to be her Representative Payee.

This was a turning point in our relationship. Her visits to HCH became more frequent and more regular. Progress on goals was slow due to her psychotic symptoms. Throughout early 2006, I explored a variety of housing and case management programs for people with SMI. Each time an opportunity arose, Ms. Harper declined it. She was not interested in group home settings and rejected programs that required a significant portion of her SSI check toward rent. She also rejected programs that required transferring care from HCH. Staff at shelters where she stayed before would not allow re-admittance until her psychotic symptoms were more controlled. Ms. Harper remained on the street for much of the winter. She spent her days in the HCH waiting room, using the client bathroom to attend to her hygiene.

In early 2006, Ms. Harper agreed to meet with a staff psychiatrist. Ms. Harper was guarded and declined medication, informing the psychiatrist that she had received an injection of Haldol that would last 15 years. I scheduled another appointment; with my prompting, Ms. Harper kept the appointment and agreed to try an anti-psychotic. The psychiatrist and I enlisted HCH's nursing staff to administer Ms. Harper's medication daily.

Ms. Harper's visits to the nurses were sporadic and required frequent reminders from me. I used her struggle to secure shelter as an opportunity to discuss medication compliance, which was required by most shelters and supportive housing programs. The psychiatrist simplified Ms. Harper's medication regimen and Ms. Harper kept her appointments more consistently and became notably calmer and more able to modulate her emotions. During one encounter she grew angry with me but then stopped herself, stating "I don't need to speak that loud." She demonstrated increased insight, making statements such as, "Will you see if [the shelter] will let me in if there is an attitude adjustment [on my part]?" and strategized about how to handle potential conflicts with fellow shelter residents. She expressed an optimism that had been absent before.

Ms. Harper continued to struggle with psychotic symptoms, such as disorganized thoughts and auditory hallucinations. Mid-2006, Ms. Harper was again hospitalized after a heated argument during which she threatened another client in the HCH waiting room. Upon discharge, Ms. Harper returned to HCH, lucid, calm and goal-oriented. I found a low-cost rental room and Ms. Harper agreed to take it. She finally had permanent housing. Securing housing and achieving the correct medication regimen constituted another turning point for Ms. Harper. After moving into the rental room, she had no further psychiatric hospitalizations, became less guarded and was able to have more relaxed, spontaneous interactions with others. Her thoughts were more organized and her memory improved. Her appearance and hygiene improved and she purchased new clothing. Perhaps most notable was her growing ability to tolerate conflict and have insight.

In September, Ms. Harper traveled out of state to see her family for the weekend and, on her return, she said, "My father wanted me to stay longer, but I had to come back to get my medicine." She had many successful visits to her family over the next couple of years. Ms. Harper began reporting trouble with her landlady who made inappropriate requests such as asking Ms. Harper to buy alcohol for her and clean for her. The electricity was shut off several times because the landlady did not pay the utility bill. Despite efforts to address these problems, they persisted until Ms. Harper decided to move out and stay in emergency shelters until she could find another place. I contacted Safe Haven, the low-demand shelter, and they agreed to consider Ms. Harper's application once she became homeless. Within a month of becoming homeless again, Ms. Harper was accepted. From there, she moved to a transitional housing program where she now shares a house with three other women with SMI.

Practice decisions

Definition of the client

Homelessness definitions include people living on the streets; staying in emergency shelters, missions, single room occupancy facilities, abandoned buildings or vehicles; or doubling up with a series of friends and/or extended family members (Health Resources and Services Administration, 1999). HCH understands that the transition to stable housing is complicated and can take time, and we work with clients for up to a year after they have become stable and permanently housed.

Goals

Ms. Harper's primary goal was permanent independent housing. While that goal never changed, it evolved. Initially she only wanted certain emergency shelters or a rental room in the private market. She was minimally interested in psychiatric care and too disorganized and paranoid to maintain medication compliance for long. Only when Ms. Harper finally engaged in psychiatric treatment could she understand that the housing she sought was unavailable, unaffordable, or inadequate. She then modified her goal and was open to public housing or supportive housing programs. I explicitly agreed to her goal of housing and defined my role as helping her access resources such as income, identification, and, when she was ready, psychiatric care. My initial objective was to allow Ms. Harper to determine the pace and character of our relationship. This honored her overarching goal of maintaining independence and allowed me to take the time needed to earn her trust.

Contract and objectives

It is challenging to discuss treatment planning with a client who has SMI but who does not yet consider herself to be in treatment. For Ms. Harper, a more clinically oriented approach to treatment planning would have undermined the relationship rather than enhance it. We focused on securing shelter, obtaining a mailing address, and getting access to income, clothing and food. As Ms. Harper became more comfortable with me, we talked more about other objectives, such as applying for supportive housing programs and engaging in psychiatric treatment to reduce her psychiatric symptoms. Our initial contracts were verbal and short-term, as Ms. Harper had difficulty tolerating a more formal approach. Our working contract was renegotiated at every session; themes of the work included housing, income, help communicating with the outside world (through access to mail and the telephone), and access to tangible necessities (such as toiletries and clothing). Ms. Harper now participates in a more formal contracting process regarding her goals for treatment as well as our Representative Payee relationship. We budget and create an appointment schedule at the end of each month; periodically we develop a formal treatment plan outlining goals for the next six months.

Meeting place

Ms. Harper and I generally meet in my office at HCH. Initially, HCH outreach workers approached Ms. Harper on the street. When she started seeing me, she sometimes tolerated brief visits in the office. Other times, I met with her briefly outside or on the first floor near the building entrance. She was uncomfortable with the large, crowded waiting room, and often waited for me outside across the street from the clinic.

Ms. Harper gradually stayed longer and began using the clinic waiting room as a kind of day shelter, spending much of the morning there before going to lunch at a local soup kitchen. Now, Ms. Harper is very comfortable both in the clinic and in my office for extended periods of time. She is well known to staff and has friends among the HCH clients.

Use of time

The frequency and duration of our sessions varied. Initially, our encounters were brief and sporadic. I scheduled appointments, as I would for any client. When she did not keep these appointments, I began to see her whenever she arrived. My goal was to have some kind of interaction with Ms. Harper to build the relationship even if it was brief and only involved checking mail and giving her some snacks and toiletries.

Once Ms. Harper began receiving SSI and I became her Representative Payee, her visits were more frequent, longer and we scheduled appointments. Prior to SSI approval, Ms. Harper visited HCH two or three times a month; after she received SSI, she visited an average of 11 times per month. As she secured stable housing and gained more control of her SSI funds, we reduced the frequency of her visits. She sees the adherence nurses daily and I see her twice a month; HCH is an important source of social support for her.

Strategies and interventions

Just as effective case managers nurture the therapeutic alliance with their clients (Chinman, Rosenheck & Lam, 2000; Howgego, Yellowlees, Owen, Meldrum & Dark, 2003), mental health practitioners recognize that attending to a client's immediate practical needs, such as shelter, is a priority (Kirsh & Tate, 2006). HCH collapsed these two functions and created the position of Therapist Case Manager. The Therapist Case Managers at HCH can tailor their interventions to the needs and capacities of each client. I am convinced of the effectiveness of this combined role. My becoming SSI Representative Payee presented both a risk and an opportunity. On one hand, research suggests that for severely mentally ill SSI beneficiaries with no family members, clinical professionals are the best equipped to carry out the Representative Payee role (Brotman & Muller, 1990; National Research Council, 2007). Mentally ill individuals who participate in agency-based Representative Payee programs spend fewer days in the hospital than before participation (Luchins, Hanrahan, Conrad, Savage, Matters & Shinderman, 1998), experience fewer days of homelessness (Rosenheck, Lam & Randolph, 1997), and make greater use of psychiatric services (Rosen, McMahon & Rosenheck, 2007).

Nevertheless, engaging clinicians as Representative Payees raises ethical issues about whether this constitutes a dual relationship. When clients perceive clinicians using the payee role as leverage to compel treatment compliance, the therapeutic alliance can suffer (Angell, Martinez, Mahoney & Corrigan, 2007; Elbogen, Soriano, Van Dorn, Swartz & Swanson, 2005; Luchins et al., 1998). Yet, studies suggest that such relationships become more satisfactory to clients over time, as the relationships are negotiated and clinicians maintain a client-centered and non-coercive stance (Dixon, Turner, Krauss, Scott & McNary, 1999; Elbogen et al., 2005). I never made access to Ms. Harper's funds contingent on appointment or medication compliance. I used the Representative Payee relationship as a therapeutic tool, involving Ms. Harper in decisions about her SSI benefits, promoting financial autonomy, and attending to the conflicts that arose in the context of our Representative Payee-beneficiary relationship.

Stance of the social worker

My initial stance was one of acceptance and responsiveness, designed to reduce barriers to her engagement with HCH as a clinic and me as a provider. In addition to being flexible about the timing and location of encounters, I focused connections by being responsive to her requests, respectful of her privacy, and holding back my thoughts and opinions unless she asked me for them. I avoided declarative statements that sounded judgmental and gave her time to express anger.

Once I was designated SSI representative payee, my stance became more active. I proposed applying to supportive housing programs and we talked about the role of mental health treatment in gaining access to these programs. She declined these suggestions; I reviewed them periodically in case she changed her mind. This was a challenging period for me, since Ms. Harper would not be likely to find housing or receive psychiatric treatment as long as she declined both. If HCH and I had given up too early, we would have missed an opportunity for Ms. Harper to come to her own decision to engage in psychiatric treatment and find housing.

I am now in a maintenance role; I make sure Ms. Harper's rent is paid, that she has reliable access to her funds and medication, and is aware of upcoming appointments. Ms. Harper asks me to advocate for her or uses me as a sounding board when she is upset about housemates or other personal matters. She is reserved about her personal affairs, and I do not press, although I make suggestions more freely now.

Use of resources outside social worker/client relationship

I used resources outside of HCH, including shelter providers, supportive housing managers, Social Security staff, bank managers, lawyers, landlords, case managers, and psychiatric crisis unit staff. I maintain contact with Ms. Harper's treatment team at HCH, including her psychiatrist, her physician, and two adherence nurses. Our team approach helps us share observations and develop strategies to resolve problems as they arise.

Reassessment and evaluation

Reassessment and evaluation takes place formally when Ms. Harper and I complete six-month treatment plans. We discuss her progress and make adjustments in between those meetings. Case conferences about Ms. Harper's mental and physical health allow me to respond to concerns. My long-term relationship with Ms. Harper allows me to recognize patterns over time. I recently noted that Ms. Harper's psychotic symptoms increase during the early fall months, around the anniversary of a traumatic incident in her life, and I shared this information with her treatment team to help us anticipate periods of decompensation.

Transfer or termination

HCH provides services to homeless individuals for up to a year after they have become permanently housed. I raise the issue of transfer of care to other clinics early. Ms. Harper and I talked about transitioning to another clinic several months ago. She knows that once she secures stable independent housing, we will look for other sources of mental and physical health care and case management. We gradually increased her responsibility for managing her funds. Transition is a difficult time for clients who have been coming to HCH for a long time. Just as engagement in services takes time, so does the process of termination.

Differential discussion

Today, Ms. Harper is doing remarkably well. She has safe and reliable shelter, has developed friendships, is in close contact with her family, and has not been in a psychiatric hospital for nearly three years. One of the most striking aspects of Ms. Harper's case is how long it took for her to obtain shelter; even after engagement with HCH services. This is not uncommon for chronically, mentally ill individuals who are unable or unwilling to comply with requirements of supportive housing or shelter programs.

An alternative housing and treatment model has emerged to address the needs of this population. "Housing first" is a model that offers individuals housing regardless of their sobriety, psychiatric state or interest in treatment. Medical care, mental health services, and substance abuse treatment are offered to clients, but they are not compelled to use them. As explained by Sam Tsemberis, an early proponent of this model: "Once housed, individuals' priorities shift from ensuring their survival to improving the quality of their lives and that's when they become interested in the other services we offer" (HCH Clinicians Network, 2003, p. 5). Evaluations of housing first programs have yielded positive results (Gulcur *et al.*, 2003; Stefancic & Tsemberis, 2007) The housing first approach has been identified as a best practice by the U.S. Interagency Council on Homelessness and is now a centerpiece of Baltimore City's Ten Year Plan to End Homelessness (Baltimore Homeless Services, 2008). HCH developed Homeward Bound, the first "housing first" program in Baltimore City. Homeward Bound has housed 33 chronically homeless people in permanent independent apartments. Ms. Harper was not eligible because she had entered transitional housing by then, but this would have been beneficial for her.

References

Angell, B., Martinez, N., Mahoney, C. & Corrigan, P. (2007). Payeeship, financial leverage, and the client-provider relationship. *Psychiatric Services*, 58 (3): 365–72.

Baltimore Homeless Services.(2008). *The journey home: Baltimore city's ten year plan to end homelessness.* Retrieved from Baltimore City website: http://www.baltimorecity.gov/mayor/downloads/0108%2010%20 Year%20Plan.pdf

Baltimore Homeless Services & Baltimore City Health Department. (2007). *The 2007 Baltimore city homeless census.* Retrieved from Baltimore City website: http://www.baltimorehealth.org/info/2007%20 BaltimoreCityHomelessCensus_9_14_07.pdf

Brotman, A. & Muller, J. (1990). The therapist as representative payee. *Hospital and Community Psychiatry*, 41 (2): 167–71.

Chinman, M., Rosenheck, R. & Lam, J., (2000). The case management relationship and outcomes of homeless persons with serious mental illness. *Psychiatric Services*, 51 (9): 1142–7.

Culhane, D. P., Metraux, S. & Hadley, T. (2002). Supportive housing for homeless people with severe mental illness. *LDI Issue Brief*, 7 (5): 107–163.

Davis, J. M., Chen, N. & Glick, I. D. (2003). A meta-analysis of second-generation anti-psychotics. *Archives of General Psychiatry*, 60 (6): 553–64.

Denning, Patt (2000). *Practicing harm reduction psychotherapy: An alternative approach to addictions.* New York: The Guilford Press.

Dixon, L., Turner, J., Krauss, N., Scott, J. & McNary, S. (1999). Case managers' and clients' perspectives on a representative payee program. *Psychiatric Services*, 50 (6): 781–6.

Draine, J., Salzer, M., Culhane, D. & Hadley, T. (2002) Role of social disadvantage in crime, joblessness, and homelessness among people with serious mental illness. *Psychiatric Services*, 53 (3): 565–73.

Elbogen, E., Soriano, C., Van Dorn, R., Swartz, M. & Swanson, J. (2005). Consumer views of representative payee use of disability funds to leverage treatment adherence. *Psychiatric Services*, 56 (1): 45–9.

Glazer, W. M. & Byerly, M. J. (2008). Tactics and technologies to manage nonadherence in patients with schizophrenia. *Current Psychiatry Reports*, 10: 359–69.

Gulcur, L., Stefancic, A. Shinn, M. Tsemberis, S. & Fischer, S. (2003). Housing, hospitalization, and cost outcomes for homeless individuals with psychiatric disabilities participating in continuum of care and housing first programmes. *Journal of Community & Applied Social Psychology*, 13 (2): 171–86.

HCH Clinicians' Network. (2003). Supportive housing helps break the cycle of homelessness. *Healing Hands*, 7 (6). Retrieved 6/11/09, from: http://www.hhchc.org

HCH Clinicians' Network. (2005). Closing the door to homelessness: How clinicians can help. *Healing Hands*, 9 (5). Retrieved 6/11/09, from: http://www.hhchc.org

Health Resources and Services Administration. (1999). *Program assistance letter 1999–12: Principles of practice—A clinical resource guide for health care for the homeless programs.* Retrieved from: http://bphc.hrsa.gov/policy/pal9912.htm

Homeless Resource Center. (2008). *Expert panel on evidence-based practices in homeless services: Summary of proceedings.* Retrieved from Homeless Resource Center website: http://homeless.samhsa.gov/ResourceFiles/fvbqj4m2.pdf

Howgego, I., Yellowlees, P., Owen, C., Meldrum, L. & Dark, F. (2003). The therapeutic alliance: The key to effective patient outcome? A descriptive review of the evidence in community mental health case management. *Australian and New Zealand Journal of Psychiatry*, 37 (2): 169–83.

Interagency Council on Homelessness. (2006). *Good ... to better ... to great. Innovations in ten year plans to end homelessness in your community.* Retrieved from Interagency Council on Homelessness website: http://www.ich.gov/slocal/Innovations-in-10-Year-Plans.pdf

Keith, S. (2009). Use of long-acting risperidone in psychiatric disorders: Focus on efficacy, safety and cost-effectiveness. *Expert Review of Neurotherapeutics*, 9 (1): 9–31.

Kirsh, B. & Tate, E. (2006). Developing a comprehensive understanding of the working alliance in community mental health. *Qualitative Health Research*, 16 (8): 1054–74.

Lindamood, K. & Singer, J. (2008). Ending homelessness with Maryland's Health Care for the Homeless, Inc. *Maryland Medicine*, 9 (4): 9–11.

Luchins, D. J., Hanrahan, P., Conrad, K. J., Savage, C., Matters, M. D. & Shinderman, M. (1998). An agency-based representative payee program and improved community tenure of persons with mental illness. *Psychiatric Services*, 49 (9): 1218–22.

MAPS-M.D.. (2008). *Maryland's Public Health System.* Retrieved 11/02/07, from: http://www.maps-md.com/forproviders/providermanual.htm.

McMurray-Avila, M., Gelberg, L. & Breakey, W. (1999). Balancing act: Clinical practices that respond to the needs of homeless people. In Fosburg, L. B. & Dennis, D. L. (ed.), *Practical lessons: The 1998 national symposium on homeless research.* Washington, D.C.: U.S. Department HUD and HHS.

National Low Income Housing Coalition. (2008). *Out of Reach 2007–2008.* Retrieved from: http://www.nlihc.org/oor/oor2008/

National Research Council. (2007). *Improving the Social Security Representative Payee Program: Serving beneficiaries and minimizing misuse.* Washington, DC: The National Academies Press.

Newman, Sandra J. (2005). *Low-end rental housing: The forgotten story in Baltimore's housing boom.* Retrieved, from: http://www.urban.org/UploadedPDF/311222_rental_housing.pdf

Oliver, K. A. (1998) State Health Care Reform: Maryland Medicaid Reform: Design and Development. *Psychiatric Services*, 49 (6): 735–8.

Rosen, M. I., McMahon T. J. & Rosenheck, R. (2007). Does assigning a representative payee reduce substance abuse? *Drug and Alcohol Dependence*, 86 (2–3): 115–22.

Rosenheck, R., Lam J. & Randolph, F. (1997). Impact of representative payees on substance use by homeless persons with serious mental illness. *Psychiatric Services*, 48 (6): 800–6.

SAMHSA (Substance Abuse and Mental Health Services Administration) (2003). *Blueprint for change: Ending chronic homelessness for persons with serious mental illnesses and co-occurring substance abuse disorders.* Rockville, M.D.: Center for Mental Health Services, SAMHSA.

Social Security Administration (SSA). (2007). *SSI Annual Statistical Report.* Retrieved from: http://www.socialsecurity.gov/policy/docs/statcomps/ssi_asr/

Stefancic, A. & Tsemberis, S. (2007). Housing first for long-term shelter dwellers with psychiatric disabilities in a suburban county: A four-year study of housing access and retention. *Journal of Primary Prevention*, 28 (3–4): 265–79.

14 Social work in a for-profit renal dialysis unit

Betsy C. Blades

Introduction

Social work in a dialysis unit offers an opportunity for long-term involvement with patients who have evolving issues. The Council of Nephrology Social Workers (CNSW) has identified three periods of high involvement: the initial crisis, adjustment to chronic fluctuating illness, and decline in health to death. Interspersed between these, and which need to be addressed, are periods of stability as well as life-altering events such as job loss, divorce, and death or illness of a family member (Frank, Auslander & Weissgarten, 2003). Concurrently evolving organizational and policy changes shape the social worker's condition of work and provide opportunities.

Context

Policy

The single most important policy shaping the availability and delivery of dialysis treatments is the coverage of dialysis by Medicare as an entitlement. Those with sufficient work credits to qualify for Medicare are eligible for coverage, regardless of whether they are eligible for or interested in Social Security Disability. For most others, Medicare is available only by virtue of age or after two-and-a-half years from the time of disability determination. Medicare Part B covers 80% of the Medicare allowed rate for dialysis and certain approved medications.

Prior to 1972, the availability of dialysis was limited by the cost and the scarcity of resources, and the majority of patients were breadwinners. In some cases, approval by selection committees was required. Providers were generally a few teaching hospitals relying on insurance reimbursement and grant funding, and the majority of treatments were done at home (Blagg, 2008). With limited opportunity to expand the availability of treatment, the early pioneers turned to the federal government. In a dramatic demonstration, a patient was dialyzed briefly before the House Ways and Means Committee in 1972, which contributed to the inclusion of the coverage for dialysis in the Medicare amendments of that year. The promise here was that young, otherwise healthy patients could be rehabilitated and remain a part of the workforce.

With the change from dialysis as a limited resource to dialysis as an entitlement, there has been rapid growth in the patient population as well as the proportion of the Medicare resources devoted to end-stage renal disease (ESRD). Initially, in-center dialysis was much more highly compensated by Medicare than was home dialysis (Giles, 2003). As a result, the number of dialysis units initially operated by hospitals and later by individual and groups of nephrologists grew rapidly. A composite rate included the cost of treatment supplies and staffing, a standard battery of laboratory testing and medications. Prior to 1972, there was no experience of treating patients who were older than 45–50 at the onset of ESRD, and patients with diabetes had not been dialyzed due to their perceived limited lifespans. Currently, diabetes is the most frequently underlying cause of ESRD, and patients in their 80s and with multiple complex medical diagnoses are now routinely admitted to dialysis units.

The 1976 Medicare ESRD Conditions of Coverage required multidisciplinary care teams that included social workers with master's degrees (41 Fed. Reg., 1976), (Conditions of Coverage, 2008). Social workers' delineated responsibilities included participation in care planning, assessment, individual and group counseling, and referral to community resources. How this was to be done or with what frequency was left unstated until 2008. Although social workers were required in all dialysis units, they were usually working alone with little guidance from the federal regulations. The Council of Nephrology Social Workers (CNSW) was established as a professional group under the umbrella of the National Kidney Foundation (NKF) in an effort to provide education and advocacy for often isolated social workers. They provided outlines for what should be included in assessments, sample job descriptions, and later staffing calculators for determining appropriate caseloads based on patient acuity. Calculators were designed to help social workers advocate for themselves with administrators. CNSW also established guidelines for local chapters to provide a peer group for professional development, the opportunity to develop and disseminate information about local resources, and to advocate for the profession at the local level.

As ownership of dialysis units shifted to for-profit, ever larger chains, maximizing profit became important. This seems like a cat and mouse game with the government continuing to try to close loop holes discovered by dialysis providers to enhance reimbursement. The basic composite rate of reimbursement set by Medicare has actually shrunk because the initial rate of reimbursement was high. As for-profit units have merged forming ever larger chains, the ability to economize on the cost of providing treatments has improved. There are also opportunities to enhance reimbursement due to charges for medications outside the composite rate. Also, by law, for many patients covered by employer group health insurance plans (EGHP), the private plan is primary payer for up to 33 months and usually at a higher rate than Medicare.

Social workers are often squeezed in efforts to enhance profits. For-profits eliminated financial counselors transferring their functions to social workers, and increasing caseloads resulted in assessments that were little more than corporate established checklists. Over the years, efforts to request exceptions to the requirement that social workers have master's degrees have been rebuffed. In the absence of federal requirements to retain a meaningful role for social workers, local CNSW chapters attempted to work with the states. A study by the Maryland chapter quantified the fact that social workers were spending insufficient time on the required tasks assigned by federal regulation (Maryland Commission ..., 2008). The result was new state regulations requiring initial assessments within 30 days and annual updates (Maryland Commission..., 2008). Notes are required quarterly for stable patients or monthly for those who are unstable. Several areas to be covered in assessments are delineated, and there is a list of conditions that would define instability. Caseload limits were not addressed in this State. The reasoning for seeking more regulation has been that companies would need to allow more time to assure that essential tasks were being met, either by decreasing caseloads or by assigning non-social work tasks to others (Giles, 2003; Widmann, 2006).

Because the federal government is the major payer, it and its intermediaries have become increasingly involved in setting rules and monitoring the provision of care at the local level.

Maryland has a Kidney Disease Program (KDP) that pays for dialysis-related treatments and hospitalizations, as well as renal-related medications as the payer of last resort. Participation by dialysis units with the KDP involves an annual re-certification inspection by the state Kidney Commission. Participation with Medicare requires inspections at a lesser frequency, which are conducted by a state agency designated by CMS. As part of these unannounced inspections, social work assessments and notes are reviewed and patients are interviewed.

In effect in 2008, new Medicare Conditions for Coverage (CfC) represent the most comprehensive conditions change since amendments were enacted. During the comment period, the largest number of comments by any professional group was from social workers, and the conditions relating to social work reflect the outcome-driven practice model advocated by CNSW. While we had hoped for a definition of caseload limits, the government supported only professional standards relating to acuity. Still, tasks to be done only by social workers are defined, and those that can be done by social work assistants—such as financial or social security applications, and transportation—are specified. The requirement that social workers have master's degrees has been retained (Browne, 2008; Council of Nephrology Social Workers, 2008). Still, we must find ways to prove our contribution (Beder, 2000; Beder, Mason, Johnstone, Callahan & Lesage, 2003; Callahan, 2007).

Social workers are responsible for specific content required for comprehensive multidisciplinary assessments to be completed according to precise schedules and timetables. Care plans arise from the assessments. Goals and plans are individualized and outcome based with timelines and measurable outcomes. After the initial crisis and adjustment periods, assessments are completed annually for patients who are stable, and monthly for those who are not. There are clear criteria for deeming a patient unstable. All team members must attend care planning meetings. Although patients and/or their representatives must be invited, their attendance is optional. Another element introduced in the new conditions is the use of a tracking instrument to quantify quality of life from the time of the three-month assessment and repeated at least annually. Social workers are responsible for meeting both state and federal regulations. While state and federally mandated inspectors have traditionally been nurses, in light of the new CfCs, some states are assembling review teams that include social workers. Each change supports our contribution to achieving positive outcomes for the renal patient (Bordelton, 2006; Dobrof, Dolinko, Lichtiger, Uribarri & Epstein, 2001).

Technology

Dialysis is a treatment for kidney failure known as Stage V chronic kidney disease or ESRD (National Kidney Foundation, 2009). While patients may have some renal function, the kidneys are not filtering effectively enough to prevent toxins from building up in the blood. Left untreated, the patient develops uremia and in some cases excessive fluid retention, which will ultimately result in death. The three general treatment options for ESRD are hemodialysis, peritoneal dialysis, and transplant. Hemodialysis, the most common modality in this country, involves the use of a dialysis machine to pump blood through an artificial kidney to remove fluids and cleanse the blood of toxins. Typically, patients dialyze three times per week for treatment times of 3–4 hours each. In-center hemodialysis, the only treatment offered at our facility, is provided in two or more shifts each day. Patients spend their dialysis time in reclining chairs, sleeping, watching TV, reading, interacting or any activity that allows them to be as comfortable as possible in one general position for the duration of the treatment period.

Important here is information regarding access, medication, diet and fluid control. The vascular access is the means by which the patient's blood supply is connected to the dialysis machine. The three access types are an external catheter, a synthetic graft connecting a vein and an artery, and a fistula created by a direct surgical connection between a vein and an artery. For each type of access, advantages and disadvantages often differ for patients and staff. An external catheter usually enters the chest and tunnels under the skin with the end in the heart. Many patients prefer catheters because the needles enter external ports so the discomfort of needle sticks is avoided. Disadvantages are that they can easily become infected, and long-term damage to the vessels can occur. Catheters are most often used in new patients who need dialysis quickly, such as when diagnosis is made late in the course of the disease or when a patient delays surgical follow-up. Both a graft and fistula require needle sticks through the skin. The graft has been the easiest for the surgeon to place and is still used in less than optimal vessels. Grafts are also easier for inexperienced staff to cannulate (that is, make a cavity in), and patients often regard them as less unsightly than a fistula. They are more likely to become clotted or damaged to the point that further surgery is required for replacement. The fistula is the preferred type of access, yielding the best quality dialysis, and there is considerable pressure on dialysis facilities by Medicare intermediaries to increase the number of patients dialyzing by that means.

A number of medications have been developed to compensate for some lost functions, such as the kidney's role in red blood cell production. Others are prescribed to minimize complications of long-term dialysis such as bone loss. Some are given intravenously during treatment, while others are to be taken by the patients at home. Diet and fluid control are also important. Despite the length of the dialysis treatment, the process can only partially replace natural kidney function. Thus, the patient must support the process with fluid and diet control to avoid the build-up of certain harmful electrolytes in the blood. One of the most difficult changes for many patients is the recommended restriction of salt intake, which increases thirst and subsequent fluid intake. Excessive fluid can overtax the heart, for example, and it is often difficult to safely remove rapidly. Foods with high potassium content—including oranges, bananas, nuts, potatoes, greens, milk products, chocolate, and tomatoes—must also be limited. These have been favorite foods for much of many patients' lives. While the patient has a passive role in the actual treatment, with home medications, diet and fluid control, attendance, and to a lesser extent access, the patient or caretaker has to take responsibility. The ability of the patient to assume this responsibility is subsumed under the general heading of compliance (Auslander, Dobrof & Epstein, 2001).

Organization

Established in 1987 as a community site of an urban hospital's large dialysis program, the facility is located in a suburban business complex where its census fluctuates between 60 and 68. In 2004, the hospital sold the unit to a small, rapidly growing for-profit chain. The staff was not "sold" with the unit, but the new company had first option on retaining employees. I have been the facility social worker since 1987. Registered nurses and technicians provide direct patient care with a minimum staff-patient ratio of 1:3. An on-site administrator, clinical nurse manager, and administrative assistant work full-time; the dietitian and I, part-time. Three nephrologists, solo practitioners, are partners with the owner/company and rotate as medical director.

The company was founded by two businessmen experienced with the larger for-profit chains. Its boutique branding model is to locate physician partners with the potential to refer patients and then build a unit with features such as electric fireplaces in well-appointed waiting rooms. Since our unit pre-existed, we do not fit the boutique model, but the company website refers to our inner-city location as an example of their commitment to serve under-served areas. We were the 11th unit in the company, and it grew in less than five years to 70 facilities, with more coming. The two large national chains which own more than two-thirds of all facilities in the Baltimore metropolitan area dialyze more than 100,000 patients each. Our company will remain midsized with a goal of exceeding the quality of care of the larger chains.

Within the company, regional executive vice presidents are rewarded by development of new units and by profitability. While the corporate goal is to compete with the large chains, there is competition between regions within the company. Quality ratings are determined monthly. It is difficult for the non-administrative staff to identify with the parent company as we are so isolated. While our parent hospital and all support services were formerly all in one place five miles away, our present human resources department is now two time zones away, and key people operate from laptop and cellphones from any number of places throughout the country.

Social workers within the company do not have a hierarchy. The vice president for finance, whose position was created as the company grew, is assisted by a cadre of regionally assigned insurance management specialists (IMS), who are interested in patients with employer group health plans (EGHP), as well as underinsured and uninsured patients. The IMS orient new social workers about financial policies and issues. Making quarterly visits, IMS maintain frequent contact with social workers by phone and email and are available by phone to talk with patients with EGHPs about their insurance. There is no consistent approach to educating inexperienced social workers and no ongoing mechanism for social workers to communicate with one another.

All committees/task forces at the unit level are multidisciplinary; I am therefore involved in each effort (Ravani, Marinangeli, Tancredi & Malberti, 2003). Generally, all committees are essentially composed of the same people, and this provides an opportunity for the social worker to be involved and assume leadership roles. For example, I have coordinated committees on adequacy of dialysis and a project to increase the number of patients dialyzing by AV fistula.

The staff of our facility is stable, and the relatively small unit enhances opportunities for staff and patients to get to know each other. We observe patient birthdays, play monthly bingo, and serve holiday meals several times a year. Even in a large metropolitan area, the dialysis world can be very small, and staff and patients find they have other connections through church, community or mutual friends. Also, through the ongoing treatment, close personal relationships develop, and boundary issues often need to be addressed. While some units emphasize a family-like relationship between staff and patients, we formalize the difference by addressing and referring to our patients by title and last name.

Description of the client situation

Patricia Addo, a 56-year-old African American woman with two adult children, began dialysis four years ago. A large woman, she takes extraordinary care with her appearance. Her clothes, accessories, and jewelry are all color coordinated, and her hair, nails, and make-up are cared for meticulously. When she started dialysis, she had been married to her second husband for six years. He is an African immigrant, working towards citizenship. On public assistance following the end of her first marriage, she took advantage of work study programs to earn bachelor's and master's degrees in education. Having resigned from full-time teaching due to her health, she continued to teach as a substitute but no longer had health insurance. While hospitalized for a diabetic crisis about five months earlier, she learned that her kidney failure was progressing.

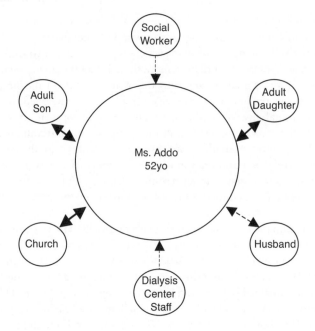

Figure 14.1 Before ecomap for Ms. Addo.

Medical assistance (MA) for which she applied on the basis of her hospital bills, took several months to become effective. Her medical care was therefore episodic. Because she could not have a permanent access created, she started dialysis with an external catheter.

The ecomap for Ms. Addo at the onset of dialysis treatment can be seen above.

Crisis period

Ms. Addo was anxious, tearful and talkative on her first day of outpatient dialysis. As I responded to her concerns she became more relaxed. Over the next few weeks, I completed my assessment and assisted with education including information about treatment options. She described good social supports through family and church (strong beliefs had helped her weather past crises), was able to articulate her concerns, and expressed an interest in learning compliant behaviors. All of these are important predictors of a good long-term adjustment to dialysis.

Ms. Addo hated the treatments, describing a morbid fear of needles that led to her delaying having a permanent access placed. She thought her best option was a transplant, and her son agreed to be considered as a donor. As long as she thought she had a way out she did not have to begin to make peace with dialysis. About four months after beginning treatment she and her son went for an initial pre-transplant appointment. The upshot was most traumatic for her: she was advised to lose 60 pounds to reduce the depth of her abdomen where the transplanted kidney would be placed. She became so emotionally distraught when the surgeon told her this that the social worker took her to her office to help her regain her composure (Wiebe, 2004; Wolfe, 2003). When she voiced how much she hated dialysis, the social worker suggested she consider a psychiatric evaluation as psychotropic drugs might help her to better manage her situation. At that point she ran from the social worker's office, grabbed her son and rushed out of the building. She has never told her son what transpired on that day.

Following that appointment, she was angry and did not believe she would ever achieve the surgeon's expectation (Wolfe, 2003). Not only did she know it would be difficult to lose the weight, she stated that her anatomy was such that she would still have a large abdomen even if she lost 100 pounds. She talked with the dietitian about weight loss, but said that offered little hope for her as she is convinced "the love of salt and grease is cultural." She also sought information about stomach surgery for weight loss. Application for the surgery yielded no response. She refused to consider having an evaluation of the need for psychotropic medications because she did not want that to be part of her medical record.

Growing to accept that there was no shortcut to end dialysis, Ms. Addo yielded to pressure to have a permanent access, and a synthetic graft was placed in her lower right arm. As the time for cannulation approached, she became more anxious at the thought of needing needle sticks. When the arm had finally healed to the point that cannulation was possible, she delayed and delayed. She had to take deep breaths, asked for time to get herself together, put a towel in her mouth and cried a lot. Some staff members were wearied by the time required to initiate treatment, and she was upset by comments she heard that she "should have gotten used to the sticks by now." She declared a numbing cream on the area to be ineffective. When her anxiety did not abate, her nephrologist reluctantly prescribed a more powerful numbing agent that requires a half-hour prep time and which she continues to follow scrupulously.

A family challenge

While she was at peace with dialysis, she agreed to sponsor her husband's two children, still living in their home country. Not sure she was really up to raising children again, she acknowledged finding the presence of her daughter's children trying during the times they lived with her. Getting the children here took more than six months, during which time she was able to make some plans. However, she remained anxious about sharing responsibility for them. To prepare, we changed her shift so she would be available when the children came home from school. After an initial adjustment, Ms. Addo enjoyed them and helped with language skills and school work.

This was a peaceful time. She hated but accepted dialysis. Active and independent, she no longer talked about losing weight or transplant. Attending all treatments, she was consistently late and, as a result, sometimes had to have a shortened treatment. Efforts to help her improve her timeliness were of little avail as she said being late is part of her basic personality. Her move to an early shift as well as staff's acceptance of this trait allowed her to receive her full treatment on most occasions. She continued to be involved with her church, particularly enjoyed singing at church and in the community, and was regarded as having made a good adjustment to dialysis.

Insurance issues

Always in the background were insurance concerns. She began dialysis with temporary medical assistance (MA). I assisted her to apply for the state Kidney Disease Program (KDP), which requires disclosure of family income including copies of federal income tax forms. In the first year this was not a problem as she had earned income from the previous year of teaching, but I did note that although the income tax was filed jointly with her husband, no income was claimed for him. Her response was, "My husband is not a citizen." She also applied for Medicare and Social Security Disability Insurance. Between the Medicare and KDP, she had full coverage for the costs of her treatments and her medications. When KDP needed to be renewed the following year, she had no tax forms as she had not had any earnings aside from her disability income, and her husband declared no income. KDP denied coverage until she obtained MA. At that point, she was responsible for the cost of her medications. Of less concern was the 20% of the cost of her dialysis. I gave her an application for MA for Medicare Beneficiaries, but she did not want to complete it. She had once had Medical Assistance when she was desperate with hospital bills and the knowledge that she needed to start dialysis, but this time the circumstances were not desperate. Her only legal recourse was to do nothing, pay for her own medications, and let the dialysis unit absorb their loss. She knew that her husband should be filing taxes. Signing a false application for Medical Assistance conflicted with her being honest, and there was also the fact that her husband was applying for citizenship. Although it took a few months for the dialysis billing company to learn that she no longer had KDP, they were insistent she have a secondary insurance, and it was the social worker's responsibility to follow up with the patient. On financial matters patients look to me to give them information and recommend a course of action. In this case, however, this was the patient's decision entirely, as I was unwilling to advise her to compromise her integrity or to take action that might jeopardize her future. Our administrator understood my conflict and her commitment to the company's mission, so she took over communication with the patient on this matter. Ms. Addo did apply for Medical Assistance as a single person, but she continued to worry about whether she had done the right thing.

A family crisis

After another period of peace, Ms. Addo experienced a shock when her husband sent the children to stay with relatives for the weekend. When she returned from dialysis, he had also moved out. After months of minimal interaction between us, Ms. Addo needed my help. She called the police, had the locks changed, and wrote letters to the INS because, as the sponsor of the children, she had assumed responsibility for them. Once these first actions were completed, reality hit. Although they had been married for eight years, she perceived that her husband had used her to get permanent residency status for himself and his children and then abandoned her. She was left angry and grieving, and although he is still living and working in the area, she has not spoken with him again. She believes he sent the children back to their home country.

Of immediate concern was how she would live. Her income was not sufficient to rent at market rates, and no family members were in a position to take her in. She identified some immediately reducible expenses, and I assisted her in exploring potential housing. An emergency grant from the National Kidney Foundation (NKF), and a loan from her church provided two months of rent, which assured her shelter and time to develop an alternate plan. Once she was appropriately sheltered in a senior housing building that accepts disabled residents under 60, her anxiety began to abate. She then entered another period of psychosocial stability.

Decisions about practice

Definition of the client

The patient was the only client. Although over the time of our involvement her husband, his children, her daughter and grandchildren lived with her, there was no indication that they were concerned about her dialysis. In some cases, I would hold at least one family meeting to help the others appreciate her experience and express their concerns. However, Ms. Addo and I decided the way the dialysis was affecting her was the only concern. The unit has its own culture, and staff members often need to be reminded that what seems routine to us is totally new and often overwhelming to the patient. For example, when her fear of needle sticks did not abate and some staff members made demeaning comments about her, we had a meeting that resulted in the staff creating a plan for limit-setting carried out with sensitivity to her fears. The staff members were frustrated, and for that moment, they became part of the client definition.

Goals, objectives and contracting

Within the overall goal of adjustment to dialysis and the associated changes so the highest quality of life can be achieved, specific goals change over time depending on the patient's process. In my work with Ms. Addo, the objectives have been more implied than defined, and there was no stated contract. An initial five objectives were meant to help her to maximize the benefits of dialysis: to help her to reduce her anxiety and negotiate the crisis of beginning dialysis, begin to regain a sense of control, know that her feelings and concerns were normal, define and express her concerns, and help her understand my role in the process. The next goal, which was painful for her, was to help her to recognize that she had no avenues for the escape she wanted and to accept the need for treatment.

Meeting place and use of time

The meeting place varies with the patient's need for privacy and available time. There are standards about the distance between chairs that allow a private interaction at chair-side with someone who has normal hearing. However, the unit looks public, and it is sometimes hard to keep the technicians at a distance and not interjecting comments. When a patient is uncomfortable talking in the unit, we have the option of using my office. However, when transportation services are used, the time between treatment and departure may be insufficient to talk. Initially, Ms. Addo and I talked in the unit. However, when she started to drive her own car, we moved to meeting in the office after treatment. Although she does not seem to have any problem with talking in the unit, she spends most of her treatment time sleeping soundly. My involvement with Ms. Addo is ongoing, and because of the long-term nature of our relationship, it has been fluid to this point. With the introduction of Medicare's new Conditions for Coverage (CfCs), social workers must set timelines to achieve objectives.

Strategies, interventions and the stance of the social worker

I frequently use a problem-solving approach; however, as I am part of an interdisciplinary team, my interventions may extend beyond the traditional social work arena. CNSW has identified appropriate interventions for each of three periods. Ms. Addo is a great talker; I just introduce a topic and she begins. However, her insurance situation necessitated my being more directive. I reframed this in part by highlighting resources to help her to reduce the costs of her medications while downplaying the interests of the dialysis company.

Use of resources outside of the helping relationship

I assisted Ms. Addo to access a number of resources, some specifically for the renal patient and others related to need and Medicare status. Before she was comfortable driving to treatment, she was referred to transportation resources; she was assisted with re-certification for KDP and MA for Medicare beneficiaries; and I helped her to enroll in a Medicare Part D prescription plan. For other resources such as Medicare and Social Security Disability, some direction enabled her to follow through on her own. When she needed time to plan how she would live after her husband left, I obtained a grant from the NKF to assist with her rent. In her quest for subsidized housing, I provided resource information, but she actually accomplished this much faster on her own with some behind-the-scenes intervention by a fellow church member.

Reassessment and evaluation

State regulations set the reassessment schedule requiring quarterly notes on stable patients and then annual assessments. Federal regulations require reassessment after three months and then annually. I find it useful to spend some time with patients about two months after beginning dialysis to help them to appreciate the changes in their health status and activity level. Often patients are so preoccupied with how much has changed in their lives that they find it difficult to appreciate how much their lives have improved since pre-dialysis. I usually prepare the patient for this reevaluation early in the relationship when they seem so hopeless.

My most recent annual reevaluation with Ms. Addo was about six months ago—a year after her husband left her. She was feeling very positive, settled in her new apartment, teaching a Bible class in her building; financially secure and at peace with her marital situation. She is still angry enough with her husband that she intends to ask for alimony if he ever files for a divorce, but she has no intention of pursuing the matter herself. Recounting the events of the year, she noted that the beginning of things turning good had been my work with her to help her to develop a plan and then jumpstart the process with the emergency grant from the NKF.

The current ecomap for Ms. Addo can be seen below.

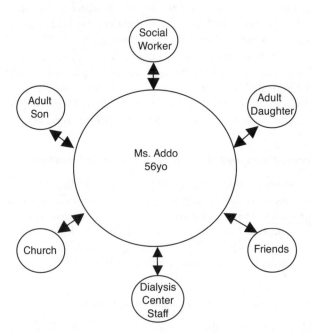

Figure 14.2 After ecomap for Ms. Addo.

Transfer and termination and case conclusion

Social work involvement with the patient goes on at some level as long as the patient is treated in the unit. Occasionally, the patient transfers to another unit, and there is an opportunity to end with the patient and to pass on information so that the focus of the social worker can also be transferred. Most often, patients leave the unit due to death, transfer to a nursing home with in-house dialysis, or receive a transplant.

My involvement with Ms. Addo is ongoing. At this point, she has found new friends in senior housing, teaches Bible study in her building, continues her church involvement and singing. Driving herself to treatment, she still arrives late. Recently she has raised the possibility of working again but does not think she can go back to classroom teaching. She talked about transferring to a facility closer to her home, and I gave her a list and encouragement; however, she could not find another unit where she thought she could be as comfortable. Crises continue to arise periodically; recently, she required a temporary catheter while recovering from surgical intervention due to access problems. For these small crises, she requires minimal intervention to help her to order her thinking so that she can follow through on her own. Overall, she is stable at this point with respect to dialysis, her health, and social situation.

Differential discussion

The essential goals were addressed with the patient. However, without timelines and measurable outcomes, it has been difficult to justify the role of social work as a "cost center" in a for-profit dialysis unit. It was therefore easy for corporate providers to justify turning us into "productive" contributors to the revenue stream. Although somewhat overwhelming initially, the new CfCs based on an outcome-driven model of social work practice promise improved patient service as well as my own satisfaction. I have also appreciated the willingness of the facility administrator to address financial/insurance issues when they present an ethical conflict for me. While these issues are not a problem when they promise to assist the patient, at other times the company policy threatens to put me in the position of an adversary rather than a patient advocate and to divert attention from the task of supporting the patient's compliance.

References

Auslander, G., Dobrof, J. & Epstein, I. (2001). Comparing social work's role in renal dialysis in Israel and the United States: The practice based research potential of available clinical information. *Social Work in Health Care*, 33, (3/4):129–51.

Beder, J. (2000). Social work research in nephrology: A necessity, not a luxury. *Dialysis & Transplantation*, 29 (4): 208–14.

Beder, J., Mason, S., Johnstone, S., Callahan, M. B. & LeSage, L. (2003). Effectiveness of a social work psychoeducation program in improving adherence behavior associated with risk of CVD in ESRD patients. *Journal of Nephrology Social Work*, 22:12–22.

Blagg, C. R. (2008). The renaissance of home dialysis: Where we are, why we got here, what is happening in the United States and elsewhere. *Hemodialysis International*, 12:S2–S5.

Bordelton, T. D. (2006). An outcome study of a piloted ESRD patient and staff symposium. *Social Work in Health Care*, 43 (1): 75–89.

Browne, T. (2008). Psychosocial aspects of the 2008 end-stage renal disease. *Journal of Nephrology Social Work*, 29 (Fall). http://www.kidney/org/professionals/cnsw/JNSWonline/jnswArchive.cfm?id=29

Callahan, M. B. (2007). Begin with the end in mind: The value of outcome-driven nephrology social work. *Advances in Chronic Kidney Disease*, 14 (4): 409–14.

Conditions for Coverage. Conditions for Coverage (2008). 42CFR Parts 405,410,413, *et al.* Medicare & Medicaid Programs: Guidelines for coverage for end stage renal disease facilities; Final Rules Arp 15, 2008. http://edocket.access.gpo.gov/2008/pdf/08-1102.pdf

Council of Nephrology Social Workers (2008). Psychosocial aspects of the 2008 dialysis conditions for coverage. *Journal of Nephrology Social Work*, 29 (Fall). http://www.kidney/org

Dobrof, J., Dolinko, A., Lichtiger, E., Uribarri, J. & Epstein, I. (2001). Dialysis patient characteristics and outcomes: The complexity of social work practice with the end stage renal disease population. *Social Work in Health Care*, 33 (3/4): 105–8.

Frank, A., Auslander, G. K. & Weissgarten, J. (2003). Quality of life of patients with end-stage renal disease at various stages of their illness. *Social Work in Health Care* 38 (2): 1–37.

Giles, S. (2003). Transformations: A phenomenological investigation into the life-world of home dialysis. *Social Work in Health Care*, 38 (2): 29–50.

Maryland Commission on Kidney Disease (2008). Retrieved 5/8/09: http://www.dsd.state.med.us/comar.htm

National Kidney Foundation (2009). Retrieved 11/06/09, from http://www.kidney.org

Ravani, P., Marinangeli, G., Tancredi, M. & Malberti, F. (2003). Multidisciplinary chronic kidney disease management improves survival on dialysis. *Journal of Nephrology*, 16 (6): 870–7.

Standards for Practice for Nephrology Social Work (5th ed.). (2003). New York: National Kidney Foundation, Inc.

Widmann, A. (2006). Outcomes driven social work: Repackaging the wheel. *Journal of Nephrology Social Work*, 25:59–60.

Wiebe, H. W. (2004). Reluctance towards transplantation: Factors influencing patient attitudes towards organ transplantation. *Journal of Nephrology Social Work*, 23:19–39.

Wolfe, W. A. (2003). Achieving equity in referrals for renal transplant evaluation with African-American patients: The role of nephrology social workers. *Social Work in Health Care*, 37 (3): 75–87.

15 Returning veterans, traumatic brain injury, and Veterans' Administration services

A War Related Illness and Injury Study Center

Patricia A. Findley

Context

The War Related Illness and Injury Study Centers (WRIISCs) work with veterans who have post-deployment-related health concerns or difficult to diagnose illnesses or injuries (WRIISC, 2006). The centers (in Washington, D.C., East Orange, NJ, and Palo Alto, CA), evolved from the Gulf War Referral Centers that were initiated by the Veterans Administration (VA) in the 1990s, specifically for Gulf War veterans with health concerns. Legislation in 1998 directed the VA to create centers that specialized in all combat-related unexplained illnesses and injuries regardless of conflict (e.g. Korean War, Vietnam, Afghanistan).

The NJ WRIISC is housed on the East Orange campus of the VA New Jersey Health Care System. The VA is broadening mental health services to meet the specific needs of the veterans of Operation Iraqi Freedom and Operation Enduring Freedom (OIF/OEF), the military conflicts in Iraq (Batten & Pollack, 2008). The WRIISC is a specialty program that hosts an interdisciplinary team comprising physicians with occupational health and internal medicine specialty training, nurses, psychologists, neuropsychologists, and social workers. It interacts with all of the services of the main facility and the VA at-large.

The WRIISC is an outpatient program that offers services to combat veterans, families, and health care professionals, and provides clinical care, education, and risk communication. To perform its mission, it uses a multidisciplinary team whose goals are to:

- provide clinical services to veterans with deployment-related health concerns and illnesses to improve their health-related quality of life;
- advance knowledge of ways to care for veterans with medically unexplained symptoms to improve their health-related quality of life;
- advance knowledge of and improve communication among veterans, the health care community and researchers regarding deployment-related health concerns and illnesses;
- advance knowledge of medically unexplained symptoms in veteran and other populations.

At the WRIISC, veterans are seen for a one-day individualized and comprehensive medical assessment of their health, with a focus on suspected deployment-related health issues and unexplained symptoms such as anxiety, depression, exposure concerns, dizziness, and memory loss. The evaluation consists of a review of the medical record, an extensive history and physical examination, a psychological interview, neuropsychological screening, exposure assessment, fitness testing, a social work assessment, and health education. If available, spouses or parents may accompany the veteran for his/her evaluation.

In order to be eligible for the program, patients must have unexplained symptoms after adequate primary and secondary work up, including a psychiatric evaluation, concerns related to their deployment to a hostile area, not abused substances for at least six months, a stable living arrangement, and the capacity to travel safely to the WRIISC. The evaluation culminates in a pre-final meeting where the interdisciplinary team discusses findings and develops treatment recommendations. At this meeting, which includes the veteran and accompanying family members, the team provides recommendations for further care and testing. As the team social worker, I am responsible for helping the veteran connect to the recommended resources.

As of late 2008, the U.S. has seen approximately 1.64 million deployed into Iraq or Afghanistan. Nearly 300,000 veterans suffer from post-traumatic stress disorder (PTSD) or major depression, and 320,000 soldiers experienced a probable traumatic brain injury (TBI) during their tours of duty (Moran, 2008). In fact, mild TBI (mTBI) has become the "signature" injury characterizing the key injury of this conflict due to blast injuries resulting from improvised explosive devices (IEDs) (Jones, Fear & Wessely, 2007).

Policy

President Hoover signed the executive order establishing the VA on 21 July 1930, joining the Veterans' Bureau, the Bureau of Pension and the National Homes for the Disabled Volunteer Soldiers into one federal agency called the Veterans Administration. The VA provides care to veterans who were honorably discharged from active military service and reservists who were called to active duty by Federal order and completed their assigned tour of duty. The VA uses priority groups to balance the distribution of health care resources across eligible veterans based on level of service-connectedness. The highest priority is for those with 50% or more service connectedness and the lowest is for non-service connected veterans who have a household income and/or net worth above the VA's national income threshold, but whose income is below the geographically based income threshold for their place of residence. If a veteran requires services but is above the income threshold, a co-payment is charged.

As the nation entered the OIF/OEF conflict, returning veterans were allowed two years of health care services within the VA system upon discharge from active duty and enrollment into the VA. The National Defense Authorization Act (NDAA) of Fiscal Year 2008 (Public Law 110–81) was signed by President George W. Bush on 28 January 2008 to increase the years of coverage from two years to five years post-military discharge. This policy shift is notable, as many veterans do not immediately enroll in the VA upon discharge, and many of the issues related to deployment may not surface until more than two years after return. Symptoms of PTSD, TBI, concerns over exposure to chemicals and other environmental factors in the combat zones, or other medical issues may evolve over time, and seeing a doctor is fairly uncommon in this younger population (Marcell, Klein, Fischer, Allan & Kokotailo, 2002). Furthermore, many veterans do not want to admit to psychological issues because of the stigma attached (Hoge *et al.*, 2004). Therefore, each VA has an OIF/OEF Coordinator whose role is to work with each OIF/OEF veteran to facilitate negotiation of the overall health care system, paying special attention to those veterans with TBI.

Technology

A brain injury occurs when an individual experiences a blow or jolt to the head (i.e. closed head injury) or a penetrating head injury (i.e. open head injury) that disrupts the function of the brain. Injuries can range from "severe" (i.e. an extended period of unconsciousness or amnesia after the injury) to "mild" (i.e. a brief change in mental status or consciousness). Common features of TBI can be seen across physical, cognitive, and emotional levels of functioning (Centers for Disease Control and Prevention, 2008). Frequently reported physical issues include disruptions of speech, vision and/or hearing, paralysis, headaches, seizure disorder, muscle spasticity, and reduced endurance. On the cognitive side, problems reported include difficulties with concentration, attention, perceptions, planning, communication, writing skills, short-term memory, long-term memory, judgment, sequencing, reading skills, and orientation. Behavioral and emotional changes can include fatigue, anxiety, low self-esteem, restlessness, agitation, mood swings, excessive emotions, depression, sexual dysfunction, lack of motivation, inability to cope, and self-centeredness. A TBI can also impact one's ability to sleep or cause one to sleep too much.

With an mTBI a patient generally experiences at least one of the following:

a   any period of loss of consciousness;
b   any loss of memory for events immediately before or after the accident;
c   any alteration in mental state at the time of the accident (e.g. feeling dazed, disoriented, or confused);
d   focal neurological deficit(s) that may or may not be transient.

The severity of the injury should not exceed the following post-traumatic amnesia (PTA) criteria: the incident is not greater than 24 hours; an initial Glasgow Coma Scale (GCS) score of 13–15 is exhibited; and the loss of consciousness is 30 minutes or less (Mild Traumatic Brain Injury Committee of the Head Injury Interdisciplinary Special Interest Group of the American Congress of Rehabilitation Medicine, 1993). Despite what seem to be clear criteria, it is difficult to diagnose mTBI, particularly as mTBI can lead to "post-concussion syndrome" that can include headaches, dizziness, mild mental slowing, and fatigue. For some people, symptoms may last only a few months; for others, problems may persist indefinitely.

This diagnostic difficulty makes it hard to provide treatment for these individuals. A screening tool is used to identify some of the symptoms that may present themselves in the veteran. However, many of the symptoms can relate to conditions such as PTSD and depression, causing the brain injury itself to be overlooked. The symptoms may be so subtle they are missed by the injured person, fellow soldiers, or even medical personnel. Furthermore, symptoms may take days or weeks to appear. It has been reported that as many as 18% of the OIF/OEF soldiers have incurred an mTBI (Hoge *et al.*, 2008), a yet complicating factor is that 18.5% of returning service members meet criteria for PTSD or depression (Tanielian & Jaycox, 2008). Additionally, barely half of those who require care for these conditions actually seek out care, but only half of those individuals receive adequate care; there are tremendous gaps in need for mental health services and the receipt of that care (Tanielian & Jaycox, 2008). Therefore, the WRIISC screens again for TBI when the veteran is evaluated.

Treatment for mTBI differs from treatment for a moderate or severe TBI: a more severe injury generally includes a hospital stay followed by several weeks of inpatient rehabilitation with therapy from an interdisciplinary team. Incurring an mTBI generally does not require hospitalization, but may require some of the therapies indicated for those with more severe brain injuries at lesser intensity. Neuro-ophthalmologic examination may also be indicated to address issues the individual has with vision such as diplopia (double-vision) and blurring or difficulty in reading.

Some individuals benefit from medications following an mTBI. Anti-anxiety and/or antidepressants may be prescribed. Sleep medications are prescribed to re-establish regular sleep patterns. Medications are generally quickly tapered off with the support of the manual therapies (e.g. physical and occupation therapies), environmental supports (e.g. the use of an alarm clock to assist in the re-establishment of a sleep schedule), and social support (e.g. family members, social work, psychology) to reduce anxiety and depression.

Electronic Medical Record System and My HealtheVet

The VA has moved to an electronic medical record. Health care professionals within the VA are able to review veteran medical records, laboratory results, prescription history, and demographic and eligibility information from security-enabled desk top computers through a system called the Computerized Patient Record System (CPRS). It allows the clinician to check on orders for services regardless of where the veteran was seen. The system can also provide clinical reminders (e.g. complete TBI screen).

In 2005, as a complement to CPRS as a provider-based system, the VA introduced My HealtheVet (MHV), an e-health web-based portal. Veterans are able to manage their health care through this page by recording and tracking blood pressure, body weight, lab results, etc. This health history journal allows the veteran to record exercise, sleep, and dietary habits, and the results can be graphed to see progress. There are links to VA resources, record information on the providers seen, the treatment locations, and health insurance information. The most widely used section of MHV is the online pharmacy where veterans can refill prescriptions online and arrange for their home delivery.

Organization

The VA's vast health care system has shifted its focus from inpatient to outpatient programs that are more fiscally viable and outcome focused. VA's fiscal year 2009 spending is projected to be approximately $93.4 billion with $40 billion of that to health care alone. This covers programs and services in the VA's 153 medical centers (at least one in each state, Puerto Rico and the District of Columbia) divided into 23 separate but coordinated Veterans Integrated Service Networks (VISNs) or regions that provide care across the nation with more than 1,400 sites of care, including 909 ambulatory care and community-based outpatient clinics, 135 nursing homes, 47 residential rehabilitation treatment programs, 232 Veterans Centers and 108 comprehensive home-care programs (Department of Veterans Affairs, Office of Public Relations, November 2008). Almost 5.5 million people received care in VA health care facilities in fiscal year 2008, with 773, 600 being seen in VA inpatient facilities and the outpatient clinics registered over 60 million visits (Department of Veterans Affairs, Office of Public Relations, November 2008). The WRIISC evaluates about 125 veterans annually.

Decisions about practice

Description of the client

Captain Andy Long, a veteran of the OIF/OEF Conflict, served in Iraq for one tour of duty. He is a 47-year-old married white male who lives with his wife (Jean) of 20 years, and two children, Tim, age 17, and Beth, age 16. Prior to deployment, Andy was a police officer, but post-deployment he is unable to serve as a police officer; his memory lapses render him unable to hold any regular job. His wife is involved and supportive; however, she needs to work full-time to pay the mortgage and household expenses.

Andy learned about the WRIISC while he was attending an adjustment support group run by the VA for returning veterans. He self-referred to the program when he realized he met all of the criteria for admission. Andy continued to experience unexplained symptoms such as ringing in his ears, fatigue, and pain in different parts of his body after medical evaluation. Following an earlier psychiatric evaluation, he was diagnosed with PTSD; he experienced flashbacks of disturbing combat images, particularly one in which he killed an insurgent and another where an improvised explosive device hidden in a garbage can exploded near him. He reported nearly causing a traffic accident after his return home when he swerved to avoid a garbage can while experiencing a flashback. He also reported hypervigilance, irritability, and insomnia. Previous medical records were requested and staff noted some of the symptoms Andy reported that met the criteria for PTSD also met the criteria for TBI. Andy also was concerned that his ongoing pain and fatigue was related to his deployment-related experiences. Although he used prescribed medication for that pain, he reported no substance use for six months prior to the scheduled evaluation. He lived in a stable environment with the support of his family and was able to travel easily to the WRIISC for the evaluation.

Despite this, it took Andy nearly a year to agree to the evaluation at the WRIISC. He was proud of his experiences and leadership in the army and hoped he would be called for a second tour of duty in Iraq. He voiced a sense of responsibility for the unit he left in Iraq when he returned home following his injuries. He stayed in email and cellphone contact with those active duty soldiers, as well as some of the veterans who returned with him. Andy did not seem to realize that the constant contact with soldiers in Iraq and his overdeveloped sense of responsibility could be making his symptoms worse. His wife expressed concern about him. Also, his daughter Beth was "hanging out" with teens who were frequently in trouble with school administrators because of their defiant behaviors. Both Beth's and Tim's grades declined. Andy was concerned about his children. Having a parent deployed to an active combat area without a known date of return may be one of the most stressful experiences a child can have (Lincoln, Swift & Shorteno-Fraser, 2008); furthermore adolescents particularly may seem angry or act out (Stafford & Grady, 2003), as Andy and Jean observed with Beth.

Andy missed the "brotherhood" that existed with his police department colleagues. His fellow officers were concerned about his deployment, but were even more concerned when he returned from Iraq with physical injuries that would limit Andy's role as a police officer, as well as cognitive issues that further interfered. Andy was assigned a desk job, and, although unhappy in that role, he was aware of his deficits and that led to sadness and a sense of hopelessness. The chronic pain he dealt with from his injuries, coupled with his depression, led to alcohol abuse. Andy began drinking with friends and former co-workers in the evenings and weekends so he could still feel a part of his former world, and the numbing effects of the alcohol helped to reduce the physical and emotional pain he was feeling. He reported abstaining from all substances except his prescribed pain medication for six months prior to evaluation at the WRIISC as required, but this abstinence has been questioned.

Contracting, developing objectives and outcome measures

Following the comprehensive interdisciplinary team evaluation, objectives were set with Andy and his wife for further care. Because of Andy's inconsistent memory and awareness of deficits, I helped Andy address and follow through on the recommendations. Due to the delay in evaluation, Andy had adopted a new lifestyle around his deficits, challenging goal accomplishment. We recommended that Andy seek further evaluation of his back pain to assure the appropriateness of the dosage of his pain medication, and that he register for MHV so he could use that system to record and monitor his symptoms, particularly because of his concerns about his memory. We also discussed the symptoms of PTSD and recommended that he be seen in the specialized PTSD clinic. In addition, we educated Jean on PTSD and suggested that she might consider a support group for herself. Couples therapy was recommended at an earlier point, Jean reports, but they decided to stop and she chose not to share the reason. We suspected it may be that mTBI issues required some special attention and education, extending the usual period of reconnecting after deployment and forming a newer relationship (Erbes, Polusny, Macdermid & Compton, 2008).

Andy knew he had hit his head, but neither he nor his wife understood the potentially long-term consequences of that injury. Both believed time would return all of Andy's cognition and awareness, but the team needed to explain the etiology and the longer-term consequences of brain injury beyond the physical damage to the head, including effects on behavior, attitudes, and cognition. We presented this information knowing I would follow up with Andy and Jean

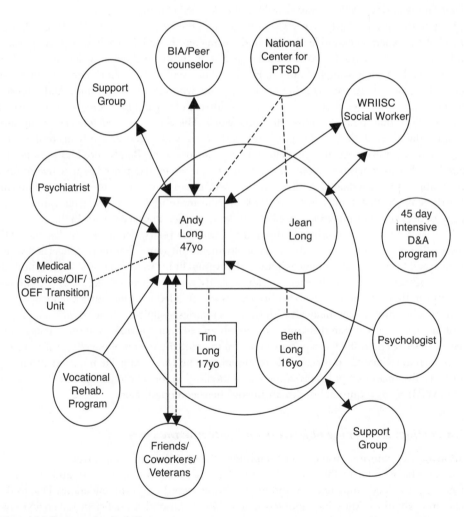

Figure 15.1 Ecomap for Andy Long.

to ensure they were connected to appropriate resources for support and ongoing education. The team internist recommended a referral to a psychiatrist to manage the medications for simultaneous treatment of the PTSD and the accompanying anxiety and depression, as well as the symptoms of brain injury that may sometimes be managed through medications. I was very concerned about Andy's vocational trajectory and recommended referral to vocational services within the VA. Also, I was concerned about Andy's children; I suggested that Jean follow up with the school district to see if she could find some support for them there.

Outcome measures for the WRIISC focus on how successfully the patient is able to follow up on recommendations made by the team. I am responsible for helping the veterans to negotiate any barriers that would inhibit their ability to achieve a goal or complete a recommendation. A full written report outlining the evaluation findings and recommendations from the inter-disciplinary team was sent to Andy within a week. The report is written in lay language to increase readability. With Andy's permission, the medical records were released to his other health providers, most importantly to his primary care physician. I called Andy to review and discuss the report, to answer any questions, and to reconnect Andy with the other team members as necessary. Smoking cessation was a team recommendation. From experience, I knew that when recommendations are not something the veteran wishes to comply with—such as smoking cessation, weight loss, or further counseling—I had to be prepared to reinforce the team recommendations and emphasize the benefits of compliance on health and wellbeing.

Many veterans live long distances from the VA, and commuting back may be difficult, so much follow-up contact is done by phone. Since Andy lived near the VA and was able to come to my office, we arranged for follow-up visits in my office. I find an office visit is particularly helpful if paperwork needs to be completed, resources need to be shared, or I want to have a better opportunity to interact with the veteran and his/her spouse. I often schedule these visits when the veteran has another appointment within the hospital center. It is during the telephone contacts or visits that I assess the veteran's progress towards treatment goals. This is documented in CPRS so the entire team can be aware of the progress.

Use of contract

The contract formed with WRIISC patients consists of the team recommendations in the summary evaluation record. Since they are recommendations, they are open to discussion and clarification, and they provide the roadmap to begin work. The actual contract to work with the social worker is verbal and implied as appointments or times for telephone contacts are established and the veteran follows up. This makes the initial contract fairly undefined, but following the first meeting after the receipt of the report, more specifics can be attached with respect to next steps. Andy had some immediate needs to attend to with respect to making appointments for medical and psychiatric follow-up; however, work with the couple about the meaning of the brain injury would need to evolve as I was able to explore their relationship more and to provide more education on brain injury and get them involved with a support group. My goals are to involve them both in support groups (separately), make a referral for Andy for vocational counseling, and to continue to educate him on his mTBI and provide other case management as necessary for Andy to meet the other team recommendations.

Meeting place

Andy liked to come into the VA to meet with me. He was being followed by a psychologist on a weekly basis so he would schedule time to see me when he came to see her. It seemed having the outside appointments gave him the structure in his day that was lacking because of his inability to work. Also, being able to come to the VA gave him a chance to potentially run into a fellow veteran for lunch, a cup of coffee, or just to catch up. This met his need for affiliation, even though his coming to my office met with some challenges; occasionally Andy would forget about the appointment, the location of my office, and one day had to call his wife for her to remind him of my name. This was very frustrating to him, but with the help of the psychologist, he was learning to write things down in a notebook to help his memory. Although he admitted to being embarrassed, he would tell me of his memory lapses which seemed to help him disassociate this new way of being from his old "normal" self. He was also hoping his memory would return to the way it was prior to the injuries. However, Andy's denial over his functional losses frequently found him angry, something Jean would complain about when we met. This type of coping through denial and anger is very common in those with mTBI (Rosenthal, 1999).

Use of time

Time at the WRIISC is limited by the one-day face-to-face evaluation period; however, given the use of the telephone as a main source for follow-up, time becomes much more flexible for the social worker and the client. During the day of evaluation, I complete a 30-minute evaluation with the veteran. I am able to review any medical records in CPRS and any of the intake materials completed by the veteran. The overall period of relationship with many of the WRIISC veterans may be just 30 minutes of evaluation time and a final team meeting, but others require some intermittent or ongoing contact. It is important to note that, if the veteran appears to need intensive case management services (i.e. impending homelessness, extreme family dysfunction), the case would be referred to a social worker/case manager within the VA who specifically is able to provide those intensive services. Follow-up with WRIISC veterans is at one week, three months, and six months, generally via the telephone.

Strategies and interventions

Overall, I take an integrative, pragmatic case management approach in working with the WRIISC-evaluated veterans that involves interdisciplinary team collaboration. On the day of evaluation I serve as the team member who follows up and ties the pieces of the evaluation together for the veteran as recommendations are reviewed. However, my role becomes the leader in the follow-up, facilitating service brokering and coordination.

Stance of the social worker

Working with a client with a TBI and PTSD is complex. Bryant (2008) suggested damage of the prefrontal cortex in TBI and the disturbance in the neural networks that facilitate regulation of anxiety may contribute to enhanced emotional reactions to trauma. Furthermore, Bryant also notes mTBI can increase the incidence of PTSD because the brain injury can reduce the cognitive resources needed to employ appropriate cognitive strategies to cope with psychological trauma, such as being able to assess a situation for its true threat. Additionally, the literature suggests many of the ongoing sequelae of mTBI (e.g. headache, depression, poor attention span) may also be attributed to psychological stress (Rosenthal, 1999). These are important pieces of information for me be aware of with a case like Andy's.

Reframing helps the client with a TBI to integrate the old self-concept with the new realities of his or her life (Baker, Tandy & Dixon, 2002). For Andy this meant he had to learn to accept help when he needed it, keep a memory book for recording important dates and information, and to have a more realistic sense of goals for himself, knowing his reactions are different now with his mTBI. Learning to do some of these tasks helps Andy cope with his situation better which, in turn, helps his wife and family. Consistency and keeping the process as simple as possible (Folzer, 2001), being careful not to demean or treat the client in a child-like manner, frequent use of positive feedback on steps taken towards the therapeutic goals are also helpful. Keeping a "memory book" or notebook of thoughts, appointment schedules, and other details helps to focus Andy and reduce his anxiety when he can quickly look up something rather than struggle to remember. Together, the psychologist and I work on reinforcing the use of the memory book.

Overall, I keep a directive stance with lots of points in clarifying agreements with respect to goal achievement because Andy would frequently forget steps we had agreed on. A significant concern was his starting to drink again as he struggled to cope with his deficits. In conversation with the psychologist, his physician, and the OIF/OEF coordinator, it was concluded that a referral to a substance abuse program would be a good next step but that program also needed to be familiar with working with someone with mTBI. Fortunately, the VA system supports such a program, so he was referred to a 45-day intensive substance abuse program. His next step will be that program once a slot opens for him to attend.

Use of outside resources

A referral to the Brain Injury Association of America (BIA) (Brain Injury Association, 2008), a valuable resource for ongoing education and support needs, was made immediately, to supplement the VA-based resources. Nearly every state has a BIA office, or at least a contact for further information. Another very valuable resource is the National Center for PTSD (Department of Veterans Affairs, 2007), which offers a toll-free hotline and website filled with information for veterans and their families, as well as for professionals, including information on PTSD and TBI combined.

Andy continues in the same initial support group, with that group setting allowing him the opportunity for reality orientation and to practice his psychosocial skills (e.g. holding conversations where he might have to look up an item in his memory book). Research shows that someone like Andy may feel a greater incentive to change when he sees others share common issues (Folzer, 2001). Jean was also referred to a support group where she is able to gain support, receive information, ventilation, and learn new coping mechanisms (Folzer, 2001) when dealing with some of the issues related to TBI she is experiencing in Andy and within her family; both will receive counseling within the intensive substance abuse program.

Reassessment, transfer or termination

Reassessment of the therapeutic work occurs after nearly every session with Andy as he visits about once a month. I review my last entry in CPRS where I note my progress on my goals of referral for vocational counseling, support groups for Andy and Jean, and any education I provide on brain injury and other resources I use or referrals I make. I also review any new notes prepared by other providers for my next meeting with Andy. I open the sessions with Andy with a careful review of the last session. The more careful review is needed due to Andy's memory problems. Andy has kept his notes in his memory book as he prepares for each session.

Together we review his notes and discuss mutually agreed upon goals for the current session. Termination of our relationship will come when the original goals are met, and when he attends the substance abuse treatment program. He is also receiving some additional support now from a peer-counselor through the BIA, who is also a veteran with a TBI.

Differential discussion

Working with Andy and his family was somewhat limited by the policy of the VA and the mission of the WRIISC. Family therapy may have worked well in addressing issues Andy and Jean might have had with their teenage children. The role of the family in helping an individual adjust to the injury is an important one, with the role of the social worker providing adjustment counseling and referrals of community support and resources (Degeneffe, 2001). I needed to be aware of the multifaceted nature of mTBI as it is experienced within a family system, as I mediate between care systems. I frequently find myself educating the referral sources I'm in touch with regarding mTBI.

References

Baker, K. A., Tandy, C. C. & Dixon, D. R. (2002). Traumatic brain injury: A social worker primer with implications for practice. *Journal of Social Work in Disability & Rehabilitation*, 1 (4): 25–42.

Batten, S. V. & Pollack, S. J. (2008). Integrative outpatient treatment for returning service members. *Journal of Clinical Psychology*, 64 (8): 928–39.

Brain Injury Association. (2008). Brain injury association of America. Retrieved 12 November 2008, from http://www.biausa.org/index.html

Bryant, R. A. (2008). Disentangling mild traumatic brain injury and stress reactions. *New England Journal of Medicine*, 358 (5): 525–7.

Centers for Disease Control and Prevention. (2008). *Facts for physicians*. Retrieved 10 November 2008, from http://www.cdc.gov/ncipc/tbi/Facts_for_Physicians_booklet.pdf

Degeneffe, C. E. (2001). Family caregiving and traumatic brain injury. *Health & Social Work*, 26 (4): 257–68.

Department of Veterans Affairs. (2007). National center for PTSD. Retrieved 4 December 2008, from http://www.ncptsd.va.gov/ncmain/index.jsp

Department of Veterans Affairs, Office of Public Relations. (November 2008). Facts about the Department of Veterans Affairs. Retrieved 13 November 2008, from http://www1.va.gov/opa/fact/docs/vafacts.doc

Erbes, C. R., Polusny, M. A., Macdermid, S. & Compton, J. S. (2008). Couple therapy with combat veterans and their partners. *Journal of Clinical Psychology*, 64 (8): 972–83.

Folzer, S. M. (2001). Psychotherapy with "mild" brain-injured patients. *American Journal of Orthopsychiatry*, 71 (2): 245–51.

Hoge, C. W., Castro, C. A., Messer, S. C., McGurk, D., Cotting, D. I. & Koffman, R. L. (2004). Combat duty in Iraq and Afghanistan, mental health problems, and barriers to care. *New England Journal of Medicine*, 351 (1): 13–22.

Hoge, C. W., McGurk, D., Thomas, J. L., Cox, A. L., Engel, C. C. & Castro, C. A. (2008). Mild traumatic brain injury in U.S. soldiers returning from Iraq. *New England Journal of Medicine*, 358 (5): 453–63.

Jones, E., Fear, N. T. & Wessely, S. (2007). Shell shock and mild traumatic brain injury: A historical review. *American Journal of Psychiatry*, 164 (11): 1641–5.

Lincoln, A., Swift, E. & Shorteno-Fraser, M. (2008). Psychological adjustment and treatment of children and families with parents deployed in military combat. *Journal of Clinical Psychology*, 64 (8): 984–92.

Marcell, A. V., Klein, J. D., Fischer, I., Allan, M. J. & Kokotailo, P. K. (2002). Male adolescent use of health care services: Where are the boys? *Journal of Adolescent Health*, 30 (1): 35–43.

Mild Traumatic Brain Injury Committee of the Head Injury Interdisciplinary Special Interest Group of the American Congress of Rehabilitation Medicine. (1993). Definition of mild traumatic brain injury. *Journal of Head Trauma Rehabilitation*, 8 (3): 86–7.

Moran, M. (2008). Independent report spotlights war's MH devastation. *Psychiatry News*, 43 (10): 1–24.

Rosenthal, M. (ed.). (1999). *Rehabilitation of the adult and child with traumatic brain injury.* Philadelphia: FA Davis.

Stafford, E. M. & Grady, B. A. (2003). Military family support. *Pediatric Annals*, 32 (2): 110–15.

Tanielian, T. & Jaycox, L. H. (eds.). (2008). *Invisible wounds of war: Psychological and cognitive injuries, their consequences, and services to assist recovery.* Santa Monica, CA: Rand Corporation.

WRIISC. (2006). War related illness and injury study center. Retrieved 11/13/08, from http://www.wri.med.va.gov/index.html

Part 1.4

INDIVIDUAL AND FAMILY WORK

The elderly

16 The case of Junior

A study of collaboration, boundaries, and use of self

Renee C. Cunningham-Ginchereau
and Carol Perrot

Context

Policy

Junior was a consumer in the In Home Support Program (IHSP) at Center in the Park (CIP). The IHSP is a 10-year-old program created by the Philadelphia Corporation for Aging (PCA), the Area Agency on Aging for Philadelphia and administered through five senior centers of which CIP is one. According to a nationwide, independent evaluating and consulting group, it is the only program of its kind in the country. PCA controls the program's procedures, eligibility criteria, and administration, and it audits sites regularly to ensure compliance regarding intake procedures, documentation, appropriateness of services, timeliness and accuracy of paperwork, proper fiscal management of the Discretionary Fund budget and the overall contract budget. PCA gives us our mandate to practice.

Important federal policies that relate to Junior's care are those of the Department of Housing and Urban Development (HUD)'s rules and regulations that govern the eligibility and occupancy requirements of Section 202 buildings; Medicare, in relation to the length of time, terms and conditions under which he could stay in the hospital; and Medicaid in relation to the conditions of payment for nursing home care.

Technology

PCA's database holds information regarding demographics, contacts, care plans, program use, care managers, and home visit schedules for every PCA client. Each care manager must enter client contact information within 24 hours. All contact logs and tracking dates are monitored. This is a relatively new process, and, at the time of my work with Junior, only the demographic information was entered into the database. All contact logs, assessments, and care plans were done manually and maintained in the case file.

Organization

CIP is a nationally accredited non-profit senior community center whose mission is to promote positive aging and foster community connections for older adults whose voices are critical instruments in shaping our activities and direction. We provide programs and classes for older adults who are physically able to come to the Center and social services for older adults who are homebound and in need of assistance maintaining their independence in the community. This is accomplished through a variety of programs such as the IHSP, Housing

Counseling Program, Service Coordination at two area senior housing buildings, and Center Counseling.

CIP has over 6,000 members ranging in age from 55 to 102, including 500 who are homebound. We draw the majority (over 77%) of our membership from the six immediately surrounding zip codes, as well as the Greater Philadelphia area. Approximately 40% of older adults in the neighborhood live alone, compared with about 30% of all Philadelphia elders; about 25% live in poverty (double the statewide average). Current demographics show that a little over 95% of CIP's participants served during the last year were 60 + years of age and 90% are African American. With regard to gender, 82% are female and 18% are male.

The demographics of IHSP consumers closely mirror those of the Center participants. Its goals are to help older adults to "get back on their feet," maintain independence in their homes and prevent further deterioration (Alkema, Reyes & Wilber, 2006; Cantrell, 2007). To qualify for IHSP services, older adults must be over 60 years old, homebound, and able to independently perform their own activities of daily living, i.e. bathing, dressing, grooming, etc. Services can be short-term or ongoing, as needed.

The program uses a "discretionary fund," provided by PCA and managed by each site, to deliver those services the consumer and care manager agree are needed. All services need approval by the CIP supervisor who first seeks approval of the IHSP Specialist at PCA. Consumers are reassessed for continued appropriateness on a yearly basis and events-based reassessments are done on an as-needed basis.

Each IHSP site has its own Intake Worker. A prospective consumer is screened for appropriateness and the case is assigned to a care manager for an initial assessment conducted in the consumer's home. Contact patterns vary according to the estimated length of time a case will be open; consumers whose cases are deemed to be long-term must be called every three months at minimum and visited twice per year, with an annual reassessment.

I consult and coordinate closely with the Visiting Nurse Association of Greater Philadelphia (VNA), an independent non-profit home care agency serving Philadelphia and its surrounding areas (Polivka & Zayac, 2008). This Medicare-approved agency employs a Community Liaison whose job it is to identify isolated individuals who need home care services in order to safely stay in their residences as long as physically possible. To do this, the liaison assembles as many community resources as necessary. Clients are often referred by community social workers like me, family members, and neighbors. Services are provided with clients' consent and authorization from their physicians and medical insurance. Often these entities are not in agreement. Once services can be arranged they are offered to the client. Clients like Junior often reject service with the intention of trying to maintain their independence for as long as possible. When clients are discharged from the VNA's home care program, the agency keeps touch with the client and is ready to resume services when appropriate.

Description of the client situation

Junior, a consumer in the IHSP, had been receiving home-delivered meals, occasional housekeeping services and financial assistance with past due bills for three years. Since I had supervised his previous care manager, I was very familiar with his situation, had met him and reviewed his file. When I became his care manager, I was the Senior Supervisor of CIP's Social Services Department supervising six IHSP social workers, the Family Caregiver Support Program supervisor and the secretary, and I followed a small caseload of consumers with complicated issues needing specialized attention and multi-system coordination.

Decisions about practice

Definition of the client

Junior was a 72-year-old homebound African American man who suffered from non-insulin-dependent diabetes, hypertension, mild short-term memory loss, arthritis, allergies, and lower extremity edema which was a direct result of congestive heart failure (CHF). He smoked cigarettes and had been in alcoholism recovery for many years. During the time we worked together, he admitted he also battled a crack addiction, and until recently had been actively smoking crack for years. Junior received a modest amount of social security income and lived by himself in a senior housing complex. A retired sanitation worker, he was forced to leave his job due to a leg injury he sustained while working. The apartment that Junior lived in was an HUD 202 building. As a consequence, his rent (with most utilities included) was subsidized and could never exceed 30% of his income.

Family was vitally important to Junior. His older brother Thomas was in his 80s, wheelchair bound, and lived in a nursing home. He and Junior spoke on the telephone every morning and, until Thomas had several toes amputated due to complications from diabetes, he would stay with Junior on the weekends. Junior was also close to an older sister, Thelma, with whom he spoke regularly, and to Thelma's children, especially one son, John.

Junior had been divorced for many years and had fathered five children. He had been close to his only son who died of a drug overdose two years prior to our working together. Now, he was only close to one daughter, Sandra, to whom he spoke regularly. She lived out of state, visited him monthly, and had often asked Junior to move in with her and her family so that she could better assist him with meal preparation, laundry, and other activities that were difficult for him. Junior continually declined her offer. Sandra and John provided the most support urging Junior to keep medical appointments, and providing emotional support and socialization. Because Junior's basic needs were not being met he was referred to our program, to which Sandra had referred him years before for home-delivered meals.

During my work with Junior, I spoke to Sandra several times on the telephone and worked closely with John. Both confided their frustrations with Junior. He was a proud man who relished his independence and was reluctant to accept help from family and outside entities. Junior and I developed a strong bond and had an excellent rapport. His faith in me and trust in our relationship made it possible for me to have a significant impact on his life. Because of our relationship, I was able to convince him to make positive changes.

Junior and I began our work together with many barriers to our relationship. Junior was an older African American man and I was a white woman who was young enough to be his grandchild. There were great differences in our education and life experience, as well (Isaacs & Schroeder, 2004; Nath, Hirschman, Lewis & Strumpf, 2008). In order to work effectively with Junior, I had to have an understanding of the effects of oppression, discrimination, the impact of the Civil Rights Movement and life before it, the role and dynamics of family, and the importance of kinship; religiosity, church affiliation and pastoral relationship; and the physical and mental health disparities that exist for African American older adults (Institute of Medicine, 2003; Nelson-Becker & Canda, 2008) because they affect a person's life and decision making.

The other key to establishing a positive relationship with Junior was authenticity and a sincere desire to help. Junior trusted me because he knew I was invested in his health and wellbeing, that I believed he could overcome the challenges facing him, and that I would do whatever I could to help him. We worked together in an equal and friendly partnership, discussing things of mutual interest such as sports and music, and I used self-disclosure to help him to feel less like a client and more like a partner (Dewane, 2006). My role as Junior's advocate was a central part of our work, and my efforts on his behalf helped to strengthen his trust in me. Junior often made poor decisions and neglected his own health and environment, yet he was competent to make those choices. I agreed Junior would be better off in a more structured environment, such as his daughter's home, where someone could prompt him to take his medicine, eat properly, and generally care well for himself (Lauder, Roxburgh, Harris & Law, 2009).

I had to remember that when Junior made a bad decision it did not mean he lacked the capacity to make a good one. Despite the fact the decisions he made were often poor and in direct conflict with his objectives, he had the right to choose how he wanted to live. Although I did not agree with some of his decisions, I respected his right to make them and defended that right whenever it was threatened. That said, I also knew it was my responsibility to point out to Junior occasions when his decisions conflicted with his own objectives and how they jeopardized his ability to live independently. I also used his trust in me and respect for my position to try to convince him to make better choices.

Goals

Junior lived alone, and the goal that was most important to him was maintaining his independence. All of the objectives set forth by his family, physicians and me had in some way to further this goal. My goal as his social worker, however, was conditional; I could only support his living in the community as long as I knew it to be safe for him to live independently. As Junior's health and circumstances deteriorated, I had to amend this goal.

Junior's other stated goals were to stay in the IHSP and retain me as his care manager. Junior had worked with three different IHSP care managers prior to our work together. I was careful to make sure Junior understood the parameters of the IHSP and that he knew he would be in the program as long as he continued to be eligible. I assured him I would maintain our relationship and would always do whatever I could to advocate for him and assist him in any way possible. This response showed poor disengagement; however, I felt justified in doing so, because, in addition to being Junior's case manager, I was also the supervisor for the program and had more latitude and authority, and also because I felt genuine feelings of friendship toward Junior and wanted to do whatever I could for him, whether inside or outside the confines of the program. *boundaries*

Developing objectives and contracting

Various objectives were established and addressed. The main objectives were to keep his apartment clean, better maintain his health, ensure he received proper nutrition, and make sure his bills were paid in a timely fashion. All of these objectives, if met, would ensure the achievement of his goal to maintain his independence. Many significant crises and challenges were barriers to reaching those objectives. Each time a crisis arose he and I would contract verbally and assign specific tasks and responsibilities to get back on track. For example, I would agree to negotiate a payment arrangement for a past-due utility company bill and he would agree to make a doctor's appointment. This was done on an as-needed basis.

In the time his case was active, Junior was able to meet many objectives. When we first opened his case we ordered home-delivered meals because he was unable to prepare his own meals. We also purchased furniture for his apartment because he was sleeping on a mattress on the floor and had only milk crates to sit on. At the time I began working with Junior, he had been mugged while walking several blocks to purchase money orders to pay his bills. To cover the stolen money I was able to have his rent and utilities paid through the IHSP.

Junior's health and functional ability began to deteriorate and his ability to remain safely in the community was called into question. He often visited me in the office, which would have jeopardized his eligibility for the IHSP had his case been reviewed by PCA. On one particular day, Junior arrived nearly breathless, his vision was blurred and his legs were swollen such that he could not get his socks on and had to leave his shoes untied. He told me he had two doctor's appointments on this day (cardiologist and optometrist) and wanted my opinion on which appointment he should keep. Junior was reluctant to go to the cardiologist because he was afraid he would be admitted to the hospital. He was adamant he did not want to be admitted and had signed himself out against medical advice on previous occasions.

Furthermore, Junior was afraid that he would be forced to go into a nursing home. Junior had been told by doctors during previous hospital stays that they were concerned about his capacity to make decisions and felt he was unable to live on his own. His nephew John also threatened to "put him away" in a nursing home. I was able to convince him to go to the cardiologist but had to promise I would advocate for him should anyone call his competency into question. Afraid he would not make it to the appointment in his current state, I drove him to the cardiologist and informed them of his current condition, noting I was afraid he had CHF. The doctor determined Junior was indeed in severe congestive heart failure. He was not admitted to the hospital and was instead sent home with a very complicated regimen of medications, mostly diuretics. Given his state when he arrived at the cardiologist, his complex medical conditions and new diagnosis, I was incredulous that he was not admitted.

When he arrived home, he called and said he could not read the medication bottles he had been given because his vision was still very blurry, likely a sign that his blood sugar was unstable. I contacted Carol Perrot, RN, Community Liaison from the VNA for consultation, support, and to try to get an emergency home care visit from a nurse to assist him in setting up his meds. Carol agreed Junior should have been admitted and contacted the cardiologist to get an order for home care so she could go to Junior's home, check his vitals, and set up his medications. The cardiologist refused to approve the order, stating that she "went against her better judgment by allowing him to leave and not admitting him," said he needed to be in the hospital, and advised that he go to the emergency room. In over 15 years as a home visiting nurse, this was the first time Carol ever experienced a doctor refusing to approve home care.

I attempted to convince Junior to go to the emergency room and, given the urgency, advised he take an ambulance. He refused, wanting to protect his privacy and not wanting the people who lived in the building to think he was frail. Carol and I both tried unsuccessfully to reach Junior's primary care physician to approve the home care. Junior was not speaking to his nephew John and would not allow me to call him, vaguely mentioning that they were having "problems." His daughter was also unavailable. I called Junior's neighbor, Ernestine, and asked her to read me the medication bottles and I instructed her about which pills to give him immediately and which pills to set out on the counter for the evening. Junior said he felt okay and promised he would call 911 if he started to feel sick. Ernestine promised to look in on him.

When I called him the next day, there was a woman yelling in the background. I asked him who was there and he indicated that it was the woman who "cleaned the apartment" and that she wanted money and drugs. I told Junior to instruct her to leave. He did, she refused, and I told him I was on my way to the apartment. I do not know what I thought I was going to do when I got there, but she left before I had to find out.

I had a talk with Junior about his deteriorating health and his need to get immediate medical treatment. I spoke frankly to him and told him if he did not get treatment he was going to die. He agreed to go but only if I took him. It was on our ride to the ER that he confessed to me that he smoked crack and that his nephew, John was the person who gave it to him. John allegedly gave crack to both Junior and the "woman who cleaned the apartment" so she would "look after" him. We spent the day in the emergency room and he was admitted.

After his stay in the hospital, Junior required oxygen and a higher level of care than we could provide. I facilitated his transfer to a long-term care program through PCA, and continued to work with him and his new social worker informally and, shortly after his transfer, it became clear he was no longer able to live safely on his own. We discussed nursing home placement and he agreed to enter a facility, provided he could be with his brother Thomas.

Meeting place

Because IHSP clients are homebound, we are required to do home visits. Homebound does not mean the client is completely unable to leave the home, but that it is difficult for them and they require assistance to do so. Because Junior often took the bus to CIP and walked from the bus stop to my office he would, by pure definition, not be appropriate for the IHSP. If, at the time of my work with him, the contact logs were done in the PCA database, they would have been closely monitored by PCA and it is most likely that I would have been forced to close his case. The lack of a computerized tracking database at the time worked in my favor and I made the decision to keep Junior's case open, knowing I would have a lot of explaining to do if that case was ever audited.

If I had given in to the urge to do Junior's reassessment in my office during one of his "drop in" visits and had not visited his home, I would have never gotten a clear picture of his situation. My initial visit shocked me: his apartment smelled strongly of urine, there were blood stains on his sheets, he had no food in his cabinets and the only thing in his refrigerator was a plate of rotten food and a few frozen meals from the IHSP. These are things he would have been ashamed to admit if we had only met in my office.

Use of time

Junior's case had been open for approximately four years and I worked with him for approximately one year. Though the IHSP requires phone contact every three months and two home visits per year, a client's circumstances often dictate more frequent contact. I spoke to Junior weekly, sometimes daily, and, when in crisis, several times a day. In the year we worked together, he probably visited me in my office four times, and I visited him in his home three times, and twice at the hospital. The average length of our visits was about an hour, with some visits only lasting 30 minutes and others lasting several hours.

Strategies and interventions

The IHSP employs a strengths-based model (Greene & Cohen, 2005; Lietz, 2009) and, primarily, short-term, solution-focused work (Fast & Chapin, 2000). Thus, I drew on Junior's past experiences in overcoming difficult circumstances in order to help him make positive changes to maintain his independence. When he was going through a difficult situation, I asked him what had been done in the past when a similar situation arose. In order to help Junior draw on his strengths, I had us discuss previous situations where he was able to overcome an obstacle.

Unfortunately, Junior's old ways of coping were maladaptive. For example, he noted that when he had faced difficult situations in the past he often drank or did drugs in an effort to avoid the conflict and its potentially painful resolution. We discussed more functional solutions and, in that way, Junior was able to actively participate in the decision-making process, arrive at solutions that would improve his situation, and to the extent possible, remain in control of his circumstances.

Stance of the social worker

I took on many roles in my work with Junior: conciliator, when he was at odds with his family; mediator, when he was in danger of eviction; interpreter, when I explained his medical conditions and medications; and advocate, when the hospital staff wrongfully said he was incompetent. I thought I was a police officer when I sped to his apartment to remove a crack addict from his apartment, and I organized his bills, arranged to have his apartment cleaned, and delivered messages to his brother Thomas, who worried when Junior did not answer the phone. In many regards, what Junior and I developed was a friendship, what felt to me to be a natural byproduct of helping even though questions of inherent authority and power mitigate against real equality (Schwartz & Williams, 1998). At the time I was working with Junior, I was still developing my professional identity. I found it difficult to remain professional at all times. I liked Junior and I felt a personal stake in his wellbeing. It was important to Junior that I was a "real person" and not just a service provider (Cooper & Lesser, 2002; Raines, 1996).

Use of resources outside of the helping relationship

Junior's extended network of family and service providers was both helpful and problematic: in some cases these individuals and agencies truly helped him, in other cases they provided little concrete support and some created barriers to Junior's goals and objectives. In the ecomap on page 200, solid lines indicate an active helping relationship, and dashed lines indicate a problematic relationship. The presence and/or direction of arrows show the flow of information and/or support.

It may seem unusual to show the primary care physician (PCP) and cardiologist relationships as problematic; however, both physicians made it very difficult for Junior to maintain his wellbeing. The cardiologist chose not to admit Junior. After allowing him to leave, and knowing he lived on his own, she gave him a regimen of medications Junior was clearly not capable of following. Realizing the mistake, she refused to authorize home care for Junior when that could have made a great difference in his ability to comply and remain independent. During this time I also made many emergency calls to the PCP's office in an effort to relay Junior's rapid physical decline. The PCP showed no appreciation of the urgency and severity of Junior's health crisis, provided no advice or support to either Junior or me and, by the time he authorized home care through VNA, Junior was already hospitalized.

As mentioned above, I worked very closely with Carol Perrot, the Community Liaison nurse from the VNA. In the situation that precipitated Junior's hospitalization, she affirmed that the health care system was failing Junior. If I had not intervened and taken him to the emergency room, Junior would have died. Carol educated me about his medical conditions and how the lack of medical attention, improper nutrition, drug use and poor self-care were impacting his overall health. She tried desperately to help me to navigate the health care system by speaking with his doctors and the hospital social workers. We had worked closely on several cases and her guidance was always invaluable. In my work with Junior she provided

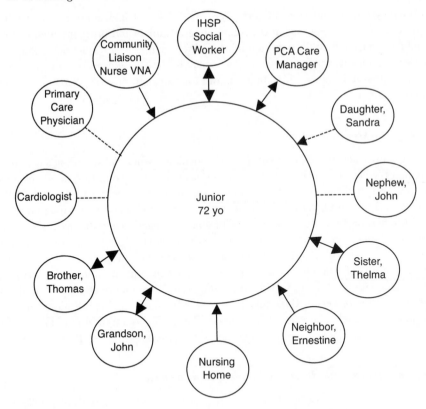

Figure 16.1 Ecomap for Junior.

me the greatest support.

When it became clear he should no longer live on his own, I knew a nursing home was the safest, most suitable place for Junior. Although I had already closed his case, I worked with his new social worker at PCA to give Junior all the information, pro and contra, to make that decision. Junior was willing to go into a nursing home if he could be with his brother. My mother worked there and spoke to the admissions department and helped facilitate Junior's admission to the nursing home. Junior was comforted to know he would be with his brother, and was pleased to know my mother would be there to look in on him.

Reassessment and evaluation

During my work with Junior I conducted one official reassessment, within the timeframe specified by the IHSP. Junior and I were able to meet all of his objectives which were concrete and measurable, making it easy to determine what needed to be done in order to achieve them. While he did eventually go into a nursing home, we met his goal for as long as we could.

Transfer and termination

When Junior was released from the hospital, it was clear his needs had changed and a higher level of care was warranted. I had to refer him to PCA for a long-term care program. I was clear in our ongoing discussion of his needs that this may happen and, though he did not want to lose me as his social worker, he understood and agreed he needed more assistance than the IHSP could provide. PCA assessed him and assigned him to an appropriate program. After his services began, I closed the case.

Reviewing his closed file would only give you a taste of what Junior went through, and what I went through with him. No question in the assessment asks about the client/care manager relationship. No form captures the fact that I sat in the emergency room with Junior all day, or that this man, who was in serious congestive heart failure and in withdrawal from crack, offered to give me his seat. There is no place to write that Junior touched and broke my heart with his hardships and his ways. Closing his case was difficult for me.

Case conclusion

Junior remained in the community for approximately one month before he entered the nursing home. He did well and lived there with his brother Thomas for another three years before he died as a result of complications from CHF.

Differential discussion

If I had been asked when I closed Junior's case if I would have changed anything, in my hubris I would have said there was nothing I would do differently. Nevertheless, experience, training and education have given me a new perspective. I should have looked into whether or not he was eligible for disability income as a result of his work-related injury. I should have conducted a home visit much sooner than I did. I would have had a better understanding of the severity of Junior's situation and could have begun adding services sooner. I should never have driven to his apartment to chase out the cantankerous crack addict; I should have had Junior call the police to have her removed for trespassing. As a supervisor, I would never have allowed my social workers to conduct themselves in that way. It was a rash decision, showing poor judgment, a lack of professionalism, a lack of boundaries, and a lack of regard for my own safety. When I found out Junior's nephew John was supplying him with crack, I could have called the police, and I could have called Older Adult Protective Services. I did not do these things because I allowed my relationship with Junior to cloud my professional judgment. He asked me not to report John, and I was afraid of how it would affect him. I was concerned for his safety when John found out, and I was afraid it would do irreparable damage to my relationship with Junior.

What I think about most in this case is my use of self and the setting of boundaries. I believe my self-disclosure and the posture I took with Junior, coupled with my genuine desire to help him, is what made our bond so strong. Furthermore, I credit this bond with the successful outcome of the case. I truly believe Junior would have died if he had not come to see me the day I took him to the hospital (another breach, as we have a rule against transferring clients in our own vehicles). In an effort to show Junior friendship, I compromised some of my authority and professionalism. I should have been more aware of myself, more in tune with how Junior made me feel, and what impact our working relationship had on me. Had I been more aware of these triggers, I would likely have conducted myself differently and would not have become so personally involved with him. As it is, Junior and I had a profound effect on each other, both personally and professionally. I learned much from our work together.

References

Alkema, G. E., Reyes, J. Y. & Wilber, K. H. (2006). Characteristics associated with home and community-based service utilization for Medicare managed care consumers. *The Gerontologist*, 46 (2): 173–82.

Cantrell, R. L. (2007). Common care: Toward a more acceptable option of care for the frail elderly. *Social Work in Public Health*, 23 (1): 61–73.

Cooper, M. & Lesser, J. (2002). *Clinical social work practice: An integrated approach*. Needham Heights, MA: Allyn & Bacon.

Dewane, C. (2006). Use of self: A primer revisited. *Clinical Social Work Journal*, 34 (4): 543–58.

Fast, B. & Chapin, R. (2000). *Strengths-based care management for older adults*. Health Professions Press, Inc.

Greene, R. R. & Cohen, H. L. (2005). Social work with older adults and their families: Changing practice paradigms. *Families in Society*, 86 (3): 367–74.

Institute of Medicine (2003). *Unequal treatment: Confronting racial and ethnic disparities in health care*. Washington, D.C.: National Academies Press.

Isaacs, S. L. & Schroeder, S. A. (2004). Class—The ignored determinant of the nation's health. *New England Journal of Medicine*, 35 (11): 1137–42.

Lauder, W., Roxburgh, M., Harris, J. & Law, J. (2009). Developing self-neglect theory: An analysis of related and atypical cases of people identified as self-neglecting. *Journal of Psychiatric and Mental Health Nursing*, 16 (5): 447–54.

Lietz, C. A. (2009). Establishing evidence for strengths-based interventions? Reflections from Social Work's research conference. *Social Work*, 54 (1): 85–7.

Nath, S. B., Hirschman, K. B., Lewis, B. & Strumpf, N. E. (2008). A place called LIFE: Exploring advance care planning of African American PACE enrollees. *Social Work in Health Care*, 47 (3): 277–92.

Nelson-Becker, H. & Canda, E. R. (2008). Spirituality, religion and aging research in social work: State of the art and future possibilities. *Spirituality and Social Work*, 20 (3): 177–93.

Polivka, L. & Zayac, H. (2008). The aging network and managed long-term care. *The Gerontologist*, 48 (5): 564–9. IA.

Raines, A. C. (1996). Self disclosure in clinical social work. *Clinical Social Work Journal*, 24, 357–75.

Schwartz, M. & Williams, J. (1998). Treatment boundaries in the case management relationship: A clinical case discussion. *Community Mental Health Journal*, 34: 1–13.

17 A framework for working with people with early-stage dementia

A relationship-focused approach to counseling

Phyllis Braudy Harris
and Kathleen "Casey" Durkin

> *"One of the things about this [Alzheimer disease] is—it's in the family and the family has not only me and my wife, but we have our children and the children have their spouses"*
>
> (Henderson & Andrews, 1998, p. 65).

Context

Over the last 15 years, the approach of health care professionals working with people in early-stage dementia and their families has evolved from first working mainly with family members, to then focusing on the needs of the person, to now working with the whole family structure in a relationship-centered (versus a caregiver-centered or person-centered) approach (Harris & Keady, 2006). This chapter discusses the clinical case of a man who referred himself to counseling for assistance in dealing with the impact of a diagnosis of Alzheimer's disease (AD) on himself and his family. Dementia is a clinical syndrome and an all-encompassing term used to connote a loss of memory and other cognitive abilities. It is caused by a variety of conditions, with AD being the most common cause of dementia. AD is a progressive irreversible dementia estimated to affect 5.2 million people currently in the U.S. and 11–16 million by 2050, if prevention or effective treatment is not possible. The prevalence of AD doubles every five-year interval beyond the age of 65, and the U.S. Census Bureau estimated that beginning in 2006 the baby boomer population started to turn 60 at a rate of 330 persons every hour (Alzheimer's Association, 2008a; Herbert *et al.*, 2003; NIA, 2006). Thus AD is a significant and mounting concern for older adults, their families and the community and The National Institutes of Health has labeled this disease a "Looming National Crisis."

Policy

Working with dementia sufferers and their families takes place within this growing public concern and national awareness about AD; when listening to older adults one of their biggest admitted fears is "losing their memory" (Patrick, Starks, Cain, Uhlmann & Pearlman, 1994; Phinney, 2002). However, unlike the European Union (EU), there is no policy effort on the part of the U.S. government to make Alzheimer's disease and other dementias a public health priority. On 18 December, 2008, the Council of the EU drafted a policy statement calling for European countries to make Alzheimer's disease a top public health priority and to provide resources and support to people with dementia, their families and caregivers (Council of the

European Union, 2008). Without such national recognition and support, American families often shoulder much of the burden of health care costs for dementia. In 2007, the economic cost of providing dementia care by family members alone was estimated to be $89 billion (Alzheimer's Association, 2008a). Nine million people care for a family member with dementia and 75% of dementia care is provided solely by family members (Uhlenberg & Cheuk, 2008). Medicare and Medicaid cover some of the costs of medical, nursing home, and drug prescription costs. However, with the rapid graying of the U.S. population, Medicare and Medicaid costs are estimated to increase in the 10-year period from 2000–10 by 54.5% and 80% respectively (Alzheimer's Association, 2001), straining the already strained American health care system.

Technology

Also, over the last 15 years there have been major biomedical technological advances in the diagnosis of AD, such as using brain imaging technology that includes magnetic resonance imaging (MRI), computed tomography (CT), and positron emission tomography (PET scanners). This allows a person to be diagnosed much earlier in the disease trajectory (Alzheimer's Association, 2008b; Harris, 2002). AD is often described in three stages: early, middle, and late. The symptoms of early-stage (the focus of this chapter) are: impairment of recent memory, and sometimes difficulty with reasoning, language, concentration, disorientation, and poor judgment (Kuhn, 2003).

There are four accepted anti-dementia drugs, three for the early stage: aricept, exelon, and razadyn, and nemenda for middle- to late-stage dementia. For some people, for a limited time, one or a combination of these drugs may slow down the symptoms. However, given that the cause of AD is still unknown, there is no effective treatment that stops the deterioration of brain cells (Alzheimer's Association, 2008b). This leaves people with AD and their families in something of a Catch-22. With earlier diagnosis, people can be more involved in the short- and long-term decisions that will affect their lives, giving them more control; however, the progression of the disease, as of now, cannot be stopped.

In addition, through early detection there is now a new and somewhat controversial category of memory loss not associated with impairments in activities of daily living, called mild cognitive impairment (MCI). MCI may be a transitional condition between normal aging and early AD (Peterson, 2003). However, there is much controversy about the benefit of knowing such a diagnosis, as some persons with the label may progress to dementia, some may remain stable, and a few may improve (Whitehouse & Moody, 2006).

Though there are no biomedical cures for AD, people with dementia and their families, especially in the early stages, are urged to use psychosocial interventions to maintain the quality of their lives. People can still have meaningful lives with dementia. These interventions include counseling, support groups, environmental modifications, adult daycare, and keeping physically, mentally and socially active (Alzheimer's Association, 2008a; Woods & Clare, 2008).

The case study discussed below takes place within a loose organizational structure; one of the aging and memory assessment units of a well-known local hospital where Mr. Adams was diagnosed with early-stage AD. As stated earlier, he was the one who noticed the changes in himself and self-referred. Once he had received the diagnosis, which confirmed his suspicions, he referred himself to the local chapter of the Alzheimer's Association to further his education about the disease, its trajectory, its treatment, and its impact. After meeting a few times with the staff at the Association he was referred for private counseling, as the staff thought he would benefit from this type of intervention and the Association did not offer this service.

Thus except for the restraints of third party insurance providers, the social worker (CD, co-author of this chapter) did not have many organizational restraints on her provision of service to Mr. Adams.

Decisions about practice

Client description

Mr. Adams is a college-educated African American gentleman and a long-time community activist and engineer. He describes himself as a leader, from beginning as student body president in junior high school, to college fraternity president and becoming the director of a Civil Rights program. He held the distinction of becoming the first African American to become a member of a distinguished group of corporate professionals. Mr. Adams was very proud of his children's accomplishments: all three children graduated from college, with his son holding a master's degree from a prestigious university and one daughter holding a master's degree from a local private university. The remaining daughter had proved herself to be an accomplished business person and mother. This background serves to describe the fabric of Mr. Adams's personality (as well as his family's): a self-starter and a highly motivated man who throughout life demonstrated proactive thinking and planning. About four years ago, he began to notice changes in his behavior, which precipitated his making an appointment with a memory and aging clinic. He had been separated from his wife for many years.

Meeting place and appointment time

It is optimal, before meeting with a person who is experiencing memory loss, to make sure s/he has had a neurological evaluation. If this has not occurred, then part of the counseling "contract" *must* be a referral for a neurological evaluation. There are times when an individual who is concerned about his or her memory will seek counseling and through the counseling will gain the support to make the appointment. This allows individuals to begin to feel secure that they will not need to weather a possible diagnosis of dementia alone. Then, when agreeing to work with a person with dementia (PWD), or any type of memory loss, it is critical for the social worker to identify a regular time and place (e.g. same time and day weekly). This provides the opportunity for the person to develop a set routine and ensures her/his ability to keep appointments. Also, meeting in the same location (office) can provide a sense of comfort and familiarity, which is especially important for a person with memory loss. In this case example, I (CD, co-author of this chapter) provided a welcoming environment: plants, objects for fidgeting, comfortable chairs and sofas, as well as bottled water to increase a sense that Mr. Adams and his family's comfort were held in high regard. Research suggests providing counseling within the home setting may also be an option to consider, as the PWD or carers may experience difficulties with transportation or other unforeseen complications (Hill & Brettle, 2006).

Stance of the social worker

Dementia and the journeys each person and her/his family members move through vary greatly. Bowers (1987) and Harris (2007) review different styles of care that daughters and sons (respectively) provide for parents with dementia. Bowers identified 'preservative care' which supports this relationship-focused approach in psychotherapy. Bowers' 'preservative care,' although initially defined as occurring later in the disease, neatly fits our concept of working with PWD and their families through the early stages of the disease. This type of care is defined as maintaining the PWD's family connections, dignity, hope and sense of control. This will be further illustrated through the discussion of goals and strategies below. In addition, Keady and Nolan (2003) identify stages perceived by the PWD. These include slipping, suspecting, covering up, revealing, confirming, surviving, disorganization, decline, death. The first eight stages and the 'preservative care' concept are pertinent to keep in mind in this relationship-focused approach.

My stance is similar to the office décor: warm, yet respectful, valued and accepted. This helps the people with dementia and their carers to develop the comfort needed, not only to express their thoughts, feelings, and fears but also to join the therapist and one another in developing a plan and approach to preserve one another's dignity, resiliency and allow for successful adaptation and integration. A social worker must remain at all times flexible to the ever-changing needs of this specialized population, as the disease varies greatly (Hill & Brettle, 2006). In addition, it is critical for the therapist to take the lead in the first meeting to discuss confidentiality, both when working with the PWD alone as well as with the family group.

The vast majority of people with dementia are from a generation that was taught not to voice its concerns, fears or even desires. Their adult children, many of whom are baby boomers, have a different mindset and believe talking therapies are a helpful and a sometimes necessary tool. For this reason, the stance of the social worker needs to set the stage initially by respecting the older adult's perspective but, through psycho-educational discussions, can help the older adult come to understand that therapy will greatly add to the goal of preserving independence and control. The authors have found individual counseling (with inclusion of carers) using the relationship-focused approach described in this chapter to be very effective. Previous research provides evidence that counseling is effective and helps in the improvement of quality of life with older adults (Hill & Brettle, 2006).

Goals, developing objectives, and contracting

The goals when working with a person with memory loss are similar and yet differ from typical psychodynamic psychotherapy. The similarities lie within representative goals for this modality; including but not limited to enhancing self-esteem, developing good coping skills, developing a trusting relationship and working through previous issues, including loss (Hausman, 1992). The differences are significant with particular focus on the need to involve family members during the course of treatment. The rationale for involving family members needs to be clearly explained to the people with dementia as a method of validating their sense of self and perspective of their reality. The social worker needs to engage the person in the belief that sometimes, due to this destructive disease, there may be times when s/he may be missing some crucial facts. In order to best serve the person, having family members share critical information will help the person to better maintain control in her/his life, as well as better identify the coping strategies that will preserve her/his sense of personhood.

As the social worker begins to work with the PWD and the family members, this team can serve to identify and reinforce any opportunities to foster resiliency (Harris & Durkin, 2002). Table 17.1 on page 209 illustrates ways in which the social worker can efficiently help the person and engage family members to support the development of valuable coping strategies. The underlying purpose is to assist the person to preserve a positive sense of self and promote an acceptance of a realistic independence.

When goal-setting with the person and any family members, maintaining a positive sense of personhood (Kitwood, 1997) should always remain a focal point. Goals should include focusing on helping the person manage as much control over their lives as possible. People with dementia in the early stages often struggle with grief over their losses of independence and heightened fears of further incapacitations (Kasl-Godley & Gatz, 2000).

The initial goals for Mr. Adams and his family members were: (1) better open and honest communication among them, and (2) the development of positive coping strategies for Mr. Adams to enhance his positive sense of self and promote an acceptance of a realistic independence. Together, if we (the therapist and family) could create a safe environment for Mr. Adams to *not* cover up the difficulties that were causing him internal stress, he would become more likely to move towards revealing where he needed help and assistance. This would improve his quality of life and allow his family to meet his needs and feel secure in knowing their father was safe.

Mr. Adams came to his first session with his son and two daughters in tow. In the waiting room I explained that I would first meet alone with Mr. Adams and I would then invite the adult children to join us. I felt it was essential for Mr. Adams to meet me alone first. This allowed Mr. Adams the opportunity to state his wishes and to "have an objective person to talk with." This individual time with Mr. Adams allowed me to explain that I would respect his wishes and thoughts, and together we would decide how to weave his family members in and out of the therapy. I conveyed to Mr. Adams that I saw him as a person who had made many contributions to our society and who I believed could continue to so.

During this first session, Mr. Adams assumed control as he informed me of his current situation with his diagnosis of AD, his involvement as a participant in an AD research center, and his recent completion of an educational lecture series at the Alzheimer's Association. It was clear from our discussion that Mr. Adams prided himself on his ability to be realistic and proactive on his own behalf. I voiced these observations to Mr. Adams and he concurred. After close to 25 minutes with Mr. Adams, I suggested we invite his son and daughters to join us, so they too could be supportive of him. Before I left the office I clearly stated what I planned to tell his children and asked him if this was acceptable, and if there was something he would prefer me to leave out or add. I purposefully wanted Mr. Adams to understand he and I needed to be partners in how and why we involved family members in this relationship-based modality.

As the three children settled in, I teased Mr. Adams that he was obviously a VIP, as an entourage had accompanied him. The entire group chuckled and this purposeful use of humor allowed an ease to exist within the group. I sat the son and both sisters facing their father so he could see them and me from his seat. I took the lead and gave a thumbnail sketch of my discussion with Mr. Adams. I asked the son and daughters if this was their "take" on Mr. Adams's situation or had we missed any important details. They agreed I had an accurate summary and commended their father for seeking professional help. The children explained to their father that they wished to be as supportive as possible and felt some added safety themselves in having a "professional" walk them through some difficult situations.

Mr. Adams had explained to me earlier that there had been a situation where he had mixed up his medications, and thus his family had safety concerns. Although Mr. Adams had a complete rationalization for how he mixed up his medications, he added he would feel more secure with a new and safer medication plan. Together with his son and daughters, we devised a new medication schedule that identified who would stop by Mr. Adams's apartment daily to monitor his medication. Two of the three children could add this into their own daily routines. All agreed that this would support Mr. Adams in his wish to remain living alone in his apartment and give the children "some peace of mind." I also mentioned that there probably were other areas of his life where working together like this with his family could assist him in remaining independent as long as possible, and we could discuss these at future meetings.

I contracted with Mr. Adams that we would meet for six sessions, which would also allow for family members to join us for parts of our sessions. I explained that at the end of these six sessions, together we would evaluate if Mr. Adams wished to continue or if together we thought we might take a break and he could use me on an as needed basis. This would allow both Mr. Adams and his children some predictability and control. I explained that at all times in our lives, it is helpful to do things in a planful manner and that contracting in this way we would be planful of our time together.

Strategies and interventions

Table 17.1 on page 209 shows interventions for social workers to assist the person with dementia to develop positive coping strategies for preserving a sense of self and to promote a realistic independence. It uses a strengths-based philosophy. Some of these strategies were used with Mr. Adams and his family; the authors have used others with other clients. This table illustrates how the social worker in a relationship-focused approach should remain inclusive of PWDs and their carers in the treatment approach. Previous research on ways health care professionals and family members can help persons with dementia develop positive coping strategies (Harris & Durkin, 2002) has prompted these same authors to develop this relationship-focused approach.

Mr. Adam's words below exemplify the development of these positive coping strategies. Acceptance of diagnosis:

> As I thought about my situation, as I move through the twilight years, I do so with neither dread nor apprehension, I do so with the quality assurance that the quality of life is going to be good for me. Good for me because of my attitude as I grew up, good for me because I'm surrounded by a really loving and devoted family that I can depend on … it is these forces plus my attitudes that will get me through this.

> … being angry and not accepting reality is not going to change the fact that you've got a problem …

Role transition acceptance:

> One of the things I learned is it's [dementia] not gonna go away. Whatever the problem is, it's not going to get better by being left to its own devices. This is why I try to be honest with my kids. They can help me stay strong. I think the family needs to accept that this individual is not handicapped or has his mental capacity just diminished and be able to accept that, adjust to that instead of becoming upset about it, accommodate that difference. It certainly makes a lot of difference that I am blessed with my son and daughters … So, I'm blessed and even when I'm feeling a little sorry for myself, and worry, I remember that they are making lots of arrangements for me …

> It ain't what happens to you that really matters, it's what you decide to do about it.

Proactive approach: taking control:

> Seriously, I've decided I'm going to have a very highly regimented life. In other words, what to do, who to see, why, it's very simple. That's the way I'll organize. You know: 8:00 shower, shave, blahblahblah, breakfast, etc …

Table 17.1 Relationship focusing approach to develop positive coping strategies

Coping Strategy	Social Work Action Steps for Working with a Person with Dementia (PWD)	Social Work Action Steps for Working with Family Members to help PWD
Acceptance of diagnosis	• Allow PWD to share what brought him/her to the session, symptoms and concerns, and actions taken to deal with them • Allow time for questions and discussion of physician's diagnosis • Provide opportunities in a safe environment for expression of feelings including frustration, anger, guilt, blame, hopelessness and humiliation • Help PWD move toward acknowledgment of the dementia diagnosis • Discuss how diagnosis has affected family relationships • Make referrals to Alzheimer's Association local chapter or Internet Support Groups for: education, and early-stage support groups	• Help family to hear the PWD's account and concerns • Listen to major caregiving concerns • Make referrals to another therapist to help individual family member(s) with issues related to changes in their relationship, role transition, anticipatory losses and caregiver stress • Encourage family to secure accurate information on etiology of the diagnosis • Help family members to acknowledge that the PWD can be a partner in making decisions • Encourage PWD and family to discuss together possible actions steps to handle mutual concerns.
Disclosure of diagnosis	• Discuss privacy and how to choose who to tell • Suggest keeping a journal • Develop opportunities during sessions to practice new skills for talking about the diagnosis	• Help family to develop understanding that PWD in early stages needs to have control and they should decide together who, when and how significant people need to be told • Encourage family to anticipate out loud what any potential reactions may be and how to respond • Suggest keeping a journal
Role transition acceptance	• Address feelings related to loss of career/family and/or social roles and independence • Evaluate and refer for treatment of depression and/or anxiety • Reframe loss as a relief and an opportunity vs. failure (e.g. *This is your time to be taken care of...*) • Refer for possible inclusion in clinical drug trials (allows for feelings of altruism) • Help PWD consider meaningful volunteer work or early-stage adult daycare or clubs • Discuss still possible meaningful roles in the family	• Help family member(s) identify roles/tasks so that the PWD can continue meaningful participation in the family and elsewhere • Identify roles of primary carer(s) and other supports needed • Help family identity people in their lives who can take on caregiving tasks to lessen their stress (examples include who helps with medication, transportation, meals, cleaning, etc.) • Prepare for breakdowns in plans and discuss the need to be understanding of one another

(continued)

Coping Strategy	Social Work Action Steps for Working with a Person with Dementia (PWD)	Social Work Action Steps for Working with Family Members to help PWD
Strengths identification	• Help PWD to identify lifelong strengths as well as new strengths—look for examples of resiliency and adaptation • Explore, discuss and help PWD identify previous positive coping strategies	• Encourage family to focus on and reinforce the strengths of the PWD • Help family to identify lifelong strengths and new strengths of PWD—look for examples of resiliency and adaptation • Work with PWD and family member(s) to compose a list of their individual and family strengths and accomplishments and read these together regularly
Proactive approach taking control	• Engage the PWD as a capable person and partner in the treatment planning process • Encourage PWD to take a proactive stance • Promote PWD putting together a file of all medical, financial and legal documents to share with family member(s)	• Encourage family to include PWD in all levels of planning; demonstrate this in sessions • Discuss openly the desires of the PWD; encourage PWD or family to arrange for durable power of attorney, advance directives or living will; organize all financial documents, medical information, and legal documents

Words from Mr. Adams's family also illustrate themes in this relationship-focused approach: Strengths identification:

There's a lot, Dad, that I know you struggle with, like sometimes writing out your checks, but I still want to talk about my business proposals with you. You still offer words of wisdom and I appreciate your listening …

Role transition acceptance:

As Dad points out, we are stepping in and helping out in areas, and sometimes there's somewhat of a feeling of role reversal in a way that's kind of awkward. Sometimes we disagree but it doesn't seem like it's really a big deal.

Use of time

The social worker needs to be mindful that the person with dementia may sometimes (but not always) lose track of time. The social worker should begin each session—again mindfully—using routine with a verbal cueing of warm-up techniques. In this case, I would ask Mr. Adams to bring me up to speed with how his week had gone, specifically repeating the coping strategies he had planned to practice during the week.

If there was a visible concern, I would respectfully register this with Mr. Adams. One example of this occurred when, for the second week in a row, I noticed Mr. Adams was wearing clothes that appeared to have small food stains on them. His appearance was always important to him, which reinforced his positive sense of self. I shared with him my concern that maybe he just wasn't getting the chance to keep up with his laundry and perhaps we could involve his children in helping out.

Use of outside resources

As described earlier, Mr. Adams was a proactive, "take the bull by the horns type of person," as he liked to describe himself. As an engineer, he had always prided himself on being able to fix almost anything in his home. He confided that following a "snafu" where he almost made a grave mistake in repairing his hot water heater; he immediately enlisted help from the local senior center. He began with home repair help and gradually enlisted other supports through this resource. After confiding in his long-term internist about his suspicions that he may have some cognitive decline, as evidenced by his home repair debacle, coupled with experiencing moments of complete confusion, he was referred to the memory assessment center of a local hospital, as discussed earlier in the chapter. His suspicions were confirmed and he accepted the referral to the local chapter of the Alzheimer's Association. Refer to Table 17.1 on page 209, as this chart specifically addresses how the social worker in a relationship-focused approach can encourage the use of outside resources that promote role transition acceptance, strengths identification and most importantly, proactive approach taking control. The ecomap on page 212, Figure 17.1, illustrates the strong network this individual has at his disposal.

Reassessment, evaluation, and termination

This specialized dementia population requires termination to begin, as with most clients, in the first meeting. In addition, due to the unknown speed and trajectory of this disease, reiterating

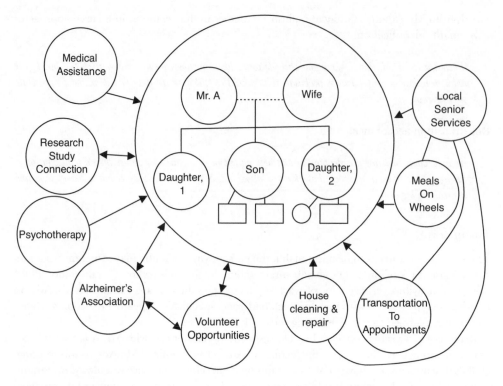

Figure 17.1 Ecomap for Mr. Adams.

the contracted number of sessions each time, and the ability to re-contract for additional sessions is critical. The ethical considerations of the capacity of the PWD cannot be overlooked. At the point when the social worker feels the PWD can no longer use the counseling session to reduce emotional stress and aid in developing positive coping strategies, the need for termination is fundamental.

In order to be cognizant of when termination is appropriate, reassessment and evaluation need to be a constant part of the weekly counseling sessions. This consists of comparing the agreed-upon goals and action steps to the PWD's weekly progress. Given the PWD's memory loss, this reassessment and evaluation needs to be an important part of every session. The PWD should be encouraged to record the counseling session and to listen to it during the week. Use of the recording provides a "supplemental memory aid," reminding the PWD of the goals that need to be accomplished. The family can assist by reminding the PWD about the recording.

As part of the reassessment, certain questions relevant for this specialized population need to be asked, such as:

1 Given the PWD's strengths and his/her disease process; do the agreed-upon goals continue to be realistic?
2 Have the goals been broken down in small enough steps and been explained in understandable terms?
3 Do family members' observations support the reported outcomes?
4 What can family members do to support these outcomes?

When the decision to terminate has been reached, the stance of the social worker shifts to helping the PWD know that the social worker will always be there for him/her and their carers, should future needs develop.

Case conclusion

A diagnosis of dementia dramatically changes the lives of sufferers and those of their family members. It is a devastating disease with an irreversible negative trajectory. Yet, people can still live lives of quality and of meaning. Social workers working with people in the early stages of the disease and their family members can make a difference in the lives of their clients through the use of counseling. The relationship-focused approach discussed above allowed the person with dementia and his carers to become partners in the future decision making and planning of their lives. Together they all felt as if they were sharing control, preserving Mr. Adams's dignity and sense of selfhood, and coming to an acceptance of necessary interdependence upon each other. All of this was being undertaken with the aim of maintaining a realistic independence for Mr. Adams as long as possible. Together they mapped out how they planned to cope through the next stages of this journey of dementia.

Mr. Adams reflected: "I feel like I'm Chairman of the Board and I have the best board of directors one could wish for."

References

Alzheimer's Association. (2001). *Medicare and Medicaid costs for people with Alzheimer's disease.* Retrieved 12/30/08, from http://www.alz.org/national/documents/alzreport.pdf

Alzheimer's Association (2008a). *Alzheimer's disease facts and figures.* Washington D.C.

Alzheimer's Association (2008b). Steps to diagnosis. Retrieved 1/1/09, from http://www.alz.org

Bowers, B. J. (1987). Inter-generational caregiving: Adult caregivers and their aging parents. *Advances in Nursing Science*, 9 (2): 20–31.

Council of the European Union. (2008). Council conclusions on public health strategies to combat neurodegenerative diseases associated with aging and in particular Alzheimer's disease. Retrieved 1/1/09, from http://www.consilium.europa.eu/newsroom.

Harris, P. B. (ed.). (2002). *The person with Alzheimer's disease: Pathways to understanding the experience.* Baltimore: The John Hopkins University Press.

Harris, P. B. & Durkin, C. (2002). Building resistence through coping and adapting. In Harris, P. B. (ed.). *The person with Alzheimer's disease* (pp. 165–186). Baltimore: John Hopkins University Press.

Harris, P. B. & Keady. J. (2006). Editorial. *Dementia: The International Journal of Social Research and Practice*, 5 (1): 5–11.

Hausman, C. (1992). Dynamic psychotherapy. Retrieved 01/21/09, from http://www.alzforum.org/dis/tre/drt/dynamic.asp

Henderson, C. & Andrews, N. (1998). *A partial view: An Alzheimer's journal.* Dallas, TX: Southern Methodist University Press.

Herbert L. E. *et al.* (2003). Alzheimer's disease in the U.S. population: Prevalence estimates using the 2000 census. *Archives of Neurology*, 60 (8): 1119–22.

Hill, A. & Brettle, A. (2006). Counseling older people: What can we learn from research evidence? *Journal of Social Work Practice*, 20 (3): 281–97.

Kasl-Godley, J. & Gatz, M. (2000). Psychosocial interventions for individuals with dementia: An integration of theory, therapy, and a clinical understanding of dementia. *Clinical Psychology Review*, 20 (6): 755–82.

Keady, J. & Nolan, M. (2003). The dynamics of dementia: Working together, working separately, or working alone. In Nolan, M., Lundh, U., Grant, G. & Keady, J. (eds). *Partnerships in family care: Understanding the caregiving career* (pp. 15–32). Maidenhead: Open University Press.

Kuhn, D. (2003). New horizons. Early diagnosis of Alzheimer's means new implications for care. *Contemporary Long Term Care*, 26 (7): 25–6.

National Institute on Aging. (2006). *Journey to discover: 2006–2005 progress report on Alzheimer's disease.* Washington D.C: U.S. Department of Health and Human Services.

Patrick, D. L., Starks, H. E., Cain, K. C., Uhlmann, R. F. & Pearlman, R. A. (1994). *Medical Decision Making*, 14 (1): 9–18.

Peterson, R. C. (ed.) (2003). *Mild cognitive impairment: Aging to Alzheimer's disease.* New York: Oxford University Press.

Phinney, A. (2002). Living with the symptoms of Alzheimer's disease. In Harris, P. B. (ed.). *The person with Alzheimer's disease: Pathways to understanding the experience* (pp. 49–74). Baltimore: The John Hopkins University Press.

Uhlenberg, P. & Cheuk, M. (2008). Demographic change and the future of informal caregiving. In M. E. Szinovaz & A. Davey (eds). *Caregiving contexts: Cultural, familial, and societal implications* (pp. 9–33). New York: Springer Publishing Company.

Whitehouse, P. J. & Moody, H. R. (2006). Mild cognitive impairment: A 'hardening of the categories'. *Dementia: The International Journal of Social Research and Practice*, 5 (1): 13–25.

Woods, B. & Clare, L. (2008). *Handbook of the clinical psychology of aging.* England: John Wiley and Sons, Ltd.

18 Autonomy—friend or foe in the health care center

A social worker's perspective

Jennifer Bell

Context

Description of setting

Roland Park Place (RPP) is a Continuing Care Retirement Community (CCRC) located in Baltimore, Maryland. A not-for-profit organization, RPP is managed by a board of directors, organized around the services provided to its residents. It provides three levels of care: independent living, assisted living, and nursing home. People move to RPP for the many amenities and benefit from the continuum of care philosophy. They do not generally leave RPP but move through the different levels of care as the need arises. The Health Care Center (HCC), a federally regulated nursing home, provides both short- and long-term residency. Some people come for a short period of rehabilitation or even respite care; whereas others are here indefinitely because they are no longer able to reside in Independent or Assisted Living. Those living in the HCC, whether temporarily or long-term, are provided opportunities to interact with one another through activity programming and rehabilitation opportunities. We, along with family members, try to make the HCC as home-like as possible, bringing in items from home, becoming close with staff and other residents, and promoting relationship. The goal is to make the stay as comfortable as possible.

Policy

Structured federal nursing home regulations have only existed for about two decades. In 1965, the institution of Medicare and Medicaid services initiated federal regulations in skilled nursing facilities and "although federal regulations were enacted once Medicare and Medicaid began to pay for nursing home care, they were inadequate in design, poorly implemented and often unenforced by the federal and state agencies that shared regulatory responsibility" (Walshe, 2001, p. 129). After a report by the Institute of Medicine (IOM), Congress decided major changes were needed to improve care in nursing facilities and passed new regulations in the Omnibus Budget Reconciliation Act (OBRA) of 1987 (Kane, 2001). Prior to that reform, regulations were sparse, and there was no way to identify or track issues within a nursing home. The Omnibus Budget Reconciliation Act (OBRA) and the subsequent regulations (USDHHS, 1988, 1989, 1994, 1995a, 1995b) mandated uniform comprehensive assessments of all nursing facility residents at admission and periodically thereafter; developed quality indicators that were more outcome-oriented than process-oriented; and changed federal survey procedures to interview and assess residents, rather than simply reviewing medical records (Walshe & Harrington, 2002).

The new regulations allow oversight to assure that America's seniors are being provided the best care possible. The Minimum Data Set (MDS), an assessment format developed through OBRA, is designed to "identify a resident's strengths, preferences, and needs in key areas, and provide a holistic and comprehensive picture of the resident's functional status" (as cited in Hawes *et al.*, 1997). In addition to providing a snapshot of the resident's functional, cognitive and emotional capabilities, the MDS guides nursing home staff in creating the resident's plan of care. Care plan meetings typically occur on a quarterly basis with the intent of discussing care issues with the resident and his/her family. The meetings also provide the resident and his/her family a venue to discuss concerns with the entire interdisciplinary team.

Additional supervision occurs via annual state surveys conducted by the Health Care Financing Administration (HCFA). Although these surveys are to be conducted on an annual basis, the survey window falls between nine and 15 months (Harrington & Carrillo, 1999). In addition to the annual survey, HCFA investigates any complaints made about the facility. With the goal of making sure nursing homes are in compliance with the federal guidelines, the MDS surveyors examine documentation from charts, interview residents, families and staff, and observe care. If a nursing home is deemed out of compliance, the facility will be issued a deficiency that may result in monetary fines, a halt to admissions and possibly even closing the facility. Despite many improvements in regulations (Decker & Adamek, 2004), there are growing concerns that seniors may still be receiving poor care.

The Patient Self-Determination Act (PSDA)

I have dual roles in the HCC, as both admission coordinator and social worker. In my admissions role, I supply newly admitted patients with information about resident rights and advance directives. Here, a key policy is the Patient Self Determination Act (PSDA) (Galambos, 1998), which requires health care organizations receiving Medicare or Medicaid payments to provide written information to all patients informing them of their rights to refuse treatment and to use advance directives (Bradley & Rizzo, 1999).

Social workers are often thought of as advance directive experts, as we are typically the professionals who address end-of-life issues (Berkman, 2006; Black, 2005; Geriatric Social Work Initiative, 2009). Such issues can be daily occurrences in nursing homes (Lacey, 2005). We need to understand residents' present situation and help them to look into the future, making sure conversations with family members about future plans—including palliative care or comfort measures—are held prior to any crisis. This kind of prior planning clarifies with family members what the resident wants and provides some comfort to those who may need to make those decisions in the future.

Residents consider many questions when discussing advance directives, including how they want their life to end; for example, "would they want a feeding tube or artificial hydration?" or "would they want a machine to breathe for them?" Other questions regard the use of a durable power of attorney for health care, a living will (Osman & Perlin, 1994), or other forms of instruction recognized under state law that address the provision of health care in situations where a person is unable to make medical treatment decisions (Mezey & Ramsey, 1994). Living wills specify what a person desires for life-sustaining treatments when he/she is nearing death, for example, in a terminal condition, end-stage, or a persistent vegetative state (Living Will, 2009). A Health Care Power of Attorney is a document in which people designate a specific individual who will make medical decisions for them when they are no longer able.

Although the PSDA started a societal life conversation, some felt there was more to be accomplished. The PSDA does not address capacity determination, surrogacy choice, dispute mediation, frequency of review of decisions, and arrangements for staff (and community) education (Mezey & Ramsey, 1994). Several of the issues have been addressed in state laws, specifically surrogacy choice. In Maryland, the Health Care Decisions Act (HCDA) provides the much needed direction for the mandated PSDA. This act provides guidance on how to implement the PSDA. It breaks down information about advance directives, how someone is deemed incapable of making decisions, explains surrogacy and defines the hierarchy levels, and it also touches on Do Not Resuscitate orders (DNRs) and the forms that must accompany the orders. The HCDA is updated periodically to add new information. Therefore, social workers must stay aware of any changes.

Upon admission to a nursing facility, seniors are faced with a great deal of information about advance directives, including being told a decision is needed about their code status; that is, whether they would want cardiopulmonary resuscitation (CPR) if their heart were to stop beating. I have to be able to explain the complexities of CPR and its results in a way that the resident can understand (Vandrevala, Hampson, Daly, Arber & Thomas, 2006).

When discussing code status, end-of-life care issues and advance directives, I am cognizant of potential cultural barriers to these conversations (Smith, 2004). Knowing a person's values, beliefs, faith and cultural background can help guide my discussions. For instance, some religions—such as Orthodox Jews and Catholics—encourage life-sustaining treatments, whereas other religions are neutral on the subject (Ejaz, 2000). Although understanding people's perspective is important, I also remember people do not always fit into a neat mold. When facing death, people can surprise me; although their faith, culture, race, gender, etc. might indicate a belief for or against end-of-life care, code status or advance directives, I have to be prepared for any answer they give, to hear what is and is not being said during these discussions and ask for clarification when uncertain. These decisions are too important to get wrong.

I have to be able to see the big picture but also be able to explain some of the smaller details such as a specific regulation and how it affects residents. Understanding how regulations have come to be and knowing their impact today will help me to influence future laws for nursing home residents.

Technology

Specific kinds of technology serve both to extend the lives of the elderly, and to support them in living as independently as possible. Examples in the HCC include the many medications for managing blood pressure, high cholesterol levels, depression, and GERD (gastroesophageal reflux disease); those that are prescribed for specific conditions; and electronic devices, ranging from emergency alert buttons, hearing aids, enlarged displays and buttons to pacemakers/ defibrillators and power wheelchairs (Bruder, Blessing & Wandke, 2007). For example, one resident, Mr. Atkinson, lived independently but was in and out of the HCC for fatigue. We realized he needed a pacemaker, but he really didn't want to have the operation. After many discussions in which I helped him to see he was feeling great each time he left the HCC because he had been waited on, and that he became exhausted after a few days at home because he had to do everything for himself, he decided to get the pacemaker. What a difference there was. He told me he wished he had done it sooner.

End-of-life care technology, in particular, can range from artificial nutrition and hydration to the use of morphine and other drugs to manage pain. Discussing advance directives typically entails conversation about artificial nutrition or hydration, and I must be familiar enough with these options to help residents make decisions for living wills. For example, feeding tubes, which can be used as the supplemental or primary source of an individual's nutrition, can be short- or long-term solutions for those with nutritional deficits (Amella, Lawrence & Gresle, 2005). Prior to making decisions for their living wills, residents have all of this information including how feeding tubes are placed (e.g. through the nose, abdomen or small intestine). When the time comes for intense discussions about feeding tubes, the physician typically facilitates the decision-making process.

Organization

Continuing Care Retirement Communities (CCRCs) are growing in number as the aging population increases. Many desire CCRCs for their amenities (e.g. fitness center, activities/ trips, library, multiple eating venues, etc.) and the promise of support through the levels of care as one requires more help. In theory, this sounds perfect; however, many never consider the fact that they would be the ones needing to move through the continuum of care (e.g. independent living, assisted living and nursing home). Often, when people are encouraged to move to a higher level of care, it is a shock because they never thought it would happen to them. They believed their days would be filled with trips to museums, lectures, concerts, participation in local activities, resident councils, all from the coziness of their independent living home/apartment. To leave independent living may mean giving up all of that, as well as their independence, though many continue to lead active lives in the other levels of care. Social workers benefit from the ongoing relationships with residents and the ability to build stronger relationships over the years. These longstanding relationships allow social workers the opportunity to work with residents on various issues, while building trust that can be used in future circumstances.

Many CCRCs are mission-driven; the mission is the backbone of an organization. From that, services are delineated and provided to the clients or residents of the facility. As times change, so do the services. Constantly working towards improving services to the residents is what keeps the organization thriving. Typically, a board of directors helps to keep the organization moving within the mission through strategic planning. Social workers need to be aware of the internal structure of the organization but also need to be aware of outlying resources in the community. One main role of the social worker is discharge planning both back into the CCRC community, or back to home in the community at large. It is imperative to know how the other levels of care operate and what their expectations are in order to provide the best guidance and discharge planning to the resident. By knowing the separate levels of care criteria, the ongoing dialogues between the resident and other staff can be guided.

When residents return to their homes in the outside community, social workers must be aware of the resources to help. Becoming familiar with outpatient therapy services, home health care agencies, private duty agencies, etc. is crucial for effective discharge planning. Also knowing how those services are paid for is another area of required knowledge. The interdisciplinary team works to develop and implement a plan of action for the resident's expected care. Social workers need to pull together all the pieces from each discipline to see the full picture and relay it to the resident. To be a good resident advocate, requires a solid working relationship is needed with all disciplines. When the team disagrees, the social worker needs to step in and help assess the entire picture to include the resident's wishes. Understanding an organization's mission, beliefs and values guides a social worker in his/her role as advocate. Organizations as a whole are complex but understanding the nuances of the company as well as the individual players helps make advocacy possible.

Decisions about practice

Description of the client situation

Mrs. Gertrude Jacobs, a 94-year-old widow, was admitted to our nursing home following a stroke with dysarthria, difficulty in articulating words, caused by impairment of the muscles used in speech. Due to her dysarthria, communicating was difficult for her and the staff. Her functional ability had greatly declined since her latest stroke, as well.

Prior to coming to the nursing home, Mrs. Jacobs had been living in an independent living apartment receiving help with dressing and bathing. She used a power wheelchair for mobility, as her leg muscles were weakened from a childhood polio episode. Although she could not walk, she had retained the capability of transferring into her power chair and toileting herself. This last stroke took those capabilities. Mrs. Jacobs was completely dependent on staff to provide for her activities of daily living (ADLs) such as bathing, dressing, toileting, and mobility. She was completely discouraged by her circumstances and quickly fell into a depression. Although she made suicidal statements, she was not actively pursuing suicide, just wishing for death.

Within two weeks, the depression became apparent. The first few weeks after admission to a nursing home involve a tough adjustment for most people and I visit to help with this transition. Mrs. Jacobs needed a little more intervention. At first she was willing to vent her frustrations when she could but, due to her dysarthria, even our visits began to be problematic for her. Being unable to communicate, she felt she was a burden, especially to her two children, despite their complete devotion. After a while she started to defer to her children to make decisions because she did not want to be bothered, just one of many symptoms of her depression. She stopped eating and had difficulty sleeping. She fatigued quickly which caused her to become excessively frustrated and to sink even lower into a depression. This fatigue was so burdensome that she cut her therapy times in half, as she was too tired to participate. The nurse practitioner met with her and decided to increase her depression medication. Within several weeks her mood had improved, she was getting sleep and her appetite had increased. Since she was feeling better, Mrs. Jacobs was more adept at working with therapy and saw improvements.

With the depression managed, she was willing to work with me a little; although by this time her total focus was on physical, occupational, and speech therapy, which took most of her time in between a nap or two and meals. Her speech was improving, giving her the ability to become her own advocate. She still encouraged her children to speak for her, yet she also listened to their input. Mrs. Jacobs' cognition, poor upon arrival, had cleared given her a renewed sense of self.

In a nursing home, therapy schedules may be very fluid. Trying to set up a schedule to meet with a resident is nearly impossible, especially with someone like Mrs. Jacobs, who had at least three hours of therapy daily. It was agreed that I would try and visit with her several times a week. Try was the key word as she was rarely in her room. The plan was to meet in her room to focus on her goal of returning to her independent living apartment and what steps needed to be accomplished for this to occur.

Since her room was private, there was no need to find another spot to talk. Depending on her mood, our sessions could last 10 or 15 minutes, just giving me the highlights of her day, or up to 45 minutes. Our meetings never lasted more than 45 minutes because typically by the time we met, she was either in between therapy sessions or had finished for the day. Either way, she was exhausted and needed rest. She also knew that if she needed to see me on a particular day she had several avenues to find me, including my phone number or having a nurse page me.

In order for her to return to her independent living apartment, she had to accomplish four tasks. The first was to work with her various therapies, no matter how frustrating or tiring they were. Refusing therapy was not an option unless she was sick. Second, she had to be able to transfer herself on the toilet, her prior level of functioning. Third, her safety awareness needed to improve. Fourth, with that needed improvement she would be able to use her power wheelchair again. It had been taken from her when she ran into walls and almost hit staff and residents. Having her power wheelchair would allow her to again go to meals and activities by herself.

Although these tasks were functionally based, together we used those as measurable criteria for getting her closer to her goal of going back to her apartment. Using the strengths perspective to keep her focused and helping her feel empowered were our main areas of concentration. I knew she had lived a long time, seen a lot, was resilient and relied on coping strategies to see her through difficult times. In these ways, I showed respect for Ms. Jacobs and encouraged self-determination and autonomy (Chapin & Cox, 2001).

Seniors of today have lived through a lot, including the Great Depression, World War II, and the Korean War. They may remember hardships but not see their survival as a strength. Helping them to focus on how they made it through the difficult times, and finding their coping strategies, opens their eyes to the possibility of dealing with their current situations. Encouraging them to reminisce helps them to recognize that this is just one more era in their life, with positives and negatives. Often, reminiscence will open the discussion to include thoughts about aging and death. Geriatric social workers are among the few who will listen to these issues (Greene, 2000).

As Mrs. Jacobs progressed in rehabilitative therapy and her depression lifted, she was able to look back over her life. She found there were many times when life seemed unfair and exceptionally difficult, but she was able to gain strength from family, friends, and her faith. During this time she was regaining her inner strength, but her ability to self-toilet and her safety awareness were not progressing. Mrs. Jacobs continued to reach for things way out of her reach, increasing her likelihood of falling. She was not able to process some of the simple steps needed for toileting and therefore consistently needed help. Because these abilities were not improving, it became clear that returning to her independent living apartment was not appropriate. As we continued to meet, we discussed the possibility of not being able to return to her apartment. At first she refused to consider the thought, but with discussion she admitted she was not progressing as she hoped. We again used reminiscence to help her focus on times when things did not go as planned but how she found hope regardless.

Since Mrs. Jacobs felt she was losing everything if she could not return to her apartment, I continued to try to empower her within the realm of having to live in the HCC (Kelchner, 2001, p. 119). We looked at the fact that her children would always be a support to her no matter where she lived. I tried to have her become more active in choices for herself, as she had relinquished a lot of that responsibility to her children during her depression and had never regained it. We looked at ways to keep her more autonomous even in the HCC.

Unfortunately, she was not interested in working with me much because all she would focus on was improving to go home; she would not even consider the possibility of staying in the HCC.

A family meeting was arranged to discuss her progress and the decision about her level of care. When staff indicated her progress was not enough for her to return safely to her independent living apartment (IL), Mrs. Jacobs and her family were enraged. They indicated that no one had ever mentioned that returning to her apartment may not be an option and believed that staff had set up false hope for Mrs. Jacobs. The varied therapists and I had been speaking with Mrs. Jacobs throughout her two months in the HCC about the possibility of needing another level of care and yet she acted as though this was the first time. The therapists had also been having many impromptu meetings with Mrs. Jacobs' children as they inquired about their mother's progress. None of what was said at the meeting was new and yet the reaction was surprising. At that point, Mrs. Jacobs' ecomap looked like Figure 18.1 below.

Officially hearing that Mrs. Jacobs was recommended that to stay in the HCC is very different from the "possibility" of her staying. Her children refused the recommendation and insisted we become creative and find other ways to help her accomplish these goals. The therapists who had been a great resource to me in my work with Mrs. Jacobs prior to this, now became crucial. We met daily to brainstorm new approaches; unfortunately, Mrs. Jacobs had great difficulty in carryover. Although her cognition had improved several weeks into her stay at the HCC, she still had trouble with processing and remembering. These were the culprits keeping her from returning to her apartment. Without these abilities, no new interventions or strategies stood a chance. Mrs. Jacobs was kept informed about staff concerns regarding her lack of progress and potential options.

Finally, after a month of no improvement, Mrs. Jacobs and her family met with us again. We continued to explain that the safest environment for her was the HCC. Mrs. Jacobs had told us often she did not like the HCC, due to the lack of privacy and always having people around, so it was uncertain how she would take a new approach. Since the family would not relent about her returning to IL but did concede she had not made progress, we suggested she return to her apartment and receive 24-hour support. Surprisingly, everyone was in agreement with the plan. The family even believed, once in her apartment and surrounded by her own things, she would make the final progress needed and then the 24-hour support could be weaned back. Since they were still focused on her making improvements, we decided once she returned home, another meeting would occur to determine her progress.

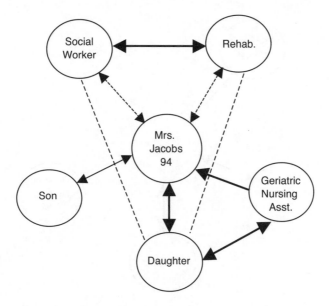

Figure 18.1 Ecomap for Mrs. Jacobs' first HCC stay.

Because I work in a retirement community, I see residents move from one level of care to another and must take great care not to sever or destroy relationships. During Mrs. Jacobs' termination from the HCC, we discussed the importance of autonomy and choices. She felt much better being able to choose where she would live. Mrs. Jacobs returned home to her independent living apartment with 24-hour help. The geriatric nursing assistants who provided the 24-hour care kept a careful journal in which they noted every activity with which Mrs. Jacobs needed assistance. Her family read the journal, talked to the assistants, watched Mrs. Jacobs struggle over the next period of time and realized the hours of help could not be weaned back. They made the decision to return her to the HCC. Mrs. Jacobs moved back to the HCC permanently within a month of her discharge. She was content with the decision because she had proven to herself that she could not live the kind of life she wanted; she commented that she actually had more privacy in the HCC (where staff buzz in and out) than she did at home with 24-hour support. Thus, in the HCC, Mrs. Jacobs was less isolated and more comfortable and content.

Differential discussion

Looking back, it is obvious that some issues could have been handled differently. The biggest problem was the family's "buy-in." Not including the family in discussions prior to the family meeting, or even assessing their ability to handle their mother's decline, set the staff up for the catastrophic blow-up meeting. In retrospect, I would have prepared the family for her changed circumstances. Because of the resident's desire to pass all decisions to her children, she was in fact making them part of her system and making them a client. Having buy-in from the family would probably have helped me to empower the whole family. The family was a great resource that was not used to its full potential. In the future, when working with a resident who is extremely close with her family, I will encourage the family to participate in or at least have knowledge of goal-setting and implementation. Tapping into a resident's support system also

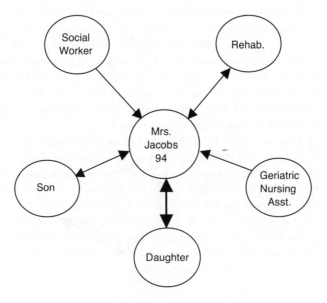

Figure 18.2 Ecomap for Mrs. Jacobs' move to the HCC.

helps improve her mood and gives the worker another view of the resident with information that perhaps the resident did not care to divulge. I will take my cues from the resident about whether family should be included, but when it is OK, that resource should be used.

In addition, when she was highly depressed, it would have been beneficial to try cognitive or cognitive-behavioral therapy with Mrs. Jacobs. That has been proven to be helpful with depression. No intervention is perfect or foolproof. The benefit to this case was Mrs. Jacobs' self-determination to return home with help, followed by coming to her own conclusion that the HCC was the best place for her. Had Mrs. Jacobs stayed in the HCC, her adjustment would have taken longer, as she would never have seen for herself how much support she needed. By going home, she was able to see and accept her decline, then choose the level that actually gave her more independence, the HCC.

Allowing residents to have a voice and the autonomy to make choices, even poor ones, can be empowering and provide guidance to better decisions later. Even though I may not agree with certain decisions, the fact that residents made them reminds me I have done my job and supported their autonomy. There is no greater advocacy skill than promoting autonomy.

References

Amella, E. J., Lawrence, J. F. & Gresle, S. O. (2005). Tube feeding: Prolonging life or death in vulnerable populations? *Mortality*, 10 (1): 69–81.

Berkman, B. (2006). *Handbook of social work in health & aging*. New York: Oxford University Press.

Black, K. (2005). Advance Directive communication practices: Social workers' contributions to the interdisciplinary health care team. *Social Work in Health Care*, 40 (3): 39–55.

Bradley, E. H. & Rizzo, J. A. (1999). Public information and private search: Evaluating the Patient Self-Determination Act. *Journal of Health Politics, Policy and Law*, 24 (2): 239–73.

Bruder, C., Blessing, L. & Wandke, H. (2007). Training the elderly in the use of electronic devices. In Stepenidis, C. (ed.). (2007). *Universal access in human-computer interaction* (pp. 637–46). Berlin: Springer-Verlag.

Chapin, R. & Cox, E. O. (2001). Changing the paradigm: Strengths-based and empowerment-oriented social work with frail elders. *Journal of Gerontological Social Work*, 36 (3/4): 165–79.

Decker, C. L. & Adamek, M. E. (2004). Meeting the challenges of social work research in long-term care. *Social Work in Health Care*, 38 (3): 47–65.

Ejaz, F. K. (2000). The influence of religious and personal values on nursing home residents' attitudes toward life-sustaining treatments. *Social Work in Health Care*, 32 (2): 23–39.

Galambos, C. M. (1998). Preserving end-of-life autonomy: The Patient Self-Determination Act and the Uniform Health Care Decisions Act. *Health & Social Work*, 23 (4): 275–81.

Geriatric Social Work Initiative (2009). Retrieved 6/7/09, from http://www.gswi.org.

Greene, R. R. (2000). Serving the aged and their families in the twenty-first century using a revised practice model. *Journal of Gerontological Social Work*, 34 (1): 43–62.

Harrington, C. & Carrillo, H. (1999). The regulation and enforcement of federal nursing home standards, 1991–7. *Medical Care Research and Review*, 56 (4): 471–94.

Hawes, C., Mor, V., Phillips, C. D., Fries, B. E., Morris, J. N., Steele-Friedlob, E., Greene, A. M. & Nennstiel, M. (1997). The OBRA-87 Nursing home regulations and implementation of the resident assessment instrument: Effects on process quality. *Journal of the American Geriatric Association*, 45 (8): 977–85.

Kane, R. A. (2001). Long-term care and a good quality of life: Bringing them closer together. *The Gerontologist*, 41 (3): 293–304.

Kelchner, E. S. (2001). Social work with older adults in health care and residential settings in the new millennium: A return to the past. *Journal of Gerontological Social Work*, 36 (3/4): 115–25.

Lacey, D. (2005). Nursing home social worker skills and end-of-life planning. *Social Work in Health Care*, 40 (4): 19–40.

Living Will (2009). Retrieved 6/7/09, from http://www.mayoclinic.com/health/living-wills/HA00014

Mezey, M. & Ramsey, G. C. (1994). Making the PSDA work for the elderly. *Generations*, 18 (4): 13–18.

Osman, H. & Perlin, T. M. (1994). Patient self-determination and the artificial prolongation of life. *Health & Social Work*, 19 (4): 245–52.

Smith, S. H. (2004). End-of-life care decision-making processes of African American families: Implications for culturally-sensitive social work practice. *Journal of Ethnic & Cultural Diversity in Social Work*, 13 (2): 1–23.

USDHHS (1988, 1989, 1994, 1995a, 1995b). Omnibus Budget Reconciliation Act (OBRA). Retrieved 11/06/09, from www.kff.org/medicare/7717.cfm

Vandrevala, T., Hampson, S. E., Daly, T., Arber, S. & Thomas, H. (2006). Dilemmas in decision-making about resuscitation—a focus group study of older people. *Social Science & Medicine*, 62: 1579–93.

Walshe, K. (2001). Regulating U.S. nursing homes: Are we learning from experience? *Health Affairs*, 20 (6): 128–44.

Walshe, K. & Harrington, C. (2002). Regulation of nursing facilities in the United States: An analysis of resources and performance of state survey agencies. *The Gerontologist*, 42 (4): 475–86.

19 Geriatric social work in a community hospital

High-touch, low-tech work in a
high-tech, low-touch environment

Sarah L. Maus

Context

Description of the setting

Memorial is an independent 570-bed, acute care teaching hospital located in a suburb just outside of a large east coast city. The county in which we are situated is quite wealthy and has the third highest percentage of older adults in our state, which has one of the highest percentages of older adults in the nation. We serve parts of two adjoining counties, one of which includes a large, metropolitan area. While our patients are overwhelmingly Caucasian, we have significant Spanish, African-American, Portuguese and Korean populations.

Forty-seven percent of our inpatient population is over 60 years of age. Our statistics reflect those of the nation, in that the old-old, those over 85, are the fastest growing segment of this older population. A large home care department provides services to our patients in the community, and we work closely with our Area Agency on Aging and a local network of over 60 extended care facilities.

Policy

Several policies influence the work we do. Perhaps the most significant is the Health Insurance Portability and Accountability Act of 1996 ("HIPPA") (HIPAA, 2009). Also referred to as the "Privacy Rule," HIPPA defines the kind of communication we are allowed to have with regard to our patients' health information. A second policy, Advance Health Care Directives, Act 169, signed into state law late in 2006, provides a comprehensive statutory framework governing advance health care directive and decision making for incompetent patients (Studer, 2004). It makes available a set of standards for use in the health care setting to define incompetence and to seek determination from the courts for such (Baker, 2000; Doukas & Reichel, 2007). Included in this Act is a hierarchy created by the legislature that sets the order in which family and friends are to be used as health care representatives (American Bar Association, 2006). This is especially helpful to our medical staff, who feel more comfortable with decisions made with proper legal backing. In addition, our hospital has its own policy for patient rights and responsibilities. Given to every patient upon admission, this brochure describes, in detail, the rights afforded all hospital patients, as well as the responsibilities of patients as partners in their care. It directs patients who have any questions or concerns to our patient relations department.

Technology

The primary function of a social worker in an acute care hospital is discharge planning (Auslander *et al.*, 2008; Leahy & Lording, 2005). Communication tools are our main forms of technology. Our medical record is accessible in both paper and electronic form. Physicians continue to document on paper charts, while many other professionals enter their work on computers found throughout the hospital. All social workers are equipped with cellular phones and have access to email. We frequently use copiers and fax machines to share pertinent information with institutions to which we are referring our patients. The hospital employs a courier service to transport time-sensitive materials. In addition, the hospital has created various forms—both paper and electronic—which we use to communicate among ourselves and with outside agencies. Those pertinent to our case study include professional consults, the patient transfer form, patient discharge forms, and the formal application for a court competency hearing with essential medical interrogatories (Moye, Butz, Marson & Wood, 2007; Qualls & Smyer, 2007).

Communicating with our geriatric patients often involves other forms of technology. Because of the effects of aging, it is very important that we assess our geriatric patients to determine their ability to see, hear and comprehend what we are telling them (Brink & Stones, 2007). It is also important to ensure their ability to be involved, to whatever degree they choose or are able, in their own medical care (Giordano, 2000; LeJeune, Steinman & Mascia, 2003). We do this by making sure eye glasses are available and clean, hearing aids are available and have working batteries, and patients are well oriented to their surroundings with the use of orientation boards in each room and engagement in careful conversation.

Organization

Approximately 10 years ago, Memorial combined its social work and case management departments and chose, as the director, a registered nurse (Naleppa & Reid, 2000). The administration believed that since both departments were responsible for discharge planning, it would be more efficient to have one director. Those who were left out of the transition were tapped to create a geriatric service line, and I am the Manager of Geriatrics. The mission of this entity is to improve and maintain the health status of our elderly community through both inpatient and outpatient geriatric and geropsychiatric services. Our one inpatient program is the Hospital Elder Life Program, in which we collaborate with the Department of Nursing to assure specialty geriatric inpatient care to our "at risk" patients. This program has succeeded in creating a greater awareness throughout the staff of the special needs of the frail elderly.

The nature of hospital social work has changed dramatically since the introduction of Diagnosis Related Groups (DRGs) and our hospital's Case Management Department reflects these changes (Auerbach *et al.*, 2000; Sulman, Savage & Way, 2001). With length of stay becoming a primary concern, and with complicated and problematic discharges occurring more frequently within the elderly population, many of the less measurable social work functions fell to the geriatric service (Keigher, 2000). The social workers who are affiliated with the geriatric service line have fewer time constraints and more flexible ways of measuring success than those within the case management department because of the nature of our role within the hospital (Cantrell, 2007). For this reason, coordination of decision making in relation to questions of patient competency is centered in our Senior Service Department as opposed to Case Management (Veeder, 2002).

We work closely with our attending and consulting physicians as well as floor nurses, to ensure clear and timely communication. When medical concerns from patients and families are made known to us, we facilitate conversations to address these concerns. Also, we are in communication with the physical therapists, as they help to determine what level of care our patients will need upon discharge. Open communication with the clinical staff guides our ability to inform patients and families and to secure an appropriate and timely discharge.

Decisions about practice

Description of the client situation

Mrs. Esposito is a 79-year-old widowed woman who lives alone in her two-story row home in a city neighborhood. She has three grown children, all of whom are married and live close by, as well as seven grandchildren. Mrs. Esposito was a homemaker during her working years. She depends on her deceased husband's social security check for financial support. Until several months ago when Mrs. Esposito was diagnosed with lung cancer, she was independent in all her activities of daily living. She attended church every morning, kept a spotless house and welcomed visits from family and friends. Recently, however, the family had begun to notice increased confusion, impaired short-term memory and a change in her normally pleasant demeanor.

Mrs. Esposito was brought to the emergency room by one of her daughters. She was experiencing a tingling in her arms and legs and had a brief loss of consciousness. Because of her known history of cancer, Mrs. Esposito was admitted to the oncology unit for further tests and observation. Unfortunately, at some time during her first night, she fell out of bed. While she did not experience any serious injury, she did have some pain and bruising. She was placed on a low bed with a bed alarm.

Over the course of the next few days Mrs. Esposito became more confused. She was not oriented to time and could neither identify that she was in a hospital, nor imagine why that would be so. She had taken an anti-anxiety medication in the past and this was restarted, in the belief that some of her confusion might be due to withdrawal. Otherwise, her confusion was attributed to delirium, not a rare occurrence in hospitalized elderly persons, especially those who have already begun to experience some dementia (Scott & Barrett, 2007). As her anxiety and confusion worsened, she made attempts to leave the hospital. She had frequent angry outbursts and refused care. Mrs. Esposito was placed on 1:1 observation, where a staff member is assigned to sit with a patient at all times.

Once it became clear to Mrs. Esposito's physician she would not be able to return to her previous living situation, social work was consulted. At first, Shelley, an oncology social worker from the case management department, attempted to meet with Mrs. Esposito, but she became hostile and was not willing or able to participate in her discharge plans. Either Pam or Rita, the patient's daughters, was often in her room, so Shelley arranged a time to meet with them together (Levine & Kuerbis, 2002). Both daughters confirmed that their brother, Rich, was an active alcoholic and had not been interested in becoming involved in the past. He did not return phone calls so the meeting went on without him.

As the discussion began to focus on the changes that would need to be made in Mrs. Esposito's living situation, it became clear that both Pam and Rita were distraught (Raveis, 2007; Wolff & Kasper, 2006). They believed that, aside from minor changes in memory and mood, their mother had been independent before coming to the hospital and they were not ready to accept as permanent the changes they now saw. They were unwilling to participate in a discussion of discharge planning, so the meeting adjourned with the idea that another one would take place later in the week.

Mrs. Esposito stabilized medically, and though she was still confused she did go to physical therapy. Her confusion became intermittent and her doctors felt she could go to a skilled nursing facility. She had been in bed for many days; her legs were weak, her balance bad and her stamina non-existent. When Shelley next met with Pam and Rita, she gave them the names and phone numbers of several skilled nursing facilities with good rehabilitation programs, asking that they visit these facilities and choose one. She told them she would take care of the discharge arrangements once they had decided on a destination.

When Pam and Rita returned with their decision, they met in Mrs. Esposito's room and told her of the visits made on her behalf. Her daughters assured her this was a temporary placement and they had chosen a good facility. Mrs. Esposito became angry and hostile, insisting she be allowed to go to her own home immediately upon discharge. She was adamant in refusing to go to a skilled nursing facility. When questioned about how she would be able to care for herself she simply stated she would manage (Dwyer, 2005).

At this point, we decided any further discussion with Mrs. Esposito would only cause undue distress. We exited her room and reconvened in a conference room down the hall. Pam and Rita were in tears. They began to talk about their own health issues; Rita had been diagnosed with multiple sclerosis five years earlier, Pam had had lupus since early adulthood. Both of these chronic medical conditions had been under control until the stress of Mrs. Esposito's condition had caused an exacerbation of symptoms. Pam was in pain much of the time; Rita's mobility became more limited. They wanted to make their mother happy—she had done so much for them, often putting their wants and needs before her own while they were growing up. They knew if Mrs. Esposito went home she would need care that they could not provide.

The possibility of hiring help at home was investigated. No one had the financial wherewithal to provide this, and while Mrs. Esposito would probably be eligible for home services through the local office of aging, she would need 24-hour care, which is not available. Mrs. Esposito was still intermittently confused; we hoped she would see the wisdom of our plan in time.

Unfortunately, after several days, Mrs. Esposito was still confused and refusing to consider placement. She no longer needed acute care; a fact our case manager, who is responsible for utilization review, reminded us of daily. Shelley, the case management social worker, spoke with the attending physician and it was determined Mrs. Esposito would need a guardian (Crampton, 2004). It was at this point that I was asked to become involved.

A geropsychiatrist was consulted, who determined Mrs. Esposito lacked the mental capacity to make informed decisions regarding her care. Pam and Rita held joint power of attorney; however, this did not allow them to make decisions she vehemently opposed. I coordinated the petition process with our legal department, making sure the interrogatories by the psychiatrist and medical doctor were completed. The use of interrogatories allows the physician's opinion to be considered by the judge of the Orphan's Court without the physician having to attend the proceedings. It was agreed that Pam would seek to be made guardian. Along with the hospital attorney, I would attend the hearing to represent the testimony.

It took a few days to gather the documentation necessary to petition the court. As we prepared our case, Mrs. Esposito grew sicker. Her cancer had spread and her prognosis was poor. Her attending physician did not believe she had long to live. We arranged for Pam and Rita to meet with our palliative care team. In the end, Mrs. Esposito went home with hospice care. This service was mostly covered by her insurance. Additionally, since her care would be time-limited, her daughters believed her needs could be met among the extended family.

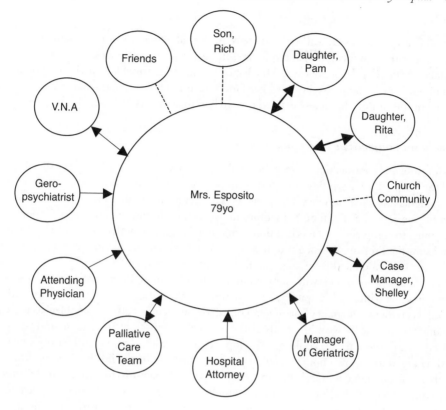

Figure 19.1 Ecomap for Mrs. Esposito.

Definition of the client

Social workers employed by the hospital serve several different clients. Initially, one would think of the patient as our client. More often than not, the patient comes with a family who can assist us in our work with the patient. Sometimes, however, the family serves to make our job more difficult. We must also work within the hospital system, being mindful of our relationships with physicians, nurses and other health professionals. Insurance carriers can also be seen as our clients, as they have very direct influence on the hospital stay and discharge arrangements. In our case, Mrs. Esposito is at the center of our client system. We also worked with her children to assist us in assuring a safe discharge for their mother. We are responsible to the hospital administration for providing good quality client satisfaction while efficiently managing our patient's case to avoid a discharge delay and thus assure reimbursement.

Mrs. Esposito was referred for social work intervention by the attending physician when he began to anticipate her discharge. After our initial meeting, it was clear she would need help in planning for her discharge. Pam and Rita were readily available and interested in providing assistance; therefore, they became an integral part of the client system. Their provision of background information and family history helped us not only to plan for their mother's discharge, but also to understand who she was before she became our patient. Working with them gave us insight into the relative ability of the family to support our patient and helped to explain their emotional reactions throughout the discharge planning process.

Goals

Our goal as hospital social workers is to coordinate a safe discharge for our patients. We provide them with the information and resources necessary to make choices. Patients are allowed to make unsafe choices; but because Mrs. Esposito was clearly unable to make a rational decision about her discharge, we involved her family. Our goal of a safe discharge remained the same, but the cast of characters with whom we had to coordinate this discharge grew.

Developing objectives and contracting

The only formal contract that exists in hospital social work is the one between the social worker and the hospital. Our job description determines the role we play with other staff and with our patients and their families. The patients' satisfaction with our work has become a large part of our annual evaluation. Sometimes in opposition to this, but equally as important, is our ability to complete our tasks in a timely manner. Hospital length of stay is a closely monitored statistic. Pressure is brought to bear on a social worker who cannot effectuate a timely discharge when a patient is no longer in need of acute care.

Our unofficial contract is with our patients and their families. Representing ourselves as patient advocates within the hospital system, we promise them their voices will be heard and that we will keep them informed of arrangements made on their behalf. We often feel as if we are walking a tightrope between the goals of the hospital and those of the patient and family.

In the case before us, we could not develop a contract with our patient. Her objective—to be discharged to her own home—could not be met because of the hospital's commitment to assure a safe discharge to those who are deemed to lack capacity to make informed decisions. The contract we did develop was with her daughters. They were in agreement regarding our objective which was to create a safe discharge destination but, in order to make this a working relationship, we had to respect the time they needed to process all of the changes in their mother's condition while moving them forward towards a decision about her care.

Meeting place

Hospital social workers are often assigned to patients by floor or medical specialty. The initial meeting with Mrs. Esposito occurred in her room, which is typical. Subsequent meetings continued in her room until it became clear that this was causing her undue stress and anxiety. When we met separately with Pam and Rita we were able to find a conference room on her floor that was not in use. Finding available space in the hospital for family meetings is often difficult. Once found, however, the ability to close the door protects us from interruption. Though medical staff—physicians, in particular—are getting better at respecting the existence of a meeting in a patient's room into which they have entered, it is often only a seasoned social worker who has the temerity to insist on acknowledgement and etiquette in these situations.

Use of time

We saw Mrs. Esposito approximately every other day throughout her 12-day hospitalization. The length of the interaction depended upon her mood. When she seemed interested in engaging, we stayed for perhaps 20 minutes but when she was angry or agitated by the tenor of our conversation, we left rather quickly. Meetings with Pam and Rita lasted anywhere from 20 minutes to more than an hour, depending on the nature of the discussion and their ability to engage in the issues at hand. We met with them five times during their mother's stay.

Because of the confusing and conflictual nature of Mrs. Esposito's situation, I spent a lot of time coordinating the consultations needed to file for guardianship. Trying to catch up with busy physicians is difficult and a certain amount of telephone tag is to be expected. At one point, when Mrs. Esposito was less confused, the attending physician questioned the need for guardianship. During a particularly lucid conversation, she convinced him and his residents that it would be possible for her to return to her home with appropriate home care. The following day, I arranged a meeting in the patient's room with the physician and the case management social worker. We allowed the physician to lead the interview, but when we had information that would underscore Mrs. Esposito's irrationality, we gently exposed it. In this way we were able to show the wisdom of our plan without offending our patient. Had it been determined that Mrs. Esposito would go to a skilled nursing facility, Shelley would have spent time contacting the facility, faxing the chart copy and arranging transportation.

Strategies and interventions

Working with older adults in an acute care hospital demands patience and constant "checking in." It was important at our first meeting that I take the time to get to know Mrs. Esposito— who she was before she became a patient, and what resources, including family, financial and internal, were available to her. To do this, I make a pronounced effort to respect each patient's space. I introduce myself and explain my role in the hospital. I ask if it is all right if I sit near her bed as it is important that I am at face level. I make sure she can see and hear me and I intersperse our conversation with questions to ascertain her level of comprehension.

Without this very intentional effort, it is easy to make the assumption that Mrs. Esposito understands and agrees with everything we are saying. If that assumption proves false, our plans for the patient can unravel, often at the last minute. As Mrs. Esposito was only one of many patients to be seen, I had to make this interview as comprehensive as possible in a short span of time without making her feel rushed. An efficient but personal and respectful assessment contributes to a successful intervention. "Checking in" with older adults to be sure they understand what is going on around them is very important. Mrs. Esposito neither saw nor heard well and often seemed to agree with medical staff, either because she didn't want to bother them or because she didn't have the energy to care to understand. When she became angry and combative, it was important to recognize when our interaction was no longer helpful and to exit the room gracefully.

It was necessary to convene a meeting with the physician, his residents, Shelley and me with Mrs. Esposito in her room to make sure we were all in agreement with the plan. We were not interested in taking our patient's independence away from her, but after meeting with Pam and Rita, Shelley and I did not believe that Mrs. Esposito would be able to care for herself, and we knew the strain this would put on her daughters. With careful questioning, we were able to expose Mrs. Esposito's unrealistic expectations of both her and her daughter's abilities to manage in her home.

Stance of the social worker

As a patient advocate, I try to help the patient and family process the medical information they are being given in a way that allows them to make appropriate decisions about their future (Freeman, 2005; Kane, 2004). It was important that Pam and Rita felt as if they were being respected and treated like partners in the care of their mother. Although Shelley would have liked to have left the first meeting knowing a choice would be made about a skilled nursing facility within the next few days, neither Pam nor Rita was nearly at this point. We always work to "meet clients where they are." To try to rush them into making a decision almost never works, and when it does it is often fraught with anxiety and doubt. Patients and caregivers are expected to process a lot of information in what may seem to them to be a short amount of time. Shelley and I have intimate knowledge of the discharge process and the choices that need to be made; however, this was all new to Pam and Rita. Additionally, we as professionals have no emotional connection to these decisions or their consequences—we go home to our own lives at the end of the day—so we must always be mindful of the process for others.

Resources outside of the social worker/client relationship

We have both internal and external customers and resources available. Internally, the medical staff greatly influences our work in the timeliness and appropriateness of referrals, in their interactions with patients and families we might be called on to explain, and in their cooperation with paperwork and administrative functions necessary to accomplish the discharge. The social workers in our home care department can be a great resource, both in their prior knowledge of the patient and for follow-up. We frequently request consultation with our palliative care and hospice teams as well as our pastoral care and physical therapy departments. Each of these entities helps us to advocate for our patients and craft a comprehensive discharge plan. In guardianship cases we work closely with our legal department. They submit the petition to the Orphans Court and schedule the hearing times. This is only one of many responsibilities assigned to the legal department, so there are times when we have to assert our agenda.

Our relationship with agencies outside the hospital, our external customers, is important to maintain, as this maximizes good communication and ease of referral. Shelley works closely with the clinical admissions liaisons who represent the extended care facilities in our area. Her interaction with them determines her ability to place patients with challenging circumstances.

Because of their discretion and professionalism, our legal department maintains a good relationship with the Orphan's Court, which makes it easier to obtain optimum hearing times. Meals on Wheels is another outside agency with which we interact regularly. Religious organizations, including the patient's individual place of worship, are a great resource. Had Mrs. Esposito been less delirious, we might have called on her parish priest to help in negotiating a safe aftercare plan for her. We have several faith-based thrift stores in our area and we rely on them for clothing, furniture and food donations when necessary.

Reassessment and evaluation

With each new development in Mrs. Esposito's health status, we were required to reassess and revise our interventions. Initially, we thought we could work with our patient in selecting a rehabilitation facility for discharge. Next, we endeavored to work with Pam and Rita, but we realized they would need to be given more time than we had anticipated to concur with our plan. Once they agreed with our plan and it became evident Mrs. Esposito never would, we needed to begin the guardianship process. When the physician questioned this plan, we had to re-evaluate and test our assumptions. Finally, when Mrs. Esposito became gravely ill, we had to transfer her care to the case manager.

Transfer, termination, and case conclusion

Once it was decided Mrs. Esposito would go home, the case manager became responsible for discharge arrangements; including hospice, home care and transportation. We did stay in touch with her and her daughters until she left. We always encourage patients to call us, even after discharge. Sometimes we hear from patients and/or relatives almost immediately after discharge, sometimes months or years later, and sometimes never. There doesn't seem to be any logic to this; the families I've worked the hardest for might never call, while those for whom I felt I was able to do very little make the grandest expressions of gratitude. Mrs. Esposito died in her home two weeks after discharge. Pam and Rita came to the hospital with an assortment of chocolates for the nurses on her floor to thank the staff for their kindness toward their mother. They asked to speak to Shelley and me, thanking us and saying that their mother had died peacefully with family around her.

Differential discussion

Often, it is only in retrospect that we know whether or not we've done a good job. I felt the Esposito family had a good outcome, but this was not without anxiety and tension throughout. We wanted to fulfill Mrs. Esposito's wish to go home. Her daughters, Shelley, and I did not want to send her to a skilled nursing facility against her will. However, we had to consider her safety and the fact she was no longer thinking clearly. We also had to deal with the reality that her funds, as well as Pam's and Rita's ability to help, were limited. Though it was, eventually, her advanced cancer that allowed her to do this, I believe her last days were more peaceful than months more in a facility would have been. I was happy to see Pam and Rita again and to hear, from them, of their mother's death. Even after the best of outcomes, families can feel they were pressured to make choices they didn't want to ever have to make and they can blame the social workers for that. Sometimes, as visible representatives of the hospital, we can become the targets of anger and blaming due to unresolved grief. We can also be the scapegoat of a health care system that is often neither fair nor equitable.

Though there is not a proven correlation—social work is, after all, a soft science—I believe the way in which we relate to our patients and their families throughout the hospital stay has direct consequences for their ability to adapt to the overwhelming changes in their lives. The respect for their circumstances and empathy for their feelings—as well as an understanding that life is a process—allows them a safe space to absorb these changes and participate positively in their health care. In our case, Mrs. Esposito could not make good use of our interventions. Her dementia and subsequent delirium would not allow this. Though it meant additional stress on and patience from us, we were able to advocate for Pam and Rita and allow them the time they needed to make appropriate decisions. The fact they came back and thanked us seemed to be evidence they benefited from our intervention.

References

American Bar Association (2006). *Legal guide for Americans over 50* (2nd ed.). New York: Random House Reference.

Auerbach, C., Rock, B. D., Goldstein, M., Kaminsky, P. & Heft-Laporte, H. (2000). A department of social work used data to prove its case. *Social Work in Health Care*, 32 (1): 9–23.

Auslander, G. K., Soskoine, V., Stanger, V., Ben Shahar, I. & Kaplan, G. (2008). Discharge planning in acute care hospitals in Israel: Services planned and levels of implementation and adequacy. *Health & Social Work*, 33 (3): 178–88.

Baker, M. E. (2000). Knowledge and attitudes of health care social workers regarding advance directives. *Social Work in Health Care*, 32 (2): 61–74.

Brink, P. & Stones, M. (2007). Examination of the relationship among hearing impairment, linguistic communication, mood, and social engagement of residents in complex continuing-care facilities. *The Gerontologist*, 47 (5): 633–41.

Cantrell, R. L. (2007). Common care: Toward a more acceptable option of care of the frail elderly. *Social Work in Public Health*, 23 (1): 61–73.

Crampton, A. (2004). The importance of adult guardianship for social work practice. *Journal of Gerontological Social Work*, 43 (2–3): 117–29.

Doukas, D. J. & Reichel, W. (2007). *Planning for uncertainty: Living wills and other advance directives for you and your family*. Baltimore: Johns Hopkins University Press.

Dwyer, S. (2005). Older people and permanent care: Whose decision? *The British Journal of Social Work*, 35 (7): 1081–92.

Freeman, I. C. (2005). Advocacy for aging: Notes of the next generation. *Families in Society*, 86 (3): 419–23.

Giordano, J. A. (2000). Effective communication and counseling with older adults. *International Journal of Aging & Human Development*, 51 (4): 315–24.

HIPAA. (2009). Retrieved 2/18/09, from http://www.HIPAA.org.

Kane, R. A. (2004). The circumscribed sometimes-advocacy of the case manager and the care provider. *Generations*, 28 (1): 70–4.

Keigher, S. M. (2000). *Aging and social work*. Washington, DC: NASW Press.

Leahy, D. A. & Lording, P. (2005). Impact of a social work residential care team on the discharge of hospitalized patients. *Australian Social Work*, 58 (3): 285–300.

LeJeune, B. J., Steinman, B. & Mascia, J. (2003). Enhancing socialization of older people experiencing loss of both vision and hearing. *Generations*, 27 (1): 95–7.

Levine, C. & Kuerbis, A. (2002). Building alliances between social workers and family caregivers. *Journal of Social Work in Long Term Care*, 1 (4): 3–17.

Moye, J., Butz, S. W., Marson, D. C. & Wood, E. (2007). A conceptual model and assessment template for capacity evaluation in adult guardianship. *The Gerontologist*, 47 (5): 591–603.

Naleppa, M. J. & Reid, W. J. (2000). Integrating case management and brief treatment strategies: A hospital-based geriatric program. *Social Work in Health Care*, 31 (4): 1–23.

Qualls, S. H. & Smyer, M. A. (2007). Changes in decision making capacity in older adults: Assessment and intervention. In Moye, J. & Braun, M. (eds.). *Assessment of medical consent capacity and independent living* (pp. 205–36). Hoboken: John Wiley & Sons.

Raveis, V. H. (2007). The challenges and issues confronting family caregivers to elderly cancer patients. In Carmel, S., Morse, C. A. & Torres-Gil, F. M. (eds.). *Lessons on aging from three nations, Volume II. The art of caring for adults* (pp. 85–97). Amityville: Baywood Publishing Company.

Scott, K. R. & Barrett, A. M. (2007). Dementia syndromes: Evaluation and treatment. *Expert Reviews of Neurotherapeutics*, 7 (4): 407–22.

Studer, Q. (2004). *Hardwiring excellence: Purpose worthwhile work making a difference*. Gulf Breeze: Fire Starter Publishing.

Sulman, J., Savage, D. & Way, S. (2001). Retooling social work practice for high volume, short stay. *Social Work in Health Care*, 34 (3/4): 315–32.

Veeder, N. J. (2002). Care management as management. *Care Management Journals*, 3 (2): 68–76.

Wolff, J. L. & Kasper, J. D. (2006). Caregivers of frail elderly: Updating a national profile. *The Gerontologist*, 46 (3): 344–56.

20 Hospice services

The dilemmas of technology at the end of life

Michelle K. Brooks

Context

From medieval times to the present, hospice has been a place where the weary could find shelter and refuge. Linguistically the word *hospice* shares the same root as hospitality, and hospice has come to mean compassionate relief from the weariness of illness and a specialized level of care at life's end. In 1967, Dame Cecily Saunders started the modern hospice movement in England. Saunders' vision included a holistic approach focused on symptom management and emotional support for the families of the dying individual. The first hospice care was provided at the inpatient setting of St. Christopher's Hospice in England, and the movement sparked a shift in the way we think about dying.

In 1969, Dr. Elisabeth Kubler-Ross published her bestselling book, *On Death and Dying*, which significantly influenced both the medical community and the general public. Kubler-Ross's humanizing of the dying process supported deinstitutionalizing the care of dying patients and led to the introduction of hospice as a specialized level of home care. By 2007, nearly 70% of all hospice care was provided in the patient's home (National Hospice and Palliative Care Organization, 2008). Combining symptom palliation and emotional support offers people who are dying an opportunity to experience the end of their life on their own terms (Gazelle, 2007). Hospice empowers caregivers to tackle the difficult task of physically caring for those they love.

Policy

The holistic approach to care includes an interdisciplinary team (IDT) of professionals consisting of medical professionals (the patient's physician, the hospice medical director, registered nurses, social workers, spiritual counselors, home health aides, bereavement counselors), and volunteers who focus their attention on the entire unit of care, the patient and his/her support system. Prior to a hospice admission, many patients have experienced themselves as body parts, with specialists probing, irradiating, surgically removing, and chemically bombarding sick cells—all with hope of a cure. Patients are referred to hospice when all aggressive disease-fighting efforts have either been exhausted and/or failed. Eligibility for hospice care requires that the patient have a terminal diagnosis with a life expectancy of six months or less. Medicare establishes guidelines of eligibility specific to various disease trajectories. Patients may remain on hospice service beyond six months if there is evidence of continual decline. Patients receiving hospice care do not return to hospitals for treatment; instead all care is provided in the patient's residence. A residence is defined as a private home, an assisted living facility, a nursing home or an inpatient hospice unit. The Medicare hospice benefit does not cover room and board charges of residential facilities. Medicare will provide limited coverage for patients receiving hospice care in hospitals, but that benefit is time sensitive (typically two weeks) and meant for symptoms that require continual care.

The Medicare hospice benefit was instituted in 1987, and when a patient chooses hospice care, Medicare becomes the primary insurer. The majority of hospice patients are over the age of 65 and in 2007, Medicare reimbursements accounted for 83% of all hospice revenues (NHPCO, 2008). The 2009 Medicare reimbursement rate is a capped daily rate of $154.09 per day. There are no co-pays or additional fees for hospice Medicare patients; the benefit provides 100% coverage. In addition to professional services provided by the IDT, the hospice benefit also covers durable medical equipment (DME), supplies (diapers, gloves, etc.) and includes coverage of all medications used for symptom palliation. Patients have access to care 24 hours a day, seven days a week. Medicaid and private insurers provide participants a hospice benefit with most plans following Medicare's guidelines. Unlike Medicare, some private insurers provide an inpatient hospice benefit that covers room and board charges.

Medicare's Conditions of Participation (COPs) sets standards of care for the hospice team. Patients referred to hospice are expected to be evaluated by a hospice nurse within 48 hours, and social workers are required to assess the patient and family within the first five days. In addition, chaplain and bereavement services are considered core services of care.

The hospice movement has grown tremendously since the 1970s. The National Hospice and Palliative Care Organization (NHPCO) reported 4,700 hospice providers in the United States in 2007 (NHPCO, 2008). In the same year, the Center for Disease Control (CDC) reported over 1.4 million terminally ill patients received hospice care accounting for 38.8% of all U.S. deaths. While the majority of hospice providers are not-for-profit agencies, in recent years there has been an increase of hospice providers from the for-profit sector (NHPCO, 2008).

Technology

While the concept of hospice care is slowly being embraced, medical technology has transformed many once deadly diseases into serious chronic illnesses (Rando, 1984; Van der Maas, 2006). Medication and devices applied to, or inserted into, a person's body, can manage and regulate numerous symptoms and body functions. Patients and families now confront decisions about withholding and/or withdrawing technology at the end of life. One of the more complex discussions in hospice regards nutrition and hydration, especially when Artificial Nutrition and Hydration (ANH) are being provided by a feeding appliance (often referred to as a feeding tube or peg tube). Deeply held religious and cultural beliefs may guide decisions regarding ANH (Cicivelli, MacLean & Cox, 2000; Hoefler, 2000; Morrison, Meier & Cassel, 1999; Repenshek & Slosar, 2004). What is often missing from the dialogue, particularly for people with neurobiological disorders, is the understanding that a feeding tube does not improve survival rates (Alters, 2009; Hoefler, 2000). The emotional connection to food is powerful. Food is the fuel of life, it heals and sustains; however, food has little power to derail the course of a terminal illness. Feeding appliances, while useful in many short-term circumstances, can enhance the suffering of the terminally ill. At the end of life, ANH is responsible for symptoms such as aspiration, pneumonia, diarrhea, and can increase gastrointestinal discomfort (Buiting et al., 2007; Casarett, Kapo & Caplan, 2005; Hoefler, 2000).

Patients naturally decrease food intake as they get closer to death. Decreased intake supports the body in its effort to shut down. It is normal for loved ones to be alarmed when witnessing this change in nutritional intake, and the presence of an ANH appliance complicates these emotions. Fears of starvation and dehydration often cloud the reality that death is approaching because of the terminal illness. The chief complaint and observable result of decreased hydration is dry mouth and thirst (Casarett, Kapo & Caplan, 2005). Both symptoms can be managed with ice chips, swabs, and mouth care. A study conducted at St. Christopher's Hospice indicates that dry mouth and thirst are the result of mouth breathing (typical during active dying), medications, and conditions related to the disease progression (Ellershaw, Sutcliffe & Saunders, 1995).

Organization

Keystone Hospice is a not-for-profit independent hospice in Philadelphia, Pennsylvania, which had 511 new hospice admissions in 2008. These patients were cared for in their homes, care facilities, hospitals, and at Keystone House (an 18-bed inpatient residential hospice unit located in Wyndmoor, Pennsylvania). Keystone House is a Victorian mansion with an atmosphere akin to a bed and breakfast. Uniquely, while most inpatient hospice units located within hospitals have restricted lengths of stay (usually under two weeks), residents have the opportunity to remain at Keystone House for the remainder of their lives. The agency is Medicare certified, CHAP (Community Health Accreditation Program) accredited, approved by Medicaid providers, and participates with nearly all private insurers. Keystone Hospice provides care to those in need, regardless of their ability to pay. We are committed to the creative and complementary therapies and offer Music Therapy (MT), Art Therapy (AT), Movement Therapy (MovT), as well as Acupuncture and Chinese Herbal therapies.

Patients referred to Keystone Hospice are admitted on the day of the referral or upon hospital discharge. The admission team consists of a hospice nurse and social worker who will continue to follow the case. This unique approach introduces the social worker to the patient and family at the difficult moment of consenting to hospice care. Through a comprehensive plan of care, the social worker directs the allied team (consisting of Chaplains, MT, AT, MovT, Complementary Therapies, Bereavement Counselors, and Volunteer Director) regarding the psychosocial needs and desires of the patient/family. Plans are reviewed and updated weekly.

Decisions about practice

Definition of the client

Hospice views the "client" as the patient and the patient's support system and the hospice social worker therefore offers support and counseling to the patient as well as to anyone in the patient's support network. Let me introduce Liza, a 69-year-old Caucasian female with two adult children, three grandchildren, and James, her partner of more than 10 years. Liza was an artist; she dabbled in real estate, and is described as a person with a magnetic personality. Her commitment to physical health included daily exercise, yoga, and dance classes. While Liza never participated in any formal religion, she is described as a spiritual person. Three years ago, Liza was diagnosed with a rare neurological disease, Progressive Supranuclear Palsey (PSP), which has no known cure. Brain cells deteriorate causing movement impairment, and common symptoms include: postural instability, dysarthria (muscles of the mouth, face, and respiratory system weaken, eventually the inability to move these muscles, drooling is common), dysphagia (difficulty swallowing), bradykinesia (slowed ability to start and continue movement or inability to adjust the body's position), and visual disturbances and cognitive impairment (www.emedicine.medscape.com). Eye movement impairment causes the patient to have a fixed vertical gaze.

PSP symptom progression is different for everyone. Liza's early symptoms were dysarthria and dysphagia. As Liza's swallowing difficulties escalated, discussions ensued regarding ANH. Liza feared that a feeding tube would extend her life beyond a meaningful existence. It had value in the present but not necessarily in her future. At the time, Liza was still able to walk and communicate. Liza and her physician (PCP) discussed options and Liza agreed to a peg tube with a plan to withdraw ANH toward the end of her life.

I met Liza shortly after she had moved to her daughter Monica's home. Liza's care needs had escalated beyond her partner's physical abilities. The move was hard for Liza who left behind her beach home, James, and her pets. Monica, a single mother of 10-year-old Annie, altered her work schedule to care for her mother, and private caregivers were hired to assist Liza. She used a walker (with occasional episodes of falling backwards) and is now in advanced stages of PSP. Her cognitive processing is delayed but she appears alert and oriented. Her ability to communicate has diminished significantly and she now communicates by rocking her torso. Her gaze is fixed with facial muscles frozen in a flat expression. She is dysphagic, has a history of pneumonia, and is nourished via a feeding tube. Periodically Liza cries out, a common symptom of PSP, however Monica feels the crying is an effort to communicate needs. Monica has been involved in her mother's care since the diagnosis. I sense a deep connection between the women. Liza's other daughter, Sharon, lives on the West Coast. Monica and Sharon have communicated daily. Sharon planned to visit with her sons (Sam and Jack).

This is a well-educated, white, middle-class family that is open to support. Monica selected Keystone Hospice because of the agency's progressive mission, and she believes the options in complementary services support her mother's curiosity about alternatives to western medicine. With the family's input, social work coordinated IDT support. The plan of care includes art therapy, music therapy, chaplaincy, and acupuncture treatments.

The hospice social worker's role involves supporting families navigating the death of a loved one. We work to identify strengths and coping skills, keeping a keen eye on helping individuals maintain healthy relationships with the patient and each other. The social worker strives to create an environment where participants feel safe to express feelings. My work with Liza and her family intensified when Liza made the decision to withdraw ANH.

Goals

The initial goal for Liza's family was relatively typical of most hospice families: support the patient and family through the dying process. Liza's diminishing ability to communicate had the potential to compromise the family's ability to relate to her, and modeling communication would be important. Time was scheduled with Sharon when she arrived. The creative arts team would work with the children in the household, and art and music therapies would use creative expression as a tool for the children to explore their feelings and grief about their grandmother's approaching death.

The work, and the goals, shifted once Liza and Sharon visited Liza's PCP, who was struck by how compromised Liza had become. The disease was progressing and the feeding appliance was beginning to fail (increased episodes of diarrhea and gastrointestinal discomfort). This prompted the PCP to revisit Liza's original concerns; Liza had been clear about her wishes of not wanting ANH to trap her into a lifeless existence. The PCP initiated the conversation. With only the ability to move her torso, Liza was able to communicate with the PCP who knew her well. She was ready to withdraw ANH (Drazen, 2003).

Witnessing Liza's interaction with her PCP, Sharon left the appointment ready to honor her mother's request—discontinue ANH. For Sharon, there was no question about what to do next but Monica was not quite ready. There were a lot of questions—would it be painful, would she feel hunger, is it OK to do this? Monica felt uncomfortable and scared. Tension built between the siblings as Monica grappled with her mother's decision. I now focused on helping the family negotiate this decision.

Contracting and developing objectives

The hospice contract begins during the admission process, which provides an opportunity to explore how folks are coping with the shift to comfort measures. A hospice admission signals death is approaching. At this meeting, I assess how prepared the group is to deal with impending loss; this helps to develop the plan of care designed uniquely for the patient and/or family. Patients and/or their caregivers sign a contract agreeing to the terms of hospice care. There are four major points to the contract. First, the focus of care shifts from cure to comfort measures. Second, at the time of death no heroic lifesaving measures will be employed. The goal is a peaceful death. The team then prepares the family about what to do at the time of death. Third, the family must understand that hospice patients do not return to the hospital, other than if they experience an unexpected trauma (i.e. a fall). Fourth, information is provided about all IDT services. Families are informed there is open communication amongst team members regarding the patient and family.

Hospice social work allows goals and objectives to be flexible enough to evolve to match the changes occurring within the family system. Changes in physical symptoms affect the patients and those caring for them. The social worker's role is supportive, and the work may change as the patient's physical condition changes. Liza's decision to withdraw ANH sent shock waves through her family; the work shifted to accommodate the impact on relationships.

Meeting place

The meeting place for a hospice social worker is typically wherever the patient is at any given time. Most of my work takes place in the patient's home where there are so many opportunities to do good work. Clues such as photographs, a calendar a few months behind, unread mail and newspapers give unspoken evidence about what has been happening, and these clues often direct the visit. It can be challenging to create intimacy when a caregiver is hovering, so the work becomes inclusive. Caregivers may hover from a desire to protect the patient, but most often, they hover because they need support. My experience suggests when patients need a private space, they will create it; if I sense they want it but are hesitating, I will ask for them. Social workers must honor the patient as a person, trusting them to know what they need. The holistic approach of hospice invites us to see the person behind their diagnosis.

Working in an inpatient facility and/or hospital setting makes creating intimacy difficult. There is far less environmental control in these settings where interruptions are frequent, schedules of personal care are important, and social workers must be flexible. Institutional settings produce interruptions, and sometimes offer opportunities to explore a patient's feelings about accepting personal care. All the work with Liza took place in Monica's home. While the space was adequate, it became crowded and sometimes chaotic after Sharon arrived with her sons. The space became tighter as the tension increased between Sharon and Monica.

Use of time

Typically, meetings are planned at the patient's residence. The length of an appointment can be anywhere from one to two hours depending upon the needs. Time is precious for hospice patients and their loved ones. I prepare to spend as little or as much time as necessary to facilitate an environment of support, encouragement, and most importantly—communication. Talking about the end of a life is delicate work. My role is to operate as a catalyst of movement and movement requires space and time. Hospice social workers start with no expectations or agendas but rather with a willingness to meet our clients in the present moment. This is consistent with the hospice philosophy, which differs in many ways from traditional medical models. Our goal is to help patients not to die alone. Dying alone does not mean that people are present when someone takes their last breath, but rather, that the experience of dying is shared.

The length or amount of time spent with any one hospice patient correlates to the disease progression and is responsive to the needs of the patient and family. I spent eight weeks with Liza and her family. During that time I visited the home five times and had numerous phone conversations with Monica and Sharon. Unlike other areas of social work practice, visits do not require pre-approval from insurers or Medicare.

Strategies and interventions

The initial strategy is to understand the person in his/her environment, and then to allow the work to develop in the present. I tend to start the assessment with, "Tell me what has been going on." This invites the patient and family to tell their story, typically beginning with a medical historiography. While the nurse manager is interested in the details of the illness, I am curious about the experience. I gently guide the patient and family into a discussion of life prior to the illness. I want to know the people. Who have they been throughout their life? What is, or who is, significant to them? Terminal illness can reduce individuals to a diagnosis. This process of 're-membering' (Morgan, 2000) provides the possibility for the patient and/or family to experience themselves as whole, while they reflect on better times. In order to understand the loss, I must understand what they are each losing. Liza's family was losing a vibrant, significant member of the family. PSP had taken bits and pieces of Liza—they lost more of her each day.

Withdrawal of ANH complicated this family's process. I met with the family after the visit to the PCP. Monica was conflicted and frightened. My intervention was a combination of education and re-framing. Technology had interfered with and delayed Liza's dying, but the disease continued to progress. I encouraged Monica to express her fears and feelings. This was an important moment in Monica's grief process. If Monica perceived her role as a participant in her mother's death, the trajectory of her grief could potentially be long and arduous (Davis, C., 2001; Davis, M., 2006; Fleming & Belanger, 2001; Rando, 1984, 1993). Monica feared her mother would die a painful death from starvation, although medical evidence does not support her fears (Buiting, *et.al.*, 2007; Casarett, Kapo & Caplan, 2005; Ellershaw, Sutcliffe & Saunders, 1995; Ganzini, Goy, Miller & Harvath, 2003). I shared my knowledge of ANH withdrawal and the natural dying process. Monica's fears eased but she was not quite ready to start the process. Meanwhile, Sharon was anxious to stop the ANH feedings. We planned to meet again.

I returned the following week. ANH feedings were decreasing and Liza was declining. She was in a hospital bed in the dining room. Telephone conversations throughout the week had prepared me for these changes. Monica was comfortable with a gentle withdrawal of ANH.

Sharon was angry with the pace. The tension between the siblings was escalating.

When I arrived for our scheduled meeting, I was greeted at the door by Annie (Monica's daughter), while Jack and Sam ran around the house in their pajamas. Liza slept in the dining room. Sharon was in the backyard tending to a stray cat and Monica was in the shower. About 10 minutes after my arrival Sharon bounced into the house, headed straight for the front door—she was going for cappuccino, did anyone want one? I declined. Monica remained upstairs. I elected to sit with Liza. Liza could not respond but she could take in her environment. I continue to verbally communicate with patients even if they are unable to respond. This was particularly important for Liza who had a neurological disease that was locking her in (information came in but she was unable to respond). I told Liza, "This is a hard time for your girls—we need to let them do this, they will be OK." I felt certain this family could negotiate this stressful situation because at their core they all loved and respected each other—a good place to start. My goal was to get them back to their core—together.

Understanding and using resistance is critical to hospice social work. Resistance can take many forms ranging from avoiding a discussion to delaying an interaction (Brandell, 1997). Resistance was an important part of our work together. Monica and Sharon were resisting each other; together they resisted me. Oddly enough, I could appreciate that the women were at least doing one thing together—resisting me. Somehow this resistance felt hopeful for our work. Allowing the women to "waste my time" assured them that I would not abandon them, I was willing to wait. I realized that the women were struggling with feelings of abandonment by their mother. It was important that I not abandon them and that I not allow them to abandon each other (Bowlby, 1980). Working inside the resistance provided each of them the space they needed. This was scary—they knew we were going to confront their conflict. Underneath everything was the reality that Liza was dying and leaving them. "Waiting it out" is a technique often used in mediation work (Beer & Stief, 1997), but I have found it adaptable to hospice social work practice. Approximately 45 minutes after my arrival, the women were ready. Our work began.

The sisters were fighting and frustrated with each other. As the conflict escalated, it seemed Liza was increasingly isolated, and I was concerned. Monica who once seemed so confident and connected to her mother was absorbed by the conflict with her sister. Liza's decision was resulting in a premature detachment from her daughters.

I had worked with Liza's family for six weeks. This was enough time for me to be able to observe each daughter's attachment to their mother. Bowlby (1979) warns that disruption of affectional bonding can elicit loss responses of anger and anxiety. Living over 3,000 miles away for many years, Sharon had physically separated from her mother. Monica and Liza had a different relationship. Liza had been Monica's birth coach and a co-parent to Annie. She was part of Monica's daily life. In my assessment, one element of the conflict stemmed from a shared belief that their loss was the same, but their individual loss was reflective of their individual, and very different, relationships with their mother. It can be difficult for family members immersed in their own loss to recognize the loss for the other. My goal was to help them to give each other room for their individual feelings and grief.

It seemed the current struggle between the siblings had less to do with stopping the feedings than it did with the changes in the family system. A recurring theme was that they had always been able to talk with one another until now. Sharon felt Monica was being 'negative'; Monica felt Sharon would not allow her to express her feelings. Monica believed Sharon was rushing the process in order to get home sooner. Listening to them as they went back and forth in their argument, I was overwhelmed by how much they were missing each other. Liza's approaching death was not only separating them from Liza, but from each other.

As I listened to Monica and Sharon, an image came to me of two people running around a track. Neimeyer (2000) suggests the use of metaphor as an "economical" expression of understanding. I offered the following image: "The two of you are running around the same track but Sharon, you are a much faster runner. It's not that the race wasn't hard for you, but you have reached the finish line and you now know how good it feels to be there. You look back and Monica is moving at a much slower clip and seems to be working very hard. Monica has no idea what it is like to be where you are, and you, having reached the finish line, are beginning to forget the pain of the last several yards. Sharon, you now have two choices: you can wait for Monica and greet her at the finish line, or you can return to the locker room." I asked the women not to respond immediately but to give the image a moment. After a few moments, I invited each woman to share her experience, and each was able to connect with this image. The conclusion of the discussion that followed was that it was easier for them to think of the other ahead but they could not imagine not being there for each other at the finish line.

There remained one more important order of business—reconnecting Monica and Sharon to Liza. They were struggling with Liza's declined state and I asked if the music therapist could visit to help them with the process of connecting to her. They agreed.

Stance of the social worker

My role is often that of a witness and sometimes of translator. Using social work tools, I borrow and blend interventions to meet the needs of the patient and/or family. Hospice social work necessitates working in the 'here and now' (Yalom, 2005). I listen to family and personal history in an effort to understand the family system—not with the intent of changing the system. My role is to work within the existing family system and to support the system's strengths.

Resources outside the helping relationship

I frequently locate and engage resources outside of the agency to help families with financial problems, transportation, additional care-giving needs, etc. and I need a working knowledge of resources within each family's geographical area. Understanding the etiology of a patient's illness is also important. By the time I meet patients, they have often been living with their disease for years; their job is not to educate us, but rather to enhance our understanding of how they have been coping.

In the last session with Liza's family, I helped the sisters reconnect with each other but not with Liza. The daughters realized they had stopped connecting with Liza, and Liza was dying. The MT met with the family later that day, and through a songwriting exercise, she encouraged each member of the family to write lyrics to the melody of one of Liza's favorite songs. With her guidance, they were able to connect with each other and then, most importantly, the music allowed them to re-connect to Liza. Liza's family received support from multiple members of the allied team: art therapy working with the children, acupuncture for Liza, and spiritual support from the hospice chaplain.

Reassessment and evaluation

Reflection on process prior to and following a visit allows for the work to develop and mature. For example, Monica and Sharon's resistance was not immediately understood. The last intervention prior to Liza's death was not the first time I had encountered resistance from the women. After each of my first few visits, I left the family home feeling annoyed, believing the women were wasting my time. I felt disrespected. Whenever I begin to have feelings of annoyance and/or anger it is a signal for me to pull back and reflect on what is happening during these encounters. The practitioner's emotional responses are tools in the therapeutic relationship. Without reflection, opportunities to gain greater understanding can be missed. If I had not spent time reassessing the work, I may have believed the women did not want to work on their conflict, and I would have forfeited my role. In this case, I joined with the resistance rather than fighting it, with fruitful outcomes.

Transfer and termination

When a hospice patient dies, the hospice social worker transfers the case (surviving family members) to Keystone's bereavement services. The bereavement department maintains contact with the family for the next 18 months (six months longer than mandated by Medicare).

Case conclusion

During the following week, the family spent more time gathered at Liza's bedside telling stories, sharing memories, and listening to music. Monica extended invitations to family and friends to visit. Early one morning, with her daughters at her bedside, Liza died. Her death was described as both peaceful and quiet. The nurse manager and I went to the home. After the RN pronounced the patient's death, we all gathered at the kitchen table to talk about the experience. Monica and Sharon were connected in the experience and openly supported one another. The women were grateful to have shared this journey together.

Differential discussion

Several months have passed since I worked with Liza's family. I appreciate how willing Monica and Sharon were to confront their conflict and follow their mother's wishes. Not all families are so willing to engage. Reflecting on the work, I must consider how the work would have unfolded had I explored Liza and Monica's emotional relationship with the feeding appliance initially. At the time of admission, we discussed the symptoms contributing to the decision for ANH, but I never explored the meaning attached to it. Hindsight provides 20/20 vision; I believe exploring the emotional connections to ANH would have been a valuable tool. I missed the initial opportunity to discover if Liza had shared her feelings regarding ANH with her daughters. There was an element of shock in Monica's response. It is not clear if Monica's reaction was due to the realization that Liza would die, or because the news was unexpected. Liza's limited ability to communicate prevented any opportunity to explore her feelings. The majority of patients fed via ANH are cognitively compromised, thus inhibiting such a discussion. ANH decisions are influenced by personal beliefs and recommendations from medical practitioners and/or institutions (Bloche, 2005). Patients with head, neck, and throat cancers frequently have feeding appliances and seldom have cognitive impairment. Lessons from this case suggest exploring the emotional experience of a feeding appliance is a viable and important early intervention.

I often consult with families as they question the insertion of a feeding tube. Withholding treatment is less charged than the decision to withdraw feedings. Yet when one views a feeding tube as an appliance, the shift in language creates a shift in meaning. Appliances do not always work and may outgrow their usefulness. Perhaps it is time to view this technology through a different lens, allowing ourselves to understand ANH for what it is. Technology can extend a life, but in memory of Liza, does it take you beyond a life worth living? Perhaps that should always be the question.

References

Alters, S. M. (2009). *Death and dying: End-of-life controversies*. New York: Gale.

Beer, J. E. & Stief, S. (1997). *The mediator's handbook*, (Rev. 3rd ed.). Gabriola Island, Canada: New Society Publishers.

Bloche, M. G. (2005). Managing conflict at the end of life. *The New England Journal of Medicine*, 352 (23): 2371–3.

Bowlby, J. (1979). *The making and breaking of affectional bonds*. New York: Routledge.

Bowlby, J. (1980). *Attachment and loss. Volume 3: Loss sadness and depression*. New York: Basic Books.

Brandell, J. R. (1997). *Theory and practice in clinical social work*. New York: Simon & Schuster Inc.

Buiting, H. M., van Delden, J. J. M., Rietjens, J. A. C., Onwuteaka-Philipsen, B. D., Bilsen, J., Fischer S., *et al.* (2007). Foregoing artificial nutrition or hydration in patients nearing death in six European countries. *Journal of Pain and Symptom Management*, 34 (3): 305–14.

Casarett, D., Kapo, J. & Caplan, A. (2005). Appropriate use of artificial nutrition and hydration—Fundamental principles and recommendations. *The New England Journal of Medicine*, 353 (24): 2607–14.

Cicivelli, V. G., MacLean, A. P. & Cox, L. S. (2000). Hastening death: A comparison of two end-of-life decisions. *Death Studies*, 24 (5): 401–19.

Davis, C. G. (2001). The tormented and the transformed: Understanding responses to loss and trauma. In R. A. Neimeyer (ed.), *Meaning reconstruction and the experience of loss* (pp. 137–55). Washington, D. C.: American Psychological Association.

Davis, M. P. (2006). A palliative ethic of care: Clinical wisdom at life's end. *The New England Journal of Medicine*, 354 (15): 1653–4.

Drazen, J. M. (2003). Decisions at the end of life. *The New England Journal of Medicine*, 349 (12): 1109.

Ellershaw, J. E., Sutcliffe, J. M. & Saunders, C. M. (1995). Dehydration and the dying patient. *Journal of Pain and Symptom Management*, 10 (3): 192–7.

Emedicine. Retrieved 6/11/09, from http://emedicine.medscape.com.

Fleming, S. J. & Belanger, S. K. (2001). Trauma, grief, and surviving childhood sexual abuse. In R. Neimeyer (ed.), *Meaning reconstruction and the experience of loss* (pp. 311–29). Washington, D. C.: American Psychological Association.

Ganzini, L., Goy, E. R., Miller, L. L. & Harvath, T. A. (2003). Nurses experiences with hospice patients who refuse food and fluids to hasten death. *The New England Journal of Medicine*, 349 (4): 359–65.

Gazelle, G. (2007). Understanding hospice—An underutilized option for life's final chapter. *The New England Journal of Medicine*, 357 (4): 321.

Hoefler, J. M. (1997). *Managing death: The first guide for patients, family members, and care providers on foregoing treatment at the end of life*. Boulder, CO: Westview Press.

Hoefler, J. M. (2000). Making decisions about tube feeding for severely demented patients at the end of life: Clinical, legal, and ethical considerations. *Death Studies*, 24: 233–54.

Kubler-Ross, E. (1969). *On death and dying*. New York: Scribner.

Morgan, A. (2000). *What is narrative therapy?* Adelaide, South Australia: Dulwich Center Publications.

Morrison, S. R., Meier, D. E. & Cassel, C. K. (1999). When too much is too little. *The New England Journal of Medicine*, 335 (23): 1755–9.

National Hospice and Palliative Care Organization (NHPCO). (2008). *NHPCO facts and figures: Hospice care in America*. [Brochure].

Neimeyer, R. A. (2000). *Lessons of loss: A guide to coping*. Memphis, TN: University of Memphis.

Rando, T. A. (1984). *Grief, dying, and death: Clinical interventions for caregivers*. Champaign: Research Press Company.

Rando, T. A. (1993). *Treatment of complicated mourning*. Champaign: Research Press.

Repenshek, M. & Slosar, J. P. (2004). Medically assisted nutrition and hydration: A contribution to the dialogue. *The Hastings Report*, 34 (6): 13–16.

Van der Maas, P. J. (2006). End-of-life decision making: A cross-national study. (Book review.) *The New England Journal of Medicine*, 354 (15): 1654.

Yalom, I. D. (2005). *The theory and practice of group psychotherapy*. (5th ed.). New York: Basic Books.

Part 2

GROUP, PROGRAM
AND/OR ADVOCACY WORK

21 We Are Not Alone

A support group for loss after diagnosis of fetal anomaly

Judith L. M. McCoyd

Context

WANA, the We Are Not Alone support group came into being in 1995, as the result of women experiencing perinatal bereavement after having prenatal screening and testing that diagnosed a fetal anomaly (either a genetic or chromosomal disorder or some structural abnormality of the fetus). As screening for fetal anomalies by alpha-feto-protein (AFP) blood screenings became ubiquitous, usually followed by amniocentesis in the early 1990s and now typically by the Chorionic Villus Sampling (CVS) prenatal test or ultrasound, women and their partners were faced with decisions about whether to continue a pregnancy known to be affected by some sort of fetal anomaly. A variety of fetal anomalies (Down syndrome, cystic fibrosis, hypoplastic left heart syndrome to name just a few from chromosomal to genetic to structural respectively) are diagnosable, yet the severity and phenotypical impact are not always known.

With these uncertainties, women and their partners may elect to terminate an affected pregnancy rather than carry it to term. When these desired pregnancies are terminated (medically considered an abortion—here referred to as TFA, termination for anomaly), women and their partners typically experience grief of varying severity. In 1995, few resources were available to support people in this circumstance. When the bereaved attended support groups for perinatal loss they often felt ostracized and isolated, as those who experienced spontaneous loss often blamed the women for their loss due to the decision to terminate the pregnancy. These women found their way to my private practice for individual support and the idea for WANA was born.

Policy

Aspects of policy that impact women who are pregnant are the guidelines about prenatal screening and testing as developed by the American College of Obstetricians and Gynecologists (ACOG) (www.acog.org). In the U.S., women who are pregnant are urged to have maternal blood serum screening (variously named over time the AFP test, triple screen, quad screen, sequential screening) and most receive this screening without an awareness that its purpose is for fetal health screening (Browner & Press, 1995; McCoyd, 2003; Rapp, 1999; Santahlahti, Hemminki, Latikka & Ryynaen, 1998). When screening shows an increased risk of fetal anomaly, testing is recommended by use of amniocentesis, CVS or high-resolution ultrasonography (ACOG, 2005). This usually allows diagnosis of the disorder. Genetic and chromosomal disorders cannot be remedied, though some structural disorders can be ameliorated, either in utero via fetal surgery or after birth. Nevertheless, the first decision a woman or couple must make is whether the mother intends to continue the pregnancy or terminate.

This decision is itself impacted by federal and state policy (as well as insurance policies). In 1973, the U.S. Supreme Court decided abortion policy should follow a trimester timeline with focus on the woman's right to privacy and self-determination growing more limited, as the states have an ever increasing right to create policy that limits access to abortion later in pregnancy (*Roe v. Wade*, 410 U.S. 113, 1973). Many states do limit access to abortion after 22–24 weeks of gestation (Alan Guttmacher Inst). Further, coverage for termination of pregnancy is determined by one's insurance. Federal policy mandates that no federal funds can be used for pregnancy termination; therefore, women who have their health insurance through Medical Assistance, CHAMPUS (for the armed services), the Public Health Service and other federal insurance programs may not have pregnancy termination covered by their insurance. Private insurers' policies vary, with some fully covering diagnosis and termination and others (particularly religion-based policies) not covering termination procedures.

Technology

As indicated above, much of the decision making around fetal diagnosis is due to a rapid development of prenatal screening and diagnostic technology, combined with little communication about what its findings may yield (AFP3/Afp4, 2004; Bernhardt *et al.* 1998; Chorionic Villi Sampling, 2005; Leithner *et al.*, 2006). The consumption of technology occurs both because it produces what many view as authoritative knowledge (Browner & Press, 1997; Davis-Floyd & Sargent, 1997) and also due to factors such as norms about prenatal bonding (Georges, 1997; McCoyd, 2007, under review).

The technology of ultrasound is particularly illustrative (Georges, 1997). Initially showing only external details, ultrasound technology has advanced to the degree that small structures internal to the fetus can be viewed on ultrasound for diagnostic purposes and even the nuchal fold (as the neural tube of the embryo transforms to the brain and spinal cord of a fetus) can be measured early in pregnancy to assess whether there is a high degree of risk for trisomy conditions. Along with this diagnostic development, pregnant women were increasingly encouraged to "see the baby" via the ultrasound viewer and given "pictures" of faces and bodies; some are now given a CD of the entire ultrasound process (multiple communications from clients). This promotes a sense of connection with the fetus and may actually complicate the emotions when decisions have to be made about whether to terminate or continue an affected pregnancy (Georges, 1997; McCoyd, 2007, 2008b; Rapp, 1999).

Another technology associated with this population is the intervention strategy of support groups. It has been suggested that support groups are particularly useful for disenfranchised losses (Doka, 2002), where people feel isolated and different from others. This seems to be the case for women after TFA (McCoyd, 1997, 2008a, in press). Support groups are said to fulfill several primary goals: "to foster mutual aid, to help members cope with stressful life events and to revitalize and enhance members' coping abilities so they can adapt to and cope with future stressful life events" (Toseland & Rivas, 2009, 20).

Critical factors in support groups are acceptance and a sense of connection to one another. Many women who came to WANA had the experience of rejection and feeling "othered" when they attended a Perinatal Bereavement Group. Part of the reason for this is that the process of loss and the available defenses differ between perinatal loss, due to miscarriage or stillbirth, and loss due to TFA. The fact of having to make a decision to terminate the pregnancy is a complicating factor that leaves many who have had spontaneous losses feeling judgmental that the women who had TFA had "had a choice" while they had not. Further, the stigma of abortion tended to be felt by the women who had TFA more strongly during group interactions. Notably, one of the defense mechanisms encouraged in support groups for typical perinatal loss is to get in touch with the fact that the loss came through no fault of the mother and with no control. This defense seems less applicable for women who TFA and there is often a middle strategy that requires women who TFA to get in touch with the out-of-control nature of the occurrence of the anomaly before they can gain reassurance that they too had a loss through no fault of their own. These differences mean each population benefits from having its own support group rather than one that blends all types of perinatal loss.

Organization

The WANA group is part of a solo private practice structure and typically receives referrals directly from clients who are referred by their obstetricians or genetic counselors, due to the referral source's awareness of the specialty practice of the author. Fees are kept minimal and on a sliding fee basis and there is a slight discount for couples to attend the support group together.

Description of the client situation

Most clients are referred to the group after they have already had termination procedures and have returned for the obstetrical follow-up appointment or have contacted the genetic counselor due to emotional difficulties. They are then told about the group and urged to contact me directly. Many genetic counselors also call me to let me know a client may be calling (providing initials only) and what the fetal diagnosis entailed. I generally talk with clients for a pre-screening interview to assure the client is likely to be able to make effective use of group support. I inform them groups run for six to eight weeks, comprising between three and four couples, and follow a structure. The structure includes a brief presentation about a specific topic area each week, followed by time for discussion and mutual support. Groups are usually most beneficial after the initial numbness and then extreme grief have started to subside (four to six weeks post-TFA), and I work hard to form groups where there is similarity around diagnosis. This is done by separating couples into different groups where the diagnosis was inconsistent with life as compared with those where the fetus could have been brought to birth but there was a diagnosis that would interfere with customary life and/or function. Most women and couples are still actively grieving and questioning themselves and their decisions when they arrive for the first group session.

Decisions about practice

Definition of the client

The client system is the group as a whole, yet the facilitator must also attend to each individual within the group. One of the first decisions that must be made is whether the woman who is referred will benefit most from individual work or from the support group. Since most women feel quite isolated, and as if they are the only one who experienced this trauma, the group is often the most effective intervention. When women have little control over their active grieving and are unable to articulate their concerns other than to cry, they may benefit more from individual work.

Once a set of women and couples have been pre-screened and selected for the group, arrangements are made to meet on a weekly schedule that fits the needs of that particular group (i.e. weekday evenings, weekend afternoons). This is the transition to viewing the client more as the group and less as a constellation of individuals. This is further consolidated after the first session when the group members introduce themselves and begin to invest in the goals of the group.

For the purposes of this case example, I will introduce Susan and Carl. Susan is a pretty, bright woman of 35 who terminated a pregnancy affected by Down syndrome about six weeks prior to our first session. She was quite tearful on the phone during the pre-screening call, particularly because she has a two-year-old daughter and they had learned the fetus had been male and she wanted a child of each gender. She is a psychologist who had mixed feelings about how bonded she had been to "the baby," but also felt she "d[id]n't have it in [her] to parent a child with those problems." Her husband, Carl, is 38 and fairly reserved. He did not understand why she was so upset because he felt they'd decided to "do something about it" if they had prenatal testing and it came back with a poor result. Further, he believed Susan "would be much better once we're pregnant again." They were having some tensions around their varied responses to this event.

Goals

As noted above, support groups are most focused on promoting supportive relationships among the group members, promoting coping capabilities and providing strategies for coping with stressful events in the future. Yalom (2005) asserts that there are a number of therapeutic factors involved in group work; support groups often focus on two specifically: universality and the instillation of hope. For Yalom, these two factors are related. Universality is a dynamic of groups that mediates individuals' sense of being "unique in their wretchedness" (p. 6) and feeling alone and isolated. Support groups allow this myth to be broken by this

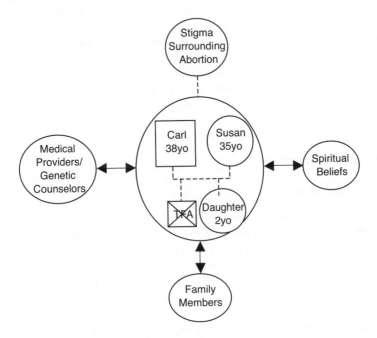

Figure 21.1 Ecomap for Susan and Carl before group.

sense of universality, which allows people to feel supported in the fact that they are not alone in their struggles; further, this can instill hope, as they see and hear about others who have survived and even thrived after the experience. Indeed, after attending her first group session a member of WANA said she was relieved to "lay eyes on other people who have made the same decision and they're normal and they don't have three heads" (personal communication, October 1996). These goals are true of most support groups. There are also goals that are specific to this type of group.

Because some group members come after having been rejected within a typical perinatal support group structure, I use both the prescreening phone call and the first session to be explicit that the members all share the experience of having a prenatal diagnosis, making a decision to TFA, and doing so. Therefore, part of the goal for the group is to revisit the decision-making process, rework it when not in crisis, learn about grieving and begin to transition to understanding how to continue bonds (Klass, Silverman & Nickman, 1996) with the child they lost while also beginning to consider a future pregnancy if this is intended. For instance, Susan created a Christmas ornament that reminded her of the son she did not give birth to and she puts it on her tree each Christmas to remember his presence in their lives. This represents a unique and nuanced understanding; although Susan and Carl decided not to continue the pregnancy with their son, they did not reject *him*. They continue the loving, parental relationship with him despite feeling they could not allow him to be born with his impairments. Indeed, their decision was predicated on their parental love as they choose to keep him from suffering the physical and psychological wounds they foresaw for him should he be born with Down syndrome.

Developing objectives and contracting

During the first group meeting, I encourage members to share only first names to protect their privacy as they begin to learn one another's stories. The objective of the first group session is to promote a beginning rapport among members of the group and to have them recognize they are not alone in their situation or their responses to it. The objective for the second group session is to re-visit the decision-making process in two ways. First, they are helped to consider the "expert" literature on decision making to see how they were not able to have the time or the level of certain information that decision-making theorists posit as ideal. Second, they are urged to share with their partner (and with the group to the extent that they feel comfortable) what factors went into their decision making at the time and how they believe those factors continue to operate in their lives currently. This is often a scary proposition (explained at the end of the first session as "homework" to discuss with their partner) because people are afraid they may discover that they regret their choice. Nevertheless, this seldom happens; most couples benefit from having the decision revisited in calmer circumstances and tend to share that with the group in the second session.

Weeks three to five are characterized by grief-related objectives, including psycho-education about normal grief trajectories (both longer and more variable than most assume); gender differences in grieving; and rituals and holidays as opportunities for active grieving to promote healing. An implicit objective of these sessions is to promote ways the group members offer one another suggestions and support. It was during one of these sessions that Susan was able to share an insight. Another group member was struggling with whether their decision was "right or wrong." Susan said, "I've come to believe that right or wrong can't characterize our decision—but it was the wise decision."

By the sixth session, termination of the group is an implicit and explicit topic and looking toward the future is the objective. This session is usually used for a "group graduate" (someone who has gone through the group and has gone on to have a successful pregnancy and birth) to come and speak with the group. Explicitly, the objective is for that person to share strategies that helped them to cope with the anxiety of a future pregnancy, while implicitly the objective is to enhance hopefulness about the future. A final session is used to summarize and explore the meanings of the ending of the group and the new meanings they have about the experience of diagnosis and TFA in their lives.

Meeting place

The practice is located in a central suburban area easily accessed by the metropolitan and suburban areas nearby. There is a small free parking lot next to the building and bus and train lines come within a three-block walking distance. The office is within a building that had been a residence and the office is in the room that was the living room, with a (non-working) fireplace, mantle and sofa and chairs to promote a non-hospital-like atmosphere. Although cozy, the room is large enough to hold eight to nine comfortably and usually coffee, tea, and small snacks are provided.

Use of time

Group members are told that sessions will last for one-and-a-half hours and run weekly for six to seven weeks. The weekly nature works to promote the intensity within the group-support relationships, while also assuring women and couples that the commitment to the group is not ongoing or very burdensome in terms of time. Some groups elect to complete in six sessions, some prefer to allot a last session for processing the ending of the group itself. I very consciously manage time, making sure to start the educational part promptly when all members have arrived or within five minutes of the start time, whichever comes first. Approximately 15 minutes is used to address a topic area and then I facilitate discussion among the group members. Although I begin to use non-verbal messages to draw the session to a close about 10 minutes before the scheduled end time, I will allow the group to continue past the end time if the group is doing productive work and if I comment on that and gain every member's consent to continue for a specific amount of time (no longer than half an hour).

Strategies and interventions

Group facilitation is predicated on helping group members feel safe, to speak openly about their own emotions and experiences, and offer feedback to other group members. An important intervention as part of the first session is to identify "group climate rules" that will allow the members to feel safe within the group. Members are helped (via questions) to articulate fears about confidentiality, judgment and exposure and to identify acceptable group behaviors; for example, nothing from the room goes outside the room; no judgments of others, only questions helping one to understand the other's position; and an understanding that we will provide tissues and the nearest person may offer a hand on the shoulder, etc. if someone is crying.

The first session is also used to get each group member talking (breaking the ice). As the first session is slightly more directive, I usually request that the partner tell the story of how they came to know about the diagnosis of their baby, and ask that the mother talk about what she hopes to gain from participating in the group (which assists in clarifying and contracting). Women often add to the story after their partners finish and then they discuss what they hope to get from group participation. This allows each to have a specific role to play when going around the group and allows each to talk as much or little as is comfortable for them.

Another intervention used frequently in group work is to recognize themes and comment upon them. For instance, in a session on gender differences in grieving, I commented, "It sounds like Jean is saying something similar to Susan. Jean was talking about how she thought her husband didn't care because he kept staying long hours at work and Susan was saying she's annoyed by Carl's time away at ball games, but I guess I'm hearing a need for the guys to get some time away, a sort of break from the action and the women are feeling left alone with the grief they can't get away from … Does that seem right?" This intervention inspired the third couple to talk about their tensions through that lens and the other two couples clearly resonated and spoke more about how the gender differences affected them and their perceptions of one another. Drawing out themes, commonalities and highlighting strategies are some of the intervention methods used most commonly in group work. Validation and normalization are also used frequently.

Stance of the social worker

Although I provide some information at the beginning of each group session and may periodically share information about coping strategies that have benefited prior clients and group members, I consciously avoid being perceived as the "expert" or becoming the "point of contact." By arranging the first group session as one where the group does a "round robin"

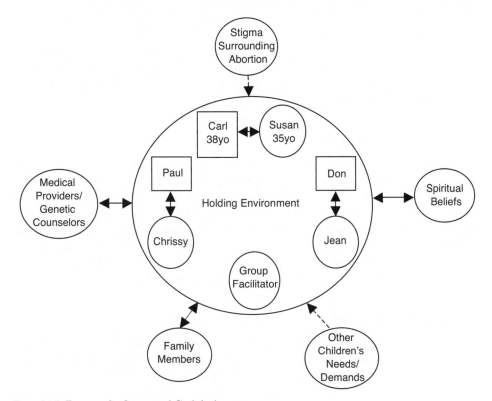

Figure 21.2 Ecomap for Susan and Carl during group.

where everyone talks in turn, the expectation is formed that each group member actively participates. I place myself as part of the group circle without any spacing that would hold me above or at a central point in any way.

As I comment on themes and draw connections, the stance is also one of pulling back from the action when the members are directly interacting with one another. Indeed, it is important for any group facilitator to model scanning the group when speaking and avoiding talking to any one group member. This provides a role model for others on how to share their stories with the group. Occasionally a group member starts with a tendency to direct all communication toward the group facilitator. Non-verbal interventions like looking away from the speaker and looking around the group to model a different behavior can stimulate full group interaction. Sometimes, a minimal prompt such as "can you say that to Susan?" or some other re-directing comment can help promote full group interaction. Seldom does this fail to work, but if it should, I talk with the member afterwards and encourage him or her to look around the group when speaking and avoid talking directly to me.

Use of resources outside of the helping relationship

I keep resources for support and information available and share information about those resources during group. The availability of a support website (ahc.org) is discussed early in each group and several books pertinent to this type of loss are available for group members to borrow during the weeks of group meetings. Further, group members are encouraged to share information about resources that they learn about for support or future care. They often share information about physicians who are particularly supportive (or not so).

Another set of resources includes strategies to avoid difficulties. For instance, many obstetrician offices register women into formula and baby picture companies' databases early in their pregnancy. Women who terminate approach their original due date and their mailboxes are suddenly filled with baby product coupons and endorsements. Sharing knowledge about getting off of these lists is part of moving outside the parameters of the typical helping relationship, yet offering useful information.

Reassessment and evaluation

At the last session, I distribute an evaluation sheet requesting feedback about whether the group was helpful on criteria ranging from my knowledge and skills to the space and the effects on the individual and their relationship. Though these are evaluated with a five-point Likert scale-type rating, respondents are also urged to provide comments and suggestions. Generally, respondents express satisfaction and report they have improved on both individual and couple parameters. Most express a readiness to move forward and be done with therapeutic intervention. Most also offer to return as a group graduate at a later date. The male partners often write comments such as "this saved our marriage" or "I thought I was losing my wife."

Transfer and termination

When the group completes its sessions, there are sometimes individuals who remain distressed and decide to continue individual work. The nature of having the group as part of my private practice allows easy transfer to individual or couples work, if they elect that, or referral to another practitioner if the couple elects that. Additionally, sometimes psychiatric assessment for medication is indicated if depression or anxiety symptoms continue to be disabling after the group intervention. Referral to a psychiatrist who has expertise in childbearing issues is part of the service offered to group members if it seems appropriate.

Case conclusion

Due to the time-limited nature of the group, the "case" of the group is closed when the final session occurs. Whether allotted its own session for processing the end, or given a time at the end of the session on future pregnancy, the ending of the group is explicitly discussed. We identify the positive things that evolved from the group, and the wishes for continuation are discussed. Areas of growth are explicitly recognized. The relationships that developed are acknowledged and recognized as forces for healing that allow group members to move forward toward their prior goals of growing their families.

Susan had been able to talk at length during group sessions about her questions about their decision and about their different modes of grieving. Carl, too, had been open and used discussion with the other fathers to discover that each was somewhat afraid they "lost the wife they knew," to her immense grief. They were able to transition their sense that their wives "were nuts" and begin to see how this was a common reaction to grieving the loss and one that their wives (and they) could survive. Further, Carl was able to recognize some of his own behaviors as a form of grieving behavior, and this helped Susan to feel closer to him. She began recognizing her grief was expectable and not something that made her "crazy—diagnosable," a fear she had expressed in an early session. They were able to feel their partnership once again in moving toward healing and consideration of another pregnancy.

Differential discussion

The provision of a support group such as WANA would ideally be done within the context of the hospital or obstetrical and genetics group that provides the medical care. In that way, everyone would be offered the chance of support around this difficult experience and, hopefully, the cost of the service would be covered by the medical practice or the hospital. The chanciness of who actually is referred and manages to get connected to a group leaves many who are likely in need and not receiving support.

That said, this particular group gelled quite well and all three couples seemed to gain support from one another. The discussions among the group members about the gender differences in grieving were particularly useful in helping to defuse tensions that were growing between members of two of the couples. Group work provided the ideal intervention in that the couples could see that they were playing out dynamics in a very similar way to the others and could learn by seeing it in the others, rather than hypothetically hearing it in an individual session. The universality of the group allowed them to see that the marital tensions were not specific to them, but part of a larger dynamic of disenfranchised grief (Doka, 2002) and gender differences in grieving (Versalle & McDowell, 2004–5).

Women and their partners typically arrive at the first group with strong feelings, feeling stigmatized and alone (McCoyd, 2008a). The power of universality (Yalom, 2005) is seen as the group helps to assuage these feelings, while also promoting relationships with others who understand. This is particularly pertinent in the United States context where abortion is controversial. Many legislative and political regulations about abortion exist, yet the technology continues to develop in ways that allow slight differences in genetics or physiology to be identified. It is not always clear what those differences may entail. The level of uncertainty of medical outcomes for women and their partners—combined with their assessment of the burdens they believe they can bear—leave women and couples making decisions with major emotional and ethical implication. Providing support for the ramifications of these experiences is not just what women say they want (McCoyd, in press), it is the socially just thing to do.

References

AFP3/AFP4: the facts and the options for your care. (2004). Genzyme Genetics: Self.

American College of Obstetricians and Gynecologists (2009). Retrieved 11/06/09, from www.acog.org

Bernhardt, B. A., Geller, G., Doksum, T., Larson, S., Roter, D. & Holtzman, N. A. (1998). Prenatal genetic testing: Content of discussions between obstetric providers and pregnant women. *Obstetrics and Gynecology* 91: 648–55.

Browner, C. H. & Press, N. A. (1995). The normalization of prenatal diagnostic testing. In F. D. Ginsberg and R. Rapp (eds.), *Conceiving the new world order: The global politics of reproduction* (pp. 307–2). Berkeley: University of California Press.

Browner, C. H. & Press, N. A. (1997). The production of authoritative knowledge in American prenatal care. In R. E. Davis-Floyd and C. F. Sargent (eds.), *Childbirth and authoritative knowledge: Cross-cultural perspectives* (pp. 113–31). Berkeley: University of California Press.

Chorionic Villi Sampling. (2005). Genzyme Genetics: Cambridge, MA. Self.

Davis-Floyd, R. E. and C. F. Sargent (eds.). 1997. *Childbirth and authoritative knowledge: Cross-cultural perspectives.* Berkeley: University of California Press.

Doka, K. J. (ed.) (2002). Disenfranchised Grief: New Directions, Challenges and Strategies for practice. Berkeley: University of California Press.

Georges, E. (1997). Fetal ultrasound imaging and the production of authoritative knowledge in Greece. In R. E. Davis-Floyd & C. F. Sargent (eds.), *Childbirth and authoritative knowledge: Cross-cultural perspectives,* (pp. 91–112). Berkeley: University of California Press.

Klass, D., Silverman, P. R. & Nickman, S. L. (eds.). (1996). *Continuing bonds: New understandings of grief.* Washington D.C.: Taylor & Francis.

Leithner, K., Assem-Hilger, E., Fischer-Kern, M., Loffler-Stastka, H., Thien, R. & Ponocny-Seliger, E. (2006). Prenatal care: the patient's perspective: A qualitative study. *Prenatal Diagnosis,* 26: 931–7.

McCoyd, J. L. M. (1997). Perinatal bereavement: It's not all the same. *NAPSW Forum,* Autumn, 7–9.

McCoyd, J. L. M. (2003). *Pregnancy interrupted: Non-normative loss of a desired pregnancy after termination for fetal anomaly* [unpublished dissertation]. Bryn Mawr (PA): Bryn Mawr College. Available from: Proquest, Ann Arbor, MI; 3088602.

McCoyd, J. L. M. (2007). Pregnancy interrupted: Loss of a desired pregnancy after diagnosis of fetal anomaly. *Journal of Psychosomatic Obstetrics and Gynecology,* 28: 37–48.

McCoyd, J. L. M. (2008a) Women in no man's land: The U.S. abortion debate and women terminating desired pregnancies due to fetal anomaly. *British Journal of Social Work.* Published online 28 May 2008 pending journal publication: doi:10.1093/bjsw/bcn080

McCoyd, J. L. M. (2008b). I'm not a saint: Burden assessment as an unrecognized factor in prenatal decision making. *Qualitative Health Research,* 18 (11): 1489–1500.

McCoyd, J. L. M. (In press). What do women want? Experiences and reflections of women after prenatal diagnosis and termination for anomaly. *Health Care for Women International* 30(6): 507–35.

McCoyd, J. L. M. (under review). Betrayed and disillusioned: Prenatal technology and women's experience.

Toseland, R. W. & Rivas, R. F. (2009). *An introduction to group work practice* (6th ed.). Boston: Allyn & Bacon.

Versalle, A. & McDowell, E. E. (2004–5). The attitudes of men and women concerning gender differences in grief. *Omega,* 50 (1): 53–67.

Yalom, I. (2005). *The theory and practice of group psychotherapy* (5th ed.). New York: Basic Books.

22 Spina bifida and physical activity

Group-centered care

Kim Lyons Garver

Context

At the State University of New York's (SUNY) Upstate Medical University's Center for Development, Behavior and Genetics (CDBG), Wednesday is Spina Bifida Clinic day. On any given Wednesday, six to 10 children with spina bifida and their families/caregivers come to Spina Bifida Clinic (the Clinic), where they are greeted, registered and weighed, a health history is taken, and any concerns the patient or family/caregiver have are listed. Then, a parade of providers enters and exits the patient room, bringing expertise and assessment skills. A multi-disciplinary report is produced a day or two after the visit and distributed to the family and to the primary care physician. The patient may also travel for various tests to other clinics at SUNY Upstate Medical University and other sites. Professionals who are typically involved with the care of a child with spina bifida include social workers, nurse specialists, physical therapists, occupational therapists, orthotists, developmental pediatricians, and surgeons in urology, orthopedics and neurosurgery.

Spina bifida is the number one permanently disabling birth defect in the United States. There are approximately 70,000 individuals with spina bifida living in the U.S.; seven of every 10,000 babies are born with the condition, and 60,000,000 women are at risk of having a child with spina bifida (Boulet, *et al.*, 2009). Taking folic acid supplements during childbearing years can reduce the incidence of this birth defect by 70% (CDC, 1992). Advances in medical treatment have allowed a majority of children born with spina bifida today to live active and productive lives (Bowman, McLone, Grant, Truita & Ito, 2001). Learning to be active at a young age is a key predictor of ongoing physical health and fitness level throughout the lifespan (Dosa, *et al.*, 2008).

SUNY Upstate Medical University (University Hospital) has approximately 370 inpatient beds. In 2008, we admitted over 18,000 patients, saw more than 50,000 patients in the Emergency Department, and our 77 outpatient clinics had over 200,000 visits. With over 3,000 outpatient appointments in 2008, the CDBG includes the Child Development Clinic, Genetics and Metabolic Clinics, Physical Disabilities Clinic, Fit Families Program, and the Spina Bifida Clinic which serves approximately 220 patients and their families/caregivers. The Clinics at the CDBG generally serve patients using a traditional single- or multi-disciplinary approach. A pilot program using a group visit modality was conducted for children with visual impairments and their families, and, based on that, group visits were started for Spina Bifida Clinic patients.

Individuals with developmental and physical disabilities often struggle with loneliness and isolation, especially as they transition from school age to young adulthood (Appleton *et al.*, 1997). A question I ask patients as part of my psychosocial assessment is what they like to do in their spare time. For greater than 80% of those over the age of 10, the number one answer is solitary activities, e.g. reading, knitting and playing on the internet or computer games. Group visits were instituted to help address this tendency toward social isolation.

The spina bifida group is scheduled once a month in the evening at a state of the art gym facility and is open to all school-aged patients (ages five to 18) and their families/caregivers. The group visits begin like a conventional spina bifida center visit, with registration and nursing assessment. The entire group enjoys a dinner together and splits into two groups: adaptive physical activities for the children and an educational lecture for the parents or other family members, followed by time to address medical concerns. This group is facilitated not only by the Clinic staff but also by SUNY Cortland's Adaptive Physical Education (APE) professors and their students. In her letter of invitation to families, our director, Dr. Nienke Dosa, introduced the group visit project: "The use of group visits is growing around the country. Health care providers have found that these visits allow health care to be provided in ways that cannot be done during the usual office visit. The group visit program is a different way for families and children to meet with their health care providers and to learn how to deal with common issues."

Policy

The trans-disciplinary medical model approach is the current standard of care for children with spina bifida. Having multi-disciplinary professionals interact with the patients and those accompanying them means decisions and actions regarding patient care are influenced by many perspectives. The group visit model of care is considered the standard of care for other complex chronic conditions, such as diabetes care in the adult population. Research studies have demonstrated cost savings and improvements in medical and social outcomes (Kawasaki *et al.*, 2007). Managed care influences whether or not physical therapy and occupational therapy see certain patients due to insurance constraints. Because my work as the Spina Bifida Clinic social worker is not a billable service at this time, I am free to see every patient.

Initially the group visits were not being billed and were being financed through a grant from American Legion Post #113 and from private donations to the SUNY Spina Bifida Fund. More recently, the team has begun billing insurance companies for these group visits by documenting nursing assessment and medical care that occur in the group visit setting. Given the medical issues addressed, including medical equipment needs, the team has found these visits to be an effective supplement to the traditional medical model office visit. The continuity offered by monthly group visits allows staff to monitor effectiveness of recommendations and to fine tune adjustments to adaptive equipment and mobility aids.

Technology

Spina bifida ("split-spine"), one of a number of conditions called "neural tube defects," is a complex birth defect affecting motor, cognitive, sensory, psychological, and emotional development. It is a very old condition, in that archeological discoveries have identified its characteristic spinal deformities in 7,000-year-old skeletons. In spina bifida, the developing baby's central nervous system fails to form at some point along its length, and the location at which the defect occurs determines the extent of the disability. This may include paralysis, hydrocephalus, mental retardation, bladder/bowel dysfunction, and musculoskeletal deformity. When the brain is not completely developed, the condition is called "anencephaly." In the most common and innocent form of spina bifida, spina bifida occulta (occurring in 10 to 15%

of the general population), only the bones of the spinal column are incompletely developed, and the nervous tissue beneath is normal. It usually occurs at the lower end of the spine and rarely causes medical problems. Meningocele is another abnormality, identified by a mass that contains cerebrospinal fluid and does not affect the spinal cord and nerves. Myelomeningocele, the most severe form of spina bifida, appears at birth as an open cyst or mass, usually located in the thoracic or lumbar area. Myelomeningocele involves the incompletely developed lining of the spinal cord and nerves, and children born with this form of spina bifida have varying degrees of physical disability. Over 90% have some degree of weakness of their legs, inability to control the bowel or bladder voluntarily, and a variety of orthopedic deformities. After birth, almost all babies with myelomeningocele are treated with an operation to cover the opening of the spine, which does not restore function of the abnormal nerve tissue. Once the back has been closed, hydrocephalus (accumulation of serous fluid within the cranium) then may be evaluated through head circumference measurements, brain ultra-sound, or computed tomography. Management of the hydrocephalus usually involves a shunting procedure whereby cerebrospinal fluid is internally diverted to another place in the body for better absorption (National Institute of Neurological Disorders and Stroke, 2009).

The cause of spina bifida is still not completely understood. It occurs during the first 28 days of pregnancy, while the spine is developing. About 20 years ago, researchers discovered that supplements of folic acid, a common B vitamin, can reduce the statistical risk of having a baby with a neural tube defect, and now women who take folic acid daily for at least one month before becoming pregnant and who continue to take it daily during the first three or four months of pregnancy reduce their chances of having a baby with spina bifida. At present, a blood test during early pregnancy can establish risk, ultrasound can detect spina bifida, and amniocentesis can establish the presence of spina bifida. Women can decide then whether to abort the pregnancy or carry it to term. In the future, we may learn how to eliminate this complex birth defect, but for the moment, children born with spina bifida and their families rely on a range of medical and social services.

Special wheelchairs make it possible for many young people with spina bifida to play team sports. Generally, Medicaid pays for a person with a physical disability to receive a wheelchair every five years. The APE staff has brought to these groups wheelchairs that can skate, some that can sled, and some for basketball. A professor is fond of saying, "We do not have one pair of shoes in our closet" (Cortland, 2009); similarly, people with disabilities should not be limited to one wheelchair for all occasions. This technology has been eye-opening for patients and their parents/caregivers.

Organization

The mission of SUNY Upstate Medical University is to improve the health of the communities we serve through education, biomedical research and health care. This effort between APE staff and students and the Clinic staff addresses all three components. We are educating one another about the role of physical education and health care in our patients' lives, evaluating our practice through feedback from patients and families/caregivers to look at ways to enhance patients' lives by focusing on their abilities rather than their disabilities, and revisiting how we provide health care in ways that prevent social isolation and enhance physical fitness and prevent obesity (Dosa *et al.*, 2008; Schultz & Liptak, 2007).

Description of the client

Robert is a six-year-old with spina bifida. Specifically, he has a high lumbar level myelomen-gocele with shunted hydrocephalus, neurogenic bowel and bladder, symptomatic Chiari II malformation, obesity, and a history of spinal cord de-tethering at age four. He is an only child of married parents, who both work. Robert's parents state he is more excited about coming back to the spina bifida monthly meeting than he has ever been about anything in his life, except possibly Christmas. At the December group, when I announced that the next meeting would be in February because January weather is so unpredictable here, it was evident that Robert was close to tears and could not understand why the group would not meet next month. Robert's parents have struggled together, but more so separately, to make sense of what it means to have a child with a disability (Lutkehoff, 1999). Robert's mother states that his father has struggled to have a son who cannot do the physical sports any father would want his son to engage in with him. Robert's father states that his mother cannot let him go, and cuddles him. When she leaves for work, she will call and speak with Robert, which increases Robert's anxiety at her absence, according to the father.

Through this group, the Clinic staff has seen this couple view Robert more realistically. Robert's mother was in tears listening to JoAnn Armstrong describe at the first group how she became a member of the Paralympics team and now trains young people with disabilities. JoAnn stresses that part of the training is training the parents to let go. "We let the mothers help their children take their coats off at the first practice," JoAnn shared. "At the second practice, we ask the parents to please wait outside. It is amazing what kids can do!" (Hughes, 2006).

Decisions about practice

Description of efforts to market the group

Referrals to the group initially came from the Clinic staff. We went through our 220 patients and listed all those who are in kindergarten through high school and are wheelchair ambulators. Additionally we invited local wheelchair athletes to come as mentors. Since the start of this group, its reputation has grown, and families from as far as three hours away have come for the two- to three-hour sessions. These families have not had children with spina bifida but, rather, children with other disabilities who could benefit from the camaraderie of seeing other kids like them in wheelchairs engaging in physical activities such as soccer and "Indiana Jones," a modified dodgeball game (one of Robert's favorites).

As social workers, we are trained to be sensitive and aware of cultural stereotypes and to address them as they arise and to advocate for fair treatment for everyone, regardless of race, religion, sexual orientation, or disability. This is a tenet of being a social worker. I must admit that my own beliefs about what wheelchair ambulators can and cannot do have been challenged. Robert's mother has not been the only adult in tears during our groups (Wheel Chair Back Flip). It is interesting to note that the sports focus of the group visit has resulted in far greater participation of fathers than the conventional spina bifida center visits.

In order to expand further, the plan is to advertise in other venues that reach school-age children with physical disabilities and that warrant the use of a wheelchair. One distinction is that this group is for the physically but not the mentally disabled. The Special Olympics is geared toward the population which have both physical and mental disabilities. The Games for the Physically Challenged are available to children who have primarily motor disabilities.

Goals

The goals of this group are many, and the ones discussed here relate to preventing isolation. Being around other children who are in wheelchairs allows children to recognize they are not alone. Most of the kids who are participating in this group are the only children in their schools who are permanent wheelchair ambulators (AHRQ, 2005). In the past, the medical model isolated families and patients. Built into the group is the opportunity for families to interact, to break bread together and to talk about their struggles as parents and as advocates. Prior to group interactions, those between families and patients with spina bifida were limited to brief waiting room encounters before clinic appointments. Thus, prevention of isolation in young adults is a primary goal of this group.

The Syracuse Flyers is a local wheelchair basketball team. Members of the team, including Tammy Delano, have come to our group as mentors. Tammy was recently chosen as the sixth member alternate of the five-member Paralympics curling team for the Winter Paralympics. Her success has inspired younger wheelchair ambulators at group. After they've gotten clarity as to what curling is ("sitting on the ice and sweeping" is how Tammy defined it for the group), they remember watching the Olympics on TV, never considering how they could aspire to that level of competition themselves. Tammy and other Flyers basketball players are hoping to develop future athletes for the team. Team sports build relationships and decrease a sense of isolation (Hughes, 2006). The physical activities learned at the group can be translated and modified and played at home, and it is hoped this education will decrease computer usage and TV viewing, both in the present and in the future for these individuals.

Developing objectives and contracting

The objective of the group visits is to focus on sports, physical activity, and wellness. Each session focuses on a particular topic decided upon by the group. Families are given the chance to learn from experts in the field, including other families who are dealing with similar health issues and to get their needs met and their questions answered. The group visit program is a different way for families and children to meet with their health care providers and to learn how to deal with common issues. Although these group visits will not replace the child's regular appointments at the spina bifida center, they are an adjunct opportunity for families.

Meeting place

The group meets at the SUNY Upstate Medical University's Institute for Human Performance. This state of the art building encompasses a city block. The parking lot is extremely accessible and parking is free at the hour that the group convenes. The group begins downstairs, where patients are weighed, vital signs are taken, and patients are registered. A classroom with tables and chairs provides a space for families to eat with other families and with Syracuse Flyers athletes, SUNY Cortland professors and students, and with Spina Bifida Clinic staff. Then the elevators and stairs allow access to the spacious gymnasium with a walking track circling the oval-shaped room. The center of the room is open and surrounded on either side by weightlifting equipment. The parents remain in the room where the dinner was shared or in another classroom next to the gymnasium while the children and their siblings enjoy the gym space. Having the extra wheelchairs SUNY Cortland provides allows the children with spina bifida to be on equal playing ground with their able-bodied siblings who also participate in the physical activities in wheelchairs.

Use of time

Meetings occur monthly with the exception of January, as noted earlier. Each meeting is scheduled to last for two hours from 5:30–7:30pm. However, we have observed that families do not want to leave. Again, this is often the first opportunity they have had to lean on other families who are also treading the road of a parent of a child with spina bifida. The two staffs debrief after the group. This time of evaluation and review is incredibly valuable. Debriefing has gone as late as 9:30pm, due again to families' reluctance to leave at the end of the group session and subsequent late start to the debriefing time. It is hoped these groups will be ongoing. The Spina Bifida Clinic business staff is pursuing the feasibility of reimbursement through insurance companies.

Strategies and interventions

We are employing an educational group modality approach as well as role models within the group context. Robert's parents state that in gym he is the only person in a wheelchair. He is often given an alternative activity to do, usually in the hall outside of the gym, away from his peers. Several of the children have stated how incredible it would be if the SUNY Cortland staff could take the wheelchairs to their school and then have their gym class play soccer, all in wheelchairs. Similarly, parents/caregivers share how they have advocated in their children's Individualized Educational Plan (IEP) Committee on Special Education (CSE) meetings and what has worked and what has not worked. This ability to share and to learn has increased both knowledge and confidence. With groups, the stages are informally known as forming, storming, norming, and performing (Tuckman, 1965).

One unexpected benefit of this modality has been the inclusion of patients' fathers. Typically in the office, the fathers of newborn patients will come to initial Spina Bifida Clinic visits. After the first one to two office visits, it is typically only the mother who comes with the patient. With few exceptions, we have found that both parents are attending group. We have speculated that there are multiple reasons for this change. SUNY Cortland APE professor, Tim Davis, commented on how predominantly female the Spina Bifida Clinic staff are and how the APE professors and students are predominantly male. The group is offered in the evening after the work day (i.e. 5:30–7:30pm). The group offers physical activities, which is a draw for some fathers. Offering food at any event tends to increase attendance, so maybe just the inclusion of box dinners has increased the number of participants within each family.

Stance of the social worker

This modality has changed how patients and families view me. Usually, during their office visits, I enter the patient room with my psychosocial assessment in hand and ask questions relative to the services involved in their day-to-day life, including school. I ask what financial resources the family has and what resources they may be eligible for, e.g. SSI, Medicaid waiver program; assess whether the patient and, if applicable, his or her parents/caregivers are stressed or depressed; and entertain any questions the patient and/or his or her family may have for me. I anticipate developmental stages and what this family and this patient may experience between now and their next annual clinic visit. I obtain Releases of Information (ROIs) as needed so that I can follow up with systems already in place to advocate for patient's needs that may not be at the level this family and patient need. Then, I may follow up on the

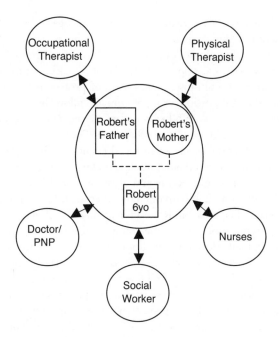

Figure 22.1 Traditional medical model office visits.

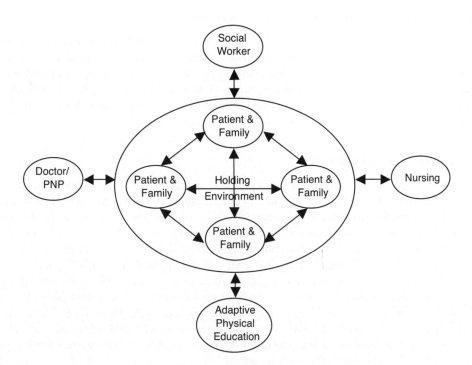

Figure 22.2 Group visits.

telephone with the family days or weeks after their office visit to see how things are going or how goals we have identified during their office visit are being met.

I carry no paper assessment to dinner or in the gym during our group visits. As a matter of fact, I come in dress-down pants as opposed to the business casual attire at the Clinic. With my social work voice among a multi-disciplinary team of professionals, I encourage patients to go beyond what they thought possible. And, of course, I allow them to dream beyond their chair, and to laugh and to connect with other children and teenagers who are similarly bound to the ground by wheels. I high five, and verbally praise effort.

During the group visit, Robert was pushed by an APE student. He used his smooth six-year-old parlor chatter to state that he could not ambulate that wheelchair himself. He praised and flattered the student who helped him. At the end of the session, his father stated that Robert could and should ambulate himself. It is an ongoing process, and Robert may not be as fast as some of the other group participants, but Robert is learning to ambulate himself, even though he gets tired. Several parents, especially of the younger group participants, have stated their children are very tired and fall asleep en route home in the car, even in the Institute's parking lot. Robert is learning self-determination and control. His efforts are praised by me and by the other group facilitators who have watched the gains he is making.

One of the great pleasures of the group visits is to see patients meeting each other. Often these are the only children in their schools who are in a wheelchair. This is like gym class except they are not the minority—their able-bodied siblings are! Also, the group visit model, with many ages of patients and families/caregivers, is a great way for families and professionals to take a "lifespan" approach to medical care, to be proactive about preventing complications, and to be positive and ambitious about the future rather than passive.

Use of resources outside of the helping relationship

I partner with many professionals to make these groups successful: APE professors and students, nurses, occupational therapists, social work students, physicians, and paraprofessionals. Additionally, two adults with spina bifida volunteer during our Wednesday Spina Bifida Clinic days and with the groups. We encourage parents to invite their children's physical education (PE) teachers to come to our groups to learn about how to adapt PE to include the child with a physical disability and the other students in games together.

Reassessment and evaluation

As mentioned previously, we spend time at the end of each group reflecting and processing. During this time, we ask parents to fill out their perceptions as well as what topics they would like presented at future groups. The informal feedback from patients has been positive. Robert is not the only patient who anxiously looks forward to these visits. Michael, a teenager with cerebral palsy (CP), did not want to come to this group. He walks with difficulty and has a wheelchair at home. He grumbled through dinner, and reluctantly went upstairs to the gym with his sister and twin brother. After about 10 minutes, he and his siblings got into wheelchairs, and after another 20 minutes of activity, he asked me where his parents were. When I told him they were downstairs at a talk, he looked disappointed. Then, I asked him if he needed them, and he said with pride, "Yes. I want them to see all the things I am doing!" The change in his demeanor over the course of group was astonishing. His positive reaction is very typical of all the school-age children who attend.

Transfer and termination

It is hoped children will stay engaged in this group as long as they need to, and that relationships between patients, siblings and families will be long-lasting and continue both between the monthly meetings and beyond the group. The members of the Syracuse Flyers are hopeful the physical activities the children are engaging in will transfer into an even more successful wheelchair basketball program in the local Syracuse area.

Case conclusion

Robert continues to count the days between groups. His parents continue to struggle with his disability and the impact it has on their day-to-day life, but they have found hope in other families who also have children with spina bifida. The family that traveled three hours each way to attend the group plans to trek 100-plus miles again next month to give their son a sense of what PE can be like for someone who is differently abled. The financial support for continuing group medical visits is being sought through Medicaid and other insurance providers, and it is hoped this modality will not only continue but expand. Maybe a new group will form of young adults, ages 18–25, to look at issues of transition and independence among patients with spina bifida.

Differential discussion

Children with spina bifida need opportunities to teach others and to volunteer their services just as their able-bodied siblings and peers do. Having role models already in group will allow the group participants to transfer into roles of greater responsibility as the group participants age. Facilitating less formal means of ongoing mutual support would benefit group participants. To that end, group participants and SUNY Cortland staff have asked about sharing email and IM addresses, and creating a blog as a means to allow patients and families to stay connected to each other, using today's high-tech means of communication. Possibly our group invitation letters can be emailed or put up on a blog in the future.

As the Spina Bifida Clinic social worker, I can evaluate and share the scope of my involvement in this new modality and ensure ways this modality is shared with other social workers. Bringing together clients with similar conditions or diagnoses, though not new, is underutilized. The success of our group can be generalized far beyond spina bifida to many other health conditions.

References

Agency for Healthcare Research and Quality (AHRQ). (2005). *Next steps after your diagnosis: Finding information and support.* Retrieved 2/2/09, from www.ahrq.gov/consumer/diaginfo.htm.

Appleton, P. L., Ellis, N. C., Mincham, P. E., Lawson, V., Boll, V. & Jones, P. (1997). Depressive symptoms and self-concept in young people with spina bifida. *Journal of Pediatric Psychology* 22 (5): 707–22.

Boulet, S. L., Gambrell, D., Shin, M., Honein, M. A. & Matthews, T. J. (2009). Racial/ethnic differences in the birth prevalence of spina bifida—United States, 1995–2005. *Morbidity & Mortality Weekly Report.* Retrieved 2/2/09, from http://www.cdc.gov/Morbidity & Mortality Weekly Report/preview/Morbidity & Mortality Weekly Reporthtml/mm5753a2.html

Bowman, R. M., McLone, D. G., Grant, J. A., Truita, T. & Ito, J. A. (2001). Spina bifida outcome: A 25-year prospective. *Pediatric Neurosurgery*, 34: 114–20.

CDC. (1992). Recommendations for the use of folic acid to reduce the number of cases of spina bifida and other neural tube defects. *Morbidity & Mortality Weekly*, 41: #RR-14.

Chrionic villi sampling (2005). Genzyme Genetics, Cambridge, MA. Self.

Cortland, T. (2009). Personal communication.

Dosa, N. P., Foley, J. T., Eckrich, M., Woodall-Ruff, D. & Liptak, F. S. (2008). Obesity across the lifespan among individuals with spina bifida. *Disability and Rehabilitation*, 30 (25): 1–7.

Hughes, L. T. (2006). *Getting into disabled sports*. Retrieved 2/2/09, from the Rochester Rookies website: http://www.tswaa.com/ESRRookies.htm and http://sbonlineroc.org

Kawasaki, L., Munter, P., Hyre, A. D., Hampton, K. & DeSalvo, K. B. (2007). Willingness to attend group visits for hypertension treatment. *The American Journal of Managed Care* 13 (5): 257–62.

Lutkenhoff, M. (ed.) (1999). *Children with spina bifida: A parent's guide: The special-needs collection*. Bethesda: Woodbine House.

National Institute of Neurological Disorders and Stroke. (2009). Retrieved 6/9/09, from http://www.hinds.nih.gov/disorders/spina_bifida/spina-bifida.htm

Schultz, A. W. & Liptak, G. S. (2007). *Obesity, insights factsheet*. Spina Bifida Association of America. http://www.sbaa.org

Tuckman, B. (1965). Developmental sequence in small groups. *Psychological Bulletin*. 63: 384–99. Retrieved 11/10/08. Reprinted with permission in *Group Facilitation*, 3, Spring 2001. http://dennislearning-center.osu.edu/references/group group%20dev%20article.doc

Wheel Chair Back Flip. Retrieved 6/12/09, from http://www.youtube.com/watch?V=7NjvgT60-mk&feature=related

23 Group interventions for adults with HIV/AIDS

Meeting the needs of Latino patients living with HIV/AIDS at a comprehensive care center in New York City

Vanessa Norris

Context

More than 25 years into the AIDS epidemic, the need remains vital for treatment and prevention interventions targeting vulnerable populations, such as the Latino population in the United States. The group intervention discussed in this chapter involves Latino patients living with HIV/AIDS (PLWH) in New York (NYC). The intervention took place at the Center for Special Studies (CSS), a comprehensive care center dedicated to the treatment of adult PLWH affiliated with Weill Cornell Medical Center (NYP/Cornell), an acute care hospital located on the Upper East Side of Manhattan. NYP/Cornell, along with Columbia University Medical Center, comprises the New York-Presbyterian Hospital, a comprehensive university hospital with 2,242 certified beds. The New York-Presbyterian Hospital is affiliated with two medical institutions, Columbia University College of Physicians & Surgeons and Weill Medical College of Cornell University, and provides primary and specialty care services in all medical specialties.

Policy

Despite dramatic shifts in the HIV/AIDS epidemic, the prevalence and incidence of HIV/ AIDS in the U.S. underscores the severity of this public health issue (Center for Disease Control and Prevention [CDC], n.d.a.). The CDC estimates 1,039,000 to 1,185,000 people are living with HIV/AIDS in the U.S., 74% of whom are male. A breakdown by risk factor indicates 45% of those infected are men who have sex with men (MSM); 27% are persons infected through high-risk heterosexual contact; 22% are those infected through intravenous drug use (IVDU); and 5% are those who were exposed through MSM and IVDU. Analyses by race and ethnicity indicate that communities of color, such as the Latino population in the U.S., bear a disproportionate impact of HIV/AIDS. While Latinos accounted for 15% of the U.S. population in 2006, this ethnic group accounted for 17% of all new HIV infections during the same year. In 2006, the rate of new HIV infection among Latinos was three times that of whites; and, in 2005, HIV/AIDS was the fourth leading cause of death for Latino men and women ages 35–44 (CDC, n.d.a.).

Among the 50 states, New York (NYS) bears a significant burden of the HIV epidemic in the U.S., with a comparable impact on communities of color. In an analysis of cumulative AIDS cases across the U.S. through 2006, NY ranked the highest with 17.8% of cases reported (Kaiser Family Foundation [HKFF], 2008). In an analysis of cumulative AIDS cases in NYS by race and ethnicity through 2006, Latinos accounted for the second-highest number of cases reported (29%) second to blacks (44%). Within NYS, the HIV epidemic is felt profoundly in NYC. Between 2004 and 2006, NYS reported a total of 13,861 cases of HIV per 100,000 population. In this same timeframe, cases reported in NYC accounted for 80.2% (11,118 cases per 100,000 population) of cases reported in the state (NYC Department of Health, 2008).

Access to treatment

Multiple factors contribute to the Latino community's vulnerability to HIV/AIDS, including poor access to health care, delays in seeking health care services, linguistic barriers, and factors related to this ethnic group's perception of and behavior around sexual roles, practices, and education (Van Servellen *et al.*, 2003; Zambrana, Cornelius, Boykin & Lopez, 2004). For Latino PLWH, access to testing and treatment is complicated by the extreme stigma within the Latino community around HIV/AIDS and the behaviors associated with infection (particularly, MSM and IVDU). Cultural norms regarding sex and sexuality, as well as gender role, inhibit patients' interest in and willingness to seek treatment (VanOss Marín, 2003; Van Servellen *et al.*, 2003). Access to medical insurance is another factor that influences health outcomes for Latino PLWH, particularly those who are undocumented.

Government-sponsored insurance programs such as Medicaid and Medicare adequately provide treatment options for persons of lower socioeconomic status and for those who are disabled. An additional, state-funded public insurance program called AIDS Drug Assistance Program (ADAP) exists for PLWH. Eligibility criteria and coverage vary from state to state. In NYS, ADAP provides several insurance options for patients who do not qualify for Medicaid or Medicare, and eligibility is means tested. The program assists NYS residents living with HIV whose income exceeds the Medicaid threshold, yet is below $44,000 for an individual and $59,200 for a two-person household (NYC Department of Health, n.d.). ADAP also provides insurance to undocumented individuals who would not qualify for Medicaid due to their immigration status. Originally instituted to provide access to antiretroviral drugs (ARV), ADAP has expanded to provide coverage for primary care services in ambulatory care settings through ADAP Plus. In addition, NYS's ADAP has developed a program called ADAP Plus Insurance Continuation (APIC) whereby PLWH pays for private insurance premiums given that the patient meets the means test. In an effort to ensure appropriate care, NYS's ADAP also pays Medicaid spend-downs, and Medicare co-pays for patients who meet the criteria for ADAP. One of the greatest limitations of ADAP coverage is that it does not pay for emergency room care or inpatient hospitalization.

Technology

HIV, also known as the Human Immunodeficiency Virus, is the virus that causes AIDS (Acquired Immunodeficiency Syndrome). It is a retrovirus that attacks cells in the human immune system (the system in the body that fights disease) called T-cells or CD4 cells. A measure of these cells, called a T-cell count, is an indication of the strength of the immune system. The danger of the HIV virus is that it uses T-cells to replicate throughout the body while simultaneously destroying these cells. As a result of this process, patients infected with HIV experience a compromised immune system, which impairs the body's natural ability to fight disease. A patient is given an AIDS diagnosis when his/her immune system falls below a specified point (i.e. the patient's T-cell count is below 200) or the patient contracts an infection indicative of a compromised immune system, known as an opportunistic infection.

HIV is transmitted through the exchange of bodily fluids during sexual intercourse, the exchange of blood products, and mother-to-child transmission during child birth and breastfeeding. While HIV remains present in the body and replication continues, patients can remain un-symptomatic for as long as 10 years after initial infection. HIV/AIDS can be prevented and treated; however, there is currently not a cure for HIV/AIDS or vaccine to prevent against HIV infection. The risk of transmission can be diminished by eliminating high-risk behaviors.

HIV and AIDS significantly impair the human body and its functioning, and also result in significant emotional and psychological distress. Having HIV/AIDS induces numerous emotional reactions and psychological responses that have a profound impact on an individual's wellbeing (Smiley, 2004). Common emotional reactions to having HIV/AIDS include anger, depression, and anxiety, and feelings of fear, shame, guilt, and hopelessness.

Treatment

The advent of highly active antiretroviral therapy (HAART) has resulted in a remarkable shift in the mortality, morbidity, and quality of life of PLWH. HAART has made HIV/AIDS, once perceived as a death sentence, a more chronic and manageable disease. It must be stressed that HAART is a treatment, not a cure. Through various biological mechanisms whose description is beyond the scope of this chapter, HAART works to inhibit the HIV ability to replicate, allowing the immune system to strengthen and improve the body's ability to fight against disease. Currently there are five classes of HAART, each of which blocks HIV replication through a different mechanism. The treatment goal of HAART is to reduce the amount of HIV in the body and thus strengthen the immune system. HAART is typically prescribed as a combination of at least three different ARVs, also referred to as a "cocktail" or "regimen." These regimens must be taken in combination on a fixed and rigid schedule (i.e. every day, at the same time of day). Failure to adhere to this schedule can result in the virus becoming resistant to a given combination of ARVs, eliminating some drugs as treatment options. Adherence to HAART is a significant issue for PLWH in the U.S. and globally (CDC, 2007).

Organization

Founded in 1988, CSS strives to provide high-quality, specialized care to adult PLWH, primarily those who are indigent. CSS prides itself on two distinguishing characteristics; namely, providing care according to an interdisciplinary team approach and adhering to a continuity of care model. Serving as the outpatient and inpatient HIV/AIDS service for NYP/Cornell, CSS has two outpatient clinical sites, the Glenn Bernbaum Unit housed inside NYP/Cornell and the Rogers Unit, a satellite clinic in the Chelsea section of Manhattan. Both are overseen by a single program director; however, each has its own clinical and administrative staffs. Patients at both clinical sites are seen by appointment.

Services are provided by a team of professionals who specialize in HIV/AIDS including: primary care physicians, psychiatrists, an OB/GYN (specialist in obstetrics and gynecology), social workers, nurses, nutritionists, dentists, and a chaplain. Every patient is assigned to one primary care physician and a social worker who serve as the "backbone" of the clinical team. Patients are referred to other specialties based on individual need. CSS has 20 social workers (10 at each unit) who report directly to CSS Senior Staff. Each social worker is responsible for approximately 100–110 patients. On an outpatient basis, we are responsible for ensuring patients have access to essential resources such as housing, food, transportation, and medical insurance and provide counseling services regarding issues such as: crisis intervention, adjustment to HIV diagnosis, adjustment to illness progression, disclosure, relationships, social isolation and stigma, and education about adherence to HAART and safer sex practices. We also participate in committees focusing on special projects, provide outreach, and facilitate support groups. On an inpatient basis, we provide the services previously listed, in addition to assisting with negotiating and implementing discharge plans. All discharge-planning is done in collaboration with a member of the CSS nursing staff, who is responsible for arranging all home care needs (i.e. visiting nurse and home health aide services, prescriptions, and equipment).

In 2007, CSS treated a total of 2,409 patients (1,709 male, 609 female, seven transgender, and three unknown/unreported). Consistent with statistics for NYC, Latino patients account for the second-largest group treated at CSS, with 35% of patients identifying as Hispanic/Latino, second to Black/African American (39.8%). As previously indicated, CSS treats a primarily indigent population that depends on public health insurance, namely Medicaid, Medicare, and ADAP. An analysis of patients by expected payer shows 53.9% Medicaid, 11.7% Medicare, 20.3% ADAP, 5% both Medicaid and Medicare, 2.1% private insurance, and 6.8% other/unreported.

Decisions about practice

Description of the client

The Latino Support Group (LSG) is a group of Latino patients with whom I worked at CSS. Routine clinical interventions revealed Latino patients at CSS faced issues common to PLWH (i.e. stigma, social isolation, disclosure of serostatus, prevention and the use of safer sex practices, and adherence to complex HAART regimens). However, consistent with well-documented phenomena indicating culture impacts health experience and behavior (Spector, 2004; VanOss Marín, 2003; Van Servellen *et al.*, 2003), these issues took on a distinctive quality and had unique ramifications for these patients, given the cultural beliefs and values of the Latino community. In order to demonstrate the relationship between culture and health experience and behavior, the following example will illustrate how the issues of social isolation and stigma, when viewed from a cultural context, can influence health outcomes for Latino PLWH.

In the Latino culture, family is the primary unit. According to the cultural concept of *familialism*, Latinos identify with "attachment to one's family, strong feelings of familial loyalty, and the obligation to support the family emotionally and materially" (Mason, Marks, Simoni, Ruiz & Richardson, 1995, 7). Given the stigma of HIV/AIDS in the Latino community, many Latino PLWH fear and/or experience isolation and rejection due to their serostatus. It is not uncommon for Latino patients to feel as if their HIV infection is a means of punishment for having engaged in socially unacceptable behaviors and lifestyles. For example, a member of the LSG, Ms. Andres, is a monolingual, Spanish-speaking woman who identified a risk factor of unprotected heterosexual sex with a former boyfriend and referred to the terror she felt about losing her family in the face of her HIV. She was convinced that if her brother learned of her HIV status he would throw her out of the house and ostracize her from her mother, her only true support. This is common for Latino PLWH, as the stigma embedded in the Latino community often deters patients from learning or disclosing their HIV status, for fear they will lose their family or burden them with the shame of an HIV diagnosis or their sexual orientation.

The ecomap for Ms. Andres, Figure 23.1 below, depicts the systems integral in the life of a PLWH.

The size of the LSG varied between five and eight members at any given time, with a total of nine members participating. (Throughout the life of the group some members were lost due to life events and new members were added to replace them.) Four members participated throughout the lifespan of the LSG. Of the nine members in total, three were women and six were men. All of the men had a significant history of IVDU. Two of the men were gay, one was bisexual, and three were straight. All of the women were straight, reported a risk factor of unprotected heterosexual sex, and denied a history of IVDU. Their ages ranged from 36 to 61.

Goals and objectives

Given culture's direct influence on health experience and behavior, the primary goal of the LSG was to create a safe and culturally sensitive environment where patients could explore issues related to their HIV disease, their experience of illness and medicine, and the multiple psychosocial stressors in their lives within a cultural context. Addressing the social isolation experienced by Latino PLWH at CSS was a primary objective for the LSG. In addition, the LSG offered a venue for education and the exploration of common issues through sharing personal experiences among peers. Some primary issues discussed included: stigma, disclosure, adherence to HAART, safer sex practices, and patient-provider communication.

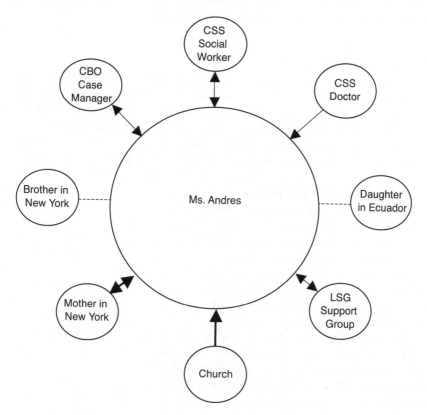

Figure 23.1 Ecomap for Ms. Andres.

Contracting

In order to ensure the success of the LSG, I created contracts on the organizational level with CSS staff and on the individual level with patients. During the planning phase, I negotiated successfully with CSS administrators for meeting space and for financial resources for the group's operation. It was also necessary to establish contracts with staff members (i.e. social workers, doctors, nurses) who approved of the need for the LSG and agreed to provide referrals.

Contracting with patients began early in the LSG's development and continued throughout the life of the group. During the recruitment process, I screened each patient who expressed interest in participating. The purpose of the screening interviews was multifaceted. While I was concerned with assessing each individual's appropriateness for the group and building a suitable group composition (Smiley, 2004; Yalom, 2005), I also began contracting with patients. In our discussions about expectations, structure, and purpose, we contracted for a commitment to regular attendance, the meeting time and place of the group, using Spanish as the language of group process, etc. Given the language barrier facing many Latino PLWH seeking medical and psychosocial services (Van Servellen et al., 2003), I felt it was important to hold the LSG in Spanish, giving participants—many of whom turned out to be monolingual (Spanish-speaking)—the opportunity to discuss issues in their native tongue. Screening interviews also recognized the cultural concept of *personalismo*, which guides interpersonal relationships and highlights Latino patients' desire for intimate, personal relationships and individualized attention (Galanti, 2003). Once the LSG began, contracting continued among the individual group members. In addition to the initial items to be decided, additional items included if and how to add new members, and termination.

Meeting place and use of time

The LSG met in the conference room at CSS's Bernbaum Unit. In a clinic where space and privacy is the highest of commodities, particularly for social workers, the conference room adequately provided the privacy and freedom from distraction that is recommended for group meetings (Yalom, 2005). For many patients who receive care at CSS, the clinic serves as a haven of familiar faces and support; for this reason, holding the group at CSS was advantageous.

The LSG met for 90 minutes, once a week. Yalom (2005) explains that 90 minutes is usual for group therapy, as it allows sufficient time for the warm-up interval and for the major themes of the session to unfold. Likewise, it avoids entering the two-hour timeframe, which he describes as the "point of diminishing returns" when the group can become weary, repetitious, and inefficient. Each session was divided into two segments, with 60 minutes devoted to group process, and 30 minutes during which the group shared a meal (lunch) provided by CSS. My decision to include a meal as part of the session was calculated. Food, in Latino culture, represents a sense of welcoming, a sense of camaraderie, and a sense of support. In Latino households, holidays, celebrations, or mere social gatherings always center on food. So, including a meal within the session served as a means of bringing the members together and recognizing an important part of their culture. The group members contracted to the agenda during the first session. They decided to dedicate the hour to group process and the last half-hour to sharing lunch. While the tone of the group usually lightened during the meal, group process did not end, as discussion of issues and themes continued.

Throughout the life of the LSG, members successfully created a "family-like" environment within the group that extended beyond the LSG's existence, as I learned that several members maintained contact even after the group terminated. My relationship with group members varied. Several were patients I routinely followed at CSS. With these patients, I was careful to make clear distinctions between our relationship in and outside of the group. For patients I did not follow outside of the group, the relationship was clearer. It extended from recruitment to termination and focused solely on issues relevant to the LSG.

Strategies and interventions

A variety of theoretical principles and models guided the strategies and interventions employed to attain group goals. A peer support model paired with the use of culturally competent practice principles (CCPP) (Lu, Lum & Chen, 2001) served as the underpinning of the entire group experience. Psycho-education and problem-solving techniques were also utilized to address themes, relationships, and concrete issues that emerged in group process. Historically, social work interventions with groups have successfully met the multifaceted needs of PLWH (Wiener, 2003; Willinger, 2003). These interventions have served to negate the isolation felt by this population, while providing a supportive network that offers positive affirmation, adaptive coping, and increased social support (Heckman *et al.*, 2001; Smiley, 2004). Peer support groups specifically provide a unique opportunity for PLWH (Molassiotis *et al.*, 2002; Sandstrom, 1996). Through discussions with peers, these interventions allow PLWH to reinforce coping skills and self-esteem and address issues such as the existential challenges evoked by having HIV/AIDS, how to combat stigma, how to build social support, and how to live with the uncertainty and the possibility of death. In addition, these groups allow patients to explore issues through mutual experience and commonality with peers.

The concept of *culturally competent* practice implies that, within the act of providing care, practitioners "understand and attend to the total context of the patient's situation" (Spector, 2004, p. 47). Lu, Lum, and Chen (2001) define *cultural competency* as a clinician's "acceptance and respect of cultural differences, self analysis of one's own cultural identity and biases, awareness of the dynamics of difference in ethnic clients, and the need for additional knowledge, research, and resources to work with clients" (p. 3). CCPP were embedded in the development, recruitment, and engagement tasks that established the framework for the LSG. For example, including a meal and making Spanish the language of group process directly supported Latino cultural values. In addition, prescreening interviews recognized the cultural concept of *personalismo*, and the idea of *familialism* drove the need to create a safe and cohesive, family-like environment within the LSG. Within group process, CCPP shaped the context within which themes were explored. The following will demonstrate how the issue of adherence to HAART, a prominent issue for all PLWH, took a unique path given the cultural beliefs of a Latino PLWH.

The efficacy of HAART strongly depends on patients maintaining 95% or greater adherence. Traditionally, issues of health and disease in Latino culture are thought of according to a system of folk beliefs and practices that use folk healers (*curanderos, santeros*) and natural or herbal remedies for the treatment of disease (Castro *et al.*, 1996). In many cases, these practices are used in conjunction with biomedical interventions; however, sometimes the two conflict with one another as the following shows.

Ms. Baez is a middle-aged woman originally from Central America who was infected by her husband, who had a history of IVDU and died of AIDS. She described longstanding difficulty with adherence to HAART. At the same time, she and her doctor recognized her past recovery from a severe acute episode of HIV-related illness was a result of HAART. Group discussion revealed Ms. Baez strongly believed herbal and natural supplements were integral to promoting and maintaining good health. As such, she routinely took a variety of these agents each morning in the form of vitamins, blended drinks, and/or teas. Further exploration revealed Ms. Baez's HAART regimen called for taking the medication with food each morning. Ms. Baez's practices led to inconsistent adherence, as she reported being too full to take her HAART after consuming all of her herbal treatments.

Education and problem solving were an integral part of the LSG. While I provided didactic/concrete knowledge, group members worked through individual issues reaching feasible and culturally sensitive solutions. In this case, they reinforced the importance of adherence and helped Ms. Baez find a suitable compromise that allowed her to improve her adherence to HAART, while not abandoning her cultural beliefs. Thus, she was simultaneously able to hold on to her folk medical model while also adhering to more Western biomedical interventions.

Stance of the social worker

My role as group facilitator began with the tasks of "creation and maintenance" and "culture building" (Yalom, 2005, 118–21). Creation and maintenance began during the planning and development of the LSG when I assessed the need for the LSG, sold the idea of the group to the stakeholders (i.e. staff and patients at CSS), and constructed an intervention that met the needs of Latino patients at CSS while maintaining the institution's standards of care. Once the group began, I assumed the role of clinician and gatekeeper; as such, my function was to promote group process, while preventing member attrition, maintaining membership stability, and fostering and preserving group cohesiveness (Yalom, 2005). In establishing an appropriate culture for group process, my priority was to create an environment that was safe, reliable, and sustainable. This creates a "space" allowing members to spontaneously express opinions, comment on reactions to the group and/or individual group members, and discuss feelings honestly. Throughout the phases of the group, my interventions were rooted in fundamental psychodynamic techniques such as active listening, interpretation, and meeting the patient where he/she is by hearing and understanding the patient's narrative as he/she perceived it (Lukas, 1993). Collectively, these skills allowed me to assess, engage, and build a therapeutic alliance with members. Given the peer support model on which it was based, the LSG had a less formal and less structured atmosphere. As such, I assumed the role of keeping the group on track and ensuring the focus, content, and progress of group process (Molassiotis *et al.*, 2002). While I did not set an agenda for each group session, I ensured the group did not stray too far from its goals. In addition, when necessary, I stepped in using interpretation and confrontation to assist in resolving conflict between group members and clarifying issues.

Much of the education that occurred during the group occurred among members. While I did assume the role of "technical expert" by providing psycho-education around issues like depression, anxiety, interpersonal conflict, and concrete information about HIV/AIDS and HAART, I also worked to foster interactions between members who offered knowledge, experience, and support. This dynamic is demonstrated by the case of Mr. Cortes, a heterosexual man with a risk factor of IVDU. During one group session, Mr. Cortes discussed his loneliness and his fear about intimacy with an HIV-negative individual. In the ensuing discussion about safer sex practices and HIV prevention, I provided technical information about transmission, the function of condoms, and psycho-education about the feelings and emotions that accompany this issue. Reflecting on their own experiences, values, and beliefs, group members were able to provide valuable information about their experience with disclosing to an intimate partner. They discussed the use of condoms with a partner, the actual experience of using a condom, and their emotional response to such an experience.

Use of resources outside of the helping relationship

A great advantage of working on this kind of a team is the ability to collaborate and share resources, knowledge, and expertise across disciplines. At CSS, the cohesive nature of these interactions provides a unique opportunity for this. On many occasions, I tapped into the expertise of my colleagues as a source of information and a referral network for members seeking specialized care. In addition, internet-based fact sheets, books, and pamphlets provide information and a basis for group discussion. Personal experience gained through individual members' experiences with community based organizations and external systems (i.e. Medicaid, Medicare, public assistance) also served as a resource to group members.

Reassessment and evaluation

To measure outcomes of the LSG, I assessed overall and individual change, observed clinically, and gathered reports of members. Reassessment of clinical strategies and the overall effectiveness of the LSG was an ongoing process. I kept detailed documentation of each session outlining themes discussed, the reaction of members, and plans for upcoming sessions. Reassessment and evaluation led to one significant change during the life of the group. While the LSG was originally designated a "closed group", or one that does not admit new members once the group has started, it was necessary to deviate from this structure when several group members were lost due to life events (i.e. returning to work, childcare, etc.). During this transition, I felt it was appropriate to add new members. Doing so ultimately turned out to be a favorable change as new ideas and perspectives brought a new vitality into group process.

Termination

The LSG terminated after 18 months. The decision was based on membership, group process and my clinical assessment. At the time of termination, the energy of the group had begun to fade. The group had successfully worked through issues achieving the goals originally set forth; however, content became repetitive, members appeared to be getting tired and frustrated, and productivity diminished. More than anything, members were clinging to the camaraderie of the group above the need to work through additional issues. During the last sessions of the LSG members were able to speak openly about the experience, identified their progress and the struggles they experienced in the group. The group's termination meant I ended with those who were not part of my caseload and continued with those who are.

Case conclusion

Significant positive outcomes were observed relative to the goals of the LSG. Of particular significance were the social support relationships that developed amongst members. Within its natural progression, the LSG successfully evolved into a close-knit, supportive network that individual members openly referred to as a "*familia*" (family). Months after the group's termination, I still find members catching up in the CSS waiting room and have learned of others maintaining contact outside the clinic. The LSG also successfully explored the issues of stigma, disclosure, adherence to HAART, and patient-provider communication. Members seized the opportunity to explore these issues in a cultural context and, in many cases, were able to use the support and experiences of peers to better understand their own feelings and reactions. In addition, using collective problem solving, members helped each other reach concrete solutions and behavior change. For example, one group member, who spoke vividly of his struggle with starting HAART during the group, ultimately began treatment and is having a great response to his regimen. Sadly, one group member moved out of NYC after the group's termination and recently died. The news of his passing spread to former group members and affected several of them quite profoundly; they commented on his spirit, his kindness, and the supportive friendship they shared with him.

Differential discussion

Outcomes from the LSG were notably positive and demonstrated the value of recognizing culture's impact on health experience and behavior. The culturally sensitive and supportive environment that existed in the LSG provided a unique environment for the exchange of peer support and mutual experience. Permitting members to explore complex issues within a cultural context allowed them to reach solutions that integrated their cultural beliefs with practices necessary to maintain good health. In instances where concrete change was not possible, the culturally sensitive environment of the LSG allowed members to understand the dynamic between their cultural beliefs and attitudes and/or behaviors. Integrating CCPP into routine clinical practice remains imperative as a means for practitioners to better understand patients' experience and behaviors and to deliver appropriate care.

References

Castro, F. G., Coe, K., Gutierres, S. & Saenz, D. (1996). Designing health promotion programs for Latinos. In P. M. Kato & T. Mann (eds.), *Handbook of diversity issues in health psychology* (pp. 319–45). New York: Plenum Press.

Center for Disease Control and Prevention (CDC). (2007). *National center for HIIV/AIDS, viral hepatitis, STD, and TB prevention: New York 2007 profile.* Retrieved on 23 October 2008, from http://www.cdc.gov/nchhstp/stateprofiles/New_York/New_York_Profiles.htm

Center for Disease Control and Prevention (CDC). (n.d.a.). *HIV and AIDS in the United States: A picture of today's epidemic.* Retrieved on 10/22/08, from http://www.cdc.gov/hiv/topics/surveillance/united_states.htm

Galanti, G. (2003). The Hispanic family and male-female relationships: An overview. *Journal of Transcultural Nursing,* 14 (3): 180–5.

Heckman, T. G., Kochman, A., Sikkema, K. J., Kalichman, S. C., Masten, J., Bergholte, J. & Catz, S. (2001). A pilot coping improvement intervention for late middle-aged and older adults living with HIV/AIDS in the USA. *AIDS Care,* 13 (1): 129–39.

Kaiser Family Foundation (2009). Retrieved 11/06/09, from http://www.statehealthfacts.org.kff.org

Lu, Y. E., Lum, D. & Chen, S. (2001). Cultural competency and achieving styles in clinical social work practice: A conceptual and empirical exploration. *Journal of Ethnic and Cultural Diversity in Social Work,* 9 (3/4): 1–32.

Lukas, S. (1993). *Where to start and what to ask: An assessment handbook.* New York: W. W. Norton & Company.

Mason, H. R. C., Marks, G., Simoni, J. M., Ruiz, M. S. & Richardson, J. L. (1995). Culturally sanctioned secrets? Latino men's nondisclosure of HIV infection to family, friends, and lovers. *Health Psychology,* 14 (1): 6–12.

Molassiotis, A., Callaghan, P., Twinn, S. F., Lam, S. W., Chung, W. Y. & Li, C. K. (2002). A pilot study of the effects of cognitive behavioral therapy and peer support/counseling in decreasing psychological distress and improving quality of life in Chinese patients with symptomatic HIV disease. *AIDS Patient Care and STDs,* 16 (2): 83–96.

New York City Department of Health. (2008). *HIV cases per 100,000 population.* Retrieved, from http://www.nyhealth.gov/statistics/chac/general/hiv.htm

New York City Department of Health. (n.d.) *ADAP—Eligibility, enrollment process and provider information.* Retrieved 12/17/08, from http://www.health.state.ny.us/diseases/aids/resources/adap/eligibility.htm

Sandstrom, K. L. (1996). Searching for information, understanding and self-value: The Utilization of peer support groups by gay men with HIV/AIDS. *Social Work in Health Care*, 23 (4): 51–74.

Smiley, K. A. (2004). A structured group for gay men newly diagnosed with HIV/AIDS. *The Journal for Specialists in Group Work*, 29 (2): 207–24.

Spector, R. E. (2004). *Culture care guide to heritage assessment and health traditions.* Upper Saddle River, NJ: Pearson Prentice Hill.

VanOss Marín, B. (2003). HIV prevention in the Hispanic community: Sex, culture, and empowerment. *Journal of Transcultural Nursing*, 14 (3): 186–92.

Van Servellen, G., Carpio, F., Lopez, M., Garcia-Teague, L., Herrera, G., Monterrosa, F., Gomez, R. & Lombardi, E. (2003). Program to enhance health literacy and treatment adherence in low-income HIV-infected Latino men and women. *AIDS Patient Care and STDs*, 17 (11): 581–94.

Wiener, L. (2003). Group intervention in the early days of the GRID epidemic: A reflection of one social worker's personal experience. In B. Willinger & A. Rice (eds.), *A history of AIDS social work in hospitals: A daring response to an epidemic* (pp. 143–54). New York: Haworth Press.

Willinger, B. (2003). The missing support: Group intervention with AIDS patients. In B. Willinger & A. Rice (eds.), *A history of AIDS social work in hospitals: A daring response to an epidemic* (pp. 155–60). New York: Haworth Press.

Yalom, I. D. (2005). *The theory and practice of group psychotherapy* (5th ed.). New York: Basic Books.

Zambrana, R. E., Cornelius, L. J., Boykin, S. S. & Lopez, D. S. (2004). Latinas and HIV/AIDS risk factors: Implications for harm reduction strategies. *American Journal of Public Health*, 94 (7): 1152–8.

24 Woman to Woman

A hospital-based support program
for women with gynecologic cancer
and their families

Arden Moulton

Context

Description of the setting

Woman to Woman (WtoW), the Gynecologic Oncology Support Program at the Mount Sinai Medical Center in New York City, was instituted in 2003 by a survivor of ovarian cancer. Her perceived lack of emotional support and access to information throughout her cancer experience inspired her to initiate a collaboration between the Mount Sinai Department of Social Work and the Division of Gynecologic Oncology in the Department of Obstetrics, Gynecology and Reproductive Science, to create a dedicated psychosocial support program for women diagnosed with gynecologic cancer and their families (Remmer & Rosberger, 1996). This partnership led to the creation of WtoW, an adjunctive social work program that provides peer to peer mentoring to women in treatment for ovarian, uterine, cervical, vaginal and vulvar cancer. I coordinate the program and in that role, in collaboration with each woman's physician, I identify volunteers and train and support them throughout the process. As Program Coordinator, I match women who are going through the treatment process with the volunteers—all survivors of ovarian, uterine and/or cervical cancer. I determine the appropriateness of the referral (not matching women who have been diagnosed with dementia or serious mental disorders; volunteers are not mental health professionals). If the patient requests a referral and is appropriate, I match the patient with a volunteer of similar diagnosis and age. For example, a pre-menopausal 40-year-old woman newly diagnosed with ovarian cancer has likely been diagnosed at a late stage, lowering her chance of survival. She also faces loss of fertility following the standard of care treatment, radical hysterectomy, and premature menopause; the symptoms of which—hot flashes, mood swings, vaginal dryness—are typically more severe than in natural menopause. I would typically match this woman with a volunteer who has had similar experiences with the psychosocial issues around diagnosis and treatment. I also consider cultural similarities, language and family issues (Patten & Kammer, 2006). The specific concerns expressed by a patient are always considered.

Thus, throughout treatment and post-treatment, women receive support, information and advocacy training from volunteer survivors of gynecologic cancer. WtoW also provides support to the partners of women in treatment through an information guide (Moulton, 2007). Volunteers work with women in all inpatient and outpatient treatment areas. Survivor volunteers have monthly processing and continuing education meetings with me as Program Coordinator. The role of Program Coordinator was originally part-time but, as a result of both a growing number of women referred to Mount Sinai for medical care and the success of the WtoW program, the role was expanded to full-time and has allowed for an enriched partnership between the gynecologic oncology social worker, program staff and volunteers. From the inception of the program in 2003 to the present, WtoW volunteers have provided support and information to over 450 women in treatment for gynecologic cancer.

The Mount Sinai Medical Center is an academic organization comprising a large, tertiary hospital, the Mount Sinai Hospital (MSH), and a medical school, The Mount Sinai School of Medicine. Both are located between East Harlem—a very poor, culturally diverse area with a high proportion of immigrants—and the Upper East Side, one of the wealthiest areas in Manhattan and, perhaps, in the country. The Division of Gynecologic Oncology treats the largest number of women diagnosed with gynecologic cancer in the Northeastern United States. In 2007, for example, over 450 women were treated at MSH and 1,000 more received care at its affiliate hospitals. Also, in the United States in 2007, there were an estimated 9,170 women diagnosed with cervical cancer, 41,200 with uterine cancer and 20,180 with ovarian cancer. That year, an estimated 28,060 women died from gynecologic cancer (ACS, 2008). In New York State, 931 women were diagnosed with cervical cancer, 3,152 with uterine cancer and 1,700 with ovarian cancer, and there were 1,870 gynecologic cancer deaths (NYS-DH, 2009).

Policy

WtoW is funded through a grant and private donations. The women receiving support from the program are seen in the Gynecologic Oncology Clinic (GOClinic), inpatient service, and Cancer Treatment Center. Policies related to insurance plans in the three settings affect women's quality of life in a number of ways. While women in treatment receive standard of care treatment protocols depending on their diagnosis, stage of disease, etc., the setting for receiving treatment varies according to their insurance coverage. As a result of Medicaid's rules for reimbursement, while women with private insurance receive two- to five-hour chemotherapy infusions at the outpatient center, women receiving Medicaid are required to be hospitalized overnight for treatment (NYS-DH, 2008). This 24-hour commitment to treatment, versus a maximum five-hour commitment for the privately insured, affects women's work and family life. Also, lack of beds at this busy hospital often results in delays in treatment for women with Medicaid.

Women report increased anxiety as a result of treatment delays and loss of work and family time. While our volunteers cannot affect system changes in entitlement policies or hospital admissions, they reduce some stress for women in treatment through hospital visits and phone calls (Macvean & White, 2008). Knowing a valued peer, one who speaks the same language, will provide emotional support consistently throughout treatment helps ameliorate the often difficult reality of hospital protocols (Ashbury & Cameron, 1998). We also have a patient fund that can provide financial support to women whose need has been evaluated by the gynecologic oncology health care team. The fund has provided money to pay electric bills, transportation costs, and rent for a woman at risk for eviction.

In NYC, most women receiving Medicaid are enrolled in a managed care plan (NYS-DH, 2008). Only if she is enrolled in a managed care plan accepted by Mount Sinai can a woman receive care at our GOClinic. While the goal of this policy is to provide comprehensive health care services to women, long waits, lack of consistent translation services, rotating medical personnel, and the financial impact of treatment for cancer negatively impact quality of life for these women. Through the consistent caring presence of our program we attempt to assuage the effects of long waits and changing personnel.

Technology

Cervical, endometrial, and ovarian cancers characterize 95% of gynecologic cancers, and rank fourth in both incidence and mortality in cancers diagnosed in women (ACS, 2008, 2009; NCI, 2009). Although these cancers all originate in the female reproductive organs they differ in diagnosis, treatment, and prognosis. While a diagnostic tool (the PAP) exists for cervical cancer, and uterine cancer is typically detected early enough to be successfully treated, ovarian cancer, the leading cause of death from gynecologic cancer in the U.S., is most often diagnosed at stage III or IV, indicating spread of the disease to other organs. No reliable diagnostic tool exists for ovarian cancer. Women with gynecologic cancer are monitored throughout their lives with checkups starting at three months following end of treatment. CAT scans, PET scans, blood monitoring (CA 125 test) and "second look" surgery for ovarian cancer are typical options (Connor & Langford, 2003).

The 15 WtoW volunteers are survivors of at least one of the most common gynecologic cancers; 12 of ovarian cancer, and three of both ovarian and endometrial cancers. The difficult treatment protocols and often grim prognosis for women diagnosed with stage III or IV ovarian cancer resulted in a multidisciplinary decision to prioritize support for women diagnosed with the disease (ACS, 2009). Having 12 ovarian cancer survivor volunteers guarantees there will be consistent, ongoing support to newly diagnosed peers. The high recurrence rate (75%) is a difficult issue. If a woman successfully completes treatment, the longer she is categorized as NED or "no evidence of disease," the better her chance of a cure. Volunteers are required to wait two years after the end of treatment to apply, decreasing their odds of recurrence; however, the fact cancer has recurred for three of the original five volunteers and that one has died has profound implications for the volunteers and the women they mentor.

Treatment for these cancers is determined by type and stage of the disease and age and health of the patient. Women diagnosed in early stages may not require chemotherapy or radiation. Cervical cancer is typically treated with surgery, chemotherapy and/or radiation. Endometrial cancer is treated with surgery; typically, a radical hysterectomy including removal of the cervix, uterus, ovaries and fallopian tubes, followed by chemotherapy and/or radiation. Ovarian cancer is treated with surgery including a radical hysterectomy, debulking (removal of cancer cells visible in the peritoneal cavity) and chemotherapy. All the WtoW volunteers have experienced one or all of the above treatments. Their personal experiences with treatment and management of side-effects are shared, if requested, with the patients they mentor. Receiving practical advice from a woman who has had a similar experience can be comforting and reassuring.

Organization

Highly regarded in the field and with a 100-year history, the Mount Sinai Department of Social Work has 210 social workers who are an integral and necessary part of the functioning of the hospital and are accepted, valued members of multidisciplinary teams. The WtoW Program Coordinator role is both clinical and administrative. While the full-time gynecologic oncology social worker is responsible for assessment of patients, discharge planning and clinical support throughout treatment, I provide clinical support to survivor volunteers through monthly meetings and individual sessions. I maintain relationships with patients in order to follow their progress medically and psychosocially, to monitor the relationship between volunteer and patient, and to assess the efficacy of the program. As Coordinator, I manage volunteer schedules, fundraising—including grant writing and organizing benefits—write training and support materials, attend and sponsor education conferences, and do community outreach.

Decisions about practice

Description of the client

Irma Fuentes, 39 years old, was diagnosed with ovarian cancer in 2006 and has received various kinds of support from three volunteers in different settings during her cancer experience. Having emigrated from El Salvador in 1998, Irma is bilingual and is in the U.S. on a work visa. Irma's mother and eight of her 11 siblings live in El Salvador. Her father died of a stroke in 2003. Irma and three of her brothers live in Yonkers, approximately 25 miles north of NYC. From 1998 to 2004, she worked in a factory augmenting her income with a part-time job at her church. In 2004, Irma lost two fingers in a factory accident and has been on long-term disability ($350 a week) since then. From 2000–6, Irma lived with a boyfriend, and in 2006, she delivered a baby, Sofia, by Caesarian section. On returning home, Irma experienced shortness of breath and was diagnosed with a blood clot in her lung. The next day her obstetrician told Irma that she had stage III ovarian cancer. Due to her complicated medical needs, Irma was transferred to MSH, and in September 2006, she had a radical hysterectomy for removal of all reproductive organs and debulking, or removal of all visible cancer cells. Doctors also implanted a Greenfield filter in Irma's thigh to reduce the possibility of further blood clots. As a result of the hysterectomy, Irma is infertile and experiences symptoms of menopause. Following her diagnosis, Irma's boyfriend left their home telling her he was unable to manage the emotional and practical problems associated with fatherhood and her illness.

I meet with all women who express interest in WtoW. After consultation with my social work colleague and the health care team, I determined Irma's appropriateness for referral during our initial meeting and discussed the benefits of WtoW. While she was interested in meeting a peer, her principal concern was her financial situation. Her boyfriend's disappearance meant the loss of much-needed income. Also, Irma did not have medical insurance and was concerned about the cost of care for Sofia throughout her treatment. Irma sued the factory where she was working when she lost her fingers but the factory closed, making financial restitution unlikely. When diagnosed with ovarian cancer, Irma received an additional $130 a week from SS.

Definition of the client

Irma became our client and both she and Sofia benefited from our support. Because Irma needed emotional, practical and financial help, I referred her to three volunteers in two settings during her treatment (Bultz & Holland, 2006).

Goals

During our initial meeting, Irma identified her financial situation and its impact on her baby as her primary concern. While she was profoundly affected by the emotional turmoil of giving birth, facing a life-threatening clot and being diagnosed with ovarian cancer in the space of one month, Irma's fear that her sudden financial instability would affect her ability to care for Sofia overwhelmed her ability to cope. Acknowledging this I referred Irma to WtoW volunteer Valerie, a survivor of ovarian cancer and founder of WtoW. Valerie's status as a member of the Mount Sinai Auxiliary Board, a philanthropic organization that funds innovative programs within the hospital, helped her to raise the seed money to start WtoW. Her passion and dedication to helping women has contributed to the sustained success of the program.

Valerie, 67 years old, lives on the Upper East Side, has been married for over 40 years to a successful lawyer and real estate entrepreneur and is the mother of three adult children. While Irma and Valerie differ dramatically both culturally and demographically (Spector, 2004), Valerie's "founder" status and history of philanthropy became the most important qualities for an initial match with the financially devastated Irma. Sharing a diagnosis of ovarian cancer was another important criterion for the match and addressed the second goal, normalizing Irma's response to her diagnosis. Valerie's long-term survival would give hope to Irma and provide her with an advocate throughout treatment. Valerie met with Irma, and her kindness, empathy, and unique understanding of Irma's medical situation and sharing of her own history helped Irma begin to acknowledge the overwhelming fear she felt about her diagnosis and its impact on her and her daughter's future. After consultation with Irma's doctors we determined that support from the WtoW Patient Fund was warranted. WtoW covered two months of childcare. After two months, continued support was provided by Valerie and her husband through their personal foundation.

The third goal, Irma's need for advocacy, was identified during chemotherapy treatment. Being insured through emergency Medicaid meant she would be hospitalized for 48 hours three times a month for eight months. Every week, between treatments, Irma came to the GOClinic to monitor her blood levels. There, volunteers Jane, a 12-year survivor of uterine cancer, and Joyce, a survivor of breast, uterine and ovarian cancer, developed a relationship with Irma. Their advocacy efforts included informal translating, serving as liaisons with the health care staff, helping with paperwork and providing practical information about managing chemotherapy side-effects. The volunteers provided Irma with a wig when she lost her hair, made sure she understood the doctor's words, provided her with snacks while she waited and served as consistent supports throughout treatment. When Irma's emergency Medicaid ran out, the volunteers acted as liaisons with the gynecologic oncology social worker to ensure her treatments would not be delayed. The support system provided by the volunteers including emotional, financial and advocacy guidance helped Irma regain her equilibrium and learn new coping strategies.

Use of contract

A contract between volunteer and patient is established following a woman's initial agreement to be part of WtoW. First contact with a woman is made by the Gynecologic Oncology social worker who ascertains her interest in the program. The fear and confusion experienced by most women at the time of diagnosis results in a majority of women agreeing to participate in the program. Very few women refuse the program and those who do are offered it again during chemotherapy. Women uninterested in meeting with a volunteer immediately following surgery may not be physically or emotionally prepared for anything other than recovery from surgery and pain management. Irma agreed to join the Program and I met with her four days after her hysterectomy and debulking, and established a verbal contract agreeing on a visit from a survivor volunteer. I then discussed the referral with the team. Carefully reading her medical chart provided me with information necessary to determine her support needs. These included demographic information, medical status and information on Irma's family and social supports. Our verbal contract was backed up with chart notes from both the social worker and the program coordinator. A second less formal contract was formed between Irma and the survivor volunteers. The relationship formed between Irma and the volunteer survivors included agreeing to share their stories, providing consistent availability, and educating Irma on techniques for coping with gynecologic cancer, and financial support.

Meeting place

We work in all Mount Sinai treatment venues. Initial contact is made on the inpatient floor designated for women with gynecologic cancer. There are 16 beds; 13 of which are semi-private, and volunteers meet with women in their rooms, join them for walks around the floor or visit in the family waiting room. Irma first met with Valerie in her semi-private room five days after surgery and one day before discharge. Irma had a roommate at the time of each visit, but the unusually large size of the room allowed Irma and Valerie to speak privately and did not impede their interactions. Irma discussed her main fear, that she would die and leave Sofia without a mother. As time went on, especially during post-treatment, this fear receded and Irma began to feel hopeful about survival.

Irma met with Jane and Joyce weekly at the GOClinic, a large, crowded, uncomfortable space located in the basement of the inpatient building. Due to JACHO safety evacuation requirements, there is no access to private space in the clinic; all interactions must take place in the general waiting area. At times Irma requested help from Jane, who is bilingual, to help her better understand her doctor's recommendations and treatment plans. These meetings took place in the examination rooms. The lack of privacy may have impeded Irma's willingness to share personal information with Jane and Joyce, but she continued to reach out to them.

Use of time

My initial meeting with women in treatment takes approximately 15 minutes. This usually takes place during post-surgical recovery, impacting the duration of the intervention. Follow-up visits in treatment areas and the GOClinic are usually shorter; no more than five minutes. Most interventions involve WtoW volunteers who see patients in all treatment areas in the Hospital. Some volunteers meet with women outside the Hospital and on the phone, and the time structure for these interactions is open-ended and determined by volunteer and patient.

Use of time for hospital visits is determined by a number of factors. The most important consideration is always the patient's physical condition and availability. Women recovering from surgery may be unable to sustain conversations of any duration due to pain management and recovery from anesthesia. The volunteers ascertain availability by speaking to a woman's nurse to determine if she is in her room and if she is amenable to visits. Length of stay is determined by the volunteer and the patient but usually do not exceed 15 minutes. When a woman is receiving chemotherapy treatments, some of which are five hours in duration, visit times vary from a brief greeting to half-hour discussions between volunteer and patient. Again, visit times are determined by both volunteer and patient.

Valerie met with Irma at bedside for their initial meeting following Irma's surgery for ovarian cancer. Irma's physical weakness and her emotional lability limited the duration of their visit. Valerie introduced herself, explained her role and informed Irma of the financial support she would receive from WtoW. This visit lasted about 10 minutes. Longer, deeper discussions took place between Irma and GOClinic volunteers, Jane and Joyce. Irma had recovered physically at the time of these visits. She had begun to cope emotionally, and reduced anxiety allowed for longer interactions. Irma came to Mount Sinai for treatment every three weeks and was seen by a volunteer during each admission for chemotherapy. These visits varied according to issues discussed and volunteer availability.

Interventions

Interventions by the volunteers include crisis intervention and social support while group work techniques are used to help the volunteers. The timing of the initial meeting between survivor volunteer and patient, and the nature of the peer model, results in a natural use of crisis intervention. Volunteers are trained in active listening and empathic interviewing but are not professionally trained in crisis theory (Aguilera, 1998). The interaction between peers includes a sharing of experiences that normalizes a confusing, stressful environment for patients. Volunteers' active listening encourages patients to tell their cancer story, helping them to process and understand their crisis.

Providing information, emotional buttressing and advocacy assistance in both group and individual settings, social support is acknowledged to have a positive influence on health outcomes (Campbell, Phaneuf & Deane, 2003). The WtoW model offers women in treatment for gynecologic cancer social support from peers who have had similar experiences. Women newly diagnosed with cancer often feel anxious, fearful and out of control. The information WtoW volunteers give to peers increases their knowledge of their illness, producing a sense of mastery and increasing feelings of control (Edgar & Remner, 1996; Remmer & Rosberger, 1996). The emotional empathy inherent in interactions between peers creates an interpersonal bond that encourages a hopeful outcome and models positive behavior. Encouraging self-advocacy through teaching and modeling helps women navigate the health care system increasing their self-esteem and making the treatment experience more manageable. Meeting Valerie, Joyce and Jane at the time of her diagnosis gave Irma hope that she could also expect a positive outcome. The practical information they provided encouraged Irma to advocate for herself with her health care team, the insurance system and her community.

Group techniques are used for the volunteers. Established to process work with patients and further educate survivors on issues pertinent to their work—including cultural competency and teaching of additional mentoring skills—the monthly survivor volunteer group supports the powerful connection between members. Their common effort to cope with and find meaning in their illness and the practical need to problem solve around their work with patients has resulted in personal growth and group cohesiveness. Yalom's "curative factors" that evolve from group therapy are identifiable when assessing the work of the WtoW group (Yalom, 2005). Most of the volunteers seek out membership in WtoW with the goal of helping others in similar situations. The volunteers all report improvement in their own lives through their work. They are often inspired and energized by the efforts of their group peers. The group has produced significant interpersonal relationships between members, a result of their common bond of survivorship and mentoring of others. The altruism they exhibit through their work with women extends to their relationships within the group, further increasing group cohesiveness.

Stance of the social worker

My role as Program Coordinator of WtoW includes completing a brief psychosocial assessment of women in treatment who have asked for a referral to the program and who have been deemed appropriate by the gynecologic oncology social worker and the woman's doctor. The demographic, diagnostic and personal information I gather from my 15-minute interview helps me determine what needs should be addressed immediately and influences the match between patient and survivor volunteer. After meeting with Irma following her ovarian cancer surgery, I determined that her immediate need for practical support to pay for childcare for

Sofia was her primary concern. Introducing her to Valerie at this time facilitated a donation from the WtoW Patient Fund, alleviating Irma's anxiety and allowing her to address other issues arising from her diagnosis. Irma's fear that her diagnosis would result in her death was partly addressed by meeting Valerie, a woman with a similar diagnosis who is doing well physically and emotionally. Her fear that all people with cancer die of the disease was further diminished after meeting Joyce and Jane, both of whom have survived their cancers and are living active, productive lives. Meeting Jane, who is bilingual, each week at the Mount Sinai GOClinic gave Irma the opportunity to discuss her emotional and practical concerns in Spanish, her first language. I continued to assess Irma's changing needs throughout her treatment through brief one-to-one contacts, either in person or on the phone.

Ongoing consultation with the three volunteers who worked with Irma was critical to my assessments as were monthly discussions of Irma's medical progress with her health care team. Through our ongoing interactions with Irma we determined that Irma's lack of knowledge about both her illness and the Mount Sinai Hospital system impacted on her ability to self-advocate. Jane and Joyce discussed their own treatment stories with Irma teaching her about ovarian cancer through listening and example. The volunteers also discussed Irma's need for information with her doctors who then took more time during her appointments to answer her questions and concerns. They encouraged Irma to write down her questions before meeting with her doctors, and Jane translated at times to ensure Irma understood the medical information she received.

A challenge for me in my role as Program Coordinator and social worker is a tendency to micro-manage the work of the volunteers, over-involving myself in their interventions. Becoming too clinical and over-thinking each interaction could reduce the spontaneity between Irma and the volunteers and interfere with their natural bond, a bond I do not share because I have not had cancer. Irma trusted the volunteers because of the commonalities of their experiences and because they were lay persons who could remove the distance that can arise between staff and patient. Respecting the volunteers' unique and important role in Irma's recovery became a challenge for me that demanded constant monitoring of my thoughts and actions. Their support, while critical to Irma's success, augmented the medical and psychosocial support provided by the Gynecologic Oncology Interdisciplinary Team.

In my role as social work counselor to the volunteers, I lead monthly group meetings with the volunteers and meet individually with each volunteer every six months to determine her emotional wellness and discuss issues that arise from the often difficult work we do with patients in treatment. At that time, I reassess volunteer appropriateness to continue as volunteers. The group meetings are organized around the work the volunteers do with women, providing both ongoing education and training and an opportunity to process the emotional issues that inevitably arise through the intimate relationships the program creates. Volunteers may see a woman once or they may develop a long-term relationship. The real possibility that a woman with whom they have developed a relationship does not respond to treatment and dies makes it imperative that they process feelings of profound sadness and helplessness. My stance as social worker necessitates that I maintain a professional role as mediator and emotional support for the volunteers, but my own feelings of sadness have at times made stoicism difficult to maintain. The death of a volunteer or her return to treatment is especially difficult for me. I like and admire these remarkable women. When the volunteers talk about their work "protecting" them from further illness, I empathize with their "magical thinking," and I become angry and sad when these brave women succumb to their disease.

The volunteers also strongly identify with some women, seeing themselves back in the role of the patient; the fear of recurrence is never far from their consciousness. I have used the meetings to educate the volunteers about counter-transference and to normalize their feelings of anxiety and concern about their health. A strong mutual support group has evolved among the volunteers as a result of their work and the often difficult realities of their shared experiences. Volunteers have supported each other through the death of one of the original five volunteers, personal life events, health concerns, etc. One of my challenges as group leader has been re-learning group dynamics to create a safe, effective environment encouraging group attendance and cohesiveness. The changes in the size and make-up of the group over the past five years have also been challenging, but the work the volunteers do bonds them quickly and overcomes initial reticence to share feelings and experiences. Demographic differences among volunteers could present barriers, but mutual support of their shared experience as patients and as mentors emphasizes similarities more than differences.

Group discussion of the volunteers' work with Irma emphasized their various roles in providing her with practical help, emotional support and advocacy training. We discussed her excellent medical prognosis and Sofia's thriving childhood. The volunteers expressed satisfaction about their role as mentors and we talked about their need to find meaning in their own illnesses through their work supporting Irma and other women.

Use of outside resources and mapping devices

When Irma requested information about support groups for women with ovarian cancer, the volunteers and I referred Irma to the Cancer Support Team, a support and information organization near her home in Westchester. Irma has also received counseling from the priest at her home. Childcare for Sofia, paid in part by the WtoW Patient Fund and Valerie's philanthropic trust fund, was provided by a relative in her home. The ecomap, Figure 24.1 on page 289, reflects the various support systems offered to Irma throughout her treatment for ovarian cancer.

Reassessment and evaluation

Irma and I met to discuss how the survivors had impacted on the resolution of her emotional and practical issues (Dunn & Stegunga, 1999; Levine & Silver, 2007). Meeting with Irma at various times during her treatment allowed me to assess the effectiveness of the interventions of the volunteers and to make changes where necessary. At the same time, the volunteers discussed their work with Irma, its effectiveness and their own response to working with her at our monthly processing meetings.

At the beginning of her treatment, Irma stated practical issues, specifically financial concerns, were of critical importance as they involved the physical wellbeing of her daughter. The funds provided gave Irma immediate relief, allowing her to focus on her treatment and recovery. At my first meeting with Irma she was grateful and relieved as a result of the financial support and more hopeful after meeting the survivor volunteers who helped her to know that she might survive her illness, advocate for herself, and live to raise Sofia.

Irma reported feeling secure in her knowledge of ovarian cancer and ability to manage her appointments and interactions with her doctors. Her feelings of anxiety and fear lessened over time and she attributed feeling less anxious to a combination of a gradual adjustment to her illness, the support of her family and the volunteers, and her love for Sofia, her "little miracle." Her insurance issues were a continuing problem and source of anxiety. The emergency Medicaid did not pay for her outpatient visits. The volunteers and I referred Irma to a social worker who manages insurance problems.

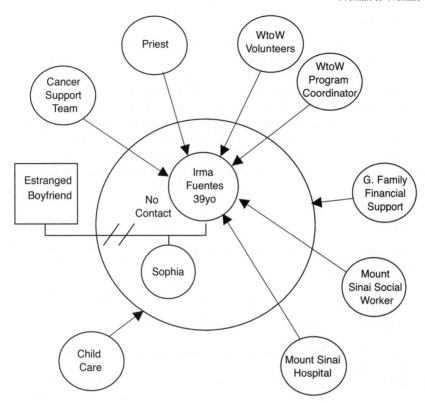

Figure 24.1 Ecomap for Irma Fuentes.

The volunteers discussed their work with Irma during our monthly meetings. Valerie was pleased to have helped, and Jane and Joyce discussed their ongoing work with Irma. While both felt their limited interactions with Irma had a positive effect on her functioning, they were frustrated by the impact of Medicaid on Irma's care.

Case conclusion

Irma's cancer is currently in remission. The WtoW volunteers continue to see Irma every three months at her follow-up appointments. At her last appointment, Irma reluctantly told Joyce and Jane she was experiencing ongoing financial problems related to her inability to find work. WtoW and the G. family provided Irma with additional financial support, enabling her to pay for childcare for Sofia during her job search. The WtoW volunteers and I will continue to provide Irma with emotional and practical support.

The WtoW volunteer group will continue to meet consistently to support its members, encourage cohesiveness and sharing, and further educate the volunteers. The group allows me to monitor progress and current functioning of group members to identify individual distress resulting from work with patients.

Differential discussion

At the time of our initial meeting with Irma, our bilingual survivor volunteer Nancy had not yet joined WtoW. Spanish is not Jane's first language and, while competent, she is not fluent. After Nancy's training, Irma was still receiving treatment and, on reflection, I think it would have augmented Irma's WtoW experience to talk with a survivor in her first language, Spanish. Nancy is also closer in age to Irma and might have engaged her in discussions about fertility and sexuality, issues of particular interest to younger women in treatment. Learning more about Irma's cultural heritage, including her extended family in El Salvador, her spiritual beliefs and her values about healing would have better informed our work and given us an even greater sensitivity to the context in which her illness occurred (Patten & Kammer, 2006; Spector, 2008).

References

ACS (American Cancer Society). (2008). *Cancer Facts and Figures*. American Cancer Society: Atlanta, ACS (American Cancer Society). (2009). *All about ovarian cancer*. American Cancer Society: Atlanta.

Aguilera, D. (1998). *Crisis intervention: Theory and methodology*. New York: Mosby.

Ashbury, F. D. & Cameron, S. L. (1998). One-to-one peer support and quality of life for breast cancer patients. *Patient Education and Counseling*, 35: 89–100.

Bultz, B. & Holland, J. (2006). Emotional distress in patients with cancer: the sixth vital sign. *Community Oncology*, 3: 311–14.

Campbell, H. S., Phaneuf, M. & Deane, K. (2003). Cancer peer support programs—do they work? *Patient Education and Counseling*, 55: 3–15.

Connor, K. & Langford, L. (2003). *Ovarian cancer: Your guide to taking control*, Sebastopol: O'Reilly

Dunn, J. & Stegunga, S. K. (1999). Evaluation of a peer support program for women with breast cancer—lessons for practitioners. *Journal of Community Applied Social Psychology*, 9: 13–22.

Edgar, L. & Remmer, J. (1996). An oncology volunteer support organization: The benefits and fit within the health care system. *PsychoOncology*, 5: 331–41.

Levine, E. & Silver, B. (2007). A pilot study: Evaluation of a psychosocial program for women gynecologic cancers. *Journal of Psychosocial Oncology*, 25: 75–98.

Macvean, M. & White, V. (2008). One to one volunteer support programs for people with cancer: A review of the literature. *Patient Education and Counseling*, 70: 10–24.

Moulton, A. (2007). Woman to Woman Information Guide for Partners, Mount Sinai Hospital.

NCI (National Cancer Institute). (2001). Report of the gynecologic cancers progress review group.

NYS-DH (New York State Department of Health). (2008). *Medicaid Program Information*. Albany, NY.

NYS-DH (New York State Department of Health). (2009). Albany: *State cancer registry, Cancer statistics.*

Patten, C. & Kammer, R. (2006). Better communication with minority patients: seven strategies for achieving cultural competency. *Community Oncology*, 3: 295–300.

Remmer, E. & Rosberger, Z. (1996). An oncology volunteer support organization: the benefits and fit within the health care system. *PsychoOncology*, 5: 331–41.

Spector, R. (2008). *Cultural diversity in health and illness* (7th ed.). New Jersey: Pearson.

Yalom, I. (2005). *The theory and practice of group psychotherapy*. New York: Basic Books.

25 The child and parent team approach

A Philadelphia interdepartmental collaborative to provide community-based services to at-risk mothers and newborns

Nick Claxton, Bozena Lamparska, and Katherine C. Maus

Context

Policy

In 2003 the Federal Child Abuse Prevention and Treatment Act (CAPTA) was amended to mandate that all child protective service (CPS) authorities throughout the country develop a system to respond to referrals of a mother determined to have used illegal drugs during pregnancy (Child Welfare Information Gateway, 2004). The primary aim of the new law is to offer services to the mother and newborn infant, in a supportive, rather than punitive framework. This 2003 reauthorization of the federal Child Abuse Prevention and Treatment Act (CAPTA) requires states receiving CAPTA grants to develop a plan for medical workers to notify CPS of infants identified at birth as affected by prenatal drug exposure. The law states that this referral, in and of itself, is not grounds for a child abuse and/or neglect determination and it cannot be used for criminal prosecution. Rather, it is intended to provide a safety screening and to link the mother to voluntary community services. The law also requires that CPS develop a safe plan for infants in this situation (Prenatal Substance Exposure, 2008).

In November 2006, Governor Ed Rendell of Pennsylvania approved House Bill 2670, amending the Title 23 Domestic Relations Act to reflect the new 2003 federal CAPTA requirements (Palm, 2006). This act took effect in Pennsylvania in May 2007. Of interest, and perhaps significance, is the wording of the state law, which could be seen as stronger than the intent of the federal law (House Bill 2670, 2006). The heading of the section amending Title 23 reads: "Mandatory reporting of infants born and identified as being affected by illegal substances" and reads, in part, "Health care providers who are involved in the delivery or care of an infant who is born and identified as being affected by illegal substance abuse ... shall immediately cause a *report* to be made to the appropriate county agency [which] shall provide or arrange for appropriate services for the infant." (*Our italics.*) Note that the federal law used the word "referral," as opposed to "report." (See also *Differential discussion* on page 301).

In anticipation of the change in state law, the Philadelphia Department of Human Services (DHS) worked closely for over a year with the Philadelphia Department of Public Health (PDPH), Division of Maternal, Child and Family Health (MCFH) to develop an appropriate response offering voluntary services to mothers found to have used illegal drugs during pregnancy. This included MCFH's developing a multidisciplinary team, known as the MCFH/

CAPTA team, to offer assessment, brief intervention, and referral to any family referred by DHS.

DHS screens all calls from hospitals referring a substance-exposed newborn and, using a set protocol, determines whether the family may be a good candidate for voluntary services. If so, one available option is to make a referral to the MCFH/CAPTA team. While federal CAPTA law and consequent state law refer only to pregnant women's illegal drug use, because of the known risks posed by mothers' alcohol use during pregnancy we decided to address alcohol use by any mother who was referred to us because of her use of illegal drugs (see *Differential discussion* on page 301).

Prevalence of substance use during pregnancy

According to the 2004 National Survey on Drug Use and Health (NSDUH), 4.6% of pregnant women aged 15 to 44 reported using illicit drugs; 11.2% drinking alcohol; and 18% smoking cigarettes in the last month of pregnancy (SAMHSA, 2005). The total number of pregnant white women using illegal drugs (113,000) has been found to be higher than African Americans and Hispanics (75,000 and 28,000 respectively), although pregnant African American women experience higher relative rates of drug use (NIDA, 2005). The NSDUH also reveals a lower frequency of illicit substance use by pregnant women compared with non-pregnant women in the same age cohort (SAMHSA, 2005). Rates of tobacco and alcohol use are also considerably lower among pregnant women compared with non-pregnant women (SAMHSA, 2005). Given the statistics, pregnancy in itself may be a deterrent to substance use. Based on estimates from the National Survey on Drug Use during Pregnancy, each year approximately 222,000 infants are born to mothers who used illegal drugs during pregnancy (NIDA, 2005). The number of children affected by prenatal substance exposure, however, is difficult to estimate for multiple reasons; including underreporting of drug use by mothers and the inconsistency of drug testing during labor and delivery (Covington *et al.*, 2002; Prenatal Substance Exposure, 2008). As a result, the actual number of infants and children prenatally exposed to substances is not precise. Estimates are that 14.5% of pregnant women reported binge alcohol use (five or more drinks on the same occasion at least once in the past 30 days), and 0.5% reported heavy alcohol use (five or more drinks on the same occasion on each of five or more days in the past 30 days) respectively (Bailey, *et al.*, 2004; Kim & Krall, 2006).

Current research findings demonstrate that the specific physiological effects of prenatal substance exposure on children are inconclusive, thereby necessitating further studies to address substance abuse among pregnant women and the long-term outcomes of their exposed children. Examination of the effects of illicit drugs on physical growth, motor skills, cognition, language skills, school performance, behavior, and attachment reveal contrary findings; some research finds a drug-related effect while other studies claim a greater environmental effect on outcomes.

Prior to the new federal and state mandates, Philadelphia DHS was not always able to respond when hospitals referred substance-exposed newborns if no other suspicions of abuse or neglect were present. This new requirement is welcomed by many hospital staff.

Technology

If technology is viewed as the means by which social groups provide themselves with the material objects of their civilization, within the MCFH/CAPTA program technology's primary manifestation is knowledge. In public health, the collection and dissemination of information is the platform upon which services are designed and implemented, resulting in improvements in health and wellbeing, certainly material objects of civilization. Our specific tools range from the scales and tapes used to weigh and measure infants and weekly urine screenings by substance abuse treatment service providers, to current best practices regarding infant and toddler development, parenting skills, feeding recommendations, and safe sleeping. In addition, we consider the relationships through which this information is provided to clients and the databases into which the information is entered to also be technological tools. In these ways, all who need to know are informed and up-to-date.

For example, the MCFH/CAPTA team includes a nurse who spends most of her time in the field. Developing a mechanism for the nurse to share information proved to be difficult during the first year of the program. Depending on the nature of the nurse's visit (initial assessment or follow-up), the appropriate form would be filled out and submitted the next time she came into the office; the confidential nature of the reports precluded the use of public fax machines. Emergent circumstances were dealt with via phone calls, or, more likely, voice mail messages to the social worker, substance abuse specialist, or supervisor. As a result, one or more team members might not have been aware of a situation. The nurse has since been provided with a laptop and an Evolution Data Only card, which made it possible for her to connect remotely to the MCFH/CAPTA server drive from anywhere in Philadelphia that got mobile phone reception. An online form was designed to allow her to write up her reports and submit them within 24 hours, thereby assuring that all team members have current data regarding our mothers and babies. Remote connectivity also enables the nurse to keep up with what is going on in the office since, for the sake of documentation, most communication occurs through email. These changes have made it possible to deliver required reports to DHS in a more timely fashion, and with more detail, allowing the DHS/CAPTA staff to be better informed as to the status of CAPTA program participants.

Organization

Philadelphia, the sixth largest city in the U.S., has a population of approximately 1.5 million residents. Since the 1950s, the City has experienced significant population losses related to deterioration in the manufacturing sector, the long-time foundation of its economic base. The loss of well-paying factory jobs and transition to a service economy, among other factors, has resulted in an increase in the proportion of Philadelphia residents living at or below the federal poverty level. Philadelphia is now the poorest of the nation's 10 largest cities. Its residents give birth to approximately 22,000 babies per year, and its infant mortality rate was 11.3 deaths per 1000 live births in 2007, the latest year for which final data is available.

The city has a well-developed public service sector including the Philadelphia Department of Public Health (PDPH) in which the Division of Maternal, Child and Family Health (MCFH) is one of six program units. Through provision of home-based family support services, public health education, and support for prenatal care, MCFH programs address the health and related social service needs of pregnant women, infants, children, and children with special health care needs. The MCFH staff of approximately 45 is comprised primarily of master's level social workers, nurses, health educators, nutritionists and others, and includes both civil service and contract employees. It is approximately 60% African American and 40% White and most staff members are women. Our offices are located in a high-rise office building in center city Philadelphia. Most MCFH program services are provided in families' homes and communities by community-based agencies under contract with MCFH, although over the past five years an increasing number of services are provided directly by MCFH staff.

MCFH services are supported by direct federal grants, federal grants channeled through the State, and City General Funds.

The PDPH and the City's child welfare agency (DHS), are independent of each other in terms of staff and funding. Although there is often an overlap in the families served by the two systems, historically there has been very limited program collaboration.

The PDPH/MCFH/CAPTA program, henceforth referred to as the program, is a collaborative effort between MCFH and DHS. If a referral is made to DHS, usually from a birth-hospital, DHS will use its standard protocols to determine an appropriate response to the referral. Depending on the circumstances and facts given to DHS, a referral for a full child abuse/neglect investigation may be warranted. However, if the case does not appear to rise to a level requiring child protective service intervention, DHS may choose to offer voluntary community-based services to the mother. The MCFH/CAPTA program falls under this category. MCFH chose to change our program's acronym to "Child and Parent Team Approach," and we use this on literature given to families.

The program offers assessment, brief intervention, and referral and works with a family for a maximum period of 90 days, which can be extended in exceptional circumstances. The MCFH team works in close collaboration with DHS, which retains primary responsibility for child safety issues, and with other services involved with the family, such as substance abuse treatment programs. Regular communication among the service providers and family is an essential component in determining how successful any intervention will be.

Decisions about practice

Definition of the client

From MCFH's perspective, our clients are both the families who receive direct services and DHS, with whom we have contracted to offer high-quality care.

From a systems perspective, the goal of the MCFH/CAPTA program is to offer DHS a service option for mothers who have used illegal drugs during pregnancy and who meet the requirements to use a short-term, voluntary program. From a practice perspective, the goal of the CAPTA program is to ensure the health, safety and wellbeing of the baby during its first few weeks of life; to ensure the health of the mother; and to support the mother in her efforts to engage in substance abuse treatment.

Developing objectives and contracting

In anticipation of the changes in both the federal CAPTA law and the Pennsylvania law, DHS approached MCFH to collaborate in developing an appropriate service response for this clientele. The development of protocols and a contract involved middle and upper level management staff from both MCFH and DHS, the City's Law Department to ensure compliance with all federal and state mandates, and several social work staff with experience in direct service, program supervision and administration, and program development. The developed protocols, policies and procedures guiding collaboration between DHS and MCFH were approved and signed by the commissioners of the two departments (DHS and PDPH).

Using their established criteria, hospital staff members determine whether a new mother or infant should be tested for the recent use of, or exposure to, illegal substances. If testing results in a determination that drugs have been used during pregnancy, the hospital is then mandated to make a referral to DHS. The DHS/CAPTA staff is notified, and a DHS worker goes to the hospital within two hours to meet with the mother and assess her appropriateness for referral to MCFH/CAPTA. Our team has no role in determining how an infant is identified as having been exposed to illegal drugs in utero, nor which mothers will be referred. MCFH becomes involved with CAPTA at the time that a referral is made by DHS. If the mother is assessed as appropriate, the referral is made to MCFH. One criterion of appropriateness is willingness to participate in the program. If the mother chooses not to participate with us, DHS refers her to another prevention program or, if necessary, for a full abuse/neglect investigation (see *Differential discussion* on page 301). Although DHS services are voluntary, the department does try to assure each CAPTA family is adequately prepared for the infant in the home by verifying the presence of a crib, car seat, supplies, etc.

Meeting place

The program is built on the belief that service within the home is more effective than office visits. Knowing the conditions in which someone lives provides important information about that individual; actually experiencing it on a weekly basis provides an insight unattainable by any other means. It is one thing to know a neighborhood is badly in need of roach extermination; it is another for the behavioral health specialist (BHS) to experience the bugs crawling on her. A mother may claim she does not smoke around her baby, but when third-hand smoke (smoke that stays in the environment after a cigarette is put out) is evident immediately upon entering the house, the nurse knows differently. At the same time, seeing the care and pride with which a home is maintained also adds to the social worker's knowledge of the client. Had home visits not been the norm, we would never have learned of the existence of a 'speakeasy' in one mother's residence. Strangers came and went frequently, smoking and drinking around the children. It was not until the client was asked about her unusual living situation that the team found out she wanted to move but had no clue how to go about doing so.

Use of time

The decision to limit our involvement to 90 days was based on our tasks of assessment, brief intervention, including education about the needs of the new baby, and referral. Three months is enough time to get a sense of the primary needs of the family, the mother's willingness to acknowledge, or not, a need for treatment, and finally to refer on to other supportive services. This time limit allows the team to work with more families over a year. Should more time be needed, however, this period can be extended.

The team is comprised of a social worker, nurse, substance abuse specialist, and supervisor. The nurse assesses and screens for immediate health issues of baby and mother; the substance abuse specialist gauges the mother's willingness and readiness to engage in some form of treatment; and the social worker addresses other issues that might affect the mother and family's ability to offer a safe and nurturing environment for the infant. Understanding that job descriptions are artificially limiting, the program hired experienced, flexible master's level staff who value intra-team collaboration. For instance, one client turned out to be the substance abuse specialist's neighbor. Although the neighbors did not know each other, to maintain as much confidentiality as possible for the client's sake and comfort, the social worker took over all client contact.

Strategies and interventions

Although the actual natural history of a CAPTA case varies according to its particular circumstances, a "typical" process could be described as follows:

- Referral made by DHS and paperwork faxed to MCFH/CAPTA via secure fax/email.
- SW checks for new referrals, prints them with copies for RN and BHS, enters spreadsheet information, and arranges the initial visit with the DHS worker, mother, child and herself.
- SW and BHS meet with mother, explain program specifics, answer questions, complete psychosocial and substance abuse assessments, get HIPAA and consent forms for release of information signed and, if possible, arrange for an intake at a drug and alcohol facility of the mother's choice after a discussion of her needs and different programs' offerings, and arrange an initial visit by the RN to assess mother and infant medically.
- SW and BHS work with the mother to develop a plan of action for the next 90 days, addressing as many of her needs as possible, particularly as they apply to barriers that may keep her from participating in and successfully completing her drug and alcohol program.
- At the nurse's first visit, after medical assessment, an action plan is developed. Standardized for the most part, this plan describes the intervention and necessary steps (e.g. baby will receive appropriate diet; baby will sleep on back in own uncluttered sleep space, without over bundling; baby will be taken to appointments and get shots on time; mother will be available for appointments with RN; mother will keep appointments for self).
- When the assessments are completed, the RN will visit the baby once a week (usually with the mother present) to weigh and measure and make sure the baby is growing appropriately. The nurse teaches the new mother about feeding, development and other areas. Once the infant has reached 10 lbs and is healthy, the nurse visits every other week. The SW or BHS may make a home visit on the off week, just to set eyes on the infant or to provide extra support to the mother. In addition they will intervene when issues arise that prevent the mother from attending her treatment program, working within and sometimes outside the system to resolve the problems.

As the team is part of a public health department, it also addresses other issues basic to family health and wellbeing, including the promotion of a non-smoking environment, safe sleep practices, healthy nutritional habits, temperament, birth control, bonding, personality and physical development, age-appropriate behaviors, discipline, PHA housing, and toilet training.

Decisions about practice

Description of the client

Addie Zen is a 30-year-old African American woman who was referred to MCFH/CAPTA due to the presence of cocaine in her system at the time of the delivery of her first child. Starting at age 15, she has over the years used alcohol, cocaine, crack, marijuana, heroin, methadone, amphetamines, benzodiazepines, PCP, Ecstasy, and opiates. She states that methadone, amphetamines, and Ecstasy were used only once or twice; her drugs of choice are crack, cocaine, and marijuana. During her pregnancy she used three times a week; prior to the pregnancy she used five days a week. She used with friends and spent around $70 a day.

She states she started when her grandfather died 15 years ago. A friend offered her a joint and she took it, having refused all offers prior to this. She continued smoking and eventually started trying other drugs, having found them to be an effective means of coping with grief and loss; she didn't have to deal with the pain. She has received inpatient treatment twice. Both parents are currently dealing with their own drug and alcohol abuse issues. Addie's mother has used alcohol, crack, and marijuana since Addie was a child; her father is an alcoholic.

Addie and her infant, Natisha, live with her 40-year-old sister, Beatrice, and her two children, a 19-year-old son and 14-year-old daughter. She is unsure who the father of the child is and has no contact with either of the possibilities. Her relationship with her mother is difficult at best, as her mother is caught up with her own addiction. Addie would like to improve the relationship, but says her mother is emotionally abusive. She maintains a good relationship with her father, another sister, and her brother. She reports a history of physical and verbal abuse by her parents, witnessed her father beating her mother, and also reports a history of depression and several hospitalizations. Due to Addie's history of relapse and disappearing, DHS has suggested that Beatrice seek joint custody of Natisha, to care for her should Addie relapse. Addie agreed to this and Beatrice is considering it.

At the time of the initial drug and alcohol assessment it was discovered that Addie did not have any medical insurance for herself or Natisha. This posed additional problems when it turned out she had no ID, either, having lost all during various moves. As a result, in order to get an intake at a drug and alcohol treatment program, Addie first had to go through an assessment with the Behavioral Health Special Initiative (BHSI), a program funded by the Commonwealth of Pennsylvania to provide assessments, referrals, and temporary funding support for individuals needing D&A treatment but lacking insurance. The BHS made the necessary arrangements to connect the client with the BHSI and got her enrolled in a program. At the same time, the SW assisted Addie with the onerous process of getting medical assistance (MA). This was especially important, as Natisha was in need of specialist care (nephrology), but could not be seen until she was covered by insurance. The process began when Addie was in the hospital delivering Natisha, but SW could not reach the appropriate individual at the hospital in order to determine the status of the application. It was recommended that Addie go to the Department of Motor Vehicles (DMV) to get a picture ID, take the picture ID to the appropriate office to get a copy of her birth certificate, and then go to her local country assistance office (CAO) to apply for benefits, which included MA.

Getting the picture ID proved more difficult than expected because Addie had a very hard time following through with directions on her own. At first there was the issue of inertia. The social worker sought the help of Addie's sister to encourage her to do the necessary tasks. Once Addie got started, different barriers popped up preventing her from following through: she didn't want to take the baby out in the cold (her sister agreed to watch the baby on her day off); she didn't have the money for the photo ID (her father gave her the money); she couldn't go on the day her sister had off (the treatment program agreed to allow her to leave the baby there while she ran the necessary errands). In the midst of all this, Addie received MA through the emergency application originally made while she was hospitalized two-and-a-half months earlier during delivery. Her D&A program was now being paid for by MA. Addie eventually got her photo ID.

Since the nephrologist would not see Natisha without insurance until additional information had been obtained from the pediatrician, the nurse helped Addie make an appointment at the local health center for interim prophylactic treatment. When Addie could not get a call back from the nephrologist scheduling an appointment, once she obtained MA the nurse intervened and made some calls until she managed to get an appointment scheduled. Since Natisha has special needs, and Addie needed support to follow-through with many tasks, the social worker made a referral to HIP and followed up with the program administrator to make sure Addie was seen by the nurse practitioner and accepted into the program.

During her 90 days with the MCFH/CAPTA program, Addie's goals of enrollment in a treatment program and getting the requisite care for Natisha were achieved. Figure 25.1 on page 299 is an ecomap of the relationship between Addie, her infant, her family, and the systems that were involved in getting her to this point.

Stance of the social worker

We—social worker, nurse and substance abuse specialist—function together as a team. The program is fortunate in that the clinical team is made up of three people who view their roles and the nature of their interventions differently. While we all have the safety of the child foremost in our minds, we work differently with the mothers. At times, one of us has seemed to want to save everyone and will do whatever it takes to accomplish that. This approach can result in difficulty for the team in maintaining appropriate boundaries. If the mother is not educated about how to use the team's services and encouraged to be independent whenever possible, termination of services at the end of 90 days will be more difficult. At the same time, this team member is non-judgmental, teaching the mothers what they need to know in order to be a good parent without making them feel as though they're bad mothers because they don't already know. Another of us believes all the mothers can be successful in dealing with their substance abuse and mental health issues and she will do what she can to bring this about. However, she also realizes that not everyone is able or ready to do so at this time, and the CAPTA intervention may be one of many in the mother's efforts toward sobriety. Our social worker believes the mother has to take responsibility for herself. He will provide her with every resource available and support her however need be, but he expects her to do as much for herself as possible.

These differing views make for interesting discussions at our weekly clinical meetings, chaired by the supervisor. For two hours every week, every referral is discussed with input invited and expected from all. What one person may view as non-compliant behavior, someone else might argue is an inability to do so as a result of early trauma. Since MCFH is committed to supporting trauma-informed services, most decisions as to outcome and intention are based on this model. However, having different approaches expressed during discussions prevents the possibility of losing perspective and becoming enablers. It should be noted that, while the specific roles and responsibilities would remain the same, the way the team works as a unit would change considerably with a change of cohort. Much is dependent on personal backgrounds and experience, so a different worker would most likely result in significantly different team dynamics. Surprisingly, there was no disagreement about how to work with Addie.

Use of resources outside of the helping relationship

As mentioned above, when issues arise that prevent the mother from attending her treatment program, working within and outside the system becomes essential to resolving the problems. This might include contacting the client's physician, treatment program provider, family members, the MCFH Healthy Start program, either for in-home case management or weekly nursing follow-up if the mother has a medical condition, to assure continuing support once the client's participation in MCFH/CAPTA has ended; the MCFH Health Intervention

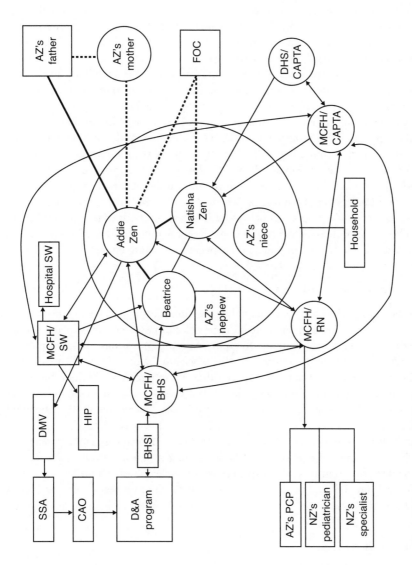

Figure 25.1 Ecomap for Addie Zen.

Program for Families (HIP), if the infant or another child in the household has a special need; the county assistance office; WIC; transportation providers; or any number of programs that meet the needs of the family.

Reassessment and evaluation

Reassessments are conducted when indicated, and every effort is made to ensure the goals are those of the mother. Even though the mother has voluntarily elected to receive our services, she has signed an agreement that says she will attend a drug and alcohol intake to determine treatment, if needed, and will provide all necessary medical care for her baby, as well as maintain communication with the team. If at any time during her participation with the program the mother does not comply with her plan of action or gives anyone on the team reason to believe her child may be at risk due to her behavior, she may be referred back to DHS. If at the weekly meetings it is agreed that the client is progressing well in her treatment, is not in need of the support of our program, and the baby is healthy and developing appropriately, we may end our work with her before 90 days. In Addie's case, there was some frustration at first on the part of the team because she wasn't doing what she said she would and needed to do. Did she not care? Was she just in the program to avoid having a DHS investigation opened? Interestingly, once the nurse helped her hook up with the local health center and realized Addie's need for support and clear-cut single instructions, rather than a list of what needed to be accomplished, Addie began to work on the different tasks. No reassessment of goals was necessary; only our approach and expectations had to change.

Transfer and termination

As the mother approaches her 90th day in the program, transfer and termination discussions take place. If the team feels the mother is doing well but needs continuing support and the mother agrees, a referral will be made to community programs that will meet those needs, as mentioned above. Once the referral has been accepted and the transfer made, the case will be closed. It is expected but not required that the mother will continue her treatment program until she has successfully completed it. It is also possible for a case to be closed not with a referral made to a specific program, but rather a recommendation that the family receives additional prevention services through DHS. Due to Natisha's special medical needs, Addie and Natisha were referred to the HIP program for ongoing case management services. This involved explaining the program to Addie, getting a signed release so a referral could be made, calling the program supervisor to make the referral, and waiting to close her case until someone from HIP had made contact, assessed the family's needs, and accepted Addie and Natisha as HIP clients.

Case conclusions

The majority of MCFH/CAPTA cases have positive terminations. That means the mother has done what was spelled out on her plan of action and there are no signs indicating she is incapable of parenting a child and providing an environment for healthy child development. Since MCFH/CAPTA is an assessment and referral program, any recommendations made as to terminations are just that: recommendations. It is at the DHS/CAPTA team's discretion to decide what the next step will be for the family. They are kept informed of what is going on with the family throughout the 90 days, via weekly reports, phone calls, and emails; most times, the MCFH/CAPTA recommendations are taken. Addie's termination was a particularly satisfying one. Addie took pride in being able to achieve her goals, especially as they applied to providing for her infant. Although it involved a lot of handholding, she did do what had to be done and felt good about her ability to do so, ultimately resulting in a greater sense of being able to care for the child. Also, when asked when she intended to continue in her treatment program, once she completed the MCFH/CAPTA 90-day portion, she responded, "I'm staying until I get my certificate [of completion]. I've got four months clean and I don't want to waste that."

Differential discussion

As noted above, the federal CAPTA law refers specifically to making *referrals* to child protective service, while the subsequent Pennsylvania law talks of making *reports*. The word "report" has long been associated with child abuse and neglect reporting. During the development phase of how to put the Pennsylvania law into effect in Philadelphia, there was significant discussion about exactly how "voluntary" this program would, or should, be. While the intent of the federal law emphasizes offering supportive services to a mother who has used illegal drugs during pregnancy, it would be difficult for a child protective service agency to ignore its primary mandate of protecting children. Hard questions then have to be addressed: how "voluntary" is voluntary? If a family is "offered services", but declines them, what should the child protective agency then do? Clearly, if there is concern about the safety of the newborn or other children in the family, the child protective agency—in this case DHS—must fulfill its obligations to investigate further to ensure the safety of the children.

In practice, the potential dichotomy of viewing the program as voluntary, while still bearing in mind child safety, can put our team in a difficult position with families. To what extent should we emphasize that service is totally voluntary, and maybe risk the family not making use of the support being offered? In practice, we walk a fine line in relationship-building between promoting the long-term value to the family of engaging with the team, while still being honest that they do not have to participate. We've developed significant skill in this area, with integrity and honesty always being paramount. Families are always told, for example, that if they choose not to work with us, they have to be referred back to DHS for further assessment, and possible investigation.

Significant discussion during the planning phase regarded the fact that both the federal and state laws address only *illegal drugs*. From a social policy perspective, then, there is a certain irony that the 2003 federal changes to CAPTA did not include use of alcohol during pregnancy. However, both DHS and MCFH staff thought alcohol use should be addressed as part of the substance abuse assessment done with each mother. Ironically, some evidence suggests alcohol is, in fact, potentially more harmful to the developing fetus than many illegal drugs. While not all the studies are unequivocal in the amount of potential damage to the developing baby from illegal drugs, there is increasing evidence that use of alcohol at any time during pregnancy can lead to lifelong problems. A range of effects, collectively known as Fetal Alcohol Spectrum Disorders (FASDs) can occur and lead, for example, to physical, cognitive, learning and behavioral problems. FASDs are thought to be the leading cause of preventable mental retardation. According to the CDC (Centers for Disease Control and Prevention) there is "no known amount of alcohol that is safe to drink" while pregnant and "there is no time during pregnancy when it is safe to drink" (CDC, 2005). A U.S. Surgeon General's Advisory in 2005 concurred, stating a pregnant woman should not drink alcohol; a pregnant woman who has already used alcohol during pregnancy should stop right away; a woman who is thinking about getting pregnant should stop using alcohol. There is also some ambiguity in the research about long-term effects of the use of illegal drugs by a mother during pregnancy:

> Current research findings demonstrate that the specific physiological effects of prenatal substance exposure on children are inconclusive ... Examination of the effects of illicit drugs on physical growth, motor skills, cognition, language skills, school performance, behavior, and attachment reveal contrary findings; some research finds a drug-related effect while other studies claim a greater environmental effect on outcomes ... Research suggests that the home environment in which the child is reared may have a stronger influence on developmental outcomes than prenatal drug exposure. In all likelihood, the direct biological effects of prenatal drug exposure and the postnatal effects of being raised by a substance using mother overlap to produce a cumulative effect on children's development (Kim & Krall, 2006, 6, 11)

The conclusion that it is the whole environment that affects a person's behavior and life choices should not come as a major surprise to any social worker. It was largely with the understanding that it is the totality of a family's experience that will contribute to a child's wellbeing or otherwise, and not just the use of drugs or alcohol by a parent, that led to a multidisciplinary approach to the intervention being chosen.

References

Bailey, B. N., Delaney-Black, V., Covington, C., Ager, J., Janisse, J., Hannigan, J. H. & Sokol, R. J. (2004). Prenatal exposure to binge drinking and cognitive and behavioral outcomes at age 7 years. *American Journal of Obstetrics & Gynecology*, 191 (3): 1037–43.

CDC (Centers for Disease Control & Prevention) (2005, February). Alcohol Use and Pregnancy http://www.cdc.gov/ncbddd/factsheets/FAS_alcoholuse.pdf

U.S. Surgeon General's Advisory on Alcohol Use in Pregnancy http://www.surgeongeneral.gov/press-releases/sg02222005.html

Child Abuse Prevention and Treatment Act (Public Law No: 108–36). Retrieved 6/11/09, from http://www.acf.hhs.gov/programs/cb/laws_policies/cblaws/capta/index.htm

Child Welfare Information Gateway (2004). *About CAPTA: A legislative factsheet*. Retrieved 4/2/09, from http://childwelfaregov/pubs/factsheets/about.cfm

Covington, C., Nordstrom-Klee, B., Templin, T., Ager, J., Sokol, R. J. & Delaney-Black, V. (2002). Growth from birth to age 7 in children prenatally exposed to cocaine, alcohol, and cigarettes: A prospective cohort study. *Neurotoxicology & Teratology*, 24 (4): 489–96.

House Bill 2670 P.N.4849. (2006). Retrieved 4/2/09, from http://www.legis.state.pa.us/cfdocs/legis/PN/Public/btCheck.cfm?txtTypes=HTM&sessYr=2005&sessInd=O&bil./

Kim, J. & Krall, J. (2006). *Literature review: Effects of prenatal substance exposure on infant and early childhood outcomes*. Berkeley: National Abandoned Infants Assistance Resource Center, University of California at Berkeley.

NIDA (National Institute on Drug Addiction) (2005). Retrieved 4/2/09, from http://www.nida.nih.gov

Palm, C. (2006). *CAPTA Compliance on Track*. Retrieved 4/2/09, from http://protectpachildren.blogspot.com/2006/06/capta-compliance-on-track.html

Prenatal Substance Exposure. (2008). National Abandoned Infants Assistance Resource Center, *UC Berkeley Fact Sheet* (April): 6–7. Retrieved 6/11/09, from http://aia.berkeley.edu/media/pdg/prenatal_subs

Pennsylvania Title 23 Domestic Relations Act (2006): Amendment to Section 6, 6386: Mandatory reporting of infants born and identified as being affected by illegal substances. http://www.dpw.state.pa.us/

Resources/Documents/Pdf/AnnualReports/OCYFPSR/AttachmentW-CAPTALegislation.pdf

SAMHSA (Substance Abuste & Mental Health Service Administration). (2004). *National Survey on Drug Abuse*. Retrived 04/02/09, from http://www.095.samhsa.gov/nsduh/reports.htmH2K4

SAMHSA (Substance Abuse & Mental Health Service Administration). (2005). *National Survey on Drug Abuse*. Retrieved 4/2/09, from http://www.samhsa.gov

26 The Young Women's Program

A health and wellness model to empower adolescents with physical disabilities in a hospital-based setting

Nancy Xenakis

Context

Policy

The Young Women's Program (YWP), which began in 2006 and is the only program of its kind in its local region, serves to teach young women with physical disabilities, aged 14–21, how to lead a healthy lifestyle. It provides a carefully planned curriculum with a variety of group classes and workshops, individual health and wellness planning, expert instruction, access to resources and a network of peers and mentors.

Over the past four decades, the nation's public health focus has shifted from acute care to long-term chronic care for persons with disabilities. The current emphasis on continuity of care is an outgrowth of a series of legislative initiatives, the most influential and widely known being the Americans with Disabilities Act of 1990 (ADA), which addressed the need and ability of persons with disabilities to function optimally in their environment.

In 1999, the Supreme Court issued a landmark decision in *Olmsted v. L.C.* that outlined a remedy for states to achieve the ADA's goal of community care in the most integrated, public settings appropriate to an individual's needs by implementing reasonable accommodations (Rosenbaum, 2000). The decision accomplished what no prior effort has achieved: the establishment of a legal standard for measuring the adequacy of publicly funded health programs designed for persons with disabilities, most notably Medicaid, the largest public health care for persons with disabilities (Rosenbaum, 2000).

Conversely, managed care has proven restrictive to persons with disabilities. Of the current 52.4 million Medicaid enrollees 16%, or about one in every six persons, can be classified as a child or adult under 65 years of age with a disability. Of the $252 billion expenditure on Medicaid benefits, 43% is for the disabled (Kaiser Commission ..., 2009). Because persons with disabilities are a costly population to serve, state Medicaid programs have begun to incorporate younger persons with disabilities into their managed care programs in an attempt to rein in spending. However, persons with disabilities are costly for a reason. On average, their need for health care services and the scope of these services are greater than those of persons without disabilities. As a population, they are particularly vulnerable in managed care programs that restrict access to services to contain costs (Regenstein & Anthony, 1998).

Social workers have assumed a major role in advocating for clients with disabilities, assisting them to find the appropriate managed care plans to meet their medical needs and to apply for exemptions when appropriate. Since funding for the YWP is provided by the Hospital's operating budget and foundation grants, and not insurance reimbursement, it is unaffected by managed care. However, during discussion groups and the program's individual health and wellness planning sessions, participants do discuss the restrictive measures of Medicaid managed care, and efforts are made to find resolutions with involved parties.

Technology

People with a range of physical disabilities should have equal access to telecommunications equipment and services that can improve their lifestyle, social interaction, security and independence (Nguyen, Garrett, Downing, Walker & Hobbs, 2007). Assistive devices for activities of daily living, such as motorized wheelchairs and augmentative and alternative communication devices, have allowed participants of the YWP to travel independently and communicate clearly. Due to technology advances and increased access, the majority of participants use both regular and cellular telephones and computers, as do able-bodied peers of their generation. To facilitate socialization and reduce feelings of isolation, a contact list is maintained. Technology is also used for presentations during class sessions and program outreach in the community. DVDs are an effective medium for communicating information and messages to participants and are used in discussion groups. Use of technology also enabled the program participants to engage in an interactive project resulting in a CD of YWP songs, with an inlay featuring their design, artwork and photography. A DVD highlighting different program sessions was developed and is played during program outreach presentations to professionals, potential participants and their parents. It allows audiences to visualize our program and fosters referrals and registration.

Organization

The YWP is a program within the Initiative for Women with Disabilities (IWD), a hospital-based center serving women with chronic physical illnesses and/or conditions, which offers accessible gynecology, primary care, physical therapy, nutrition consultations, exercise/fitness classes, wellness and social work services. The IWD is part of NYU Hospital for Joint Diseases (NYUHJD), a not-for-profit, acute, specialty teaching hospital with inpatient and outpatient services specializing in Orthopedics, Rheumatology, Neurology and Rehabilitation Medicine. NYUHJD is part of a larger academic medical center, New York University Langone Medical Center (NYULMC). NYUHJD maintains its identity with its areas of medical specialization, familiarity and accessibility among physicians, staff and patients and contained space that is easily navigated. NYUHJD also benefits from being part of NYULMC, with financial security, sharing of best practices and resources on the clinical, technological and ancillary levels. The mission of NYULMC is the relief of human suffering caused by disease and disability through patient care, education, and research. This mission resonates throughout NYUHJD and the IWD.

The IWD is a nationally known center, the only one of its kind in the New York tri-state area and is about women, for women and run by women. It was established in 1998 in response to the Office on Disability and Health (ODH) of the CDC's (Centers for Disease Control and Prevention) 1997 selection of "Women with Disabilities" as a major area of emphasis for future program activities. The ethos, or underlying character and spirit of NYUHJD, supports the mission and innovative programming of the IWD including its Young Women's Program. The senior administration of NYUHJD provides financial support, through its presence at IWD events, by sharing ideas and feedback regarding future programs and services. I am a member of an interdisciplinary team of the IWD, comprising a director, physicians, a social worker, a physical therapist, a nutritionist, wellness practitioners, a nurse's aide and support staff. Collaboratively, we develop programming, render care and provide services responsive to needs of our patients.

Description of the client situation

Young women with physical disabilities face several barriers to leading a healthy lifestyle on the social, familial and medical levels. They often face difficulty in developing a healthy image of their bodies. As they reach adolescence, there is a growing awareness of just how different their bodies are when compared with their able-bodied peers. This is often perpetuated by the perceived influence of various socio-cultural factors such as the media, peers and parents regarding thinness and body ideal (Dunkley, Wertheim & Paxton, 2001). These young women must also overcome myths that they are asexual or incapable of handling sexual relationships (Piotrowski & Snell, 2007).

Young women with physical disabilities often experience practical barriers to socialization, such as a need for special transportation, which reduces their ability to spontaneously participate in peer activities, or problems with physical access to a friend's home (Antle, 2004). This leads to problems with depression and isolation, as well as restricted career aspirations and opportunities, which result from, among many factors, a lack of socialization experiences, role models and mentors. Adolescents with physical disabilities are described as being more dependent on their parents than are adolescents without disabilities; not only in a physical sense (Blum, Resnick, Nelson & St. Germaine, 1991), but behaviorally and socially as well (Bryan & Herjanic, 1980). This can be attributed to the role families play in sheltering young women with disabilities. As a result, these young women may not become independent in sync with other teenagers. Further, parents may be unaware of, or disinclined to introduce their daughters to resources that can help them as they develop.

Girls with disabilities have few options for learning about their changing health care needs or discussing maturation issues as they move from adolescence to adulthood. These young girls often stay with their pediatricians well into adulthood, long after most young women have met with a gynecologist. As the stage is set in adolescence for many of the physical and emotional issues they will face as adults, barriers to health services and wellness activities can have an enormous impact on these young women's lives. According to an article in the *Journal of Obstetrics, Gynecologic and Neonatal Nursing*, young women with disabilities should be active partners in choosing activities to promote wellness and wellbeing, such as exercise, physical activity, nutritional guidance and stress management support groups (Piotrowski & Snell, 2007).

A 1997 study conducted by the Center for Research on Women with Disabilities (CROWD) (Nosek & Howland, 1997), reported that women with disabilities had considerable difficulty in locating physicians who were knowledgeable about their disability and the secondary conditions they were prone to, such as chronic urinary tract infections, heart disease, depression, and osteoporosis. The study highlights that obstacles to health care can be very practical. The most common problem is getting onto a doctor's exam table. Physicians can also view these young women as asexual and infantilize them well into adulthood though many have aspirations of marriage and motherhood. Only in the last 20 years has our attention started to shift away from the protective notion and toward assisting adolescents to learn self-help strategies that promote their self, competence and functional capabilities (Powers, Turner, Ellison, Matuszewski, Wilson, Phillips & Rein, 2001). Our program is aligned with this self-help philosophy and is designed to promote the "self-determination" (Powers, Wilson, Matuszewski, Phillips, Rein, Schumacher & Gensert, 1996) of its participants by exposing them to learning and empowering experiences in individual and group settings. This aims to increase their sense of self-competence, ability to achieve their personally valued goals and form new relationships.

Decisions about practice

Definition of the client

The program's clients are adolescent females with physical disabilities, primarily in high school, aged from 14 to 21. Their physical disabilities are either congenital or acquired due to accident or illness. Some have cognitive impairments secondary to their physical disability. A requirement for eligibility in the program is the ability to follow instructions, behave appropriately and function within a group structure. A telephone screening generally with a parent or legal guardian is then conducted to discuss the potential participants' level of functioning, her interests and accommodations, review program expectations and determine appropriateness of fit. The participants are either self-referrals or referred by a health care or academic professional. The participants and their parents (legal guardians) complete registration paperwork which includes a consent form that is reviewed. Parents (legal guardians) can participate in an orientation to the program but afterwards are encouraged to allow the young women to participate independently. The YWP offers separate educational and wellness workshops for parents (legal guardians) as they have a vital and often complex role in the participants' development and can benefit from a parent (legal guardian) support network.

The program's participants are from diverse racial, ethnic and socioeconomic backgrounds and although they all have a physical disability, their types of physical disability and level of functioning vary. In accordance with Lynch & Hanson's (1999) explanation that being culturally competent means respect for difference, eagerness to learn, and a willingness to accept there are many ways of viewing the world, our staff is experienced in working with different cultural backgrounds; sensitive to the participants' various needs; and willing to explore these differences to enhance the groups' overall experience. The nutrition classes focus on healthy eating, where the foods of different cultures represented by the participants are prepared and discussed. In the discussion groups, issues relating to familial relationships and parental roles are explored. During the individual health and wellness planning sessions, participants develop their own personal goals, particularly in the spiritual domain where they often share their socio-cultural and ethnic beliefs and practices.

Goals

The mission of the YWP is to provide the opportunity for girls with physical disabilities to mature into young women, through age-appropriate health, social and wellness activities. This is achieved by helping young women take charge of their health and wellness, and respect and honor their bodies. The program also serves as a bridge for young women with disabilities, helping them to meet the need for age-appropriate gynecological and medical care as they mature through referrals to the IWD. Most importantly, it provides young women an opportunity to socialize with their peers, develop friendships and share resources. Its main objectives are:

*   Introducing girls with physical disabilities to concepts of health and wellness through classes and workshops in exercise/fitness, wellness, expressive arts and discussion groups.

- Providing young women the opportunity to explore and develop friendships; share concerns and feelings with other young women with disabilities; discover new and rewarding goals/visions for their future; and develop and use self-advocacy skills.
- Introducing girls to available resources on health and wellness for persons with disabilities.
- Helping participants learn how to access appropriate medical care, both primary and gynecological.

Each participant develops an individual health and wellness plan identifying achievable goals for the coming year. The purpose of this exercise is to apply the concepts learned in the group sessions to one's own life and develop meaningful, short-term goals in the five wellbeing domains: recreational, physical, emotional, educational/vocational and spiritual. It is intended to improve one's feelings of self-worth and self-competence. Every six months, each participant reviews, evaluates and updates her goals.

Developing objectives and contracting

Contracts are established with participants, staff, vendors, and funding sources. Written contracting is completed with the transportation companies that provide transportation assistance for the program participants. The majority travels with a paratransit company that serves persons with disabilities. A subscription service was contracted between this company, the program and the participants and their parents (legal guardians), specifying the scope of services and each party's responsibility. The purpose of this contract is to provide timely, efficient transportation service. Participants who attend the same schools or reside in the same areas are scheduled on the same vehicles to enhance socialization and increase the comfort level of parents (legal guardians) to allow their daughters to travel independently. Similarly, a transportation service was contracted to bring a large group of participants who all attend a high school outside of the paratransit company's jurisdiction to the Program.

The contract between the YWP and program participants and their parents (legal guardians) stipulates our policies and procedures including attendance and a consent to participate/liability form. This ensures that participants comply with program expectations, participate safely in all program activities, and allows the hospital to be free from liability. The individual health and wellness plan each young woman develops reflects her short-term personal goals and also serves as a contract between the participant and myself. I present a typed health and wellness plan to each respective participant for her review, signature and reference, and a copy is maintained in my office. We also contract with our funding sources. When a particular grant is awarded to the YWP, the grantor designates how certain funds are to be appropriated and also provides timelines and specifications for reporting how funding was used.

Meeting place

The group sessions of the YWP are held in a large, open pediatric waiting area of the hospital that allows ample and accessible space for all program activities. A smaller, adjacent pediatric waiting area is set up for a quiet study hall at the beginning of each group session. A tutor is available to assist participants with their homework and studying. The meeting space for the individual health and wellness planning sessions is my office. It is a private and accessible space which allows the program participants to feel comfortable to discuss concerns without interruption.

Use of time

The program consists of 10 consecutive 2.5-hour sessions offered weekly after school in the fall and spring. Specialized workshops are offered on weekends and school recess. Table 26.1 below provides an overview of the after-school program structure.

This structure allows for a combination of organized class time as well as informal interactions among the participants. The 45-minute classes provide adequate time to engage participants in an activity and to hold their interest. The 10 consecutive 2.5-hour sessions in one program season allow for regularity and duration that enable the young women to meet program objectives, including learning new skills and developing friendships. The specialized workshops allow for continuity within the program year-round and provide the opportunity to offer classes that require longer duration.

Biannually, at the end of the fall and spring programming, all of the participants meet with me individually for an hour-long initial or follow-up session in my office to complete health and wellness planning. The six-month interval between sessions allows sufficient time for participants to work on achieving their short-term personal goals. During the fall and spring after-school program sessions, ongoing discussions are held with the young women on their individual health and wellness planning. This process serves as a reminder to the young women of their respective plans and gives them the opportunity to share with the group. The young women can be part of the program while they are 14–21 years old. After they age out, they can join other adult programs and services of the IWD for the remainder of their lifetime.

Strategies and interventions

The research by Stewart, Law, Rosenbaum & Willms (2001) emphasizes that the transition from adolescence to adulthood is an important developmental process in the life course of an individual. Those with physical disabilities can face additional challenges in response to unique issues and concerns. The YWP addresses these transitional challenges on two levels: concretely by offering classes, workshops and experiences related to living arrangements, independent travel, school, career, health care, community life, socialization, sexuality, taking care of one's body and financial management; secondly, by creating a bridge to adulthood for its participants in these areas, through developing their skills in advocacy, empowerment, goal setting, independence, communication, negotiation, persistence (especially when faced with adversity), navigating and being resourceful, and sharing information with others with similar needs.

The literature on persons with disabilities over the past two decades has identified the many needs of this population, the existing gaps in services and their societal perception. Some point to the types of programming and services that would make life for persons with disabilities more fulfilling professionally and personally. Empowering experiences that promote

Table 26.1 After-school program structure

Time Period	Activity
4:30–5:00p.m	Homework/studying (tutoring available), review of resource table, socialization, healthy snacks
5:00–5:45p.m.	Health and Wellness Class #1*
5:45–6:30p.m.	Health and Wellness Class #2*
6:30–7:00p.m.	Healthy dinner, guest speaker on program/service, socialization

* class categories are: Exercise/Fitness, Expressive Arts, Wellness, Discussion Groups.

self-determination and self-competence primarily include goal setting; opportunities for so-cialization with peers and mentors; exposure to community resources; and developing skills to take care of their bodies and lead independent lives (Antle, 2004; Healy & Rigby, 1999; King, Shultz, Steel, Gilpin & Cathers, 1993; Piotrowski & Snell, 2007; Powers *et al.*, 2001; Reiter & Goldman, 1999; Rimmer & Rowland, 2008; Stewart, Law, Rosenbaum & Willms, 2001; Tate, Roller & Riley, 2001; U.S. Dept of Health and Human Services, 2005; van Campen & Iedema, 2007). This literature served to inform the creation and development of the YWP and reinforced its outcomes.

A study conducted by King, Shultz, Steel, Gilpin & Cathers (1993) found that adolescents with disabilities are significantly lower in both independence (the disposition to express one's own opinions and to resist the pressure of others to conform) and persistence (the disposition to persist at tasks or goals until they are completed, despite obstacles or difficulties). Their suggested intervention strategies include involving the teenager in decision making and goal setting, encouraging problem solving and role playing around problem situations, and reinforc-ing behaviors related to the acquisition of competence.

The individual health and wellness programming is an intervention designed to serve several purposes. First, it is a means to foster open, candid communication about thoughts and feelings related to the participants' health and wellness. Second, it serves as a concrete tool by which to identify perceived strengths and gaps related to various health and wellness domains and rate the level of importance of these areas to the participant. Finally, based on these exercises, it allows the participants to develop short-term, achievable goals in identified areas. Overall, this portion of the program provides an opportunity for each participant to express herself independently and freely and feel empowered to create, attain and evaluate her own goals.

Stance of the social worker

My stance is primarily as the coordinator of this program and an advocate for persons with disabilities as well as providing counseling. Eda Goldstein (1996, 194) states, "environmental and sociocultural factors are important in shaping behavior and in providing opportunities for the development, enhancement and sustainment of ego functioning." I have found focusing on ego strengths and weaknesses with the young women, as a group and as individuals, as a function of the young women's collective system, is important in assessing and exploring is-sues. I have also found that assisting our participants to identify their strengths as a group and individually has been effective in improving their self-confidence, developing a more positive sense of self and having a more optimistic and goal-oriented attitude towards the future. My strengths perspective assumes that despite "life's problems, all people possess strengths that can be marshaled to improve their lives," (DeJong & Miller, 1995, 729). Establishing rapport by being a reflective listener reduces the level of threat and brings trust to the client/social worker relationship (Hepworth, Rooney & Larsen, 2006). In the program, this is done with parents (legal guardians), as they have a vital and often complex role in the participant's development, and with participants during our group and individual sessions. Empathic attunement involves the ability to "accurately and sensitively perceive the inner feelings of the client" (Hepworth, Rooney & Larsen, 2006, 87).

Literature on persons with physical disabilities supports a group empowerment model such as the YWP, where the emphasis is on creating opportunities for the self-reliance of participants and less dependence on the health care professional (Stewart & Bhagwanjee, 1998). Further, Antle (2004) states that in the social model of disability, social workers need to challenge dominant notions of life with disability as tragic, painful, and hard, and support parents (legal guardians) as influential players in the evolving self. The group sessions reflect this paradigm shift. We aim to help young women with physical disabilities build esteem-enhancing opportunities and broaden their supportive network beyond their families, not only individually but on a larger systems level.

Use of resources outside of the helping relationship

According to the Surgeon General's 2005 report, *Call to Action to Improve the Health and Wellness of Persons with Disabilities* (USDHHS), an important strategy is to continue to develop community-based public-private partnerships to facilitate coordinated care and services. The YWP partners with the community in several ways that mutually benefit the program, its participants and the community; first, by organizing field trips to different recreation and learning institutions and organizations as a way for the young women to learn what each offers, which are fully accessible, and how to navigate transportation; second, through collaboration with other programs that serve the disabled population and conducting cross-marketing and recruitment to maximize participation; and third, by offering joint workshops with programs that incorporate the mission and services of each.

To heighten awareness of the program in the community, ongoing outreach is conducted to students, parents, teachers, therapists and counselors at public and private accessible high schools, and presentations for professionals at medical centers, disability organizations and social service agencies. I collaborate with these individuals on referrals and feedback on a participant's performance and obtain like information.

Given the program's structure within the IWD, the young women can receive accessible gynecology and primary care services at the Center. The program emphasizes the importance of these medical services, introduces the practitioners, and facilitates the referral process. There is also a partnership with the paratransit company to ensure timely, efficient and safe transportation services for all participants to travel independently on a consistent basis. Finally, I collaborate with the IWD interdisciplinary team members and program instructors on program design, curriculum and individual participants as appropriate. The organigraph on page 312, A Hub with a Web, illustrates the functionality of the program.

Reassessment and evaluation

The group sessions provide opportunities to discuss the unique challenges faced by young women with physical disabilities and several positive results are noted. The participants engage in many forms of physical activity for the first time, brave new approaches to wellness, broaden their skills set through the instructors and their peers, discuss their feelings, and begin to connect to each other as friends.

I have observed how the participants initiate independence by parents (legal guardians) taking a less prominent role and allowing their daughters to travel and attend the program on their own. Participants who were once partially or fully dependent for eating and drinking are initiating autonomy and many young women are trying new activities they were previously hesitant about (for example, acupuncture, rowing, drama). Many parents have noted positive changes in their daughters' behavior and attitude that are reflected in this feedback:

> *My daughter has really blossomed this year through her experiences at the IWD, especially the course on healthy eating … the transportation was fabulous, thanks for arranging that and it helped her learn to travel on her own.*

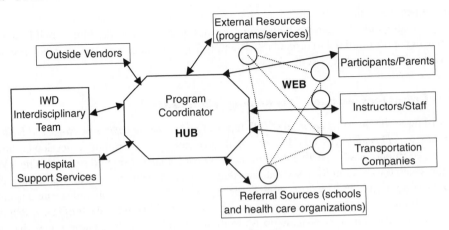

Figure 26.1 Young Women's Program organigraph: a hub with a web.
Adapted from Mintzberg & Van der Heyden, 1999.

My daughter is counting the days until the next workshop—she is really looking forward to it.

She [my daughter] really likes coming. Even when she is tired or has a lot of school work she always insists on coming. She always leaves happy.

The young women begin to develop friendships by communicating with each other and sharing thoughts, feelings, and ideas about being adolescents with physical disabilities. They listen empathically and support one another on how to cope with stressors. They exchange valuable resources on summer internships and camps, attending events at accessible venues and obtaining extra help at school. The large and growing body of theoretical and empirical evidence indicates that social support, particularly emotional support, plays an important role in enhancing health and quality of life in women with physical disabilities (Tate, Roller & Riley, 2001). This mutual support is expressed in these anecdotes:

From a participant: *"The program gets me out of the house, I learn new things and meet new people. The program is important for my development as a person."*

From a parent: *"The program helps her [my daughter] socialize and be with other young women with disabilities outside of the school setting."*

Increased participation has resulted from community outreach, through presentations to students, parents, teachers, therapists, and counselors at public and private accessible high schools; also from presentations for professionals at medical centers, disability organizations and social service agencies. Enquiries from professionals, primarily in health care and school-based settings, have grown exponentially. Participants' satisfaction has resulted in their serving as ambassadors of the program and marketing it to their peers. Several have requested and volunteered to participate in formal presentations to community organizations. Ninety-five percent of first-time attendees return to future sessions.

The classes serve many purposes for the young women. First, 45 minutes seems to be the appropriate length of time to teach a topic and hold their interest. Second, classes are diverse in subject matter and focus on experiential learning. Third, classes teach new skills and re-sources, either through the expert instructors or the curriculum. Finally, they give participants the opportunity to learn from each other and socialize in a structured, safe environment. These quotes offer a small window into the class experiences of the young women:

The exercise helps my body. The discussions teach me things.

I liked all of the classes. The talk we had on traveling with a physical disability is important; we need to know how to do that. I do yoga now at home that I learned at the program. I liked learning about how to eat healthy, especially the healthy snacks … I plan to try those and hopefully with that and exercising I can get in better shape.

Coming each week and learning better ways to take care of myself [helps me to accomplish my goals]. It [the program] gives me an outlet. I have freedom and a voice.

Exposure to our program's various health and wellness services through its classes and development of personal goals has resulted in many young women scheduling appointments for medical, wellness and social work services at the IWD. Several of the young women now see the IWD gynecologist and primary care physician regularly for preventive care and many are seeking nutrition and physical therapy consultations and individual counseling.

Program evaluations are completed at the end of each program season to inform future programming and have consistently yielded favorable results (greater than 60%) in the areas of goal accomplishment, satisfaction with classes and instructors, learning new skills and applying them to everyday situations and improved overall quality of life in areas of independence, self-confidence/competence, self-advocacy and socialization. In the individual health and wellness planning, 84% responded that they thought this was helpful in identifying and achieving their own personal goals. Of the 27 total goals, 30% were completed in their entirety, 48% were partially completed and 22% were not completed at all. In general, the participants felt comfortable communicating and did not have difficulty developing their own goals but many needed guidance in breaking them down into concrete steps towards their achievement.

The distribution of a typed, signed plan seems effective in providing the young women with something tangible that makes their goals real and a document they can refer to throughout the year. These statements from some of the young women convey their thoughts about the health and wellness planning.

It gives me something to work towards. I've never really pushed myself like this before.

I like talking about and writing down my goals. It makes it real. Even though I didn't complete all of my goals, I feel a sense of achievement.

Transfer and termination

Conferences are held with participants and sometimes their parent (legal guardian) regarding referrals and transfers to adult programming at the IWD. If the participant is interested in pursuing this, I speak with my colleagues regarding the transfer and they connect with the participant to conduct transition planning. Participants' files including their demographic and medical background and individual health and wellness plans are forwarded to the appropriate personnel.

Case conclusion

Data from program evaluations from the past two years highlight the effectiveness of the program model, as does the increase in program enrollment, retention and requests by professionals for outreach presentations for their clients/students. Individual health and wellness planning was achieved.

Differential discussion

Despite positive program evaluations and verbal sentiments from the participants and the percentage of health and wellness goals achieved, it is difficult to determine the program's efficacy. The health and wellness planning was implemented in the past year, and goal achievement needs to be measured with a large number of participants over several goal-setting/evaluation cycles. A longitudinal study following the YWP participants as they enter adulthood would enhance our knowledge of long-term effectiveness of the program. Stewart, Law, Rosenbaum & Willms' (2001) study, which examined the transition to adulthood for youth with disabilities, reported many of their youth recognized their generation is the first of its kind surviving into adulthood and remaining in its communities. Given this fact, the YWP, which is now entering its third year, certainly serves a need. The addition of other program components—such as partnering participants with adult mentors and expansion of our current cadre of community partners, including a linkage with high schools to improve academic performance—will enhance future programming.

References

Antle, B. J. (2004). Factors associated with self-worth in young people with physical disabilities. *Health and Social Work*, 29 (3): 167–73.

Blum, R. W., Resnick, M. D., Nelson, R. & St. Germaine, A. (1991). Family and peer issues among adolescents with spina bifida and cerebral palsy. *Pediatrics*, 88 (2): 280–5.

Bryan, D. P. & Herjanic, B. (1980). Depression and suicide among adolescents and young adults with selective handicapping conditions. *Exceptional Education Quarterly*, 1: 57–65.

CDC Center for Disease Control and Prevention. (1997). *Office of Disability and Health, Women with Disabilities Initiative*. Retrieved 12/22/08: http://www.cdc.gov/women/pubs

DeJong, P. & Miller, S. (1995). How to interview for client strengths. *Social Work*, 40 (6): 729–36.

Dunkley, T. L., Wertheim, E. H. & Paxton, S. J. (2001). Examination of a model of multiple sociocultural influences on adolescent girls' body dissatisfaction and dietary restraint. *Adolescence*, 36 (142): 265–79.

Goldstein, E. (1996). Ego psychology theory. In F. Turner (ed.), *Social work treatment* (pp. 191–217). New York: Free Press.

Healy, H. & Rigby, P. (1999). Promoting independence for teens and young adults with physical disabilities. *Canadian Journal of Occupational Therapy*, 66 (5): 240–9.

Hepworth, D., Rooney, R. & Larsen, J. A. (2006). *Direct social work practice: theory and skills* (7th ed.). (pp. 81–131). Pacific Grove, CA: Brooks/Cole.

Kaiser Commission on Medicaid and the Uninsured. (2009). *Medicaid: A primer*. Henry J. Kaiser Family Foundation. Retrieved 11/28/08: http://www.kff.org/medicaid/upload/keyma&mcstats.pdf

King, G. A., Shultz, I. Z., Steel, K., Gilpin, M. & Cathers, T. (1993). Self-evaluation and self-concept of adolescents with physical disabilities. *American Journal of Occupational Therapy*, 47 (2): 132–40.

Lynch, E. W. & Hanson, M. J. (1999). *Steps in the right direction in developing cross-cultural competence*. (2nd ed.). Baltimore: Paul H. Brookes Publishing Co.

Mintzberg, H. & Van der Heyden, L. (1999). Organigraphs: Drawing how companies really work. *Harvard Business Review*, (September-October): 87–94.

Nguyen, T., Garrett, R., Downing, A., Walker, L. & Hobbs, D. (2007). Research into telecommunications options for people with physical disabilities. *Assistive Technology*, 19 (2): 78–93.

Nosek, M. & Howland, C. (1997). Breast and cervical cancer screening among women with physical disabilities. *Archives of Physical Medicine and Rehabilitation*, 78 (12): 539–44.

Piotrowski, K. & Snell, L. (2007). Health care needs of women with disabilities across the life span. *Journal of Obstetric, Gynecologic and Neonatal Nursing*, 36 (1): 79–87.

Powers, L. E., Turner, A., Ellison, R., Matuszewski, J., Wilson, R., Phillips, A. & Rein, C. (2001). A multi-component intervention to promote adolescent self-determination. (Take charge field test-statistical data included.) *Journal of Rehabilitation*. 67 (1): 37–45.

Powers, L. E., Wilson, R., Matuszewski, J., Phillips, A., Rein, C., Schumacher, D. & Gensert, J. (1996). Facilitating adolescent self-determination: what does it take? In: Sands D. J. & Wehmeyer M. L. (eds.), *Self-determination across the life span: independence and choice for people with disabilities* (pp. 257–84). Baltimore: Paul H. Brookes.

Regenstein, M. & Anthony, S. E. (1998). *Medicaid managed care for persons with disabilities*. Economic and Social Research Institute, Occasional Paper 11.

Reiter, S. & Goldman, T. (1999). A programme for the enhancement of autonomy in young adults with physical disabilities: the development of a realistic self concept, individual perception of quality of life and the development of independent living skills. *International Journal of Rehabilitation Research*, 22 (1): 71–4.

Rimmer, J. A. & Rowland, J. L. (2008). Physical activity for youth with disabilities: a critical need in an underserved population. *Developmental Neurorehabilitation*, 11 (2): 41–148.

Rosenbaum, S. (2000). The Olmstead decision: implications for state health policy. *Health Affairs*, 19 (5): 228–32.

Stewart, R. & Bhagwanjee, A. (1998). Promoting group empowerment and self-reliance through participatory research: A case study for people with physical disability. *Disability and Rehabilitation*, 21 (7): 338–45.

Stewart, D., Law, M. C., Rosenbaum, P. & Willms, D. G. (2001). A qualitative study of the transition to adulthood for youth with physical disabilities. *Physical and Occupational Therapy in Pediatrics*, 21 (4): 3–17.

Tate, D. G., Roller, S. & Riley, B. (2001).Quality of life for women with physical disabilities. *Physical Medicine and Rehabilitation Clinics of North America*, 12 (1): 23–7.

Van Campen, C. & Iedema, J. (2007). Are persons with physical disabilities who participate in society healthier and happier? Structural equation modeling of objective participation and subjective well-being. *Quality of Life Research*, 16: 635–45.

United States Department of Health and Human Services (2005). *The Surgeon General's call to action to improve the health and wellness of persons with disabilities*. Retrieved 8/19/08: http://www.surgeongeneral.gov/library/disabilities/calltoaction

27 The social worker on the genetic counseling team

A new role in social work oncology

Susan A. Scarvalone, Julianne S. Oktay, Jessica Scott, and Kathy J. Helzlsouer

Introduction

Breast cancer remains the most frequently diagnosed cancer (after skin cancer) among American women, with over 192,000 diagnosed every year (American Cancer Society, 2008). It is the second leading cause of cancer death (after lung cancer), with over 40,000 deaths. Ovarian cancer is much less frequently diagnosed, with over 20,000 new cases a year, but survival is poorer than breast cancer, since it is not easy to detect at an early stage. Approximately 15,000 women die each year from ovarian cancer. The discovery that mutations in two genes (called BRCA1 and BRCA2) (Friedman *et al.*, 1994; Miki, Swensen & Shattuck-Eidens, 1994; Wooster *et al.*,1995) leads to an increased risk of breast and ovarian cancer has made it possible for women with breast cancer, and those with a strong family history of cancer, to potentially clarify their risk through genetic testing. Research has shown that approximately 10% of women with breast cancer have a strong genetic predisposition to cancer and about half of these women carry mutation in BRCA1 or BRCA2 (Lynch, Fusaro, Lemon, Smyrk & Lynch, 1997). Many cancer centers around the country have developed genetic counseling and testing services for their patient populations. Social workers have much to contribute to these services. In this chapter, the social work role on a multidisciplinary team in an oncology genetic counseling and testing program is described.

Context

Description of the setting

The Cancer Prevention and Genetics Counseling Service, part of the Prevention and Research Center (PRC) of the Mercy Medical Center, was developed for women who are at high risk of cancer, or who have cancer and have a family history suggesting that they might have a genetically based type of cancer. The team is made up of a physician with a strong background in oncology and genetics, a genetic counselor and a social worker. This service includes a complete evaluation of family history and other factors that may increase the risk of developing certain cancers, genetic counseling and testing, and development of a preventative health care plan.

The PRC is devoted to improving the health care of individuals through clinical and research programs focused on the prevention, early detection and treatment and long-term management of diseases, especially cancer. We offer clinical services, research and educational programs to promote health and wellbeing for cancer patients and their families. In addition to integrating research into clinical care, we offer a group-based mind-body medicine program

(*Be Well, Stay Healthy* ™) for breast cancer survivors who are experiencing persistent fatigue. We are also involved in research, the Fatigue Intervention Trial, which examines the impact of family participation in the *Be Well, Stay Healthy* ™ Program, and offer *Be Well, Stay Healthy KIDS* for children and teens coping with cancer in the family, a monthly group-based program offering support and education for school-age children and teenagers. Staff includes a medical director, nurse practitioner, genetic counselor, epidemiologist, biostatistician, and research nurses and research assistants, and a full-time clinical research social worker who is the primary clinician to address the social and emotional needs of patients in the PRC. She provides the full range of social work interventions to patients referred to the Cancer Prevention and Genetics Counseling Service and facilitates and participates in program design, recruitment and retention for the group programs described above.

Organization

Founded in 1874 by The Sisters of Mercy, The Mercy Medical Center, an urban community-based hospital in the city center, was initially dedicated to providing high-quality care to the poor and underserved inner-city population. Today, it is a full-service medical center providing comprehensive services across the medical spectrum. In recent years, MMC has developed a number of specialty centers that are nationally recognized for their excellence, including a particular focus on women's health. In 2003, MMC opened a beautiful new building to house the Women's Center for Health and Medicine, "designed to offer women the quality of care they expect, the comfort and concern they desire, and an atmosphere of healing from the moment they enter" (http://www.mdmercy.com/womens). We advocate strongly for women's health, with an emphasis on prevention, education and outreach. The Weinberg Center houses the PRC as well as outstanding programs for the treatment of breast cancer, radiation oncology, plastic and reconstructive surgery. In 2006, the cancer programs at MMC were consolidated under The Institute for Cancer Care. In addition to the social worker at the PRC, there are two social workers responsible for oncology care, one inpatient and one outpatient.

Policy

Several major policy issues related to insurance coverage, and also to confidentiality and potential discrimination, are relevant to the Cancer Prevention and Genetics Counseling Service (McEwen, 2006); in part because the ability of patients and families to obtain genetic testing is a fairly recent development. Genetic testing for BRCA1 and BRCA2 is currently only done by one company (Myriad Genetic Laboratories, Inc.), which has the patent (exclusive licensing) for analysis of these genes. The laws that govern patents for genetic discoveries have made this monopoly possible, although there have been challenges of the patent in Canada and in Europe (Patenaude, 2005). Currently, the cost for the sequencing of the genes for breast and ovarian cancer is over $3,000. Because a small set of mutations has been found in these genes (two mutations in BRCA1 and one in BRCA2) that explain most of the mutations for those of Ashkenazi Jewish background (Strewing *et al.*, 1997), the test for members of this population is sometimes less costly (Patenaude, 2005). Another broad policy issue is inadequacy, since genetic counseling programs are not accessible in all parts of the country.

    The cost of genetic counseling and testing is usually paid by public or private health insurance. In the U.S., for those under 65, health insurance is largely employee-based with very poor people covered by Medicaid (a State-Federal partnership), and those over 65, by Medicare, and some special groups covered by limited programs, such as the Veterans Administration.

The result is a very complex system with no universal standard for genetic programs' coverage. While genetic services are covered by most health insurance programs, coverage and amount paid vary. Also, an insurance company may require a certain family history or characteristics of cancer before it will pay for services. Medicare now covers genetic testing for breast and ovarian cancers under certain conditions, but Medicaid coverage is available only in some states. Furthermore, not all patients have health insurance, and many who do are "underinsured." Of cancer patients, 33% have difficulty paying, and 25% use all or most of their savings dealing with cancer care (Kaiser Family Foundation, 2009). Patients with health insurance pre-diagnosis may risk losing coverage, especially if employment is affected and they are not able to afford COBRA. Once insurance is lost, the cancer diagnosis may make health insurance difficult to obtain or excessively expensive for those on private health plans. Those without health insurance have limited access to genetic services. Self-pay would be the only option (unless a special program can be found for this purpose, such as a private foundation, waiver of fee by the laboratory, etc.). In addition to testing, costs could be incurred for preventative surgery, medications, and increased surveillance.

Other policy issues are related to the risk of discrimination based on genetic testing. Some results can affect one's ability to obtain insurance coverage for medical, disability, life or long-term care insurance (Oktay, 1998). Despite widespread fears of discrimination, there have been no reported cases of discrimination based on the BRCA 1 & BRCA2 genetic tests according to the Myriad Website (2009). Also, an employer or future employer could gain access to medical records, especially now that records are becoming electronic. Some women with health insurance decide to pay for the testing themselves, to prevent their insurance company from learning of testing or results. Some request that results not be placed in their medical records due to fear of discrimination. These concerns are especially salient for women who seek genetic testing because they have a family history of breast cancer, but have not been diagnosed with breast cancer themselves. A series of federal and state legislative initiatives prohibit discrimination based on genetic testing. The earliest came about through the Americans with Disabilities Act of 1990 (ADA), which was expanded in 1995 to include in the definition of "disabled" individuals with genes that put them at risk for genetic disorders. The next federal development was the passage of HIPAA, the Health Insurance Portability and Accountability Act (1996) prohibiting group health plans from using genetic information to deny coverage. Its protection does not extend to all types of employment-based health insurance. It was extended in 2000 to provide privacy for health information in medical records. While not specific to genetic information, these standards apply because they are comprehensive to all health information.

Most recently, Congress passed the Genetic Information Nondiscrimination Act (GINA) that, once implemented, will prohibit discrimination in employment and health insurance on the basis of genetic information. Also, it will prohibit employers from requiring potential employees to have genetic testing, set requirements on use and disclosure of genetic test results, and prevent health insurers from denying coverage or adjusting premiums based on the results of genetic testing (Genetic Alliance, 2009). The act was designed to encourage individuals to take advantage of available genetic services and of therapies that result from future scientific advances. Some states have also enacted genetic non-discrimination laws for their citizens. Social workers interested in genetics should learn about any legislation in their states, as well as the status of any legal challenges to such legislation.

Policies are often evaluated for their ability to provide services that are both adequate and equitable and, in that regard, policies related to genetic testing have a long way to go. Because of the large numbers of people who lack health insurance, this service is practically inaccessible to many people who could benefit from it. Because some potential for discrimination exists, and information about the long-term psychological impact of testing is lacking, there are ethical issues relating to the benefits compared with the risks of the service. Finally, because the technology in this biomedical field outpaces the ability of society to develop and implement regulations, the future will likely involve a continuous process of policy needing to "catch up" with the technological developments. Clearly, this has implications for social work service that will be discussed below.

Technology

The discovery of the structure of the DNA molecule, and later, the mapping of the human genome have allowed scientists to identify specific genetic errors, or mutations, with specific diseases. Extensive studies of the DNA of families with high rates of breast cancer led to the identification of two genes associated with it. These mutations explain about half of inherited forms of breast cancer. (Much rarer genes can also contribute to breast cancer.) Thus, about half of suspected inherited forms cannot yet be attributed to specific genetic abnormalities. Mutations in these genes affect their functions and lead to an increased risk of developing cancer. The genes are incompletely penetrant, meaning not everyone who carries a mutation will develop breast cancer. The risk of developing breast cancer depends on the mutation and can vary from a lifetime risk of 30% up to 80%. Men who carry mutations are also at increased risk of cancer, but their rates are lower. The genes are inherited in an autosomal-dominant pattern, meaning a child of a person with a mutation in one of these two genes has a 50% chance of inheriting the mutation. Both men and women inherit altered BRCA1 or BRCA2 genes and, whether or not they are ever diagnosed, they may pass on the alteration to their children. It is estimated women who inherit a BRCA1 or BRCA2 mutation have up to an 85% chance of being diagnosed in their lifetime, compared to about 12% chance in the general population (Patenaude, 2005). The risk for ovarian cancer may be 20% to 40%, compared with less than 2% lifetime risk for the general population (Ford *et al.*, 1998).

Clinical genetic testing for BRCA1 and BRCA2 mutations became available in the mid-1990s. Because test results may be hard to interpret, and testing can raise complex psychological and family issues, it is important that education and counseling be provided both before and after testing. When tests first became available, interest was high, but when women learned more about the test and what positive or negative results could mean, they were less likely to choose to have the test than they were before the education (Biesecker *et al.*, 2000; Capelli *et al.*, 2001). Even today, many women may have unrealistic expectations for testing.

Today two primary groups seek genetic testing: women diagnosed with breast or ovarian cancer and with a family history of cancer, and women unaffected but who have a family history of cancer. Those diagnosed with cancer may be referred by their physician because the preferred treatment may differ if a genetic mutation is found. Characteristics that make a genetic mutation more likely are having early onset breast cancer, bilateral breast cancer, or a family history of early onset breast or ovarian cancer. Testing may also be sought by women who have not been diagnosed but who are concerned about their own risks. They might have mothers, sisters, grandmothers, and aunts who have been diagnosed, or who have been found to carry a genetic mutation. Some women who do not have cancer in the family but are highly anxious about their risk also seek testing. To have the most informative testing, the ideal situation is to first test someone in the family who has had cancer in order to determine if BRCA1 or BRCA2 mutations can explain the family history. This is important since BRCA1 or BRCA2 mutations only explain a portion of suspected inherited forms.

There are four possible results from the BRCA1 and BRCA2 genetic testing (Miller *et al.*, 2006). A "positive" result means a patient has the same mutation known to be present in another family member who has been diagnosed. A "true negative," means the patient is not a carrier of a mutation known in the family. Both of these results require that another family member who has or had cancer was tested and a specific mutation was identified. Two other types of results can occur. When the carrier status of the family member with cancer is not known or is negative, the result may be called "indeterminate." The other possibility, a mutation of "uncertain significance," occurs when a genetic mutation is found, but it is not known if the mutation causes a problem in how the gene functions. For example, gene changes may alter the spelling of the gene but not change the function. This is analogous to the American and British ways of spelling the word color. The two different spellings, color and colour, are both understood.

One option available to women who test positive is heightened screening and surveillance designed to detect a cancer early, so that it can be treated as soon as possible. For breast cancer, surveillance includes mammography, breast MRI (magnetic resonance imaging), and clinical breast exams. For ovarian cancers, surveillance includes transvaginal ultrasound, CA-125, and clinical exams; however, this screening has not been proven effective for the early detection of ovarian cancer. Another option is to have risk-reducing surgery, removing the breasts or ovaries and fallopian tubes, which greatly reduces but does not eliminate the chances of developing cancer. A woman can choose to have preventative mastectomies (removal of healthy breasts) and/or bilateral salpingo-oophorectomy (removal of healthy fallopian tubes and ovaries). A third option is chemoprevention (Tomoxifin or raloxifine), but its effect on future breast or ovarian cancer in those with BRCA mutations may be limited.

Negative or inconclusive test results are difficult to interpret, unless the negative is a "true negative." Here, one's risk of breast cancer is not zero but is the same as the risk in the population at large. While one might think that a woman's receiving a negative result would be relieved, the reality is more complex. Some feel "survivor's guilt," especially if family members have tested positive. When the test result is "indeterminate," it means her risk cannot be clarified based on the test result. It could be a "true negative," or it could be that the type of mutation in BRCA1 or BRCA2 was not determined by the genetic test. The woman is still considered at risk because of her as yet unexplained family history.

Because the results can be difficult to interpret, and can lead to psychological consequences, such as depression, anxiety (Lerman & Shields, 2004) and family problems (Hughes *et al.*, 2002; Kenen, Ardern-Jones & Eeles, 2003; Parker & Lucassen, 2003; Tercyak *et al.*, 2001), the social worker can help women to sort through the factors affecting their decision making, consider the repercussions of the decisions, weigh the costs and benefits of genetic testing, and deal with the practical, medical and emotional implications. Life-changing decisions affecting future fertility, body image and sexuality are involved. It is also important for the woman considering testing to consider with whom she will share the results: others in the family who may be at risk, or her children? When? If not married, will she share her results with a future husband? What if she has a sister who does not want to know the results, or a mother who doesn't want her to get tested? A social worker can help patients with these difficult decisions, deal with the emotions involved, and help the family to cope with the results. Those seeking testing may be thinking about short-term decisions concerning testing, and risk-reducing procedures, but long-term needs must be considered, as well. Women at high risk may be making decisions about marriage, children and life-planning, as may their children, especially if they are young.

Decisions about practice

Definition of the client

Carla referred herself when she learned that her sister was diagnosed with breast cancer and found to be positive for a BRCA1 mutation. She and her husband, married just over a year, are both 27 and have no children. Carla is an administrative assistant for a large firm and her husband is a data systems analyst with a technology firm. They live in Baltimore, and all extended family members live out of state. The primary client in genetic counseling and testing is the individual seeking genetic services, but by definition genetics is a family matter. Other family members, including unborn children, can be affected by test results. Here, family includes the patient's siblings, parents and children and extended family. So, Carla and her husband are the primary clients, while future children and the extended family are a kind of secondary client.

Meeting place

The Genetic Counseling Services have a suite of offices at the PRC. The waiting area has comfortable chairs and lighting. The consultation room itself is designed to be comfortable and relaxing with subdued lighting and plants. It is a fairly intimate space (12' × 12') with large windows overlooking the city. In the center of the room is a round conference table and chairs.

Use of time

The consultation is for one or two sessions. At the initial one-hour consultation, the patient and any accompanying family members meet with the genetic counselor and me, the social worker, in the consultation room. After explaining the service, answering questions and completing a family history, the genetic counselor discusses the medical information and family history with the oncologist whose office is next door while I stay and talk with the patients and family. The oncologist and genetic counselor return to discuss the results of their family history analysis and any recommendation about genetic testing. At this point, the patient and family may make a decision, or they may decide to think further about their options.

If a patient decides to have genetic testing, a blood sample is taken, and sent to the lab. The genetic counselor explains that she will contact the patient by phone with the results and confirms that the patient is comfortable with this arrangement. All patients also receive a written medical visit summary and a copy of the testing results. A second session is then scheduled with the team to discuss the test result implications. In cases where the patient decides not to pursue genetic testing, and in some cases when the test results are negative (that is, no mutation is identified), a second session may not take place. At the conclusion of the consultation session(s), the team informs the patient they are available for further discussion or referral if needed.

Goals

There are six goals for genetic risk counseling: "(1) Comprehension of genetic risk information to enable an adaptive decision and to determine whether family history suggests an inherited pattern; (2) Effective decision making regarding whether to undergo genetic testing;

(3) Adjustment and minimization of the negative impact of genetic testing; (4) Adherence to surveillance recommendations; (5) Follow-up decision making regarding prevention options; and (6) Communication of test results to family members" (Miller *et al.*, 2006, 281). My role is to: help ensure that the individual understands the implications for making the decision whether to be tested for potential risk for cancer; identify the pertinent issues that may impact on the patient and family; help the patient and family consider the effect this information will have; and determine if others in the family may need additional intervention. In the first consultation, I address the social and emotional implications of cancer risk screening and family members' relationships since the information may affect their choices and decisions. I seek ways to support the decisions of the patient and to help them appreciate the complexity of their decision. I am also attentive to any barriers, both practical and psychological, which may affect the patient facing this decision. In the second session, I focus on how each individual faces living with the new information.

Contracting and developing objectives

At the initial visit I describe my role on the team, explaining that I help with the practical, social and emotional aspects of genetic testing. Because the involvement of a social worker is provided as part of the holistic care offered by the PRC, there is usually no individual contracting concerning social work services. If patients are interested in more help with this process, I am available by telephone or in-person in the two-week window between the first and second consultation sessions. If further social work assistance is required for areas beyond the scope of practice for the cancer risk consultation service, I arrange appropriate referrals.

Intervention: Session one

At the first session, Carla, a soft-spoken, articulate young woman, explained that her sister Sylvia, age 34, was recently diagnosed with breast cancer, and is currently undergoing treatment. Carla attended her first appointment alone; her husband was unable to come. The session began with a review of her family history by the genetic counselor. Carla had brought a notebook with questions and took notes as the genetic counselor reviewed what we would cover. She gave Carla an overview of the risk assessment process, and explained medical implications and options, being careful to answer Carla's questions and see that Carla understood the information. Then, she took a history of Carla's family, focusing on which relatives had a cancer diagnosis, when they were diagnosed, with which cancers, and other pertinent information about these relatives such as age at diagnosis.

The family history allows the genetic counselor and oncologist to assess any pattern of cancers related to a possible BRCA1 or BRCA2 mutation. Carla's parents, both alive and healthy, have never been diagnosed with cancer. In addition to her sister, she has a healthy 22-year-old brother. Her maternal grandmother does not have cancer at age 88, but her maternal grandfather died at age 89 with kidney cancer. Her paternal grandmother did not have cancer, but her paternal grandfather died of prostate cancer at age 62. Three paternal great-uncles all had cancer, but Carla had little information about the types of cancer or ages at diagnosis. Also, it is important to note that Carla's family originates from Eastern Europe, of Ashkenazi Jewish heritage, because this population has a higher incidence as described earlier. Carla raised questions about insurance, confidentiality, and about how the test results might affect her plans to have children if she were to test positive. Since she and her husband have good health insurance, they were not concerned about coverage for the service. However, she was concerned about the potential impact on future coverage and employment. The genetic counselor reassured her that although this is a legitimate concern, there has not been a single legal case of discrimination and the passage of the GINA law will mean stronger protection from discrimination. Once Carla's concerns were discussed, the counselor left the consultation room to meet with the oncologist to discuss the case and develop a recommendation.

I used this opportunity to ask Carla what it was like to think about being tested for this risk. She explained that she is very close to Sylvia, and was shocked and upset to hear of her breast cancer diagnosis. Aware of the increased risk for Ashkenazi Jews, she had thought of that immediately, since her sister is so young to have a breast cancer diagnosis. When Sylvia's results were positive, she said "I knew I had to do something right away," and described herself as "not the type of person to hide from events" and said that her way of coping is "to face it head first." We explored how testing positive might affect Carla, her husband, and their plans for having children, and suggested that she contemplate what she would do if there was a positive, negative or indeterminate finding, keeping in mind that no decision has been made about testing, nor had any testing taken place. I have found that this technique helps patients explore their feelings about testing, being at risk for cancer and the emotional impact not only on themselves, but also on their family members. In this case, we focused primarily on how Carla felt her husband was dealing with the uncertainty of her risk for developing cancer.

Timing of testing is an important focus for my assessment. It is often helpful for people to take some time considering the genetic testing decision, so that it is not made under stress. In Carla's case, having a sister facing cancer and testing positive was very recent, and I saw that she had given much thought to this before the initial consultation. She had explored information on the internet, talked to family and was knowledgeable about options. Carla has a loving and close relationship with her husband, and while this has been very upsetting for both of them, she was more worried about him. If recommended, she was very determined to go ahead with testing. Driving her decision to move quickly was her plan to have children someday. They had planned to hold off on this for at least four years while they concentrated on their careers and saved money but she realized that if she tests positive, the plan might change. I felt that Carla was able to make an informed decision, based on her solid understanding of the implications of the test—whether it came out positive, negative or indeterminate. She is the kind of person who has a tendency to "intellectualize" and seeks knowledge to handle her anxiety. It was my opinion that she was in a position to deal responsibly with her potential risk.

When the oncologist and genetic counselor reviewed the pattern of cancer in Carla's family with her, they noted that the cancers in Carla's mother's family (kidney and liver cancer) are not related to breast cancer risk. Her paternal grandfather's prostate cancer and her paternal uncles' cancers could reflect this pattern, were more information known. While it is often assumed that a breast or ovarian cancer is inherited through the mother, BRCA1 and BRCA2 mutations can be inherited through the paternal line. Her sister was diagnosed at a young age and tested positive for the BRCA1 gene, and that, combined with the Ashkenazi Jewish family background, suggests Carla has a 50% chance of being a carrier of this same mutation. They concluded it would be prudent for Carla to be tested, and she wanted it done as soon as possible. Since her husband supported her decision to have the genetic testing, her blood was taken immediately following the initial consultation.

Intervention: Session two

Since a specific BRCA1 mutation had already been identified in her family, Carla's blood was only tested for this known mutation. Unfortunately, Carla tested positive. The genetic

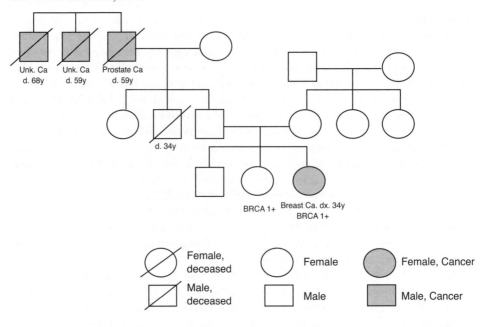

Female,
deceased

Female

Female, Cancer

Male,
deceased

Male

Male, Cancer

Figure 27.1 Genogram for Carla.

counselor contacted Carla to give her the results and set up a second appointment. Carla and her husband arrived together for that appointment, ready to hear the recommendations of the oncologist and to ask questions. As in the prior session, the genetic counselor reviewed the medical information, including what is now known about the risk for breast, ovarian and other cancers. The oncologist reviewed recommendations for increased monitoring for breast and ovarian cancer. Prophylactic surgery or hormonal medication were options the couple might want to consider at some point in the future. She did not recommend an immediate oophorectomy since Carla is only 27, and the risks of premature menopause (medical and psychosocial) have to be considered. Answering their family planning questions, she supported the idea that they might want to consider having children in the near future, rather than waiting for a few more years. She also answered questions about other family members' susceptibility to developing cancer, and told them that as of now, medical science is not able to prevent the passing of the mutation to future children, nor is any type of "gene therapy" yet available to correct the genetic mutation. Before leaving, the oncologist arranged for Carla to begin ongoing follow-up and surveillance at our Breast Center.

After the genetic counselor and oncologist left, I stayed with the young couple. My goals were to ensure they understood the meaning of the results, help them deal with the emotional impact, and assist with decision making about future surveillance and/or prevention, including the possible impact on their goals for having children. I encouraged them to identify any concerns they had about how this information might affect their relationship. The threat of a potentially life-threatening illness and the uncertainty of whether that illness will even develop, leave people with the task of living as if all were well, while knowing of the real possibility that cancer can intrude at any time (Rolland, 2006). Carla and her husband were determined to carry on "as normal." At the same time, they recognized that this news has definitely changed their priorities. Carla's husband said, "I wanted to wait at least until we were 30 before having children, but I know I can figure out a way to financially change that."

We also talked briefly about the surgical preventative measures that were discussed with the oncologist, having a bilateral mastectomy or oophorectomy. Carla said she really didn't think she needed to consider this now, and would be more comfortable thinking about these options after they had had children. She was relieved the oncologist and genetic counselor had reassured her about this recommendation. In my experience, the decision to have preventative surgery is more common with women who have already had children and consider their family size complete. For young women who have not yet had children, there is more emphasis on the need to complete a family quickly.

They were also concerned about how to communicate the news to her family, particularly her parents, since they were still in shock over Sylvia's diagnosis. In addition, we discussed how this would affect her younger brother, and whether he might be tested as well. Carla was very concerned about how her father would take the news, and whether she would tell him the oncologist recommended he be tested to determine (confirm) the BRCA1 mutation originated on his side of the family. This could help identify other relatives who could be at risk. We also discussed disclosing the results to future children, but they were not concerned about this, certain that by the time their children were old enough to be told, advances in technology would create an entirely different set of circumstances.

Stance of the social worker

The context of the service has a major impact on my stance. The team uses a biopsychosocial model of practice, as the intersection between biological (genetic, cancer in patient and family), psychological and social (including family) aspects of genetic testing are central to the intervention. To contribute to the team, I have a solid understanding about the state of knowledge of genetic testing for cancer risk, particularly for the BRCA1 and BRCA2 genes. Also, with a background in oncology social work, I am familiar with cancer treatment and the impact of cancer on family. Equally important is the knowledge I bring about the complicated dynamics for the patient and family in evaluating cancer risk. In addition, I am familiar with practical resources, insurance and financial considerations and I keep a comprehensive referral source database if additional services are needed. Because this is a two-session very specialized service, the intervention I provide is psycho-educational. While the focus is on decision making, based on understanding the risks and benefits of the testing, I also provide socio-emotional support throughout the process, and assess emotional impact and family strengths and weaknesses. Since the service is limited, if needed I make the appropriate referral for individual or family therapy.

Resources outside of the social worker/client relationship

Because genetic services are fairly new, there are not a lot of services for "previvors." Information about cancer genetics is available on the internet, and I often refer patients to the National Cancer Institute or the American Cancer Society websites for educational information. There is no support group locally for those who are considering testing or who have received positive test results. If patients have positive results, I may refer them to the FORCE organization (Facing Our Risk of Cancer Empowered) which has an extensive website with bulletin boards where patients and family members can connect with others in their situation, hear stories, and ask questions. FORCE has a monthly newsletter, and holds an annual conference where women who have had prophylactic surgeries help others making this decision. Our team often links patients to services for medical follow-up. Also, as mentioned previously,

I may refer someone to individual or couple counseling should this be needed.

Figure 27.2 below illustrates the interaction between Carla and her system, and the health system, of which the Cancer Genetics Counseling Service is a part.

Differential discussion

Our consultation was appropriate for Carla's case because, although it was limited to two sessions, she was provided with adequate information and support to make a decision about genetic testing, and she was supported as she and her husband dealt with their initial response to the testing results. This service is ideal for patients who have the ability to understand the information and have access to the medical resources needed for long-term management. Like Carla, patients/families who use this service tend to have good economic and social support. The consultation does not provide ongoing services for those who may need additional help, so screening for referral needs is a critical component here. Genetic testing has the potential to exacerbate family problems and, if not handled well, to create psychological symptoms (anxiety and depression) in those who are tested. Some testing services have provided additional services, such as support groups for those who test positive, but these are fairly rare. This is related to the lack of funding for psychosocial services in our health system. It is difficult to find support for a genetic support service that would be available to deal with issues that arise "down the road," as family circumstances change, and as new knowledge becomes available.

Practice in context

It is important to recognize that all aspects surrounding cancer prevention and genetic counseling are undergoing rapid change: this includes the technology of genetic testing, our knowledge of its meaning, social policies involving human genetics, and the structure of the health care system, including the payment system for health care services. We hope that, as the "biopsychosocial model of health and illness" gains prominence, and with the increased recognition of the value of psychosocial services, social workers will not have to struggle to "fit" a person who is at risk of an illness into a "medical model" that steers funding to those already

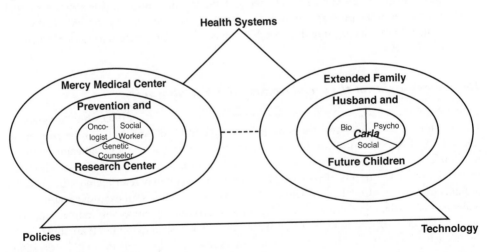

Figure 27.2 Prevention and research center organigraph.

diagnosed. As the genetic basis of more diseases is understood, it is hoped that more programs, services, and protections will be in place for those at risk. Finally, we hope and expect that medical treatments for those with cancer will continue to improve, so that cancer will be seen as chronic and will not carry the terror of a terminal illness. Also, as our understanding of the genetics of cancer improves, we will eventually be able to prevent cancer in those at risk through new technologies, such as "gene therapy." Since the technology continues to develop rapidly, it is likely that policy in this area will lag for the foreseeable future.

References

American Cancer Society. (2008). *Cancer Facts and Figures*. Retrieved 6/8/09: http://www.cancer/org

Biesecker, B. B., Ishibe, N., Hadley, D. W., Giambarresi, T. R., Kase, R. G., Lerman, C. & Struewing, J. P. (2000) Psychosocial factors predicting BRCA1/BRCA2 testing decisions in members of hereditary breast and ovarian cancer families. *American Journal of Medical Genetics*; 93: 257–63.

Capelli, M., Surh, L., Walker, M., Korneluk, Y., Humphreys, L., Verma, S., Hunter, A., Allanson, J. & Logan, D. (2001). Psychological and social predictors of decisions about genetic testing for breast cancer in high-risk women. *Psychology, Health and Medicine*, 6 (3): 321–33.

Ford D., Easton, D. F., Stratton, M., Narod, S., Goldgar, D., Devilee, P. C., Bishop, D. T., Weber, B., Lenoir, G., Chang-Claude, J., Sobol, H., Teare, M. D., Struewing, J., Arason, A., Scherneck, S., Peto, J., Rebbeck, T. R., Tonin, P., Neuhausen, S., Barkardottir, R., Eyfjord, J., Lynch, H., Ponder, B. A., Gayther, S. A., Birch, J.M., Lindblom, A., Stoppa-Lyonnet, D., Bignon, Y., Borg, A., Hamann, U., Haites, N., Scott, R. J., Maugard, C.M., Vasen, H., Seitz, S., Cannon-Albright, L.A., Schofield, A., Zelada-Hedman, M. & Breast Cancer Linkage Consortium. (1998) Genetic heterogeneity and penetrance analysis of the BRCA1 and BRCA2 genes in breast cancer families. *American Journal of Human Genetics*, 62: 676–89.

Friedman, L. S., Ostermeyer, E. A., Szabo, C. I., Dowd, P., Lynch, E. D., Rowell, S. E. & King, M. C. (1994) Confirmation of BRCA1 by analysis of germline mutations linked to breast and ovarian cancer in ten families. *Nature Genetics*, 8 (4): 399–404.

Genetic Alliance (2009). Retrieved 6/8/09: www.geneticalliance.org

Hughes, C., Lerman, C., Schwartz, M., Peshkin, B. N., Wenzel, L., Narod, S., Corio, C., Tercyak, K. P., Hanna, D., Isaacs, C. & Main, D. (2002). All in the family: Evaluation of the process and content of sister's communication about BRCA1 and BRCA2 genetic test results. *American Journal of Medical Genetics*, 107: 143–50.

Kaiser Family Foundation/Harvard School of Public Health Cancer Survey. Conducted 8/1–9/14/06. Retrieved 1/31/09: http://www.cancer.org

Kenen, R., Ardern-Jones, A. & Eeles, R. (2003). Family stories and the use of heuristics: Women from suspected hereditary breast and ovarian cancer (HBOC) families. *Sociology of Health & Illness*, 25 (7): 838–65.

Lerman, C. S., Lerman, C. & Shields, A. E. (2004). Genetic testing for cancer susceptibility: The promise and the pitfalls. *Nature Reviews: Cancer*, 4: 235–41.

Lynch, H. T., Fusaro, R. M., Lemon, S. J., Smyrk, T. & Lynch, J. (1999). Survey of Cancer Genetics. *Cancer* 80(suppl): 523–32.

Miki, Y., Swensen, J. & Shattuck-Eidens, D. (1994). A strong candidate for the breast and ovarian cancer susceptibility gene BRCA1. *Science*, 266, 66–71.

McEwen, J. (2006). Genetic testing: Legal and policy issues for individuals and their families. In Miller, S. M., McDaniel, S. H., Rolland, J. S. & Feetham, S. L. (eds.). *Individuals, families and the new era of genetics: Biopsychosocial perspectives* (pp. 506–29). New York: W. W. Norton.

Miller, S. M., Daly, M. B., Sherman, K. A., Fleisher, L., Buzaglo, J. S., Stanton, L., Godwin, A. K. & Scarpato, J. (2006). Psychosocial processes in genetic risk assessment for breast cancer. In Miller, S. M., McDaniel, S. H., Rolland, J. S. & Feetham, S. L. (eds.). *Individuals, families and the new era of genetics: Biopsychosocial perspectives* (pp. 274–319). New York, NY: W. W. Norton.

Myriad (2009). www.myriadinc.com

Oktay, J. S. (1998). Genetics cultural lag: What can social workers do to help? *Health & Social Work*, 23 (4): 310–15.

Parker, M. & Lucassen, A. (2003). Concern for families and individuals in clinical genetics. *Journal of Medical Ethics*, 29: 70–3.

Patenaude, A. F. (2005). *Genetic testing for cancer: Psychological approaches for helping patients and families*. Washington DC: American Psychological Association.

Rolland, J. S. (2006). Living with anticipatory loss in the new era of genetics: A life cycle perspective. In Miller, S. M., McDaniel, S. H., Rolland, J. S. & Feetham, S. L. (eds.). *Individuals, families and the new era of genetics: Biopsychosocial perspectives* (pp. 139–72). New York, NY: WW Norton.

Strewing, J., Hartge, P., Wacholder, S., Baker, S. M., Berlin, M., McAdams, M., Timmerman, M. M., Brody, L. C. & Tucker, M. A. (1997). The risk of cancer associated with specific mutations of BRCA1 and BRCA2 among Ashkenazi Jews. *The New England Journal of Medicine*, 336: 1401–8.

Tercyak, K. P., Hughes, C., Main, D., Snyder, C., Lynch, J. F., Lynch, H. T. & Lerman, C. (2001) Parental communication of BRCA1/2 genetic test results to children. *Patient Education and Counseling* 42: 213–24.

Wooster, R., Bignell, G., Lancaster, J., Swift, S., Seal, S., Mangion, J., Collins, N., Gregory, S., Gumbs, C. & Micklem, G. (1995). Identification of the breast-cancer susceptibility gene BRCA2. *Nature*, 378: 789–92.

28 Camp Achieve

A week-long overnight camp for teens and preteens with epilepsy

Emily Beil Duffy and Sue Livingston

Introduction

The Epilepsy Foundation of Eastern Pennsylvania (EFEPA) is one of two Pennsylvania affiliates of the Epilepsy Foundation National Office in Landover, Maryland. Founded in 1972 by local families and a neurologist who recognized a need for information and support beyond medical aspects of the disorder, EFEPA now serves 18 counties and about 65,000 individuals with epilepsy in eastern PA with a staff of six full-time and three part-time employees. Our mission is to ensure that people with seizures are able to participate in all life experiences and to prevent, control and cure epilepsy through services, education, advocacy and research. It is our vision to create a community where people impacted by epilepsy can experience the respect, support and care they deserve to live fuller lives. With dedication to quality of life for people with epilepsy/seizure disorders, EFEPA envisions the day when the stigmas associated with them are permanently erased (Kerson, in press; Kerson & Kerson, 2008; Kobau & Price, 2003; Krauss, Gondek, Krumholtz, Paul & Shen, 2000; Van Brakel, 2006). We provide education, support and advocacy in various ways; one of which, Camp Achieve, is a camping experience that is meant to build self-esteem, confidence, independence and friendships. Camp Achieve has often been these kids' only positive social experience, due to the reality that transitional services for youth with epilepsy are lacking.

Epilepsy and stigma

The mere word "epilepsy" carries a tremendous stigma that is driven by numerous myths and misconceptions (Jacoby, 2008). Despite modern science, society holds onto myths and misconception such as: epilepsy is contagious, people with epilepsy can see into the future, they are possessed by the devil, or they are mentally retarded. More than a medical diagnosis, it affects individuals and families psychosocially. The physical effects may be the most visible, but children are also affected developmentally, socially and academically. The embarrassment individuals affected by epilepsy feel forces them to suffer in silence. Children say they feel different from their peers and are afraid of being teased about having seizures when with their friends.

In a study designed by Austin and the National Epilepsy Foundation, and administered in schools selected by its regional offices, 19,441 valid surveys were collected. Of those surveyed, 59% had never known anyone with epilepsy while only 21% had. Interestingly, 31% stated they were "very" or "somewhat" familiar with epilepsy as opposed to 88% who stated they were "very" or "somewhat" familiar with asthma (Austin, Shaffer & Deering, 2002). Children with epilepsy are 1.3 to three times more likely to develop psychological problems such as poor coping skills, poor self-concept, and social withdrawal (Briery & Rabian, 1999). Social adjustment is an area of particular vulnerability for children with epilepsy and camp offers a supportive social opportunity where they can model or observe problem solving, help others, and relate to peers who share similar circumstances" (MacLeod & Austin, 2003; Plante, Lobato & Engel, 2001).

Children's perceptions of epilepsy are heavily influenced by their family, school, neurologist, and community. Perception directly affects their health behavior quality of life. Families who refuse to discuss epilepsy, seizures, or medications with their children or do not use proper medical terminology perpetuate stigma and negatively affect their child's perception of their disorder. Children are taught to be fearful, embarrassed, and not to ask questions. Imagine a young child, whose parent has told him or her not to disclose their epilepsy to anyone, who then has a seizure in public. That child is now not only embarrassed and confused but also afraid and worried that he/she has done something wrong, something the parent has said not to do. This is a tremendous burden to put on a child. We have found the Camp Achieve experience can improve the attitude towards the disorder, perceptions about epilepsy, and overall quality of life (Briery and Rabian, 1999).

Context

Technology: epilepsy, seizures and medication

Often called a seizure disorder, epilepsy is a collective term for a group of disorders affecting 1% of the population and caused by abnormal brain cell electrical activity and characterized by at least two epileptic seizures that are unprovoked by any immediate identifiable cause (Epilepsy Foundation of America, 2009). Each disorder involves some sort of seizure associated either with loss or disturbance of consciousness, an abnormal psychic experience or behavior, or abnormal motor or sensory phenomena. Seizures occur when brief, strong surges of electrical activity affect part or all of the brain. Usually, but not always, epilepsy involves convulsive movements of the body; sometimes, it involves hyperactivity or only momentary inattention or staring (Engel *et al.*, 2007; Shorvon, Perucca, Fish & Dodson, 2004; Walker & Shorvon, 2005).

Currently, of more than 20 antiepileptic drugs (AED) available, most are effective for only one seizure type. Finding the right medication and the right dosage with the least side-effects can be slow and frustrating for the patient, family, and neurologist. The seizure type determines which AED to try; then the level of effectiveness and amount and severity of side-effects is considered. For example, some medications will work best for a specific seizure type but actually worsen other types or cause unbearable side-effects. Side-effects commonly alter cognitive, emotional and behavioral functioning. Finding "control" is defined as no seizures and no side-effects. To achieve the right balance and dosage requires numerous medical tests as well as the experience and observational abilities of the neurologist.

Other treatment options include: surgery, vagus nerve stimulator (VNS) (Schacter & Schmidt, 2003) or a ketogenic diet (Freeman, Kossoff, Freeman & Kelly, 2006; Freeman, Kossoff & Hartman, 2007; Kinsman, Vining, Quaskey, Mellits & Freeman, 1992). If campers are on a ketogenic diet, we ask caregivers to pack their meals for the week. Most often these are used in combination with AEDs; rarely are AEDs completely eliminated. A few campers have undergone surgery. Surgery for children is not a typical treatment option because they often present with seizure activity that is not localized in the brain. Surgery is a last resort option for localized refractory seizures that cannot be controlled by AEDs. The plasticity of the brain during childhood development and maturation may limit the postoperative cognitive side-effects. The decision to pursue surgery is very personal, and people must weigh the possibility of being seizure-free against the risks of surgery (Freeman, Vining & Pillas, 2000).

The camp must be prepared for epilepsy-related emergencies and, for these, we have rescue medications available. One such emergency demanding immediate attention is when a camper is in status epilepticus, a period of time where seizures are repeated in clusters (short seizures that continue one after another) or a single seizure continues for longer than five minutes without recovery. Recovery is defined as being seizure-free for at least 20 minutes. Not all campers require rescue medications; some are not at risk of going into status epilepticus. The most common rescue medication administered at camp is diazepam because it is rapidly absorbed into the bloodstream. It is administered rectally by using a premeasured syringe, a procedure that can be done by a lay person. Other commonly used rescue medications are Lorazepam, which can be crushed and placed between the gum line or given whole, between seizure clusters; and Clonazepam, which is a wafer that melts when placed in the mouth. Unfortunately, status epilepticus is not a rare occurrence at camp. We do our best to remove other campers when managing it but this is not always possible. Privacy can be protected simply by having someone hold a blanket around the camper while the medication is administered. Campers often ask if another camper is OK when having a seizure, and after being reassured, go about their activities.

Organization

Most children with chronic disorders such as epilepsy are not allowed to attend traditional summer camps because they need closer medical supervision or cannot participate in certain activities (Walker & Pearman, 2009). In 1999, we began a three-day Preteen and Teen Weekend Retreat that preteens, ages 8–12, attended with one parent and teens attended on their own. In 2006, we transformed the retreat into Camp Achieve, a week-long overnight experience.

The camp is managed by a committee comprised of a medical advisor (who is a pediatric neurologist), the executive director, camp director, and camp coordinator. All volunteers (medical professionals, counselors, and junior counselors) must pass a criminal and child abuse background check as well as be granted approval by the camp committee. Three medical volunteers are always on the campgrounds, available 24 hours a day by walkie-talkies and cellphones. We have found it most effective to maintain a 3:1 counselor to camper ratio. All volunteers, both medical and non-medical, receive seizure first aid training and epilepsy education. It is common that approximately half or more of the volunteers have epilepsy. Volunteers must adhere to strict safety guidelines including the first and most important rule that no camper is ever left alone. There are three counselors for each cabin of between six and eight campers: a lead counselor, a camp counselor and junior counselor, with the lead counselor overseeing the group. Lead counselors, medical professionals and EFEPA staff communicate over walkie-talkies 24 hours a day and, most importantly, use them to radio for medical assistance. Caregivers are given EFEPA staff and lead counselor cellphone numbers to check in as needed throughout the week.

EFEPA raises money for camp through private donations, pharmaceutical donations and other grants. We also choose to keep camp costs low ($250 per camper), and we provide full financial aid to about 30% of families. A cornerstone of our cost savings is achieved by relying on a network of volunteers who serve as counselors and medical professionals.

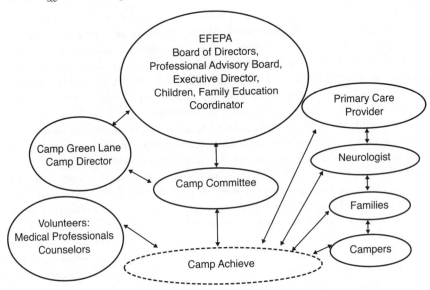

Figure 28.1 Camp Achieve organigraph.

Decisions about practice

Definition of client

The campers are our primary clients and their caregivers, secondary. Campers include children and teens, ages eight to 17 years old with a primary diagnosis of epilepsy, and who have the ability to complete activities of daily living (ADL) independently (Shaffer & Dilorio, 2006). Many individuals with epilepsy also have co-morbid disorders that affect their functional ability. We have learned over the years that we cannot accommodate campers who are unable to complete ADLs independently or have another primary diagnosis, as evidenced by our needing to send some campers home before completion of camp, due to safety concerns.

   This specific definition was made to maximize safety and potential for a positive camp experience; we include it on Camp Achieve brochures and it is addressed with all caregivers during the initial phone call. Our practice now is for the neurologist and the caregiver to each sign a document that states that potential campers are able to complete all ADLs independently and that epilepsy is their primary diagnosis. This lessens the chance for miscommunication and increases the potential that camp will be a good fit. First, all caregivers must complete an informal phone interview with the camp coordinator in order to get a better understanding of the child or adolescent's level of independence. After this initial screening process, a camper information packet is sent to the caregiver and neurologist. The packet includes camp registration, parental consent, health and seizure summary, school information, camp rules and expectations, medication schedule, a liability waiver holding EFEPA harmless, insurance coverage and a treatment authorization form from the hospital nearest the camp. A separate neurology history (accompanied by a signed medical release) is faxed directly to the appropriate provider to be completed and returned to EFEPA. Each child and caregiver is asked to sign off on having read and understood the rules form. Thus, we are provided detailed seizure history, seizure type, triggers, other medical diagnoses and a general medical background to ensure that each individual is medically, physically and behaviorally suited to attend camp. The camp committee then approves or denies all submitted camper packets.

Since campers face stigma and fear that has often resulted in social isolation (Funderburk, McCormick & Austin, 2007; Kossoff, 2005; Wagner & Smith, 2005), we strive to be as inclusive as possible, and we ask campers who have aged out to return as volunteer junior counselors when appropriate. As previously stated, campers' caregivers are our clients, too. The caregiver is the gatekeeper who, in part, determines if the child will attend camp. The idea of camp is new to them, and caregivers are often very reluctant for their child to attend. We know this kind of worry is not unusual and often complicates family relationships and produces over-protective parents. We know, too, that caregivers are placing a large amount of trust in us to care for their child's emotional, physical and medical needs for an entire week. In past years we had caregivers attend the entire camp weekend with their child but we found this inhibited the campers' growth. We also know caregivers benefit from the respite, too. We now include caregivers by inviting them to the talent show and the closing ceremony. Finally, we believe that caregivers who allow their child to attend camp foster independence, curiosity, and a feeling of psychological and physical safety.

Goals and objectives

Our goal is to increase youths' ability to live well with epilepsy. Safety is our first and the most important objective. Also important are supporting autonomy and providing positive recreational and educational activities that result in a memorable, meaningful experience for the campers. They participate in positive and enjoyable recreational activities that promote social skills, problem solving, mutual encouragement, and a sense of accomplishment. Volunteers foster relationships and appropriate levels of autonomy—two necessary ingredients for healthy self-identity (McEwan, Espie & Metcalfe, 2004). Prior to camp, these kids have been excluded from activities because of parental fear, social exclusion, and concerns surrounding their safety and perceived limitations associated with epilepsy. While at camp they freely participate in social and recreational activities. For example, one of the first recreational activities campers try is wall climbing and they cheer each other on as each one climbs to the top of the wall. Last summer, Katie, who has cerebral palsy and whose left side is her helping side, climbed to the top of the wall with the whole camp cheering. Similar to the benefits of group therapy, as campers begin to feel secure and comfortable they learn how to give and receive support, build social skills, and decrease social isolation. So when Chuck, who was afraid to go down the water slide, saw Jeff doing it he risked it as well, and it made his day.

The campers begin experiencing a new level of independence and building confidence in other ways, as well. For many, this is their first time away from home and a first for cleaning up after themselves (or not), dressing themselves, taking their medication without a caregiver's reminder, or even choosing their own food. This autonomy creates increased self-efficacy, which directly influences the development of positive health habits and behaviors (Snead *et al.*, 2004). Very often, we find the kids feel ready for camp when their parents are not so sure. We suggested that Sue try camp for one day, and she loved it so much she convinced her parents to let her stay for the whole experience. That was several years ago, and now Sue is a counselor.

Daily educational activities, informally called jam sessions, are held to arm campers with the knowledge to fight stigma, dispel myths, and feel empowered by their epilepsy—not fearful. Many campers know very little about their epilepsy and how it relates to them. Addressing these kinds of issues puts the individual in charge, not the fear and negative anticipation of the next seizure (Mittan, 2005a, 2005b). We know children desire information on how epilepsy will affect them in the future, as well as strategies to manage seizures and ways to talk with others who have seizures (Austin, Shaffer & Deerin, 2002). "Jam sessions" topics include: "dating, drugs/alcohol, and driving", "how to talk to your doctor", "understanding special education ... what are your rights?", "what are all these medications?" and "famous people with epilepsy." We also invite guest speakers who have epilepsy or another disorder to provide inspiration and motivation through their experiences. These speakers have included "Ms. Wheel Chair America", "Mighty Mike" Simmel, who has epilepsy and plays for the Harlem Wizards, and Dirk Johnson, a professional football player whose sister has epilepsy. We also hold a panel discussion called "heroes among us." The volunteers with epilepsy sit on the panel, tell their story, and take questions from campers. Access to real-life mentors and those surviving and thriving with epilepsy instills hope and inspiration.

Short-term memory is often affected by seizure activity so we try to create ways for campers to hold on to memories. Photos and videos are taken throughout camp and are posted online. Each camper is given a tee shirt, a backpack full of gifts, and a certificate of achievement to serve as positive, tangible reminders of camp. We also compile a list of campers' information to exchange and encourage campers and families to socialize throughout the school year. Each fall, we hold a "camp reunion" for campers, families, and volunteers to reconnect.

Contracts

Camp Achieve depends on effective and explicit contracts between EFEPA and the camp director, caregivers, campers, volunteers, and neurologists. Our contracts are written with the intent of maximizing the safety of our campers and providing information essential to the camp experience. We revise them annually to include critical and up-to-date information that will help us to maximize safety.

We contract annually with Camp Green Lane for use of their facilities. That contract clearly delineates specific financial obligations, insurance and safety requirements. Room remains for negotiating important aspects around which the Camp's daily schedule is built: meal times, daily menus, reserved cabins, provision of lifeguards, athletic equipment, art supplies, and rainy day activities.

Medical professionals, counselors, and junior counselors contract to volunteer their time to the foundation. Families entrust their child to us, and therefore, it is imperative that we have professional and responsible staff. All volunteers must provide detailed information and pass criminal and child abuse background checks. We provide volunteers with detailed guidelines and expectations and sign a letter of agreement to adhere to EFEPA guidelines. The information gathered also assists with pairing volunteer counselors and junior counselors, aids in assigning specific cabin groups, and helps us plan activities around particular skill sets.

Meeting place

The decision to use Camp Green Lane was made because of its convenient location in relation to the Philadelphia metropolitan area, safety specifications, the collaborative nature of the camp director, and Green Lane's familiarity with other special health care needs populations. They had significant prior experience in hosting sessions for youth with diabetes, asthma, and hemophilia. The traditional camp grounds provide a variety of activity options and adequate medical facilities: a swimming pool with two slides, an arts and crafts room, tennis courts, basketball, volleyball and Frisbee golf courses, miniature golf, an infirmary, cafeteria, athletic fields, camp fires, archery, wall climbing, a hockey rink, a ropes course, and several outdoor auditoriums. The campgrounds and buildings are accessible to differently abled campers, cabins do not have bunk-beds and are in close proximity to each other, and the infirmary contains locked areas for medications.

Use of time

Camp Green Lane and campers' school schedules determine the dates on which camp will be held each year. Camp Green Lane runs a seven-week traditional overnight camp and cannot accommodate us until after the completion of their regular camp season. Also, most campers attend summer school that runs through mid-July. Therefore, camp is always scheduled at the end of July or the beginning of August. The length of camp—five nights and six days—is determined by campers' wellbeing and budgetary challenges. Many campers have never spent time away from home and families can be very apprehensive about this new experience. Decreased sleep, excitement, and sun—all natural aspects of camp—unfortunately, trigger seizures.

Strategies and interventions

Most campers have never witnessed another person having a seizure, met another person with epilepsy, slept away from home without a caregiver, much less attended summer camp before. The overall strategy of camp is to provide therapeutic recreational activities, purposeful interventions, and appropriate medical supervision by competent medical providers (Epstein, Stinson & Stevens, 2005). We foster campers' strengths by providing them with opportunities to practice, learn, and refine their social skills—the ultimate goal being better management of the adversity they will face when they return home.

Volunteers arrive one day prior to campers, and we facilitate an orientation that focuses on epilepsy education, seizure first aid, ice-breakers (bonding activities), a tour of the facility, group and cabin assignments, and an overview of guidelines and expectations. Orientation sets the tone for the week and we want to thank the volunteers for their time. Our goal is for everyone to feel appreciated, excited, and prepared for the week. We finish the day with a "pizza party" as a token of our gratitude and an opportunity for volunteers to get to know one another.

On arrival, campers go immediately through registration, which can take several hours. The most time-intensive process is medical registration. Campers have arrived with duffle bags full of medication for *just* one week and all medications must arrive in their original prescription bottles. Together, the volunteer medical professional and caregiver organize the medications in individualized pill organizers. During registration, volunteers run an organized activity for campers to join and assist families in feeling comfortable when leaving their child.

Following registration, we all gather for camper orientation, which serves not only to familiarize the campers with their new surroundings, but also to create a sense of community. We go over camp guidelines, group assignments, play ice-breakers and watch an educational video detailing what it looks like when someone has a seizure, various seizure types, and seizure first-aid. Because so many campers have never seen a seizure or known anyone else with epilepsy, the video is a nonthreatening way for them to learn and prepare them for what they will inevitably witness throughout the week. The campers are curious but no one has seemed horrified or overwhelmed. It's just one more kind of information about epilepsy.

The remainder of the week is strategically designed to provide access to therapeutic educational and recreational activities with purposeful interventions. Every morning campers gather at the flag pole for "morning meeting." This time is used for announcements, to take attendance, and to set a positive tone for the day. Each day also includes rest and free-time, thus promoting camper interaction rather than adult-facilitated social interaction.

Counselors are instructed to encourage campers to participate to the best of their ability in all activities. Through positive modeling, campers begin to encourage and motivate one another. As camp progresses, group cohesion forms, relationship skills and comfort levels increase and the campers come truly to believe they are no longer alone. Exposure to recreational activities throughout the week promotes a sense of normalcy and mastery. One specific example is yoga because recent studies have shown a positive relationship between seizure control and practicing yoga. Yoga has been shown to alleviate stress, induce relaxation, promote a better understanding of the body, and enhance mental focus (Epilepsy Action, 2009; Yardi, 2001). Epilepsy disrupts the balance between the body and mind and yoga is a learned skill that can guide campers towards regaining control and balance. The campers thoroughly enjoy it and are given another set of coping skills through their exposure to yoga techniques.

Another purposeful intervention activity is kids creating art based upon their experience with epilepsy, or even drawing a picture of themselves having a seizure. Campers use multiple methods to create their own masterpiece and are given an opportunity to share their drawings. We've submitted campers' creations, with their permission, to Ortho-McNeil's publication *Creative Expressions*, and used others for a variety of EFEPA's publications. Music is important too, and for several years Jason, who is now 18 and a counselor, has made that his special purview, with gospel and other kinds of singing for everyone. Last summer, Jason, who had never had a seizure at camp, had a grand mal seizure. Recovering, he wanted to go home, but after resting for a short while in our infirmary, said, "I'm not here to go home just because I had a seizure," and he stayed and enjoyed the rest of camp. He is a loving and compassionate fellow, and we are so glad he stayed.

Camp concludes with a formal ceremony to acknowledge the successes of each camper as an individual. Families are invited and encouraged to attend so they can observe their child having a successful social experience. The ceremony validates different achievements during the week and, for many, this is likely the first time they have been honored for their participation in a social setting. Campers are given something tangible to take away to ease the transition home and to sustain them in what can often be an emotionally and socially difficult environment.

Prior to the closing ceremony we invite families to attend a formal educational talk. This time is used to inform families of the multiple services provided by EFEPA to support them throughout the entire year, not just one week in the summer. We strive to build a connection with the entire family because they are our clients, too. The educational talk focuses on empowering caregivers and equipping them with the knowledge to foster a positive attitude towards epilepsy in themselves and their child. It is also a time for families to connect with one another and build support networks among themselves.

Stance of the social worker

The social worker, as camp coordinator, manages all aspects of camp. I help the volunteers and staff to meet goals and objectives by clearly communicating them through written contracts and communiqués, as well as being available to all before and during camp.

Use of outside resources

Outside resources are essential to keeping up to date on how to serve our campers who are incredibly medically and psychosocially complex. Collaborative relationships with pharmaceutical companies, local pediatric neurology groups, and other epilepsy foundations help us to better meet the needs of our campers and families. These relationships provide us with up-to-date medical knowledge, new funding streams, access to volunteers, as well as innovative strategies and interventions. We also create collaborative relationships with local schools and pediatric neurology groups in an effort to increase awareness about opportunities to attend camp or serve as a camp volunteer. We educate and encourage neurology groups to provide care that goes beyond the boundaries of the commonly accepted medical model by focusing on educating children about their disorder and providing emotional support to the family (Austin, Shaffer & Deering, 2002). We would like camp to be prescribed by neurologists to patients and families as part of a treatment plan to improve the individual's and family's psychosocial functioning.

EFEPA's Board of Directors and Professional Advisory Board (PAB) serve as resources for funding and operational support. We ask the Board to assist in fundraising and to ensure the continued fiscal health of the organization. To further underscore specifically how their efforts help others, board members are asked to volunteer as counselors. This also gives them the opportunity to meet campers and better understand their unique strengths and challenges. All board members receive formal invitations to attend the annual cookout. EFEPA's Professional Advisory Board (PAB) consists of neurologists and lawyers who assist with the creation and revision of medical forms within the camper packet, help develop medication routines, ensure safety requirements are adequate and up to date, and are available to consult as needed on a variety of medical-related issues before and during camp. The medical advisor on the camp committee is selected from the PAB.

Reassessment and evaluation

Towards the end of the week, campers and volunteers complete a survey that assesses their experience, letting them know we value their opinions. These surveys collect feedback about the activities, guest speakers, educational sessions, quality of meals, orientation, and recommended changes/suggestions for next year. Camper surveys are kept very simple due to the varying levels of literacy. Campers rate activities on a scale of one to four and answer a series of yes or no questions. We encourage everyone to provide verbal feedback, too. Additionally, we ask counselors to provide feedback about campers' and junior counselors' level of "fit" and "appropriateness" at camp.

We also ask caregivers for verbal feedback about their experiences beginning with their first contact with our organization all the way through to picking their child up at camp. We strive to remain flexible and open to all feedback in an effort to improve camp and better meet our goal to empower campers, their families and caregivers to live well with epilepsy. It is also critical that we report to our various funders regarding our success in meeting identified goals and objectives. This process helps us to synthesize information and, ultimately, identify the necessary changes and areas for improvement for the following year. Finally, the camp committee meets shortly after camp ends to evaluate and assess camp in its entirety.

Termination and case conclusion

On the final day we hold a closing ceremony and families are invited to attend. Everyone gathers and the camp coordinator and executive director give speeches highlighting the fun, memorable, and positive experiences throughout the week. Each camper is called up to receive a certificate of achievement and a picture is taken to capture the moment. We encourage campers to exchange contact information and to keep in touch throughout the school year. To facilitate this we distribute a master list of everyone's contact information. All campers are invited to the reunion, held in the fall, which serves as time for former campers to reunite and for potential campers and families to become familiar with Camp Achieve.

Differential discussion

Society has taught us to fear epilepsy, and centuries of misunderstandings have supported negative social responses. Children with epilepsy still feel as though each is the only one in the world having seizures, and hold tremendous fear about disclosing their disorder or having a seizure in public. This negative self-perception directly affects their health behaviors and quality of life. When kids walk into camp it is as though they have entered a new world, a safe one, a familiar one. Sometimes you can see them take a deep breath and smile as if it is their first *real* smile. They belong here, they are free to make friends and be themselves. After attending camp, we hope children and families can reframe their fear of disclosure or having a seizure in public as an opportunity to teach others about seizure first aid and further uproot social stigma. We hope they feel empowered, informed, and have an improved attitude towards their condition. This will enhance their health behaviors (e.g. adherence to medication) and provide them with a sense of individual and family mastery.

Yearly, we face funding constraints, difficulty obtaining volunteer medical providers, and other challenges. But, despite setbacks, we are committed to providing youth with epilepsy opportunities "to participate in all life experiences" and we believe summer camp not only positively affects their life trajectory but also their families, schools, and communities. The yearly return of campers and counselors tells us we are making a difference. The growth of campers into junior counselors and then into counselors speaks volumes about the long-term value of camp and the special place it holds for participants. During the camp reunion in the fall we watch and listen to campers reminisce about camp, tell prospective campers about their experiences, and witness self-assurance and enthusiasm. It is why we do what we do.

References

Austin, J. K., Shaffer, P. O. & Deering, J. B. (2002). Epilepsy familiarity, knowledge, and perceptions of stigma: Report from a survey of adolescents in the general population. *Epilepsy & Behavior*, 3: 368–75.

Engel, J. Jr., Pedley, T. A., Aicardi, J., Dichter, M. A., Moshé, S. & Trimble, M. (2007). *Epilepsy: A comprehensive textbook* (2nd ed.). Philadelphia: Williams & Wilkins.

Epilepsy Action. (2009). Retrieved 6/3/09: http://www.epilepsy.org.uk/info/sportsandleisure/yoga.html

Epilepsy Foundation of America. (2009). Retrieved 5/27/09: http://www.epilepsy/foundation.org/about/

Epstein, I., Stinson, J. & Stevens, B. (2005). The effects of camp on health-related quality of life in children with chronic illnesses: A review of the literature. *Journal of Pediatric Oncology Nursing*, 22 (2): 89–103.

Freeman, J. M., Kossoff, E. H. & J. B. & Kelly, M. T. (2006). *The ketogenic diet: A treatment for children and others with epilepsy* (4th ed.). New York: Demos.

Freeman, J. M., Kossoff, E. H. & Hartman, A. L. (2007). The ketogenic diet: One decade later. *Pediatrics*, 119 (3): 535–43.

Freeman, J. M., Vining, E. P. G. & Pellas, D. J. (2002). *Seizures and epilepsy in childhood: A guide for parents*. Baltimore: Johns Hopkins University Press.

Funderburk, J. A., McCormick, B. P. & Austin, J. K. (2007). Does attitude toward epilepsy mediate the relationship between perceived stigma and mental health outcomes in children with epilepsy? *Epilepsy & Behavior*, 11: 71–6.

Kerson, T. S. (in press). Epilepsy and media. In Pinikahana, J. & Walker, C. *Social epileptology: Understanding the social aspects of epilepsy*. New York: Nova Science Publishers.

Kerson, T. S. & Kerson, L. A. (2008). Truly enthralling: Epileptiform events in film and on television— Why they persist and what we can do about them. *Social Work in Health Care*, 47 (3): 320–37.

Kinsman, S. L., Vining, E. P. G., Quaskey, S. A., Mellits, D. & Freeman, J. (1992). Efficacy of the ketogenic diet for intractable seizure disorders: Review of 58 cases. *Epilepsia*, 33 (6): 1132–6.

Kobau, R. & Price, P. (2003). Knowledge of epilepsy and familiarity with this disorder in the U.S. population: Results from the 2002 Health-Styles survey. *Epilepsia*, 44:1149–154.

Kossoff, E. H. (2005). Adolescents and epilepsy. *International/Pediatrics*, 20 (2): 78–85.

Krauss, G. L., Gondek, S., Krumholtz, A., Paul, S. & Shen, F. (2000). The Scarlet "E": The presentation of epilepsy in the English language print media. *Neurology* 54:1894–98.

Jacoby, A. & Baker, G. A. (2008). Quality of life trajectories in epilepsy. *Epilepsy Behaviour*. 12 (4): 557–71.

McEwan, M. J., Espie, C. A. & Metcalfe, J. (2004). A systematic review of the contribution of qualitative research to the study of quality of life in children and adolescents with epilepsy. *Seizure*, 13 (1): 3–14.

MacLeod, J. S. & Austin, J. K. (2003). Stigma in the lives of adolescents with epilepsy: A review of the literature, *Epilepsy & Behavior*, 4:112–17.

Mittan, R. J. (2005a). S. E. E. Program Parents' Manual: How to raise a child with epilepsy—part one: Coping with fear. *The Exceptional Parent*, (October): 60.

Mittan, R. J. (2005b). S. E. E. Program Parents' Manual: How to raise a child with epilepsy—part two, Coping with stigma. *The Exceptional Parent*, (November): 58.

Plante, W., Labato, D. & Engel, R. (2001). Review of group interventions for pediatric chronic conditions. *Journal of Pediatric Psychology*. 26: 435–53.

Schacter, S. C. & Schmidt, D. (eds.) (2003). *Vagus Nerve Stimulation* (2nd ed.). London: Martin Dunitz.

Shaffer, P. O. & Dilorio, C. (2006). Self-management in epilepsy care: Putting teen and families in the center. *EP Magazine*. Retrieved on 5/20/09 from www.epilepsy.com.

Shorvon, S., Perucca, E., Fish, D. & Dodson, E. (2004). *The treatment of epilepsy* (2nd ed.). London: Blackwell Publishers.

Snead, K., Ackerson, J., Bailey, K., Schmitt, M. M., Madan-Swain, A. & Martin, R. C.(2004). Taking charge of epilepsy: The development of a structured psychoeducational group intervention for adolescents with epilepsy and their parents. *Epilepsy & Behavior*, 5 (4): 547–56.

Van Brakel, W. H. (2006). Measuring health-related stigma—A literature review. *Psychology Health & Medicine*, 11 (3): 307–34.

Wagner, J. L. & Smith, G. (2005). Psychosocial intervention in pediatric epilepsy: A critique of the literature. *Epilepsy & Behavior*, 8: 39–49.

Walker, D. A. & Pearman, D. (2009). Therapeutic recreation camps: An effective intervention for children and young people. *Archives of Disease in Childhood*, 94 (5): 401–6.

Walker, M. & Shorvon, S. (2005). *Understanding epilepsy*. London: British Medical Association.

Yardi, M. (2001). Yoga for the control of epilepsy. *Seizure*, 10: 7–12.

29 YOUR Blessed Health

A faith-based, community-based
participatory research project to
reduce the incidence of HIV/AIDS
and sexually transmitted infections

*Kevin J. Robinson, Bettina Campbell,
and TaMara Campbell*

Context

Policy

African Americans have had the highest rate of HIV/AIDS infection among any U.S. racial or ethnic group for more than a decade (Steele *et al.*, 2007). While faith-based organizations have long been noted as a pillar of the African American community, the African American faith community has not met the prevention needs presented by the HIV/AIDS epidemic (Zukerman, 2000). A major barrier to an effective response by the African American faith community has been the negative religious and moral attitudes about behaviors associated with HIV transmission (i.e. sexual behavior and intravenous drug use) (Francis & Liverpool, 2009). The challenges of marrying HIV prevention with the religious and spiritual mission of faith-based institutions is an issue faith-based organizations can begin to reconcile through collaboration, training and technical assistance.

Providing health education about HIV/AIDS and sexually transmitted infections (STIs) through faith-based institutions is not new, but it has not become widespread (Francis, Hudson & Liverpool, 2009; Campbell, 2007; Hartwell *et al.*, 1990). While there are national organizations such as the AIDS National Interfaith Network, The Balm in Gilead and the National Coalition of Pastors Spouses that provide HIV/AIDS training and resources to the African American faith community, there are few examples of HIV prevention interventions conducted in African American churches that have been embraced, effective, and sustained. In a review of over 500 articles, researchers using keywords to identify faith-based approaches to HIV prevention found only four peer-reviewed articles describing faith-based HIV prevention programs (Francis & Liverpool, 2008).

African American faith-based organizations historically have been a setting for social activities, a vehicle for disseminating information, a tool for organizing the community and a conduit for providing social services, and they continue to fulfill these roles today (Billingsley, 1999; Billingsley & Caldwell, 1991; Krause, 2003). Faith-based organizations often assume service needs abdicated or inadequately met by other service institutions (Billingsley, 1991; Mattis & Jagers, 2001). Historically, churches have been involved in a variety of health interventions, and they can be an important vehicle for disseminating accurate but sensitive information regarding behaviors that parents are often uncomfortable discussing with youth (Peterson *et al.*, 1999; Coyne-Beasley & Schoenback, 2000). Parents who attend church endorse and trust faith-based institutions to teach their children about sensitive issues in the context of morals and beliefs that are congruent with their own and their community's values (Coyne-Beasley & Schoenback, 2000). While faith-based organizations are situated to play an important role in preventing HIV/AIDS in African American communities, these institutions must gain the efficacy and capacity to integrate their interpretation of religious doctrine with up-to-date, comprehensive HIV/AIDS education.

YOUR Blessed Health was conducted under the auspices of the Prevention Research Center (PRC) of Michigan. The Center builds upon existing long-term partnerships between the University of Michigan School of Public Health, community-based organizations (CBOs), local health departments, and the Michigan Department of Community Health and other statewide health associations. The PRC is governed by Community and State boards, and my work will be governed by the Community Advisory Board. The Prevention Research Center is one of 33 centers nationwide funded by the Centers for Disease Control and Prevention.

Technology: HIV testing

Although 58% of African-Americans report they have been tested for HIV—more than any other racial or ethnic group—33% of the African Americans who have been tested report they did not discuss their most recent test results with a health care professional, which could mean they did not return for their test results or that post-test counseling was optional (Aragon *et al.*, 2001). According to the Kaiser Family Foundation (2001), most African Americans don't learn they are seropositive until they are much sicker than their white counterparts. By then, they are less likely to respond to the anti-retroviral medicines and other drug combinations that control AIDS (Aragon *et al.*, 2001). African Americans are also plagued by higher incidence rates of gonorrhea, herpes, tuberculosis and hepatitis C infection than their white counterparts (CDC, 2007). Recent studies have reported that co-infection of HIV with TB or hepatitis can complicate treatment, and result in higher levels of hepatitis virus in the blood, more rapid progression of liver damage, and a greater rate of death than people with only HIV infection (Piliero & Faragon, 2002; Cotler & Jensen, 2001).

One of the most exciting outcomes of this intervention was the number of people who were tested for HIV at YBH events and affiliated activities. During the course of the intervention, 80 people were tested for HIV at YBH events. Moreover, in many instances, the ministers of the participating congregations were the FIRST in line to be tested. As one pastor acknowledged, "I think that this program is very beneficial to the community and there are people submitting to testing as a result of this presentation."

Organization: Community-Based Participatory Research (CBPR)

Community-Based Participatory Research (CBPR) is a collaborative approach to research that equitably involves all partners in the research process and recognizes the unique strengths that each brings (Israel *et al.*, 1998; Viswanathan *et al.*, 2004). CBPR begins with a research topic of importance to the community and has the aim of combining knowledge with action and achieving social change to improve health outcomes and eliminate health disparities (Israel *et al.*, 1998; Viswanathan *et al.*, 2004).

CBPR is an orientation to research that changes the role of researcher and researched, recognizes community as a unit of identity, and builds on strengths and resources. Moreover, CBPR is an applied approach with an explicit goal to influence change in community health, norms, systems, programs and policies.

There has been mounting interest in/support for CBPR as a result of the ever-increasing understanding of the importance of local context in research, growing community and funder demands for community-driven research/collaboration, and the understanding that complex health and social problems are ill-suited to "outside expert" research. These principles guided the collaborative research project, YOUR Blessed Health. The YOUR Blessed Health partnership included: YOUR Center, Flint Odyssey House Health Awareness Center, Faith Access to Community Economic Development, Pastors' Spouses of Genesee County, and The University of Michigan School of Public Health, and is funded by The Ruth Mott Foundation.

Organization: The Prevention Research Center (PRC) of Michigan

The mission of the Prevention Research Center of Michigan is to expand and share knowledge, thereby strengthening the capacity of the community, the public health system, and the university to improve the public's health. Consistent with its theme, "Closing Gaps and Improving Health in Partnership with Families and Communities," the Center conducts community-based participatory prevention research aimed at improving the health status and reducing morbidity and mortality among populations experiencing a disproportionate share of poor health outcomes. The interventions forming the basis for the research emphasize the role of families and communities in health promotion and disease prevention, and reflect the social ecological health model.

Organization: YOUR Center, Inc.

YOUR Center, Inc. was the primary Community-Based Organizational (CBO) partner in the YOUR Blessed Health collective. Founded in 1996 in Flint, MI under the leadership of Bettina Campbell, LMSW (Executive Director), YOUR Center was incorporated in response to a community-wide survey that identified gaps and barriers that have prevented Genesee County residents from transforming their neighborhoods into higher performing neighborhoods, communities, and districts. YOUR Center began addressing these needs by becoming an authority in HIV/AIDS prevention, education and outreach. In 1997, YOUR Center began collaborating with Faith Access to Community and Economic Development (FACED), Flint, MI to provide limited HIV/AIDS and STI education to churches and other faith-based organizations. In 2004, a group of Flint area pastors' spouses concerned about the increasing rate of STIs and teenage pregnancies in African American females approached YOUR Center seeking guidance regarding increasing their role in providing HIV/AIDS and STI education and outreach.

Description of the client situation

The population of the city of Flint, MI, the site of the study, is 56% African American (U.S. Census Bureau, 2006). Genesee County, where Flint is located, is one of 22 high HIV/AIDS prevalence counties in Michigan. Moreover, Genesee County is ranked fifth in the total number of reported AIDS cases, and has the seventh-highest prevalence of HIV/AIDS in the state in 2006 (Michigan Department of Community Health, 2007). The number of people living with HIV/AIDS is increasing an average of 5% a year in every age group in Genesee County. Of the 630 reported cases in Genesee County, 460 are from Flint (Michigan Department of Community Health, 2007).

In Flint, there are several agencies and programs that educate youth about sex, sexuality, and preventing STIs, yet the number of STIs, including HIV, diagnosed among area youth continues to rise (Michigan Department of Community Health, 2007). Those under age 19 living with HIV/AIDS have increased 45% in Genesee County since 2000, while the number of 20–24-year-olds living with HIV/AIDS has increased 85% (Michigan Department of Community Health, 2007). Statewide, the rate of new diagnoses among 13–24-year-olds almost doubled between 2002 and 2006, from 5.7 to 9.7 cases per 100,000. Of those, 76% are African American (Michigan Department of Community Health, 2007). Genesee County has the second highest rate of chlamydia and the second highest rate of gonorrhea in Michigan (Michigan Department of Community Health, 2007). In 2006, rates of chlamydia among African Americans were eight times higher than those in Whites, and rates of gonorrhea were over 13 times higher (Michigan Department of Community Health, 2007). Moreover, one in every 25 young adults 15–24 years old in Genesee County was diagnosed with chlamydia (Michigan Department of Community Health, 2007).

Decisions about practice

Definition of the client

The YBH approach is unique in that it seeks not only to educate youth, but to train adult faith leaders, particularly pastors' spouses, to address HIV/AIDS and youth sexual risk using a curriculum that has been endorsed by the National Coalition of Pastors' Spouses. Due to the many responsibilities and busy schedules of pastors in African American churches, this intervention seeks to build on the often untapped resource of pastors' spouses. These spouses not only understand the pastors' mission and vision for the church, they also understand the church's culture. By getting the 'blessing' of pastors to do the intervention and engaging pastors' spouses as the lead trainers, YBH gains considerable credibility and support in the host churches.

Goals, developing objectives and contracting

The primary aim of the intervention is to change the norms of churches to be more open and accepting settings, in which youth and adults can discuss HIV/AIDS and the behaviors and factors that put people at risk for contracting the disease. Central to this approach are respecting the values and beliefs of adult guardians and faith leaders and treating HIV/AIDS as not only a sexual or moral issue, but a health issue. The YBH approach provides faith-based organizations with a flexible menu of options from which faith leaders can adapt the intervention to the beliefs, doctrine and culture of their individual organizations.

The five primary outcome objectives of this pilot intervention were:

1 Conduct 10 five-week youth HIV education and skills building sessions, one per church.
2 90% of youth participants will demonstrate an increased awareness of their risk of contracting HIV.
3 75% of youth participants will self-report an increase in relationship negotiation skills, including communicating their choices to remain abstinent.
4 Train 20 pastors' spouses, ministers' spouses, and their designees to provide HIV prevention education.
5 Conduct two educational sessions per month to church members and church ministries, reaching a total of 3,500 congregants.

Ultimately, the YBH intervention pilot was designed to develop the proposed intervention into a replicable HIV-intervention model. We plan to disseminate results to all stakeholders, including the African American faith-community and state health officials.

Meeting place

YOUR Blessed Health programming was located in either the 11 participating churches or the two housing complexes (all of which were located on the north and northwest sides of Flint, MI). Analogous to considerations of cultural sensitivity, the process for developing an effective, faith-based, HIV prevention intervention must consider how HIV/AIDS and its primary modes of transmission can be effectively discussed and addressed in a way that is amenable to churches' unique organizational cultures (Resnicow *et al.*, 1999). Some researchers distinguish between faith-based and faith-placed interventions (Campbell & Hudson, *et al.*, 2007; DeHaven *et al.*, 2004). Faith-placed interventions are provided in the context of a faith-based organization. In contrast, YBH offers a faith-based intervention that emanates from the experience of a faith-based HIV/AIDS service organization that has been collaborating with these churches and this community for over a decade.

While the core materials and goals of YBH do not vary by setting, the structure, frequency and timing of the training sessions and outreach activities are determined by each church in consultation with YBH staff. Compared with faith-placed initiatives, faith-based interventions are better able to capitalize on the strengths of faith-based organizations by assuring that intervention messages and components are congruent with the doctrine and teachings of the faith leaders (DeHaven *et al.*, 2004). In this context, it is critical to provide faith-based organizations with the opportunity to address their unique perspectives in the following areas: religious beliefs regarding gender roles in relationships; cultural and gender norms regarding sexual behavior; cross-gender communication about sex, sexuality and relationships; insistence on linking HIV/AIDS with the behaviors associated with transmission; understanding of and willingness to discuss sexual identity, including bisexuality and homosexuality; willingness to discuss safer sex alternatives (e.g. condom use, masturbation, oral sex); and willingness to distribute condoms on the grounds or at the events of a faith-based organization.

Use of time and strategies and interventions (mapping device)

The YBH intervention includes five basic components: (1) a 10-hour, five-session youth training program using the HIV Outreach, Prevention and Education (HOPE) curriculum created for YBH that focuses on basics of HIV/AIDS, STIs, sexual knowledge, and communication skills, and focuses on creating individualized risk reduction plans; (2) a 10-hour, five-session training program for adults in the church and community based on the HOPE curriculum that provides basic STI and HIV/AIDS knowledge; (3) an initial (three-hour) and ongoing training and support for pastors, pastors' spouses, and other church leaders who will conduct the youth and adult training sessions that provides them with the basic knowledge, skills, and resources to lead the YBH sessions and conduct other church HIV/AIDS educational activities; (4) church-wide activities, including sermons and presentations during the primary weekly service to raise awareness of HIV/AIDS and HIV risk and to reduce stigma associated with HIV/AIDS and people living with HIV/AIDS; and (5) community-wide activities such as health fairs that educate and raise awareness about HIV/AIDS and promote collaboration between different faith-based institutions on HIV prevention. Through these multi-level efforts, YBH seeks to increase the capacity of faith-based institutions and faith leaders to more effectively address HIV/AIDS and STIs.

Reassessment and evaluation

Evaluation instruments were designed by YBH staff, in consultation with faculty and staff from the University of Michigan School of Public Health. Process and outcome evaluations were conducted, though only process data are reported here. Participants in each YBH session or event were asked to complete satisfaction surveys. Adolescents and adults completed pre-tests at the beginning of their training series and post-tests at the end. Adolescent pre- and post-tests included items about HIV risk behaviors, history of STIs and HIV/AIDS, intentions to use condoms and communicate with partners about safe sex, and self-efficacy to use condoms correctly and communicate with partners. Adult pre- and post-tests only assessed changes in knowledge and attitudes about HIV/AIDS.

Case conclusion

A pilot of YBH was conducted from October 2006 to March 2007 in 11 predominantly African American faith-based organizations and among residents residing within two public housing communities. The project was designed and implemented by YBH staff to reduce HIV-stigma in faith leaders and adults (i.e. pastors, pastors' spouses, educational leaders in the church, and parents and guardians of youth), and to increase behavioral intentions to abstain from sex or to have protected sex in 11–19-year-old African American males and females. All of the intervention settings had adult faith leaders trained to conduct the youth and adult training sessions and used the HOPE curriculum to train participating youth. Some of the intervention sites also hosted training sessions for other adults and/or church-wide educational activities. Consistent with the flexible approach of the YBH intervention, the format for implementing the program varied by site. Some of the faith leaders provided single, all-day training sessions for youth or for adults that incorporated several of the HOPE sessions, whereas others provided the training sessions over the course of five weeks. In addition, the amount of HOPE curriculum covered in the youth and adult training sessions varied according to the faith leaders' comfort level and the materials' congruence with the culture and doctrine of the faith organizations. The remainder of the results discusses findings from youth and adults, faith leaders and other adults, and each type of event.

Youth and adults

The YBH intervention was very successful in reaching youth. All 11 churches conducted youth training sessions, although only six of the churches decided to provide the complete five-session curriculum. Across the 11 churches and two community settings, 50 sessions were conducted with youth with an average of 12.8 youth per session for a total of 189 youth. There was generally low attrition between sessions. In general, the youth reported they were satisfied with the content of the curriculum. Despite their level of satisfaction with the curriculum content, youth reported that YBH, "could have been improved if more people attended the program." More than one youth reported disappointment that more of their peers were not in attendance and that they wished the sessions could be longer. The youth also wished that the "kids" would have talked more about their experiences at school and with their friends.

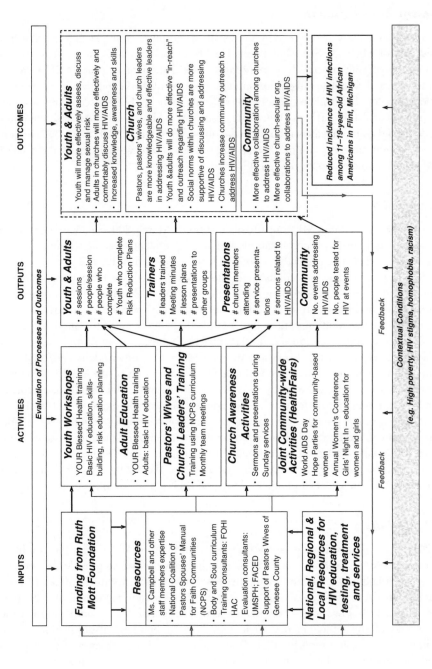

INPUTS   ACTIVITIES   OUTPUTS   OUTCOMES

Evaluation of Processes and Outcomes

Funding from Ruth Mott Foundation

Resources
- Ms. Campbell and other staff members expertise
- National Coalition of Pastors Spouses' Manual for Faith Communities (NCPS)
- Body and Soul curriculum
- Training consultants: FOHI HAC
- Evaluation consultants: UMSPH; FACED
- Support of Pastors Wives of Genesee County

National, Regional & Local Resources for HIV education, testing, treatment and services

Youth Workshops
- YOUR Blessed Health training
- Basic HIV education, skills-building, risk education planning

Adult Education
- YOUR Blessed Health training
- Adults: basic HIV education

Pastors' Wives and Church Leaders' Training
- Training using NCPS curriculum
- Monthly team meetings

Church Awareness Activities
- Sermons and presentations during Sunday services

Joint Community-wide Activities (HealthFairs)
- World AIDS Day
- Hope Parties for community-based women
- Annual Women's Conference
- Girls' Night In – education for women and girls

Youth & Adults
- # sessions
- # people/session
- # people who complete
- # Youth who complete Risk Reduction Plans

Trainers
- # leaders trained
- Meeting minutes
- # lesson plans
- # presentations to other groups

Presentations
- # church members attending
- # service presentations
- # sermons related to HIV/AIDS

Community
- No. events addressing HIV/AIDS
- No. people tested for HIV at events

Youth & Adults
- Youth will more effectively assess, discuss and manage sexual risk
- Adults in churches will more effectively and comfortably discuss HIV/AIDS
- Increased knowledge, awareness and skills

Church
- Pastors, pastors' wives, and church leaders are more knowledgeable and effective leaders in addressing HIV/AIDS
- Youth &adults will do more effective "in-reach" and outreach regarding HIV/AIDS
- Social norms within churches are more supportive of discussing and addressing HIV/AIDS
- Churches increase community outreach to address HIV/AIDS

Community
- More effective collaboration among churches to address HIV/AIDS
- More effective church-secular org. collaborations to address HIV/AIDS

Reduced incidence of HIV infections among 11–19-year-old African Americans in Flint, Michigan

Feedback   Feedback   Feedback

Contextual Conditions
(e.g. High poverty, HIV stigma, homophobia, racism)

Figure 29.1 Prevention and outreach through Flint Pastors' Wives.

When working with youth, it is important to tap into their sense of invulnerability and invincibility with accurate facts and information (Crosby, 1996). YBH youth seemed to internalize information about HIV transmission and recognize they did not know all there was to know about sex, STIs, HIV transmission, and sexual risk. For example, one participant said, "[I learned] how easy it is to contract HIV/AIDS." Another participant commented that, "[I learned] how much risk is involved in sex." These lessons are often difficult to effectively convey to youth. Other youth indicated that they learned important lessons regarding the importance of seeking support from others, the consequences of engaging in sex, and the need to responsibly manage sexual situations. These findings suggest more intensive training on communication skills and negotiating skills is needed but that the intervention helped youth understand the complexity of sexual relationships. It is noteworthy that we did not encounter the main barrier we anticipated: young people being embarrassed to talk to their pastors' spouses about sex and sexuality. In fact, the trainers of two churches reported that their young people said, "It was real cool for the pastor's wife to talk about sex."

Training youth was one goal of the YBH program, but changing the norms of faith-based institutions and eventually communities was another important goal of the intervention. One of the primary strategies employed to achieve this goal was providing training for adults. Four churches and one housing community provided 13 adult training sessions, for a total of 121 adults. There was an average of 9.3 adults participating in each educational session.

Pastors' spouses and church leaders' training

YBH was successful in gaining the support of the pastors, the participation of all 11 pastors' spouses, and the engagement of other key leaders in the churches. Fifty-five pastors' spouses, ministers' spouses, and their designees (including adult and youth leaders) from the 11 churches and two community settings were trained to deliver the YBH curriculum in their respective organizations. Following the training, participants demonstrated increased sexual health knowledge, improved facilitation skills, and a greater comfort level with discussing sexual health topics. The training proved beneficial even for those who were formally involved with health ministries or who had formal training in health service provision. For example, one trainer expressed, "I am a nurse, and the training reinforced some of the knowledge that I had and dispelled some myths that I had."

While YBH successfully provided adult and youth training and worked to create more supportive church environments for discussing sexual health, teaching youth about sex and sexuality is different than teaching them about the Bible and religious doctrine. In general, we found that most of the adults trained to lead the adult and youth sessions were satisfied with the curriculum. They felt comfortable teaching youth about the HIV/AIDS disease and helping youth to identify modes of transmission and other basic, innocuous information about HIV/AIDS and STIs. Some trainers, however, were far less comfortable discussing condom use, sexual communication, and negotiating skills, as this content is what often makes open discussion of HIV/AIDS and STIs taboo in church. Discussing behaviors that are explicitly forbidden by church doctrine and yet are a reality of the challenges today's youth face was far more difficult for the individuals implementing the intervention. Several of the churches did not discuss condoms or condom use or provide condom-use demonstrations during the training sessions.

Pastors

Overall, the pastors were pleased with the YBH program. As one pastor acknowledged, "I think that this program is very beneficial to the community, and there are people submitting to [HIV] testing as a result." Eight of the 11 pastors completed the Pastor Inventory: a brief questionnaire assessing their feelings about discussing HIV/AIDS in church and their perceptions of YBH. The pastors' comfort level discussing HIV/AIDS in church increased for 63% of the pastors and remained the same for the rest. All the pastors agreed the YBH initiative was tasteful and educational. All of the pastors also agreed YBH increased awareness of HIV/AIDS and decreased stigma regarding individuals with HIV/AIDS among their congregations. Pastors were asked to rate the overall positive impact they believed YBH had on their congregation's awareness and understanding of HIV/AIDS; six pastors reported there was a 'high' level of impact and two pastors reported a 'medium' level of impact.

There were also a number of positive actions and comments by pastors outside of the Pastor Inventory. One of the pastors, for example, infused content from one of the adult educational sessions into his Sunday morning service. A bishop reported that, "I will encourage the implementation of YBH in all the churches that are a part of my jurisdiction." Finally, one pastor stated he was ready to organize a pastors' group to establish ongoing HIV testing in their churches.

Church events

Seven hundred people participated in church services where faith leaders, pastors' spouses, and YBH staff shared information about HIV/AIDS. These activities included pastoral messages and sermons during the service, presentations during youth and adult Sunday school, and other presentations at the churches. The YBH Principal Investigator (PI) was invited by two ministers from churches participating in YBH to provide HIV/AIDS educational and skills building presentations and trainings to their congregations during the Sunday morning service. When the YBH PI asked a pastor how long her message should be, the pastor said, "Honey, tell it like it is. They need it all. If you can say it, they can hear it." Subsequently, one member of the congregation reported that, "I feel that this presentation had a positive impact on our entire congregation, especially our youth, in making them aware of the danger of risky behavior and aware that you can't just look at a person and determine their status or condition." Many of the participants came up to the YBH PI and the other trainers to indicate how much they appreciated discussion of these topics in these settings. While all congregants may not have shared these views, the support from the pastors and the pastors' spouses demonstrated the churches' commitment and helped to reinforce the educational messages and support for the intervention. As one congregant reported, "Our adults and youth are asking questions ... they are taking booklets, and asking about the YOUR Center [the local HIV/AIDS education and service agency implementing YBH]." In addition, several more requests have been made of the YBH team to provide these sessions at other Flint area churches. These findings suggest that the goal of increasing awareness was achieved.

Community events

While the church events were designed to focus on the congregants of the individual churches, the community events were designed to connect members of the faith community across churches and denominations, and to reach out to those who were not affiliated with the

11 involved churches. Four community-wide events were held to raise community awareness of HIV/AIDS. These events, which reached 480 people, included opportunities for dialogue across lay youth and adults, clergy, and faith leaders, within and across denominations. The events, which focused largely on women and girls, often included opportunities for inter-generational communication and sharing. As a result, parents, grandparents and guardians who attended YBH-sponsored community events indicated that they felt more comfortable talking with their teens about sexuality, and that they were likely to initiate a conversation about sexuality with their children. One parent stated, "In my household there has been more dialogue and more interest in safer sex practices."

Summary of results

During the six-month pilot project, YBH successfully engaged 11 churches across seven denominations and two housing communities (Campbell & Griffith *et al.*, 2007). Often denominational differences, pastoral philosophy, and the unique interpretations of the Bible within denominations can make interdenominational efforts difficult, if not impossible. The YBH intervention, however, has been successful in building positive relationships across denominations in the Flint African American faith community. The intervention staff trained 189 youth, 121 adults, and 55 pastors' spouses and church leaders. The church events reached 700 participants and the community events reached another 480 people for a total of 1,180 people. In total, the intervention directly reached 1,545 people across the 11 churches. Across the 11 churches, YBH reached approximately 4,000 indirectly during the six-month pilot. Also, during the course of the intervention, 80 people were tested for HIV at YBH events. Moreover, in many instances, the ministers of the participating congregations were the first in line to be tested.

Differential discussion

Faith-based organizations are important institutions in the African American community, and have the potential to be key agents in reducing HIV/AIDS infection rates. This pilot of YBH has illustrated that faith-based HIV prevention programs are feasible and well-received if they follow some basic principles: (1) respect the denominational doctrine and vision of the pastors, (2) engage pastors' spouses (or some other champions), and (3) build on the church leadership teams' understanding of what is appropriate and will be acceptable in their specific organizations. The YBH intervention allows for the individuality of the churches, which seemed to be a key factor in churches' comfort with participating in and enthusiasm for adopting this intervention. Like interventions for individuals, "one size" does not fit all, and it is important to meet churches where they are. Each church may have a different understanding of the issues, comfort with presenting material, and capacity to deliver the intervention. Rather than excluding those who are more conservative and uncomfortable with certain material, the YBH approach illustrates the importance of recognizing the initial intervention may only be the beginning. The goal is not to have churches conduct a one-time intervention, but to change how these issues are addressed by the faith leaders and congregants in the long-term. Faith-based organizations can balance their vision and interpretation of church doctrine and address the HIV epidemic in the African American community if they are assisted with balancing their moral and spiritual mission with this public health crisis.

References

Aragon, R., Kates, J. & Green, L. (2001). *African Americans' views of the HIV/AIDS epidemic at 20 years: Findings from a national survey*. Menlo Park, CA: Kaiser Family Foundation.

Billingsley, A. (1999). *Mighty like a river: The black church and social reform*. New York: Oxford University Press.

Billingsley, A. & Caldwell, C. H. (1991). The church, the family and the school in the African American community. 60 (3): 427–40.

Campbell, B., Griffith, D. M., Robinson, K. J. & Hobbs, D. (2007). *YOUR Blessed Health: HIV/AIDS prevention & outreach through Flint pastors' spouses*. Flint, MI: Ruth Mott Foundation.

Campbell, M. K., Hudson, M. A., Resnicow, K., Blakeney, N., Paxton, A. & Baskin, M. (2007). Church-based health promotion interventions: Evidence and lessons learned. *Annual Review of Public Health*, 28: 213–34.

Centers for Disease Control and Prevention (CDC). (2007). *HIV/AIDS Surveillance Report*.

Cotler, S. J. & Jensen, D. M. (2001). Treatment of hepatitis C virus and HIV co-infections. *Clinics in Liver Disease*, 5 (4): 1045–61.

Coyne-Beasley T. & Schoenback, V. J. (2000). The African-American church: A potential forum for adolescent comprehensive sexuality education. *Journal of Adolescent Health*, 26 (4): 289–94.

Crosby, R. A. (1996). Combating the illusion of adolescent invincibility to HIV/AIDS. *Journal of School Health*, 66 (5): 186–90.

DeHaven M. J., Hunter I. B., Wilder L, Walton J. W. & Berry J. (2004). Health programs in faith-based organizations: Are they effective? *American Journal of Public Health*, 94 (6): 1030–6.

DuBois, W. E. B., (2000). *DuBois on religion*. (P. Zukerman, ed.). NY: Alta Mira Press.

Francis S. A. & Liverpool, J. (2009). A review of faith-based HIV prevention programs. *Journal of Religion and Health*, 48 (1): 6–15.

Hartwell, V., Gaddis, P. Jr. & Fletcher, B. W. (1990). *AIDS and the African-American church*. Mississippi, USA: Jackson State University National Alumni AIDS Prevention Project.

Israel, B. A., Schulz, A. J., Parker, E. A. & Becker, A. B. (1998). Review of community-based research: Assessing partnership approaches to improve public health. *Annual Review of Public Health*, 19 (1): 173–202.

Krause N. (2003). Religious meaning and subjective well-being in late life. *Journal of Gerontology*, 58B (3): S160-70.

Mattis J. S. & Jagers R. J. (2001). A relational framework for the study of religiosity and spirituality in the lives of African Americans. *Journal of Community Psychology*, 29, 519–39.

Michigan Department of Community Health. (2007). *Natality, mortality, and other vital statistics* [internet]. Retrieved: www.michigan.gov/MDCH.

Peterson J., Atwood, J. & Yates, B. (1999). Key elements for church-based health promotion programs: Outcome-based literature review, *Public Health Nursing*, 19 (6): 401–11.

Piliero, P. J. & Faragon, J. J. (2002). Hepatitis B virus and HIV co-infection. *AIDS Reader*, 12 (10): 443–4, 448–51.

Resnicow, K., Baranowski, T., Ahluwalia, J. S., Braithwaite, R. L. (1999). Cultural sensitivity in public health: Defined and demystified. *Ethnicity & Disease*, 9, 10–21.

Steele, C. B., Melendez-Morales, L., Campoluci, R., DeLuca, N. & Dean, H. D. (2007). *Health disparities in HIV/AIDS, viral hepatitis, sexually transmitted diseases and tuberculosis: Issues, burden and response, a retrospective review, 2000–2004*. Atlanta, GA: Centers for Disease Control and Prevention.

U.S. Census Bureau. (2006). *American Fact Finder* [internet]. Washington DC: U.S. Census Bureau; c2006. Retrieved: http://factfinder.census.gov/home/saff/main.html?_lang=en

Viswanathan, M., Ammerman, A., Eng, E., Gartlehner, G., Lohr, K. N., Griffith D., *et al.* (2004). *Community-based participatory research: Assessing the evidence. Evidence Report/Technology Assessment No. 99* (prepared by RTI University of North Carolina Evidence-Based Practice Center under Contract No. 290–02–0016), AHRQ Publication 04-E022-2. Rockville, M.D.: Agency for Healthcare Research and Quality.

30 Amethyst

Integrating tobacco dependence services with long-term alcohol and other drug addiction treatment for homeless and low-income women

Gretchen Clark Hammond, Barbra Teater, and Shauna P. Acquavita

Context

Amethyst, Inc. provides long-term alcohol, tobacco and other drug addiction treatment integrated with permanent supportive housing for women and women with dependent children in Columbus, Ohio. Amethyst combines intensive alcohol and drug treatment with mental health services, trauma counseling, health and wellness services, intensive case management, economic and educational supports, emergency baby-sitting and parenting support in a comprehensive program that assists women for up to five years. Each female-headed household resides in a fully furnished apartment located within a community of recovery. The residential units are located on the bus line and are only a few miles from the main treatment facility. Women attend programming five days per week, with the most intensive period of treatment lasting two years. On any given day Amethyst houses 100 women and between 65 to 85 children. In State Fiscal Year 2008, the average length of stay for all Amethyst participants was 19 months. The average length of stay among women with dependent children residing at Amethyst was 28 months. All women are homeless at their time of entry into Amethyst.

Amethyst was founded in 1984 by nine recovering women who began as volunteers in a donated house. While at Amethyst, women are treated concurrently for alcohol, tobacco and other drugs (ATOD) through the provision of counseling, educational and case management services by staff that have licensure as social workers, counselors and chemical dependency counselors through the state of Ohio. The majority of clinical personnel hold graduate degrees.

Amethyst provides comprehensive, gender-specific treatment to assist women with addiction, mental health, physical health, family strengthening and economic stability. Critical to Amethyst's success are the extensive supportive service linkages for participants in the program. Each participant engages in a wide range of services according to her needs and the goals established on her individualized plan. Federal recommendations from The Center for Substance Abuse Treatment (TIP 2: Pregnant, Substance-Using Women) (1993) and the National Institutes on Drug Abuse Principles for Drug Abuse Treatment, Principles of Effective Treatment (1999) are reflected in Amethyst's program design. Services provided are listed in Table 30.1 on page 352.

Amethyst is recognized for innovation when it comes to gender-specific treatment for women, including the full integration of tobacco as a drug of addiction. Amethyst began the process of integration in 2002, and became a fully integrated tobacco-free facility in February

Table 30.1 Chart of service provisions

Addiction Recovery	Socioeconomic Stability	Wellness and Family Stability
Individual and group counseling services for relapse prevention and education about addiction	Intensive Case Management (ICM) for linkage to benefits and improved coordination of services for physical and mental health	Parenting education and family counseling to improve stability of the entire family
Integrated tobacco treatment including targeted relapse intervention services	ICM for life skill development, including education on finances and money management	Women's health programming for eating disorders, HIV/AIDS, STD prevention detection and treatment
Spirituality, cultural education and linkage to peer support systems for the ongoing promotion of recovery	Support for pursuing and achieving educational goals	Group and individual counseling to help children heal from the traumatic effects of living in families affected by addiction, poverty, violence and homelessness
Counseling for recovery from trauma including physical, emotional and sexual abuse as it relates to addiction and recovery	Assistance with vocational development, including volunteer placements and support for maintenance of employment in the community	SummerQuest Services: ATOD prevention, violence prevention, asset-building and social skill development; After-school programming, and emergency babysitting

2006. Amethyst's Integrated Tobacco Treatment program was awarded the 2008 Science to Service Award for the Treatment of Substance Abuse & Recovery Support Services category through the Substance Abuse and Mental Health Services Administration (SAMHSA), a division of the United States Department of Health and Human Services (HHS). The expectation for participants is that they remain abstinent from alcohol, tobacco and other drugs during treatment and throughout their recovery.

Policy

Smoke- and tobacco-free policies decrease morbidity and mortality in smokers and non-smokers alike. Smokers who are subject to smoke-free policies at work are more likely to cut down and/or stop smoking, and non-smokers are protected from second-hand smoke (Fichtenberg & Glantz, 2002). Institutional bans on smoking are not new. Maine instituted the first ban on smoking in all hospitals in 1989 (Borio, 2008). Chemical dependency programs such as the Cleveland Clinic located in Cleveland, Ohio and Gateway Rehabilitation Center in Aliquippa, Pennsylvania also instituted bans on smoking that year (Capretto, 1993; Kotz, 1993). However, challenges developed as several myths—assumed by staff and clients in treatment alike—impeded progress in this issue. These myths included: people in treatment do not want to stop smoking, they will relapse if they attempt, and they are unable to stop (Campbell, Wander, Stark & Holbert, 1995; Ziedonis, Guydish, Williams, Steinberg & Foulds, 2006). Also, with no statewide ban on tobacco in chemical dependency programs, difficulties arose around being one of the few tobacco- or smoke-free units. Ten years later, New Jersey became one of the first states to implement a statewide ban on tobacco in residential chemical dependency programs (Robert Wood Johnson Foundation [RWJF], 2008). The New Jersey Department of Health created the *Drug-Free is Nicotine-Free* manual in order to educate substance abuse treatment providers statewide and nationwide on the importance of addressing tobacco within chemical dependency treatment (RWJF, 2008). Also, training programs on becoming tobacco-free chemical dependence programs were provided to many organizations, including those in Pennsylvania, New York, Massachusetts, Alaska, Virginia, Minnesota, Nevada, Washington, D.C., and Ohio (RWJF, 2008).

Tobacco prevention and treatment came to the forefront in Ohio with the creation of the Ohio Tobacco Use Prevention and Control Foundation (TUPCF) in 2000, later changing its name to the Ohio Tobacco Prevention Foundation (OTPF). Grants became available for prevention and treatment initiatives in 2002, which encouraged entities throughout the state to apply for funding to address this public health problem. Amethyst received the first round of grants in 2002 and continued to receive OTPF funds until June 2008, at which time Ohio's governor and the state legislature decided to dissolve OTPF. At that time, all grants ceased. During those five years, Amethyst developed internal policy, procedures and treatment protocols for tobacco dependence treatment, which included curricula, professional training and a relapse intervention program.

At the state level, publicly funded treatment agencies are not required to address tobacco within treatment services, even though nicotine dependence and nicotine withdrawal are diagnosable disorders found in the *Diagnostic and Statistical Manual of Mental Disorders, Version IV-TR (DSM-IV-TR)* within the category of substance dependence (American Psychiatric Association [APA], 2000). Nicotine dependence should be part of a comprehensive addiction assessment. If a client meets the criteria for diagnosis, this information should be placed on the treatment plan and addressed within program services. Resistance to the diagnosis and treatment of tobacco dependence exists outside of formal policy and is influenced by myths and beliefs that exist about tobacco within the treatment community (Fuller *et al.*, 2007; Ziedonis *et al.*, 2006).

In addition to the absence of tobacco treatment policies for treatment providers, current health care policies in Ohio affect tobacco dependence treatment. Medical coverage for people in treatment varies, with many people not eligible for public benefits. Ohio had Disability Assistance (DA) until July 2005. It had provided many people in treatment with medical coverage and minimal cash assistance. The elimination of DA resulted in 60–70% of the women at Amethyst losing medical coverage. Medicaid in Ohio covers Nicotine Replacement Therapy by prescription but, without Medicaid, the cost must be paid out-of-pocket. Amethyst assists with the costs associated with these medications because pharmacotherapy for tobacco dependence improves chances for remaining abstinent (Fiore *et al.*, 2000). Services for tobacco dependence are integrated with other drugs of addiction and are therefore reimbursable under the public reimbursement system.

Technology

Prevalence rates for tobacco use among chemically dependent persons are high, ranging from 70–90%, as compared with 21% in the current adult population in the United States (Centers for Disease Control and Prevention [CDC], 2007; Kalman, 1998; Kalman, Morissette & George, 2005; Sharp, Schwartz, Nightingale & Novak, 2003). Developments in the diagnostic assessment of tobacco dependence and treatment of this addiction have advanced greatly over the past two decades.

Amethyst combines the Fagerström Test for Nicotine Dependence (FTND) (Heatherton, Kozlowski, Frecker & Fagerström, 1991) with the criteria found in the *DSM-IV-TR*. The FTND is a self-administered questionnaire with eight items relating to tobacco use that are scored and then totaled with a possible range of 0 to 11. A total score of six or less indicates a low to moderate dependence on nicotine and a total score of seven or more indicates a high dependence on nicotine (Fagerström & Schneider, 1989; Heatherton *et al.*, 1991). The *DSM-IV-TR* lists nicotine dependence under the category of substance-related disorders, with specific diagnostic criteria for nicotine use disorder, nicotine withdrawal disorder and nicotine-related disorder not otherwise specified (APA, 2000).

The development of numerous nicotine replacement therapies (i.e. patch, gum, lozenge, inhaler, nasal spray) and non-nicotine medications such as varenicline and bupropion have advanced the treatment of nicotine dependence by aiding with withdrawal symptoms. Behavioral counseling, including Motivational Interviewing, is recognized as effective in the treatment of tobacco dependence (Miller & Rollnick, 2003). Formalized training and certification programs for tobacco treatment exist throughout the country (please see the list at the end of this chapter). Amethyst's Tobacco Treatment Team has attended numerous trainings to become proficient in the treatment of tobacco dependence.

Tools for monitoring the compliance of clients in treatment settings include carbon monoxide monitors to measure carbon monoxide (CO) in the lungs and urine tests to measure cotinine, the metabolized version of nicotine. The CO monitor is a quick, easy to use and relatively non-invasive tool for detecting recent exposure to tobacco (about six to nine hours), or acute abstinence, as the expired CO has a short half-life (Jatlow, Toll, Leary, Krishnan-Sarin & O'Malley, 2008). Alternatively, the urine test for cotinine is more expensive, time-consuming and cannot be used with clients who are using nicotine replacement therapies, yet has a longer half-life and is therefore more sensitive in detecting abstinence from tobacco, with a window of five to seven days (Gariti, Alterman, Ehrman, Mulvaney & O'Brien, 2002; Jatlow *et al.*, 2008). Amethyst monitors for alcohol, tobacco and other drug use through urine screens and therefore uses both forms of technology, depending on the client's current tobacco cessation treatment plan.

Organization

Amethyst, Inc. ascribes to principles associated with feminism, which include collaboration, multiple viewpoints, and appreciation for the experiences of women. The CEO of Amethyst is one of the organization's founding mothers and focuses on innovative practices for women in treatment. Staff persons are valued for their skills, talents and commitment to working with women and families. The ethos of the organization is one where learning is valued, research is encouraged and creativity is supported. Amethyst's organizational size lends itself to change, as it is not a small part of a larger organization (as opposed to a program within a large hospital system), but large enough to be recognized as a major provider of services in the Columbus community. This situation affords the opportunity for all staff persons to be engaged in change processes. Amethyst's desire to treat tobacco dependence existed not only within the organization, but extended to other providers throughout the state. Amethyst worked extensively with other women's treatment providers, men's providers, youth providers, and health systems to assist them with the integration of tobacco cessation into their services. This collaborative situation is still in place through training and technical assistance provided by Amethyst.

Amethyst involved a multi-department task force for the integration of tobacco dependence treatment and took approximately 18 months to progress through the necessary steps, including creating tobacco-free grounds, exploring available curricula, training staff, assisting staff persons with quitting tobacco, and creating policies and procedures. A treatment team was designated to oversee tobacco dependence services, including a relapse intervention program.

The CEO and Project Coordinator acted as community liaisons with other service providers and supported persons not familiar with tobacco dependence, including child welfare workers, criminal justice personnel and mental health workers, as clients would now be expected to remain abstinent from tobacco. The normalization of tobacco use, especially within substance abuse, mental health and criminal justice settings, presented some challenges in working with outside providers. Through education and dialogue (i.e. presenting treatment rationales, providing training) these challenges were overcome. The program is continuously evaluated and improved, as the commitment to treating tobacco remains strong.

Decisions about practice

Client description

This discussion centers on the organization as the client, rather than a specific individual. In our experience, working with organizations to become tobacco-free was necessary in order to affect an individual client. The experience at Amethyst parallels the processes other health service organizations experience when making the conversion from tobacco-tolerant to a tobacco-free organization. However, there are distinctive aspects to the process because Amethyst is an alcohol and drug treatment agency. Commonplace in many alcohol and drug treatment facilities is a high prevalence of tobacco use and an unchecked acceptance for the use of this drug as benign or the "lesser of many evils." Amethyst was one of the early treatment centers to become a fully integrated tobacco-free facility in Ohio and remains a model program.

Goals

Organizations interested in tobacco dependence treatment often fall into one of two categories: (1) smoke-free or (2) tobacco-free. Smoke-free organizations are understood as prohibiting use of combustible tobacco indoors, but allow its use outdoors. Tobacco-free agencies view tobacco in the same context as alcohol and other drugs and prohibit the use of the products on the grounds or any time during the duration of treatment. Staff persons in a tobacco-free organization are expected to be non-identifiable as tobacco users. Amethyst determined that it would become a tobacco-free organization, as it was already smoke-free (since 1984).

Developing objectives and contracting

Organizational change involves all staff persons, regardless of position, at some time. For Amethyst, going tobacco-free represented a cultural change and affected those working in clinical and non-clinical roles. Therefore, numerous meetings were held to plan for this change. Discussion within and between departments was necessary in order to address staff concerns, dispel myths, and share the vision for the organization. Amethyst created a tobacco-free task force and began working from an 18-month timeline. Task force members represented all major departments and included current, former, and never tobacco users. The charge to the task force was to move the organization from smoke-free to tobacco-free, including the development of personnel policies and treatment protocols. Those persons who were current tobacco users were offered assistance in the process of becoming tobacco-free, including reimbursement for nicotine replacement therapy.

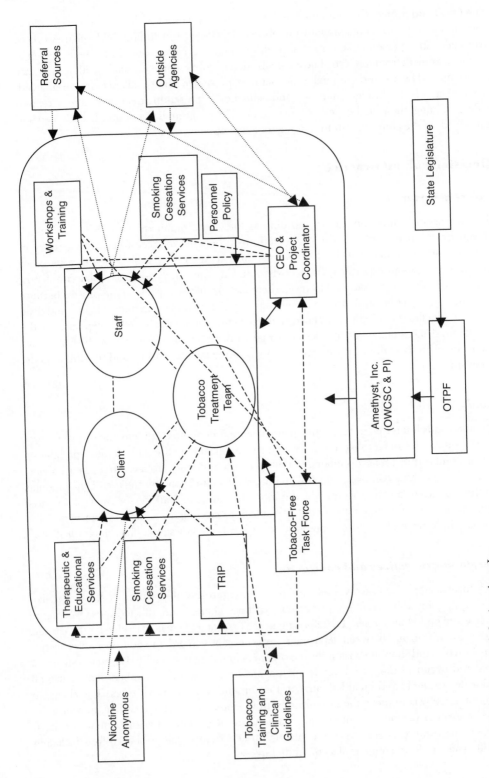

Figure 30.1 Organigraph for Amethyst, Inc.

Meeting place and use of time

The Tobacco-Free Task Force met regularly, usually on a monthly basis. These meetings were open to all interested staff and took place on-site during the lunch hour. Materials developed from these meetings were shared with the staff and information was communicated on a regular basis to keep staff apprised of the changes and also to quell any developing rumors about the conversion to a tobacco-free agency. It was important to keep the process moving in order to keep staff invested in the process.

Strategies and interventions

Hoffman and Slade (1993, 156) identify 12 critical steps in order for treatment programs to be successful in their transition to becoming tobacco-free. First, Hoffman and Slade detail how one must recognize the challenges tobacco creates for the addictions treatment community. Individuals who have mental illness and/or substance abuse diagnoses are two to four times more likely to smoke than the general population (Lasser *et al.*, 2000). This situation translates into higher morbidity and mortality among these individuals. The second step suggested by Hoffman and Slade is the creation of a committee in the organization dedicated to the tobacco-free transition; this committee should also have a commitment from the executive(s). Third, the organization develops a tobacco-free policy. The policy needs to identify consequences for use, similar to existing drug-free workplace policies. Treatment protocols for client use should mirror existing practice for relapse. Fourth, the organization should establish a policy implementation timeline with measureable goals and objectives, including transition time to address unforeseen issues and other challenges.

Conducting staff training is the fifth step. Training across departments is essential, even for individuals who do not provide clinical services, as going tobacco-free represents a cultural shift for many, and it requires education and dialogue. Additional training for those in direct services roles is recommended. Addressing the needs of tobacco-dependent staff is next on the list and includes suggestions for on-site assistance and referral. Seventh, organizations must begin to assess and diagnose nicotine dependence in clients and develop appropriate treatment goals to address this issue. Curriculum development for client education encompasses the eighth step. Communication with outside resources is discussed again in step nine. Step 10 suggests requiring staff to be tobacco-free, so this assistance early on is necessary for the success of both patients and staff. The establishment of tobacco-free grounds is step 11. Finally, the organization must implement nicotine dependence treatment throughout the program.

Amethyst's own tobacco-free process incorporated these steps, beginning first with the development of a tobacco-free task force and then followed by many sessions of staff training, smoke-out days and client workshops. Personnel policy development involved Amethyst's existing drug-free workplace policy, in which tobacco was incorporated. Discussions with referral sources and outside persons came in written and face-to-face communication. Interestingly, as Amethyst was engaged in its own process, it assisted sister agencies simultaneously. This situation presented an opportunity for collaboration and parallel learning processes for both Amethyst and the other organizations. The ability to troubleshoot, discuss and share ideas, curricula and training opportunities proved beneficial. It also created a support network for the respective executives who were met with resistance by some providers, support persons and referral sources.

Stance of the social worker

Social workers intervene with many historically oppressed groups who are vulnerable to tobacco use (Kaplan & Weiler, 1997). This situation makes them well suited to address tobacco use at micro, mezzo and macro levels. Providing tobacco dependence counseling to individuals, developing tobacco-free work environments, and advocating for health plan reimbursement for provider counseling services to pay for cessation activities, all represent opportunities for significant impact on tobacco use.

Our education and training in tobacco dependence and addictions informs our practice and our work with this case. Gretchen is a social worker, specializing in administration. Her clinical training on tobacco dependence treatment came from extensive review of literature on tobacco dependence and chemical dependency. Gretchen was also trained by Dr. Terry Rustin of Texas and Bernice Order-Connors of New Jersey, both of whom advocated for an integrated approach to tobacco dependence and addictions treatment. Gretchen is also a Certified Tobacco Treatment Specialist from the Mayo Clinic Nicotine Dependence Center. Barbra is a social worker and completed the Tobacco Treatment Specialist Certification Training through the Mayo Clinic. Shauna is a licensed clinical social worker and completed the Tobacco Treatment Specialist Certification Training through the University of Massachusetts and the American Lung Association Freedom from Smoking Clinic Facilitator Training.

Use of resources

Amethyst was (and still is) fortunate to have employed several resources for this process. Amethyst relied on the information provided in the Clinical Practice Guidelines for Treating Tobacco Dependence (2000), including the characteristics for brief and intensive interventions. Helpful to Amethyst was the Tobacco Dependence Program at the School of Public Health, University of Medicine and Dentistry of New Jersey. Their manual, *Drug-Free is Nicotine-Free: A Manual for Chemical Dependency Treatment Programs* (Hoffman, *et al.*, 1997) provided information on organizational considerations, including the need for extensive staff training. Additionally, Amethyst benefited from its work with the Ohio Women's Coalition Smoking Cessation and Prevention Initiative (OWCSC & PI) who provided a detailed timeline for organizational change. Amethyst's work was supported through a grant from the Ohio Tobacco Prevention Foundation for five-and-a-half years, during which OTPF staff persons provided expertise, suggestions and training opportunities. The community of OTPF grantees throughout the state of Ohio provided extensive support, encouragement and valuable information during this time.

Reassessment and evaluation

The major area for reassessment came in the curriculum and treatment cycle for Amethyst clients. Originally, we developed a nine-session curriculum, as many classes at Amethyst run on eight- to 12-week cycles. Client feedback indicated that this approach was insufficient for their needs, as this drug was the most normalized one in their lives and the one they had used the longest. Curriculum changes resulted in an 18-session workbook, centered on the concepts of wellness and recovery. They also began two Nicotine Anonymous meetings bi-weekly during the lunch hour to provide themselves with support and fellowship. Amethyst designated four persons as the Tobacco Treatment Team because of their expertise in tobacco dependence treatment. In addition to developing a more extensive curriculum, the Tobacco Treatment

Team proposed an intensive intervention lasting twelve months.

This intervention contains a relapse prevention/intervention component called TRIP (Tobacco Relapse Intervention Program) which includes individualized sessions for those women who relapse on tobacco or begin demonstrating relapse warning signs. Primary counselors call on the Tobacco Treatment Team for support, and assistance for clients demonstrating relapse warning signs, or to refer a client for additional services in the case of a relapse. Intervention changes included working with women in pre-treatment and engagement efforts (assumed to be pre-contemplative about quitting) 90 minutes per week. After pre-treatment completion, clients participate in a two-class series lasting between nine and 12 months: Smoke-Free Action and Smoke-Free Maintenance. The goal of this curriculum is to move the client from a sense of compliance (i.e. "I'm only quitting because you are making me") to a feeling of acceptance of nicotine and tobacco as drugs. Once this acceptance is reached, the integration of tobacco into the recovery experience follows.

Transfer and termination

The notion of transfer and termination is an interesting one in this process. Being a tobacco-free agency seems to contain an evolutionary element where we feel as though "we have it all figured out"—the clients are successful, the staff is supportive and things seem to be going smoothly. We experience bumps in the road, including the loss of funding and the dissolution of the OTPF, and work to overcome them with creativity, flexibility and perseverance. Our experience with this process has deepened our understanding of addiction, relapse and recovery, as our clients examine all their drugs of dependence rather than just some of them, as they had done in the past. They recognize their cravings for tobacco as "desires to use" and see this desire as a warning sign. Our process does not have a termination per se; rather, we operate in maintenance most of the time, pausing to review our program and make improvements.

Case conclusion

In addition to the information shared above in the reassessment and evaluation section, Amethyst compared its implementation of an intensive intervention with the recommendations provided in the Clinical Best Practice Guidelines for Treating Tobacco Dependence (2000). This assessment demonstrated that Amethyst's intervention exceeded the standards set forth in the guidelines because of service intensity and duration. Figure 30.1 on page 356 illustrates the integration of tobacco treatment services at Amethyst.

Differential discussion

Becoming a tobacco-free agency has strengthened our organization—it forced us to examine our perceptions about addiction, including the phrase "a drug is a drug is a drug." We realized that by talking about tobacco dependence and nicotine addiction, we were able to discuss the progression of the disease with our clients in a more in-depth manner. Now, when we ask them to "look back" at when their addiction started, they can begin with tobacco and they find it was the first drug they used. The focus on the basics of recovery is emphasized, including the recognition that a craving for tobacco is a craving to use a drug, which signals a relapse trigger or warning sign. We begin working with the clients during their engagement phase and discuss the process of quitting tobacco to allay their fears. We have found that this part of the work is essential and necessary, as it allows us to begin building rapport with new clients who have reservations about quitting. The core of our message centers on our perception that addiction has three components: (1) the physical process of the body and brain becoming addicted; (2) the emotional processes of replacing normal emotional coping with drug use and the significant emotional relationship that forms with the drug, making it feel like a friend and a lover; and (3) the social component where one learns to associate his or her actions with use. We discuss these components and emphasize how tobacco, alcohol and other drugs are integrated and similar. Training in motivational interviewing is also quite helpful, as it allows us to embrace ambivalence and work with the client and understand where she is in her cessation process.

Another benefit to this process is bearing witness to the physical health changes for our clients. The clients' personal attention to their own health and wellness is vastly changed, as they now can attend to their multiple illnesses without exacerbation from their tobacco use. They share with us how their tobacco-free life has impacted their children and grandchildren in positive ways and how proud they are of themselves—because they thought they would never quit smoking. Our agency focus on wellness has proliferated throughout our programming, not limited to or divided from addiction recovery services. The rewards from this undertaking will continue to be realized in the lives of our staff, the women and their children. This work is both inspiring and tiring, but at all times it is worth the effort.

References

American Psychiatric Association (2000). *Diagnostic and statistical manual of mental disorders* (4th ed. Text Revision.). Washington, D.C.: American Psychiatric Association.

Borio, G. (2008). *Tobacco Timeline.* Retrieved 11/29/08: http://www.tobacco.org/resources/history/Tobacco_History20-2.html

Campbell, B. K., Wander, N., Stark, M. J. & Holbert, T. (1995). Treating cigarette smoking in drug-abusing clients. *Journal of Substance Abuse Treatment,* 12 (2): 89–94.

Capretto, N. A. (1993). Confronting nicotine dependency at the Gateway Rehabilitation Center. *Journal of Substance Abuse Treatment,* 10: 113–16.

Center for Substance Abuse Treatment, U.S. Dept. of Health and Human Services, Public Health Service Substance Abuse and Mental Health Services Administration (1993). Treatment Improvement Protocol Series (TIP) 2: *Pregnant, substance-using women.* DHHS Publication No. (SMA) 93–1998.

Centers for Disease Control and Prevention (CDC). (2007). *Health, United States, 2007: With chartbook on trends in the health of Americans.* Hyattsville, M.D.: National Center for Health Statistics.

Fagerström, K. & Schneider, N. G. (1989). Measuring nicotine dependence: A review of the Fagerström Tolerance Questionnaire. *Journal of Behavioral Medicine,* 12: 159–82.

Fichtenberg, C. M. & Glantz, S. A. (2002). Effect of smoke-free workplaces on smoking behaviour: Systematic review. *BMJ: British Medical Journal,* 325 (7357): 188.

Fiore, M. C., Bailey, W. C., Cohen, S. J., Dorfman, S., Goldstein, M. G., Gritz, E. R., *et al.* (2000). *Treating tobacco use and dependence.* Clinical practice guideline. Rockville, M.D.: U.S. Department of Health and Human Services, Public Health Service.

Fuller, B. E., Guydish, J., Tsoh, J., Reid, M. S., Resnick, M., Zammarelli L., *et al.* (2007). Attitudes toward the integration of smoking cessation treatment into drug abuse clinics. *Journal of Substance Abuse Treatment,* 32: 53–60.

Gariti, P., Alterman, A. I., Ehrman, R., Mulvaney, F. D. & O'Brien, C. P. (2002). Detecting smoking following smoking cessation treatment. *Drug and Alcohol Dependence,* 65: 191–6.

Heatherton, T. F., Kozlowski, L. T., Frecker, R. C. & Fagerström, K. O. (1991). The Fagerström Test for Nicotine Dependence: A revision of the Fagerström Tolerance Questionnaire. *British Journal of Addiction,* 86: 1119–27.

Hoffman, A. L., Kantor, B., Leech T., *et al.* (1997). *Drug-free is nicotine-free: A manual for chemical dependency treatment programs.* New Brunswick, NJ: The Tobacco Dependence Program.

Hoffman, A. L. & Slade, J. (1993). Following the pioneers: Addressing tobacco in chemical dependency treatment. *Journal of Substance Abuse Treatment*, 10: 153–60.

Jatlow, P., Toll, B. A., Leary, V., Krishnan-Sarin, S. & O'Malley, S. S. (2008). Comparison of expired carbon monoxide and plasma cotinine as markers of cigarette abstinence. *Drug and Alcohol Dependence*, 98: 203–9.

Kalman, D. (1998). Smoking cessation treatment for substance mis-users in early recovery: A review of the literature and recommendations for practice. *Substance Use & Misuse*, 33: 2021–47.

Kalman, D., Morrisete, S. B. & George, T. P. (2001). Co-morbidity of smoking in patients with psychiatric and substance abuse disorders. *American Journal on Addictions.* 14: 106–123.

Kaplan, M. S. & Weiler, R. E. (1997). Social patterns of smoking behavior: Trends and practice implications. *Health and Social Work*, 22: 47–52.

Kotz, M. M. (1993). A smoke-free chemical dependency unit. *Journal of Substance Abuse Treatment*, 10: 125–131.

Lasser, K., Boyd, J. W., Woolhandler. S., Himmelstein, D. U., McCormick, D. & Bor, D. H. (2000). Smoking and mental illness: a population-based prevalence study. *JAMA*, 284: 2606–10.

Miller, W. R. & Rollnick, S. (2003). *Motivational interviewing: Preparing people for change* (2nd ed.). The Guilford Press: New York.

National Institute on Drug Abuse (1999). *Principles of drug addiction treatment: A research based guide.* NIH Publication No. 99–4180.

Robert Wood Johnson Foundation (RWJF). (2008). *N.J. Drug and alcohol treatment providers learn to kick butts, too. Grant results.* Retrieved 12/01/08: http://www.rwjf.org/reports/grr/027022.htm

Sharp, J. R., Schwartz, S., Nightingale, T. & Novak, S. (2003). Targeting nicotine addiction in a substance abuse program. *NIDA: Clinical Perspectives*, August, 33–9.

Ziedonis, D. M., Guydish, J., Williams, J., Steinberg, M. & Foulds, J. (2006). Barriers and solutions to addressing tobacco dependence in addiction treatment programs. *Alcohol Research & Health*, 29 (3): 228–35.

Other resources

Campbell, B. K., Krumenacker, J. & Stark, M. J. (1998). Smoking cessation for clients in chemical dependence treatment: A demonstration project. *Journal of Substance Abuse Treatment*, 15 (4): 313–18.

El-Guebaly, N., Cathcart, J., Currie, S., Brown, D. & Gloster, S. (2002). Smoking cessation approaches for persons with mental illness or addictive disorders. *Psychiatric Services* (Washington, D.C.), 53 (9): 1166–70.

Internet resources

Association for the Treatment of Tobacco Use and Dependence (ATTUD). http://www.attud.org/index.php

Drug-free is nicotine-free: A manual for chemical dependency treatment programs can be ordered at http://www.tobaccoprogram.org/educationalman.htm

Implementing a Smoke-Free Environment Tobacco Consultation Service. http://www.med.umich.edu/mfit/tobacco/freeenvironment.htm

Making your workplace smoke free: A workplace guide. http://www.cdc.gov/tobacco/secondhand_smoke/guides/workplace_guide.htm

Implementing a Tobacco-Free Campus Initiative in Your Workplace Toolkit. http://www.cdc.gov/nccdphp/dnpa/hwi/toolkits/tobacco/index.htm

Training to become a tobacco treatment specialist

Mayo Clinic: http://www.mayoclinic.org/ndc-rst/tts-certification.html
University of Massachusetts: http://www.umassmed.edu/tobacco/training/index.aspx
University of Medicine and Dentistry of New Jersey: http://www.tobaccoprogram.org/tobspeciatrain.htm

31 Advocacy and compensation programs for radiation exposure claimants

Susan E. Dawson and Gary E. Madsen

Context

During the Cold War period of the 1940s through the 1980s, the United States and the Soviet Union developed massive nuclear industries. In the U.S. the Atomic Energy Commission (AEC) was created in 1946 to regulate this new industry and also to control the procurement of uranium ore from privately owned mining companies. Mechanical ventilation technology, while readily available, was not mandated early on for the underground uranium mines. Until the early 1970s, a serious lack of health and safety regulations led to the illnesses and deaths of thousands of workers. Workers' compensation was not generally available due to the extended latency period between uranium exposures and disease onset. It was only in 1990, with the passage of the Radiation Exposure Compensation Act (RECA), that uranium workers began to receive federal compensation because of this negligence on the part of the uranium industry and the government (Advisory Committee on Human Radiation Experiments, 1996).

In the 1940s there were no large-scale epidemiologic studies of uranium miners in the U.S. from which to develop an adequate health and safety radiation standard; however, the dangers of radiation were known in the scientific community as a result of uranium miner studies conducted in the 1800s in Europe. A large number of uranium miners who died of lung cancer worked in the Erzgebirge Mountains which bordered today's Czech Republic and Germany. The studies' results indicated that the miners' lung cancers were related to radon exposures in the mines. Unfortunately, these results were debated among U.S. scientists, delaying the development of effective regulations in the U.S. (Advisory Committee on Human Radiation Experiments, 1996). It was not until 1955 that the states adopted a radiation standard as a guideline, and the Environmental Protection Agency (EPA) did not establish a more stringent federal radiation standard until 1971.

Policy and technology

In this chapter, we will discuss the Radiation Exposure Compensation Act (RECA) of 1990 (P.L. 101–426), the RECA Amendments of 2000 (P.L. 106–245), and the Energy Employees Occupational Illness Compensation Program Act (EEOICPA) of 2000 (P.L. 106–398, Title XXXVI). It is important to note that U.S. veterans who witnessed atmospheric nuclear testing have separate radiation compensation legislation and may be eligible under RECA; however, they will not be discussed in this chapter.

The nuclear fuel cycle has four main components: mining, milling (leaching uranium concentrate from the ore), enrichment (further refinement), and fuel fabrication. Because our research for the past 20 years as an occupational and environmental health social worker (Susan Dawson) and an environmental sociologist (Gary Madsen) has focused on uranium miners and millworkers, we will limit our discussion largely to these two groups and their families. We will also discuss organizing activities among advocates, beneficiaries, and claimants, and issues concerning the present resurgence in uranium mining and milling due largely to the worldwide expansion of nuclear power.

Underground Uranium Miners Studies

In the U.S., uranium mining and milling were concentrated in the states of Arizona, Colorado, New Mexico, Utah, and Wyoming. In 1950 the U.S. Public Health Service (PHS) began the first large-scale mortality study of underground uranium miners employed on the Colorado Plateau. To secure compliance from the mining companies, the PHS had an unwritten agreement not to inform the workers that any radiation-related illnesses were work-related. The PHS simply informed the workers to contact a physician, ultimately denying them the right to apply for workers' compensation. Duncan Holaday, an industrial hygienist and the study's principal investigator, stated:

> ... and when we reported the information that we found, it would be done in such a way that the facilities where a particular set of samples were taken would not be identified and that we would not inform the individual workers of what data we found. (Advisory Committee on Human Radiation Experiments, 1996, p. 360)

As in the European studies, the PHS study found a similar average latency period of about 20 years between exposure and disease onset. It did not begin to establish a statistically significant excess of lung cancer deaths among the U.S. miner population until the early 1960s. As time went on, the researchers found that lower and lower cumulative levels of exposure were related to the development of lung cancer and also elevated levels of certain nonmalignant respiratory diseases (NMRD) (Archer, 1983; National Institutes of Health, 1994). Other researchers, primarily in New Mexico, produced medical studies of Navajo and non-Indian miners, which further established the connection between exposures and illnesses. (For a review of worldwide underground uranium miner radiation studies, see National Institutes of Health, 1994).

From a social work perspective, evidence of how underground miners and their families dealt with these uncompensated illnesses and/or deaths was largely anecdotal. In 1989, Susan conducted a study on the Navajo (Diné) Nation, interviewing 55 Navajo underground miners and their survivors (Dawson, 1992). She was invited to testify about mental health impacts of uranium mining at a RECA congressional field hearing in Shiprock, New Mexico, on the Navajo Nation. She reported that at no time did the government inform the workers of the inherent health risks of uranium mining or provide compensation to the workers and their families for the deaths and illnesses of the uranium workers. Because of a lack of risk notification, workers could not make decisions regarding their behaviors at the worksite. The government also did not address ecological damage created by the industry, which resulted in further health hazards. Moreover, workers brought home their soiled work-clothes and were worried about radiation contamination of their families (U.S. Senate, 1990). The study results also indicated that a majority of miners had lung cancer, other types of cancer, and nonmalignant respiratory diseases (NMRD), and those who were not ill indicated how worried they were about being the next to contract an illness. Until the 1980s there were no uranium education programs directed toward miners on the largely rural reservation, and many workers did not understand the relationship between lung cancer and other illnesses and their employment.

Uranium millworker studies

The uranium millworkers were not studied as intensely as the miners. It was believed that underground mining, in general, was more hazardous because of the closed conditions of the underground mines and the resulting high levels of radon gas exposure. The millwork process did involve exposure to uranium ore and yellowcake dust (uranium concentrate). There were two comprehensive epidemiologic studies that involved non-Indian participants (Archer, Wagoner & Lundin, 1973; Waxweiler *et al.*, 1983). The Archer *et al.*, (1973) study found a significant excess of cancer of lymphatic and hematopoietic tissue and Waxweiler *et al.*, (1983) found excesses of certain nonmalignant respiratory diseases (NMRD). The hearings for the 1990 proposed RECA bill focused on the underground uranium miners and largely ignored the millworkers, even though these studies were published well before the hearings. After testifying at the miners' hearing, a group of millworkers approached Susan about conducting a millworkers' study, since they were excluded from the proposed RECA legislation. At that time only underground uranium miners, Nevada Test Site (NTS) workers, and atomic downwinders (people exposed to Nevada's atomic testing) were being considered for compensation. Gary had participated as a photographer during some of the mining interviews and was shocked by the plight of the Navajo workers and their families. Working together in 1990, we received funding to study millworkers on the Colorado Plateau.

This study involved 170 workers including Indian (mostly Navajo) and non-Indian millers (Dawson, Madsen & Spykerman, 1997; Madsen, Dawson & Spykerman, 1996). The results paralleled those of the miners'. Most of the millworkers had never been warned about radiation hazards at work. A majority identified working in areas containing high amounts of ore dust or yellowcake dust at some point in their employment. The most often reported health problems were respiratory symptoms or diseases. Many former workers reported emotional stress, including anxiety and depression, concerning present or future work-related health problems. We supplied key activists with these study reports which they passed on to former millworkers whom they had identified. The dissemination of this information led to invitations to testify in 1995 before The President's (W. J. Clinton) Advisory Committee on Human Radiation Experiments and twice in 1998 before congressional committees about the possible inclusion of the millworkers in RECA.

We will now discuss the Radiation Exposure Compensation Act (RECA), its Amendments of 2000, and the Energy Employees Occupational Illness Compensation Program Act (EEOICPA) of 2000. Within this context, we will identify some of the major inadequacies of the programs and how they were addressed or not addressed by Congress.

RECA 1990

Congress passed RECA in 1990 and the Department of Justice (DOJ) was charged with administering the program. The Act provided a one-time compassionate payment of $50,000 for individuals living "downwind" from nuclear fallout, $75,000 for the workers who participated in the Nevada Test Site (NTS) aboveground nuclear weapons tests, and $100,000 for underground uranium miners. The compensable diseases for underground uranium miners included primary lung cancer and certain nonmalignant respiratory diseases (NMRD). RECA required that workers had been employed between 1947 and 1971 in Arizona, Colorado, New Mexico, Utah, or Wyoming.

The majority of claimants were soon aware that the requirements for compensation were so stringent that they could not meet the criteria for eligibility. Native American workers made up a significant number of the claimants. Some of the major impediments to receiving compensation were especially onerous to these Native American groups. For example, traditional marriage ceremonies were not recognized as legal proofs of marriage for miners' widows. Other blocks to compensation included the requirement to produce original birth and death certificates.

For Indian and non-Indian claimants, even meeting the minimum exposure requirements was difficult. Often claimants and many companies did not have copies of employment records because companies were out of business by the time claimants needed both employment and exposure documentation. Also, medical records had to be officially certified and in their original forms. Claimants generally had only copies of these records, and this again created major delays in the application process. Regarding diagnosis of compensable illnesses, the majority of the claimants lived in rural areas, including Indian reservations, which had neither health specialists nor adequate screening facilities for diagnostic testing. Eventually many of these obstructions to compensation were addressed through administrative orders prior to the 2000 Amendments.

A claimant also had to establish certain levels of radiation exposure to be compensated; however, the exposure criteria were significantly higher than established by previous scientific studies. The requirements were also different for those who smoked cigarettes compared with those who did not smoke; even though it was also known that radiation exposures caused lung cancer regardless of smoking behavior. The standard measurement for radiation exposure is called the working level (wl) and cumulative exposures are identified as cumulative working level months (cwlm). If a worker is exposed to 1 wlm for a year, this would result in a cumulative exposure of 12 cwlm. The minimum cumulative exposure requirement was identified as 200 cwlm for nonsmokers, 300 cwlm for smokers up to age 45, and 500 cwlm for smokers after age 45. This high level of cumulative exposure was demanded, even though research published in 1987 found that mine workers receiving only 120 cwlm exposure over their careers had more than a doubling of risk of death from lung cancer (Hornung & Meinhardt, 1987).

RECA Amendments of 2000

In 2000 the Amendments to the Act (RECA) were passed, addressing many of the deficiencies of the 1990 legislation. For the miners, the states were expanded to include Idaho, North Dakota, Oregon, South Dakota, Texas, and Washington. The occupational categories were enlarged also to include uranium millworkers, open-pit (surface) miners, and ore transporters. For the uranium miners, they must have been employed at least one year at some time between 1942 through 1971, or had an exposure level of at least 40 cwlm during that same time period. These requirements were consistent with research results that kept finding lower and lower cumulative exposures still resulting in elevated levels of illnesses (National Cancer Institute, 1997). Regarding the millworkers and ore transporters, they were required to have worked a minimum of one year during the same time period. Disease categories for millworkers and ore transporters include primary lung cancer and renal cancer, certain NMRDs, and other chronic renal diseases. As with the 1990 legislation, the 2000 Amendments exempted workers who were employed after 1971. This date was tied to the end-date of the federal uranium procurement program. In addition, since the federal exposure standard for miners was set at 4 wlm/yr by the Environmental Protection Agency (EPA) in 1971, many policymakers believed these standards provided adequate safety, even though the research literature indicated otherwise (National Institute for Occupational Safety and Health, 1980).

Currently, downwinders and onsite test participants qualify for RECA if they have one of several types of cancers. Fallout victims need to have lived in certain counties in Arizona,

Nevada, and Utah for at least two years from 1951 to 1958 or during 1962 to be eligible. Onsite test participants must have been present during the detonation of an atmospheric nuclear device and within the official boundaries of the following test sites: Nevada, Pacific, Trinity, or the South Atlantic. *EEOICPA 2000* A companion act to RECA for those in the uranium industry is the Department of Labor's (DOL) Energy Employees Occupational Illness Compensation Program Act (EEOICPA). It was passed in 2000, originally under the Department of Energy (DOE), and providing payment of $150,000 and medical expenses to uranium industry workers and their survivors who qualify for compensation. A further extension of the program, passed in 2004, compensates and pays medical expenses for qualified employees of DOE contractors and subcontractors. The DOE workers needed to have been exposed to beryllium, silica or radiation and have contracted certain diseases, including cancer, chronic beryllium disease (CBD), chronic silicosis, and beryllium sensitivity (medical benefits only).

Workers also needed to have been employed in one of 362 DOE-covered facilities, which is considered a work in progress and updated twice a year. Nuclear workers, for example, employed at the NTS from 1951 to the present are one of the most recent groups able to qualify for both RECA and EEOICPA, since the NTS was added recently to the facilities list. In addition, uranium miners, millworkers, ore transporters, or eligible survivors who qualify under RECA could also receive an additional $50,000 lump sum payment and medical benefits under EEOICPA.

The atomic downwinders who have received the $50,000 RECA payment are ineligible for EEOICPA. This is the only group ineligible for additional compensation and medical benefits under the program. Another issue concerning RECA and the downwinders involves geographic designation of fallout exposure. A 1997 National Cancer Institute (NCI) study identified certain counties in Colorado, Idaho, Montana, South Dakota, and Utah as having the highest per capita thyroid doses from the NTS's nuclear tests (National Cancer Institute, 1997). Grassroots activists are now advocating that RECA broaden the geographic regions for compensation based upon this study.

Organizations

In this section we will present advocacy groups and governmental agencies associated with the RECA and EEOICPA programs beginning with the pre-RECA era in which activists sought redress legislation and ending with those presently involved with modifying or implementing these two programs. A timeline for advocacy groups and legislation is presented in Figure 31.1 on page 368.

Advocacy groups

In the 1980s one of the first support groups for underground uranium miners emerged among the Navajo, whose activists worked early on to educate and organize uranium workers and their families. In 1984 the Uranium Radiation Victims' Committee (URVC) was formally organized in Red Valley, Arizona. Before it was created, it was a small grassroots group of Navajo miners and their widows. Another group, the Mexican Water Uranium Committee, was also created in 1985. Both of these groups were instrumental in advocating for RECA and for disseminating information across the Navajo Nation at chapter houses (governmental units). It was common for several hundred people to attend these meetings, which updated participants on the proposed RECA legislation and upcoming events. The Red Valley group also developed a uranium worker registry which eventually became the Office of Navajo Uranium

Pre-RECA Atomic Downwinders Groups

    1978 Utah Citizen's Call

    1980 Downwinders

Pre-RECA Miners' Groups

    1984 Uranium Radiation Victims Committee (URVC)

    1985 Mexican Water Uranium Committee

1990 Radiation Exposure Compensation Act (RECA)

    RECA Reform Groups 1992 Four Corners' Millers Association 1992 Western Navajo

    Agency Millers 1999 Dependents of Uranium Workers 1999 Western States

    RECA Reform Working Group

2000 Energy Employees Occupational Illness Compensation Program Act (EEOICPA)

    EEOICPA Reform Group 2003 Alliance of Nuclear Worker Advocacy Groups (ANWAG)

2000 [RECA] Amendments Act

    Amendments Reform Group 2007 Post-'71 Uranium Workers Committee

Figure 31.1 Radiation compensation advocacy timeline*.
* This timeline does not include all advocacy groups.

Workers (ONUW) at the Indian Health Service (IHS) hospital in Shiprock, New Mexico. The Red Valley area, which included Cove, Arizona, on the Navajo Nation had been impacted greatly by uranium mining and the miners from there had significant health problems. An early organizer, Michael Begay from Cove, worked to assemble a group from the Red Valley/ Cove area which was populated by a growing number of miners' widows. The ONUW was grassroots-initiated and eventually supported by both tribal and State of New Mexico funds (Charley *et al.*, 2004). At the same time, atomic downwinder groups, such as Citizen's Call and Downwinders, were involved with advocacy on behalf of their members. Utah's Citizen's Call was organized in 1978 in southern Utah for downwind victims of fallout by Janet Gordon, Mary Lou Milberg, Preston Truman, and Elisabeth Bruhn Wight. The Downwinders, formed in Salt Lake City, Utah in 1980 by Preston Truman, was a concerned citizens' group about the new generation of nuclear weapons.

After RECA was passed in 1990, two Navajo millworker support groups were formed around 1992: the Four Corners' Millers Association of Shiprock, New Mexico, which assisted millworkers and their families from the Northern Navajo Agency, and the Western Navajo Agency Millers of Tonalea, Arizona, which assisted people in Tuba City and nearby areas. Another support group, the Dependents of Uranium Workers (NNDUW) was organized in 1999 to assist with information about uranium impacts community-wide. The group developed a needs assessment survey of family members and health status. Other groups have formed and disbanded, including the Western States RECA Reform Working Group, a coalition of smaller reform groups formed in 1999. It disbanded after the passage of the 2000 Amendments, though many of its grassroots groups are still in existence, e.g., Diné Care, Eastern Navajo Uranium Workers, and Utah Navajo Downwinders.

These groups were instrumental in rural community organizing around RECA and carried over to advocate for the passage of the 2000 Amendments. Activists on the Navajo Nation, including such people as Timothy Benally, Perry Charley, Phil Harrison, and many others, traveled often to Washington, D.C., to testify and worked tirelessly with workers and their families, legislators and scientists to pass RECA. In our research, we found that the Navajo uranium workers and activists established a tightly-knit grassroots effort in support of the legislation. In addition, their clan-based, matrilineal, group-oriented culture supported a collectivist orientation not often found in Anglo communities. Off the reservation, Anglos tended to support a more individualistic orientation often blaming themselves for not taking precautions against radiation on-the-job, even though they had not been informed about the hazardous conditions.

More recently, the Post-71 Uranium Workers' Committee grassroots group, formed in 2007, is centered in the Grants, New Mexico area. It is their contention that they should also be included in RECA and EEOICPA. It was during the 1970s and 1980s that several hundred women production workers were hired as miners, millworkers, and ore transporters (Madsen *et al.*, 1999). Many of them are now active in this advocacy group. They have an online survey for workers which, to date, has included more than 1,100 participants. In addition, the Alliance of Nuclear Advocacy Groups (ANWAG) was created in 2003 to monitor the implementation of EEOICPA. This coalition of people, who are referred to as the "sick worker advocacy groups," includes activists from such diverse states as California, Colorado, Illinois, New Mexico, and Tennessee.

Government Compensation Agencies

Regarding health monitoring, workers who are applying for RECA may receive medical services at one of the five Radiation Exposure Screening & Education Program (RESEP) clinics in Arizona, Colorado, New Mexico, Nevada, and Utah. RESEP was created under the 2000 Amendments to RECA to award grants to health care providers in the 12 states most affected by the nuclear weapons industry, including Arizona, Colorado, Idaho, Nevada, New Mexico, North Dakota, Oregon, South Dakota, Texas, Utah, Washington, and Wyoming. These clinics are funded through the Health Resources and Services Administration (HRSA) and apply to downwinders, onsite participants, uranium miners, millers, and ore transporters, helping to establish eligibility for RECA. The National Institute for Occupational Safety and Health (NIOSH) also conducts dose reconstruction for workers and their survivors eligible for the EEOICPA program. To apply for either RECA or EEOICPA, claimants may access forms from the Department of Justice (DOJ), the Department of Labor (DOL), and RESEP clinics (see Resource section for information).

Description of the client situation

It is unknown how many people were exposed to radiation at work or through nuclear testing; however, we can identify the client base for the RECA and EEOICPA compensation programs. As of 31 October 2008, the following claimants were approved: downwinders (12,604), onsite (testsite) participants (1,251), miners (4,947), millworkers (1,183), and ore transporters (243) for a total of 20,228. The total value of approved claims is $1,356,119,396. (U.S. Department of Justice, 2008).

The EEOICPA website does not list the occupational categories of claimants (U.S. Department of Labor, 2008). However, the amount of approved claims for compensation and medical benefits as of 28 October 2008 is $4,294,029,529. There are two categories of general claimants in the program referred to as cases and claims. *Cases* refer to employees only and *claims* refer to these same employees who may have one or more claims plus family survivor benefits. The first category includes 33,748 employees who have been paid compensation, and the second includes 45,615 total claims (U.S. Department of Labor, 2008). When compensation payments for RECA and EEOICPA are combined, the result is more than $5.6 billion.

Differential discussion

One of the problems that has developed between the RECA compensation program beneficiaries and the EEOICPA program is lack of notification about program eligibility. For instance, if a millworker has received compensation from RECA, s/he is then eligible for compensation under EEOICPA. Due to confidentiality restrictions under RECA, the beneficiaries' names may not be supplied to the EEOICPA program. Therefore, the EEOICPA has established an outreach program in which public meetings are held in communities known to have uranium workers.

We suggest that one way to further facilitate such an outreach program is to create a social network analysis and map, resulting in a list of people representing organizations who would likely network with claimants and beneficiaries, e.g. activists, attorneys, physicians, etc. Social network analysis examines social relations among a set of actors, focusing on relationships between the actors. Social workers, in using a network map, could play an important role in notifying community key individuals who are associated with these compensation programs. The network map identifies key players, key players' contacts, and the flow of information among them all.

Using a snowball technique, first key informants in a community are identified for their expertise in compensation activities. They are then contacted and asked to identify their contacts, about whom they share information concerning compensation programs. The network then snowballs as contacts are interviewed and each one provides their contact names. The resulting network map, which could be composed of such contacts as activists, lawyers, medical personnel, and social workers, is then a list of inter-connected persons who are involved in compensation issues in the community. This map allows for a broad coverage of possible contacts within the community who may identify and notify future claimants. *UCINET for Windows, Version 6: Software for Social Network Analysis* creates the network map which provides an overall view of network ties and the strength and density of network relationships (Borgatti, Everett & Freeman, 2002).

Given the complexity of the application process for these compensation programs, it is important for practitioners to be aware of the latest developments in each program. For example, up until July 2008 the EEOICPA DOE Facilities List of 362 facilities did not include the Nevada Test Site (NTS). While workers could apply for RECA, they were ineligible for the extra benefits under EEOICPA; however, given the recent listing of their facility, they may apply now. These workers are not notified directly about facilities list updates by the DOL because of RECA confidentiality provisions. The main avenue for them to learn about the list is to know about it themselves, through other workers, DOJ/RECA program, DOL outreach programs, or other informed professionals.

Present uranium resurgence and recommendations

Uranium mining and processing came to a virtual standstill by 1990 when the price of uranium declined to $7/pound and there were significant stockpiles available. Recently, however, the price of uranium spiked to $140/pound before dropping off to current levels of less than $80/pound. The surge is largely attributed to the global demand for nuclear power plants in the face of global warming (Dubner, 2008). In the United States, there is an intensive effort in the Southwest to open up uranium mining and milling to meet this demand. The Navajo Nation Tribal Council has already banned uranium mining and processing on the reservation because of their concerns about future health problems. Western states, however, are currently in negotiations with uranium companies to develop mining sites and processing mills.

In response to the demand for uranium production, we have several concerns and recommendations for people associated with present and future uranium workers, downwinders, and their families. It is important that workers and downwinders hire attorneys or access government agencies where there are experts in the area of radiation compensation. Because of the difficulty in applying to RECA and EEOICPA, it is paramount that claimants do not employ attorneys or other professionals unfamiliar with these programs.

Given the past history of the uranium industry and its attendant health problems, we anticipate future health issues among workers and citizens living in close proximity to uranium sites. A second generation of activists and advocates will need to understand this past history of exposures and illnesses and to monitor the upcoming uranium industry. It will also be important to be vigilant regarding future compensation legislation to ensure that future workers and their families are given due consideration. Because there have been few large-scale studies of communities in close proximity to uranium mining and milling sites, we recommend that further studies in uranium-impacted communities be conducted.

Regarding uranium workers and future employment in the industry, all new employees need to be screened and monitored regularly for radiation dosages and any health problems. Health screenings provide worker baselines that are instrumental in determining compensation eligibility. Uranium workers and their families also need to keep copies of all employment and medical records, including chest x-ray films if taken, and original birth and death certificates. Complete documentation of work and health histories proves useful in expediting any cases brought before RECA and EEOICPA. In addition, people working with claimants and beneficiaries need to be aware of uranium activist groups that monitor government compensation agencies and inform workers and their families about key compensation issues.

In conclusion, the history of the uranium industry reveals the slow response of government regulatory agencies to scientific studies that documented radiation-related exposures and illnesses. This impeded the development of health and safety standards. It also demonstrates the importance of grassroots efforts on the part of uranium workers, downwinders, their families, activists, and professionals to establish the need for redress and the passage and eventual modification of compensation legislation. For social work practitioners, there are important implications for practice regarding advocacy and activism on behalf of their clients who may be eligible for compensation. The uranium industry's resurgence indicates that there will be future waves of possible claimants and their survivors. Maintaining vigilance regarding radiation compensation legislation, regulatory agencies, and compensation programs is paramount to best assist uranium workers, downwinders, and their families.

References

Advisory Committee on Human Radiation Experiments (ACHRE). (1996). *The human radiation experiments: Final report of the President's Advisory Committee.* New York: Oxford University Press.

Archer, V. E. (1983). Diseases of uranium miners. In Rom, W. M. (ed.), *Environmental and occupational medicine* (pp. 687–91). Boston: Little, Brown.

Archer, V. E., Wagoner, J. K. & Lundin, F. E. (1973). Cancer mortality among uranium mill workers. *Journal of Occupational Medicine*, 15 (1): 11–14.

Borgatti, S., Everett, M. & Freeman, L. (2002) *UCINET 6 for Windows: Software for social network analysis*. Harvard: Analytic Technologies.

Charley, P. H., Dawson, S. E., Madsen, G. E. & Spykerman, B. R. (2004). Navajo uranium education programs: The search for environmental justice. *Applied Environmental Education and Communication*, 3: 101–8.

Dawson, S. E. (1992). Navajo uranium workers and the effects of occupational illnesses: A case study. *Human Organization*, 51 (4): 389–97.

Dawson, S. E., Madsen, G. E. & Spykerman, B. R. (1997). Public health issues concerning American Indian and non-Indian uranium millworkers. *Journal of Health and Social Policy*, 8 (3): 41–56.

Dubner, S. J. (2008). Why did the price of uranium skyrocket? *New York Times*. 24 March 2008. Retrieved 3/8/09: http://freakonomics.blogs.nytimes.com/2008/03/24/why-did-the-price

Hornung, R. W. & Meinhardt, T. J. (1987). Quantitative risk assessment of lung cancer in U.S. uranium miners. *Health Physics*, 52 (4): 417–30.

Madsen, G. E., Dawson, S. E. & Spykerman, B. R. (1996). Perceived occupational and environmental exposures: A case study of former uranium millworkers. *Environment and Behavior*, 28 (5): 571–90.

Madsen, G. E., Dawson, S. E., Spykerman, B. R., Coons, T. A. & Gilliland, F. D. (1999). Women uranium workers: A case study of perceived hazardous exposures and health effects. *New Solutions: A Journal of Environmental and Occupational Health Policy*, 9 (2): 179–94.

National Cancer Institute (NCI). National Institutes of Health (NIH). (1997). *Estimated exposures and thyroid doses received by the American People from Iodine 131 in fallout following Nevada atmospheric nuclear bomb tests*. Washington, DC: GPO.

National Institutes of Health (NIH). (1994). *Radon and lung cancer risk: A joint analysis of 11 underground miners studies*. NIH Publication No. 94–3644, January 1994, Washington, DC: U.S. Department of Health and Human Services, Public Health Service, National Institutes of Health.

National Institute for Occupational Safety and Health (NIOSH). (1980). *The risk of lung cancer among underground miners of uranium-bearing ores*. NIOSH Study Group Report. 30 June 1980. Unpublished report.

U.S. Department of Justice (DOJ). (2008). *Radiation Exposure Compensation System. Claims to Date Summary of Claims Received by 10/30/2008. All Claims*, page 1. Retrieved 10/31/08: http://www.usdoj.gov/civil/torts/const/reca/

U.S. Department of Labor (DOL). (2008). *EEOICP Program Statistics. Data as of 10/28/2008*. Retrieved 10/31/08: http://www.dol.gov/esa/owcp/energy/regs/compliance/weeklystats.htm

U.S. Senate. (1990). 101 Congress, Second Session, on the Impacts of Past Uranium Mining Practices. Hearing before the Subcommittee on Mineral Resources Development and Production of the Committee on Energy and Natural Resources. (13 March 1990). Congressional Field Hearing. *Mental health effects on uranium workers from radiation exposure during uranium mining*, pp. 147–57. Shiprock, New Mexico. Washington: USGPO.

Waxweiler, R. J., Archer, V. E., Roscoe, R. J., Watanabe, A., and Thun, M. J. (1983). *Mortality patterns among a retrospective cohort of uranium mill workers*. Proceedings of the Sixteenth Midyear Topical Meeting of the Health Physics Society, Inhalation Toxicology Research Institute, 428–35.

Government compensation resources

Energy Employees Occupational Illness Compensation Program Facilities List http://www.hss.energy.gov/HealthSafety/fwsp/Advocacy/faclist/showfacility.cfm [This website lists all 362 DOE-covered facilities for EEOICPA.]

National Institute for Occupational Safety and Health (NIOSH) Office of Compensation Analysis and Support 4676 Columbia Parkway Cincinnati, OH 45226 Mailstop C46 877-222-7570 www.cdc.gov/niosh/ocas

Radiation Exposure Screening and Education Program Clinics (RESEP) Health Resources and

Services Administration (HRSA) 5600 Fishers Lane Rockville, M.D. 20857 888-ASK-HRSA http://ruralhealth.hrsa.gov/radiationexposure/default/htm

Department of Justice Radiation Exposure Compensation Program (RECA) PO Box 146 Ben Franklin Station Washington, DC 20044-0146 800-729-7327 www.usdoj.gov

Department of Labor Office of Workers' Compensation Programs (OWCP) Energy Employees Occupational Illness Compensation Program (EEOICPA) Frances Perkins Building 200 Constitution Avenue, NW Washington, DC 20210 866-888-3322 www.dol.gov/esa

32 Fighting cancer in India

Implementing cancer control strategies at a national level

Navami Naik

Context

Cancer is a leading cause of death globally. The World Health Organization estimates 7.6 million people died from cancer in 2005 and 84 million people will die in the next 10 years if action is not taken. More than 70% of all cancer deaths occur in low- and middle-income countries, where resources available for prevention, diagnosis and treatment of cancer are limited or nonexistent (WHO, 2006).

Organizations based in the U.S. with long histories of working in cancer control realize cancer is a global health problem and if they want to help eradicate this problem, they need to implement their programs on a global scale rather than just focusing on the United States. At a press conference held at the American Cancer Society Center in December 2008, leaders from the American Cancer Society, Susan G. Komen for the Cure, and the Lance Armstrong Foundation announced they would team up with the International Agency for Research on Cancer (IARC) and the National Cancer Institute of Mexico to focus attention on the growing international cancer problem. According to the IARC's World Cancer Report, also unveiled at the briefing, while cancer death rates and incidence are dropping in the U.S., global cancer incidence rates are expected to climb about 1% each year with larger increases in China, Russia, and India. Given that many large U.S.-based businesses now have their offshore operations in India and that Asian Indians continue to account for a large number of the immigrant population in this country, the non-profit I work for has made India a country of focus in its cancer control activities.

There are an estimated 2.5 million cases of cancer in India at any given time (National Cancer Registry Programme, 2006). Nearly 800,000 cases were diagnosed in the year 2000 with 550,000 deaths due to cancer. Tobacco-related cancers account for almost a third of cancers diagnosed in head, neck, lung and esophagus. Cancers of the breast and cervix are the two most common for women and account for half the cancer burden in Indian women. The heavy cancer toll is due to the fact that 70% present in clinically advanced stages T3–T4 with catastrophic impact (Dinshaw, 2002).

No wonder, then, that the diagnosis of cancer is viewed almost as a death sentence by patients in India. Interviews conducted by this author with cancer patients in India revealed that all were overwhelmed when first diagnosed, which led to severe anxiety and depression. Many had not told parents or partners of the diagnosis until hospitalization became inevitable. Almost none had told their extended family of their diagnosis. Interviews with caregivers revealed that cancer impacts not only the patient but also his family. Taking care of the patient, loss of income associated with an advanced stage patient, and accompanying the patient to distant medical facilities for cancer treatment often drains families' physical, emotional and financial resources.

Policy

The primary objectives of India's National Cancer Control Programme, begun in 1975–6, are: (1) primary prevention through education about the hazards of tobacco consumption and the importance of genital hygiene for prevention of cervical cancer, (2) secondary prevention by early detection and diagnosis of cancers, (3) strengthening existing cancer treatment facilities, and (4) offering palliative care in terminal stages (Joranson, Rajagopal & Gilson, 2002; Rao, Gupta & Agarwal, 2002). In the past decade, India has issued two important policy statements regarding tobacco control. Signed into law in 2003, the India Tobacco Control Act (ITCA) has the goal of reducing tobacco consumption and protecting citizens from exposure to second-hand smoke. In 2005, India ratified the World Health Organization Framework Convention on Tobacco Control and in this same period conducted the Global Youth Tobacco Survey (GYTS) in an effort to track tobacco use among adolescents.

The India Tobacco Control Act includes provisions prohibiting smoking in public places, direct or indirect advertisement of cigarettes and other tobacco products on billboards and in all media excluding point of sale; the sale of tobacco products to minors (less than 18 years of age), and within a radius of 100 yards of any educational institution. Currently, the Government is finalizing rules regarding placing specified health warning labels on all tobacco product packaging, including details of the nicotine and tar content (Reddy & Gupta, 2009; Sinha *et al.*, 2008). While the Act is definitely a step in the right direction, the public is often unaware of the provisions, and thus does not demand proper implementation. Therefore, one task on which we concentrate is to spread awareness about both the harmful effects of tobacco and provisions of the Act.

Cancer Control: Knowledge into Action, WHO Guide for Effective Programmes (2006) is a series of six modules that provides practical advice for program managers and policy-makers on how to advocate, plan and implement effective cancer control programs, particularly in low- and middle-income countries. In response to the World Health Assembly resolution on cancer prevention and control, adopted in May 2005, the guide calls on member states to intensify action against cancer by developing and reinforcing cancer control programs. It builds on various WHO policies that have influenced efforts to control cancer.

The guide indicates that: (1) prevention of cancer integrated with the prevention of chronic diseases and other related issues offers the greatest public health potential and the most cost-effective long-term method of cancer control, and (2) early detection detects the disease at an early stage when it has a high potential for cure (the two strategies for early detection are: early diagnosis, involving patient's awareness of early signs and symptoms leading to a consultation with a health provider—who then promptly refers the patient for confirmation of diagnosis and treatment—and national and regional screening of asymptomatic and apparently healthy individuals to detect pre-cancerous lesions or an early stage of cancer, and to arrange referral for diagnosis and treatment), (3) treatment aims to cure disease, prolong life, and improve the quality of remaining life after the diagnosis of cancer is confirmed by the appropriate available procedures, and (4) palliative care meets the needs of all patients requiring relief from symptoms and psychological and supportive care, particularly those with advanced stages who have a very low chance of being cured or who are facing the terminal phase of the disease (WHO, 2006). We used this guide as a framework for planning our program in India.

Technology

When an organization based in the U.S. wants to implement cancer control measures in a country thousands of miles away, there has to be a strong reliance on basic technology. You need the telephone to organize frequent teleconferences for keeping your partners on the ground engaged, computers to maintain databases of all your contacts in the country, the internet to research trends in that country and to email your in-country advisors, your partners, and other key stakeholders, and airplanes to be able to travel to and within the country as you conduct various program planning, monitoring, and evaluation visits. Successful efforts require that the media spread awareness about cancer, its risk factors, prevention, and early detection.

Another sort of technology is the established guidelines we use to formulate, implement and evaluate a cancer control plan. In its guide for effective programs, WHO advocates a stepwise approach for planning and implementing interventions for cancer control, based on local considerations and needs. The planning steps include asking:

1 Where are we now? Investigate the present state of the cancer problem, and cancer control services or programs.
2 Where do we want to be? Formulate and adopt policy. This includes defining the target population, setting goals and objectives, and deciding on priority interventions across the cancer continuum.
3 How do we get there? The planning phase is followed by the implementation phase in which the steps needed to implement the policy are identified in relation to core (implement interventions in the policy that are feasible now, with existing resources), expanded (implement interventions in the policy that are feasible in the medium term, with a realistically projected increase in, or reallocation of, resources) and desirable (implement interventions in the policy that are beyond the reach of current resources, if and when such resources become available) possibilities (WHO, 2006).

Organization

The non-profit I work for is a U.S.-based voluntary health organization with over 50 years of experience. It is dedicated to eliminating cancer as a major health problem by educating people on the need for prevention and early detection measures, having programs in place to help diminish suffering from cancer, funding research to find a cure, and advocating for laws that will help eliminate cancer. The India program is one among many international efforts undertaken by this organization. Its international mission concentrates on capacity building in developing cancer societies through collaboration with other cancer-related organizations. A key strength of this organization is providing information to cancer patients and their caregivers about cancer and about various resources available to cancer patients and their caregivers.

Description of the client situation

In India, 21 Regional Cancer Centers (RCCs) have been established under the National Cancer Control Programme. Cancer care facilities are also available in a number of medical colleges and some private and charitable hospitals in the country. The program however has mainly contributed to the development of radiation oncology services rather than making any headway in the direction of prevention and early detection (Dinshaw, Shastri & Patil, 2005).

As per a 2008 report submitted to the Government of India by the National Cancer Control Task Force, there is no uniform cancer prevention strategy for the entire country. Awareness programs have been undertaken in a few places, but there is no uniform standardized Information, Education and Communication (IEC) strategy for cancer prevention. There is no education on risk factors, early warning signals and their management. Cancer screening is not practiced in an organized fashion in any part of India. There are sporadic attempts at opportunistic interventions and small-scale research studies for field interventions.

In this situation, the client is all those people in India who have been diagnosed with cancer, as well as those people who are at potential risk of developing cancer, and their caregivers. As per the WHO guideline, a public health expert was engaged to investigate the present state of the cancer problem and cancer control services or programs in the country. The report submitted by this expert stated that nearly 150 non-government organizations (NGOs) in the country offer awareness and early detection, treatment and care, rehabilitation and terminal care (Sanyal, 2005). However, the distribution is not even across the states. A majority of these organizations are run by cancer survivors or those families who have lost a loved one to cancer. While they may have fine intentions, they often lack non-profit management or fundraising skills. It was felt that their efforts could be optimized by strong central leadership and capacity building.

The private medical sector remains the primary source of health care for the majority of households in both urban areas and rural areas (Ministry of Health & Family Welfare, 2007). Many treatment facilities for cancer are run by the private sector; however, private treatment is expensive and unaffordable for most. Private facilities also have a regional imbalance just like government facilities. Supportive and palliative care is absent, except for a few states, which is a concern because more than 80% of patients come to hospitals with late-stage cancers. Around one million patients with cancer are in need of palliative care. Morphine is a highly controlled commodity in India (Sharma, 2008). Major barriers to access opioids are complicated regulations and problems related to attitude and knowledge regarding pain relief from opioids among professionals and the public (Rajagopal, Joranson & Gilson, 2001; Rajagopal & Joranson, 2007). Also, tobacco use in India is a much greater public health challenge compared with other countries, due to the many variations in which tobacco is consumed. This includes smoking (such as bidis and cigarettes), smokeless forms (such as gutkha and mawa for chewing), and direct application of tobacco (e.g., Mishri) (Arora, Reddy, Stigler & Perry, 2008). According to the WHO- and CDC-supported Global Youth Tobacco Survey (GYTS), prevalence of tobacco use among 13–15-year age group school students in 2000–4 was 17.5% in some form, the rates being much higher in north-eastern states.

During my travels to India and my visits to the RCCS, the one thing that kept hitting me again and again is the late presentation of the disease. The lack of awareness about cancer as a disease and its symptoms, and the many myths surrounding the disease and its treatment, mean most patients wait until the suffering gets unbearable before going to the doctor. This results in a majority of the cancer patients being diagnosed at a stage when it is too late for any effective treatment. Given the lack of palliative care services, these patients then have to live without hope and die after a lot of suffering. When I saw the level of awareness in the U.S. and how this has resulted in cancer being caught earlier and people surviving longer, the high number of deaths in India was very hard for me to accept.

Decisions about practice

Definition of the client

Cancer control aims to reduce the incidence, morbidity and mortality of cancer and to improve the quality of life of cancer patients in a defined population through systemic implementation of evidence-based interventions for prevention, early detection, diagnosis, treatment and palliative care. Comprehensive cancer control addresses the whole population, while seeking to respond to the needs of the different subgroups at risk (WHO, 2006). In this case, the client is ultimately all those people in India who have been diagnosed with cancer or are at potential risk, and their families and caregivers. With a population of over one billion people, it is not possible to provide direct services to all those affected by cancer. Also, given that the situation in the U.S. varies greatly from India in terms of the awareness, incidence, treatment, and post treatment, it is not possible to take a successful program from the U.S. and transport it to India in the same format. Additionally, given the fact that almost every state in India has its own language, culture, customs and norms, it is neither possible, nor feasible to have a standardized intervention for all states. Often, the best way of making an impact in situations such as this is to partner with local organizations. The difficult part is going into a country that is culturally different from the country of operations with a completely different medical structure and to identify potential partners who are transparent in their dealings and sincere in their efforts.

Goals

As described earlier, India has a number of NGOs dedicated to fighting cancer. It was decided to offer representatives of leading NGOs some training in areas that would benefit them in their work. At the end of the training, the participating organizations would be asked to submit proposals for a small project that would help them implement something they had learned during the training. To be able to achieve the long-term goals of spreading awareness about cancer in India and promoting healthy lifestyles and early detection to downstage cancer, it is necessary to institute the short-term goal of providing NGOs in India with the technical know-how and the financial resources to implement cancer control measures. The hope was that the funding would enable organizations to undertake novel and experimental projects, that the experience they gained during the year-long funding would allow them to streamline the project with lessons learned, and also give them time to look for alternate sources of funding to carry on the project beyond the first year.

Developing objectives and contracting

1   Invitations were sent to leading NGOs throughout the country. NGOs from Kerala in south India, Lucknow in north India, Gujarat in western India and Assam in north-eastern India were all asked to send their representatives to the training. Additionally, NGOs from the key metropolises in the country such as Delhi, Kolkata, Mumbai and Chennai were also invited. Representatives from 30 leading NGOs participated in the week-long training provided in India's capital city. The curriculum was based on perceived gaps identified in the national profile submitted by the public health expert. The language of delivery was English, a language in which most educated people in urban India are

fluent. The topics for the curriculum were: Cancer Early Detection: Information on what constitutes early detection and early detection methods for the cancers that cause the highest mortality and morbidity—cervical, breast and oral (Okonkwo, Draisma, der Kinderen, Brown & de Koning, 2008). Participants were also trained in how to develop and implement early detection programs.

2 Cancer Pain Policy in India: Information on what is palliative care, how to treat pain, barriers to pain relief, the current Indian scenario and the role of strategic advocacy.

3 Patient Services: Training on how to help cancer patients, their families and caregivers to navigate the complex health system and identify financial and community resources.

4 Advocacy for creating smoke-free places: Training in working with the media to educate the public on the health hazards of secondhand smoke, creating smoke-free workplaces and public spaces through legal means and ensuring compliance with the laws.

5 Advocacy: Training in principles of advocacy, what are the steps in the advocacy process, how to develop a successful message, meeting with decision makers and using the media for advocacy.

6 Program planning: Training in the basics of activity planning, carrying out a SWOT analysis, clarifying the problem and identifying outcomes, outputs, activities and inputs, developing an activity program delivery plan, budgeting, monitoring and evaluation.

7 Organizational Strategic Planning: Preparation in the basics of planning, what is organizational strategic planning, who should be involved in it, what are the basic steps, articulating the organization's mission and vision, developing goals, strategies, objectives and a framework for planning programs, writing an operational plan, and developing a system for monitoring and evaluating the effectiveness of the plan.

8 As planned, participants were taught how to write project proposals and then were asked to submit one proposal each, based on one of the past week's areas of training. These proposals were carefully scrutinized by experts within the organization for scope, feasibility, clarity of expected outcome, and resources needed. A total of 12 proposals were selected, and seed funding ranging from $5,000 to $10,000 was provided to each of them, based on their need and scope. The funding was divided into two installments, with part of the funding to be paid after the contract was signed and the remaining amount to be released after we received a mid-term report from the grantees. A contract was drawn up with each organization stating that they would be expected to provide a mid-term report describing their progress towards meeting the objectives of their seed grant project, the unforeseen obstacles that they had encountered while executing their project, their plans for tackling those obstacles, and a brief description of how their project had contributed towards cancer control in India. They would also have to submit a monthly expense report outlining how the seed grant money had been utilized for the project. The NGOs would also be expected to submit a similar report at the end of their project with additional information on their plans for sustaining the project beyond the period covered by the seed grant. The NGOs were also assured that as the organization's manager for India programs based in the U.S., I would be available as a point person for them not only for regular check-ins and updates but also to ensure they received any technical assistance required from experts within the organization.

Meeting place

Given the nature of the program, it was far more economical and practical for me to visit each seed grant project. I visited each seed grant organization only once during its 12-month grant period, and I wanted to make the most of each visit. Therefore, it seemed best to visit the organizations once they had finished at least six months of their project to give them the time not only to implement the project but also begin to get a fair sense of the impact of their work. All grantees were expected to submit mid-term reports. Once these reports had been submitted, I planned a site visit with each organization to monitor whether programs were indeed being run as per the report and evaluate the progress on each project. I also requested that at each site visit, I would like to meet at least one person who had been directly impacted by the seed grant.

Use of time

My goal was to conduct all my site visits during my one visit to India. I caught the direct flight to Mumbai and then caught a domestic flight to the southern-most state in India to begin my site visits. Given the distances and how far-flung our grantees were, my schedule went mostly like this: arrive at night, meet with representatives of the NGO at breakfast to discuss their project, discuss their mid-term report, discuss their plans for overcoming potential hazards and outline the support and resources that they needed from me. Then we would proceed to where the project was being conducted. We would either tour the actual project or watch a presentation of activities conducted, followed by a meeting with the staff involved in the implementation of the project. This would be followed by meeting with people impacted by the project. During each visit, I was also trying to capture human interest stories that would assure the donors of the grants' impact when I reported on the project after returning to the U.S. I would be finished with all the meetings by late afternoon and would catch an evening flight to the next destination on my list to begin the same itinerary again in a different city with a different NGO.

I devoted more time to projects that had reported facing unforeseen difficulties in their mid-term reports, to help the grantees problem-solve and get a fair idea of additional supports or resources they would need. One grantee had reported spending less than a quarter of the initial grant installment. This was a matter of concern as we could not release the next installment. This grant was for conducting workshops on palliative care among doctors, nurses, medical students and the lay public. It turned out that this grantee had actually conducted more workshops than it had committed to in its proposal. However, staff there had encouraged each of the institutions where the workshops were organized to take part-responsibility for funding the workshop. Their reasoning was that this way they could organize more workshops with the grant amount, thus creating more awareness. I had to explain to them that the donors for this project expected their funding to be made use of in the period covered by the grant. I also helped facilitate a consultation with an expert in the field of palliative care in India, for possible suggestions on how best to use the remaining grant amount.

Despite the time constraints, I believe actually visiting each project and seeing our partners at work in their settings gave me a unique understanding of their strengths, weaknesses and sincerity, which I would not have been able to gain from only telephone and email contacts with them. What I saw everywhere were very committed, very sincere individuals who had managed to make an amazing impact while working with very few resources. One such site visit was to a hospice where I met a 24-year-old woman who had been diagnosed with very late-stage breast cancer. She had been abandoned by her husband and his family, as well as by her own family, and was essentially waiting to die far away from home, all alone. She said the staff at the hospice was her only family now.

Strategies and interventions

Due to the report submitted by the public health expert and through our own meetings with government officials and cancer control experts in India, we had a fair idea of the key issues around cancer control in India. So, while accepting proposals for seed grants, we had to be sure that the projects undertaken would tackle some of these issues. We divided them into three broad categories—palliative care, patient services and advocacy—and made sure that each of the grants given aimed at making an impact in at least one of these areas. So a grant was given to an NGO in Delhi that would educate children about the tobacco control law and the harmful effects of smoking and then use these children as advocates to ensure that hotels in the city implemented the ban on smoking in public places. Another project recruited volunteers from the community to help cancer patients navigate the medical system and help them identify available medical, community and financial resources. A third taught fourth-year medical students and nursing students about palliative care. Another funded nutritional supplements, headscarves, caps and activity kits for children affected with cancer. A fifth funded the position of a social worker and a palliative care nurse for a cancer hospital. Yet another funded training of voluntary health workers to educate women from lower socio-economic backgrounds on methods for prevention and early detection of breast and cervical cancer.

Stance of the social worker

I have had the experience of living in India for most of my life and of working there for 10 years. I also have sufficient experience living in the U.S. and working in an atmosphere of diligent paperwork, frequent meetings or conference calls to keep everyone on the same page, promoting knowledge-sharing and maintaining a transparency in all dealing. Work in India often happens at its own unique pace with its own unique style. I see myself as a resource person and support for our grantees in India and as a bridge between the two cultures. I do not want to be seen as a representative of an American organization who walks in and feels she knows better just because that organization has dollars to invest. However, I do have to make sure all deadlines are adhered to and all relevant paperwork is submitted well within deadlines. I am accountable to my supervisors and the donors, and it is expected that I also demand the same kind of accountability from our partners in India. This means I am often walking a tightrope between diplomacy and professionalism. For example, I feel that the concept of time is much more flexible in India than it is in the U.S. So, most of our grantees had to be sent two to three reminders that a report was overdue before I would actually receive the report. Unfortunately, that is perceived as a very lax professional standard in the U.S.

Managing a program in a country thousands of miles away from where you are based provides enough problems without the additional challenge of working in an economy in recession. The telephone and internet are big blessings. As the lead staff for our India programs, I used email and telephone calls to stay in touch with all our grantees at least once a month. In the fourth month of their project, the grantees were provided with templates for the mid-term reports. They were sent reminders one month before the reports were due, and there were frequent follow-ups with those organizations who had not submitted their reports by the due date. If the NGOs were facing any difficulties either in the implementation of their project or compilation of their report, I tried to provide them with resources from within our organization to help them problem-solve.

Use of resources outside the helping relationship

What we hope to do as an organization is to take the evidence-based programs and practices that we have successfully implemented here in the U.S. and adapt them in a culturally sensitive way for India. As we have a number of in-house experts on different programs and topics related to cancer care, we often consulted them on various aspects related to developing a cancer control program for India and for any subject-matter expertise needed by our grantees in India. We have also developed strong relationships with the government of India's health ministry, with the WHO staff in India working on cancer control and with several of the leaders in cancer control in India. These relationships have been extremely helpful in deciding the nature and scope of our program and for providing valuable insights and advice into our programs. Our grantees have also benefited from these relationships.

Reassessment and evaluation

The mid-term reports proved to be useful for evaluating the progress of the project, understanding what the problem areas were and how these could be tackled. A representative of the donor foundation accompanied me on most of the visits. We had already provided the donors with the mid-term reports and an agenda for the visit, including topics to be discussed, prior to each visit. Actually seeing the progress on each project and being able to evaluate the relationship between the grantees and our organization first-hand helped the donor identify with each program on an individual basis. After the site visits, a conference call was set up with representatives of the donor foundation, my supervisor and me to re-evaluate the progress on the projects. The donor foundation was satisfied with the progress on each of the projects to the point of wanting to continue funding several of the grantees for the next year.

Transfer and termination

Each of the seed grant projects was for 12 months. An email reminder with a template for their final grant report and expenses was sent to each of the grantees a month before the end of the grant period. For the final report, we stressed on the importance of two questions: "How would they quantitatively or qualitatively evaluate their projects?" and "What measures had they taken to ensure that the project was sustainable beyond the period covered by the grant?" Once the NGO submitted its final report, I sent them an acknowledgment of receipt stating that the report met the criteria and that they had been able to take some concrete steps in the fight against cancer through their seed grant project. I assured them that, although the grant period had come to an end, the grantees were welcome to reach out to us if they needed any technical input. I also made a point of sending them e-greetings during major Indian festivals and asked them to keep me informed about any new projects they have undertaken. What I hope to achieve from this is the smooth transfer of their role from that of a grantee to a partner in the fight against cancer in that region.

Case conclusion

Given the size and diversity of India, we decided that the best way to make an impact would be to empower organizations on the ground to implement cancer control measures in their regions. Each of the seed grant projects tackled different aspects of cancer control in India.

Grantees worked hard to make a difference within the limited resources they had and managed to achieve some incredible results.

One NGO has succeeded in getting its district declared as smoke-free, at another children's hospital I visited, a four-year-old girl's father told me with tears in his eyes how the activity kits kept his daughter occupied during the five-hour bus journey to reach her place of treatment. He smiled proudly as he said not only was his daughter benefitting from the treatment she received at the hospital but was also looking healthier, thanks to the nutritional supplement provided. A woman restaurateur told me she had been unaware of the ill-effects of smoking or chewing tobacco until she attended a workshop organized by a grantee working in tobacco law advocacy. Now, she has a no-smoking section in her restaurant and also does her best to dissuade her family, friends and employees from smoking by talking to them about the ill-effects of tobacco use and by handing out relevant literature. This is evidence that little by little, through our various projects, we have been able to make an impact on the lives of people affected by cancer or those at risk.

Differential discussion

As mentioned earlier, it is not an easy task to manage a program for a country that is thousands of miles away. Without any staff in India, and coming in as a foreign organization, it would not have been a manageable task for us to implement any of our signature, evidence-based programs in India. Also, we had decided on a bottom-up approach, preferring to work directly with NGOs rather than funneling money through the government. I believe that this gave us a good exposure to the situation on the ground.

One of the issues in working in such a way relates to measuring impact. How do you know whether you have managed to make any substantial difference to the situation in the country? The term *seed grant* brings to mind a vision of a farmer scattering seeds in a field and hoping that at least some of them thrive in the soil and become plants. To me, distributing seed grants seems to be a similar process. So when you are working in a large country the important questions become, is it worthwhile to give small grants spread across the country, or would it make for a better impact to build capacity, city by city, region by region? Given the nature of the economy and the inevitable fight for the same dollars to support similar causes, is it even feasible to make a sustained impact region by region? These questions are those that most program planners struggle with as they formulate cancer control strategies at a national level.

References

American Cancer Society. Leading cancer organizations team up for global cancer fight. Retrieved 3/15/09: http://www.cancer.org/docroot/NWS/content/NWS_1_1x_Leading_Cancer_Organizations_Team_Up_For_Global_Cancer_Fight.asp

Arora, M., Reddy, K. S., Stigler, M. H. & Perry C. L. (2008). Associations between tobacco marketing and use among urban youth. *American Journal of Health Behavior*, 32 (3): 283–94.

Dinshaw, K. A. (2002). Addressing the cancer agenda: How have we measured up? *Fifty years of cancer control in India*. Government of India: National Cancer Control Programme.

Dinshaw, K. A., Shastri, S. S. & Patil, S. S. (2005). Cancer control programme in India: Challenges for the new millennium. *Health Administrator*, 60 (1): 10–13.

Joranson, D. E., Rajagopal, M. R. & Gilson, A. M. (2002). Improving access to opioid analgesics for palliative care in India. *Journal of Pain and Symptom Management*, 24 (2): 152–9.

Ministry of Health and Family Welfare. (2007). *2005–06 National Family Health Survey (NFHS-3) Report*. Government of India.

National Cancer Registry Programme. (2006). *Consolidated report of the population based cancer registries 2001–2004*. Indian Council of Medical Research. Retrieved 3/1/2009: http://icmr.nic.in/ncrp/report_pop_2001-04/Initial%20Pages.pdf

Okonkwo, Q. L., Draisma, G., der Kinderen, A., Brown, M. L. & de Koning, H. J. (2008). Breast cancer screening policies in developing countries: A cost-effectiveness analysis for India. *Journal of the National Cancer Institute*, 100 (18): 1290–1300.

Rao, Y. N., Gupta S. & Agarwal, S. P. (2002). National Cancer Control Programme: Current status & strategies. In Agarwal, S. P. (ed.) *Fifty years of cancer control in India*. Government of India: National Cancer Control Programme.

Rajagopal, M. R. & Joranson, D. E. (2007). India: Opioid availability—an update. *Journal of Pain and Symptom Management*, 33 (5): 615–22.

Rajagopal, M. R., Joranson, D. E. & Gilson, A. M. (2001). Medical use, misuse, and diversion of opioids in India. *The Lancet*, 358: 139–43

Reddy, K. S. & Gupta, P. C. (2009). *Report on tobacco control in India executive summary*. Ministry of Health and Family Welfare Government of India, Center for Disease Control and Prevention USA, World Health Organization. Retrieved 3/2/2009: http://www.whoindia.org/LinkFiles/Tobacco_Free_Initiative_Executive_Summary.pdf

Sanyal, B. (2005). Role of the private sector in health care in India with special role in cancer. *Health Administrator*, 42 (1): 143–7.

Sharma, D. C. (2008). Special report: National poor palliative care in India. *The Lancet*, 9, 515.

Sinha, D. N., Gupta, P. C., Reddy, K. S., Prasad, V. M., Rahman, K., Warren, C. W., Jones, N. R. & Asma, S. (2008). Linking Global Youth Tobacco Survey 2003 and 2006 data to tobacco control policy in India. *Journal of School Health*, 78 (7): 368–73.

WHO (World Health Organization). (2006). *Cancer control: Knowledge into action. WHO guide for effective programmes, planning*. World Health Organization.

World Health Organization. *Tobacco Control Legislation*. Retrieved 3/2/2009: http://www.whoindia.org/en/section20/section25_928.htm

Index

Text in **bold** indicates a table or figure

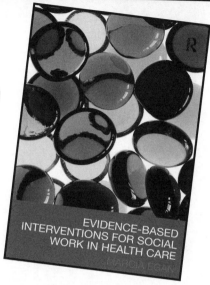

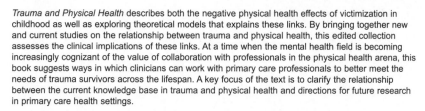